MW00712057

IBM   International Technical Suppc

EJB 2.0 Development with WebSphere Studio Application Developer

April 2003

SG24-6819-00

Note: Before using this information and the product it supports, read the information in "Notices" on page xix.

First Edition (April 2003)

This edition applies to Version 5 of WebSphere Studio Application Developer and WebSphere Application Server and to the Enterprise JavaBean specification 2.0.

This book is similar to the redbook *EJB Development with VisualAge for Java for WebSphere Application Server*, SG24-6144, but uses WebSphere Studio Application Developer as the development tool.

© **Copyright International Business Machines Corporation 2003. All rights reserved.**
Note to U.S. Government Users Restricted Rights -- Use, duplication or disclosure restricted by GSA ADP Schedule Contract with IBM Corp.

Contents

© Copyright IBM Corp. 2003. All rights reserved.

Notices

This information was developed for products and services offered in the U.S.A.

IBM may not offer the products, services, or features discussed in this document in other countries. Consult your local IBM representative for information on the products and services currently available in your area. Any reference to an IBM product, program, or service is not intended to state or imply that only that IBM product, program, or service may be used. Any functionally equivalent product, program, or service that does not infringe any IBM intellectual property right may be used instead. However, it is the user's responsibility to evaluate and verify the operation of any non-IBM product, program, or service.

IBM may have patents or pending patent applications covering subject matter described in this document. The furnishing of this document does not give you any license to these patents. You can send license inquiries, in writing, to:
IBM Director of Licensing, IBM Corporation, North Castle Drive Armonk, NY 10504-1785 U.S.A.

The following paragraph does not apply to the United Kingdom or any other country where such provisions are inconsistent with local law: INTERNATIONAL BUSINESS MACHINES CORPORATION PROVIDES THIS PUBLICATION "AS IS" WITHOUT WARRANTY OF ANY KIND, EITHER EXPRESS OR IMPLIED, INCLUDING, BUT NOT LIMITED TO, THE IMPLIED WARRANTIES OF NON-INFRINGEMENT, MERCHANTABILITY OR FITNESS FOR A PARTICULAR PURPOSE. Some states do not allow disclaimer of express or implied warranties in certain transactions, therefore, this statement may not apply to you.

This information could include technical inaccuracies or typographical errors. Changes are periodically made to the information herein; these changes will be incorporated in new editions of the publication. IBM may make improvements and/or changes in the product(s) and/or the program(s) described in this publication at any time without notice.

Any references in this information to non-IBM Web sites are provided for convenience only and do not in any manner serve as an endorsement of those Web sites. The materials at those Web sites are not part of the materials for this IBM product and use of those Web sites is at your own risk.

IBM may use or distribute any of the information you supply in any way it believes appropriate without incurring any obligation to you.

Information concerning non-IBM products was obtained from the suppliers of those products, their published announcements or other publicly available sources. IBM has not tested those products and cannot confirm the accuracy of performance, compatibility or any other claims related to non-IBM products. Questions on the capabilities of non-IBM products should be addressed to the suppliers of those products.

This information contains examples of data and reports used in daily business operations. To illustrate them as completely as possible, the examples include the names of individuals, companies, brands, and products. All of these names are fictitious and any similarity to the names and addresses used by an actual business enterprise is entirely coincidental.

COPYRIGHT LICENSE:
This information contains sample application programs in source language, which illustrates programming techniques on various operating platforms. You may copy, modify, and distribute these sample programs in any form without payment to IBM, for the purposes of developing, using, marketing or distributing application programs conforming to the application programming interface for the operating platform for which the sample programs are written. These examples have not been thoroughly tested under all conditions. IBM, therefore, cannot guarantee or imply reliability, serviceability, or function of these programs. You may copy, modify, and distribute these sample programs in any form without payment to IBM for the purposes of developing, using, marketing, or distributing application programs conforming to IBM's application programming interfaces.

© Copyright IBM Corp. 2003. All rights reserved.   **xix**

Trademarks

The following terms are trademarks of the International Business Machines Corporation in the United States, other countries, or both:

Redbooks(logo)™	DB2 Universal Database™	Lotus®
Redbooks™	DB2®	MQSeries®
AIX®	Encina®	Redbooks™
Cloudscape™	Informix®	SP™
CICS®	IBM®	VisualAge®
Domino™	IMS™	WebSphere®

The following terms are trademarks of other companies:

ActionMedia, LANDesk, MMX, Pentium and ProShare are trademarks of Intel Corporation in the United States, other countries, or both.

Microsoft, Windows, Windows NT, and the Windows logo are trademarks of Microsoft Corporation in the United States, other countries, or both.

Java and all Java-based trademarks and logos are trademarks or registered trademarks of Sun Microsystems, Inc. in the United States, other countries, or both.

C-bus is a trademark of Corollary, Inc. in the United States, other countries, or both.

UNIX is a registered trademark of The Open Group in the United States and other countries.

SET, SET Secure Electronic Transaction, and the SET Logo are trademarks owned by SET Secure Electronic Transaction LLC.

Other company, product, and service names may be trademarks or service marks of others.

Preface

This IBM® Redbook provides detailed information on how to effectively use WebSphere® Studio Application Developer for the development of applications based on the Enterprise JavaBeans (EJB) architecture, and deployment of such applications to a WebSphere Application Server.

Throughout the book, we provide examples based on a simple banking application with an underlying relational database.

In Part 1, we introduce EJBs as a part of Java 2 Enterprise Edition (J2EE) and cover the basic concepts and the architecture. In particular we point out the new functions introduced with the EJB 2.0 specification that provide, for example, enhanced functionality for container-managed persistence entity beans and message-driven beans. We also provide best practice guidelines for successful implementations of EJBs.

In Part 2, we introduce the sample banking application and then implement entity beans, session beans, and message-driven beans using WebSphere Studio Application Developer. We also implement finder methods, different mapping strategies, and simple clients that use the EJBs. At the end, we describe how to deploy EJB applications to a WebSphere Application Server.

© Copyright IBM Corp. 2003. All rights reserved.

The team that wrote this redbook

This redbook was produced by a team of specialists from around the world working at the International Technical Support Organization, San Jose Center.

| Ueli | Wouter | Lars | Deborah | Martin |

Ueli Wahli is a Consultant IT Specialist at the IBM International Technical Support Organization in San Jose, California. Before joining the ITSO 18 years ago, Ueli worked in technical support at IBM Switzerland. He writes extensively and teaches IBM classes worldwide on application development, object technology, VisualAge® for Java, WebSphere Application Server, and lately WebSphere Studio products. In his ITSO career, Ueli has produced over 25 Redbooks™. Ueli holds a degree in Mathematics from the Swiss Federal Institute of Technology.

Wouter Denayer is an IT Architect with IBM Belgium. He currently focuses on application architecture within the WebSphere family while using existing open source components and tools wherever possible. Wouter started working with Web technology in 1993 and has since acquired knowledge of many different platforms and products. This experience allow him to better understand the client environment on application integration projects.

Lars Schunk is a Consultant IT Specialist in IBM Global Services Germany. He has three years of experience in design and development of Internet and intranet application solutions. He holds a degree in business informatics from the University of Applied Sciences in North-East-Lower-Saxony, Germany. His areas of expertise include J2EE, EJB, WebSphere, and Tomcat.

Deborah Shaddon is an IT Architect in the IBM Global AMS Delivery Group based in Chicago, Illinois. She is a co-author of the redbook *Developing Servlets and JSPs with VisualAge for Java and WebSphere Studio*, SG24-5755. She has over 15 years of application development and architecture experience, including mainframe, client/server, and e-business technology solutions. Deborah works closely with IBM customers on application and enterprise architectural solutions, across multiple industry sectors including retail, banking, insurance, real estate management, and credit. Her current areas of expertise include distributed component-based architectures, primarily J2EE, service-oriented architectures, J2EE application and integration frameworks, and agile development techniques. She works with many IBM products, including WebSphere Application Server, Application Developer, WebSphere MQ, and Lotus® Domino™. Deborah holds a degree in Business Information Systems from Bradley University, Peoria, Illinois, and is currently pursuing a Masters in Software Engineering from DePaul University, Chicago, Illinois.

Martin Weiss worked in IBM Switzerland for more than 20 years, most recently in the field of WebSphere application development. In 2001 he established his own company, Martin Weiss Informatik (www.mw-informatik.ch). Martin has sound experience in Enterprise JavaBeans technology and has been working with the WebSphere development tools since the early days of EJBs. He is a Certified WebSphere Specialist and provides consulting services and education in Switzerland. Martin is a co-author of the Redbooks *Design and Implement Servlets, JSPs, and EJBs*, SG24-5754, and *Enterprise JavaBeans Development Using VisualAge for Java*, SG24-5429.

Thanks to the following people for their contributions to this project:

► Daniel Berg, Chuck Bridgham, Justin Hill, and Kevin Williams of the Application Developer team in IBM Raleigh

► Chris Brealey and Timothy Deboer of the Application Developer team in IBM Toronto

► Karri Carlson, Eric Erpenbach, Todd Johnson, Albert Lee, and Michael Schmitt of the WebSphere team in IBM Rochester

Become a published author

Join us for a two- to six-week residency program! Help write an IBM Redbook dealing with specific products or solutions, while getting hands-on experience with leading-edge technologies. You'll team with IBM technical professionals, Business Partners and/or customers.

Your efforts will help increase product acceptance and customer satisfaction. As a bonus, you'll develop a network of contacts in IBM development labs, and increase your productivity and marketability.

Find out more about the residency program, browse the residency index, and apply online at:

ibm.com/redbooks/residencies.html

Comments welcome

Your comments are important to us!

We want our Redbooks to be as helpful as possible. Send us your comments about this or other Redbooks in one of the following ways:

► Use the online **Contact us** review redbook form found at:

    ibm.com/redbooks

► Send your comments in an Internet note to:

    redbook@us.ibm.com

► Mail your comments to:

    IBM Corporation, International Technical Support Organization
    Dept. QXXE Building 80-E2
    650 Harry Road
    San Jose, California 95120-6099

Part 1

EJB architecture and concepts

In Part 1, we introduce Enterprise JavaBeans as part of J2EE. We describe the EJB architecture and concepts, and introduce the different types of EJBs.

We discuss in detail each type of EJB and point out what is new with the EJB 2.0 specification. In each chapter we conclude with best practice guidelines for successful implementation of EJB-based applications.

© Copyright IBM Corp. 2003. All rights reserved.

1

Introduction to Enterprise JavaBeans

This chapter introduces Enterprise JavaBeans and shows how they are integrated in the J2EE platform.

Readers who are already familiar to the EJB standard can skip this chapter.

© Copyright IBM Corp. 2003. All rights reserved.

Server-side component architecture

Enterprise JavaBeans (EJB) is an architecture for server-side component based distributed applications written in Java.

Since its introduction a few years ago, Enterprise JavaBeans technology has gained momentum among platform providers and enterprise development teams. This is because the EJB component model simplifies development of business components that are transactional, scalable, and portable. Enterprise JavaBean servers reduce the complexity of developing business components by providing automatic support for system-level services, such as transactions, security, and database connectivity, thus allowing the developers to concentrate on developing the business logic.

The EJB specification describes a server-side component-based architecture:

> The EJB architecture is a component architecture for the development and deployment of component-based distributed business applications

The specification has been created by different companies. They are mentioned in the first pages of the EJB specification.

The goal of this specification is to define a standard, so that different vendors are able to implement these standards. Because this standard defines every essentially detail of the architecture, an application written using the Enterprise JavaBeans architecture is scalable, transactional, and multi-user secure. Such an application may be written once, and then deployed on any server platform that supports the Enterprise JavaBeans specification.

Figure 1-1 gives an overview for a basic EJB environment:

► The EJB components are running inside the container of an EJB server.

► The container has the connection to the database or to other components.

► An EJB client can access the EJBs from the same Java Virtual Machine (JVM) or from another JVM over remote interfaces. The EJB home component is comparable to a factory for the EJB objects. The EJB objects retrieved from the home components can be also local or remote objects.

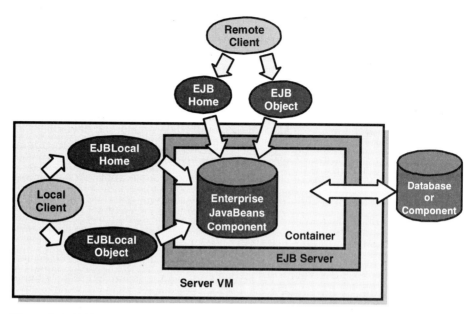

Figure 1-1   EJB environment

Background

Architectures have undergone several major evolutionary shifts. The shift from one-tier, mainframe-type systems to two-tier client/server based systems, addressed the need to separate out application tier from the resource tier. During the early 90s, traditional enterprise information system providers began responding to customer requirements by shifting from the two-tier, client/server application model to more flexible three-tier and multi-tier application models. This n-tier model is the current model whereby we distribute our software over a set of machines, all of which comprise a part-of the total application.

The new models separated business logic from system services and the user interface, placing it in a middle tier between the two. The evolution of new middleware services—transaction monitors, message-oriented middleware, object request brokers, and Web application servers—gave additional impetus to this new architecture. In addition, the growing use of the Internet and intranets for enterprise applications contributed to a greater emphasis on lightweight, easy-to-deploy clients that run in Web browsers.

Multi-tier design simplifies developing, deploying, and maintaining enterprise applications. It enables developers to focus on the specifics of programming their business logic, relying on various back-end services to provide the infrastructure, and client-side applications (both stand-alone and within Web browsers) to provide the user interaction.

Once developed, business logic can be deployed on servers appropriate to existing requirements of an organization. However, no standard component architecture existed for the middle tier, and forced developers to focus on plumbing details specific to the particular mix of platform, operating system, and middleware services. This limited developers to deploy a single application on a wide variety of platforms, or to readily scale applications to meet changing business conditions.

Why EJBs?

Numerous Web sites are up and running using Java without any EJB technology. Developers have been using servlet/JSP models and managing transactions themselves using commit and rollback functionality that is built into JDBC without the help of application servers.

But when doing so, the application developers are confronted with many challenges. Some of the most important ones are managing concurrency, persistence and transactions. As a result, the developers have to either develop proprietary code or buy supporting frameworks.

These problems are solved by using enterprise beans. The use of enterprise beans allow developers to focus on the business logic and release them from coding infrastructure and middleware logic, and developers become more productive and efficient.

As with most other technologies, enterprise beans do not provide the unique solution to all problems. Using enterprise beans has advantages and disadvantages. However, the advantages outweigh the disadvantages, especially for more complex applications that require a sophisticated robust and distributed persistent model.

Once again, not every application environment may benefit from using enterprise beans. To help you decide whether this technology is appropriate, this section provides some reasons to consider using it.

Object distribution

When using Enterprise JavaBeans, distributed objects are used for building an enterprise-scale system. In short, this means that the parts of your program can be deployed to as many different physical machines and in as many separate OS processes as appropriate to achieve the performance, scalability, and availability goals of your system.

Portable component-based architecture

For many forward-looking customers, the key issue is that they have to achieve independence from platform, vendor, and application-server implementation. The EJB architecture, which is an industry-standard component architecture, can help achieve these goals. Enterprise beans developed for WebSphere can usually be deployed on non-IBM application servers, and vice versa. This was demonstrated at the June 1999 JavaOne conference where the same car dealer application was deployed on multiple enterprise bean application servers vendors. While in the short-term it is often easier and faster to take advantage of features that may precede standardization, standardization provides the best long-term advantage.

Also, customers must consider the increasing availability of tools and optimized implementations of the EJB standard that you would not get with home-grown managed object frameworks. Because most customers are not in the middleware business, their efforts can be more effectively targeted at activities that are more directly related to their business.

Object persistence

Making an object persistent means that its state (the values of its variables) can be preserved across multiple invocations of a program that references that object. In most cases, the state of a persistent object is stored in a relational database.

Unfortunately, objects and relational databases differ a lot from each other. Relational databases have limited modeling capabilities, such as object inheritance and encapsulation, compared to Java. Additionally, SQL data types do not exactly match Java data types, leading to conversion problems. All these problems are solved when using CMP entity beans.

Independence from database schema

EJB technology enables a clear separation of business logic from database access. The business logic is independent of the database schema and can be deployed into organizations with different or changing database schemas.

Transaction management

Concurrent access to shared data can be one of the biggest headaches to a developer. The consideration of all the related issues as database locking, concurrency, or even loss of data integrity can lead to the creation of highly complex schemes for managing access to shared data at the database level.

Enterprise beans automatically handle these complex threading and simultaneous shared data issues. As mentioned previously, the EJB container provides all the necessary transaction services to enterprise beans for control access to back-end data in a transactional manner.

Multiple data sources with transactional capabilities

Many applications require the ability to access multiple data sources. For example, a program may use data in both a middle-tier DB2® or Oracle database and a mainframe CICS® or IMS™ system accessible through WebSphere MQ. The key is that some applications require that this access is fully transactional—that data integrity is maintained across the data sources.

For example, an application may demand that placing a user order will consist of storing the detailed order information in an Oracle database and simultaneously placing a shipment order with a CICS system through WebSphere MQ. If either the database update or the MQ enqueuing fails, then the entire transaction should roll back.

In the past, the only choices with which to build systems like these were transaction monitors such as Encina®, CICS, or Tuxedo, which used non-standard interfaces and required development in such languages as COBOL, C, or C++.

Enterprise beans support multiple concurrent transactions with full commit and rollback capabilities across multiple DB2 data sources in a full two-phase commit-capable environment.

Middle-tier architecture

Very often companies consider their application software, particularly the business rules and data structures that make up the business logic, as corporate assets. Therefore, they are concerned with protecting these assets from the public Internet.

Enterprise beans enable a company to use a middle-tier architecture so that presentation logic can be separated from business logic. This separation makes possible the use of a second firewall between these two different layers for higher isolation of all application components that contain business logic.

Multiple client types accessing shared data

Often, a single application will have multiple client types that need access to the same set of information. For example, an application may have a Web-based HTML front end for external customers, and a more complete Java application front end for internal users. Traditionally, this problem has been solved by writing two versions of the same application that share the same data sources (database tables). However, this is not efficient either in programming time or utilizing the database, if multiple database locks could be held at one time.

The EJB solution to this problem is to put common data and business logic in a single set of EJBs that are accessed by different client types (for example, HTML/servlet and application). EJBs control access to the back-end data and internally manage the current transactions and database locking. This reduces the total programming effort by removing duplicate code in the application and by reducing the amount of effort spent in writing database control logic.

Concurrent read and update access to shared data

Traditionally, fat client solutions require the application to manage access to shared data at the database level. This often results in highly complex schemes to deal with database locking and concurrency, or alternatively, with the loss of data integrity when these issues are not considered.

Enterprise beans automatically handle these complex threading and simultaneous shared-data issues. As mentioned previously, enterprise beans control access to back-end data and manage the current transactions and database locking internally.

Method-level object security

Certain types of applications have security restrictions that have previously made them difficult to implement in Java. For example, certain insurance applications must restrict access to patient data in order to meet regulatory guidelines. Until the advent of enterprise beans, there was no way to restrict access to an object or method by a particular user. Previously, restricting access at the database level, and then catching errors thrown at the JDBC level, or by restricting access at the application level by custom security code would have been the only implementation options.

However, enterprise beans now allow method-level security on any enterprise bean or method. Users and user groups can be created that can be granted or denied execution rights to any EJB or method. In WebSphere, these same user groups can be granted or denied access to Web resources (servlets, JSPs, and HTML pages), and the user IDs can be in a seamless way passed from the Web resources to the EJBs by the underlying security framework.

Multiple servers to handle throughput and availability

Over the past several years, customers have found that fat client systems simply do not scale to the thousands or millions of users that Web-based systems may have. At the same time, software distribution problems have led to a desire to trim down fat clients. The 24-hour, seven-day-a-week nature of the Web has also made uptime a crucial issue for businesses. However, not everyone needs a system designed for 24x7 operation or that is able to handle millions of concurrent users. Developers should be able to design a system so that scalability can be achieved without sacrificing ease of development, or standardization.

What customers need is a way to write business logic that can scale to meet these kinds of requirements. WebSphere's EJB support can provide this kind of highly scalable, highly available system. It does this by utilizing the following features:

► Object caching and pooling: WebSphere Application Server automatically pools enterprise beans at the server level, reducing the amount of time spent in object creation and garbage collection. This results in more processing cycles being available to do real work.

► Workload optimization at server: WebSphere Application Server Network Deployment features EJB server cluster management. Using Network Deployment you can create server groups that span nodes. In addition, you can configure and run multiple instances (called clones) of a WebSphere server on one machine, taking advantage of multiprocessor architectures. You can administer a set of nodes running WebSphere servers using a single administration facility. A setup using multiple nodes improves availability and prevents a single point of failure in the application server.

► Cloning supports automatic failover: With several clones available to handle requests, it is more likely that failures will not damage throughput and reliability. With clones distributed to various nodes, an entire machine can fail without producing devastating consequences. All of these features happen without specifically being programmed into the system. No changes to the server-side code are necessary to take advantage of this kind of scalability.

Note that WebSphere Application Server Network Deployment supports distribution, cloning, and automatic failover of other server-side Java technologies, such as Java servlets and JSPs. However, these are more presentation-oriented technologies and serve as a complement to EJBs rather than as a competitor to EJBs. When uptime and scalability are key, EJBs should be a part of the overall solution.

Integration with CORBA

Enterprise beans are built on technology that is a combination of Java Remote Method Invocation (RMI) and Component Object Request Broker Architecture (CORBA). Clients access an enterprise bean using RMI over IIOP. This allows pure CORBA clients to access enterprise beans as EJB clients.

Development roles

Developing and running components with a well-defined mapping between tasks and roles allows the right person to do the right job. The various tasks within a EJB development and production process are assigned to different roles, which are part of the specification. The EJB architecture therefore defines six roles. From a technical point of view, each role may be performed by a different person. To ensure this, the roles are described in the specification. In a real-life scenario, more than one role may be performed by one person.

In our book you are the bean provider, because you are about to develop beans with WebSphere Studio Application Developer, and IBM are a server vendor performing the roles of the container and server provider.

While testing and deploying your beans several times to the test servers, you are performing more than one role, but several, as follows:

► Enterprise bean provider
► Application assembler
► EJB deployer
► EJB server provider
► EJB container provider
► Systems administrator

For a detailed description of the roles see "EJB roles" on page 34.

Java 2 Platform, Enterprise Edition (J2EE)

The Java 2 Platform, Enterprise Edition (J2EE) is a robust suite of middleware application services for server-side application development. J2EE is an extension of the Java 2 Platform, Standard Edition (J2SE).

J2EE makes all Java enterprise APIs and functionality available and accessible in a well-integrated fashion. This helps to simplify complex problems in the development, deployment, and management of multi-tier, server-centric enterprise solutions. Let's look at the technologies included with J2EE.

J2EE services summary

Table 1-1 shows the technologies provided by the J2EE specification.

Table 1-1   Technologies of J2EE specification

	J2EE specification
Web	Servlets, JSPs
EJB	Enterprise component architecture
Database	JDBC
Naming and directory	JNDI
Messaging	JMS
e-mail	Java Mail, JAF
Distributed objects	JavaIDL, RMI, RMI-IIOP
Transactions	JTA, JTS

Java servlets and JavaServer Pages (JSP)

A servlet can be thought of as an applet that runs in the server side. Servlets provide a component-based, platform-independent method for building Web-based applications without the limitations of CGI programs.

JSP technology is an extension of servlet technology created to support authoring of HTML and XML pages. It enables combining fixed template data with dynamic content data and is a good alternative to servlets.

Servlets and JSPs are suited for simple request/response Web models. We recommend that applications developed with EJB follow the model-view-controller (MVC) design pattern. This pattern defines an architectural three-way split for an application, separating data elements (the *model*) from the data presentation (the *view*) and from the manipulation of the data into the presentation (the *controller*).

The J2EE relies heavily on JSPs as the view part of the MVC pattern to bridge the gap between EJB and HTML code, placing JSPs at the key boundary between data and presentation. Similarly, servlets are used as the controller and EJBs as the model part of the MVC pattern, respectively.

Enterprise JavaBeans (EJB)

EJB defines how server-side components are written and provides a standard architectural contract between the components and the application servers and containers that manage them. The EJB specification provides a solution for a clear separation of the business logic and the intricacies of dealing with persistency, transactions, and other middleware-related services.

JDBC

JDBC provides uniform access to a wide range of relational databases. JDBC enables Java programmers to represent database connections, SQL statements, and retrieving results in a portable way. JDBC 2.0 has built-in support for database connection pooling.

Java remote method invocation and RMI-IIOP

RMI is a mechanism for invoking methods remotely on other machines. EJB relies on Java RMI as a communications API between components and their clients. Sun Microsystems with IBM and others has recently developed a more portable version of RMI, which uses the Object Management Group's (OMG) Internet Inter-ORB protocol. IIOP is necessary for J2EE deployments to be interoperable with CORBA systems.

Java Naming and Directory Interface (JNDI)

JNDI is a standard for naming and directory services. In EJB-based applications when the client code requests access to an EJB component, JNDI is used to locate and retrieve the component to service the client. JNDI enables writing portable directory and naming service code that works with multiple directory services, such as LDAP and CosNaming.

Java Messaging Service (JMS)

By combining Java technology with enterprise messaging, the JMS API provides a new, powerful tool for solving enterprise computing problems. The JMS API improves programmer productivity by defining a common set of messaging concepts and programming strategies that will be supported by all JMS technology-compliant messaging systems.

Java Mail

The Java Mail API provides a platform- and protocol-independent framework to build Java-based mail and messaging applications. It basically allow the applications to have e-mail capabilities. Java Mail depends on Java Activation Framework to encapsulate message data and to handle interactions.

Java Activation Framework (JAF)

JAF enables developers to determine the type of an arbitrary piece of data, to encapsulate access to the data, to discover the functional operations available on it, and to instantiate the appropriate bean to perform the operation(s). It also enables you to dynamically register types of arbitrary data and actions associated with particular kinds of data. Additionally, it enables a program to dynamically provide or retrieve JavaBeans that implement actions associated with some kind of data.

Java Transaction API (JTA) and Java Transaction Service (JTS)

JTA is a high-level transaction API that allows applications and J2EE servers to manage transactions. JTS specifies the implementation of a transaction manager, which supports JTA and implements the Java mapping of the OMG Object Transaction Service (OTS) 1.1 specification at the level below the API.

Java IDL

Java Interface Definition Language (IDL) is an implementation of the CORBA specification and enables interoperability and connectivity with heterogeneous objects. It is basically an object request broker provided with JDK 1.2. The Java IDL enables distributed Web applications to transparently invoke operations on remote network services using the industry standards IDL and IIOP from OMG.

J2EE architecture overview

Figure 1-2 shows an overall view of the different J2EE technologies.

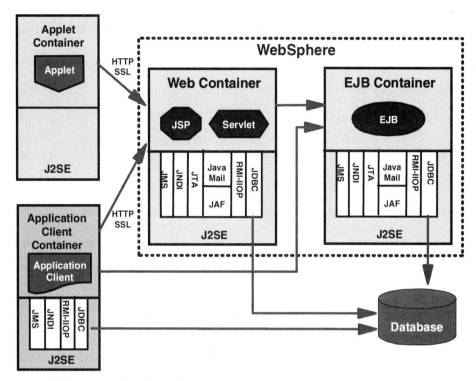

Figure 1-2   J2EE architecture diagram

Web containers and EJB containers

Containers are basically runtime environments that provide components with specific services. For example, as shown in Figure 1-2, Web containers provide runtime support to clients by processing requests through invoking JSPs and servlets and returning results from the components to the client. Similarly EJB containers provide automated support for transaction and state management of EJB components, as well as lookup and security services.

IBM products and J2EE

Table 1-2 shows the support in WebSphere Version 5 for the various J2EE technologies.

Table 1-2 Support of J2EE technologies by WebSphere products

Technology	Version	Comments
JDK	1.3	Fully supported
JDBC	2.0	WebSphere adds a unique prepared statements cache implementation.
JMS	1.0.1	WebSphere MQ supports native JMS and can be used by WebSphere.
JNDI	1.2	WebSphere 3.5 supports most of the JNDI 1.2. It uses `CosNaming` as a service provider.
EJB	2.0	WebSphere supports EJB 2.0 plus: Access beans: Simplify client application using EJBs Inheritance: Support polymorphism and reuse
Servlet	2.3	Fully supported
JSP	1.2	It also has high-quality tool support through WebSphere Studio.
JTA and JTS	1.0	Supported with (two-phase commit) distributed transactions
RMI-IIOP	1.0	Fully supported
JAF	1.1	Fully supported
Java Mail	1.1	Not supported
XML DOM/SAX		Fully supported
HTTP	1.1	Fully supported

EJB specifications

The Enterprise JavaBeans (EJB) specification is a foundation for the Java 2 Platform, Enterprise Edition (J2EE) defined by Sun. Vendors use this specification to implement an infrastructure in which components can be deployed, and use a set of services such as distributed transactions, security, or life-cycle management. As a developer, you just reuse the services detailed in the specification. For example, you do not need to include any code in your components to make them transactional. This lets you concentrate on the business logic of the application.

Enterprise beans are designed to be portable from one vendor's execution environment to another, independent of the choices made by the vendor to implement the services described in the specification. The quality of service required by an enterprise bean is described outside of the component in a deployment descriptor. The deployment descriptor is analyzed at deployment time by a tool provided by the vendor. This feature provides a great level of flexibility for reusing your component. For example, if you wish to change the transactional behavior of an enterprise bean, you have to change only the transaction attribute stored in the deployment descriptor, not the EJB business logic. Changes are taken into account when you re-deploy the enterprise bean in the container.

Enterprise JavaBeans architecture

The Enterprise JavaBeans specification defines the architecture shown in Figure 1-2 on page 15.

In this section, we describe the features and limitations of the different EJB versions that have been specified by Sun and the Java community.

EJB 1.0

Here are the features and limitations of EJB 1.0.

Features

EJB 1.0 introduced the following features:

► Enterprise bean instances are created and managed at runtime by a container.

► An enterprise bean can be customized at deployment time by editing its environment properties.

► Client access is mediated by the container and the EJB server on which the enterprise bean is deployed.

► Flexible component model.

► Support for component distributions and security.

► Stateless and stateful session beans are defined and must be supported.

► Container-managed persistence and bean-managed persistence entity beans are defined and are not mandatory in this version.

▶ For transaction support, either the original javax.jts package or the new `javax.transaction` package can be used.

Limitations

Although some of the features are attractive, there are some limitations as follows:

▶ Entity bean support is not mandatory.

▶ Java RMI-IIOP support is not mandatory, which defies interoperability with other heterogeneous components.

▶ The deployment descriptor is not available in text format.

▶ Requires a separate deployment file for each enterprise bean, causing large applications composed of many beans to slow down.

▶ Interoperability between containers is not defined.

▶ No standard container API.

EJB 1.1

EJB 1.1 attempts to provide a high degree of application compatibility for enterprise beans that were written for the EJB 1.0 specification.

Differences over 1.0

EJB 1.1 addresses many of the limitations and loopholes found in EJB 1.0. The most significant changes include:

▶ Entity bean support, both container- and bean-managed persistence, is required.

▶ Java RMI-IIOP argument and reference types must be supported. That is, the client API must support the Java RMI-IIOP programming model for portability, but the underlying communication protocol can be anything.

▶ The `javax.ejb.deployment` package has been dropped in favor of an XML-based deployment descriptor.

▶ Declarative security authorization (access control) is now more role driven.

▶ Isolation levels are now managed explicitly through JDBC (BMP), the database or other vendor-specific mechanisms.

▶ The bean-container contract has been enhanced to include a default JNDI context for accessing properties and resources, for example, JDBC and JMS.

▶ The basic EJB roles have been expanded and redefined to better separate responsibilities involved in the development, deployment, and hosting of enterprise beans.

- Allows using `java.lang.String` as a primary key type.
- Allows a session bean instance to be removed upon a timeout while the instance is in the passivated state.
- Allows enterprise beans to read system properties.

The EJB 1.0 enterprise bean code has to be changed or recompiled to run in an EJB 1.1 container, in the following situations:

- An enterprise bean that uses the `javax.jts.UserTransaction` interface needs to be modified to use the new `javax.transaction.UserTransaction`.
- An enterprise bean written to the EJB 1.0 specification has to be modified to use the `getCallerPrincipal()` and `isCallerInRole(String roleName)` methods instead of the deprecated `getCallerIdentity()` and `isCallerInRole(Identity)` methods to work in all EJB 1.1 containers.
- An enterprise bean with container-managed persistence written to the EJB 1.0 specification has to be recompiled to work with all EJB 1.1 compliant containers, because the required return value of `ejbCreate(...)` in EJB 1.1 is different from its value in EJB 1.0.
- An entity bean in EJB 1.0, whose finders do not define the `FinderException` in the methods' throws clauses, must be changed. EJB 1.1 requires that all finders define the `FinderException`.
- In EJB 1.1, an entity bean must not use the `UserTransaction` interface.
- The enterprise bean in EJB 1.0 uses the `UserTransaction` interface and implements the `SessionSynchronization` interface at the same time, which is not allowed in EJB 1.1.

Limitations

In spite of many added features over EJB 1.0, EJB 1.1 still faces the following limitations:

- Data modeling capability is very simple.
- Mapping of the CMP beans to the database schema is outside of the specification.
- Relationships and inheritance are not supported.
- Specification of finder methods is not in the specification.

EJB 2.0

EJB 2.0 is the latest version of the specification. The most important changes in the specification are those made to container-managed persistence (CMP) and the introduction of a completely new bean type, the message-driven bean.

New features supported in EJB 2.0

EJB 2.0 provides these enhancements:

► Integration of EJB with JMS.

► Message-driven beans.

► Implement additional business methods in the home interface that are not specific for bean instance.

► EJB query language (EJB QL), which enables searches based on the object schema instead of data schema.

Changes in EJB 2.0

EJB 2.0 contains these changes over EJB 1.1:

► The new CMP component model is radically different from the old CMP model, because it introduces an entirely new participant, the *persistence manager.*

► There is a completely new way of defining container-managed fields, as well as relationships with other beans and dependent objects.

► The introduction of message-driven beans provides a component model for the enterprise beans acting as JMS clients, allowing them to be deployed in the rich and robust environment of the EJB container system.

Limitations

Even with EJB 2.0 we face some limitations:

► Inheritance is not supported.

► The mapping of entity beans to relational databases is vendor specific.

General restrictions of EJB

EJB development places some restrictions on the developers for better component management and easier service. The restrictions include the following:

► An enterprise bean must not use read/write static fields. Therefore, we recommend that all static fields in the enterprise bean class are declared as *final.*

- An enterprise bean must not use thread synchronization primitives to synchronize execution of multiple instances.

- An enterprise bean must not use the AWT functionality to attempt to output information to a display, or to input information from a keyboard.

- An enterprise bean must not use the `java.io` package to attempt to access files and directories in the file system.

- An enterprise bean must not attempt to listen on a socket, accept connections on a socket, or use a socket for multicasting.

- The enterprise bean must not attempt to query a class to obtain information about the declared members that are not otherwise accessible to the enterprise bean because of the security rules of the Java language.

- The enterprise bean must not attempt to create a class loader, obtain the current class loader, set the context class loader, set the security manager, create a new security manager, stop the JVM, or change the input, output, and error streams.

- The enterprise bean must not attempt to set the socket factory used by `ServerSocket`, `Socket`, or the stream handler factory used by URL.

- The enterprise bean must not attempt to manage threads.

- The enterprise bean must not attempt to directly read or write a file descriptor.

- The enterprise bean must not attempt to obtain the security policy information for a particular code source.

- The enterprise bean must not attempt to load a native library.

- The enterprise bean must not attempt to gain access to packages and classes that the usual rules of the Java programming language make unavailable to the enterprise bean.

- The enterprise bean must not attempt to define a class in a package.

- The enterprise bean must not attempt to access or modify the security configuration objects (`Policy`, `Security`, `Provider`, `Signer`, and `Identity`).

- The enterprise bean must not attempt to use the subclass and object substitution features of the Java serialization protocol.

- The enterprise bean must not attempt to pass *this* as an argument or method result. The enterprise bean must instead pass the result of `SessionContext.getEJBObject` or `EntityContext.getEJBObject`.

EJB 2.0 overview

In this section, we have a short look at the new and changed function in EJB 2.0. More details are presented in Chapter 2, "EJB architecture and concepts" on page 33.

Local interfaces

An EJB client never directly interacts with an EJB object. The client uses the component interface, which defines the methods that are available to the client. The implementation of this interface is provided by the container.

Without having the new local interfaces, the container has to provide only one implementation of this component interface—an implementation for invocations over a network protocol, because the EJB client has to be a remote client. If the EJB client and the EJB object itself are in the same Java Virtual Machine (JVM), an avoidable overhead arises because of the communication layers.

To avoid this overhead, one type of component interface is being added to the EJB specification 2.0: the *local component interface*.

There are now two types of component interfaces: a local and a remote interface. We can now choose the type that suits our needs.

Container-managed persistence (CMP)

An EJB container and an EJB have to interact with each other. In the case of an CMP entity bean, this interaction is quite complex. This communication is called a contract.

The EJB specification 2.0 establishes new contracts for CMP. These new contracts are fundamentalsfor the new functionality and they support more efficient vendor implementations.

The new contracts themselves are transparent to an EJB programmer. From a programmer's point of view, there are only some changes in the implementations. One change that may catch the attention of a programmer is that the bean class is now an abstract class without fields. The getters and setters of the bean class describe the attributes of the bean. It is then the job of the container to generate a concrete class for this bean and to implement the fields and the relationships between entity beans.

The two new primary CMP functions are relationships and EJB QL.

Container-managed relationships (CMR)

The main principles of CMR and CMP are comparable. In CMP, we describe our container-managed fields and the container is responsible for persistence. In CMR, we describe the relations between our entity beans and the container is responsible for maintaining the referential integrity.

What a container does in different situations is clearly described in the specification. For example, if we create a one-to-many relationship between bean A and bean B and invoke a set method on instance A2 passing the instance B1, the container has to remove the previous relationship between A1 and B1 because of the 1:n relationship definition. B1 can only belong to one instance of bean A. The container has to remove the prior relationship in the same transaction context to maintain the referential integrity.

The descriptions of the relationships are based on the abstract persistence schema. The abstract schema and the description of the relationships are part of the deployment descriptor.

The members of a container-managed relationship must have a local interface.

The container-managed relationships support one-to-many (1:m), one-to-one (1:1), and many-to-many (m:m) relationships.

EJB query language

The finder methods in the home interfaces are responsible for locating particular entity objects, but the name and the declaration of the methods are not sufficient information for the container to generate an implementation of the finder method. Therefore, the bean provider has to provide a description of the finder method. The EJB Architecture Version 1.1 does not specify the format of the finder method description. So every vendor (that is, every container provider) must offer a way to do this.

There are some obvious drawbacks with this approach. Every container provider offers a different way to describe and implement the finder methods, but all the different implementations have a big drawback in common. Since the EJB 1.1 beans have no object schema, they have to implement and describe the finder methods based on the data schema.

The EJB Query Language (EJB QL) enables us to describe the finder methods based on the object schema in an independent manner. Now our finder methods are supported by every EJB 2.0 compliant container. We do not have to customize our finder methods if we are using another database or another EJB container.

The EJB QL uses an SQL-like syntax to select objects or values. It is a typed expression language.

EJB home methods

EJB 1.1 allows only create and finder methods in the home interface of an entity bean. The business logic has to be implemented in the bean class and can be accessed over the component interface. Since we can invoke a method over the component interface only if there is a concrete implementation of this interface, we have to invoke this on a particular entity object.

If we have business logic that is dedicated to a bean class and in addition independent of a particular entity object, we can now place this code in a method of the bean class and declare this method in the home interface of this entity bean. In this method, we can find or create entities and access them over their component interfaces, as we do from a session bean method or any other EJB client.

If we invoke this method on the home interface, the container selects an instance of the bean and invokes the method independent of any particular entity object. In an EJB home method, no access is allowed to the attributes of the bean.

Message-driven bean

This EJB type is added in the EJB 2.0 specification. A message-driven bean is an asynchronous message consumer, implemented as a Java Message Service (JMS) consumer.

In prior EJB specifications, it was very hard to implement an asynchronous service running inside the container. The handling of threads is especially subject to restrictions inside of every EJB container. If we need multiple instances of a service class acting as one asynchronous service to meet the demands of a growing message load, we have to handle the instances ourselves, having regard to the lifetime of the different instances and to many other issues.

Dependent value classes

A dependent value class is an entity bean attribute that is a concrete serializable Java class containing a number of data fields. The data fields are stored in serialized format in a table column, or they can be mapped to individual columns using a composer. The internal structure of the dependent value class is not specified in the deployment descriptor.

A brief look at history

In this section, we explain how the EJB technology developed from a combination of CORBA and RMI, as well as the basic concepts of using EJBs.

Distributed component-oriented applications

A number of distribution technologies are available today. Some of the most well-known are the Object Management Group (OMG) Component Object Request Broker Architecture (CORBA), Sun Java Remote Method Invocation (RMI) protocol, and the Microsoft Distributed Component Object Model (DCOM). In the Java world, only the first two technologies stand out as especially important. In the next section, we briefly describe CORBA and RMI and show how they relate to the more recent technology of EJB.

CORBA overview

CORBA was developed by a consortium of companies (the Object Management Group) during the early 1990s to provide a common, language- and vendor-neutral standard for object distribution. CORBA as an architecture has been well accepted and successfully used in many projects.

The CORBA architecture is built around a special layer, the object request broker (ORB), that facilitates communication between clients and objects. The ORB is responsible for handling the object requests from a client and passing over the parameters from method invocations.

Low-level communication between different object spaces (ORBs) is done by using the Internet-Inter ORB Protocol (IIOP). By using this standard protocol, a CORBA-based program from any vendor, on almost any computer, operating system, programming language, and network can interoperate with a CORBA-based program from the same or another vendor, on any other computer, operating system, programming language, and network.

Apart from the ORB, there are two other key building blocks in the CORBA model, the Interface Definition Language (IDL), which normalizes the differences caused by language or operating system dependencies; and the CORBA services, which provide standard ways for CORBA objects to interact, such as naming and transaction.

The greatest advantages of using CORBA is that it is a standard interface that enables interoperability between different vendors' products, and that CORBA is language neutral. CORBA clients and servers can be written in a variety of computer languages, including Java, C++, C, Smalltalk, and Ada. This is possible by implementing remote interfaces for the CORBA distributed objects in IDL.

But when using CORBA to build distributed systems in Java, the development effort is higher, because many parts of the system have to be implemented in two languages: IDL and Java.

Additionally, the development tools and runtime environment for CORBA applications can also be expensive and may not fully implement the CORBA services. All these, in combination with the fact that developers started to look for simpler solutions, raised the interest in Java RMI.

RMI overview

Remote Method Invocation (RMI) enables the programmer to create distributed Java applications, in which the methods of remote Java objects can be invoked from other Java Virtual Machines, possibly on different hosts.

A Java program can make a call on a remote object once it obtains a reference to the remote object, either by looking up the remote object in the naming service or by receiving the reference as an argument or a return value. RMI uses object serialization to marshal and demarshal parameters, something that allows RMI programs to pass by value objects so that the server can operate on a local copy. Another advanced feature of RMI is the distributed garbage collection, a feature that is not available in CORBA today.

However, there are some known deficiencies of RMI, such as multiple-language support, and the lack of all of the services that CORBA supports. For example, RMI supports a naming service, but no transactions or persistence services as CORBA does. Java RMI does not even contain any provision for application level security. Also, the configuration of RMI ports in firewalls can be very difficult. All these limitations led to the combination of the two technologies.

RMI over IIOP

The two previous sections showed that neither CORBA nor Java RMI were sufficient enough to address all the issues that a Java developer faces when building enterprise applications. Although these two technologies have some holes, they can complement each other in a unique way.

RMI over IIOP (RMI-IIOP) combines the best features of RMI with those of CORBA. Like RMI, RMI-IIOP allows developers to use only Java. Developers do not have to develop in both Java and IDL. RMI-IIOP allows developers to build classes that pass any serializable Java object as remote method argument or return value. By using IIOP as communication protocol, RMI-IIOP applications are interoperable with other CORBA applications. The synthesis of these two technologies results in a unique combination of power and ease of use, the *Enterprise JavaBeans*.

From CORBA to EJBs

CORBA as an architecture has been well accepted and successfully used in many projects.

However, CORBA has some drawbacks:

► CORBA has a steep learning curve. In many cases the low-level APIs are too complex for enabling rapid application development.

► The different CORBA infrastructures were less portable than expected. Until the introduction of EJB in 1998, CORBA had no complete server-side component model and distributed object framework. The CORBA vendors (or developers) had to integrate the CORBA services with a own, non-standard application layer.

  In 1999, a year after the introduction of Enterprise JavaBeans 1.0, the OMG group has published the CORBA Component Model (CCM). However, the application server market has been focusing on EJB component solutions.

The announcement of EJB was a big hit for the CORBA community. EJB was designed to be 100% CORBA-compliant and augments CORBA with a server-side component model by defining interfaces between the components (EJBs) and the managed object framework (EJB container). All the major CORBA vendors were heavily involved in the development of the EJB specifications published by Sun Microsystems.

The EJB technology complements CORBA quite nicely. CORBA provides a great standards-based infrastructure on which to build EJB servers. EJB technology makes it easier to build applications on top of a CORBA infrastructure. With EJB the burden of low-level APIs has been shifted from the application developer to the application server infrastructure (EJB container).

Enterprise JavaBeans

Enterprise JavaBeans provided a way to improve the existing CORBA model by enhancing it with some of the best Java RMI features. The EJB model enables the Java developer to produce pure distributed applications in a simple manner. The key concepts of using enterprise beans are:

► EJBs are found or created by using an object factory that is inherited from CORBA. An EJB developer creates a Java interface, the home interface, which defines the ways in which remote objects are created or found. The EJB factory, which implements these interfaces, is called *EJB home*. Clients locate EJB homes through the Java Naming and Directory Service (JNDI).

► EJBs are accessed through a simple Java interface, the *remote interface*. The remote interface is inherited from Java RMI and provides to the programmer all the externally accessible methods of the remote object. In the EJB world, it is the *EJB object* that implements the remote interface, and allows the client to use the business logic that the remote object implements.

► EJBs use RMI-IIOP. This means that there is a well-defined, standard mapping of EJB interfaces to CORBA IDL. This assures interoperability between different systems that implement EJB servers or CORBA systems. This also provides firewall support to EJB applications.

► There are standard ways for building persistent EJBs, both through vendor-provided frameworks (the container-managed persistence model, or CMP), and through a user-developed persistence mechanism (the bean-managed persistence model, or BMP).

► There is a standard transaction model for EJBs offered through the Java Transaction API (JTA). The underlying transaction service allows an application to update data in multiple data sources within a single (distributed) transaction.

► EJBs are built upon a security model that allows the person deploying the EJB to determine what access should be granted to whom at an EJB or method level.

► An EJB is a component that implements business logic in a distributed enterprise application. An EJB container is where EJBs reside. The EJB container is responsible for making the EJBs available to the client. EJBs are deployed into EJB containers and run on Enterprise Java Servers (EJS).

JavaBeans versus Enterprise JavaBeans

JavaBeans is the component model for Java. Each JavaBean has properties, methods, and events. Enterprise JavaBeans also describe, among other things, a component model. However, these two component models are not identical.

JavaBeans are intended to be reusable software components that can be visually manipulated in a builder tool. Therefore, the JavaBeans specification describes in detail the APIs for connecting beans to each other through the event model, where one bean acts as an event listener and the other as an event source. Bean customization is done at assembly time by using properties. JavaBeans do not require a special container. They can exist inside a Java Virtual Machine.

Enterprise JavaBeans are strongly associated with a services framework. No event model is used by Enterprise JavaBeans. Customization is done at runtime by using a deployment descriptor. Enterprise JavaBeans do require an EJB container, in which they are deployed. This container should provide all the services defined by the framework and it must reside within an enterprise Java server.

So, the two component models are used in different ways. The JavaBeans model supports application assembly in a builder tool, while the Enterprise JavaBeans model supports a distributed object model. JavaBeans do not have their own container, so trying to locate them on a remote physical machine is theoretically impossible. Non-graphical server-side JavaBeans (for example, RMI server beans) could be also used instead of Enterprise JavaBeans, but that would require the implementation of an enterprise Java server framework.

EJB and CORBA interoperability

To ensure interoperability between EJB and CORBA technology, Sun Microsystems created a mapping between the EJB specifications and CORBA. The mapping includes object distribution, naming, and transactions.

Interoperability provides the following benefits:

► CORBA clients can access EJB components deployed in CORBA-based EJB servers.

► Client programs can mix calls to CORBA objects with calls to enterprise beans within the same transaction context.

► Transactions can span multiple beans located on multiple CORBA-based EJB servers from different vendors.

The EJB naming service, which is based on the CORBA Object Services (COS) naming service, makes EJB components available to CORBA clients. The Java Naming and Directory Interface (JNDI) provides an interface to COS for Java clients.

EJB transaction low-level support depends on the CORBA transaction service, Object Transaction Service (OTS). The Java Transaction Service (JTS) represents the Java binding of OTS. CORBA-based EJB containers must ensure transaction boundary setting from CORBA clients via OTS interface as well as transaction demarcation by Java Transaction API (JTA), which is the application-level interface to JTS. JTA also represents the Java binding of the Open Group XA interface for registering an application resource, for example a connection, to an external transaction manager (foundation for distributed transaction and two-phase commit respectively). RMI-IIOP enables distribution of EJBs and CORBA objects.

Implementing a scalable service in prior EJB specifications inside a container is similar to how the container handles enterprise beans internally. The instances of the EJB classes and the lifetime of these instances are handled by the container. This is one of the reasons for adding the message-driven bean type to the specification.

Adopting EJB technology

The EJB technology is relatively new compared to CORBA and RMI. However, it has gained a lot of attention from many organizations and companies. Today, there are many parties that are committed to this new open standard and they are doing big investments in this technology by improving and advancing the EJB specifications.

Adopting this technology is a step towards a more structured and standard way, and there should not be any hesitation in the relatively longer skill developing cycle compared to other traditional approaches. This is an investment that will be returned in many ways.

End-to-end enterprise application development

Let's go through a scenario where you, as an IT project manager, have a project where you are going to use EJBs. What steps are you going to follow to develop your application?

Application server market analysis

First, you have to analyze the market for EJB container/servers, also called application servers. The vendors or container/server providers have lots of information published on the Web. However, be aware that some companies only sell containers, not application servers, which means you will have to buy two products instead of one.

Reuse or develop

The next step is to determine which EJBs you could reuse instead of writing them yourself. Search the Internet to find companies that provide EJB (bean providers), and visit their sites.

Development

After that research, you are now finally ready to start your development and assemble the enterprise beans to form your application; you are now a bean assembler.

Deployment

After the development is done, all the enterprise bean classes are contained in a JAR file, the EJB-JAR. Before an enterprise bean can be installed in an application server, the enterprise bean must be deployed. During deployment, several application server-specific classes are generated.

Deployment descriptor

The deployment descriptor contains attribute and environment settings that define how the application server invokes enterprise bean functionality. Every enterprise bean must have a deployment descriptor that contains attributes used by the application server. These attributes can often be set for the entire enterprise bean or for individual methods of the bean.

The deployment descriptor is part of the contract between the bean developer and the bean consumer. This contract verifies that all the necessary information for assembling and deploying the application, is passed between the bean provider, the application assembler, and the application deployer.

The role of the deployment descriptor is to capture the declarative information (for example, information that is not included directly in the enterprise beans code) that is intended for the consumer of the beans.

There are two basic kinds of information in the deployment descriptor:

- *Enterprise bean structural information*—Structural information describes the structure of an enterprise bean and declares an enterprise bean's external dependencies. Providing structural information in the deployment descriptor is mandatory for the bean developer. The structural information cannot, in general, be changed because doing so could break the enterprise bean. For example, isolation levels and transaction attributes are structural information.

- *Application assembly information*—Application assembly information describes how the enterprise beans are composed into a larger application deployment unit. Providing assembly information in the deployment descriptor is optional for the bean developer. Assembly-level information can be changed without breaking the enterprise bean function, although doing so may alter the behavior of an assembled application.

Install application

At this point, the deployer still has to install the application in the container/server environment. At the end of this operation, the application is live and can be either tested or placed in production. The system administrator is now in charge.

Summary

This chapter provided a high-level overview on Enterprise JavaBeans, the underlying J2EE platform, and the EJB specification.

2

EJB architecture and concepts

EJBs provide the architecture for server-side component-based distributed computing. EJBs typically represent a business process that can be shared across applications as well as across the network.

In Chapter 1, "Introduction to Enterprise JavaBeans" on page 3, several distributed technology approaches were presented that provided the foundation for distributed objects and component-based architectures. The goals of J2EE and EJB technology were introduced, as well as the role IBM plays in providing products to support these technologies. Distributed objects are really the foundation of EJBs.

This chapter is all about EJBs. It presents at a high level all the major concepts of the EJB framework. Such topics as roles, types of EJBs, and the APIs are discussed. There is a lot of material here to cover, and it is a technical chapter geared toward the EJB architect or developer.

For more information on EJB technology, please see the following URLs:

```
http://java.sun.com/j2ee/
http://java.sun.com/products/ejb/index.html
```

© Copyright IBM Corp. 2003. All rights reserved.   **33**

Introduction

In this chapter, we introduce you to the basic building blocks of EJBs. We first discuss how the EJB server and container work together to provide the basic runtime architecture needed to house your EJBs. You need to have a basic understanding of how the services of the container are made available to the EJBs, and the contracts between EJBs and their containers, in order to take advantage of these services.

We then discuss the elements of the EJB components, which are the actual EJBs themselves. Topics such as the classes and interfaces that constitute an EJB, the different types of EJBs, and some of the APIs that support the bean-container contract are covered. This first look at the EJB architecture hopefully provides both the vocabulary and overview of EJB technology, so you can see how the major elements collaborate to provide what are ultimately your service-oriented business components. We address each type of EJB, as well as such advanced topics as transaction and security, in more detail in subsequent chapters.

We conclude this chapter by introducing you to a sample business application, and we apply the knowledge learned in this chapter to model this application as a set of EJBs. We provides some general design guidelines and best practices that can help you to make appropriate choices in designing your own EJBs. This application also provides the foundation for the detail work that is discussed in later chapters.

And finally, we recognize that many of you are already familiar with EJB 1.x technology, and are looking for an introduction to EJB 2.0. Special new EJB 2.0 features will be highlighted throughout the chapter in a shaded box as shown below. We felt that the best way to introduce you to these new features was to discuss them in the context of the topic that was being presented, as opposed to just dumping them on you all at once.

> ***New EJB 2.0:** A new EJB 2.0 feature. To help you understand the new features of the EJB specification, and which IBM technologies may have changed to support them.

EJB roles

The EJB specification defines six roles for EJB development and deployment. Each role has different responsibilities in the EJB development process, so we introduce them here first.

Bean provider

The bean provider is the developer of the code, and is responsible for converting the business requirements into actual physical code. He or she must provide the necessary classes that constitute an EJB, as well as providing the deployment file describing the runtime settings for the bean. The bean provider's final product is an EJB JAR file.

Application assembler

This may be the same as the bean provider, or a senior team lead. The application assembler's responsibility is to package all the different EJB components, along with any other application components, the final product being an enterprise application EAR file.

Deployer

This person is responsible for deploying the EJB application on the target runtime environment. The deployer should be familiar with all aspects of the environment, including transaction and security support.

Server provider

The job of the server provider is to provide a runtime EJB server environment that is compliant with the EJB specification. IBM is a server provider of the WebSphere Application Server.

Container provider

The job of the container provider is to provide a runtime EJB container environment that is compliant with the EJB specification, and is generally the same as the server provider. The server and container cooperate to provide the quality-of-service runtime environment for the EJBs.

Systems administrator

The system administrator's task is to ensure that the runtime environment is configured in such a way that the application can function correctly, and is integrated with all of the required external components.

Main EJB framework components

There are six main framework components of EJB technology (Figure 2-1):

▶ **EJB server**—Provides the actual primary services to all EJBs. An EJB server may host one or more EJB containers. It is also called generically an Enterprise Java Server (EJS). WebSphere Application Server is an EJS.

► **EJB container**—Provides the runtime environment for the enterprise bean instances, and is the intermediary between the EJB component and the server.

► **EJB component**—These represent the actual EJBs themselves. There are three types of enterprise beans: entity, session, and message-driven beans.

► **EJB interfaces and EJB bean**—The interfaces for client access (EJB home and EJB object) and the EJB bean class.

► **EJB deployment descriptor**—The descriptor defines the runtime quality of service settings for the bean when it is deployed. Many of the settings of an EJB, such as the transactional settings, are defined in the deployment descriptor. The deployment descriptor is an external entity from the bean, and therefore decouples the bean component itself from the runtime characteristics.

► **EJB client**—A client that accesses EJBs.

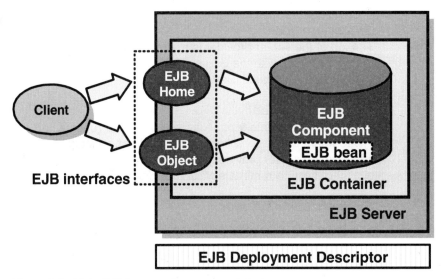

Figure 2-1   Main EJB framework components

EJB server

The EJB server is that part of the application server that hosts EJB containers. This is sometimes referred to as an Enterprise Java Server (EJS), and it is part of the application server that hosts the EJB containers. Containers are transparent to the client—there is no client API to manipulate the container, and there is no way for a client to tell in which container an enterprise bean is deployed.

The EJB server provides the implementation for the common services to all EJBs. The EJB server's responsibility is to hide the complexities of these services from the applications requiring them, thereby obtaining access to the service on behalf of the EJB, but hiding it from the EJB. The EJB specification outlines seven services that must be provided by an EJB server:

- Naming
- Transaction
- Security
- Persistence
- Concurrency
- Life cycle
- Messaging

Bear in mind that the EJB container and the EJB server are not clearly separated constructs. EJBs do not interact directly with the EJB server, but rather, do so through the EJB container, which acts as a broker to the services provided by the EJB server. So, from the EJB's perspective, it appears that the EJB container is in fact providing those services. Additionally, the specification only defines a bean-container contract and does not define a container-server contract, so determining who actually does what is a little ambiguous. The container does not actually provide the service itself; rather it communicates with the EJB server that actually implements the service, but how this is actually implemented is up the individual EJB vendors. Therefore, for the sake of simplicity, the seven services defined above will simply be referred to generically as EJB services.

EJB container

The EJB container is a system that functions as a runtime environment for enterprise beans by managing and applying the primary services that are needed for bean management at runtime. In addition to being an intermediary to the seven services above provided by the EJB server, the EJB container will also provide for EJB instance life-cycle management, and EJB instance identification. EJB containers create bean instances, manage pools of instances, and destroy them. The container provides the service level specified at deployment time in the deployment descriptor. For example, it will start a transaction or check for security policies.

All the services are well defined within the EJB framework. The framework is implemented through the bean callback methods. These methods are purely for system management purposes and they are called only by the container when it is interacting with the deployed beans, and are invoked when the appropriate life-cycle event occurs. The specification is clear on what actions trigger what events, and subsequently what callback methods are invoked, and this provides the bean developer with a predictable runtime model. All the interaction takes place in a way transparent to the bean developer and also to the client.

Remote accessibility

Ultimately, EJBs are (usually) remote, distributed objects, and the container's primary responsibility is to provide the means to access these remote objects. Remote accessibility enables remote invocation of a native component by converting it into a network component. EJB containers use the Java RMI interfaces to specify remote accessibility to clients of the EJBs.

Primary services

The responsibilities that an EJB container must satisfy can be defined in terms of the primary services. Specific EJB container responsibilities are as follows:

► **Naming**—A client can invoke an enterprise bean by looking up the name of the bean in a centralized naming space called a naming service, and this is accessed via the Java Naming and Directory Interface (JNDI) API. The container is responsible for registering the (unique) lookup name in the JNDI namespace when the server starts up, and binding the appropriate object type into the JNDI namespace.

► **Transaction**—A transaction is defined as a set of tasks that must execute together; either all must work or all must be undone. The EJB container handles the transaction operations, as well as the coordination activities between the transactions of the beans. The EJBs transaction behavior is described in the deployment descriptor, and this is also referred to as container-managed transactions (CMT). Because the container manages the transactions, applications can be written without explicit transaction demarcation.

► **Security**—The EJB container provides a security domain for enterprise beans. The container is responsible for enforcing the security policies defined at deployment time whenever there is a method call, through access control lists (ACL). An ACL is a list of users, the groups they belong to, and their rights, and it ensures that users access only those resources and perform only those tasks for which they have been given permission.

► **Persistence**—The container is also responsible for managing the persistence of a bean (all storage and retrieval of data) by synchronizing the state of the bean instance in memory with the respective record in the data source. Concurrent access to the data from multiple clients is managed through the concurrency and transaction services (entity beans only).

► **Concurrency**—Concurrency is defined as access by two or more clients to the same bean, and the container manages concurrency according to the rules of the bean type. Additionally, for message-driven beans, concurrency is defined as managing the processing of the same message.

▶ **Life cycle**—The container is responsible for controlling the life cycle of the deployed components. As EJB clients start giving requests to the container, the container dynamically instantiates, destroys, and reuses the beans as appropriate. The specific life-cycle management that the container performs is dependent upon the type of bean. The container may ultimately provide for some resource utilization optimizations, and employ techniques for bean instance pooling. Bean state-management is a type of life-cycle management, where activating and passivating of beans based on usage can be achieved. These techniques become part of the bean life cycle that the container must manage.

▶ **Messaging**—The container must provide for asynchronous messaging. Specifically, it must provide for the reliable routing of messages from JMS clients to message-driven beans.

*New EJB 2.0 - messaging service: Messaging is new in the EJB 2.0 specification. It essentially requires container providers to provide two things:

▶ Support of message-driven EJBs
▶ Support for internal messaging service

To be compliant with EJB 2.0, WebSphere Application Server Version 5 now provides both of these. The internally embedded JMS messaging that is provided with the application server is actually a lightweight implementation of IBM WebSphere MQ. Given that the messaging service is intended to only provide an internal container-level communication bus, it is not required to be a fully compliant messaging middleware implementation. However, clients wishing to integrate this messaging schema within their enterprise will find that they need more robust function, such as provided by WebSphere MQ.

EJB component (the actual EJB)

The EJB components refer to the beans themselves, and include all the classes, interfaces, and constructs that make up the enterprise bean. There are three types of enterprise beans: entity, session, and message-driven beans. The rules for bean construction (which interfaces to use, classes to extend, and so forth) are governed by the type of bean, so a quick introduction to the types of enterprise beans is presented here.

EJB types

There are three types of EJBs (Figure 2-2):

► **Entity beans**—Entity beans are modeled to represent business or domain-specific concepts, and are typically the nouns of your system, such as customers and accounts. They usually represent data (entities) stored in a database.

► **Session beans**—A session bean is modeled to represent a task or workflow of a system, and provide coordination of those activities between beans, such as a banking service, allowing for a transfer between accounts.

► **Message-driven beans**—Like session beans, message-driven beans (MDB) may also be modeled to represent tasks. However, they are invoked by the receipt of asynchronous messages. The bean either listens for or subscribes to messages that it is to receive.

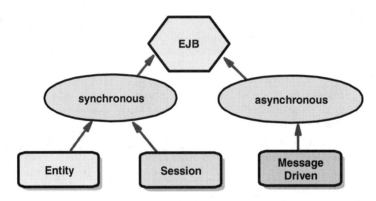

Figure 2-2   Classification of EJB types

*New EJB 2.0 - message-driven beans: Message-driven beans are new in EJB 2.0. IBM provides full support for MDBs in WebSphere Application Server Version 5, and a part of the WebSphere Studio Application Developer Version 5 development environment.

In WebSphere Application Server Version 4, message-driven beans were not available. However, similar functionality was provided in the extended messaging service support for *message beans*, which was available in the Enterprise Edition application server environment, and the Application Developer Integration Edition development environment. Although this support provided the capabilities for asynchronous message listeners, it was not an EJB 2.0 compliant implementation.

Synchronous versus asynchronous invocation

Entity and session beans are accessed synchronously through a remote or local EJB interface method invocation. This is referred to as synchronous invocation, because there is a request, and a (blocking) wait for the return. Clients of EJBs invoke methods on session and entity beans. An EJB client may be an external construct like a servlet (remote) or another EJB within the same JVM (local).

The message-driven bean is not accessible through a remote or local interface. The only way for an EJB client to communicate with a message-driven bean is by sending a JMS message. This is an example of asynchronous communication. The client does not invoke the method on the bean directly, but rather, uses JMS constructs to send a message. The container delegates the message to a suitable message-driven bean instance to handle the invocation.

EJB interfaces and EJB bean

An EJB component consists of the following primary elements, depending on the type of bean:

- **EJB component interface**—Is used by an EJB client to gain access to the capabilities of the bean. This is where the business methods are defined. The component interface is called the **EJB object**..

> ***New EJB 2.0 - component interface:** In EJB 1.x, the component interface was called the remote interface. This is because prior versions of EJBs supported only the notion of remote client accessibility. New in EJB 2.0 is the idea of local accessibility of enterprise beans. There are two types of component interfaces, local or remote.

- **EJB home interface**—Is used by an EJB client to gain access to the bean. Contains the bean life-cycle methods of create, find, or remove. The home interface is called the **EJB home.**

- **EJB bean class**—Contains all of the actual bean business logic. Is the class that provides the business logic implementation. Methods in this bean class associate to methods in the component and home interfaces. The bean class is described in "EJB bean class" on page 50.

  Entity beans also have a **primary key class**, which represents a unique entity in a database (we introduce the key class in Chapter 3, "Entity beans" on page 73).

A bean developer often develops the classes and interfaces in the above order. Therefore, we have chosen to introduce these topics in this order. The bean provider is responsible for building these elements, either directly or through the use of development tools such as WebSphere Studio Application Developer.

Terminology: We use the terms EJB object and `EJBObject` (and EJB home and `EJBHome`) interchangeably. `EJBObject` is a real Java interface that is defined by the EJB specification and that is extended by user-defined EJBs. Behind the interface is an actual class that implements the interface. This class is generated by the container when you generate the deployed code.

EJB component interface: EJB object

A component interface is used by the client of the enterprise bean to gain access to the capabilities of the bean. It defines the business methods that are visible to the client. The business methods of the component interface must have corresponding implementations in the bean class, although the bean class never implements the component interface directly (there are a lot of reasons for this, but just attribute it to one of those things about the EJB specification). A message-driven bean does not have a component interface, since it is not invoked directly by a client.

EJBs are distributed objects. An EJB client never invokes an instance of an enterprise bean class directly. A method invocation is intercepted by the EJB container that provides the services to delegate the method execution to the appropriate enterprise bean instance at the right time. An enterprise bean is therefore a passive component managed by the EJB container.

The concept of the method interceptor simplifies the component development: an EJB developer can concentrate on writing business logic. The artifact that enables the decoupling of the EJB client with the enterprise bean class is called the *EJBObject*. `EJBObjects` are part of the EJB container and are generated from the container tools during deployment. The `EJBObject` is the actual object that implements the component interface.

There are two types of component interfaces: a remote component (`EJBObject`) and a local component (`EJBLocalObject`) interface. A particular user-defined component interface may only implement one type, either local or remote, although it is possible to have one of each type per EJB (Figure 2-3).

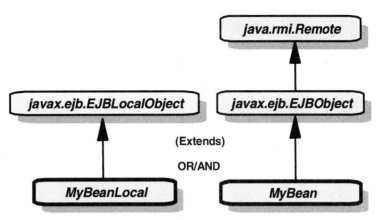

Figure 2-3   Component interface inheritance

Local versus remote interfaces

*New EJB 2.0 - local versus remote: The idea of local and remote interfaces for the home and component interfaces is new to EJB 2.0. Which one to use is influenced by how the bean itself is to be used by the client of the bean, because local and remote depict the client's view of the bean. An EJB client may be an external (remote) client, such as a servlet running on another machine, or may be an internal (local) client, such as another EJB.

Remote interfaces have always existed in EJBs, and provide the conventions for accessing distributed objects that are used by EJB clients that are *outside* of the container or JVM. In remote invocation, method arguments and return values are essentially passed via pass-by-value, where a complete copy of the object is made and serialized before being sent over the network to the remote service. Both the object serialization and network overhead can be a costly proposition, ultimately reducing the response time for the request. However, with remote interfaces, location independence can be achieved because the same call can occur whether this client is inside or outside of the container.

Local interfaces, which are new to EJB 2.0, provide a way for beans *inside* the same JVM to interact with each other locally. In local invocation, method arguments are passed by reference, and the execution is done within the same JVM, so no serialization or network overhead is assessed. However, with local interfaces, there is now location dependence, because the type of interface used will only work from clients that execute within the same JVM.

Choosing which one to provide for your beans will depend on how the beans are to be used. If entity beans are only to be called from other session beans and not directly from external clients (as recommended), then it might make sense to provide only local interfaces for your entity beans. If session facade beans are called only by external clients, then it might make sense to provide remote-only interfaces for these beans. You may provide either a local or remote interface, or both, for entity and session beans.

Although this is a new feature of the EJB 2.0 specification, and therefore provided in WebSphere Application Server Version 5, previous versions of WebSphere Application Server (V4.0/V3.5) have already provided similar local functionality (similar, but not the same). By enabling the *NoLocalCopies* setting for the server, WebSphere provided similar pass-by-reference functionality as a specific feature.

We must choose which type of component interface to extend for our own enterprise bean component interface, either `EJBLocalObject` or `EJBObject`. Remote interface methods must throw a `RemoteException`, and optionally any application exceptions. Local interface methods may only throw optional application exceptions. Both can throw an EJB exception (runtime exception).

Inherited component interface methods

Although we do not cover them in detail in this introductory discussion, the following are the methods available to us from the superclass, depending on which interface type we choose. We will see later that the existence of these methods helps our EJB clients to gain important information about our enterprise bean, and to optionally control the bean's life cycle, via the component interface. The container generates the class that implements these methods when the bean is deployed, but what is important to note now is that they are simply methods available to our client.

The interfaces are generic and intended to provide a standard component interface model for both entity and session beans. However, not all methods may be available to both types. For example, even though available, the `getPrimaryKey` methods are applicable to entity beans only. Attempts to call these methods on session beans will result in exceptions. Figure 2-4 shows the remote interface methods and Figure 2-5 shows the local interface methods.

```
public interface javax.ejb.EJBObject extends java.rmiRemote {
    public EJBHome getEJBHome() throws java.rmi.RemoteException;
    public Object getPrimaryKey() throws java.rmi.RemoteException;
    public void remove() throws RemoteException, java.rmi.RemoveException;
    public Handle getHandle() throws java.rmi.RemoteException;
    public boolean isIdentical(EJBObject ejbobject)
        throws java.rmi.RemoteException;
}
```

Figure 2-4   Remote interface methods (javax.ejb.EJBObject)

```
public interface javax.ejb.EJBLocalObject {
    public EJBLocalHome getEJBLocalHome() throws EJBException;
    public Object getPrimaryKey() throws EJBException;
    public void remove() throws RemoveException, EJBException;
    public boolean isIdentical(EJBLocalObject ejblocalobject)
        throws EJBException;}
```

Figure 2-5   Local interface methods (javax.ejb.EJBLocalObject)

Constructing the component interface: business methods

As a bean provider, we must define the business methods of our beans in our component interface. Because it is an interface, we are only defining the method. The bean class must provide the actual implementation of these methods with the exact method signature as defined in this interface (except for EJB and remote exceptions). We will see later that even though the methods in the component interface must correlate to methods in the bean class, the bean class does not actually implement this interface.

Figure 2-6 is an example of a remote component interface definition of business methods for a fictitious customer enterprise bean, and Figure 2-7 is the same example for a local component interface.

```
public interface Customer extends javax.ejb.EJBObject {
    public int getCustomerId() throws java.rmi.RemoteException;
    public String getName() throws java.rmi.RemoteException;
    public void setName(String newName) throws java.rmi.RemoteException;
}
```

Figure 2-6   Remote interface of customer entity bean

```
public interface Customer extends javax.ejb.EJBLocalObject {
    public int getCustomerId();
    public String getName();
    public void setName(String newName);
}
```

Figure 2-7   Local interface of customer entity bean

EJB home interface: EJB home

As EJBs are distributed objects, a factory service is used to create and find bean instances. The home interface provides this service, and is used by the EJB client to gain access to the bean. It defines the bean's life-cycle methods, and it provides for the basic life-cycle management capabilities of the bean, such as create, remove, and find. A message-driven bean does not have a home interface, since it is not invoked directly by a client.

Recall that a client never actually has direct access to a bean class instance. What the client of the bean actually has is an `EJBObject`, which is the interceptor to the bean instance itself. This `EJBObject` is the object that actually implements our component interface, which contains our beans business methods.

The `EjbHome object` is an object that implements the home interface. As in `EJBObject`, it is generated from the container tools during deployment, and includes container-specific code. At startup time, the EJB container instantiates the `EJBHome` objects of the deployed enterprise beans and registers the home in the naming service. An EJB client accesses the `EJBHome` objects using JNDI (Java Naming and Directory Interface).

There are two types of home interfaces: a remote home (`EJBHome`) and a local home (`EJBLocalHome`) interface. A particular user-defined home interface may only implement one type, either local or remote, although it is possible to have one of each type per EJB (Figure 2-8).

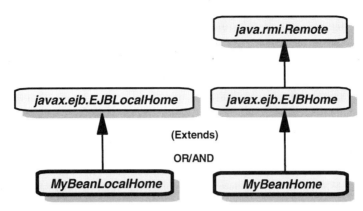

Figure 2-8   Different types of EJB home interfaces

We must choose which type of home interface to extend for our own enterprise bean home interface, either EJBLocalHome or EJBHome. And as in the component interface, remote interface methods must throw a RemoteException, and optionally any application exceptions. Local interface methods may only throw optional application exceptions. Depending on the type of home interface method, additional EJB exceptions may be thrown, such as create and find exceptions.

Inherited home interface methods

Although we do not cover them in detail in this introductory discussion, the following are the methods available to us from the superclass, depending on which interface type we choose. We will see later that the existence of these methods helps our EJB clients to gain important information about our enterprise bean, and to control the bean's life cycle through the home interface. The container generates the class that implements these methods when the bean is deployed, but what's important to note now is that they are methods which are available to our client.

The interfaces are generic and intended to provide a standard home interface model for both entity and session beans. However, not all methods may be available to both types. For example, even though available, the remove(Object obj) method is applicable to entity beans only, because the object parameter is a primary key that is applicable to entity beans only. Attempts to call these methods on session beans will result in exceptions. Figure 2-9 shows the remote home interface methods and Figure 2-10 shows the remote home interface methods.

```
public interface javax.ejb.EJBHome extends java.rmi.Remote {
    public abstract void remove(Handle handle)
        throws java.rmi.RemoteException, RemoveException;
    public abstract void remove(Object obj)
        throws java.rmi.RemoteException, RemoveException;
    public abstract EJBMetaData getEJBMetaData()
        throws java.rmi.RemoteException;
    public abstract HomeHandle getHomeHandle()
        throws java.rmi.RemoteException;
}
```

Figure 2-9   Remote home interface (javax.ejb.EJBHome)

```
public interface javax.ejb.EJBLocalHome {
    public abstract void remove(Object obj)
        throws RemoveException, EJBException;
}
```

Figure 2-10   Local home interface (javax.ejb.EJBLocalHome)

Constructing the home interface: life-cycle methods

As a bean provider, we must define the required life-cycle methods of our enterprise bean in our home interface. Exactly what type of methods we require, and their structure of the method, is governed by the type of bean and requirements for how the EJB clients need to locate the beans.

The following are the types of life-cycle methods that can be added to a home interface, and some guidelines on when to use a particular type.

▶ **Create methods**—The return value in the home is the bean's component interface. The names of create methods follow the convention of createXxxx, where Xxxx is an arbitrary suffix or empty. Beans may have zero or more create methods, depending on bean type. Although discussed in more detail later on in the book, some rules for EJB create methods are:

- Stateless session beans must have only a single no-argument create method.

- Stateful session beans must have at least one createXxxx method (with or without arguments), but can have as many distinct create methods as required.

- Entity beans may have zero or more create methods. Having no create method on an entity bean implies that the entity bean cannot be created by the client (only found through a finder method).

The behavior of what happens on a create is also dependent on the bean type. For entity beans, create implies an insert into a database. For session beans, it just means creating the bean instance.

> ***New EJB 2.0 - ejbCreate method differences:** In EJB 2.0, the `ejbCreate` methods can take the form of `ejbCreateXxxx`. This allows easier method overloading when the parameters are the same, but the methods act differently.

▶ **Finder methods**—Finder methods are only valid for entity beans, as they find the persistent data in the database that the entity bean represents. Each entity bean home interface must have a `findByPrimaryKey` method that takes the entity's primary key as an argument. Additional custom finders can be defined, for example `findAllCustomers`. The return value of a finder is the bean's component interface or a collection (representing a collection of component interfaces). The name of finder methods follow the convention of `findXxxx`, where `Xxxx` is an arbitrary suffix.

▶ **Home methods**—Home methods are valid only for entity beans. Home methods are business logic that is not specific to an entity bean instance, but for example `countCustomers`. The name of a home method can follow just about any naming convention, except it must not start with create, find, or remove. Home methods can return just about any type of serialized object, and do not actually generate bean instances.

Figure 2-11 is an example of a remote home interface and Figure 2-12 is an example of a local home interface definition for a fictitious customer enterprise bean. Notice that the remote interface methods throw a `RemoteException`, but both the local and remote interfaces throw the `CreateException` and `FinderException`, where applicable.

```
public interface CustomerHome extends javax.ejb.EJBHome {
    public Customer findByPrimaryKey(CustomerKey primaryKey)
        throws javax.ejb.FinderException, java.rmi.RemoteException;
    public java.util.Collection findAllCustomers()
        throws javax.ejb.FinderException, java.rmi.RemoteException;
    public Customer create(int customerId, java.lang.String name)
        throws javax.ejb.CreateException, java.rmi.RemoteException;
    public int countCustomers() throws java.rmi.RemoteException;
}
```

Figure 2-11 Remote home interface of customer entity bean

```
public interface CustomerLocalHome extends javax.ejb.EJBLocalHome {
    public CustomerLocal findByPrimaryKey(CustomerKey primaryKey)
        throws javax.ejb.FinderException;
    public java.util.Collection findAllCustomers()
        throws javax.ejb.FinderException;
    public CustomerLocal create(int customerId, java.lang.String name)
        throws javax.ejb.CreateException;
    public int countCustomers();
}
```

Figure 2-12   Local home interface of customer entity bean

EJB bean class

The bean class contains all of the actual business logic of the enterprise bean, and is the actual implementation of your business logic. There is no direct client view of a bean class, as clients deal directly with the component or home interface, so the idea of local and remote views do not apply when constructing this class.

There are three different types of bean classes—entity, session, and message-driven beans—and the bean class that you construct must implement one of these supertypes (Figure 2-13).

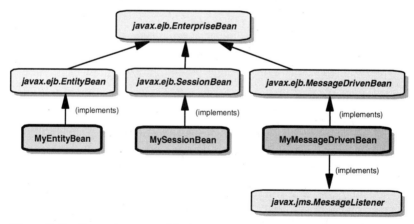

Figure 2-13   Bean classes and their supertypes

We must choose which type of interface to extend for our own enterprise bean class, either EntityBean, SessionBean, or MessageDrivenBean. Additionally, if we are constructing a message-driven bean, then we must also implement the MessageListener interface, which is the part of the JMS specification that allows us to register our class as a JMS message listener.

Inherited bean class interface callback methods

Although we do not cover them in detail in this introductory discussion, the following are the methods that we must implement depending on which interface type we choose. Because the bean class is not exposed to the client, the purpose of these methods is not to give our client control of or information about our beans, as was the case with the component and home interface super methods, but rather to provide our EJB container with a way to manage our beans.

These methods are referred to as container callback methods, and are part of the bean-container contract that we discussed previously. The container does not do anything to automatically generate behavior for these methods. We must provide the implementation for these methods in our bean class. We discuss this more in the next section on constructing the bean.

The interfaces are specific to the type of bean and what is required to support the bean-container contract depending on the type of bean. These are presented in Figure 2-14 (entity bean), Figure 2-15 (session bean), and Figure 2-16 (message-driven bean).

```
public interface EntityBean extends javax.ejb.EnterpriseBean {
    public void setEntityContext(EntityContext ctx);
    public void unsetEntityContext();
    public void ejbLoad();
    public void ejbStore();
    public void ejbActivate();
    public void ejbPassivate();
    public void ejbRemove();
}
```

Figure 2-14   Entity bean interface

```
public interface SessionBean extends javax.ejb.EnterpriseBean {
    public void ejbActivate();
    public void ejbPassivate();
    public void ejbRemove();
}
```

Figure 2-15   Session bean interface

```
public interface MessageDrivenBean extends javax.ejb.EnterpriseBean {
    public void setMessageDrivenContext(MessageDrivenContext ctx);
    public void ejbRemove();
}
```

Figure 2-16   Message-driven bean interface

Message listener interface methods

Although not really an enterprise bean construct, message-driven beans must also extend the `MessageListener` interface to allow the container to register the bean as a JMS message listener. It is really required as a hook that the container uses to invoke the enterprise bean (Figure 2-17).

```
public interface MessageListener {
    public void onMessage(Message message);
}
```

Figure 2-17   Message listener interface

Constructing the bean class: providing the implementation

We now discuss how the bean class is to be constructed. As a bean provider, you must implement all the necessary methods in the bean class. The types of methods that must be defined in the bean class are derived from the following four sources:

▶ **Component interface: business methods**—Recall that in our component interface discussion, we described how the component interface defined the business methods of the enterprise bean. The bean class must provide the implementation of the business methods defined in the component interface. As we mentioned earlier, you don't actually implement this class per se (in the Java sense), but it is up to you to make sure that each method in the component interface has a corresponding method in the bean class. These methods must match exactly the signatures in the component interface, except that the bean class methods must not throw a `RemoteException`. In the case of entity beans, these may be simple getter/setter methods, or in the case of session beans, could be task-oriented methods such as `transfer`.

▶ **Home interface: life-cycle methods**—Recall that in our home interface discussion, we described how the home interface defines the life-cycle methods of the bean, such as create and find. The EJB container and the EJB home object work closely to perform the life-cycle management of the bean. The bean class must provide implementations of these life-cycle methods defined in the home interface so that the container can do its job. Unlike the component interface methods, these bean class methods do not match exactly the signature in the home interface. However, the following conventions apply:

- **Create methods**—for each `createXxxx` method defined in the home interface, a corresponding `ejbCreatXxxx` method and `ejbPostCreateXxxx` method must exist in the bean class. The `ejbCreate` is invoked by the container prior to the bean being created, and prepares the bean for creation. The `ejbPostCreate` is invoked by the container directly after the bean instance is created, to perform any follow-up methods, just before the result is returned to the client. We discuss this life cycle in more detail in subsequent chapters. As the corresponding home create method returns a component interface, the beans `ejbCreate` method returns the type of primary key (or collection of primary keys).

- **findByPrimaryKey**—Valid only for entity beans, whether a corresponding implementation of this method must be defined in the bean class is based on whether it is a container- or bean-managed entity bean. A developer must provide implementation of the `findByPrimaryKey` only if it is a bean-managed entity. Because the corresponding home find method returns a component interface, the bean's find methods return the type of primary key (or collection of primary keys).

- **Finder methods**—For each findXxxx method in the home interface, a corresponding `ejbFindXxxx` must exist in the bean class (bean-managed entities only). The same return type rules apply.

- **Home methods**—for each home interface method (Xxxx), a corresponding `ejbHomeXxxx` method must exist in the bean class.

▸ **Container callback methods**—The final source for methods to be added into the bean class are the container callback methods. The EJB class must provide the implementation of the container callback methods that are declared in the superclass of the bean class, which is driven by bean type. For example, `ejbStore` and `ejbActivate` are types of container callback methods. A lot of the time, these methods are implemented, but left blank. When to provide meaningful implementations for these methods is discussed throughout this book.

▸ **Other methods**—If this is a message-driven bean, then the bean is required to implement the `onMessage` method, which provides meaningful logic on what to do with the message when it arrives. Other methods could be added to the bean class, for example private helper methods.

EJB deployment descriptor

The information about how beans are managed at runtime is not addressed by the interfaces and classes discussed previously. Although we did discuss in general callback methods that are part of the interfaces and are necessary for the bean-container contract for managing those beans, we did not say anything about how this is actually managed. This is the purpose of the deployment descriptor.

A deployment descriptor is an XML document describing the beans that comprise an application. It contains structural information about the beans, such as the type of bean and what interfaces and classes make up the bean, as well as any external resource dependencies that the bean has. But a deployment descriptor also contains information about how behavior should be implemented at runtime, so that this behavior may be customized at runtime independent of the bean components themselves. They describe such runtime attributes as how the bean interacts with security, transaction, naming, and other services of the container. It describes, in part, the bean-container contract for how to apply these services at runtime.

The deployment descriptor is one of the components that must be packaged in an EJB JAR file. The EJB JAR file contains all the EJB classes and interfaces comprising the application, as well as the deployment descriptor XML file that describes those EJBs.

The following XML document shows some of the basic structure of the deployment descriptor for an entity bean and a session bean. This is not the complete structure of a deployment descriptor (deployment descriptor details will be presented in subsequent chapters); it is just intended to demonstrate some of the information in the deployment descriptor.

Figure 2-18 shows an entity bean deployment descriptor example and Figure 2-19 shows a session bean deployment descriptor example.

```
<entity>
    <ejb-name>Account</ejb-name>
    <local-home>itso.bank5.cmp.AccountLocalHome</local-home>
    <local>itso.bank5.cmp.AccountLocal</local>
    <ejb-class>itso.bank5.cmp.AccountBean</ejb-class>
    <persistence-type>Container</persistence-type>
    <prim-key-class>java.lang.String</prim-key-class>
    <reentrant>False</reentrant>
    <cmp-version>2.x</cmp-version>
    <abstract-schema-name>Account</abstract-schema-name>
    <cmp-field id="CMPAttribute_1035310323213">
        <field-name>accountID</field-name>
    </cmp-field>
    <cmp-field id="CMPAttribute_1035309444670">
        <field-name>balance</field-name>
    </cmp-field>
    ......
    <primkey-field>accountID</primkey-field>
    <ejb-local-ref id="EJBLocalRef_1035426516547">
        <ejb-ref-name>ejb/TransRecord</ejb-ref-name>
        <ejb-ref-type>Entity</ejb-ref-type>
        <local-home>itso.bank5.cmp.TransRecordLocalHome</local-home>
        <local>itso.bank5.cmp.TransRecordLocal</local>
    </ejb-local-ref>
    ......
    <query>
        <description>Retrieve gold accounts ....</description>
        <query-method>
            <method-name>findGoldAccounts</method-name>
            <method-params> <method-param>java.math.BigDecimal</method-param>
            </method-params>
        </query-method>
        <ejb-ql>select object(o) from Account o where o.balance &gt; ?1
        </ejb-ql>
    </query>
</entity>
```

Figure 2-18   Entity bean deployment descriptor

```
<session>
    <ejb-name>Banking</ejb-name>
    <home>itso.bank5.session.BankingHome</home>
    <remote>itso.bank5.session.Banking</remote>
    <ejb-class>itso.bank5.session.BankingBean</ejb-class>
    <session-type>Stateless</session-type>
    <transaction-type>Container</transaction-type>
    <ejb-local-ref id="EJBLocalRef_1035497442092">
        <description></description>
        <ejb-ref-name>ejb/Account</ejb-ref-name>
        <ejb-ref-type>Entity</ejb-ref-type>
        <local-home>itso.bank5.cmp.AccountLocalHome</local-home>
        <local>itso.bank5.cmp.AccountLocal</local>
        <ejb-link>ItsoBank5CmpEJB.jar#Account</ejb-link>
    </ejb-local-ref>
</session>
```

Figure 2-19 Session bean deployment descriptor

EJB client view

As mentioned previously, from the EJB client perspective, all interactions are performed on objects that implement the home and component interfaces. The EJBHome object is the actual object that implements the home interface, and is used to manage the life-cycle methods (create, find, or remove) of the bean. The EJBObject is the actual object that implements the component interface, and is used by the client to gain access to the business methods of the bean. Both of these are part of the container artifacts created at deployment time.

Now, in reality, from a client perspective we are still invoking methods on the interfaces, and therefore, knowing that it is really an EJBHome object or an EJBObject may not be important to you. What is important to remember, however, is that we never are actually dealing with the EJB bean instance directly, since everything is managed through the EJBObject and EJBHome. This is a convention of distributed remote object brokering, but in EJBs, this is true regardless of whether this invocation is done using local or remote interfaces.

Remote versus local client views

We have already discussed the differences in motivation between the local and remote interfaces for EJB client access. Now we will continue with this discussion to show the actual client perspective, and constraints, when invoking a remote or local client view.

Figure 2-20 shows a remote invocation. The idea is that this would be executed between two different JVMs. The `EJBHome` and `EJBObject` are used to represent the remote calls that are performed on the client. The network overhead associated with invoking these operations remotely will be higher. But because the client is using the remote objects to invoke services on the bean, we achieve location independence, and the scenario will work regardless of whether the client invocation is between JVMs or within the same JVM.

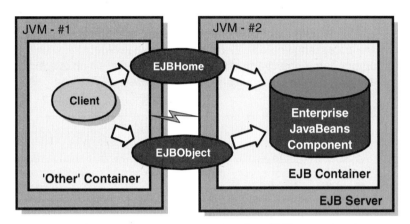

Figure 2-20   Client invocation to remote interface (EJB 1.x and 2.0)

Figure 2-21 shows a local invocation. The idea is that this would be executed within the same JVM. The `EJBLocalHome` and `EJBLocalObject` are used to represent the remote calls that are performed on the client. Because there is no network overhead involved, this will be a faster operation, but because the client is using the local objects to invoke services on the bean, we have now bound ourselves to the local only implementation, and thus we do not achieve location independence.

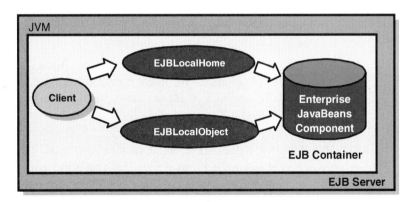

Figure 2-21   Client invocation to local interface (EJB 2.0 only)

Client EJB interaction

Client interactions to EJBs are governed by what type of EJB they are dealing with, so there is not one interaction model that applies to all types of beans. We present a simple client interaction scenario to round out the client view discussion. We continue our use of the fictitious Customer enterprise bean that we discussed in the last section.

Naming service home lookup

We mentioned that EJB home objects are bound into the naming service, and are accessed via JNDI. We use the `java.naming.InitialContext` object to look up our home object and supply it a JNDI name, which is a logical name associated with our enterprise bean (Figure 2-22).

```
InitialContext ctx = new InitialContext();
Object objHome = ctx.lookup("ejb/itso/Customer");
// Object objHome = ctx.lookup("java:comp/env/ejb/itso/MyCustomer");
CustomerHome home = (CustomerHome) javax.rmi.PortableRemoteObject.narrow
                                        (objHome, CustomerHome.class);
```

Figure 2-22   Client lookup of home interface

A couple of points about the above code snippet.

► The JNDI name is a string representing the name of the object at deploy time. This name could be a global EJB namespace element, as described above, or could be a more specific local environment namespace, such as `java:comp/env/ejb/itso/MyCustomer`. Choosing names and using environment settings will be discussed in more detail later.

► The `lookup` returns a Java type of `Object`. The client must know if the home is a local or remote home. It depends on what type the `CustomerHome` is, which is undeterminable from the above example. However, naming conventions for home interfaces seem to recommend the use of `CustomerHome` for remote, and `CustomerLocalHome` for remote interfaces.

► The `InitialContext` in this example takes no parameters. This means that it will use the default settings for whatever container runtime environment the client is running in. You have to set the appropriate properties if a different set of settings is required.

Using the home object to create or find an EJB object

Once a home object has been retrieved, we can use it to locate our bean. How we use it depends on the type of bean. Here, the Customer bean is an entity bean and we can find an existing entity bean, or create a new one (Figure 2-23).

```
Customer customer = home.findByPrimaryKey(aKey);
   or
Customer customer = home.create(aKey);
```

Figure 2-23   Finding or creating an entity bean

A couple of points about the above code snippet.

► The key is whatever is defined as the primary key for the bean. In this case, it is an `Integer`.

► If this were a stateless session bean, we would only be able to execute the create methods.

► Invoking these home methods will call the corresponding `ejbCreateXxxx` and `ejbPostCreateXxx` methods, or the `ejbFindXxxx` method, on the actual bean instance on the server.

Invoking business methods on the bean

Once we have a handle on our bean, we can execute any business methods on it that we want (Figure 2-24).

```
Integer id = customer.getId();
String name = customer.getName();
```

Figure 2-24   Invoking business methods

Bean cleanup

We can choose to remove the bean. For entity beans, this means that the actual database record is deleted from the table. There are two ways to remove the bean (Figure 2-25).

```
home.remove(customer);
   or
customer.remove();
```

Figure 2-25   Removing a bean

These remove methods are functionally equivalent. Each causes the container to invoke the `ejbRemove` method on the EJB bean instance on the server.

Remote and local interfaces: comparison

Figure 2-26 compares remote and local interfaces.

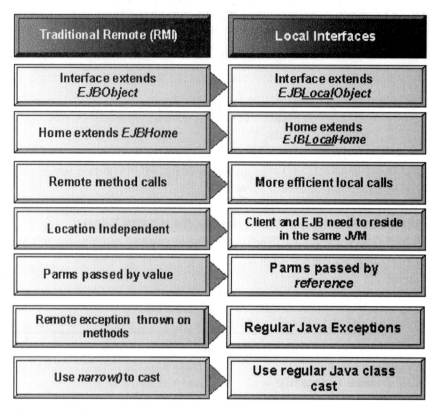

Traditional Remote (RMI)	Local Interfaces
Interface extends *EJBObject*	Interface extends *EJBLocalObject*
Home extends *EJBHome*	Home extends *EJBLocalHome*
Remote method calls	More efficient local calls
Location Independent	Client and EJB need to reside in the same JVM
Parms passed by value	Parms passed by *reference*
Remote exception thrown on methods	Regular Java Exceptions
Use *narrow()* to cast	Use regular Java class cast

Figure 2-26   Comparison between remote and local interfaces

We have discussed all the boxes in Figure 2-26 except the last. With local interfaces, the code to access the EJBHome is simplified through the use of a class cast operation (Figure 2-27).

```
InitialContext ctx = new InitialContext();
Object objHome = ctx.lookup("java:comp/env/ejb/itso/MyCustomer");
CustomerLocalHome home = (CustomerLocalHome)(objHome);
```

Figure 2-27   Client lookup of local home interface

Bean-container contract revisited

The bean-container contract describes the interactions between an enterprise bean and its container. We have already described the theory of the bean-container contract, such as the callback methods, but we now describe some of the other parties involved.

The bean contract (Figure 2-28) includes callback methods, the `EJBContext` interface, and the environment naming context.

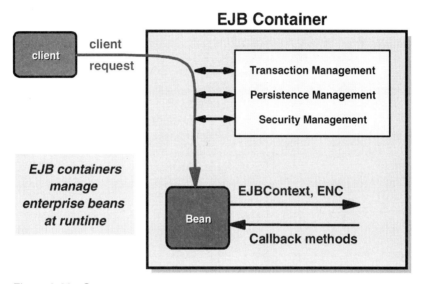

Figure 2-28   Component contracts

▶ **Callback methods**—EJBs interact with the container through a well-defined component model that is implemented by the callback methods that a bean must implement. At runtime, the container invokes the callback methods on the bean instance when the appropriate life-cycle event occurs, such as create or remove. The callback methods a bean must implement are determined by the type of bean: entity, session, or message-driven bean.

▶ **EJBContext**—Also part of the bean-container contract is the `EJBContext` interface, which provides the bean information about the container. Each bean type has its own type of `EJBContext`: `EntityContext`, `SessionContext`, and `MessageDrivenContext`, all inheriting from `EJBContext`.

▶ **Environment naming context**—Is a localized JNDI namespace for the bean that the container provides, also called the environment naming context. Contains references to environment information, resources, or other EJBs.

EJB framework summary

Figure 2-29 illustrates the message flow from a remote client to the enterprise bean class instance: the RMI-IIOP communication (stub, ORB, tie), the role of the EJB object as a method interceptor and EJB class instance wrapper, and the usage of the component contracts (callback methods, container context). The stub, tie, and EJB object implement the remote component interface provided by the EJB developer and are created from the deployment tools of the EJB container (runtime-specific classes).

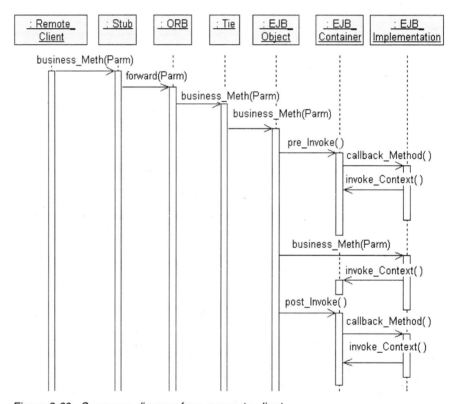

Figure 2-29   Sequence diagram from a remote client

Figure 2-30 shows the message flow from a local client to the enterprise bean class instance: the EJBLocalObject as a wrapper of the bean instance and the usage of the component contracts (callback methods, container context). The EJBLocalObject implements the local component interface provided by the EJB developer and is created by the deployment tools of the EJB container (runtime-specific class).

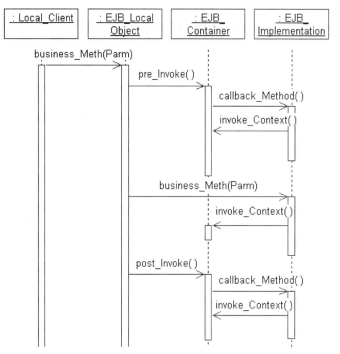

Figure 2-30   Sequence diagram from a local client

Enterprise bean types: revisited

In this section, we re-introduce the three types of EJBs: entity, session, and message-driven beans, and explore their structure, behavior, and container life-cycle relationship in more detail. Additionally, when a particular bean type might be an appropriate choice in the design, an expanded client view is also discussed. Finally, we conclude with an example application scenario that helps us to classify the usage of a particular bean type.

Bean type classification revisited

Which EJB type to choose really depends on the functionality that it should provide, what business process and behavior it represents, and how it should be invoked.

Entity beans

Entity beans are typically modeled to represent domain objects, that is, data entities that are stored in a permanent, persistent data store such as a database, and the behavior that can be performed on that data. This is sometimes referred to as objectifying the data, and the attributes of the entity object are mapped to rows in one or more database tables. Some examples of entities might be accounts or customers. Each entity is uniquely identified by its primary key. Since data in a database may be shared by multiple users, so may entity beans. Managing the concurrency of the entity bean is one of the responsibilities of the container.

Session beans

Session beans are often considered to be extensions, or agents, of the client, and perform tasks on behalf of the client. Only one client may be processing on a given session bean at a given time, so there is no concurrency of session beans. They are modeled to encapsulate process or workflow-like behavior, such as transferring funds between accounts. Although some session beans may maintain state data, this data is not persistent in the sense that an entity bean represents persistent data.

Message-driven beans

Message-driven beans are similar to session beans. They may also represent business process-like behavior, but are invoked asynchronously. They typically represent integration points for other applications that need to work with the EJB.

Additional flavors of EJB types

Although there are three explicit types of beans, there are two different flavors of both entity and session beans:

- ▶ **Flavors of an entity bean**—Remember that entity beans represent persistent data. There are two types of entity beans that govern how the persistency behavior will be managed: by the container, through *container-managed persistence* (CMP), or by the bean itself, through *bean-managed persistence* (BMP).

- ▶ **Flavors of a session bean**—Additionally, there are two types of session beans. *Stateless* session beans are beans that maintain no state, and are pooled by the container to be reused. *Stateful* session beans are beans that represent a conversational state with a client, where the state is maintained between client invocations.

Although the classifications above (CMP versus BMP, and stateful versus stateless) are often referred to as types of EJBs, they are not really different types in the sense that there are no new classes or interfaces to represent these types (they are still just session and entity beans). Rather, how the container manages these beans is what makes them different. All information regarding the way the container has to handle these different bean flavors is managed in the deployment descriptor. For entity beans, the deployment element of <persistence-type> determines if this bean is container or bean managed. For session beans, the deployment element of <session-type> determines if it is stateful or stateless. Figure 2-31 shows the types of beans, updated to show the additional types:

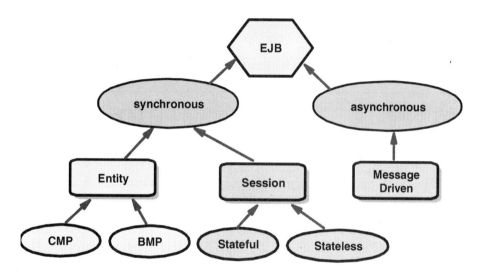

Figure 2-31   Bean types and classifications

EJB development and deployment process

In this section, we briefly the development and deployment cycle of an enterprise bean.

EJB development

The EJB developer provides for an enterprise bean:

► EJB class (has to be an abstract class for container-managed persistence in EJB 2.0).

► Home and component interface for a session and entity bean (remote or local or both).

- Primary key class for an entity bean. If the primary key is a Java class (not a primitive type, such as `int`), the primary key class is optional.

The classes and interfaces are packaged in an EJB JAR file, together with an XML-based deployment descriptor.

EJB deployment

Before an enterprise bean can be installed in an application server, the enterprise bean has to be deployed. During deployment, the container tools generate some application server-specific classes. For each enterprise bean, the tools generate:

- EJB home and EJB object implementations (the real classes that implement the home and component interfaces).
- RMI-IIOP communication classes (stub, tie) for remote interfaces.
- Concrete class for a CMP 2.0. The concrete class stores the data of the entity bean.
- Several persistence helper classes for container-managed entity beans based on mapping information that defines how the entity bean data is stored in relational tables.

The XML deployment descriptor includes information about the enterprise bean for the deployment tools and for the runtime.

We describe development and deployment for each EJB type in the sections that follow.

Developing an EJB: an example application

In this section, we present the basic components of an example application that we can use as a reference in subsequent chapters. We use this example to demonstrate the concepts of EJB development.

Although we only use a subset of the ITSO banking application that we describe in Part 2, "Developing and testing EJBs with Application Developer" on page 329, it should be noted that we discuss this application only in a very abstract sense. In fact, we skip most of the implementation details in favor of the important concepts. Therefore, the specifics of this application are reintroduced in Part 2.

Also, there is still a lot of detail that has not been introduced yet; that is coming in later chapters. This is intended to provide just the basics for how an EJB application might be constructed.

Modeling EJBs

If this were an actual application, then use cases would have been generated that outline activities that our system can perform. From this, the normal UML artifacts would have been generated, such as class and interaction diagrams. So when do we model the EJBs?

EJB modeling is generally not a separate process, but one that works in conjunction with the normal application design that is being performed. Certainly, you could produce these UML artifacts independent of whether this is an EJB application or not. Determining whether to fold EJBs into an application is more of an architectural activity than a design one. Determining the best practices and patterns to apply when constructing and interacting with your EJBs becomes a design-level activity. In the same way that general design patterns will ultimately influence how you construct your application, so will EJB design be influenced by a set of guiding principles.

In search of candidate EJBs

There are three types of EJBs, so determining what might be an appropriate candidate for EJB is determined by the type of EJB:

► **Entity beans**—We mentioned that entity beans represent business domain concepts: the *nouns* in our system. They represent data that is stored in persistent storage, such as a database. There are many similarities between entity bean modeling and data modeling. In the design of your system, anything existing in the database is a candidate entity bean. Also, the individual steps of your use cases may perform some behavior on real things. If these are likely to become database entities, they may likely become entity beans as well. Entity beans will probably map closest to the other modeling techniques, such as entity-relationship diagrams (ERD) and class-diagrams, that you may employ. The choice between CMP and BMP type entity beans is driven largely by the technology; therefore, we refer to these generally as entity beans, and leave the choice of type to later.

► **Stateless session beans**—Stateless session beans are pure business logic, and provide the services of your application. They could be used to model steps in a use case, or could be more workflow oriented (orchestrating a sequence of use cases), although they do not remember any state between interactions. Workflow is also sometimes used to describe the steps that happen within a single process, such as all the things that might be coordinated to do a transfer balance process. In any event, the *verbs* of your system are good candidates for session bean methods. Where applicable, it is better that session beans enlist the help of entity beans to perform persistence activities, as opposed to coding database access directly into the session bean.

- **Stateful session beans**—These may also be process types of beans, but are used to maintain conversational state with a user. Since session beans are owned by a single user for the length of the session, they do not perform as well as stateless session beans. They are rather the exception than the rule. Because they can remember what they did between interactions (which a stateless bean cannot), they provide some extra functionality over stateless beans, but are still business process beans, and the rules and conventions of using these are similar. An example might be an online shopping cart system that keeps track of your order as you are continuing to shop.

- **Message-driven beans**—The main difference between a stateless session bean and a message-driven bean is how each is invoked. Other than that, the pure business process that you would model for stateless session beans can also be modeled as message-driven beans. In fact, it is quite common and recommended that the message-driven bean be used to intercept the message, but then it forwards this onto a normal stateless session bean for processing. The difference is that one is invoked synchronously, while the other is asynchronous. It provides an additional technique to allow for implementation of a completely decoupled services model for your application, where the client does not have to be connected to the service in order to invoke it. Rather, they would just send a message.

Of course, we cannot think of building the EJBs as independent entities. They all work together in collaboration to provide our application. Therefore, a higher level of abstraction needs to be applied when determining the ultimate candidates, and the conventions of usage and best practices applied.

Application concepts

Here we describe a very simple online banking system. This system defines business concepts of customers, accounts, and transactions on the accounts. Additionally, the bank is responsible for coordinating all of the activity for customers and accounts, such as transferring balances, and opening new accounts. Some of these activities may be invoked synchronously and others asynchronously, while some may be invoked both ways. Periodically, various reporting of accounts may be requested, and a user is able to maintain a session while generating variations on the reports.

Candidate EJBs

The candidate EJBs are:

- **Entity beans**—Possible entity beans in this model are the nouns in our system, such as customers, accounts, and transactions.

- **Stateless session beans**—The bank that we describe has to perform certain business processes, such as transferring balances and opening new accounts. Therefore, the bank is a good candidate for a session bean, which represents the services that the bank provides.

► **Stateful session beans**—We assume that the bank can be stateless because we do not need conversational state in this simple example. However, for demonstration purposes only, we think that the process of requesting reports could be a conversational process, where the process for requesting a report will be a sequence of menus that in total will be used to generate a report.

► **Message-driven beans**—Knowing if we need message beans for an application means knowing how we choose to implement and expose the services of our application. The fact that we indicate that some of these interactions must be asynchronous is our key. For example, we might allow a transfer to be called directly by an EJB client class, or indirectly through the sending of a message. Therefore, we will use a message bean as another way in which to invoke the services that we have defined in our session bean.

ITSO banking model

The banking model consists of a few entities and relationships (Figure 2-32).

The entities and relationships in the model are:

Customer   A customer of the bank.

Account   A generic bank account. A customer may have multiple bank accounts and an account may be owned by multiple customers. A bank account is either a checking or a savings account.

Checking   A subclass of the generic bank account.

Savings   A subclass of the generic bank account.

TransRecord   A transaction record that is generated for each banking transaction, such as a deposit, withdrawal, or transfer of money between two accounts. A bank account may have many transaction records.

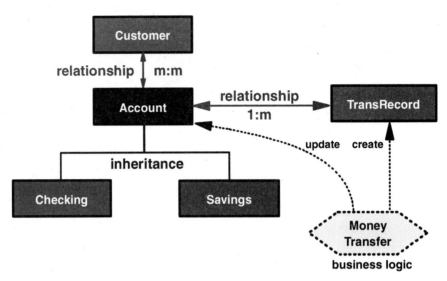

Figure 2-32   Bank model

EJB specifics

We will give the following names to the EJBs in our system:

► Entity bean—Customer, Account, Checking, Savings, TransRecord

► Stateless session bean—Banking

► Stateful session bean—Reports

► Message-driven bean—Transfer

Session bean facade

A common approach when designing EJB applications with entity and session beans is to use a facade in front of entity beans that protects the persistent data layer and controls all the client access. In this way, the session bean can tie together multiple data source accesses into a single process, and act as a single point of entry into the business layer. This allows us to have a clear separation between the business and integration tiers of our application.

There is another side benefit of using a session facade for the accessing of the entity beans. By requiring that all access to the entity beans must happen only from another EJB, we can decide to use only local home and component interfaces for our entity beans. This provides better performance for the application.

EJB interactions

And finally, we can see how each of the EJBs that we identified will work together as part of the banking application (Figure 2-33).

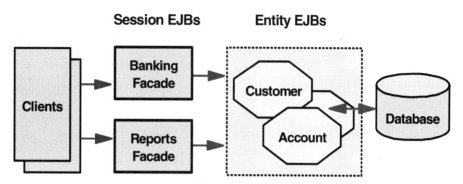

Figure 2-33   Overall banking model implemented using EJBs

Summary

This chapter described the basic architecture and concepts of EJBs by looking at the main building blocks of the EJB framework: the server, the EJB container, the EJB components and its interfaces, the deployment descriptor, and the client.

We also introduced a sample banking application as the base for further discussions.

3

Entity beans

This chapter covers the structure and features of entity beans, and describes the development process of building entity beans.

© Copyright IBM Corp. 2003. All rights reserved.

Introduction

Entity beans represent business or domain-specific concepts, and are typically the *nouns* of your system, representing fine-grained concepts such as customers and accounts. They usually represent data (entities) stored in a database. Since they represent data that is persistent in that database, changes to the bean result in changes to the database.

Entity beans allow us to objectify our data, and there are a lot of good reasons why working with objects representing the data, versus doing data access directly, is better. For example, it is a lot easier to work with objects, and they become reusable components in a system. Also, it frees us up from having to worry about developing functionality such as concurrency, transactions, security, by allowing us to leverage the services of the container. And by leveraging the persistence services of the container, we can concentrate on mapping our beans to data and providing the corresponding business methods of those beans, instead of writing SQL.

> ***New EJB 2.0 - Entity Bean features:** Most of the changes in EJB 1.x to EJB 2.0 specifications are centered around entity beans and how the container can manage and find these entities. These changes are discussed throughout this chapter and the next.
>
> The changes are so significant that EJB 2.0 beans are not backward compatible with EJB 1.1, and EJB server and container providers supporting EJB 2.0 must also support EJB 1.1. Specifying the version is a deployment option.
>
> This book addresses only EJB 2.0 development.

Why develop the entity beans first?

Entity beans are the most complex type of EJB, so why talk about the most complex enterprise beans first? Why not give us a Hello World session bean to work with first? (Hello World as an entity bean wouldn't make sense unless the words were somehow stored in a database.) We have seen that, although not required, entity beans are fine-grained objects generally used by other courser-grained EJBs, particularly session beans. Therefore, to give our session beans something ready-made to work with, we discuss developing entity beans first, and then move onto session beans.

In the real world, this work-backwards approach is a common one, and allows us to concentrate on and model the structural and behavioral aspects of our domain model, and associate process level interactions (use cases and workflow) later on. Of course, we are not saying that all your entity beans would be developed before any other parts of your system, but that they can usually be developed and tested independently from those other parts of your system. The coordinated design process that drives the definition of the remote and home interface methods must still occur, but it is sometimes common to have one part of a development team concentrate on building the entity beans, much in the same way that servlet and JSP development tasks were often separate efforts performed by different developers.

Entity bean concepts

An entity bean is used to represent a permanent object such as a customer or an account. In the most common case, the permanent data that represents the state of the enterprise bean is stored in a relational database. The attributes of the object are mapped to rows in one or more tables. Since the state is stored in a database, the state of an enterprise bean persists longer than the request, the session, or even the server or container lifetime. This is why we sometimes say that entity beans survive a server crash.

Although it is most likely a relational database, the data could theoretically come from any type of data source, and entity beans might be an appropriate choice if this data can associate to a specific concept in our domain. For example, an entity bean could be used to represent data that exists in a VSAM file accessible through CICS transactions, assuming that the row in the VSAM file somehow associates to an actual domain concept in our system. It would be inappropriate to use entity beans simply to wrap all data access, without a corresponding domain object model.

Entity beans are intended for representing business objects, or in other words domain objects (we use these terms synonymously). Business objects are the central objects in an enterprise. They are the actors in daily business processes of an enterprise. Therefore entity beans are business logic beans in addition to data access beans.

The most important properties of entity beans are:

- ▸ They represents a persistent domain object
- ▸ They support concurrent access
- ▸ The instances are container managed (instance pooling) and therefore provide scalability
- ▸ They may execute within a security and transactional context

Entity bean types

Depending on the way the persistence is managed, there are two kinds of entity beans: *container-managed persistence* (CMP) and *bean-managed persistence* (BMP) beans. Persistence can be defined as the data access protocol for transferring the state of the object between the entity bean and the underlying data source.

Container-managed persistence (CMP)

Entity beans that delegate their persistence to their EJB container are called container-managed persistence (CMP) entity beans.

What does it mean to delegate the persistence to the EJB container? Simply, as bean providers, we do not have to code any database access directly into our entity beans; we let the container do it for us. The only thing we must provide are the abstract data-to-object mappings that map the fields in our bean to a database, and the abstract methods that correlate to those fields. The container knows that data is to be persisted because the mappings are defined in the deployment descriptor, and during deployment, the JDBC code to perform the operations is generated by the container. When the beans are actually deployed, associations to real data sources can be made to dynamically bind the bean to the data. In this way, the CMPs are abstract classes that associate to data, but do not provide any implementation for accessing data themselves.

Of course, this is an oversimplification. Everything is not completely abstracted away and hidden from the developer because the developer has to have some knowledge of the underlying data sources at the time of development, to create and test the mappings in the first place. It's just that defining the deployment descriptor abstract mappings is a separate and distinct process from associating those mappings to a real data source at deployment time. One of the powers of the Application Developer is that when developing a bean, it gives you the tools and means to both define the mappings and create deployment bindings at the same time to facilitate deployment and testing.

Hiding the knowledge is not really the primary reason for having an abstraction such as this, where the definition and development of the bean and its mappings is separate from the dynamic runtime bindings of the bean. Rather, the goal is to enable the developer to work with object views of the domain data instead of data views and writing SQL. But another subtle benefit is also achieved. By having a separation of these development and persistence concerns, one is free to focus on the business logic. The CMP can be developed largely independently of the data source, allowing a clear separation of business and data access logic. This is one of the fundamental axioms of aspect-oriented programming, where the aspect of persistence can be removed from the development process and applied later, in this case at deployment time.

CMP: what was missing?

Prior versions of the EJB specifications declared the CMP as required. But a lot of essential issues were not regulated by the specification, such as standardizing the mapping to the database schema, the implementation of the finders for locating beans, or the details of how to specify relationships between entity beans.

Proprietary solutions were developed by vendors, such as IBM, to address these shortcomings of the EJB 1.1 specification. For example, IBM tools provided support for relationships, even though these were not in the specification. Essentially, these were features that addressed specific gaps and were provided above and beyond the specification. The problem with proprietary solutions is that there is no guarantee that other vendors support these solutions, or do not support them in the same way, so the beans were not portable without some re-work on the part of the developer. This defeated some of the primary goals of EJBs: to provide independency of the architecture from the implementation, and to support a portable component model. Therefore, the challenge for EJB 2.0 was to provide what was previously missing.

*New to EJB 2.0

The EJB 2.0 specification addresses some of the issues mentioned above by providing a common persistence model that CMPs are developed on. This persistent model is intended to transcend the product lines and make it standard for all EJB vendors. Specifically, the specification provides:

► An abstract persistence schema—This enables CMP mappings to be done in an abstract way for all vendor tools.

► EJB QL—A standardized query language for finding and locating beans. Although it is not actually SQL, it is an SQL-like language that supports a subset of SQL functions.

► Container-managed relationships (CMR)—Standardized how beans are related to other beans, and supports the relationship types of one-to-one, one-to-many, and many-to-many. Is actually also included as a part of the abstract persistence schema.

Application Developer and VisualAge for Java have long provided support within the tool set for building schemas and managing relationships of beans. Application Developer Version 5 provides updated tooling for the building of beans on this new, abstract model.

CMP 1.1 compatibility

The implementation of the EJB 2.0 compliant EJB container contains a compatibility mode for running EJB 1.1 components, as required by the specification. Therefore, EJBs developed on the older model can still be migrated to the newer platform without changes. This is a requirement of the specification.

Bean-managed persistence (BMP) entity bean

Entity beans that manage their own persistence are called *bean-managed persistence* (BMP) entity beans.

With a BMP entity bean, the EJB developer manages the persistent state of the bean by coding database calls, or any type of access to permanent storage, directly into the bean class. This puts the responsibility on the developer to properly manage the persistence of the bean. To do so properly requires understanding how callback methods and other bean life-cycle methods are invoked by the container as part of its persistence service, as is done automatically in CMPs, then emulating that behavior yourself in your own bean.

It is the developer's responsibility to save and restore the state of the bean when called by the container through the `ejbLoad` and `ejbStore` methods—these are the callback methods for the bean type—and to create, find, and/or remove beans through `ejbCreate` and `ejbRemove` methods—these are the life-cycle methods of the bean. We discuss each method type, and the responsibilities that the developer must perform, for both CMPs and BMPs throughout this chapter. Most of the time, the developer of BMPs uses JDBC for coding the persistence logic directly into these methods; however, other techniques can also be used, such as SQLJ or CICS transactions.

> ***New EJB 2.0 - new BMP functionality:** Although most of the new features of EJB 2.0 were for CMPs, some of the newer features are available for BMPs as well. Specifically, BMPs also may define new structures of query methods (home and select methods), although developers must code the data source logic themselves. The new EJB query language is not available for BMPs.

Choosing CMP or BMP

Given all the work that the developer has to do for BMPs, why would anybody choose BMPs over CMPs? The reality is, even with all the advances in EJB 2.0, there are still some things that CMPs cannot do. Some things that might influence your choice between entity bean types are:

▶ BMPs are much harder to develop and maintain than CMPs. All other things being equal, choose CMPs over BMPs for pure maintainability.

- There are limitations in the types of data sources that may be supported for CMPs by a container provider. Vendors such as IBM are very specific about what versions of database drivers are supported for CMPs. Also, support for non-JDBC type data sources, such as CICS, are not supported by the current CMP mapping and invocation schema. Therefore, accessing these would require a BMP.

- Complex queries might not be possible with the basic EJB QL for CMPs. Because the container is generating the SQL for you, based on a specification that is intended to address the most common types of data access (EJB QL is a subset derivative of SQL), some complex features may not be possible. For example, the specification for EJB QL supports SELECTs and joins, but not SQL date/time comparisons (in a WHERE clause). (More about EJB QL in "EJB query language (EJB QL)" on page 149.)

- IBM-specific EJB QL extensions were introduced to fill some of the gaps in the EJB QL specification, and provide for more powerful CMP solutions in the tooling for EJBs. However, using these may not give you complete 100% portability of your entity beans. This is not really a big deal if you plan to stick with WebSphere, but it is important if the beans may not be truly portable to another application server. For example, IBM provides you with an extension to do the SQL date/time comparisons, and using these will save you some of the headaches of having to do BMP development. And as before, some aspects of these extensions may actually become part of a future specification. (More on the IBM extensions in "WebSphere extensions to EJB QL" on page 157.)

- If relationships (CMR) between entity beans have to be established, then CMPs may be necessary. CMR has the ability to define and manage relationships between entity beans, and takes care of some of the more difficult relationship woes, such as referential integrity on cascading inserts. Having to do this with the BMP model is difficult, if not impossible. (More on CMR in "EJB container-managed relationships (CMR)" on page 116.)

- Additionally, the container will try to optimize the SQL code for CMPs, so they may be more scalable entity beans than the BMPs that you develop on your own. BMPs may be inappropriate for larger, more performance-sensitive applications.

So, unless you have a really good reason, stick with CMPs.

To bean or not to bean

One must use caution when developing entity beans for very large systems. A poorly architected entity bean could kill your system performance. It is not that entity beans are inherently non-performing, or that they should not be used for large systems; it is just that they are doing a lot of work for you, and you have to be aware of that as you add your own code into the callback methods. In fact, CMPs are optimized for data access against a particular type of data source, so in fact may even be faster than your own non-EJB code.

Although there are some guidelines that can be followed, choosing when to or not to use entity beans is sometimes more an art than a science. If customers and accounts are candidate entity beans, then in theory every customer and every account could become an entity bean instance. And if every instance were in use all the time, then things could get out of hand, because the container would be doing a lot of swapping in and out of the instance pool (of course, your database would probably have a problem with this too; this is just an example). System size is only one factor that could influence your decision to use entity beans; understanding the volume, concurrency, interdependencies, and transactional usage of your system will also help you to make appropriate choices. More on some specific design considerations in "Entity bean design and construction best practices" on page 109.

Bean identity - the primary key

Just as we need primary keys to uniquely identify rows in our database, so must we have primary keys to uniquely identify our entity beans. The primary key for entity beans can be any Java primitive wrapper (Integer, Double) or basic Java class (such as String). These are referred to as single-field primary keys, and this key must match one of the persistence attributes that we define.

Note that primitive Java attributes, such as int and float, must be wrapped into a primary key class.

A primary key can be any custom serializable type that we develop, with one or more fields that must also map to a subset of the persistence attributes. Undefined primary keys are also possible, such that the type is defined as java.lang.Object, but these are rarely used.

The primary key is specified in the deployment descriptor element of <prim-key-class>. The primary key is the type returned from createXxxx methods. It is also the argument used in the findByPrimaryKey method. BMPs will actually return a primary key instance from the create, but CMPs, although declared to return it, just return null.

Two entity beans are said to be identical if they have the same home interface, and their primary keys are the same. To test for this, you must use the component interface `isIdentical` method. Even if two primary keys are equal, this does not mean that they refer to the same enterprise bean instance.

Entity beans structure

Recall that entity beans implement the `javax.ejb.EntityBean` interface. Given that we know that we have two types of entity beans, we can extend the conceptual model to include these types (Figure 3-1).

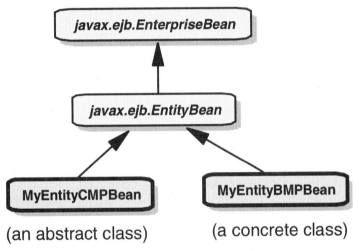

Figure 3-1   Entity bean interfaces

As you can see, CMPs and BMPs still implement the same supertype. The actual type of entity bean is declared the deployment descriptor. The `<persistence-type>` entry of the deployment descriptor may be either `Container` or `Bean`.

One further thing that distinguishes a CMP from a BMP is that a CMP must be an *abstract* class, whereas a BMP must be a *concrete* class. Because abstract classes are classes that cannot be instantiated, it is the container's responsibility to generate the concrete persistence class that contains the actual attributes. This is done at deployment time, and is based on values in the deployment descriptor.

*New EJB 2.0 - abstract class/schema: CMPs in EJB 2.0 are abstract classes, whereas they were concrete classes in EJB 1.x. BMPs remain concrete classes.

The abstract class mappings are defined in the XML deployment descriptor. This deployment mapping is referred to as the abstract persistence schema.

Callback methods

Figure 3-2 shows the callback methods that entity bean classes must implement because they extend the `EntityBean` interface.

```
public interface EntityBean extends javax.ejb.EnterpriseBean {
    public void setEntityContext(EntityContext ctx);
    public void unsetEntityContext();
    public void ejbLoad();
    public void ejbStore();
    public void ejbActivate();
    public void ejbPassivate();
    public void ejbRemove();
}
```

Figure 3-2   Entity bean callback methods

Regardless of whether the type of entity bean is a CMP or a BMP, the bean class must implement these methods because these are what the container uses to actually persist and manage the bean. The bean must also implement the life-cycle methods on the home interface—specifically, create, remove and the finders—per the conventions discussed previously. These methods define the basis of our bean-container contract.

Bean-container contract

Understanding what you as a bean developer would have to do to develop a meaningful entity bean means understanding the callback and life-cycle methods of the bean, and how this bean-container contract is enforced. This section describes various callback methods and the very basic life cycle of bean activation.

Instance pooling

One of the fundamental concepts of entity beans is that they are pooled objects, that is, they are a type of enterprise bean that may be pooled, and reused by the EJB container. Instance pooling is a service of the container that allows the container to reuse bean instances, as opposed to creating new ones every time a request for a bean is made. This is a performance optimization that is done by the container. This allows for a scalable environment, because this pool size can be increased as needed, by either adding more memory or more machines. Remember that EJB clients never deal directly with bean instances; they always do so from the container. So the container is free to pool and reuse bean instances as needed.

Moving objects into the pool and then activating them from the pool is a good place to start with understanding the entity bean life cycle.

States of an entity bean

Entity beans have three-states: *no-state*, *pooled*, and *ready* (Figure 3-3).

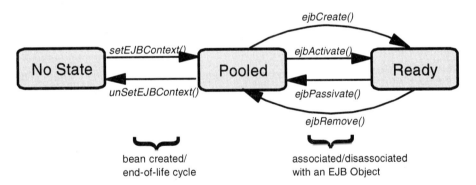

Figure 3-3   *State transitions for an entity bean*

Essentially, if the bean instance has not been created, then it is in *no-state*. Once an entity bean has been created, but not yet associated with an EJBObject, it is in the *pooled* state. It moves from pooled to *ready* when it has been associated with an EJBObject. It moves back to pooled when it becomes disassociated from an EJBObject. How, when, and if the bean is moved back to no-state is up to the container provider. It usually happens when the server is gracefully shut down.

These state transitions are important, because each state change will trigger the container to invoke a callback method appropriate to that state change. As a developer, you have to understand these transitions to know if you should apply appropriate logic in these callback methods for your bean.

Let us discuss the purpose of each callback method:

▶ **setEntityContext**—Called by the container when the bean is first added to the pool, it should be used to capture a reference to the `EntityContext` for the bean. Used most often for one-time initialization with the benefit of `EntityContext`. Figure 3-4 shows the most common form of this method.

```
public void setEntityContext(javax.ejb.EntityContext ctx){
   myEntityCtx = ctc;
}
```

Figure 3-4   setEntityContext method

▶ **unSetEntityContext**—Called by the container when the bean is removed from the pool, usually when the server is shut down. This method should clean up, or uninitialize, any resources. Figure 3-5 shows the most common form of this method.

```
public void unSetEntityContext(){
   myEntityCtx = null;
}
```

Figure 3-5   unSetEntityContext method

▶ **ejbCreate**—Called when a client creates an object through the create method on the home interface.

▶ **ejbActivate**—Called when the bean loaned out from the pool to service a request.

These methods should prepare the bean to be used, such as initializing the non-persistable fields. Be careful about defining non-persistable fields. These fields could be shared concurrently by anybody accessing this same entity bean, so although they can be specific for the bean instance itself (identity), they should not be fields specific to a particular user of the bean, because entity beans are designed to be shared among users.

▶ **ejbRemove**—Called when a client deletes an entity instance.

▶ **ejbPassivate**—Called when the bean is released back into the pool by the container.

These methods could be used to set all persistable fields to null, so that the next user of the pooled bean instance has a clean copy. Most of the time these methods are empty.

Moving between pooled and ready is what happens when the container is leveraging its instance pooling mechanism. The fact that a bean in the pool is just a bean that is not associated with an EJBObject does not mean that it is not a bean instance. It is a ready-and-waiting pooled instance, and as it moves to the ready state, the container will ensure that it has the proper data representative of that ready instance associated with an EJBObject. The container will handle synchronizing the persistent fields state, so make sure that you activate and passivate the beans non-persistent state properly; otherwise garbage left over from some other ready instance could poison the next one.

Life cycle of an entity bean

We can see that the entity bean begins its life by moving into the instance pool. This could happen, for instance, when the server starts up. At this point, it is an uninitialized bean, and it is waiting to be associated with an EJBObject (bean instance) such that it can service client requests.

There are a lot more interactions that can drive the container calling back other methods on the bean, and these may work in conjunction with the basic life-cycle methods of ejbActivate and ejbPassivate as mentioned above, or independent of them. The remainder of the discussion on life cycle focuses on what actually triggers a bean in moving from the pooled state to the ready state, or what happens when it is in the ready state, and the subsequent methods that are invoked in that sequence.

We discuss the life cycle of a bean in terms of the following interactions:

▶ **Creating an entity bean**—For entity beans, this means not only creating a new bean instance, but also inserting a new record(s) into the corresponding database. These activities usually correspond to a database INSERT.

▶ **Finding an existing entity bean**—This refers to finding an existing entity (one that already exists in a database, but not necessarily as an EJBObject). Certain container callback methods are invoked here as well, and these activities usually correspond to types of qualified SELECT statements.

▶ **Using and entity bean**—Once a reference to a bean is obtained, container callbacks occur when the client invokes a business method. Depending on the type of access, these activities usually correspond to database SELECTs and UPDATEs.

▶ **Removing an entity bean**—For entity beans, this means actually deleting rows from the corresponding database. These activities usually correspond to a database DELETE.

This will help you to determine under what conditions it is appropriate to add logic into the corresponding callback methods when doing your own bean development.

Differences in life cycles of CMP and BMP

The life-cycle sequence is the same regardless of whether or not it is a CMP or a BMP, but your responsibilities as the developer are not. For BMPs, you will have to code in data access logic directly into the methods that are otherwise generated for you with CMPs. And keep in mind that just because you are doing CMPs does not mean that you have nothing to do (even with the Application Developer). There are still many situations in which you will have to provide some form of customized behavior in these methods; it is just that the behavior is not related to data access. As in `ejbActivate` above, there may be other initialization or validations that you will have to put into the bean methods.

There are some subtle differences in how the container may choose to orchestrate the behind-the-scenes interactions with the databases, particularly where relationships are concerned. Therefore, although the sequence of events (callbacks) will be the same, what the container is actually doing behind the scenes may be different between CMPs and BMPs. Where we find some divergence in this process, we have attempted to highlight the fact.

Life cycle - creating an entity bean

We mentioned above that an entity bean create is synonymous with doing an insert into the underlying database structure.

This section describes the following:

▶ Life-cycle methods defined
▶ Bean developer's responsibilities
▶ Life-cycle sequence for entity bean create

Life-cycle methods defined

The life-cycle methods for creating entity beans are the `ejbCreateXxxx` and `ejbPostCreateXxxx` methods in the entity bean and the `createXxxx` methods in the home interface.

You can have multiple `create` methods with different signatures or different suffixes. For simplicity, we will just refer to `create`, `ejbCreate` and `ejbPostCreate` methods, but suffixes could be used to differentiate between methods that have the same signature.

Create methods

The `create` method in the home interface follows the convention of `createXxxx` and must match corresponding `ejbCreateXxxx` and `ejbPostCreateXxxx` methods in the bean class. Recall that the home create returns a component interface reference, but the bean `ejbCreate` must return a primary key. Calling the `create` method on the home interface of an entity bean means actually triggering an insert into the database. This is like a constructor for both the bean and the data. You can have as many variations on this method that you want or need, as long as they can each create a unique instance in the database. The return type is always the primary key for the bean. Create is an optional method; for read-only entity beans you would probably choose to not provide it.

The home interface `create` methods and the bean `ejbCreate` methods must throw a `CreateException`. This indicates there was a problem creating the bean. A `DuplicateKeyException` is a particular type of `CreateException` when this entity already exists.

ejbPostCreate methods

There must be a corresponding `ejbPostCreate` for every `ejbCreate` method. This method is responsible for cleaning up after the create has run. This is your last chance to do something to the bean before it is returned to the client. This is where the CMR fields can be manipulated, for example. Also, any auto-generated fields would theoretically be available from here as well. The `ejbPostCreate` method is usually empty when you do not have relationships, but this is up to the business logic of your bean.

Bean developer's responsibilities

There are two things that have to occur as a result of the `ejbCreate` method being called. The bean state must be initialized, which has to be done by the developer whether or not this is a CMP or a BMP. The other is that the actual insert to the data source must occur. For CMP, this is done for you. For BMP, the developer is responsible for hand-coding the insert logic into the method. What is returned to the client after a `create` method invocation is either an `EJBObject` or an `EJBLocalObject`.

Initialization

This refers only to any initialization of the persistent fields (remember that non-persistent fields of the bean could be done in the `ejbActivate`). Entity bean `ejbCreate` methods are responsible for initializing the bean so that the insert to the database can occur. Therefore, the `ejbCreate` must be passed in everything it needs to properly initialize the bean persistent fields for the insert. If you do not pass it in, it will either use the defaults (which are usually null or 0), or whatever you calculate it to be. Sometimes having these other attributes initially set to null is ok. This may become a problem if the fields are defined as NOT NULL in the database. In this case, you will have to set these fields to some default value or the database action will fail.

Data source insert

The following are the different behaviors/responsibilities of the entity bean types:

▶ **CMP creates**—For CMPs, the code to actually do this insert will be generated by the container based on the persistent field mappings of the bean. This could be called just as the create completes, or could even be deferred to the ejbPostCreate, since the actual time is not governed by the specification. As a developer of a CMP, this usually does not matter to you; it just happens sometime after you have done your initialization. The restriction about manipulating the CMR fields in the ejbCreate is because we cannot be guaranteed when the insert will actually occur, so we let the container take care of it for us. The developer must return null from this method.

▶ **BMP creates**—For a BMP, you must code the INSERT logic yourself into the ejbCreate method. The BMP would have to get the database (or whatever resource) connection, hand code the SQL, and perform the insert. This is where managing relationships and referential integrity can become tricky with BMPs, because BMP semantics force you to actually do the insert here, and is better left to CMPs with CMR. You are also responsible for throwing the CreateException yourself. The developer must construct and return the primary key from this method.

Things to consider

One thing that makes this whole life cycle thing a little more difficult is referential integrity on the database tables. The only fields that you are explicitly prohibited from manipulating in the create method are fields defined as part of container-managed relationships (CMR), and is typically a foreign key into another table. Because of referential integrity restrictions, they may not be available until after the insert was performed. For this reason, manipulating these fields can be done in the ejbPostCreate. Of course, only CMPs can have relationships, but trying to manage these types of restrictions can become very difficult in BMPs.

Important: WebSphere Version 5 actually defers the insert of CMP 2.0 entities in the data source until the `ejbPostCreate` method returns. In WebSphere Version 4.0, inserts for CMP entities actually occurred after the termination of `ejbCreate`.

While the specification does not govern when the insert actually takes place (after `ejbCreate` or after `ejbPostCreate`), it does imply that relationship field maintenance can happen in the `ejbPostCreate`. This is important to note when migrating beans from an older version to the newer EJB 2.0 model.

If the foreign key in a table is defined as `NOT NULL`, the bean developer must make sure that the column is initialized with a valid value. This must be done by initializing the CMR field in the `ejbPostCreate` method (it is not allowed in the `ejbCreate` method).

ejbCreate CMP example

This is all part of what you as the developer have to consider as appropriate initialization for the bean. If the create is unsuccessful, a `CreateException` will be thrown. Figure 3-6 is an example of an `ejbCreate` method for the customer bean. Here, the entity bean primary key is defined as an `Integer`.

```
public Integer ejbCreate(Integer id){
    this.setId(id); //example, because have to init at least primary-key
    this.setName(""); //example, because of non-null field
    return null;
}
```

Figure 3 6   ejbCreate method example

*New EJB 2.0 - create method: With EJB 2.0 you can use a suffix in the name of the `create` method. This allows for two `create` methods with the same parameter types but different meanings. For example, you could have two methods:

```
ejbCreateF(Integer id, String firstname)
ejbCreateL(Integer id, String lastname)
```

Life-cycle sequence - entity bean create

Figure 3-7 shows the sequence of container events when a client calls a `create` method on a home interface of an entity bean.

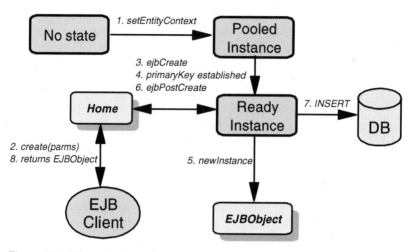

Figure 3-7 Life cycle for entity bean create

All of these life-cycle diagrams are intended to be approximations of the sequences. The general idea of how the interaction would work is depicted. It enforces what we know about the specification, such as the fact that the primary key is not truly available until after the ejbCreate executes, but before the ejbPostCreate. Some of the items, such as when the database action actually occurs, are not governed by the specification, but are shown here to give you an idea of what can occur.

Figure 3-7 is the life-cycle sequence for CMP entity beans. The major differences with the life cycle of BMPs is that the database INSERT would happen at step #5 instead of #7, because the developer must code the BMP database logic into the ejbCreate method themselves.

1. **setEntityContext**—Although probably not actually triggered by a client create, the container must populate the pool with instances at some point, so setEntityContext is called. The EntityContext is now available.

2. **create**—Client calls the create method to create a new instance of the bean.

3. **ejbCreate**—When called, prepares the bean to be inserted into the database.

4. **Primary key**—The actual primary key can now be retrieved. The ejbCreate method returns the primary key back to the container so that it can construct a new EJBObject.

5. **newInstance**—An actual EJBObject is created, which is what the will be returned to the client.

6. **ejbPostCreate**—We should now have the primary key and an EJBObject. With the EJBObject, we have access to the bean and we can manipulate CMR fields.

7. **INSERT**—The database INSERT is performed (most likely, but not always, since the specification does not really enforce where this actually occurs).

8. **EJBObject**—Is what is now returned to the client. The bean is now ready to service requests on behalf of this client.

Life cycle - finding an existing entity bean

We mentioned earlier that an entity bean find is (generally) synonymous with doing a SELECT into the underlying database structure. We would execute a find method when we want to find an existing entity that we presume already exists in our underlying persistence data store. Entity beans are typically used to refer to existing data. Entity beans are required to specify at least one type of find method, the findByPrimaryKey. As in the creates, what is returned to the client after a findByPrimaryKey method invocation is either an EJBObject or an EJBLocalObject.

This section describes the following:

▶ Life-cycle methods defined
▶ Bean developer's responsibilities
▶ Life-cycle sequence for entity bean finds

Life-cycle methods defined

The method that we describe here is the findByPrimaryKey method, which is required for each entity bean. Other finder methods exist that are discussed in Chapter 4, "Entity beans advanced: relationships, inheritance, custom queries" on page 115. The home interface defines the findByPrimaryKey method.

This method will result in a SELECT against the database, and associate the data with the bean.

Bean developer's responsibilities

The bean developer's responsibilities are dictated by the type of entity bean, CMP or BMP.

Data source SELECT - findByPrimaryKey

The following are the different behaviors/responsibilities of the entity bean types:

▶ **CMP findByPrimaryKey**—CMPs bean classes do not define a findByPrimaryKey method directly, as this is defined only in the home interface. The primary key is associated with the entity bean in the deployment descriptor, so the container is able to generate this method to the persistence class when it deploys the bean.

▶ **BMP findByPrimaryKey**—For a BMP, you must code the SELECT logic in the `ejbFindByPrimaryKey` method. The BMP would have to get the database connection, hand-code the SQL, and perform the select. Therefore, in BMPs, you code the SELECT based on the requirements and construct and return the primary key class for the bean.

Life-cycle sequence - findByPrimaryKey

Figure 3-8 shows the sequence of container events when a client calls a single entity find method on a home interface of an entity bean.

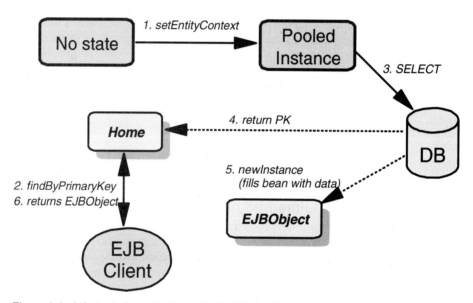

Figure 3-8   Life-cycle for entity bean findByPrimaryKey

1. **setEntityContext**—Although probably not actually triggered by a client create, the container must populate the pool with instances at some point, so `setEntityContext` is called. The `EntityContext` is now available.

2. **find**—Client calls appropriate find method.

3. **SELECT**—The database select is performed.

4. **Primary Key**—Now we have a primary key to work with. The `ejbFind` method returns the primary key to the container so that it can construct a new `EJBObject`.

5. **newInstance**—An actual `EJBObject` is created, which is what will be returned to the client (the real bean is filled with data).

6. **EJBObject**—Is what is now returned to the client. The bean is now ready to service requests on behalf of this client.

Life-cycle - using an entity bean

Once we have created or found an entity bean, and established a reference to it in the client (`EJBObject`), the EJB client can invoke the business methods. We mentioned above that invoking methods on an entity bean is synonymous with doing SELECT/UPDATE from/to the underlying database structure.

This process is called synchronization of the object data to the back-end data source. Synchronization is really about making sure that the data in the database and the state of the data in the entity bean are always equivalent. Any business method invocation can theoretically cause this synchronization to occur, but transaction management (covered in "Transactions" on page 279) influences when updates to the database occur.

This section describes the following:

- ▶ Life-cycle methods defined
- ▶ Bean developer's responsibilities
- ▶ Life-cycle sequence for entity bean usage

Life-cycle methods defined

The life-cycle methods for using entity beans are the `ejbLoad` and `ejbStore` callback methods.

ejbLoad method

There is only one `ejbLoad` method, since it is a true container-only callback method. This method is called when it is necessary to synchronize the bean with data from the database. This will most likely trigger a SELECT to occur. The `ejbLoad` is triggered when the client requests to use the bean, forcing activation to happen, thus moving it to the ready pool.

ejbStore method

There is only one `ejbStore` method, since it is a true container-only callback method. This method is called when it is necessary to synchronize the bean data with the database. This will most likely trigger an UPDATE to occur. The `ejbStore` is triggered when the bean is no longer being used by a client, and the container decides to move the ready instance back into the pooled state.

Bean developer's responsibilities

The bean developer is responsible for providing any relevant logic into these methods that should happen just after the bean is refreshed from the database (`ejbLoad`), or just before it is about to be synchronized to the database (`ejbStore`). Actually what and how depends on the type of bean.

Data source SELECT - ejbLoad

The following are the different behaviors/responsibilities of the entity bean types:

► **CMP ejbLoad**—In CMPs, `ejbLoad` is called just after the data is to be synchronized (read) from the database. This gives the developer an opportunity to do some data-level optimizations, but having any code in `ejbLoad` for CMPs is rare.

► **BMP ejbLoad**—In BMPs, the developer must code the SELECT logic to synchronize the bean with the data directly in the method.

Data source UPDATE - ejbStore

The following are the different behaviors/responsibilities of the entity bean types:

► **CMP ejbStore**—In CMPs, ejbStore is called just before the data is to be synchronized (updated) to the database. This gives the developer an opportunity to do some data-level optimizations, but having any code in `ejbStore` for CMPs is rare.

► **BMP ejbStore**—In BMPs, the developer must code the UPDATE logic to synchronize the bean with the data directly in the method.

Things to consider

Every component interface access, whether it is a read-only action, such as a get, or an update action, such as a set, can result in this `ejbLoad`/`ejbStore` cycle being triggered. This is a lot of overhead to accrue when you just want to get some information from the bean, as in read-only getter methods.

In CMP, the WebSphere container is smart enough to know if the data state in the bean has or has not actually changed, and will forego the actual `ejbStore` calls when it knows that the bean's has not changed. There is no accurate way to determine if the database itself, however, has changed, so `ejbLoad` calls will almost always be made.

For BMPs, a technique that is sometimes used is to try to manage the state change yourself, through the use of dirty flags (discussed more in Chapter 13, "Bean-managed entity bean development" on page 487). This is a tricky endeavor and requires that you have a thorough understanding of the bean-container contract so that no problems can occur.

Life-cycle sequence - usage of an entity bean

Figure 3-9 shows the usage life cycle for CMPs and BMPs. The difference here is when the `ejbLoad`/`SELECT` sequence is called.

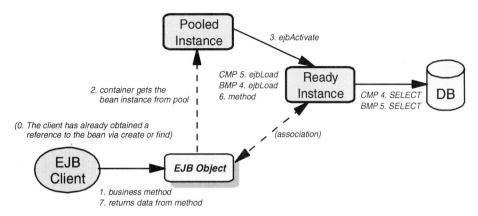

Figure 3-9   Life cycle for entity bean usage

0. The client has already obtained a reference to the bean through create or find.

1. **Business method**—The client calls a business method (from the component interface).

2. **Container**—The action triggers a bean instance to be loaded from the pool.

3. **ejbActivate**—This call makes the container activate an instance from the pool. A bean must be in ready state to process business methods. The bean may stay in the ready state for multiple calls.

CMP

4. **SELECT**—The database performs the synchronization; SELECT is performed.

5. **ejbLoad**—Is called just after the SELECT is performed.

BMP

4. **ejbLoad**—Is called.

5. **SELECT**—The SELECT is performed.

CMP and BMP

6. **Business method**—The method on the actual bean instance is executed.

7. **Returned**—The data (or none if void) is returned.

Note: In many cases the bean remains in ready state for subsequent client calls.

Life-cycle sequence - passivation of an entity bean

The container determines when it is appropriate to passivate the bean. It could be after some idle time, or when storage space in the pool becomes too large (Figure 3-10).

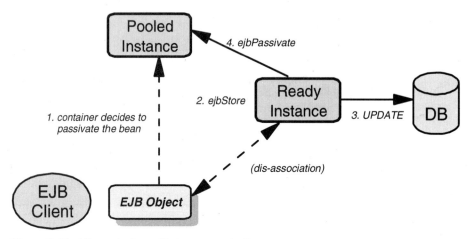

Figure 3-10   Life cycle for entity bean passivation

1. **Container**—The action triggers a bean instance that be moved back to the pool. It disassociates the bean instance from the EJB object.

2. **ejbPassivate**—This call makes the container passivate the instance to the pool.

3. **ejbStore**—Is called just before the UPDATE is performed.

4. **UPDATE**—The database is synchronized using an UPDATE.

There is no client that is actively working with the bean.

Life cycle - removing an entity bean

Once we have created or found an entity bean, and established a reference to it in the client (EJBObject), the EJB client can choose to remove it. We mentioned above that invoking the remove on an entity bean is synonymous with doing a DELETE from the underlying database structure.

This section describes the following:

► Life-cycle methods defined
► Bean developer's responsibilities
► Life-cycle sequence for removing an entity bean

Life-cycle methods defined

The life-cycle method for removing entity beans is the `ejbRemove` callback method.

ejbRemove method

This method removes (deletes) the bean, and causes the corresponding data to be deleted in the database. It is called just before the actual delete it to occur.

The remove of the home or component interface as well as the bean class throws a `RemoveException`. This indicates there was a problem removing the bean.

Bean developer's responsibilities

The bean developer is responsible for the delete logic in BMPs.

Data source DELETE - ejbRemove

The following are the different behaviors/responsibilities of the entity bean types:

▶ **CMP ejbRemove**—In CMPs, the `ejbRemove` is called just before the database delete and in most cases no code is entered.

▶ **BMP ejbRemove**—In BMPs, the developer must code the DELETE logic directly into the method.

Things to consider

There are actually two ways to remove a bean: through its home or its component interface. Either one will result in the bean's `ejbRemove` method being called.

▶ **Component interface remove**—EJB clients may invoke the remove method directly against the component interface, either from the remote (`EJBObject`) or local (`EJBLocalObject`) interface. Because this component interface corresponds to a particular EJB, the container knows what bean instance to remove. This remove method accepts no arguments. The following is the method form for the remote interface:

```
public void remove() throws RemoteException, java.rmi.RemoveException;
```

▶ **Home interface remove**—EJB clients may invoke the remove method directly against the home interface, either from the remote (`EJBHome`) or local (`EJBLocalHome`) interface. Because the home is not associated with a particular bean instance, the home must be given enough information to find the appropriate bean instance. There are two forms of this method (shown for the remote interface). Using the `remove(Handle)` method can be used against entity and session beans alike. It accepts a pointer to the bean, represented by a `Handle` object. The `remove(Object)` is valid only for entity beans. It accepts an object representing the primary key of the bean.

```
public abstract void remove(Handle handle)
                            throws RemoteException, java.rmi.RemoveException;

public abstract void remove(Object primarykey)
                            throws RemoteException, java.rmi.RemoveException;
```

Handle: Once an EJB client has a reference to a bean instance, it can use the `EJBObject.getHandle` method to return a `javax.ejb.Handle` object. The handle is a serialized pointer to the `EJBObject`. There are situations under which obtaining the handle, and saving it for later, might be useful. In the case of removing the bean, the EJB client may use this EJB `Handle` object as an argument of the `remove` method.

Note: Further attempts to use the bean will result in a `NoSuchObjectLocalException` being thrown.

> ***New EJB 2.0 - remove:** EJB 2.0 will delete the data associated with the bean in the database, and the links to other entity beans will also be removed.
>
> However, in order for the data represented by the associated bean to actually be removed as well, you must specify the `<cascade-delete>` option in the deployment descriptor. We discuss the managing of relationships in "EJB 2.0 relationships" on page 122.

Life-cycle sequence - deleting an entity bean

Figure 3-11 shows the life cycle of deleting an entity bean.

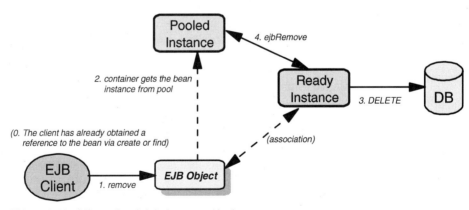

Figure 3-11   Life cycle of deleting an entity bean

0. The client has already obtained a reference to the bean through create or find.

1. **remove**—The client calls the `remove` method (from the component interface).

2. **Container**—The action triggers a bean instance to be loaded from the pool if necessary.
3. **DELETE**—The record in the database is deleted.
4. **ejbRemove**—The container moves the instance to the pool.

Abstract persistence schema mappings

The abstract persistence schema allows us to specify two things: container-managed persistence data-to-object mappings (CMP), and container-managed relationships (CMR). It is similar to the idea of how a database schema is defined, where the tables, fields, and relationships of the tables would be defined. In the EJB abstract persistence schema, these would be our entity beans, CMP fields, and CMR fields.

This section describes how CMP for persistence actually works (CMR will be covered in "EJB container-managed relationships (CMR)" on page 116r). It is one of the basic structures that a developer must understand even when developing simple CMPs.

Persistent fields

Persistent fields are the fields of our entity bean that we define as being persistable. They can be primitives or serialized Java type (this is in contrast to primary keys, which cannot be primitives). Each persistent field normally corresponds to a column in a database table.

Defining the persistent fields in the bean class

Unlike BMPs, CMPs do not actually define these fields as part of the bean. Rather, they are defined in terms of abstract getter/setter methods within the bean class (this is sometimes referred to as virtual persistent fields). Figure 3-12 is a simple example of what the `Customer` entity bean persistent field declarations looks like.

```
public abstract Customer extends javax.ejb.EntityBean {
    public abstract int getId();
    public abstract void setId();
    public abstract getName();
    public abstract void setName(String newName);
    //other methods...
}
```

Figure 3-12   Abstract class of an entity bean

The naming of the abstract methods follows the normal JavaBeans naming conventions. In the example above, we have defined two persistent fields, `id` and `name`.

Defining the persistent fields in the deployment descriptor

Each entity bean must have a corresponding entry in the EJB XML deployment descriptor. The persistent fields of the customer would be defined in the deployment descriptor as shown in Figure 3-13.

```
...
   <entity>
      ...
      <abstract-persistence-schema>Customer</abstract-persistence-schema>
      <persistence-type>Container</persistence-type>
      <cmp-version>2.x</cmp-version>
      <cmp-field>
         <field-name>id</field-name>
      <cmp-field>
      <cmp-field>
         <field-name>name</field-name>
      <cmp-field>
      ...
   </entity>
```

Figure 3-13   Deployment descriptor entry for an entity bean

Generating the persistence code

The container uses the mappings defined in the deployment descriptor to generate the actual SQL code at deployment time. It uses reflection on the bean class to determine the actual type of the field.

Things to consider

Be sure that the proper case is used when defining these fields and mappings, for instance, a field defined as `id` must match the `getId`/`setID` methods.

Every field must have the corresponding abstract methods in the bean class. However, we are not required to actually promote these fields to the component interface and allow the EJB clients visibility to these methods directly. In fact, it would be an error to promote the `setId` method because this is the primary key, and invoking it would cause an exception. We discuss design strategies to determine the appropriate methods to include in the component interface in "Entity bean design and construction best practices" on page 109.

Developing an entity bean: Customer

Application Developer provides powerful tooling to assist with the development of CMPs and BMPs alike. However, most of the tooling is geared toward CMPs. Developing all types of enterprise beans with Application Developer is discussed in great detail in Part 2 of this book.

This section brings together all the concepts discussed in this chapter, and shows how the actual beans can be constructed. We continue with the application that was presented in "Developing an EJB: an example application" on page 66, where we identified the following candidate entity beans: Customer, Account, Checking, Savings, and TransRecord.

Building entity beans

When we build an entity bean, we are concerned with the bean class, the primary key, the home and component interfaces, and the deployment descriptor:

▶ **Bean class**—The bean class must contain the getter/setter methods for the persistent fields, and implementations for the bean callback methods, implementation for the component interface methods, and any required home life-cycle methods. Differs depending on whether it is CMP or BMP.

▶ **Primary key**—For primary key fields that are Java primitives, or for composed primary keys (multiple fields), we require a special primary key class.

▶ **Home interface**—Defines the life-cycle methods of the bean.

▶ **Component interface**—Defines the client view of the bean, and the corresponding business methods.

▶ **Deployment descriptor**—The XML deployment mapping for the bean.

Expanded customer entity requirements

We use only the Customer entity bean for this example. The following are some expanded requirements and choices that we have made for this simple entity bean.

Persistent fields
We will extend the current customer that has been introduced thus far, to contain the following fields: customerID, firstName, lastName, title, userID, password, and address. For now, each of these fields will be a simple String type, except for the customerID, which will be a primitive int. A persistent field can be any of these standard Java types, or any primitives (complex types will be covered later).

Primary key

We define the primary key as `customerID`. This is defined as a persistent field of type int, but we are not allowed to have primitives for our primary key. Therefore, we have to create a custom primary key class that wraps our `int` field.

Use of local interfaces

We define only local home and component interface methods.

Home methods

We provide only a standard `create` method, and rely on the container to generate the `findByPrimaryKey` method.

Component interface methods

Each of these fields will have a corresponding getter/setter method declared in the local component interface, except for the primary key. We will not expose the primary key methods in this interface. An additional business method will be defined called `getName`, which will return a concatenation of first and last names.

Building the local component interface

This interface class looks the same for CMP and BMP entity beans (Figure 3-14).

```
public interface Customer extends javax.ejb.EJBLocalObject {
    public String getFirstName();
    public void setFirstName(String firstName);
    public String getLastName();
    public void setLastName(String lastName);
    public String getTitle();
    public void setTitle(String title);
    public String getUserID();
    public void setUserID(String userID);
    public String getPassword();
    public void setPassword(String password);
    public String getAddress();
    public void setAddress(String address);
    public String getName();
}
```

Figure 3-14   Local component interface of customer entity bean

Notice we did not define `getCustomerID` and `setCustomerID` methods. Also because this is a local interface, these methods do not have to throw a `RemoteException`. If this were a remote component interface, we would have to throw a `RemoteException`.

Primary key class

This interface class will look the same in CMP and BMP. Primary keys of entity beans may not be primitives, so we provide a wrapper for the `customerID int` field. This class must implement `java.io.Serializable` (Figure 3-15).

```
public class CustomerKey implements java.io.Serializable {
    private int customerID;
    public CustomerKey() {}
    public CustomerKey(int customerID) {
        this.customerID=customerID;
    }
    public int getCustomerID() {
        return customerID;
    }
    public void setCustomerID(int newCustomerID) {
        customerID=newCustomerID;
    }
}
```

Figure 3-15   CustomerKey class

A key class usually has additional methods, such as `equals` and `hashCode`.

Building the local home interface

This interface class looks the same in CMP and BMP (Figure 3-16).

```
public interface CustomerLocalHome extends javax.ejb.EJBLocalHome {
    public void create(int customerID) throws CreateException;
    public CustomerLocal findByPrimaryKey(CustomerKey key) throws
        FinderException;
}
```

Figure 3-16   Local home interface of customer entity bean

Notice we defined the create in terms of the actual parameters required to do the `create`, which is an `int` and not the `CustomerKey` class. The `findByPrimaryKey` method requires the primary key class as its argument. Each method throws the appropriate exceptions, `CreateException` and `FinderException`. If this were a remote home interface, `RemoteException` would also be required.

Building the bean class

We must construct the bean class differently depending on whether it is a CMP or a BMP bean. We show the CMP class first (Figure 3-17).

```
public abstract class CustomerBean extends javax.ejb.EntityBean {
    // myEntityCtx is the only actual field defined in this bean:
    private javax.ejb.EntityContext myEntityCtx;
// setting-unsetting-getting the entity context
    public void setEntityContext(EntityContext ctx) { myEntityCtx = ctx; }
    public void unsetEntityContext() { myEntityCtx = null; }
    public EntityContext getEntityContext() { return myEntityCtx; }
// basic callback method implementations
    public void ejbLoad() {}
    public void ejbStore() {}
    public void ejbActivate() {}
    public void ejbPassivate() {}
    public void ejbRemove() throws RemoveException {}
// callback method for creation
    public CustomerKey ejbCreate(int customerID) throws CreateException {
        setCustomerID(customerID);
        setFirstName(""); setLastName(""); setTitle("");
        setUserID("");    setPassword(""); setAddress("");
        return null;
    }
    public void ejbPostCreate(int customerID) throws CreateException {}
// The abstract setter-getters for the persistent fields
    public abstract int getCustomerID;
    public abstract void setCustomerID(int customerID);
    public abstract String getFirstName();
    public abstract void setFirstName(String firstName);
    public abstract String getLastName();
    public abstract void setLastName(String lastName);
    public abstract String getTitle();
    public abstract void setTitle(String title);
    public abstract String getUserID();
    public abstract void setUserID(String userID);
    public abstract String getPassword();
    public abstract void setPassword(String password);
    public abstract String getAddress();
    public abstract void setAddress(String address);
// The business method from the component interface
    public String getName() { return getFirstName() + " " + getLastName(); }
}
```

Figure 3-17 CustomerBean class as a CMP

The `CustomerBean` in Figure 3-17 provides empty implementations for most of the callback methods, but they still must exist. The `ejbCreate` method first sets all the fields to blank (non-null). If we had not done this, then the database INSERT might fail if we had database fields with `NOT NULL`. We could have defined the create methods to accept any of the input arguments required for bean creation, therefore enforcing the business rule, but in this simple case, it is not required.

All the setters and getters for the persistent fields are defined as abstract, per specification. Additionally, we have provided one business method, `getName`, which performs operations on the `firstName` and `lastName` fields using these abstract methods.

Building the BMP entity bean

We will only provide a partial implementation for the BMP methods, but you should be able to see the primary differences between these bean types. We did not actually include the database code; you will see examples of that in the development part of this book.

However, the way that this would normally work using the most brute force is to code INSERT/UPDATE/SELECT/DELETE logic directly into these methods. If this were JDBC, the normal rules would apply, such as:

▶ Finding the data source
▶ Getting the database connection from the data source
▶ Creating the SQL statement
▶ Executing the statement
▶ Traversing through the result set
▶ Closing the result set, statements, and connections

Sometimes this behavior is delegated to.a helper class.

One of the things to watch out for in BMPs is that these entity bean instances (`EJBObject`) are shared objects between EJB clients. For example, if you reference two methods in a bean, such as `setFirstName` and a `setLastName`, these may not be completely sequenced activities. Another EJB client could have performed an operation on the bean between these two operations. Therefore, if you try to cache connections between invocations, or keep connections open between method invocations, then there will be problems.

Our recommendation is to not cache open connections within the BMPs. Each method (`ejbLoad`, `ejbStore`, `ejbRemove`, `ejbCreate`, `ejbFind`) should get, use, and close connections within each invocation.

Sample BMP bean class

An extract from a customer BMP entity bean is shown in Figure 3-18. See Chapter 13, "Bean-managed entity bean development" on page 487 for a real example of a BMP.

```
public abstract class CustomerBean extends javax.ejb.EntityBean {
   private javax.ejb.EntityContext myEntityCtx;
// define the persistent fields in the bean
   public int customerID;
   public String firstName; public String lastName; public String title;
   public String userID; public String password;
   public String address;
// setting-unsetting-getting the entity context - Same as CMP:
   public void setEntityContext(EntityContext ctx) { myEntityCtx = ctx; }
   public void unsetEntityContext() { myEntityCtx = null; }
   public EntityContext getEntityContext() { return myEntityCtx; }
// basic callback method implementations
   public CustomerKey ejbFindByPrimaryKey(CustomerKey key)
                              throws FinderException {
       // code database SELECT
       // in case of errors throw ObjectNotFoundException or FinderException
       return key;
   }
   public void ejbLoad() { // code database SELECT }
   public void ejbStore() { // code database UPDATE }
   public void ejbActivate() {}
   public void ejbPassivate() {}
   public void ejbRemove() throws RemoveException {// code database DELETE }
// callback methods for creation:
   public CustomerKey ejbCreate(int customerID) throws CreateException {
       setCustomerID(customerID);
       setFirstName(""); setLastName(""); setTitle("");
       setUserID("");   setPassword(""); setAddress("");
       // code database INSERT
       // now construct and return primary key:
       return new CustomerKey(customerID);
   }
   public void ejbPostCreate(int customerID) throws CreateException {}
//The setter-getters for the persistent fields
   public String getFirstName() {return firstName; }
   public void setFirstName(String firstName) {this.firstName = firstName; }
   ...
// The business method from the component interface - same as CMP
   public String getName() { return getFirstName() + " " + getLastName(); }
}
```

Figure 3-18 CustomerBean class as a BMP

Sample BMP method with database access

Figure 3-19 shows the `findByPrimarykey` method with an example of database access through a data source.

```
// variables
    private DataSource ds = null; // cached data source
    final String dbDatasource = "jdbc/databasename";
    final String SELECT_SQL = "SELECT T1.CUSTOMERID, T1.FIRSTNAME,
                    T1.LASTNAME, ...... FROM ITSO.CUSTOMER T1
                WHERE T1.CUSTOMERID = ?";

    public itso.bank5.bmp.CustomerKey ejbFindByPrimaryKey(
                        itso.bank5.bmp.CustomerKey primaryKey)
                    throws javax.ejb.FinderException {
        boolean found = false;
        Conncetion con = null; ResultSet rs = null;
        try {
            con = getConnection();
            PreparedStatement ps = con.prepareStatement(SELECT_SQL);
            ps.setInt(1, primaryKey.customerID);
            rs = ps.executeQuery();
            found =  rs.next();
            rs.close(); con.close();
        } catch (SQLException e) {
            e.printStackTrace();
            throw new FinderException(e.getMessage());
        } finally {
            rs.close(); con.close();
        }
        If (found) return primaryKey;
        else throw new ObjectNotFoundException();
    }
// helper method
    private Connection getConnection() throws SQLException {
        if (ds == null ) {
            try {
                InitialContext ctx = new InitialContext();
                ds = (DataSource)ctx.lookup(dbDatasource);
            } catch (NamingException e) {
                throw new SQLException(e.getMessage());
            }
        }
        return ds.getConnection();
    }
```

Figure 3-19   BMP method with database access

Deployment descriptor

In tis section we describe the deployment descriptor entries for each entity bean type. We present just the entity bean elements; the complete structure of the deployment descriptor will be discussed in detail later.

Customer CMP deployment descriptor

Figure 3-20 shows the deployment descriptor entry for the `Customer` CMP.

```
<entity>
    <ejb-name>Customer</ejb-name>
    <local-home>mypackage.CustomerLocalHome</local-home>
    <local>mypackage.CustomerLocal</local>
    <ejb-class>mypackage.CustomerBean</ejb-class>
    <persistence-type>Container</persistence-type>
    <prim-key-class>mypackage.CustomerKey</prim-key-class>
    <reentrant>False</reentrant>
    <cmp-version>2.x</cmp-version>
    <abstract-schema-name>Customer</abstract-schema-name>
    <cmp-field><field-name>customerID</field-name></cmp-field>
    <cmp-field><field-name>firstName</field-name></cmp-field>
    <cmp-field><field-name>lastName</field-name></cmp-field>
    <cmp-field><field-name>title</field-name></cmp-field>
    <cmp-field><field-name>userID</field-name></cmp-field>
    <cmp-field><field-name>password</field-name></cmp-field>
    <cmp-field><field-name>address</field-name></cmp-field>
</entity>
```

Figure 3-20   Deployment descriptor of customer CMP

► We used the `<local-home>` and `<local>` declarations because we are using only local interfaces. If we used remote interfaces, we would have specified `<home>` and `<remote>` respectively.

► We define the `<abstract-schema-name>` as `Customer`, although we could use a different name.

► The `<persistence-type>` for a CMP is `Container`.

► We must have a corresponding entry for each persistent field in our abstract bean class, and the names must match and follow the JavaBean conventions of `customerID` with a `getCustomerID` method.

► Because we are using a class for our primary key that is not actually one of the persistent fields, we do not require the `<primkey-field>` tag. If our primary key was one of our persistent fields, then we would specify it here, in the format `<primkey-field>customerID</primkey-field>`.

Customer BMP deployment descriptor

Figure 3-21 shows the deployment descriptor entry for the `Customer` BMP.

```
<entity>
    <ejb-name>Customer</ejb-name>
    <local-home>mypackage.CustomerLocalHome</local-home>
    <local>mypackage.CustomerLocal</local>
    <ejb-class>mypackage.CustomerBean</ejb-class>
    <persistence-type>Bean</persistence-type>
    <prim-key-class>mypackage.CustomerKey</prim-key-class>
    <reentrant>False</reentrant>
</entity>
```

Figure 3-21   Deployment descriptor of customer BMP

Because this is a BMP, we do not specify the `<abstract-persistence-schema>` or any of the `<cmp-fields>` (they do not apply). Other than that, the only other difference with this deployment entry is the `<persistence-type>` of `Bean`. Additional tags for a BMP can refer to the data source that is used for database access (for example, the `<resource-ref>` tag).

Entity bean design and construction best practices

In this example, we introduced a couple of best practices that we want to summarize:

- **Use of local interfaces**—We modeled the entity beans to only be used within the JVM from other processes, in this case, other session beans. Therefore, we chose to define local instead of remote interfaces for our beans. This allowed us to have faster access to the entity bean.

- **Do not promote the primary key setters/getters to component interface**—Although we could have put the setters/getters into the component interface, we chose not to. Invoking the `setCustomerID` would have resulted in a runtime error, and we have other means to get the primary key that do not require the getter method.

- **Use of CMP over BMP**—In the above example, we can see that CMPs are much easier to construct. Assuming we have a supported CMP database to use, we chose CMP for this and all remaining examples.

- **Create method sets fields**—We set all the fields explicitly in the `ejbCreate` method to remove the nulls. This allowed us to support the INSERT even if we had NOT NULL columns defined in the table. Even if the fields are nullable, this technique is sometimes performed in the event that they may become non-nullable at some future time.

- ▶ **BMPs do not cache connections**—We recommend not caching open connections for a BMP within the bean class as a general rule, because a bean is shared among EJB clients. We will see later that there might be some exceptions to this with the use of transactions.

- ▶ **Primitive primary key wrapper class**—We still want the `customerID` to be an `int` so that we can perform `int` based operations in our methods, as opposed to having to make it an `Integer`. Therefore, we wrap the `int` in a custom primary key class.

- ▶ **`<abstract-persistence-schema>`**—In general, make this the same as the bean name (CMP only).

- ▶ **All other persistence setters/getters promoted**—In this case, we are working with an entity bean which only will be used locally. We have chosen to promote all the persistent fields (except for the primary key) to the local component interface. There are two different schools of thought on whether this should be done:

  - **Value object classes**—This says that the modeling of the component interface methods and those of the persistence methods in the bean should be done as independently as possible. We agree with this from an up-front design strategy, because the client view and the persistence view really are separate things.

    However, this goes further to say that to prevent the `ejbLoad`/`ejbStore` overhead that is incurred with each persistent field method invocation, these very fine-grained activities could be wrapped into a single class, and sent over as a more coarse-grained operation. For example, rather than calling a number of set methods of a bean (which cause the container to do a `ejbStore` every time), wrap these into one value object class, and pass this object as an argument in a component interface class. This strategy is most often used with remote object invocation. Also, IBM extensions provide access beans (see Chapter 15, "EJB access beans" on page 551 for more information).

  - **Use component interfaces and exploit transactional semantics**—We chose to promote each method to the component interface. Bbecause we are using local interfaces, we are working on a faster model to begin with, and therefore are not as concerned that these multiple method invocations will not perform well. If performance were a concern, we have options with transactional semantics that could allow these to execute where we could control how many times `ejbStore` is actually called (more on transactions later).

    Therefore, for us, the idea that a special component interface method be modeled just to handle this value object seems to now break our object model where we want to define and expose bean state and business methods simultaneously.

Client view of an entity bean

This section describes more of the client view for the `Customer` EJB that extends the basic client view in "EJB client view" on page 56. The examples are based on local home and component interfaces.

Looking up the bean home

Figure 3-22 shows the finding of a home interface. Because we use a local interface, we are not required to do a `PortableRemoteObject.narrow` on the object that is returned from the `lookup` method. Remember, the JNDI name is specified at deployment time, but not in the deployment descriptor.

```
InitialContext ctx = new InitialContext();
Object objHome = ctx.lookup("java:comp/env/ejb/CustomerLocalHome");
CustomerLocalHome home = (CustomerLocalHome) objHome;
```

Figure 3-22   Client local lookup of home interface

We now have a valid home factory object in which to find local component interfaces of our bean.

Client view of the entity bean life cycle

We now discuss the client view for each of the life-cycle interactions that we described previously.

Creating an entity bean

Figure 3-23 demonstrates an EJB client creating a `Customer` object.

```
try {
    int customerID = 123;
    CustomerLocal customer = home.create(customerID);
    // use bean
} catch (DuplicateKeyException dke) {
    // handle the duplicate key - may not be a serious problem
} catch (CreateException ce) {
    // handle the non-duplicate key exception..probably more series
}
```

Figure 3-23   Creating an entity bean

Here we create an entity bean with the id of 123, which causes an INSERT to be performed against the database. We could use any of the create methods defined in the home interface to create `Customer` objects. We must catch the `CreateException` and handle accordingly.

Finding an existing entity bean

Figure 3-24 demonstrates an EJB client finding a `Customer` EJB (an existing entity bean).

```
try {
   int customerID = 123;
   CustomerLocal customer = home.findByPrimaryKey(customerID);
   // use bean
} catch (ObjectNotFoundException onfe) {
   // handle the object not found - may not be a serious problem
} catch (FinderException ce) {
   // handle the other finder exception..probably more series
}
```

Figure 3-24   Finding an entity bean

Here we find an entity bean with the id of 123, which causes a SELECT against the database to be performed. We can use the `findByPrimaryKey` method, but as we will see in Chapter 4, "Entity beans advanced: relationships, inheritance, custom queries" on page 115, we may use any single-object finder method.

Using an entity bean

Figure 3-25 demonstrates an EJB client using the `Customer` entity bean.

```
String firstName = customer.getFirstName();
String lastName = customer.getLastName();
customer.setFirstName("DEBORAH");
String name = customer.getName();
```

Figure 3-25   Using an entity bean

Here we are using the entity bean. Every getter method call will cause an `ejbLoad` to be called by the container, causing a SELECT against the database to be performed. Every setter method will cause the `ejbStore` method to be called by the container, causing an UPDATE to be performed against the database. In addition to invoking the persistent field accessors, we can use any business method defined in the component interface, such as `getName`. Note that the number of `ejbStore` calls can be minimized through transaction management.

Removing an entity bean

Figure 3-26 demonstrates an EJB client removing a `Customer` entity bean.

```
try {
    customer.remove();
} catch (RemoveException re) {
    // handle the remove exception..probably more series
}
```

Figure 3-26   Removing an entity bean

Here we are using the `remove` method of the component interface to delete the bean. This will cause a DELETE against the database to be performed. We must catch and handle any `RemoveException` that could be thrown.

EJB client exception handling

Clients should explicitly catch and handle exceptions. If we use the remote interface, then we also have to catch the `RemoteException`.

We discussed some general handling of the `CreateException`, `DuplicateKeyException`, `FinderException`, and `ObjectNotFoundException`. You will have to make determinations in the code as to whether exceptions such as `DuplicateKeyException` are fatal or not. The general recommendation here is to try to never just swallow the exception, which is catching without handling or rethrowing (no {}, or { e.printStackTrace(); } catch blocks).

Other exceptions may be thrown that you have to know about, but they are of the type `RuntimeException`, so you do not have to catch them explicitly.

`NoSuchEntityException` and `NoSuchObjectLocalException` will be thrown when the EJB client attempts to access the entity bean, but the bean is not available (such as when some other EJB client removed it). Some EJB exception handling strategies are discussed in "EJB exception handling" on page 304.

Summary

In this chapter, we introduced the basic concepts of entity beans. In the next chapter, we look at advanced concepts, such as relationships, inheritance, and finder methods.

Entity beans advanced: relationships, inheritance, custom queries

This chapter extends the discussion presented in Chapter 3, "Entity beans" on page 73, to present the advanced features of EJB development available in EJB 2.0. These features include:

► Container-managed relationships (CMR)
► Inheritance (an IBM extension)
► Custom queries using EJB query language (EJB QL)

We conclude the chapter by extending the application presented in Chapter 3, to fold in examples of each topic, as well as discuss some design considerations when leveraging these new features.

© Copyright IBM Corp. 2003. All rights reserved.

Introduction

This chapter covers the following specific concepts:

▶ **EJB container-managed relationships (CMR)**—Relationships are a way to define associations between entity beans. Built-in container support is provided to support relationships in EJB.

▶ **EJB inheritance**—Inheritance is the ability of entity beans to inherit from other entity beans. It is an IBM extension already provided for EJB 1.1 by IBM products such as VisualAge for Java and WebSphere Application Server.

▶ **EJB custom query methods**—Query methods are any method in the home that is used to locate entity beans, such as `findXxxx` (called finder methods), and `selectXxxx` (called select methods). We mentioned that with CMPs, the container is responsible for generating the actual database code based on an abstract query language, EJB QL, which is a derivative subset of SQL. Custom finders are available for both CMP and BMP, but CMP can leverage the new EJB QL language.

> **Note:** IBM products, such as VisualAge for Java and WebSphere Application Server, provided support for relationships and inheritance in EJB 1.1. Relationships are now part of the EJB 2.0 specification, but inheritance is still an IBM extension provided by Application Developer Version 5 for EJB 2.0.
>
> EJB QL was already supported for EJB 1.1 by Application Developer Version 4. The official EJB QL is now supported by Application Developer Version 5.

EJB container-managed relationships (CMR)

Those familiar with relational database modeling know of an artifact called an entity-relationship diagram (ERD). The ERD defines the relationships between the tables within the relational database, and generally these relations are expressed through primary key and foreign key declarations. A foreign key in one database matches the primary key in another, and a relationship is formed.

Defining relationships for entity beans is much like the process of defining an ERD for a relational database. In fact both use the entity nomenclature, and the major reason we have to do entity bean relationships is because of the underlying database relationships. In the case of entity beans, however, we are relating objects, not tables, and objects contain both data and behavior. Therefore, the entity bean relationship semantics must transcend both the data model as well as the behavioral one.

Important: Having a foreign key on a table is a prerequisite for defining entity bean relationships in Application Developer.

We have discussed an important new feature of EJB 2.0, the ability to support container-managed relationships (CMR). CMR is defined as entity beans that are related to other entity beans, either through aggregation or composition. Until now, we have only briefly addressed the role that relationships play in the entity bean design and development process. This section introduces the relationship terminology and how relationships are defined and implemented in EJB 2.0.

Reintroducing the bank model

We feel that the best way to discuss relationships is through an actual example. Therefore, we use the ITSO banking model introduced in "Developing an EJB: an example application" on page 66 to demonstrate how entity beans relationships can be identified and built. Figure 4-1 shows the entities in our banking domain.

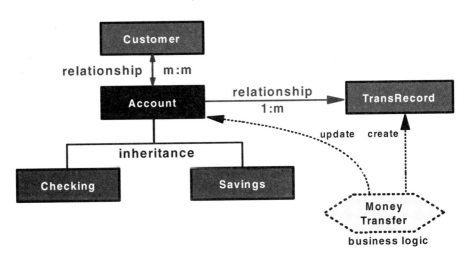

Figure 4-1   Banking model revisited

In this example, we can see that the Customer bean has relationships with the Account bean, and the Account with the TransRecord bean. This very simple diagram introduces the following relationship:

▶ **Account-TransRecord** (1:m)—This means that one account bean may have multiple transaction records, but that a transaction record can only be associated with one account.

▶ **Customer-Account** (m:m)—This means that one customer may have many accounts, and one account can be associated with many customers.

Later, we describe what all of these relationship terms mean. For now, the fact that we have two bean relationships is important. We introduce the Account and TransRecord entity bean structures here so that we can understand how they relate to the simple Customer entity bean that we have already described.

Account entity bean attributes

This bean has the following persistent fields defined: accountID, balance, interest, and accountType. The primary key is the accountID CMP field. The getter methods describing their types are shown in Figure 4-2.

```
public abstract Account extends javax.ejb.EntityBean {
    public abstract String getAccountID();
    public abstract BigDecimal getBalance();
    public abstract int getInterest();
    public abstract String getAccountType();
    //other methods...
}
```

Figure 4-2   Account bean persistent fields

TransRecord entity bean attributes

This bean has the following persistent fields defined: transID, transType, and transAmount. The primary key is the transID CMP field. The getter methods describing their types are shown in Figure 4-3.

```
public abstract TransRecord extends javax.ejb.EntityBean {
    public abstract java.sql.Timestamp getTransID();
    public abstract String getTransType();
    public abstract BigDecimal getTransAmount();
    //other methods...
}
```

Figure 4-3   Transaction record bean persistent fields

Customer entity bean attributes

We have already introduced the Customer entity bean persistent fields (Figure 4-4).

```
public abstract class Customer extends javax.ejb.EntityBean {
    public abstract int getCustomerID();
    public abstract String getFirstName();
    public abstract String getLastName();
    public abstract String getTitle();
    public abstract String getUserID();
    public abstract String getPassword();
    public abstract String getAddress();
  //other methods...
}
```

Figure 4-4   Customer bean persistent fields

EJB 2.0 and CMR

With CMP, we never actually have to program any persistence access within our beans because we rely on an abstract programming model that lets us simply declare this persistence. With CMP, we showed how we create abstract bindings of an entity bean to persistence data via the declaration of persistent fields in the deployment descriptor along with the abstract getters/setters in the bean class.

Defining CMR for entity beans is also done through an abstract programming model. We simply describe how beans relate to each other in the deployment descriptor, and let the container do the rest. Of course, what relationships we have to support will influence how we actually construct our bean classes, but to actually create the associations, we simply declare them.

Relatlonship terms

Relationships can be expressed using four key constructs:

► Relationship
► Role
► Multiplicity
► Navigability

We discuss the relationship terms based on the UML-like diagram shown in Figure 4-5. We use a 1:m (one-to-many) relationship example because this is the most common type of relationship.

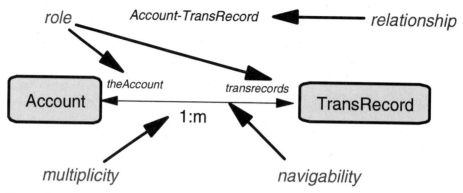

Figure 4-5 Relationship terms - an example

Relationship

A relationship represents an association between classes. The diagram in Figure 4-5 indicates an association between Account and TransRecord. Every relationship must have a name that describes the relationship; for our example we use Account-TransRecord.

Role

Each relationship has two roles, one for each direction of the association. The relationship between Account and TransRecord contains two roles: one from Account to TransRecord and a second role from TransRecord to Account. Every role has a name. In our example, the role in the direction from Account (the source) to TransRecord (the target) is called transrecords. This source/target association means that for our transrecords role, our source is the Account, and the target is the TransRecord.

Multiplicity

A role also has a multiplicity, which is an indication of how many objects may participate in the given relationship.

In our example, the 1:m multiplicity between Account and TransRecord indicates that one Account may have many TransRecord instances associated with it (following the direction of the arrow). By default, we assume the TransRecord also has a m:1 relationship with the Account, where many TransRecord beans are associated with a single Account.

We should mention that as a rule-of-thumb we define our role names in terms of their multiplicity. So, the transrecords role is defined as plural because an Account can have many TransRecord beans. The theAccount role is singular because a TransRecord may be associated with only one Account.

Navigability

Navigability is the direction of the arrow, and indicates whether a role is programmatically accessible or not. An arrow at the end of the association line means navigability. A relationship can be `bidirectional` (both roles navigable), or `unidirectional` (navigable in one direction only). The `Account-TransRecord` relationship is bi-directional.

Navigability, for either unidirectional or bidirectional, means that the beans have direct references to the related entity beans through these relationships. We will see later how navigability dictates the actual CMR fields that we have to define.

Figure 4-6 shows the complete relationship definition. Note that the multiplicity definition applies to the source (this is the way it is in the deployment descriptor).

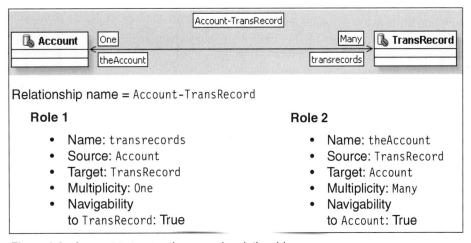

Figure 4-6   Account to transaction records relationship

Relationship types

We can discern that these entities are related, but we have not said how they are related. We now describe the basic types of relationships.

Association

An association indicates a *use* relationship; for example, an employee uses a workstation. An association manifests a loosely coupled relationship. The participants of an association have independent life cycles (Figure 4-7).

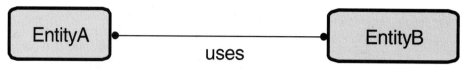

Figure 4-7 Association

Composition

Composition is a form of aggregation, with a strong ownership and coincident lifetime as part of the whole. Parts may be created after the composite itself, but once created they live and die with it. Such parts can also be explicitly removed before the death of the composite (Figure 4-8).

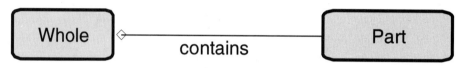

Figure 4-8 Composition

EJB 2.0 relationships

In this section, we discuss the relationship support in EJB 2.0.

Relationship scope

EJB 2.0 supports relationships among container-managed entity beans (CMP 2.0) **within the same EJB module**. An EJB module is defined as all the EJBs that are in an EJB JAR file.

Multiplicity

EJB 2.0 relationships includes the following association types:

1. **One-to-one**

   In a one-to-one relationship, an instance of one bean can have at most a single relationship with an instance of another bean, and the inverse is true. If we said that an `Account` has only one `TransRecord` (unlikely, but this is an example), then this one-to-one relationship would look as shown in Figure 4-9.

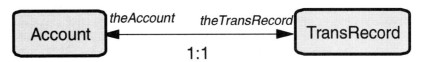

Figure 4-9   One-to-one relationship

2. One-to-many

In a one-to-many relationship, an instance of one bean can be related with many instances of another, but that other bean has at most a single relationship with the first bean. If we said that an Account has many TransRecord (more likely), but that the TransRecord could only belong to one Account, then this one-to-many relationship would look as shown in Figure 4-10.

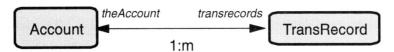

Figure 4-10   One-to-many relationship

3. Many-to-many

In a many-to-many relationship, an instance of one bean can be related with many instances of another, and vice versa. If we said that an Account has many TransRecords, and a TransRecord belongs to many Accounts (unlikely, but this is an example), then this one-to-many relationship would look as shown in Figure 4-11.

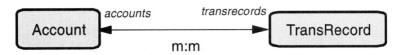

Figure 4-11   Many-to-many relationship

Direct many-to-many relationships are rare. In the real world, these relationships are usually resolved by creating intermediate associative tables, and having two 1:m relationships as shown in Figure 4-12.

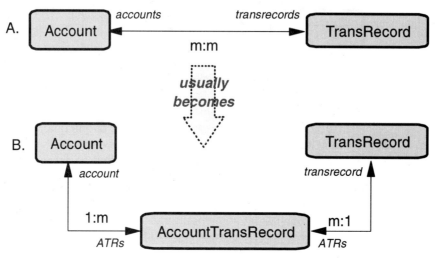

Figure 4-12   Many-many relationship with an intermediary bean

Although what is depicted in example B above is still a logical many-to-many relationship between `Account` and `TransRecord`, it is also two different one-to-many relationships.

Whether you represent your entity bean relationships as example A (direct many-to-many) or example B (two one-to-many) depends on the identity of the `AccountTransRecord`. If the `AccountTransRecord` exists solely to resolve the association, and there are no data elements associated with it, then we can go with defining a direct relationship as in example A, many-to-many. This allows for direct navigability from `Account` to `TransRecord`.

If, however, the `AccountTransRecord` is an entity within its own right, with its own data elements, then we would have to define two different relationships, which means we now have two navigation paths. Therefore, finding all the `TransRecords` for an `Account` requires two different navigations to occur: one from `Account` to `AccountTransRecord`, then from `AccountTransRecord` to `TransRecord`.

Navigability

EJB 2.0 relationships may be:

► Bidirectional—Means the relationship can be traversed in both directions, that is methods are generated to retrieve related entity beans

► Unidirectional—Means the relationship can be traversed in one direction only

Note: We should mention that multiplicity defines the three basic types of relationships in EJB: one-to-one, one-to-many, and many-to-many. Navigability further refines this relationship, but in itself is really not a separate relationship.

Navigability and local interfaces requirements

Navigability of a role requires a *local interface* of the related bean. In our example diagram for the one-to-many relationship, Account-TransRecord, the transrecords role is navigable from Account to TransRecord. Therefore, we require the TransRecord to support a local interface. This is also true for the role of theAccount. However, as we mentioned earlier, local interfaces for entity beans are a good idea in general. As we will see, the get methods that are defined for CMR fields require the return types of local interfaces or collections of these interfaces.

An entity bean that does not have a local interface can have only unidirectional relationships from itself to other entity beans with local interfaces. The lack of a local interface prevents other entity beans from having a relationship with it.

Cascade delete

Beans with relationships put new restrictions on operations such as creating and removing of the bean. Recall that a remove operation will actually delete the underlying data in the data source. If an Account is to be deleted (as in the 1:m relationship), it might mean that the associated TransRecords beans also are to be deleted (this is dependent on the business rules and constraints of the database). To have the container automatically delete all TransRecord when an Account is deleted means specifying the <cascade-delete> option to true on the Account-TransRecord relatlonshlp.

Declaring the relationship in the deployment descriptor

Relationships are declared in the deployment descriptor. First we look at the structure and then at the Account-TransRecord example.

Structure of relationship deployment descriptor

Figure 4-13 shows the basic structure of the deployment descriptor for a relationship.

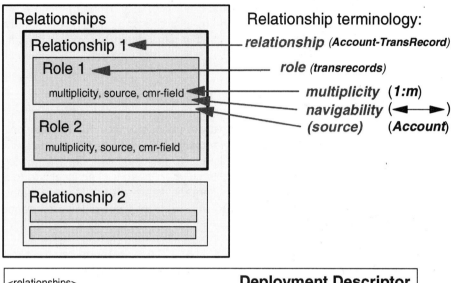

Figure 4-13 Relationship deployment descriptor structure

Entity bean definition in the deployment descriptor

The `Account-TransRecord` relationship is between `Account` and `TransRecord` entity beans.

The bean definitions for entity beans are generic beans with no relationships applied. Although the definition of the beans is a completely separate construct from the definition of the relationships within the deployment descriptor, we will see later that the definition of the relationships refer to the entity beans.

This simple example defines two bean names (`<ejb-name>`) to be `Account` and `TransRecord`. The CMP field mappings describe the persistent fields used.

Figure 4-14 show the deployment descriptors of these two entity beans.

```
<enterprise-beans>
    <entity>
        <ejb-name>Account</ejb-name>
        <local-home>mypackage.AccountLocalHome</local-home>
        <local>mypackage.AccountLocal</local>
        <ejb-class>mypackage.AccountBean</ejb-class>
        <persistence-type>Container</persistence-type>
        <reentrant>False</reentrant>
        <cmp-version>2.x</cmp-version>
        <abstract-schema-name>Account</abstract-schema-name>
        <cmp-field><field-name>accountID</field-name></cmp-field>
        <cmp-field><field-name>balance</field-name></cmp-field>
        <cmp-field><field-name>interest</field-name></cmp-field>
        <cmp-field><field-name>accountType</field-name></cmp-field>
        <primkey-field>accountID</primkey-field>
        <prim-key-class>java.lang.String</prim-key-class>
    </entity>
```

```
    <entity>
        <ejb-name>TransRecord</ejb-name>
        <local-home>mypackage.TransRecordLocalHome</local-home>
        <local>mypackage.TransRecordLocal</local>
        <ejb-class>mypackage.TransRecordBean</ejb-class>
        <persistence-type>Container</persistence-type>
        <reentrant>False</reentrant>
        <cmp-version>2.x</cmp-version>
        <abstract-schema-name>TransRecord</abstract-schema-name>
        <cmp-field><field-name>transID</field-name></cmp-field>
        <cmp-field><field-name>transType</field-name></cmp-field>
        <cmp-field><field-name>transAmount</field-name></cmp-field>
        <primkey-field>transID</primkey-field>
        <prim-key-class>java.sql.Timestamp</prim-key-class>
    </entity>
</enterprise-beans>
```

Figure 4-14   Entity deployment descriptor

Deployment descriptor for Account-TransRecord (m:m)

Figure 4-15 shows the relationship entries for a one-to-many
`Account-TransRecord` in the deployment descriptor:

```
<relationships>
  <ejb-relation>
    <ejb-relation-name>Account-TransRecord</ejb-relation-name>
    <ejb-relationship-role>
      <ejb-relation-role-name>transrecords</ejb-relation-role-name>
      <multiplicity>One</multiplicity>
      <relationship-role-source>
        <ejb-name>Account</ejb-name>
      </relationship-role-source>
      <cmr-field>
        <cmr-field-name>transrecords</cmr-file-name>
        <cmr-field-type>java.util.Collection</cmr-file-type>
      </cmr-field>
    </ejb-relationship-role>
    <ejb-relationship-role>
      <ejb-relation-role-name>theAccount</ejb-relation-role-name>
      <multiplicity>Many</multiplicity>
      <relationship-role-source>
        <ejb-name>TransRecord</ejb-name>
      </relationship-role-source>
      <cmr-field>
        <cmr-field-name>theAccount</cmr-file-name>
      </cmr-field>
    </ejb-relationship-role>
  </ejb-relation>
</relationships>
```

Figure 4-15   Deployment descriptor of a relationship

Description of the XML elements: one-to-many relationship

The XML tags for relationships are:

► Every relationship requires an `<ejb-relation>` element with an optional `<ejb-relation-name>` within the `<relationships>` section.

► Every `<ejb-relation>` has two `<ejb-relationship-role>` elements. The first role in our sample is `transrecords` with `Account` as the relationship source. The second role, `theAccount`, has `TransRecord` as the relationship source. Each `<ejb-name>` element in `<relationship-source-role>` must have an equivalent `<ejb-name>` element in the `<enterprise-beans>` section.

► The `<relationship-role>` element also defines the multiplicity, which can be `One` or `Many`. In the role with `Account` as source, multiplicity is `One`, which means that a `TransRecord` (the related entity bean) has at least a single association with an `Account`. In the role with `TransRecord` as source, the cardinality is `Many`: an `Account` has many `TransRecords`.

- If the role is navigable, as they are for both of our roles, the source entity bean maintains a reference (in the case of a `One` multiplicity) or a collection of references (`Many` multiplicity). A navigable role requires a container-managed relationship field in the form of a `<cmr-field>` element. This is a virtual field, and does not match an existing CMP field.

  In our case, we can navigate in both directions, so we have a corresponding cmr-field for both roles. This means that we have a bidirectional relationship. In our sample, we have a bidirectional relationship. The `transrecords` role is navigable, as is the `theAccount` role.

  For a one-to-many relationship, we may have navigable roles that are unidirectional or bidirectional. At least one side of the relationship must be navigable. If the role was not navigable, then we would not include any `<cmr-field>` mappings.

- The CMR fields manage the relationship. We only have to define them in the direction of navigability. It is required that this name begins with lowercase, and we usually just make this the same as the role name.

  For every `<cmr-field-name>`, there must be a matching abstract getter/setter accessors in the bean class. For example, we defined the `transrecords` CMR field, so we must have corresponding `getTransrecords` and `setTransrecords` methods in the `Account` bean class.

  Because there are many related `TransRecord` beans, these methods work with a Java type of `java.util.Collection` or `java.util.Set` (no duplicates). The type is defined in the `<cmr-field-type>` tag.

  Note that no type is defined for the `theAccount` role, because there is only one result object (and it must be an `Account`, actually an `AccountLocal`).

Description of the XML elements: one-to-one relationship
In a one-to-one relationship, both multiplicity tags would be `One` and no CMR types would be defined.

Description of the XML elements: many-to-many relationship
In a many-to-many relationship, both multiplicity tags would be `Many` and both CMR types would be defined as collection or set.

CMR programming model

As we have seen in the previous section, a navigable relationship role requires a `<cmr-field>` entry in the deployment descriptor. In this section, we describe the programming aspects of relationships.

We will use as the basis of this programming model the `Account-TransRecord` relationship with 1:m multiplicity and bidirectional navigation.

Relationship accessor methods

We mentioned that the name of a <cmr-field> in the deployment descriptor specifies a virtual relationship field in the abstract entity bean. The term *virtual* implies that we do not have to define a relationship field in the abstract bean class. This is also how we define our CMP persistent fields. However, for every cmr-field there must be a pair of matching abstract accessor methods in the bean class.

Naming conventions for the accessor methods:

▶ get<cmr-field-name>, with the first letter of the CMR field name changed to uppercase.

▶ set<cmr-field-name>, with the first letter of the CMR field name changed to uppercase.

▶ The return type of the getter method and the parameter type of the setter must be the same: local interface of the related bean (One relationship) or java.util.Collection or java.util.Set (Many relationship), according to the <cmr-field-type> element in the deployment descriptor.

A navigable relationship role requires a local component interface for the target entity bean. Relationships are expressed in term of local interfaces. And of course, all business methods callable from an EJB client, for example a session bean, have to be exposed in this local interface.

Figure 4-16 shows sample methods in the bean classes and in the local home interfaces.

```
AccountBean:
    public abstract java.util.Collection getTransrecords();
    public abstract setTransrecords(java.util.Collection aCollection);

AccountLocal:
    public java.util.Collection getTransrecords();
    public setTransrecords(java.util.Collection aCollection);

TransRecordBean:
    public abstract AccountLocal getTheAccount();
    public abstract setTheAccount(AccountLocal anAccount);

TransRecordLocal:
    public AccountLocal getTheAccount();
    public setTheAccount(AccountLocal anAccount);
```

Figure 4-16   Relationship accessor methods

Semantics of relationship accessor methods

A getter method of a single-valued relationship returns the local interface of the related bean or `null`. A getter methods of a collection-valued relationship returns a collection type with zero, one, or many references (local interfaces) of the related bean.

EJB roles and responsibilities for relationships

We discuss the responsibilities in terms of the EJB roles.

Bean provider - defining the relationships

The bean developer must model and define all of the relationships in the deployment descriptor according to the conventions above.

Application developer support for relationships

Defining relationships seems like a lot of work, so to simplify the relationships development process and to shorten the development cycle, the Application Developer provides support for defining these relationships as follows:

► Provides UML-based user interfaces to capture the relationship metadata.

► Generates the `<relationships>` elements in the deployment descriptor. The EJB developer does not have to understand the deployment descriptor details.

► Generates the abstract getter and setter methods in the abstract bean class to programmatically navigate and manipulate the relationships.

► Promotes the getter and setter methods to the local component interfaces. The EJB developer should carefully check whether the invocations of a setter cause database problems in the case of non-nullable foreign keys. If so, the setter method should be manually deleted from the interface.

► Provides a user interface (mapping editor) to map the relationships to the underlying database foreign keys. The definition of foreign key constraints is a prerequisite for the relationship mapping.

EJB container support for relationships

The EJB container supports relationships in two ways:

► The deployment tools generate the concrete bean class, which includes the implementation of the getter and setter method for a CMR field and support for the relationships.

► During runtime, the container enables the navigability of the related beans and maintains the relationship's referential integrity within the same unit of work.

EJB 2.0 relationship issues

Maintaining relationships when adding new entity bean instances must be investigated in detail if the underlying foreign key is defined as NOT NULL.

For example, the NOT NULL specification for the ACCID (accountID) column in the TRANSRECORD table prohibits the creation of a new TransRecord instance without setting the related Account instance.

This restriction can be solved by following the principles outlined here:

▶ It is mandatory to modify the ejbCreate and ejbPostCreate methods to include the Account as a parameter so that the relationship can be established using the setTheAccount method.

▶ EJB 2.0 has the restriction that CMR fields cannot be manipulated in the ejbCreate method.

▶ Setting of the related Account must therefore happen in the ejbPostCreate method. This is possible because WebSphere Version 5 issues the actual database INSERT after the ejbPostCreate method (and not after the ejbCreate method).

▶ Sample code for the ejbCreate and ejbPostCreate methods is shown in Figure 4-17.

```
public void ejbCreate(String type, BigDecimal amount, AccountLocal acct)
              throws CreateException {
    setTransID(...create an SQL timestamp...);
    setTransType(type);
    setTransAmount(amount);
    return null;
}
public void ejbPostCreate(String type, BigDecimal amount, AccountLocal acct)
              throws CreateException {
    setTheAccount(acct);                    // set the relationship
}
```

Figure 4-17   Setting a CMR field in the ejbPostCreate method

EJB inheritance

Defining an enterprise bean as a subclass of another enterprise bean is not part of the Enterprise JavaBeans specification. However, in real-life applications, we need this essential feature of object-oriented programming. Direct inheritance is specific to WebSphere Application Server and Studio Application Developer.

Application Developer provides different mapping approaches for an inheritance hierarchy: a single table approach, and a root/leaf approach with foreign key related tables.

In addition, entity beans can inherit from regular Java classes.

> **Note:** The support for EJB inheritance in the IBM tools is not new, and has been around since VisualAge for Java Version 3. EJB 2.0 still does not provide formal support for EJB inheritance, and support in Version 5 is through proprietary IBM extensions.

Bank example

In our original bank model, we saw that there were actually two additional types of entity beans, Checking and Savings, that are actual types of accounts (Figure 4-18).

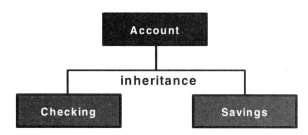

Figure 4-18   Account types modeled using inheritance

Inheritance overview

In this section, we describe the different types of inheritance and the pros and cons of these different approaches. Application Developer supports two types of inheritance: EJB inheritance and Java inheritance, which we will discuss here.

EJB inheritance

In EJB inheritance, an enterprise bean inherits properties, such as CMP fields and relationship roles, methods, and method-level control descriptor attributes from another enterprise bean that resides in the same EJB module. Because EJB inheritance is possible only within the same EJB module, the Savings and Checking beans must be located in the same module as the Account bean.

Characteristics of EJB inheritance

EJB inheritance, in respect to developing EJBs, has the following characteristics:

- For CMP entity beans, there is support for single table and root/leaf table mapping.
- The deployment descriptor will list all of the CMP fields, including those fields that have been inherited.
- Home interface classes cannot inherit from other home interface classes. Therefore, we have to promote all the related methods ourselves.
- Remote interface classes can inherit from other remote interface classes. This means that we can directly inherit all the business methods defined in the parent bean in the remote interface of the child beans. In addition, we have to promote the business methods written specifically for the child bean.
- The bean class of the child bean extends the bean class of the parent bean.
- Key classes are shared among all enterprise beans in the inheritance model. This means that the key class in the child bean is identical to the key class of the parent bean.
- For BMP entity beans, you can use any mapping model, because you write the JDBC access code yourself.

Java inheritance

In Java inheritance, an enterprise bean class inherits properties and methods from a superclass that is not itself an enterprise bean class, and the remote interface extends from an interface that defines the business methods and is implemented by the superclass. This is often done to achieve reuse, and to further classify beans as types, but these supertypes are not entity beans in their own right.

Characteristics of Java inheritance

The general characteristics of Java inheritance, with respect to the EJB development, are:

- Only distinct table mapping is supported in Java inheritance.

- The bean class extends from a superclass A, which implements the interface B. The remote interface can extend from the interface B, which defines the business methods.

- The derived classes from the same superclass are entirely different beans and they have different mappings and schemas respectively.

- The derived bean classes have different key classes characterizing them.

- If the superclass contains state, make sure that the state is persisted.

The Java inheritance model is useful when we have a Java class that already implements the logic of the bean. So, as a general merit of inheritance, it helps in code reusability. But this model is not useful for the database mapping point of view, because the underlying tables do not reflect the inheritance. This lacks the advantage of the root/leaf or single table model, which can make use of an existing database schema with one table or foreign key relationships.

Mapping schemes for inheritance model

In this section, we describe mapping schemes related to an inheritance hierarchy.

Single table mapping

All the classes in the inheritance model map to a single table (Figure 4-19). A discriminator column is used to specify the type of the instance in the hierarchy. The discriminator column is not an attribute of any enterprise bean; it is only used for mapping purposes.

Table ACCOUNT

accID	balance	discrim	minAmount	overdraft
101-1001	1495.00	SAVINGS	100.00	
102-2003	223.57	CHECKING		50.00
103-3001	675.82	CHECKING		50.00

Discriminator column

unused space in table

Figure 4-19   Single table inheritance mapping

In this mapping model, the table is not fully normalized, that is the columns specific to one bean will be unnecessarily tied up with other beans and remain not utilized. But this model provides easy access to the tables. One practical limitation to this mapping is that, when we create a new enterprise bean by extending the existing beans of the model, we have to alter the definition of the table. This is to accommodate the new columns specific to the bean.

Therefore, single table mapping should only be used when there are more CMP fields in the parent enterprise bean than in the child beans.

Root/leaf table mapping

In root/leaf table mapping, you create one table per enterprise bean in the inheritance hierarchy (Figure 4-20).

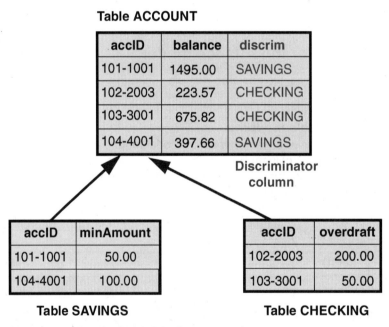

Figure 4-20   Root/leaf table inheritance mapping

The *root* table contains the parent bean specific columns and the discriminator column. Since some of these columns are related to properties inherited by the child class beans, this table will also contain the state of these properties of the child beans.

A *leaf* table is created for each child bean. Each child bean's leaf table has a foreign key pointing to the primary key of the root table and columns for fields specific of the child bean. Using root/leaf mapping is more efficient, because it does not waste space in the tables. On the other hand, two tables must be accessed to instantiate an entity bean and queries on accounts must join all the tables.

Distinct table mapping

Each class in the inheritance hierarchy maps to a different table. In this model, the tables are not likely to be normalized, because each table contains all the columns. Because of data consistency problems between the unrelated tables, it is difficult to automate the data access for this model.

Distinct table mapping is not supported by Application Developer for CMP beans.

Implementing EJB inheritance

The EJB inheritance model is specific to the IBM EJB development environment of Application Developer. This is an extension of the EJB specification. In this section, we describe EJB inheritance as implemented in the IBM tool set.

Requirements for EJB inheritance

The inheritance implementation for entity beans implies providing the following function:

► Specifying an `is-a` relationship among entity beans, such as a `Savings` is an `Account`.

► Implementing the `findByPrimaryKey` method in the home interface of the parent bean in such a way that the target base class along with its subclass is returned. For example, a search for an `Account` returns either a `Savings` beans or a `Checking` bean.

► Implementing custom finder methods so that they return collections of `Savings` and `Checking` bean instances.

► Relationship finders also return heterogeneous results, containing instances of the related class and its subclasses.

Limitations

There are some practical limitations on EJB inheritance:

► Session beans cannot inherit from entity beans and vice versa.

► Stateless session beans cannot inherit from stateful session beans and vice versa.

Home interface specifics

The home interface of the child bean, for example, SavingsHome, must not extend the parent home interface, BankAccountHome. However, the relationship between the methods of these two interfaces have to be maintained. When a method is added to the home interface of the parent bean, it is automatically copied to the child beans.

A create method of the parent home interface can only create the parent bean instance. However, a create method of the child home interface creates both the parent bean instance and the child bean instance.

A client may not work directly with an instance of the parent bean but only with the child bean, which is more specific to the client's requirements. (This assumes that there are no instances of the parent bean that are not instances of one of its children.)

Developing the inheritance hierarchy

In this section, we develop two enterprise beans, Savings and Checking, which inherit from an Account bean. We discuss developing the inheritance hierarchy using the EJB inheritance model.

Component interface

The component interfaces of the child beans define the business methods specific to them. They also extend the component interface of the Account.

Account bean

The Account bean, which is the superclass for our example hierarchy, is an entity bean. This bean does not have a create and the associated ejbCreate methods, because we assume that each account must be either a checking or a savings account. (In real applications, there can be models where instances of the superclass exist.) The Account bean can have finder methods. Using these finder methods, we can retrieve the corresponding subclass beans. This class also includes business logic method that is independent of the account type, for example, deposit of funds.

Beans and interfaces

In the bank scenario, we implement two beans, Savings and Checking, which inherit from the Account bean (Figure 4-21).

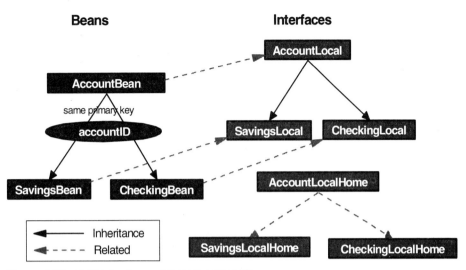

Figure 4-21   EJB inheritance hierarchy example

Mapping scheme

For our example, we employ the single table inheritance mapping model. In this mapping scheme, we have one table for all the attributes.

We will also show the root/leaf inheritance model when we discuss mapping in more detail (see Chapter 12, "Mapping strategies for CMPs" on page 467).

Deployment descriptor for inheritance

Because support for inheritance is an IBM extension, there is no place in the standard EJB deployment descriptor to specify the inheritance hierarchy. The entity beans are specified in the deployment descriptor with all the attributes, the inherited attributes and the specific attributes.

The information about the inheritance hierarchy is stored in an IBM-specific extension file called `ibm-ejb-jar-ext.xmi`. Figure 4-22 shows the content of that file for our example.

```
<?xml version="1.0" encoding="UTF-8"?>
<ejbext:EJBJarExtension xmi:version="2.0"
    xmlns:xmi="http://www.omg.org/XMI" xmlns:ejbext="ejbext.xmi"
    xmlns:ejb="ejb.xmi" xmi:id="EJBJarExtension_1035485965330">
  <ejbJar href="META-INF/ejb-jar.xml#ejb-jar_ID"/>
  <generalizations xmi:id="EjbGeneralization_1035485965330">
    <subtype xmi:type="ejb:ContainerManagedEntity"
        href="META-INF/ejb-jar.xml#Checking"/>
    <supertype xmi:type="ejb:ContainerManagedEntity"
        href="META-INF/ejb-jar.xml#Account"/>
  </generalizations>
  <generalizations xmi:id="EjbGeneralization_1035485965331">
    <subtype xmi:type="ejb:ContainerManagedEntity"
        href="META-INF/ejb-jar.xml#Savings"/>
    <supertype xmi:type="ejb:ContainerManagedEntity"
        href="META-INF/ejb-jar.xml#Account"/>
  </generalizations>
</ejbext:EJBJarExtension>
```

Figure 4-22   Deployment information for inheritance

EJB custom query methods

Query methods are any method in the home that is used to locate entity beans, such as `findXxxx` (called finder methods), and `selectXxxx` (called select methods).

*New EJB 2.0 - query methods: In EJB 1.x, finder methods were the only type of custom query method available, and these were just referred to as custom finder methods. In EJB 2.0, select query methods were added, so we refer to this category of methods as query methods, because referring to them as finder methods would not be completely accurate.

Note: They are called custom query methods for both CMPs and BMPs, because it is a definition of method function rather than an actual implementation detail of the method. CMPs can rely on the EJB query language, so are in fact true query methods. However, for BMPs, the underlying data source may or may not be one that supports a formal query-based language (as in SQL). It does not matter; such methods are still referred to as query methods.

Custom query methods defined

Query methods are used to locate existing entity beans, by interacting with the persistence layer to find the corresponding row in the database that matches the entity bean. They may return one or many beans. These query methods are located in the home interface of the entity bean. A query method can be part of the local home interface, the remote home interface, or both.

There are single object query methods that return one bean type, and multiple object query methods that return a collection.

For bean-managed persistent (BMP) entity beans, all the code to do the actual queries must be provided by the bean provider, such as the corresponding SQL SELECT code for the query method. For CMPs, this is generated by the container. Otherwise, the other conventions of query method usage, such as the way that query methods are invoked and used, is the same regardless of whether it is a BMP or CMP entity bean type. This chapter focuses only on the query method development for the CMP entity bean model.

If you are using CMP entity beans, you can use the new EJB query language (EJB QL) for your queries. EJB QL is used to specify a query for CMP entity beans using their attributes (CMP fields) and relationships (CMR fields) for navigation and qualification. The language is similar to SQL. An EJB query is independent of the bean's mapping to a persistent store. We describe the language in "EJB query language (EJB QL)" on page 149.

> ***New EJB2.0 - EJB QL:** EJB QL is a declarative query language similar to SQL, but not the same. EJB QL queries are defined in terms of the abstract persistence schema for entity beans, not the underlying data store, so they are portable across containers. The EJB QL is defined in the deployment descriptor, and when the beans are deployed, the EJB container generates the actual SQL code based on the EJB QL.
>
> Note that you can also use the "old" ways of specifying custom query even in EJB 2.0, but we describe only the "new" way with EJB QL in this document.
>
> WebSphere's EJB query language is compliant with the EJB QL defined in Sun's EJB 2.0 specification, but also provides additional capabilities that extend the basic specification. For example, the WebSphere query language supports important constructs such as date/time comparisons, subselects, and ORDER BY, whereas the Sun specification does not. These differences are described in "WebSphere extensions to EJB QL" on page 157.

An EJB QL query can be used in three situations:

- To define a finder method of an entity bean (findXxxx)
- To define a select method of an entity bean (selectXxxx)
- To dynamically specify a query using the executeQuery dynamic API

Note: Dynamic queries (executeQuery) require the interface provided by WebSphere Application Server Enterprise Edition.

Finder and select method queries are specified in the bean's deployment descriptor using the <ejb-ql> tag. Queries specified in the deployment descriptor are compiled into SQL by the container during deployment of the bean.

> **Important:** Finder methods have been part of the specification since EJB 1.0, and have always been defined on the home interface. Custom finders in EJB 2.0 introduce a couple of improvements over the custom finder method structure of EJB 1.0, for instance, the use of EJB QL.

Although support for EJB QL in the home methods is not supported, developers may choose to implement home methods by calling select methods.

CMP entity bean finder and select methods defined

There are two types of query methods: findXxxx (finder) methods and selectXxxx (select) methods.

Comparing finder and select methods

Table 4-1 lists the differences between finder and select methods.

Table 4-1   Differences between finder and select methods

Criteria	Finder methods	Select methods
Where declared	In remote and/or local home interface	Abstract method in the bean class
Method name	findXxxx - home ejbFindXxxx - bean class	ejbSelectXxxx - bean class
Visibility	Exposed to client	Internal to entity bean class to be used by other bean methods
Instances	Any arbitrary bean instance in the bean pool	Current instance, but if invocation from home method: any arbitrary instance

Criteria	Finder methods	Select methods
Return value	home: Single object or a Collection. Either `EJBObject`(s) or `EJBLocalObject`(s) of this bean type. bean: primaryKey	Single or multiple (Collection or Set) objects. `EJBObject`(s) or `EJBLocalObject`(s) of this bean type or a CMR related type, or a CMP field, a collection of CMP fields, or a CMR field.
Exception handling	`FinderException` or `ObjectNotFoundException`	`FinderException` or `ObjectNotFoundException`

Finder methods in home interface and bean class

The purpose of these finder methods are the same as for the finder methods in the prior specification. Finder methods are defined in the home interface of the EJB, are accessible by EJB clients, and they may return one or more component interface objects (`EJBObject`).

The characteristics of find methods:

► The method signature is declared in the home interface.

► The method name must start with `findXxxx` (for example `findAllCustomers`).

► If the finder is declared in the local home interface, no `RemoteException` is thrown. If it is defined in the remote interface, then `RemoteException` is thrown.

► All finder methods must throw a `FinderException`.

► Each finder method (except the `findByPrimaryKey` method) is mapped to an EJB QL element in the deployment descriptor. The container already knows how to provide the implementation for the `findByPrimaryKey` method.

► All `findXxxx` methods (except the `findByPrimaryKey` method) must match the corresponding `ejbFindXxxx` method in the concrete bean class. These methods must return either a single `EJBObject`, or a collection of `EJBObjects`.

► If the same finder is declared in the remote and in the local home interface (same name and same signature), both finders can be mapped to one EJB QL statement.

► The `findXxxx` method can return subtypes of `EJBLocalObject` (local interfaces) if defined in the local home, or `EJBObject` (remote interfaces) if defined in the remote home, or a collection of those interfaces. The bean provider specifies the result type mapping as local or remote.

Single object finder methods

Single object finders return the entity bean's component interface. Remote interfaces (EJBObject) are returned if the method is declared in the remote home interface; otherwise local interfaces are returned.

The bean provider must ensure that only one object is returned from the EJB QL statement. If it returns more than one row, the container throws a FinderException. Therefore, caution should be exercised when declaring the primary key of an object (for findByPrimaryKey), or the corresponding query statement of the method, to ensure that only unique entries are returned.

If an object is not found, then an ObjectNotFoundException will be thrown. ObjectNotFoundException is a subtype of FinderException.

Multiple object finder methods

Multiple object finders return a java.util.Collection of component interfaces (remote or local, dependent on where the method is declared).

The collection may contain duplicates if a DISTINCT clause is not used in the EJB QL select statement. The collection will not contain duplicates if the DISTINCT clause is used in the EJB QL select statement.

The client must use the PortableRemoteObject.narrow method to convert the members of the collection if the finder is declared in the remote interface. This is similar to converting a home interface from a JNDI lookup method.

Multiple object finders do not throw ObjectNotFoundExceptions when no items are found. Rather, they should return an empty collection. A FinderException would indicate a serious finding error has occurred.

Select methods in bean class

Select methods are also sometimes called private finders. These methods are accessible only within a bean class. In combination with the new home methods (see "Developing a home method" on page 463) you have a useful capability to implement quite complex methods operating on more than one entity bean of a type.

*New EJB 2.0 - select methods: Select methods are new in EJB 2.0. They allow privatizing of query methods that can be used internally by the bean class, as in helper methods, without having to expose this functionality to EJB clients through the home interface, yet allow these methods to be built using the same abstract persistence schema model, such as using EJB QL, as with external finder methods. In this way, there is a single consistent programming model that the developer can use for both the internal and external query methods.

The characteristics of select methods:

▶ The method signature is declared only in the bean class.

▶ The method name start with `ejbSelectXxxx` (for example `ejbSelectNumberOfAccounts`).

▶ All select methods must throw a `FinderException`.

▶ As in finder methods, each select method is mapped to an EJB QL element in the deployment descriptor.

▶ As in finder methods, a select method can return subtypes of `EJBLocalObject` (local interfaces) or `EJBObject` (remote interfaces), or a collection of those interfaces. The bean provider specifies the result-type-mapping as local or remote.

▶ A select method can also return a single CMP or CMR field, or collection or set of these fields.

▶ These methods are not based on the identity (key) of the bean instance that they are executing on. If you want to use the key in the EJB QL implementation you must pass the key value to the `ejbSelectXxxx` method as a parameter.

Single object select methods

Single object select methods return the entity bean's component interface. Remote or local interfaces are returned depending on how the method is defined in the deployment descriptor. If the method is to be called by a remote home finder method, for instance, then the select method return type would be defined in terms of the remote component interface. If the method is to be called by a local home finder method, then the local home component interface would be returned.

Additionally, select methods may declare return types of a CMP or CMR field, that is, a select method either returns a complete EJB or just one field (CMP or CMR).

The bean provider must ensure that only one object is returned from the EJB QL statement. If it returns more than one row, the container throws a `FinderException`. Therefore, caution should be exercised when declaring these query methods, to ensure that only unique entries are returned.

If an object is not found, then an `ObjectNotFoundException` will be thrown. `ObjectNotFoundException` is a subtype of `FinderException`.

Multiple object select methods

Multiple object finders return a `java.util.Collection` or a `java.util.Set` of component interfaces (remote or local, dependent on the method specification and how it is to be used).

Additionally, select methods may declare return types of collections or sets of a CMP or CMR field. For example, a select method could search for entity beans of another type to retrieve the beans that should be added to a relationships.

```
select object(t) from Account a, in (a.transactions) t where ....
```

The collection may contain duplicates if no `DISTINCT` clause is used in the EJB QL select statement. A `java.util.Set` result implies that `DISTINCT` is specified, because a set cannot contain duplicates.

Multiple object selects do not throw `ObjectNotFoundExceptions` when no items are found. Rather, they should return an empty collection. A `FinderException` would indicate a series finding error has occurred.

Life cycle sequence - query methods

In Chapter 3, "Entity beans" on page 73, we described the life cycle of an entity bean for the `findByPrimaryKey` query method. We extend this for all types of query methods.

Life cycle for query methods

Finder methods always execute on an arbitrary instance in the bean pool. However, select methods may execute on either a pooled or ready instance. Because select methods are always internal to the bean that is executing them, this is all handled internal to the container, but the important thing to remember about select methods is that they do not execute with the identify of the bean. So even though a particular bean is executing the select method, it is not executing on behalf of that bean.

The major difference with multiple object query methods is in how they behave in the container. The responsibilities of the developer are the same, and CMP versus BMP implementation specifics still apply, other than to say that the BMP developer will most likely look through a result set creating the collection themselves. CMPs will always return collections, while BMPs may return collections or enumerations, although it is recommended that they return collections for consistency.

Life cycle for finder methods

We update the diagram from "Life-cycle sequence - findByPrimaryKey" on page 92 (Figure 3-8) to show the life cycle of general finder methods (Figure 4-23).

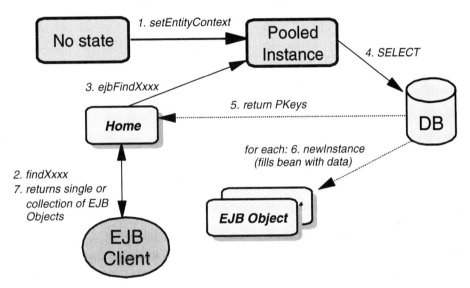

Figure 4-23   Life cycle for finder methods

Life cycle for select methods

Figure 4-24 shows the life cycle for select methods.

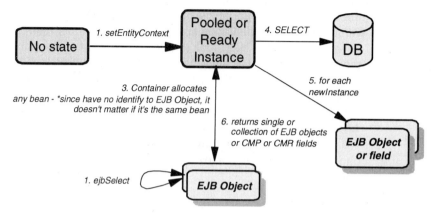

Figure 4-24   Life cycle for select methods

Adding query methods to the bean class

The construction of the entity bean class for query methods is dependent on the type of bean:

- **CMP**—For finder methods, the `ejbFindXxxx` method of the bean class is not actually added to the bean class by the developer. Instead, the `ejbFindXxxx` methods are added to the persistence class that is generated by the container at deployment time by mapping the method in the home interface with the EJB QL defined in the deployment descriptor. For select methods, the bean provider must add abstract `ejbSelectXxxx` methods to the bean class, and as in finder methods, the actual methods will be added to the persistence class by the container when the code is deployed based on the method to EJB QL mappings in the deployment descriptor.

- **BMP**—For finder methods, the `ejbFindXxxx` methods must be added to the bean class and the implementation provided by the bean developer. For `ejbSelectXxxx` methods, these methods must not be declared `abstract`, and their implementations must be provided by the bean developer.

New Customer bean requirements

We extend the `Customer` entity bean discussed in "Developing an entity bean: Customer" on page 101, to include the following query methods:

- `findByLastName`
- `findAllCustomers`
- `ejbSelectAllCustomerLastNames`

Figure 4-25 shows a sample `Customer` bean with some finder and select methods defined.

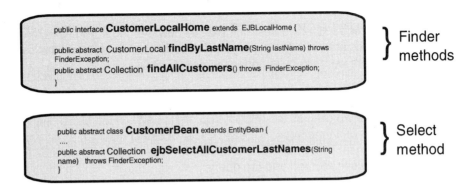

Figure 4-25   Customer finder and select methods

EJB query language (EJB QL)

EJB QL is a query specification language for the finder and select methods of entity beans with container-managed persistence (CMP). The EJB QL statements are part of the deployment descriptor, and each statement is mapped to a corresponding finder and select method.

Abstract persistence schema

In Chapter 3, "Entity beans" on page 73, we saw that the abstract persistence schema allowed us to specify two things: define CMP data-to-object mappings and container-managed relationships (CMR). It is similar to the idea of how a database schema is defined, where the tables, fields, and relationships of the tables would be defined. In the EJB abstract persistence schema, these would be our entity beans, CMP fields, and CMR fields.

When defining EJB QL, we are limited to referring only to elements described in this schema. The abstract persistence schema governs how you must define names in the EJB QL. Everything that must be mapped for an EJB QL statement must be something defined as part of this schema. You cannot use any names other than these defined above. The following summarizes these rules:

► Names of the entity beans defined in the abstract schema. Each bean by default is given the schema name of the bean (such as `Customer`, which is defined in the `<abstract-schema-name>` xml tag).

► CMP field names within these beans (such as `firstName`, anything in a `<cmp-field>` tag).

► CMR field names within these beans to navigate along relationships (such as anything defined in a `<cmr-field>`, of which we have not yet defined any).

Bean and deployment descriptor mappings

In this section, we describe exactly how the finder and select methods are associated with the deployment descriptor to understand the constraints under which we must build and implement EJB QL.

Associating the method to the query

Here we discuss the relationship of the fields in the deployment descriptor to the EJB bean methods. For each finder or select method, a corresponding `<query>` element in the deployment descriptor must exist. This creates the binding between method and the query.

Figure 4-26 shows a simple definition of the `findByLastName`, `findAllCustomer`, and `ejbSelectAllCustomerLastNames` query methods in the deployment descriptor.

The name of the abstract-persistence-schema is defined as `Customer`. This normally matches the `<ejb-name>` name (because we can only define one schema name per bean and cannot have duplicate bean names per ejb-jar), but does not have to.

A `<query>` must exist for all finder and select methods. What we see above is the `<query-method>` definition; the EJB QL statement definition will be discussed below. The name of the finder or select methods must be declared in the `<query-method>` field. Also, `<method-params>` must be defined for each parameter of the method, and the order of these must match the order of the parameters. Only select methods must define the type of result, either `Local` or `Remote`, as defined in the `<result-type-mapping>` definition.

If local and remote home interfaces have the same method names, they can both share this query definition. The container is smart enough to figure this out.

> **Note:** We should mention that the `findByLastName` method is only used as an example of a single object result. It is likely that last name is not a unique identifier for the table, and therefore, we could get a `FinderException` if more than one object is returned from the query.

```
<entity>
   <ejb-name>Customer</ejb-name>
   ....
   <abstract-schema-name>Customer</ejb-name>
   <query>
      <query-method>
         <method-name>findByLastName</method-name>
         <method-params>
            <method-param>java.lang.String</method-param>
         </method-params>
      </query-method>
      .....
   </query>
   <query>
      <query-method>
         <method-name>findAllCustomers</method-name>
         <method-params/>
      </query-method>
      .....
   </query>
      ...
   </query>
   <query>
      <query-method>
         <method-name>ejbSelectAllCustomerLastNames</method-name>
         <method-params/>
      </query-method>
      <result-type-mapping>Local</result-type-mapping>
      .....
   </query>
   ....
</entity>
```

Figure 4-26   Finder methods in the deployment descriptor

EJB QL statement declaration

The EJB QL statement must also be part of the `<query>` definition. The statement is defined using the `<ejb-ql>` tag. There must be one `<ejb-ql>` tag per `<query>` definition for each finder and select method.

Figure 4-27 shows the EJB QL statement for the `findByLastName` method.

```
    ...
  <entity>
    <ejb-name>Customer</ejb-name>
  ....
    <abstract-schema-name>Customer</ejb-name>
    <query>
      <query-method>
          <method-name>findByLastName</method-name>
          <method-params>
              <method-param>java.lang.String</method-param>
          </method-params>
      </query-method
      <ejb-ql>
        SELECT OBJECT(c) FROM CUSTOMER C WHERE c.lastName = ?1
      </ejb-ql>
    </query>
  </entity>
}
```

Figure 4-27   EJB QL definition in the deployment descriptor

We will discuss in more detail the structure of the statement language. However, notice that we only use as variables in our EJB QL statement those things that are part of our abstract schema: the `Customer` (from the abstract persistence schema name) and the `lastName` (from the CMP field definition). The rest of this is just the structure of the language. Notice that `?1` is a query parameter. There must be as many query parameters (`?1`, `?2`, ...) as there are `<method-param>` tags in the definition of the method.

Finder method schema mapping

Figure 4-28 shows how a method in the `CustomerLocalHome` interface associates to the deployment descriptor mapping.

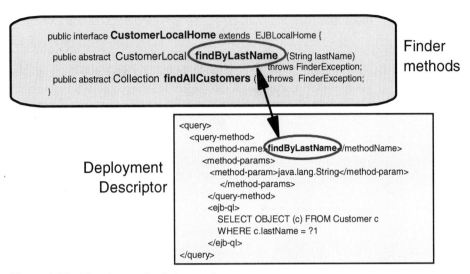

Figure 4-28 Mapping methods to queries

EJB QL syntax

The EJB QL is very similar to SQL (actually the syntax is a subset of SQL 92).

A query statement must contain a SELECT clause and a FROM clause. Like an SQL expression it can optionally contain a WHERE clause.

> EJB Query ::== *select_clause from_clause [where_clause]*

To describe the QJB QL more precisely, we use a customized Backus Naur Form (BNF) as shown in the box above. Table 4-2 gives a short BNF primer.

Table 4-2 BNF primer

symbol	meaning
::=	"is defined as"
|	"or"
[ ]	optional items
{ }	groups elements
*	repetitive items (zero or more times)
expr **AND** expr	**bold** distinguishes terminals, while non-terminals are in normal font without brackets (<>)

A _d suffix will be used as the abbreviation for declaration in our samples. For more information about BNF, see the Web page of the University of Geneva at:

```
http://cui.unige.ch/db-research/Enseignement/analyseinfo/AboutBNF.html
```

Important: Even if the EJB QL syntax looks like SQL, it is a new typed expression language. A QL expression is a query based on objects. An EJB QL select statement returns objects of a component interface type or of a CMP/CMR field type; it never returns a row from a (relational) database.

In the following sections, we describe the most important elements of EJB QL. Every expression is also described in a shaded box in BNF format.

Reserved words

Reserved words are SELECT, FROM, WHERE, DISTINCT, OBJECT, NULL, TRUE, FALSE, NOT, AND, OR, BETWEEN, LIKE, IN, AS, UNKNOWN, EMPTY, MEMBER, OF, IS and ?.

SELECT clause

The SELECT clause defines the objects that are returned from a query.

```
select_clause ::==
    SELECT [DISTINCT] {single-valued-path-expr} | OBJECT(ident_var)
```

The SELECT clause must always return a single value. This value can be either a single-valued-path-expression or a stand-alone identification qualified by the Object() operator:

```
SELECT cust.lastName FROM Customer AS cust
SELECT OBJECT(cust) FROM Customer AS cust
```

The first example returns a collection of the CMP fields of type lastName (a collection of Strings). The second example returns a collection of CustomerLocal instances.

The optional keyword DISTINCT effects a removal of duplicates in the returned collection. As mentioned previously, a finder method can also return a java.util.Set. As this class is defined as a collection that contains no duplicate elements, the DISTINCT option is implicitly added if the finder method returns the type java.util.Set.

Note: The SELECT clause is not required in WebSphere Version 5 and can be omitted. For compatibility with WebSphere 4.0 and other EJB QL providers, it should be specified anyway.

FROM clause

The FROM clause defines the set of beans from which the query results are formed and which are used in the WHERE clause.

> from_clause ::== **FROM** ident_variable_d {,ident_variable_d}

Similar to SQL, the EJB QL treats the FROM clause as a cartesian product to build this set. For example, the FROM clause for a `findAllCustomers` method would be:

```
SELECT OBJECT(customer) FROM Customer AS customer
```

Identifiers

Identifiers are the character strings in a query. To identify something, you can choose a character sequence of unlimited length. The identifiers are case insensitive. You must not use one of the reserved words.

> **Tip:** As you can read in many books and in the specification itself, it is recommended that you not use one of the reserved words from SQL. Until now, it is possible to use any other than the reserved words, but in further versions the functionality of the EJB QL will increase and more SQL words become reserved.

Identification variable declaration

> ident_variable_d ::= collection_member_d | range_variable_d

Identification variables can be either declared by using a range variable declaration (`AS`) or a collection member declaration (`IN`).

Identification variables can only be declared in the FROM clause. Keep in mind that the statement is evaluated from the left to the right side. This is important for referencing within declarations to other variable declarations; referenced identifiers must already be declared.

Range variable declaration

> range_variable_d ::= abstract_schema_name [**AS**] identifier

The AS keyword is optional. It is assumed if we omit it.

```
SELECT OBJECT(cust) FROM Customer AS cust
SELECT OBJECT(cust) FROM Customer cust
```

Collection member declaration

```
collection_member_d ::== IN collection_valued_path_expr [AS] identifier
```

A collection member declaration declares an identification variable that represents an entity that is reached by navigating a CMR field in one-to-many or many-to-many relationships:

```
SELECT OBJECT(cust) FROM Customer AS cust, IN(cust.accounts)
SELECT OBJECT(acct) FROM Account AS acct, IN(acct.transrecords)
```

The IN specification enables us to use attributes of related entities in the WHERE clause of the EJB QL statement.

Path expressions

With a path expression, we can address a CMP or a CMR field of a specified type. With path expressions, we are able to navigate along the container-managed relationships between entity beans. The navigation operator dot separates the type from the attribute, for example `customer.accounts`.

There are two kinds of path expressions:

► Single-valued path expression—A single-valued path expression points at one object. Such a path expression navigates to a CMP field or to a CMR field in a 1:1 or m:1 relationship. It contains always one object.

► Collection-valued path expression—A collection-valued path expression points to more than one object. Such a path expression navigates to a CMR field in a 1:m or m:m relationship.

WHERE clause

```
where_clause ::== WHERE conditional_expr
```

As in SQL the WHERE clause contains a conditional expression. The WHERE clause is optional in a query statement.

Conditional expressions

```
conditional_expr ::==
    conditional_term | conditional_expr {OR | AND} conditional_term
```

A conditional expression consists of other conditional expressions, logical or comparison operations or path expressions. At the end they have to evaluate to boolean values or boolean literals.

Conditional expressions can use:

- operators (+ - * /)
- comparisons (= > >= < <= <>), for strings only = and <>
- NOT
- BETWEEN arithmetic-expression AND arithmetic-expression
- IN: value IN (value1, value2, ...)
- LIKE, using wild card characters _ and %
- null comparison: IS NULL
- empty comparison: collection-valued-path-expr IS EMPTY
- collection member expression: MEMBER OF collection-valued-path-expr
- functional expressions: `concat`, `substring`, `locate`, `length`, `abs`, `sqrt`

Parameters

To pass parameters to the query statement, the declared parameters of the finder method are accessible in the query statement as a question mark followed by a number, such as, ?1, ?2, ?3. The number is the position of the declaration in the finder method's signature. This is similar to the parameter handling in a JDBC prepared statement.

For example, matching finder method declaration and EJB QL statements are:

```
findCustomerByName(String lastName, String firstName);
SELECT object(x) FROM Customer x WHERE x.lastName = ?1 OR x.firstName = ?2
```

The type of the parameter in the statement is defined by the declaration of the correspondent parameter in the finder method signature. Parameters can be primitive types (`int`), wrapper classes (`Integer`) or EJB objects.

Using a parameter is only allowed in the WHERE clause within a conditional expression that involves a single-valued path expression, such as `x.lastName`.

WebSphere extensions to EJB QL

WebSphere Application Server provides extensions to EJB QL to make it more specific and flexible. Although all of the WebSphere extensions are presented here, they may cover topics that we have not yet discussed, such as relationships and navigation.

Note that you are using vendor-specific extensions. If you have to reuse this EJB in another EJB 2.0 compliant container, you should not use these extensions.

Table 4-3 shows a comparison of the EJB 2.0 specification and the extensions of the WebSphere query language. We show the usage of the relevant extensions with a short example.

Table 4-3   EJB QL extensions in WebSphere

Item	EJB 2.0 specification	WebSphere query
SELECT clause	required	optional
Delimited identifiers	no	yes
String comparisons	= and <> only	= <> > <
Scalar functions	yes (limited set)	yes
Order by	no	yes
Calendar comparisons	yes	yes
SQL date/time expressions	no	yes
Subqueries, aggregations, GROUP BY, and HAVING clauses	no	yes
EXISTS predicate	no	yes
Dependent value attributes	no	yes
Inheritance	no	yes

SELECT clause

The SELECT clause is not required in a WebSphere EJB QL statement. For compatibility with WebSphere 4.0 and other EJB QL providers, it should be specified anyway.

Delimited identifiers

WebSphere supports delimited identifiers, that is identifiers in quotes that are reserved words:

```
select  object(o) from MyBean o where o."select" = ?1
```

String comparisons

WebSphere supports the use of < and > for string comparisons within WHERE clauses.

Scalar functions

EJB QL supports `concat`, `substring`, `locate`, `length`, `abs`, `sqrt`. These functions are valid for all DBMS supported by WebSphere.

WebSphere supports in addition type conversion functions (char, decimal, bigint, double, float, integer, smallint, real, date, time, timestamp), string functions (lcase, ucase, digits), and date/time functions (days, year, month, day, hour, minute, second, microsecond). These functions are supported only or DB2.

ORDER BY

The ORDER BY clause specifies an ordering of the objects in the result collection.

> **ORDER BY** [order_element ,]* order_element
>
> order_element ::= { path-expression | integer } [**ASC** | **DESC**]

- ► The path expression must specify a single valued field that is a primitive type (int) or a wrapper type (Integer).
- ► ASC specifies ascending order and is the default. DESC specifies descending order.
- ► integer refers to a selection expression in the SELECT clause.

Example:

```
SELECT OBJECT(a) FROM Account c ORDER BY a.accountID, a.balance DESC
```

SQL date/time expressions

WebSphere with a DB2 data store supports date/time comparisons and expression, for example:

```
t.transID > '1990-02-24'
DATE('3/15/2000') - '12/31/1999'
```

Subqueries, aggregations, group by, and having clauses

A subquery can be used in quantified predicates, EXISTS predicates or IN predicates. A subquery should only specify a single element in the SELECT clause.

When a path expression appears in a subquery, the identification variable of the path expression must be defined either in the subquery, in one of the containing subqueries, or in the outer query.

A scalar subquery is a subquery that returns one value. A scalar subquery can be used in a basic predicate and in the SELECT clause of a dynamic query.

Aggregation functions are avg, max, min, sum and count(*). Aggregation functions can only be used in subselect and HAVING clauses, but not in the top-level SELECT clause.

Examples:

▶ Accounts that have more than the average balance:

```
SELECT OBJECT(e) FROM Account e
    WHERE e.balance > ( SELECT AVG(e1.balance) FROM Account e1 )
```

▶ Largest transaction of each account:

```
SELECT object(t) FROM TransRecord t WHERE t.transAmount =
    ( SELECT MAX(u.transAmount) FROM IN (t.theAccount.transrecords) u )
```

EXISTS predicate

The EXISTS predicate tests for the presence of certain objects.

EXISTS (subselect) | collection-valued-path-expression

The result of EXISTS is true if the subselect returns at least one value or the path expression evaluates to a nonempty collection; otherwise the result is false.

To negate an EXISTS predicate, precede it with the logical operator NOT.

For example, return customers that have at least one account with a large balance, or accounts that have no transaction records:

```
SELECT object(c) FROM Customer c WHERE EXISTS
    ( SELECT 1 FROM IN (c.accounts) a WHERE a.balance > 10000 )

SELECT object(a) FROM Account a WHERE NOT EXISTS a.transrecords
```

Dependent value attributes

With a path expression you can access the attributes of a dependent value class:

```
SELECT object(c) FROM Customer c WHERE c.address.state = 'California'
```

This is only valid if the Address object is mapped to individual columns in a table using a composer ("Using composers" on page 480).

Inheritance

The data model for container-managed persistence does not currently support inheritance. This is written in the EJB Specification Version 2.0 as a restriction of the EJB QL definition in Chapter 11.2.11. It is not supported in a July 2002 draft version of the EJB Specification 2.1 either. With this restriction, entity objects or value classes of different types cannot be compared.

WebSphere extensions to EJB QL enable us to query the type of an entity bean in an inheritance hierarchy:

► The IS OF TYPE predicate is used to test the type of an EJB reference. It is similar in function to the Java instanceof operator.

► The ONLY option can be used in addition to specify that the reference must be exactly this type and not a subtype.

identification-variable **IS OF TYPE** (**[ONLY]** type)*

To illustrate EJB QL for inheritance we use an extended hierarchy (Figure 4-29).

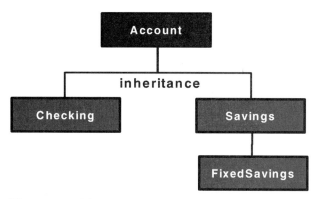

Figure 4-29   Inheritance hierarchy for EJB QL examples

Examples:

► To retrieve all the types from the inheritance hierarchy:

```
SELECT object(account)FROM Account account WHERE account.balance > 100
```

Returns instances from Account, Checking, Savings and FixedSavings where the balance is more than 100.

► To retrieve only Savings accounts:

```
SELECT object(a) FROM Account a WHERE a IS OF TYPE (Savings)
```

Note that this statement returns instances of Savings and FixedSavings, because FixedSavings is a subclass of Savings.

► To retrieve only instances of Savings without the subtype:

```
SELECT object(a) FROM Account a WHERE a IS OF TYPE (ONLY Savings)
```

WebSphere Enterprise extensions

WebSphere Application Server Enterprise Edition provides more extensions to EJB QL.

Dynamic query API

The dynamic EJB query service provides J2EE applications a way to search CMP entity beans using an extension of the EJB query language. The query can return either EJB references or values of CMP and CMR fields.

The dynamic query API is also called dynamic query service (DQS):

▶ DQS allows queries to be created and executed during runtime. Queries do not have to be statically predefined. Queries can involve a number of abstract schema types.

▶ DQS complies with the EJB QL 2.0 and the WebSphere extensions. You can compare dynamic queries with the preparation and invocation of a prepared statement in JDBC, but you are operating on the abstract schema types of the underlaying entity bean set.

Dependent value methods

We described dependent value attributes as those attributes of dependent classes of an entity bean. Dependent value methods are the methods of those classes. You can use any serializable Java class to be used in a CMP field. With dependent value methods you can address the fields and methods of a dependent object directly on the EJB QL statement:

```
SELECT object(e) FROM Customer e
WHERE e.address.distance('San Jose') > 10 AND e.address.zipcode = 95120
```

This query invokes the `distance` method of the `Address` class:

```
public double distance(String start_location) { ... }
```

EJB bean methods

A path expression can also navigate to a method of an entity bean. The method must be defined in either the remote or local bean interface. You cannot mix both remote and local methods in a single query statement:

▶ If the query contains remote methods, the dynamic query must be executed using the query remote interface. Using the query remote interface causes the query service to activate beans and create instances of the remote bean interface.

▶ Likewise, a query statement with local bean methods must be executed with the query local interface. This causes the query service to activate beans and local interface instances.

The characteristics of bean methods are:

▶ Methods must have non-void return types and method arguments and return types must be either primitive types (`int`) or wrapper types (`Integer`).

▶ Do not use get methods to access CMP and CMR fields of a bean.

▶ If a method has overloaded definitions, the overloaded methods must have different number of parameters (having different types is not enough).

▶ If any input argument to a method is NULL, it is assumed that the method returns a NULL value and the method is not invoked.

Multiple element SELECT clauses

In the specification it is allowed to return a CMP or CMR field. The EJB Query extension allows multiple elements and expressions in the SELECT clause:

```
SELECT e.name, e.salary+e.bonus as total_pay from EmpBean e
```

Quick tour on dynamic query

Here are a few examples of dynamic queries:

▶ Employee ID and maximum salary:

```
select e.empid, max(e.salary) from Employee e
```

▶ Name, total pay, and an EJB reference for all employees:

```
select e.name, e.salary+e.bonus as total_pay, object(e) from Employee e
```

▶ Invoking an object method (`print` must be defined on the address CMP field):

```
select e.address.print() as address from Employee e
```

▶ Number of employees in each department:

```
select e.dept.deptno as dept, count(*) as employee_count from Employee e
  group by e.dept.deptno
  order by 2
```

Dynamic query interface basics

The dynamic EJB query service is an EJB bean with a remote interface name of `com.ibm.websphere.ejbquery.Query` and a local interface name of `com.ibm.websphere.ejbquery.QueryLocal`.

▶ Use the remote `Query` interface if you are accessing the query service from a remote client or you want the query to return remote EJB references in the query result.

▶ The `QueryLocal` interface must be called within a transaction context and returns a demand-driven iterator. Any EJB references returned will be local references.

The main method to use is executeQuery. A reference to the Query object must be obtained from the QueryHome. A transaction context is required; if none exists, the EJB container starts a transaction upon calling executeQuery.

Figure 4-30 shows an example of a remote dynamic query.

```
import com.ibm.websphere.ejbquery.*;
  ...

 try {
   String query =
       "select e.name as name , object(e) from Employee e where e.salary < 50000";

   InitialContext ic =  new InitialContext();
   Object obj =  ic.lookup("com/ibm/websphere/ejbquery/Query");
   QueryHome qh = (QueryHome) PortableRemoteObject.narrow(obj, QueryHome.class);
   Query qb = qh.create();

   // You must specify a maximum size of the query result set (99)
   QueryIterator it = qb.executeQuery(query, null, null ,0, 99 );

   // Each tuple contains a name and an employee object reference
   while (it.hasNext() ) {
       IQueryTuple tuple = (IQueryTuple) it.next();
       String s = (String) tuple.getObject(1);
       System.out.println(it.getFieldName(1)+" "+s);
       Employee e = (Employee) PortableRemoteObject.
                             narrow( tuple.getObject(2), Employee.class );
       System.out.println(it.getFieldName(2)+" "+e.getPrimaryKey().toString());
   }
 } catch (QueryException qe) {
       System.out.println("Query Exception "+ qe.getMessage() );
   }
```

Figure 4-30 Dynamic query example

Other methods of the dynamic query interface are prepareQuery and executePlan, where a statement is prepared once and executed multiple times with different parameters:

```
String query = "select e.name from Employee e where e.salary < ?1";
QueryIterator it = null;
Integer[] parms = new Integer[1]; parms[0] = new Integer(0);
String queryPlan= qb.prepareQuery(query, parms, null );
parms[0] = new Integer(50000);
it = qb.executePlan(queryPlan, parms, 0, 99);
......
parms[0] = new Integer(60000);
it = qb.executePlan(queryPlan, parms, 0, 99);
```

Developing entity beans with advanced concepts

In this section, we expand the banking application to describe how we might add the following new features to our beans:

- ▶ Relationships
- ▶ Inheritance
- ▶ Custom query methods
- ▶ EJB QL examples

Relational database mapping

As in the CMP persistent fields, the CMR relationship fields must also be mapped to an actual database element at deployment time, so that the concrete code can be generated. Therefore, each CMR field is mapped to a foreign key on the table that we are relating to.

Expanded banking entity requirements

The following are the new features that we will add to our banking system:

- ▶ **Support for new entity bean Account**—This bean has the following persistent fields defined: `accountID` (primary key), `balance`, `interest`, and `accountType`. This bean must support the business methods of `deposit` and `withdrawal`.

- ▶ **Support for a new entity bean TransRecord**—This bean has the following persistent fields defined: `transID` (primary key), `transType`, `transAmount`.

- ▶ **Add 1:m relationship**—`Account-TransRecord`.

- ▶ **Add m:m relationship**—`Customer-Account`.

- ▶ **Account subtypes**—Add two subtypes of `Account`, `Checking` and `Savings`, using the IBM extension of inheritance.

- ▶ **New business and query methods**—We can now exploit relationships and define new business (component) and query (home) methods. Using EJB QL we can formulate quite complex queries to find beans that satisfy certain requirements. For example, we can find accounts that have a large balance (we call those gold accounts).

Entity bean relationship requirements

The relationships that we support are shown in Figure 4-31.

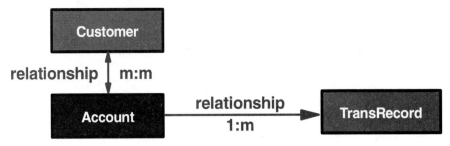

Figure 4-31 Relationships of the bank model

Because of these relationships, our beans will support the following new methods:

▶ **Customer**

- CMR accessor methods—setAccounts, getAccounts
- Business methods to exploit relationships—addAccount, removeAccount
- Query methods—findGoldCustomers, findHighInterest, findAllCustomers
- Home method—findAllCustomers (just the last names)

▶ **Account**

- CMR accessor methods—getCustomers, setCustomers, getTransrecords, setTransrecords
- Business methods to exploit relationships— addCustomer, removeCustomer
- Business methods—deposit, withdraw (throws application exception)
- Query methods—findAllAccounts, findGoldAccounts, findTransferAccounts, findLargestAccount

▶ **TransRecord**

- CMR access methods—getTheAccount, setTheAccount
- Create method to exploit relationships—create(with account parameter)

Entity bean structures

The following describes what the new entity beans of Account and TransRecord would look like. Not all details are provided (such as all the callback methods), but you should get a feel for how these new relationships can be exposed. We conclude with a client view that shows the actual usage of these new methods later. For each bean (new and old), we show the following:

▶ Component interface

- ► Home interface
- ► Bean class

Customer entity bean updates

The `Customer` entity bean requires some small updates.

Changing the Customer local component interface

Figure 4-32 shows the component interface we define for the `Customer` entity bean. We know that `Customer` is related to `Account` through a many-to-many relationship. We are required to define a local component interface because we use this bean in a bidirectional relationship.

```
public interface Customer extends javax.ejb.EJBLocalObject {
//cmp field accessors the same as before

//new methods available because of relationships
   public Collection(getAccounts();
   public void addAccount(AccountLocal anAccount);
   public void removeAccount(AccountLocal anAccount);
}
```

Figure 4-32   Local component interface of customer entity bean

Changing the Customer home interfaces

Figure 4-33 shows the new home interfaces we define for the `Customer` entity bean. Some additional finder methods are declared to demonstrate how we can traverse relationships.

```
public interface CustomerLocalHome extends javax.ejb.EJBLocalHome {
   public void create(int customerID) throws CreateException;
   public CustomerLocal findByPrimaryKey(CustomerKey key)
                                              throws FinderException;
   public Vector getAllCustomers() throws FinderException;
   public Collection getGoldCustomers() throws FinderException;
}
public interface CustomerHome extends javax.ejb.EJBHome {
   public void create(int customerID)
                             throws CreateException, RemoteException;
   public CustomerLocal findByPrimaryKey(CustomerKey key)
                             throws FinderException, RemoteException;
   public Collection findHighInterest(int interest)
                             throws FinderException, RemoteException;
}
```

Figure 4-33   Local home interface of customer entity bean

Updating the Customer bean class

Figure 4-34 shows the new `Customer` bean class and the new methods that it supports. There is a home method and two select methods declared here as well.

```
public abstract Customer extends javax.ejb.EntityBean {
   //new methods only

   //fields used for CMR
   public Collection getAccounts();
   public void setAccounts(Collection accounts);

   //new business methods
   public void addAccount(AccountHome anAccount) {
      getAccounts().add(anAccount);
   }
   public void removeAccount(AccountHome anAccount) {
      getAccounts().remove(anAccount);
   }
//new select methods:
public abstract Set ejbSelectAllCustomerNames() throws FinderException;
public abstract Collection ejbSelectNumberOfAccounts(String)
                                          throws FinderException;
//home method
   public Vector ejbHomeGetAllCustomers() throws FinderException {
      //implementation not shown
   }

   //other lifecycle methods not shown, but they exist!
}
```

Figure 4-34   Customer bean class

Account entity bean

The account entity bean represents a bank account.

Building the Account local component interface

Figure 4-35 shows the component interface we define for the `Account` entity bean. We know that `Account` is related to `Customer` and `TransRecord`, so we expose the CMR accessors. We are required to define a local component interface because we use this bean in a bidirectional relationship.

In addition, we define the business methods of `deposit` and `withdraw`.

```
public interface AccountLocal extends javax.ejb.EJBLocalObject {

    public BigDecimal getBalance();
    public void getBalance(BigDecimal balance);
    public int getInterest();
    public void getInterest(int interest);
    public String getAccountType();
    public void setAccountType(String accountType);

    public Collection getCustomers();
    public void addCustomer(CustomerLocal customer);
    public void removeCustomer(CustomerLocal customer);
    public Collection getTransrecords();

    public BigDecimal deposit(BigDecimal amount);
    public BigDecimal withdrawal(BigDecimal amount);
}
```

Figure 4-35   Account local component interface

Building the Account local home interface

Figure 4-36 shows the home interface we define for the Account entity bean.
Some additional finder methods are declared to demonstrate how we can
traverse relationships.

```
public interface AccountLocalHome extends javax.ejb.EJBLocalHome {

    public void create(String accountID)                 throws CreateException;
    public void create(String accountID, BigDecimal balance, int interest)
                                                         throws CreateException;
    public AcountLocal findByPrimaryKey(String key) throws FinderException;
    public Collection findAllAccounts()                  throws FinderException;
    public Collection findGoldAccounts(BigDecimal balance)
                                                         throws FinderException;
    public Collection findTransferAccounts(int customerID,
                               String accountID) throws FinderException;
    public AccountLocal findLargestAccount(int customerID)
                                                         throws FinderException;
}
```

Figure 4-36   Account local home interface

Building the Account bean class

Figure 4-37 shows the new Account bean class and the new methods that it
supports.

```
public abstract AccountBean extends javax.ejb.EntityBean {
    //fields used for CMP
    public abstract String getAccountID();
    public abstract void setAccountID(String accountID);
    public abstract BigDecimal getBalance();
    public abstract void getBalance(BigDecimal balance);
    public abstract int getInterest();
    public abstract void getInterest(int interest);
    public abstract String getAccountType();
    public abstract void getAccountType(String accountType);

    //fields used for CMR
    public abstract Collection getCustomers();
    public abstract void setCustomers(Collection customers);
    public abstract Collection getTransrecords();
    public abstract void setTransrecords();

    //business methods:
    public void addCustomer(CustomerLocal aCustomer) {
        getCustomers().add(aCustomer);
    }
    public void removeCustomer(CustomerLocal aCustomer) {
        getCustomers().remove(aCustomer);
    }
    public BigDecimal deposit(BigDecimal anAmount) {
        setBalance(getBalance().add(amount));
        return getBalance();
    }
    public BigDecimal withdraw(BigDecimal anAmount)
                                    throws InsufficientFundException {
        if (getBalance().compareTo(amount) == -1)
            throw new InsufficientFundException("Not enough finds");
        else setBalance(getBalance().subtract(amount));
        return getBalance();
    }

    //other lifecycle methods not shown, but they exist!
}
```

Figure 4-37   Account bean class

TransRecord entity bean

The TransRecord entity bean represents a transaction on a bank account.

Building the TransRecord local component interface

Figure 4-38 shows the component interface we define for the TransRecord entity bean.

```
public interface TransRecord extends javax.ejb.EJBLocalObject {

    public String getTransType();
    public void setTransType(String transType);
    public BigDecimal getTransAmount();
    public void setTransAmount(BigDecimal transAmount);

    public AccountLocal getTheAccount();
    public void setTheAccount(AccountLocal theAccount);
}
```

Figure 4-38   TransRecord local component interface

Building the TransRecord local home interface

Figure 4-39 shows the home interface we define for the TransRecord entity bean. An additional create method is declared to add a transaction record to an account.

```
public interface TransRecordLocalHome extends javax.ejb.EJBLocalHome {

    public void create(Timestamp transID) throws CreateException;
    public void create(String type, String amount, AccountLocal account)
                                        throws CreateException;
    public TransRecordLocal findByPrimaryKey(Timestamp key)
                                        throws FinderException;
}
```

Figure 4-39   TransRecord local home interface

Building the TransRecord bean class

Figure 4-40 the new TransRecord bean class and the new methods that it supports.

```
public abstract TransRecord extends javax.ejb.EntityBean {
    //fields used for CMP
    public abstract java.sql.Timestamp getTransID();
    public abstract void setTransID(java.sql.Timestamp transID);
    public abstract String getTransType();
    public abstract void setTransType(String transType);
    public abstract BigDecimal getTransAmount();
    public abstract void setTransAmount(BigDecimal transAmount);

    //fields used for CMR
    public abstract AccountLocal getTheAccount();
    public abstract void setTheAccount(AccountLocal theAccount);

//showing how ejbCreate and postCreate now work with the relationships
    public String ejbCreate(Timestamp transID, ..., AccountLocal theAccount)
                                                throws CreateException {
        setTransID(transID);
        setXxxxxx(.....);
        return null;
    }
    public void ejbPostCreate(Timestamp transID, ..., AccountHome theAccount)
                                                throws CreateException {
        setTheAccount(theAccount);
}
    //other lifecycle methods not shown, but they exist!
}
```

Figure 4-40   TransRecord bean class

Checking and Savings entity beans

The Checking and Savings beans are subclasses of Account.

Building the Checking local component interface

Figure 4-41 shows the component interface we define for the Checking entity
bean. It includes only its own attribute and inherits all other methods from the
Account bean.

```
public interface CheckingLocal extends AccountLocal {
    public java.math.BigDecimal getOverdraft();
    public void setOverdraft(java.math.BigDecimal newOverdraft);
}
```

Figure 4-41   Checking local component interface

Building the Checking local home interface

Figure 4-42 shows the home interface we define for the Checking entity bean. It includes only the findByPrimaryKey method and a tailored create method.

```
public interface CheckingLocalHome extends javax.ejb.EJBLocalHome {
    public CheckingLocal findByPrimaryKey(String key)
                                        throws javax.ejb.FinderException;
    public CheckingLocal create(String accountID, BigDecimal balance,
        int interest, BigDecimal overdraft) throws javax.ejb.CreateException;
}
```

Figure 4-42   Checking local home interface

Building the Checking bean class

Figure 4-43 shows the bean class for the Checking entity bean. It includes only the additional accessor methods, a tailored ejbCreate method, and an overwrite for the withdraw method that checks for the overdraft amount.

```
public abstract class CheckingBean extends AccountBean {
    // new accessor method
    public abstract java.math.BigDecimal getOverdraft();
    public abstract void setOverdraft(java.math.BigDecimal newOverdraft);
    // tailored create method
    public String ejbCreate(String accountID, BigDecimal balance,
            int interest, BigDecimal overdraft) throws CreateException {
        super.ejbCreate(accountID, balance, interest);
        setAccountType("CHECKING");
        setOverdraft(overdraft);
        return null;
    }
    // overwrite withdraw method to check for overdraft amount
    public BigDecimal withdraw(BigDecimal amount)
                                    throws InsufficientFundException {
        if ( getBalance().add( getOverdraft() ).compareTo(amount) == -1)
            throw new InsufficientFundException("Checking: Not enough funds");
        else setBalance( getBalance().subtract(amount) );
        return getBalance();
    }
}
```

Figure 4-43   Checking bean class

Savings interfaces and bean

The implementation of the interfaces and bean class for the Savings bean would be similar to the Checking bean.

Deployment descriptor updates

In this section, we outline the deployment descriptor entries for some of the entities, relationships, and finders that we have defined. This is a scaled-down version of this descriptor. A full copy can be found in Chapter 11, "Container-managed entity bean development" on page 397.

Beans

We have already seen the deployment descriptor entries for the Customer, Account, and TransRecord entity beans in "Entity bean definition in the deployment descriptor" on page 126.

The Checking and Savings bean are similar to the Account bean. Note that the CMP fields include the fields of the Account bean and their own fields.

Relationships

We have already seen an example of the Account-TransRecord 1:m relationship. Figure 4-44 shows the Customer-Account deployment descriptor entry.

```
<ejb-relation>
   <ejb-relation-name>Customer-Account</ejb-relation-name>
   <ejb-relationship-role>
      <ejb-relation-role-name>accounts</ejb-relation-role-name>
      <multiplicity>Many</multiplicity>
      <relationship-role-source>
         <ejb-name>Customer</ejb-name>
      </relationship-role-source>
      <cmr-field>
         <cmr-field-name>accounts</cmr-file-name>
         <cmr-field-type>java.util.Collection</cmr-file-type>
      </cmr-field>
   </ejb-relationship-role>
   <ejb-relationship-role>
      <ejb-relation-role-name>customers</ejb-relation-role-name>
      <multiplicity>Many</multiplicity>
      <relationship-role-source>
         <ejb-name>Account</ejb-name>
      </relationship-role-source>
      <cmr-field>
         <cmr-field-name>customers</cmr-file-name>
         <cmr-field-type>java.util.Collection</cmr-file-type>
      </cmr-field>
   </ejb-relationship-role>
</ejb-relation>
```

Figure 4-44   Customer-Account relationship in the deployment descriptor

Query language examples

In this section, we outline some of the queries implemented using EJB QL and how they are defined in the deployment descriptor.

Customer queries

We describe only one query in detail, `findGoldCustomers` (Figure 4-45).

```
<query>
    <description>Retrieve gold customers (large balance).</description>
    <query-method>
        <method-name>findGoldCustomers</method-name>
        <method-params>
            <method-param>java.math.BigDecimal</method-param>
        </method-params>
    </query-method>
    <ejb-ql>select distinct object(c) from Customer c, in(c.accounts) a
            where a is of type (Savings) and a.balance &gt; ?1
    </ejb-ql>
</query>
```

Figure 4-45   Customer finder method in the deployment descriptor

This query starts with a customer instance, follows the relationship to accounts, then tests the type of account, and compares the balance to the parameter. The query illustrates the use of a relationship, using `in(c.accounts)`, where `accounts` is the CMR field for all related account of a customer. The query also shows the use of inheritance, using `is of type (Savings)`, to select only savings accounts.

The `findHighInterest` query returns customers that have accounts with a high interest rate and at least one transaction record of type credit. This query follows two relationships from customer to accounts to transaction records:

```
select distinct object(c) from Customer c, in(c.accounts) a,
                                in(a.transrecords) t
where a.interest &gt; ?1 and t.transType = 'C'
```

The `ejbSelectAllCustomerNames` query retrieves the collection of last names of all customers. This is an example of a select method that returns a collection of CMP fields:

```
select o.lastName from Customer o
```

The `ejbSelectNumberOfAccounts` is a select method that retrieves all the account numbers for one customer:

```
select a.accountID from Customer o, in(o.accounts) a
where o.lastName = ?1
```

Account queries

The `findAllAcounts` query returns all accounts:

```
select object(o) from Account o
```

The `findGoldAccounts` query return accounts with a high balance:

```
select object(o) from Account o where o.balance &gt; ?1
```

The `findLargestAccount` query returns the account with the largest balance for one customer. This query uses a subselect to retrieve the largest balance, follows the relationship to customers to check for the given customer key, and then follows the relationship from the customer to all accounts to find the account with the largest balance. This means that the `Customer-Account` relationship is traversed twice.

```
select object(a) from Account a, in(a.customers) c
  where c.customerID = ?1 and a.balance =
        ( select max(a1.balance) from in (c.accounts) a1 )
```

The `findTransferAccounts` query returns all the accounts to which a customer can transfer money from a given account. This query also traverses the `Customer-Account` relationship twice, from the account to customers and from the given customer to all accounts. Finally, the original account is discarded from the list to only return other accounts of the customer.

```
select object(b) from Account a, in(a.customers) c, in(c.accounts) b
  where c.customerID = ?1 and a.accountID = ?2
        and a.accountID &lt;&gt; b.accountID
```

These query examples show the power of EJB QL. Such queries were not easily done with the implementation provided by EJB 1.1.

Home method

In the `Customer` class, we can implement a home method that uses the two select methods to return the list of customers and their accounts.

The `ejbHomeGetAllCustomers` method is implemented in the `Customer` bean to return a vector of customer information. First the `ejbSelectAllCustomerNames` method is called to retrieve all the names. For each name, the `ejbSelectSumberOfAccounts` method is called to retrieve the account numbers of the customer. The information is returned as an array of strings that is added to the result vector.

The actual implementation of the method is shown in "Developing a home method" on page 463.

Entity bean design and construction best practices

In this example, we introduced a couple of best practices that we want to summarize in relation to the advanced entity bean concepts:

- **Use of local interfaces**—We modeled the entity beans to be used only within the JVM from other processes, in this case, other beans. Note that this is now a requirement of our beans because of the navigability in our relationships.

- **Tailored accessor methods for many-to-many relationships**—To simplify client programming, we suggest you define tailored add and remove methods to add and delete instances of m:m relationships (for example, addAccount for the Customer bean).

Client view of advanced entity bean concepts

In this section, we look at the client view when dealing with relationships, inheritance, and custom finders.

Relationship programming

We have promoted some relationship-based methods to the component interface and added some additional finders to the home interfaces that provide us with additional business logic that we can expose to the customer.

Although we understand that behind the scenes these relationships exist and there were complex mappings to establish them, in reality, to the EJB clients, these CMR fields just look like collections of other EJBOjbect references.

Let us look at client programming for a 1:m relationship.

Traversing a "one" relationship

When looking at the Account-TransRecord relationship from the TransRecord side, the theAccount is just another field (actually a CMR field).

The CMR access method of getTheAccount and setTheAccount are now accessible from the TransRecord. If we have a TransRecord instance, we do not require the accountID to get the Account that this transaction is related to; we just use the accessor method of the TransRecord:

```
AccountLocal account = transrecord.getTheAccount();
```

Traversing a "many" relationship

When looking at all the transaction records for an account then the accessor method of the account retrieves a collection and we have to iterate through the collection to access each related transaction record:

```
AccountLocal account = accountHome.findByPrimaryKey(accountID);
Collection coll = account.getTransrecords();
Iterator collit = coll.iterator();
while ( collit.hasNext() ) {
    TransRecordLocal tr = (TransRecordLocal)collit.next();
    String timestamp = ((java.sql.Timestamp)tr.getPrimaryKey()).toString();
    String creditOrDebit = tr.getTransType();
    java.math.BigDecimal amount = tr.getTransAmount();
    ...
}
```

Note that you have to cast the items in a collection to the correct type.

Traversing in any direction of an m:m relationship is the same as traversing in the many direction of a 1:m relationship. A collection of related beans is returned and iteration through the collection is required.

Programming with a collection

Here is a subset of the methods that you can use on a Java `Collection`:

▶ `size`—Returns the number of elements

▶ `isEmpty`—Returns true if the collection has no elements

▶ `iterator`—Returns an iterator to go through the collection

▶ `toArray`—Returns an array containing all the elements

▶ `contains(Object o)`—Returns true if the object is contained in the collection

Inheritance programming

Programming against an inheritance structure requires dealing with different types of beans that are handled or retrieved using the same methods.

Testing the object type

With an inheritance hierarchy, one of the most common programming tasks is to test what kind of object is returned from a retrieval.

For example, when we retrieve an Account by primary key we want to know if we got a Checking or a Savings account. The instanceOf construct is used to check the object type:

```
AccountLocal account = AccountLocalHome.findByPrimaryKey(...keyvalue...);
if (account instanceOf CheckingLocal) {
    CheckingLocal checking = (CheckingLocal)account;
    BigDecimal overdraft = checking.getOverdraft();
    ...
}
```

When we follow a relationship to Account (for example from Customer), we may also have to investigate what kind of accounts are returned:

```
CustomerLocal cust = CustomerLocalHome.findByPrimaryKey(...keyvalue...);
Collection coll = cust.getAccounts();
Iterator collit = coll.iterator();
while ( collit.hasNext() ) {
    AccountLocal account = collit.next();
    if (account instanceOf CheckingLocal) {
        CheckingLocal checking = (CheckingLocal)account;
        ...
    } else if (account instanceOf Savings) {
        SavingsLocal savings = (SavingsLocal)account;
        ...
    }
}
```

Creating objects

When creating an object within an inheritance structure, it is important to create the correct type of object and to initialize the superclass fields and the subclass fields.

The best way to handle this is to have tailored create (ejbCreate) methods for each type of bean. For example, the ejbCreate method of the Checking bean calls the ejbCreate method of the Account bean before setting its own data:

```
public String ejbCreate(String accountID, BigDecimal balance,
                        int interest, BigDecimal overdraft) throws ... {
    super.ejbCreate(accountID, balance, interest);
    setOverdraft(overdraft);
    return null;
}
```

Note that if all accounts must be either Checking or Savings accounts, then the superclass Account should not have a public create method in the home interface. Only subclass beans can be created by using the create method on the subclass home interfaces.

Using custom finder methods

Custom finder methods return either a single `EJBObject` or a collection of `EJBObjects`. Single `EJBObject` are handled as in the `findByPrimaryKey` method.

When retrieving a collection, the programming is identical to traversing a many relationship. For example, the `findGoldCustomers` method returns a collection of `Customer` objects:

```
Collection coll = customerHome.findGoldCustomers(balance);
Iterator collit = coll.iterator();
while ( collit.hasNext() ) {
    CustomerLocal cust = (CustomerLocal)collit.next();
    int customerID = ((CustomerKey)cust.getPrimaryKey()).getCustomerID();
    String name = cust.getName();
    ...
}
```

Summary

In this chapter, we covered the advanced concepts of entity beans: relationships, inheritance, and finder methods using the EJB query language.

Session beans

This chapter describes the concepts of session beans, and introduces the two types of session beans: stateful and stateless. We then expand the requirements of the online banking example presented in Chapter 2, "EJB architecture and concepts" on page 33 to show how to develop a session bean. Finally, some best practices for session bean development and the client view of a session bean are discussed.

At the conclusion of this chapter, you should have a good understanding of when session beans are appropriate choices for implementing business logic in your EJB applications.

© Copyright IBM Corp. 2003. All rights reserved.

Introduction

Session beans are business logic beans that implement the tasks or workflow of a system, and provide coordination of those activities between other beans. An example is a banking service that allows for a transfer between accounts (or account entity beans). Sometimes session beans act as a facade that hides an entity bean from its client, as discussed in previous chapters. Session beans often are seen as extensions to the client programming model, in that they provide the objects. Often, session beans are used to model use-case interactions of an application. Unlike entity beans that represent concrete domain concepts, or nouns of a system, the session beans can represent the verbs, or processes, of the system.

As we saw in the previous chapter, entity beans allow us to *objectify* shared data that is stored persistently, often in a database. The container manages the concurrency of access to this shared data in a safe way. Session beans may also directly access data in a database, to complete the particular task at hand, or may interact with entity beans that access the data. Choosing to access data using entity beans or session beans depends on the context, and we provide some guidelines later on in this book.

*New EJB 2.0: EJB2.0 has introduced no significant changes to the session bean component model itself, with the exception of remote and local home and component interfaces, and create method signatures, which are applicable to all enterprise bean types. Readers familiar with EJB 1.1 concepts may choose to skim over this chapter. However, the examples presented here will form the basis for the future discussion on MDBs, transactions, and security.

Session bean concepts

Session beans are non-persistent enterprise beans, in that they do not survive software or hardware crashes, as is the case with entity beans. There are two types of session beans, *stateful* session beans and *stateless* session beans.

Session beans may coordinate the work between entity beans, and provide a context for which entity bean access is performed. For example, the task associated with transferring money between two bank accounts—represented by entity beans—can be implemented in a session bean. Such a transfer session bean has to find two instances of the account entity bean (by using the account IDs), and then subtract a specified amount from one account and add the same amount to the other account.

Session bean types

As we mentioned, there are two types of session beans: stateful and stateless. Structurally, these bean types may appear similar, but what distinguishes them is how they are intended to be used, and whether a conversational state is maintained between the bean and the client of the bean. Stateful session beans represent a conversational state with a single client, and are active for the life of that conversation. Stateless session beans are not dedicated to a particular client, and are intended to be reused across multiple clients.

The significant difference between these two types is in how the container manages their life cycle. Stateless session beans may be instance pooled and reused as needed among many different clients. Conversely, stateful session beans are not instance pooled, in that the container must allocate the same bean instance for each method invocation on the bean. Your responsibilities as a bean developer are influenced by the life-cycle requirements of the session bean type that you are developing.

Stateless session beans

Stateless session beans do not maintain conversational state with a client. They are pooled instances reused by the container to service multiple clients. Their identity to the client is the same regardless of which bean instance is loaned out from the pool to service that client. We describe these concepts in more detail below.

Non conversational state

A stateless session bean holds conversations that span a single method call, which is the same as saying they have no conversational state.

After each method call on a stateless session bean, the container releases the bean back into the pool and the bean instance becomes available so that it can serve a new request. This bean has no client memory of the previous method invocation. Even if the same client invokes another method on this same `EJBObject`, there is no guarantee that the exact same bean instance will be used. When the same client is invoking another method, a different stateless session bean instance may actually service the new request. Therefore, stateless session beans are not allowed to store any conversational state from method to method.

For example, if a client calls `methodA` on a stateless session bean, and then immediately calls `methodB` on that same bean, those requests may be served by a different bean instance. A stateless session bean does not maintain any state on behalf of a client. This is important to remember, because one of the most common mistakes people make when developing stateless session beans is in trying to incorrectly cache data that is reused between methods invocations.

Other member variable state

Although session beans may not store any instance state data that is specific to a particular client, the bean is allowed to store other instance variable state between method invocations, if needed. The rule here is that this data cannot, or should not, be dependent on any particular client.

This is common with data that might be needed to initialize the bean, or with data such as an open database connection, where the connection could be used between method invocations. The thing to remember, however, about open database connections is that they must be eventually closed if the bean goes away. Therefore, the bean provider must remember to provide the means to close this connection when the bean is removed from memory, such as in the bean's `ejbRemove` method.

> **Note:** We have not mentioned it yet to this point, but no EJB (stateful, stateless, message, entity) may have static variables. So although the member variable initialization may be copies of the same data between instances, they must still be regular variables, not static variables. This is because the use of static variables interferes with the container's ability to properly manage the EJBs. The EJB specification describes this, and other, restrictions on EJB behavior that should be avoided.

Stateless session identity

All instances of stateless session beans created from the same home object are identical from the client perspective, and the container can use any available instance to satisfy a client request.

If a client has handles to two different copies of a stateless session bean created from the same home object, the `isIdentical` method of the component interface always return `true`.

Instance pooling

Stateless session beans are efficient because the container can use a small number of pooled instances to serve a large number of clients.

Recall that entity beans were an enterprise bean type that could be instance pooled. Stateless session beans may also be pooled by the container, and reused and managed in a way similar to that of entity beans. Instance pooling is a service of the container that allows the container to reuse bean instances, as opposed to creating new ones every time a request for a bean is made. This is a performance optimization that is done by the container. This allows for a scalable environment, because this pool size can be increased as needed, by either manipulating the cache size of the container, adding more memory, or more machines. Remember that EJB clients never deal directly with bean instances; they always do so from the container (through the EJBObject). The container is free to pool and reuse bean instances as needed and hide the implementation specifics from the clients.

> **Note:** Session bean instance pooling is not explicitly required by the EJB specification. WebSphere Application Server supports stateless session bean instance pooling.

Stateful session bean

Stateful session beans maintain conversational state with a client. They must belong to one and only one client, in fact, concurrent access to the same stateful session bean will result in exceptions being thrown by the container. They are not pooled instances to be reused by the container, because the container must keep that one instance servicing the same client for the length of the conversation. The container may still choose to optimize access to stateful session beans through the use of passivation and activation. The identity of individual stateful beans is not the same to the client, even if their instance state is the equivalent. We describe these concepts in more detail below.

Conversational state

A stateful session bean holds conversations that can span many method calls. A typical application holds conversations with clients at various levels. A conversation is the interaction between a client and an application, and it can represent one or more business processes. This interaction often requires that conversational data between the client and the application should be stored and accessed, whenever needed. An example of conversational data is a shopping cart that contains all the products that a customer wants to purchase. This data is also known as session data.

All the method calls that come from a single client are served by the same bean. During this conversation, the bean holds conversational state for that client. In advanced cases, the conversational state may contain open resources, such as open database connections. The conversational state of a stateful session bean is stored in the bean instance fields. For the most part, this data must be serializable (more on this later).

With stateful session beans, the container must allocate the same bean instance for each method call. A new instance is created each time a client invokes `create` on the home interface. With stateful beans, you can save data in the bean instance so that this data will still be available on the next method call.

Other member variable state

There is no distinction between the role of member variable types, as there is with stateless session beans. Any instance member variable is part of the conversational state, even if this variable is not directly dependent on the client. Therefore, such things as open database connections may also be part of the state of a stateful session bean, as in the stateless example above.

The caveat here is that open database connections are not serializable. As we will see later, it is the bean provider's responsibility to ensure that the container can serialize its member variables when it passivates the bean. This can be achieved, for instance, by making these fields `transient`, and/or by setting them to null. It is up to the developer to ensure that the bean state can be properly passivated, or prepared for serialization, as well as activated, that is, rebuilding from serialization.

Stateful session identity

All instances of stateful session beans created from the same home object are unique from the client perspective.

If a client has handles to two different stateful session beans created from the same home object, the `isIdentical` method of the component interface will always return `false`.

Activation and passivation

Entity beans participate in the activation and passivation life cycles, when entity beans are loaned out of the pool and associated with an `EJBObject`. The purpose of activation and passivation was to prepare the entity bean to be associated with the actual data, and allowed for any initialization of the bean to occur.

The activation and passivation transitions also occur for stateful session beans, although the purpose is slightly different from entity beans. Passivating of session beans occurs when the state of the stateful session bean is saved to a secondary storage, so that the container can conserve or free up resources. This generally occurs if the bean has been idle for some amount of time. After passivation, the memory occupied by the bean instance can be reclaimed. If the bean is needed again (and before it times out) by the original client, then it is activated back into the container's memory. The container may activate and passivate stateful session beans as necessary to manage its resources.

The container cannot passivate an instance if that instance is involved in a transaction. The transaction has to complete first. We describe transactional considerations for session beans in "Transactions" on page 279.

> **Note:** Stateless session beans do not participate in activation and passivation, but must still implement the activate and passivate callback methods.

Serialization

We have already discussed some guidelines to follow when determining if the stateful session beans member variables can be passivated. We describe some additional scenarios here.

In order for a container to manage efficiently a large number of bean instances, it can take an instance out of memory and store it in permanent storage. The container uses object serialization to convert the bean state into a binary stream or BLOB (binary large object). It can then write the serialized data to permanent storage. As we mentioned, this is called *passivation*.

When this bean is invoked again, the container creates a new instance and initializes it with the data saved during passivation. This is called *activation*. Therefore, if the session bean contains a conversational state that must be preserved between method invocations, the session bean indicates stateful management mode.

It is the bean provider's responsibility to not only ensure that this data can be passivated, but activated as well. Let's use as an example the stateful session bean that has to maintain an open database connection. Most likely, this connection was obtained when the bean was first created, for instance, in ejbCreate. Before the bean is passivated, the developer must make sure the connection is closed (whether the field is transient or not), and set to null. If the bean is reactivated, the developer must reestablish this open connection. The container provides the callback methods to allow us to do the necessary destruction and initialization of passivated objects.

Not all stateful session beans actually end up getting passivated, because the container has not determined that some resource optimization is required. Sometimes they are just directly removed when the client no longer needs them, such as when the bean times out. Therefore, the bean provider must remember to provide the means to close the connection when the bean is removed from memory (as we will see, in the `ejbRemove` method).

Choosing stateful or stateless session bean

The following are some guidelines to follow when choosing between stateful and stateless session beans in your application.

Comparing stateless and stateful session beans

When designing an enterprise application, many times the developer has to make design decisions on what type of session bean should be used. This decision may not always be simple. The goal of this section is to simplify the decision-making process.

Table 5-1 gives a summary comparison of stateless and stateful session beans.

Table 5-1   Stateful versus stateless session beans

Stateful	Stateless
► Can retain state between method invocations ► Can service business processes that span multiple methods or transactions ► Can be aware of any client history	► Cannot retain state between methods ► Typically used for single request, single method invocation ► Anonymous method provider, not aware of any client history or state

The type of session bean to use could be determined by trying to answer these two questions:

► Does the bean have to know the state of the client to perform business logic?

► Does the bean have to maintain state between method calls?

If the answer to either of these questions is yes, then you should consider using stateful beans. If the answer is no to both questions, then using stateless beans should be fine for your application.

However, consider these two points when you intend to use stateful beans:

► The state may be lost if a failure occurs (for example, network or system failure, system reboot).

► Stateful EJBs cannot easily be replicated, leading to poor performance in a clustered environment.

Choose to use stateful session beans carefully, and only when absolutely necessary, because they require much more system overhead to maintain. However, if the business problem readily lends itself to a stateful session bean implementation, such as maintaining a shopping cart, then certainly consider them. But keep in mind that the developer must take steps to help ensure that the life cycle of these beans, such as creating, using, and removing, are clearly spelled out, so that the workflow can be expressed through the bean.

Common usage

The EJB specification describes stateful session beans to be regular session beans, and stateless to be more of a derivative. We believe this is only because of the emphasis on the term *session*, which seems to denote state that is associated with a client, which is in fact what stateful session beans are intended to represent. Stateless session beans do not have any session in this sense (we do not consider method-level conversational state truly a session). In fact, some believe that the phrase stateless session is in fact a contradiction.

We do not believe stateful session beans to be the regular beans that most developers have adopted. If anything, stateless session beans appear to be the predominant choice, mostly because of their stateless nature in supporting service-oriented system interactions (not to mention ease of use and low overhead). Therefore, we believe that most of the time, developers will choose to implement stateless session beans that express the reusable, distributed, component-based, business-level services of their applications. Stateful session beans certainly have a place in a design, but should be used more conservatively. In the end, there is no cookie-cutter guideline here, and what really matters is whether the business problem can be expressed along the lines of one model or the other.

Session bean type structure

Recall from Chapter 2, "EJB architecture and concepts" on page 33, that session beans implement the `javax.ejb.SessionBean` interface. Given that we know that we have two types of session beans, we can extend the conceptual model to include these types (Figure 5-1).

The distinctions are more logical than physical. As you can see, stateful and stateless session beans still implement the same supertype. The actual type of session bean is declared in the deployment descriptor. The `<session-type>` entry of the deployment descriptor may be either `Stateful` or `Stateless`. Other than the actual implementation specifics depending on the bean type, the physical structure of stateful and stateless session beans are almost the same.

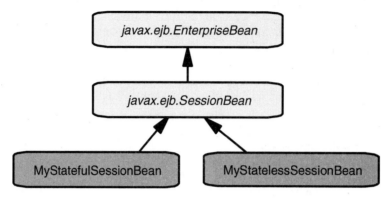

Figure 5-1 Session bean type structure

Callback methods

Figure 5-2 shows the callback methods that session bean classes must implement because they extend the `SessionBean` interface.

```
public interface SessionBean extends javax.ejb.EnterpriseBean {
    public void setSessionContext(SessionContext ctx);
    public void ejbActivate();
    public void ejbPassivate();
    public void ejbRemove();
}
```

Figure 5-2 Session bean callback methods

Regardless of whether the type of session bean is stateful or stateless, the bean class must implement these methods because these are what the container uses to actually manage the bean. The bean must also implement the life-cycle methods on the home interface, specifically, `create` and `remove`. These methods define the basis of our bean-container contract.

ejbCreate

A session bean must have at least one `ejbCreate` method. For stateless session beans, this is a single, no-argument method. A stateful session bean, on the other hand, may have multiple `ejbCreate<suffix>` methods that each define a unique way to initialize the conversational state of the session bean.

Bean-container contract

Understanding what you as a bean developer would have to do to implement a meaningful session bean means understanding the callback and life-cycle methods of the bean, and how this bean-container contract is enforced. As we mentioned, this contract is different depending on the type of session bean: stateful or stateless. This section describes the basic concepts of the bean-container contract, such as instance pooling for stateless session beans, and activation-passivation for stateful session beans. The life cycle of each session bean type is discussed.

For the purposes of this discussion, `EJBObject` will be used to refer generically to the object that implements the component interface, regardless of whether it is actually a remote `EJBObject` or a local `EJBLocalObject`.

States of a session bean

Stateful and stateless session beans have different states that define their life in the container. These are described below.

States of a stateless session bean

Stateless session beans have two-states: *no state* and *ready pool* (Figure 5-3).

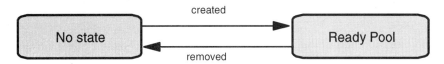

Figure 5-3   State transitions for a stateless session bean

Essentially, if the bean instance has not been created, then it is in *no state*. Once the container decides it needs a stateless session bean, it moves to the *ready* state. The bean will remain in this ready state until the container decides it no longer needs it.

Moving between pooled and ready is what happens when the container is leveraging its instance pooling mechanism. The fact that a bean in the pool is just a bean that is not associated with an `EJBObject` does not mean that it is not a bean instance. It is a ready-and-waiting pooled instance, and as it lives in the ready state, the container will ensure it associates with an `EJBObject` when a client requests services of the bean.

Note: As we will see, a client calls `create` and `remove` methods on stateless session beans, but it is really up to the container to manage the life cycle of the bean. Calling create from a client is just a way to tell the container to allocate one from the pool, the actual creation of the bean instance may have already occurred. A client calling the `remove` method on a stateless session bean does not have any impact, because it is still up to the container when to remove the bean from the pool. With stateless session beans, client calls to create will actually create new instances of `EJBObject` (the object which implements our remote interface), and a `remove` call will remove an `EJBObject` instance, not the actual session bean instance itself.

The container will retain the number of instances required to service the current client workload (without exceeding some container maximum). This workload is not measured in terms of how many actual clients there may be, because clients only need the session bean for the length of a method invocation. The actual number is stateless session beans required in a pool is usually much, much smaller than the actual number of active clients.

These state transitions are important, because each state change will trigger the container to invoke a callback method appropriate to that state change. As a stateless session bean developer, you have to understand these transitions to know how you should apply appropriate logic in these callback methods for your bean.

Let us discuss the purposes of each callback method for stateless session beans:

▶ **setSessionContext**—Called by the container when the bean is added to the ready pool, it should be used to capture a reference to the `SessionContext` for the bean. Figure 5-4 shows the most common form of this method.

```
public void setSessionContext(javax.ejb.SessionContext ctx){
   mySessionCtx = ctc;
}
```

Figure 5-4   Session bean setSessionContext method

▶ **ejbCreate**—This method is called when the container creates an instance of the stateless session bean. Recall that a stateless session bean must have only a single no-argument `create` method. Unlike the other enterprise bean types, this method is not called when the client invokes the create method of the home object. Rather, the container calls this once when a new instance is added to the ready pool. The client must still invoke the home method create, however, in order to get a reference to the `EJBObject`.

This method is used to do one-time initialization of the bean. This might include such activities as initialization of any resources used by the bean, such as database connections, that are safe to be shared among different method invocations of the client (Figure 5-5).

```
public void ejbCreate() throws CreateExceptions{
    //do some initialization, if any
}
```

Figure 5-5   Stateless session bean ejbCreate method

- **ejbRemove**—Called by the container when a bean instance is no longer needed in the pool. Like `ejbCreate`, `ejbRemove` is not invoked when a client calls the `remove` method on the home object. Rather, it is called when the container decides to remove it from the pool, such as when the container is cleaning up some unused instances to preserve resources. Theoretically, any resources that were obtained in the `create` method should be cleaned up here.

> **Note:** The container is not guaranteed to always call the `ejbRemove` method. For example, if the server itself crashes, `ejbRemove` would not be called. The problem, then, is that orphaned open resource connections might not be able to be closed properly.

- **ejbPassivate**—Although it must be implemented, it is not called in the stateless session bean life cycle.
- **ejbActivate**—Although it must be implemented, it is not called in the stateless session bean life cycle.

States of a stateful session bean

Stateful session beans have three-states: *no state*, *in use*, and *passivated* (Figure 5-6).

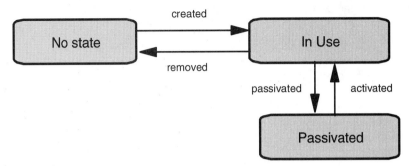

Figure 5-6 State transitions for a stateful session bean

If the bean instance has not been created, then it is in *no state*. Once a client decides it needs a stateful session bean, it will call the home object's `create` method, which will move the bean to the In Use state. The bean will remain in this ready state as long as the client is maintaining a conversation with the bean.

While the bean is in use, it may periodically be passivated. Moving between the In Use and Passivated states is what happens when the container is leveraging its passivation and activation mechanism. This happens when the container has to conserve some resources.

These state transitions are important, because each state change will trigger the container to invoke a callback method appropriate to that state change. As a developer you have to understand these transitions to know if you should apply appropriate logic in these callback methods for your bean.

Let us discuss the purposes of each callback method for stateless session beans:

▶ **setSessionContext**—Called by the container when the bean is first created and just before it moves to In Use, it should be used to capture a reference to the `SessionContext` for the bean. The purpose is the same as with stateless session beans.

▶ **ejbCreate**—This method is called when a client invokes the `create` method on a session beans home interface. There must be at least one `ejbCreate` method for each stateful session bean, although you can have multiple `create` methods with different signatures or different suffixes, such as `ejbCreateXXX`, as well as different method arguments. Unlike entity beans, there is no `ejbPostCreate` method.

This method is used to do one-time initialization of the bean. This might include such activities as initialization of any resources used by the bean, such as database connections, that are safe to be shared among different method invocations of the client, as with stateless session beans. However, a stateless session bean is now created on behalf of the client, so any initial conversational state initialization should also be done here as well.

The following is a common example of an `ejbCreate` method where the client is initializing the state of the bean (Figure 5-7).

```
public void ejbCreateCart(String userName) throws CreateExceptions{
    this.userName = userName;
    shoppingCartID = //do some randomization for a uniqueID, for instance..
}
```

Figure 5-7   Stateful session bean ejbCreate method

▶ **ejbRemove**—This method is called when a client invokes the `remove` method on a session beans home interface. Session beans have timeouts associated with them that determine when idle beans can be evicted from the container. Any resources that were acquired by the bean, such as open database connections, should be cleaned up here. Calling `remove` is a signal to the container that the bean can now be cleaned up and removed from the container's memory. You should ensure that your logic guarantees that `remove` will be called at the natural completion of a user's session of activity, and do not rely on the container to do the cleanup for you.

> **Note:** The container is not guaranteed to always call the `ejbRemove` method. For example, if the server itself crashes, `ejbRemove` would not be called. Additionally, if the bean simply times out and is in passivated state, `ejbRemove` is not called. This should be considered when designing EJBs when using resources.

▶ **ejbPassivate**—This method is called when the container decides to passivate the bean. When passivating, it will serialize the bean to some secondary storage and evict it from memory. It is called just before the serialization occurs, giving the developer the opportunity to ensure that the state of the bean can be serialized. The client has no control over when this occurs, and the container uses some internal caching algorithm to decide which beans are the best candidates for passivation.

▶ **ejbActivate**—This method is called when a client calls a method on the bean that is currently passivated. `ejbActivate` is actually called just after the bean has been deserialized from secondary storage, and gives the developer the opportunity to reinitialize any data needed to continue the operations of the bean.

Life-cycle sequence of session beans

In the previous section we described the responsibilities of each callback method, and how they are used in transitions of beans between the states.

We extend that discussion to describe the actual sequence of events that occur when a session bean is created, used, or removed. We also have to consider the passivate and activate life cycles as well. We want to show how the container actually manages the beans based on either container or client-based events, and the order in which those activities occur. Stateless and stateful session beans conform to a completely different set of container-bean contract rules, so these will be discussed independently.

Stateless session bean life cycle

We discuss the life-cycle sequence of a stateless session bean in terms of the following interactions:

▶ **Creating/removing an stateless session bean**—This is entirely a container responsibility.

▶ **Using a stateless session bean**—This is when a client invokes a method on a bean obtained through the home object.

Life cycle—creating/removing a stateless session bean

Figure 5-8 shows the sequence of container events when a container creates, and subsequently destroys, the stateless session bean instance.

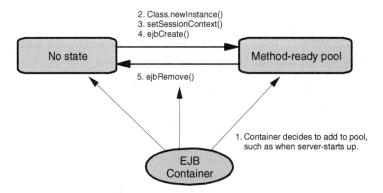

Figure 5-8   Create/remove life cycle of a stateless session bean

The above interactions are between the container and the bean. The bean provider must ensure that the appropriate logic is included in the callback methods.

1. **Container decides to create bean**—The container decides, maybe on startup, or maybe when it has to allocate more beans to the pool, to create some bean instances. Generally, an initial pool of beans is created when the server first starts up.

2. **newInstance**—The container first creates a new instance of the bean class.

3. **setSessionContext**—Container sets the session context on that bean.

4. **ejbCreate**—Allows for initialization, if any, of the bean to occur.

5. **ejbRemove**—The container now decides to evict the bean from memory to conserve resources, allowing for cleanup of the beans resources to occur.

Life cycle—using a stateless session bean

Figure 5-9 shows the sequence of client events when a client has to use a stateless session bean.

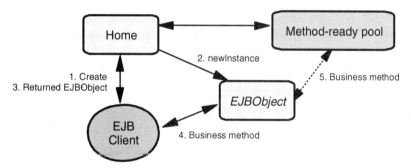

Figure 5-9   Using a stateless session bean

The above interactions are between the container and the bean. The bean provider must ensure that the appropriate logic is included. We assume that **newInstance, setEntityContext, ejbCreate** have already been called by the container, so they are not really part of this interaction.

1. **create**—Client calls the create method on the home interface, which causes the container to associate a bean instance from the pool with the client.

2. **newInstance**—The EJBObject is created.

3. **ejbObject**—The EJBObject is returned to the client.

4. **Business method**—The client calls the business method(s) on the bean through the EJBObject.

5. **Business method**—The EJBObject calls the method on the instance in the pool. The EJBObject is only associated with instance for the length of the business method.

When we described the entity bean life cycle, we did not actually show this implied interaction. What is important to note, however, is that the association between the EJBObject and the bean instance is maintained only for the life of this method.

Stateful session bean life cycle

We discuss the life-cycle sequence of a stateful session bean in terms of the following interactions:

► **Creating an stateful session bean**—This is a client-initiated activity that is invoked with a call to the home object, and involves creating a new stateful session bean.

► **Finding an existing stateful session bean**—This involves how an existing session bean is reassociated with a client. It is really a client interaction, which we describe briefly below.

► **Using and stateful session bean**—This is when a client invokes a method on an existing bean.

► **Passivating/activating a stateful session bean**—This is when the container decides to passivate and then re-activate the session bean.

► **Removing a stateful session bean**—This is also a client-initiated activity that is invoked with a call to the remove method.

Life cycle—creating a stateful session bean

Figure 5-10 shows the sequence of client events when a client creates a new stateful session bean.

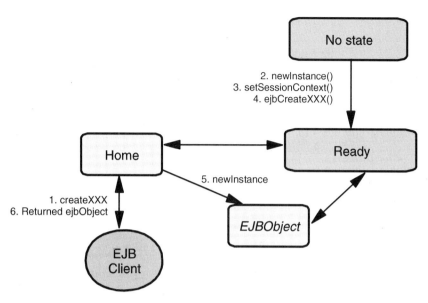

Figure 5-10   Creating a stateful session bean

The above interactions are between the container and the bean. The bean provider must ensure that the appropriate logic is included.

1. **create**—Client calls the `create` method on the home interface, which causes the container to begin building the bean instance and `EJBObject`.

2. **newInstance**—A new instance of the stateful session bean is created.

3. **setSessionContext**—Sets the session context.

4. **ejbCreateXXX**—The bean instance's corresponding `ejbCreateXXX` method is called, which may initialize the state of the session bean.

5. **newInstance**—The `EJBObject` is created.

6. **ejbObject**—The `EJBObject` is returned to the client.

Life cycle—finding an existing stateful session bean

A stateful session bean remains active until it is either removed by the client, or it timed out in the container. A client may need to gain access to an existing stateful session bean, for example, between multiple servlet invocations where the `EJBObject` has gone out of scope. Therefore, there exists a way in which to find an existing stateful session bean that a client has been working with, but does not currently have a reference to its `EJBObject`. To do this, the client must have a reference to a handle of the bean.

Entity beans have finder methods in which to locate existing entity beans. The identity of a stateful session bean, however, is not dictated by a primary key, or some other unique identifier. Therefore, they are not found through finder methods. Rather, stateful session beans are associated with a client, and the client can gain access to its session beans through a handle to the component interface. This handle can be serialized and used to refind the bean at a later time.

Figure 5-11 shows the sequence of client events when a client needs to find an existing stateful session bean by a handle to that bean.

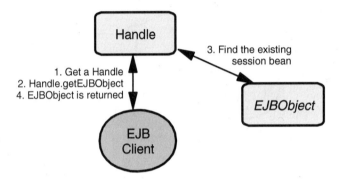

Figure 5-11   Finding an existing stateful session bean

The above interactions are between the container and the bean. The bean provider must ensure that the appropriate logic is included.

1. **get Handle**—The client gets the handle object that can be saved, for example in HttpSession. A new Handle object is created.

2. **getEJBObject**—The getEJBObject method is called on the handle.

3. **finds bean**—The container reassociates the EJBObject with the client.

4. **ejbObject**—The EJBObject is returned to the client.

Life cycle—using a stateful session bean

Figure 5-12 shows the sequence of client events when a client has to use a stateful session bean.

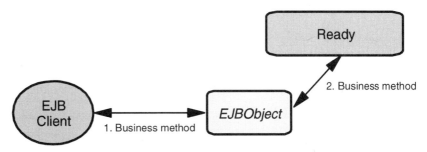

Figure 5-12   Using a stateful session bean

There really isn't much interaction here worth mentioning, just the execution of business method.

1. **Business method**—The client invokes a business method on the EJBObject.

2. **Business method**—The EJBObject delegates to the bean instance, possibly updating its state as it goes along.

Life cycle—passivating/activating a stateful session bean

Passivation occurs on a stateful session bean when the container has to release some container resources. Activation occurs when a client invokes an operation on a bean that is passivated. Each of these is a container-managed activity.

Figure 5-13 shows the sequence of container or client events when the container has to passivate or activate a stateful session bean.

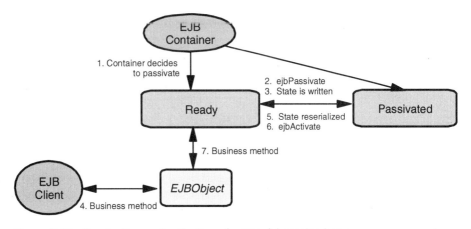

Figure 5-13   Passivation and activation of a stateful session bean

1. **Passivation trigger**—Based on some caching algorithm, the container determines that the bean is a candidate for passivation.

2. **ejbPassivate**—The `ejbPassivate` method is called on the bean, to prepare it to be serialized.

3. **State is written to secondary storage**—The state of the bean is written to some secondary storage, such as a database or file directory.

4. **Business method**—The client invokes a business method on the bean.

5. **State is rebuilt from secondary storage**—The state of the bean is rebuilt.

6. **ejbActivate**—The `ejbActivate` method is called to reinitialize any non-serializable state data that is necessary.

7. **Business method**—The actual business method on the bean instance is executed.

Life cycle—removing a stateful session bean

Figure 5-14 shows the sequence of client events when a client asks to remove a stateful session bean. Additionally, the container may also decide to remove a bean when its timeout expires, either from a passivated or ready state. When this occurs, the `remove` method is not actually called.

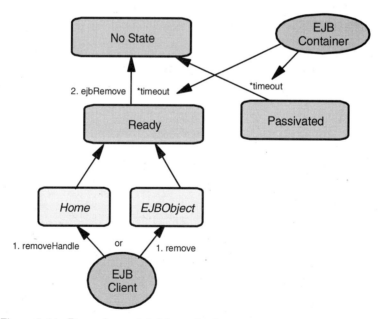

Figure 5-14   Removing a stateful session bean

1. **remove**—The client initiates a remove, either by calling the `EJBObject remove` method, or by calling the `removeHandle` on the `EJBHome`. Both methods produce the same result.

2. **ejbRemove**—The `ejbRemove` method is called, giving the bean one last chance to cleanup any open resources.

3. **timeout**—Stateful session beans may also be removed by the container when they time out, either from the passivated or ready state. When these stateful session beans time out in passivated state, their `ejbRemove` method is not called. The developer should help to ensure that a use-case sequence terminates with a call to the `remove` method of the session bean.

Developing a session bean

Tools such as Application Developer provide powerful tooling to assist with the development of session beans. Developing within the Application developer tool is discussed in detail in the second part of this book.

This section brings together all the concepts discussed in this chapter, and shows how the actual session beans can be constructed. We continue with the application that was presented in Chapter 2, "EJB architecture and concepts" on page 33, where we identified the two candidate session beans: `Banking` and `Reports`.

Building a session bean

When we build a session bean we are concerned with the bean class, the home and component interfaces, and the deployment descriptor:

- ▶ **Bean class**—The bean class must contain the bean callback methods, implementation for the component interface methods (business), and any required home life-cycle methods. The implementation of these callback methods is different depending on whether it is a stateful or stateless session bean.

- ▶ **Home interface**—Defines the life-cycle methods of the bean. There are no finder or other home interface methods of session beans, just create and remove.

- ▶ **Component interface**—Defines the client view of the bean, and the corresponding business methods.

- ▶ **Deployment descriptor**—The XML deployment descriptor for the bean.

Expanded online banking requirements

In our banking example, we described two candidate session beans: `Banking`, as a stateless facade session bean for our banking system, and `Reports`, as a potential stateful session bean candidate. The following is a review of the criteria that we used to help us classify these as session beans:

► **Stateless session beans**—The bank that we describe has to perform some business processes such as transferring balances and opening new accounts. Therefore, the bank is a good candidate for a session bean, which represent the services that the bank provides. This can be stateless, because each function represents a distinct service or activity to the client, and therefore requires no conversational state in order to be implemented.

► **Stateful session beans**—We assume that the bank can be stateless because we do not need conversational state in this simple example. However, for demonstration purposes only, we think that the process of requesting reports could be a conversational process, where the process for requesting a report will be a sequence of menus that in total will be used to generate a set of reports.

Banking stateless session bean

This main purpose of the `Banking` bean is to provide a facade layer of our system, and hides the details of the entity bean interactions from the EJB clients (Figure 5-15), and also to allow us to express the core business functions of our system. This session bean will ultimately support such business functions as querying customer data from the bank, getting a particular customer's balance, withdrawal from a customer's account, depositing to a customer's account, and transferring between customers' accounts.

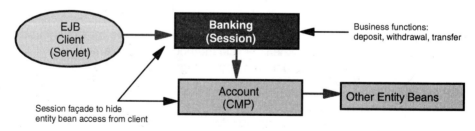

Figure 5-15   Banking session bean application example

Reports stateful session bean

The Reports bean we described as being a candidate for a stateful session bean because we want to maintain some conversational state with the client as reports are requested and produced. We recognize that this is a slightly contrived example, and that there are lots of other ways to generate reports and maintain the request state between interactions, but this is only an example. Some report business functions that we want to support include creating lists of all customers, gold customers, accounts, gold accounts, balances, etc.

The Reports session bean is represented in Figure 5-16.

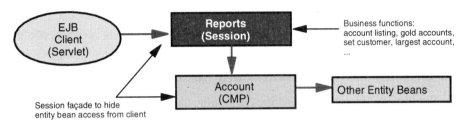

Figure 5-16   Reports session bean application example

Stateful beans and state transitions

Stateful beans are often an extension of the client, and are not completely decoupled from their clients as with stateless session beans. We cannot just define a bunch of generic, unrelated methods without knowing their relationship or the order in which they are supposed to be executed. The business methods, generally, have no independent meaning except in the context of the order in which they are to be executed, which is dictated by the contract the bean has with its client.

For example, you could not call the method called listLargestAccount unless the currentCustomer has already been set, because the listLargestAccount method depends on the state of the session bean, that is currentCustomer, to have been set.

Stateful session beans are most often modeled in terms of state transition diagrams, where each state change *to* is determined by a previous transition *from*. A particular state cannot usually be reached out of sequence. It is up to the bean developer to ensure that the bean is in the proper state in order to execute the current method and transition to the next state.

Additional requirements

The following are some expanded requirements and choices that we have made for these simple session beans.

Use of remote interfaces

We expect these beans to be used by clients. Therefore, we will define only remote home and component interface methods for our beans.

Component interface methods

We have chosen to use a remote interface for our session beans, because these are coarse-grained business processes that will be executed from outside of the EJB container.

For example purposes only, we will show how to implement the following methods on our component interfaces:

▶ **Banking**—deposit, withdraw, transfer

▶ **Reports**—listLargestAccount, setCurrentCustomer, setCurrentAccount

Building the remote component interface

The remote interface represents the business methods that we expose to our client.

Figure 5-17 shows the remote component interface of the Banking stateless session bean.

```
public interface Banking extends javax.ejb.EJBObject {
    public BigDecimal deposit(String accountID, BigDecimal amount)
        throws FinderException, RemoteException;
    public BigDecimal withdraw(String accountID, BigDecimal amount)
        throws FinderException, InsufficientFundException, RemoteException;
    public BigDecimal transfer(String accountID1, String accountID2,
                               BigDecimal amount)
        throws FinderException, InsufficientFundException, RemoteException;
    ......
}
```

Figure 5-17   Remote component interface for Banking stateless session bean

Notice that we extended EJBObject instead of EJBLocalObject—as with our entity beans—because this is a remote component interface. Also, we must ensure that the parameters and return values of each method are valid Java RMI-IIOP types.

Figure 5-18 shows the remote component interface of the Reports stateful session bean.

```
public interface Reports extends javax.ejb.EJBObject {
    public setCurrentCustomer(int custId) throws RemoteException;
    public setCurrentAccount(String accountID) throws RemoteException;
    public String[] listLargestAccount()
        throws FinderException, RemoteException, ReportInconsistentException;
    ......
}
```

Figure 5-18   Remote component interface for Reports stateful session bean

Because these are remote interfaces, we must throw RemoteException in our methods. Additionally, we are propagating the FinderException to the client, as well as custom application exceptions InsufficientFundException (not enough money) and ReportInconsistentException (customer or account not set). We describe exceptions in more detail in Chapter 8, "Additional concepts: transactions, exceptions, security" on page 277.

Building the remote home interface

The remote home interface represents the life-cycle methods of our bean for clients to create a new instance of our bean, as with stateful session beans, or to locate an existing bean instance in the pool, as with stateless session beans. From the client perspective, each appear to be creating a bean.

Figure 5-19 shows the remote home interface of the Banking stateless session bean.

```
public interface BankingHome extends javax.ejb.EJBHome {
    public Banking create() throws CreateException, RemoteException;
}
```

Figure 5-19   Remote home interface of Banking stateless session bean

Figure 5-20 shows the remote home interface of the Reports stateful session bean.

```
public interface ReportsHome extends javax.ejb.EJBHome {
    public Banking create()
        throws CreateException, RemoteException;
    public Banking createByAccount(int customerID, String accountID)
        throws CreateException, RemoteException;
}
```

Figure 5-20   Remote home interface of Reports stateful session bean

Notice that we extended `EJBHome` instead of `EJBLocalHome`—as with our entity beans—because this is a remote home interface.

For the `Banking` bean we defined only one no-argument `create` method, which is all that we are required to, and can, define for a stateless session bean. This restriction on stateless session beans ensures that every stateless session bean instance is the same as every other instance of the same type (as defined as being created from the same home object).

For the `Reports` stateful bean we show two different forms of the `create` method that allow us to create the state of the bean different ways. We must not create any finder methods with our beans, because session beans do not support finder methods. The argument types of the create methods must be valid Java RMI-IIOP types.

Because this is a remote interface, we must throw `RemoteException` in our methods. Additionally, the `CreateException` must be thrown that indicates an error on the create. We describe exceptions in more detail in "EJB exception handling" on page 304.

Building the bean class

The session bean class implements the business methods of the bean as defined in our component interface, and implements the callback methods used by the container as defined in our home interface.

So far, the only significant difference we saw in the construction of stateless and stateful session beans is in how we define `create` methods in the home interface. Other than that, everything has been pretty much the same.

This will no longer hold true as we move onto the construction of the bean class itself. The differences are so big that we will cover each in its own section.

Stateless session bean class

Figure 5-21 shows a skeleton of the stateless session bean with the `create` and callback method implementations, and an implementation of one business method, `deposit`.

```java
public class BankingBean implements javax.ejb.SessionBean {
    private SessionContext mySessionCtx = null;
    private AccountLocalHome      accountHome = null; // entity home fields
    private TransRecordLocalHome trecordHome = null;
    private CustomerLocalHome    customerHome = null;
//getHomes is a convience initialization method
    protected void getHomes() throws EJBException {
        try {
            InitialContext initCtx = new InitialContext();
            accountHome = (AccountLocalHome)initCtx.lookup
                                    ("java:comp/env/ejb/Account");

            ...
        } catch (NamingException ex) {
            ex.printStackTrace();
            throw new EJBException("Error looking up home: "+ex.getMessage());
        }
    }
    public void ejbCreate() throws CreateException {
        getHomes();
    }
    public void ejbRemove() {
    } //nothing to cleanup here, but this is where it would go
    public void ejbPassivate() { }
    public void ejbActivate() { }
    public SessionContext getSessionContext() {
     return mySessionCtx;
    }
    public void setSessionContext(SessionContext ctx) {
     mySessionCtx = ctx;
    }
    public BigDecimal deposit(String accountID, BigDecimal amount)
                        throws FinderException {

        try {
            AccountLocal account = accountHome.findByPrimaryKey(accountID);
            TransRecordLocal tr = trecordHome.create("C", amount, account);
            return account.deposit(amount);
        } catch (FinderException ex) {
            throw new FinderException("Account "+accountID+" not found");
        } catch (CreateException ex) {
            throw new EJBException("Account "+accountID+" Transrecordfailed");
        } catch (EJBException ex) {
            throw new EJBException("Account deposit failed for "+accountID);
        }
    }
}
```

Figure 5-21   Banking bean implementation (extract)

Chapter 5. Session beans

ejbCreate method

A stateless session bean can have only one ejbCreate method, which must return void and contain no arguments.

When a container invokes ejbCreate at session bean instance creation time, we take the opportunity to get the home interface objects of the entity beans used by our session bean. This way, we can do the JNDI lookup once for all instances of this bean. This is an example of a common activity in stateless session bean create methods.

Callback methods

We have left the ejbActivate and ejbPassivate methods blank, since they do not affect the stateless session bean behavior. Additionally, since we have no resources to clean up when the bean is removed from memory, we have also left the ejbRemove method blank. In the setSessionContext, we made sure that we maintained a local reference to our context object.

Business method

We have chosen to show only the **deposit** method for this bean. In this method, we find the Account entity bean, create a TransRecord instance, then use the account to update the balance based on the amount passed as a parameter. As you can see, no client state is attempted to be saved in this method.

Stateful session bean class

Figure 5-22 and Figure 5-23 show a skeleton of the Reports stateful session bean, and some work that we choose to do in the other callback methods.

```
public class ReportsBean implements javax.ejb.SessionBean {
    private SessionContext mySessionCtx = null;
    // home fields of our entity beans
    private transient AccountLocalHome accountHome  = null;
    private transient CustomerHome custRemoteHome = null;
    private transient CustomerLocalHome customerHome = null;
    // stateful fields
    private int currentCustomer = 0;
    private String currentAccount = null;
    ......

//getHomes is a convience initialization method
    protected void getHomes() throws EJBException {
        // same as for stateless session bean
    }
```

Figure 5-22   Reports bean implementation (part 1)

```
...continued...
   public Reports ejbCreate() throws CreateException {
      getHomes();
   }
   public Reports ejbCreateByAccount(int customerID, String accountID)
                     throws CreateException {
      getHomes();
      setCurrentCustomer(customerID);
      setCurrentAccount(accountID);
   }
   public void ejbRemove() { }
   public void ejbPassivate() {
      accountHome = null; customerHome = null; custRemoteHome = null;
   }
   public void ejbActivate() {
      getHomes();
   }
   public SessionContext getSessionContext() { return mySessionCtx; }
   public void setSessionContext(SessionContext ctx) { mySessionCtx = ctx; }

   public void setCurrentCustomer(int custId) {
      currentCustomer = custId;
   }
   public void setCurrentAccount(String accountID) {
      currentAccount = accountID;
   }
   public String[] listLargestAccount()
                     throws FinderException, ReportInconsistentException {
      if (currentCustomer == 0) throw new ReportInconsistentException("..");
      try {
         AccountLocal account =
                  accountHome.findLargestAccount(currentCustomer);
         if (account == null) {
            return new String[] { "No largest account", "", "" };
         } else {
            return new String[] { (String)account.getPrimaryKey(),
               account.getAccountType(), account.getBalance().toString() };
         }
      } catch (FinderException ex) {
         throw new FinderException("LargestAccount error"+ex.getMessage());
      }
   }
.....
}
```

Figure 5-23   Reports bean implementation (part 2)

ejbCreate methods

A stateful session bean must have at least one `ejbCreate` method, but can have multiple unique create methods for each way in which you want to instantiate your session bean's state. Each `ejbCreate` method must correspond to a `create` method in the bean home interface. The return type of a create method on a stateful session bean must always be the component interface bean class (in our case, `Reports`), because it is a remote bean. If this were a local bean, we would return a `ReportsLocal` corresponding to an `EJBLocalObject`. Note that there is no `ejbPostCreate` method in a session bean, as there is in an entity bean.

As with our stateless session bean, we use the create to also initialize instances to home entity bean objects for later use. This example shows that the state of the bean can also be initialized through the `create` methods, as in the case of the `createByAccount(int customerID, String accountID)` method. Each method sets the current state of the reports differently. Which one to call is up to the client.

Callback methods

Implementing meaningful callback method logic is important to properly maintaining the stability of stateful session beans:

► The `ejbPassivate` method should ensure that the state of the bean can be passivated, or serialized.

► Additionally, the `ejbActivate` should ensure that the bean state is reconstituted.

In our case, we defined the references to our entity bean home objects as being transient. This means that this data will not be saved when the bean is passivated. We are required to set these fields to null in the `ejbPassivate` method. When the bean is reconstructed, we must get the home interface objects once again.

► The `ejbRemove` method should make sure that the resources used by the bean are cleaned up. This is most important for open resources such as database connections. Sometimes developers will set fields to null to help trigger garbage collection, but this really is not required.

> **Note:** Recall that `ejbRemove` is not guaranteed to be called, for instance, if the bean has a timeout.

Developers are cautioned from doing any finalization type business logic in the `ejbRemove` method, such as an update to save data, because this method will most likely execute in an unspecified transactional context for session beans with container-managed transactions (CMT). So, although the specification says that you can access resource managers in `ejbRemove` (and ejbCreate for that matter), you must not make assumptions about how the container would handle the transactional context (such that rollback or commit might not be guaranteed if the remove fails). Put this type of save logic into your own business method to be called before a call to ejbRemove.

This unspecified transactional context is also true for ejbCreate, but as long as the ejbCreate only reads initialization data that is not part of a transaction, you should be OK.

Business method

We have chosen to show three methods of the reports bean to show that the third method (listLargestAccounts) is called based on the state that would have already been set in the first method:

▶ We first call the setCurrentCustomer method, which sets the current customer (alternatively, we could have called the ejbCreate(int customerID, String accountID) method to do the same thing).

▶ Next, we show the listLargestAccounts method. This method returns a String[] of the account number, type, and balance for that customer. This same logic could have theoretically been implemented in a stateless session bean, because we could have passed the customerId to the listLargestAccount method. But this is just a demonstration that one method's execution is dependent on another method, or state, having been set.

The method checks that the current customer has been set and throws an application exception if not.

Transactions and stateful session beans

We have started a discussion about transactions, even though we keep saying that transactions are covered in "Transactions" on page 279. But there are some fundamental aspects of the transactional semantics that you want to consider when developing your stateful session beans that do not require knowing everything about transactions yet:

▶ We have already discussed the unspecified transactional context of the ejbCreate and ejbRemove methods. This will influence what types of activities you can, or should, do in these callback methods.

▶ Another issue to consider is that the session bean instance's conversational state is not transactional, and may have to manually reset its state if a rollback occurred. So, for instance, if a bean had updated its own conversational state, and then tried to do a transactional database update, and that database update failed, it would be up to the bean developer to ensure that the state of the bean is reset properly when this occurred. By implementing the SessionSynchronization interface, stateful session beans can be notified when these events occur, and can take the necessary steps to reset its state.

Developers must ensure that the proper logic is implemented. See "Session synchronization interface" on page 300 for more information.

Deployment descriptor

Figure 5-24 shows the deployment descriptor entries for the Banking stateless session bean. For brevity, we do not show the Reports deployment descriptor.

```
<session>
    <ejb-name>Banking</ejb-name>
    <home>mysessionpackage.BankingHome</home>
    <remote>mysessionpackage.Banking</remote>
    <ejb-class>mysessionpackage.BankingBean</ejb-class>
    <session-type>Stateless</session-type>
    <transaction-type>Container</transaction-type>
    <ejb-local-ref>
        <ejb-ref-name>ejb/Account</ejb-ref-name>
        <ejb-ref-type>Entity</ejb-ref-type>
        <local-home>myentitypackage.AccountLocalHome</local-home>
        <local>myentitypackage.AccountLocal</local>
    </ejb-ref>
...
</session>
```

Figure 5-24   Deployment descriptor of a stateless session bean

The following are some important points regarding this deployment descriptor:

► **<session-type>**—This determines if this bean is stateful or stateless.

► **<home>, <remote>**—Because we are defining this bean to use remote interfaces, we must define the home interface class as <home> (vs. <local-home>), and the component interface as <remote> (vs. <local>). Recall that a bean could have both types if needed.

► **<transaction-type>**—We have defined this bean as container-managed transaction (CMT). The alternative is bean-managed transaction.

► **<ejb-ref>**—This is an optional entry that allows us to define a local reference to another EJB. By defining local references, the EJB can be retrieved through the local JNDI namespace for this bean.

This is why in our code we were able to reference the EJB using "java:comp/env/ejb/Account". If we did not do this, then we would have to search the cell or server JNDI namespace for the deployment name of this bean. This allows us to create a logical binding to an associated EJB's JNDI name that can remain constant for the life of our EJB, and allows us to not be dependent upon the real JNDI name that the associated bean may have actually been deployed under. For example, the `Banking` bean can always refer to the `Account` bean under the `ejb/Account` name. However, at deployment time, a runtime binding is made that links the `ejb/Account` to the real name that the bean is deployed under. Now we do not have to change our bean's view of things based on some deployment setting.

Session bean design and construction best practices

In our example we introduced a couple of best practices that we want to summarize, and introduced a few additional items for you to consider. These are guidelines, rather than rules, so let your experience guide you in these matters.

▶ **Do not store conversational state in stateless session beans**—This is pretty much the definition of a stateless session bean, but it bears repeating. A methods execution should not rely on any previous client or conversational state having been set in order to execute.

▶ **Use ejbCreate to initialize non-conversational stateless variables**—Take advantage of this method to initialize resources that are used throughout the life of the stateless session bean.

▶ **Release open resources on stateless ejbRemove**—Use the `ejbRemove` method to clean up any open resources acquired by a stateless session bean.

▶ **Do not implement logic in stateless bean ejbPassivate and ejbActivate**—Stateless beans are not activated or passivated, so this behavior is not called.

▶ **Do set transient and other non-serializable fields for passivation**—Be sure that you clean up and reconstitute your state data properly in the `ejbPassivate` and `ejbActivate` methods for stateful session beans.

▶ **Validate state in stateful beans**—Although it is extra work, we think that the stateful bean should check its state to ensure that the bean is in a valid state in order to execute the current operation—for example, checking that the `customerID` is not null before trying to list the largest accounts. This way you do not have to rely solely on the client's interactions (which might not be known) to determine the impact of a change on the system.

▶ **Ensure your stateful bean use case logic calls ejbRemove**—You should ensure that your logic guarantees that remove will be called at the natural completion of a user's session of activity. Do not rely on the container to do the cleanup for you.

▶ **Watch out for unspecified transactional context methods**—Methods such as `ejbCreate` and `ejbRemove` may execute in an unspecified transactional context, and so behavior that might have to be transactional should be avoided, such as database updates.

- **Be aware to manually synchronize session state with transactions**—Be aware that your bean could move to an unstable state if a transaction it was executing failed, and you do not take measures to set the state back to something safe, by being notified of the `SessionSynchronization` events.

- **Do not call a session bean from multiple clients**—Ensure that your logic will prohibit (even from the same client) the stateful session bean being called from two different clients (as defined as two separate threads).

- **Reentrancy**—Ensure that your beans do not call each other's methods in cycles. Reentrant beans are prohibited.

- **Exception handling**--Certain exceptions cause the bean to be evicted from memory.

- **Keep the beans relatively short lived**—Although session beans can span a client's conversation, this conversation should not last forever (or even very long, say, a work day). The longer the bean instance lives, the more chances it has of something bad happening to it (such as the container removing it). Try to keep the client conversational state finite and manageable, for example, the length of a transaction of some sort. If necessary, break big, long-running session beans into multiple, smaller lived ones that are easier to manage.

- **Coarse-grained vs. fine-grained objects**—Session beans should be coarse-grained business processes, such as deposit and withdrawal. Try to keep fine-grained activities hidden—that is, do not expose all the methods of an entity bean through a session bean wrapper.

- **Session facade**—The EJB session facade pattern provides a stable, high-level gateway to the server-side components. An EJB session facade hides the entity bean interfaces to the clients. All access to entity beans must go through methods of a session bean. In EJB 2.0 entity beans are defined with local interfaces only. Session beans are defined with remote and possibly local interfaces. Because all access is through session bean methods, transaction management is within the session bean and all entity accesses are performed within the same transaction.

  See "Using a session facade to entity beans" on page 262 for more information.

- **Caching of EJB homes**—We have seen one way that we are caching EJB homes in our session bean create methods. Although this is more efficient than no caching alternatives, we are still doing the lookups and the cache for every bean instance.

Client view of a session bean

This section describes more of the client view for the `Banking` and `Reports` EJBs that extends the basic client example in "EJB client view" on page 56. The examples are based on remote home and component interfaces.

We highlight where the client view changes depending on whether the bean is stateful or stateless.

Looking up the bean home

Figure 5-25 shows the finding of a home interface of a session bean.

Because we use a remote interface, we are required to call `PortableRemoteObject.narrow` on the object that is returned from the `InitialContext lookup` method. Remember, the JNDI name is specified at deployment time and not in the actual deployment descriptor file.

```
InitialContext ctx = new InitialContext();
Object objHome = ctx.lookup("itso/BankingJNDIName");
BankingHome bankingHome = (BankingHome)javax.rmi.PortableRemoteObject.narrow
        (objHome, BankingHome.class );
```

Figure 5-25   Client local lookup of home interface for a remote session bean

We now have a valid home object in which to find remote component interfaces of our bean.

Client view of the session bean life cycle

We now discuss the client view for each of the life cycle interactions that we described previously.

Creating and using a stateless session bean

Figure 5-26 demonstrates an EJB client creating a `Banking` object. Because this is a stateless session bean, create does not actually create the bean instance, but rather allocates one from the instance pool.

```
try {
   Banking bank = bankingHome.create();
   String accountID = "101-1001";
   BigDecimal amt = new BigDecimal(99.00);
   bank.deposit(accountID, amt)
} catch (RemoteException ce) {
   // series problem using the bean
} catch (OtherException ce) {
   // other problem using the bean?
}
```

Figure 5-26   Creating a stateless session bean

Creating and using a stateful session bean

Figure 5-27 demonstrates an EJB client creating a Reports object. Because this is a stateful session bean, create actually creates a new bean instance. In this example, we are using one of the alternate forms of the create method of the bean.

```
try {
   int customerID = 123;
   String acountID = "123-4567";
   Reports reports = reportsHome.create(customerID, accountID);
   // use bean
   reports.listLargestAccount();
   reports.listGoldAccounts();
   ......
} catch (CreateException ce) {
   // series problem creating the bean
}
```

Figure 5-27   Creating a stateful session bean

Finding an existing stateful session bean

We mentioned that an existing stateful session bean can be retrieved if we have a handle to the bean. This is done, for instance, when a servlet stores the handle of the stateful session bean in HttpSession between servlet invocations, and subsequently has to retrieve the handle in the next servlet invocation. The handle can be serialized to any secondary location; the servlet session is the most common because servlets are a common client of EJBs.

We first show how to store the handle to the stateful session bean. Figure 5-28 demonstrates an EJB client retrieving a handle to a stateful session bean, and storing this in an HttpSession.

```
try {
    ...//already retrieved bean and httpSession...
        Handle rptHandle = reports.getHandle();
        httpSession.setAttribute("MyReportsHandle", rptHandle);
}
```

Figure 5-28   Creating an stateful session bean handle

Now we want to find our existing stateful session bean using the handle.
Figure 5-29 demonstrates an EJB client retrieving the handle from the
HttpSession, and using it to find an existing stateful session bean.

```
try {
    ...//httpSession...
        Handle rptHandle=(Handle) httpSession.getAttribute("MyReportsHandle");
        Reports reports = (Reports) javax.rmi.PortableRemoteObject.narrow
                (rptHandle.getEJBObject(), Reports.class );
    // use bean
...
}
```

Figure 5-29   Retrieving a stateful session bean from a handle

We should note that you cannot use this technique with stateless session beans
(nor would it make any sense to try to, because a call to the home create method
does essentially the same thing).

Removing a stateful session bean

Figure 5-30 demonstrates an EJB client removing the Reports stateful session
bean. Because it really does not matter if we call remove on a stateless session
bean (because all it would do is clean up the EJBObject, not the bean itself), we
do not show it here.

```
try {
    reports.remove();
} catch (RemoveException re) {
    // handle the remove exception..probably more serious
}
```

Figure 5-30   Removing a stateful session bean

This remove will actually cause the stateful session bean to be removed from
memory, and any final cleanup of the bean could occur.

Session EJB client exception handling

Clients should explicitly catch and handle exceptions. Because we use the remote interface, our clients must catch the `RemoteException` on many of these bean interactions.

Additionally, we will get a `CreateException` if there is a problem in the session bean's `create` method, or `RemoveException` from a `remove` method. These exceptions are both considered application-level exceptions, as would be any custom exception that a bean developer may optionally choose to throw on a methods clause. EJB exception handling strategies are discussed in "EJB exception handling" on page 304.

Summary

This chapter described both stateful and stateless session beans, their contract with the container, and how to build one. How to build each bean using Application Developer is discussed in detail in Part 2 of this redbook.

We revisit the session beans discussed here in future chapters in the context of exceptions, transactions, and security.

6

Message-driven beans

This chapter describes a new feature available in EJB 2.0: message-driven beans.

We start with the concepts of JMS-based messaging in general, then describe the concepts of message-driven beans, and finally outline the banking example extended with a message-driven bean.

© Copyright IBM Corp. 2003. All rights reserved.

Introduction

Message-driven beans (MDB) are an exciting new feature of the EJB 2.0 specification. They open up a whole new realm of application architectural and integration alternatives not previously available in J2EE. This chapter describes the concepts and structure of message-driven beans and MDB development, and introduces some new integration patterns and best practices when you are considering utilizing MDBs in your design.

> ***New EJB 2.0 - Message-driven beans:** Message-driven beans are new in EJB 2.0, and, therefore, are new to WebSphere Version 5.
>
> Developers were able to achieve MDB-like functionality in WebSphere Version 4 Enterprise Edition with *message beans*. These message beans were a specialized class of stateless session beans, and ran as a custom service of WebSphere Enterprise, such that they were associated and registered as application server services, and although packaged in an EAR, were not associated with the runtime context of a particular application or EAR. Although these message beans were like MDBs, they were simply a convenient way to implement a JMS listener in WebSphere Version 4. They could not completely benefit from the messaging services provided by the server, notably, message beans that lost connections to their JMS destinations could not gracefully recover, and the entire application server process had to be restarted. Because these are now manageable J2EE services of the application server, this type of recovery can now be detected and handled more safely in WebSphere Version 5.

Asynchronous messaging

Asynchronous messaging is described as a method of communication where messages are sent one-way, that is, where a request is sent, but no reply is received. Synchronous messaging is analogous to request/reply. Asynchronous messaging is one way to communicate between applications, or between components within the applications.

We have already seen that application clients may communicate with application EJBs through RMI/IIOP. Inter-application communication can be achieved any number of ways: RMI, COM/DCOM, CORBA, Web services/SOAP, asynchronous messaging, among others.

Asynchronous messaging can be an alternative communication mechanism for invoking EJBs, where message producers (the EJB clients) and message consumers (the message-driven beans) communicate via a third-party construct, the message-oriented middleware (MOM) provider, such as WebSphere MQ. In this way, the MOM intercepts all messages between producer and consumers, such that they are decoupled processes.

JMS and the role of the JMS provider

Java Message Service (JMS) is a Java API for accessing message-oriented middleware (MOM) services. All EJB 2.0 compliant application servers must support asynchronous messaging as a method of communication based on the JMS programming interface. JMS provides a common way for Java programs (clients and J2EE applications) to create, send, receive, and read asynchronous requests, as JMS messages.

Like any of the J2EE APIs, however, JMS is just an abstraction of a common and portable programming model. It does not actually provide the runtime implementation or underlying service of the messaging, such as would be provided by the MOM. Therefore, to be EJB 2.0 compliant, application servers must also provide for a new type of service: JMS messaging server.

*New EJB 2.0 - Internal JMS server: To be EJB 2.0 (and really, J2EE 1.3) compliant, the application servers must provide two things:

▶ Support for MDBs for an automatic asynchronous messaging programming model.

▶ Provide an implementation of a JMS messaging server. This now means that the JMS server abilities are built into the application server, and therefore can be used by MDB and non-MDB-based solutions alike.

WebSphere Application Server Version 5 provides an internal JMS messaging server as part of the base WebSphere product to meet the second requirement. The internal JMS server is essentially a lightweight implementation of WebSphere MQ that allows for the exchange of messages between applications within the same WebSphere instance. Although it is possible to remotely send messages into the WebSphere embedded messaging service, the queue manager of the service cannot communicate (send) messages outside of WebSphere (or, between queue managers within WebSphere). Therefore, the server itself has limited ability for external integration. Luckily, WebSphere also allows for WebSphere MQ (or other generic providers) to be used instead of the internal JMS server as the JMS provider when a higher quality of service is expected.

The internal JMS provider is not intended to be a full-blown MOM or a viable option for enterprise application integration (EAI). It simply provides the JMS server as required by the specification, and allows for some creative application-level communication solution alternatives. It is expected that most applications will require actual WebSphere MQ for true application interoperability.

Message-driven bean introduction

Message-driven beans are used for the processing of asynchronous JMS messages within J2EE-based applications. The are invoked by the container on the arrival of a message. In this way, they can be thought of as another interaction mechanism for invoking EJBs, but unlike session and entity beans, the container is responsible for invoking them when a message is received, not a client (or another bean). Although MDBs are sometimes said to not have a *true* client, the client actually is the original producer of the message. We use this idea of MDB client throughout this chapter.

The most important properties of message-driven beans are:

► They have no identity to the client, but execute anonymously.

► They are completely managed by the EJB container.

► They are not exposed directly to the EJB client.

► They are stateless, in that they do not maintain any state on behalf of a client.

► They must implement `javax.jms.MessageListener` in addition to `javax.ejb.MessageDrivenBean`.

► They have no home or component interfaces.

Java messaging service concepts

Java Messaging Service (JMS) is a Java API for accessing message-oriented middleware systems. JMS is to messaging what JDBC is to database access, in that it abstracts away the vendor-specific aspects of the messaging provider, so that they can be accessed in a vendor-neutral way.

MDBs really are just EJBs that are invoked by the arrival of JMS messages. Because JMS is the backbone of MDBs, it is important to understand the fundamental concepts of JMS. JMS is a powerful messaging structure that can be used by any type of EJB, or any other Java class or application, not just MDBs.

JMS messaging models

There are two types of JMS messaging models: point-to-point and publish-and-subscribe.

Point-to-point (P2P)

In point-to-point, messages are sent via queues. Messages are put onto the queues by the message producers (the clients). The message consumer is responsible for pulling the message from the queue. Point-to-point is typically used when a given message must be processed (received) only once by a given consumer. In this way, there is only one consumer of the given message.

Publish-and-subscribe (pub/sub)

In publish-and-subscribe, messages are sent through topics. Messages are published to topics by the message producers. The messages may be received by any consumers that subscribe to the given topic. In this way, a message may be received, or processed, by multiple consumers.

Message-driven beans and messaging models

Message-driven beans can be either queue or topic message consumers. The choice of messaging model really depends on what is supposed to happen to the message itself, such as whether it is intended to be consumed by more than one consumer or not. Additionally, queues are typically associated with a single producer. The behavior of any model can be simulated by the other by adopting creative (and sometimes abusive) patterns. In our opinion, P2P is the most common for inter-application communication, where the producers and consumers are known entities. In this book, we use point-to-point for all the messaging examples.

JMS components

Applications interact with the messaging service through the JMS API. The application server consists of the following high-level components providing this service (Figure 6-1).

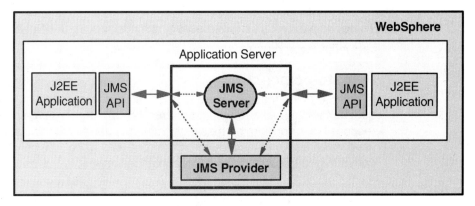

Figure 6-1   Internal JMS provider implementation

JMS provider

A JMS provider is a base messaging system and related Java classes that implement the JMS API. The resources of the JMS provider are accessed through JMS connection factory and destination objects. The provider may either be the internal JMS provider (as depicted above) provided with WebSphere, or may be an external provider such as WebSphere MQ.

JMS server

The JMS functions of the JMS provider are accessed by the JMS server within the application server. This JMS server is responsible for managing the following services:

► **Queue manager**—Responsible for providing the queue service when using point-to-point based messaging.

► **Broker**—Responsible for providing the publish/subscribe service when using pub/sub based messaging.

JMS administered objects

In JMS a number of objects are created by the WebSphere administrator and stored in a directory. The Java Naming and Directory Interface (JNDI) namespace is used to hold references to JMS administered objects, encapsulating settings necessary for connecting to and using the queues and/or topics of messaging systems. The JMS administered objects are connection factories and destinations.

JMS connection factories

A connection factory is used to create connections with the JMS provider for a specific JMS queue or topic destination. Each connection factory encapsulates the configuration parameters needed to create a connection to a JMS destination. Storing the connection details in JNDI makes the application connection code vendor independent. There are two types of JMS connection factory:

► **QueueConnectionFactory**—Encapsulates the settings necessary to connect to a queue-based messaging system.

► **TopicConnectionFactory**—Encapsulates the settings necessary to connect to a topic-based messaging system.

JMS destinations

A JMS destination provides a specific endpoint for messages. There are two types of JMS destination types:

► **Queues**—A JMS destination used for P2P.

► **Topics**—A JMS destination used for pub/sub.

Example JMS interaction

To show how these JMS objects are used by a regular Java class, we introduce a simple point-to-point example, where a simple text message is sent to a queue by a JMS message producer or client and is received by a JMS message listener.

JMS message producer

Figure 6-2 show sample Java code to send a message to a JMS queue.

The coding sequence is fairly straightforward. The connection factory is looked up, a connection is retrieved, and it is used to obtain a session. The session is used to create a sender object on a queue, and then the message is sent.

```
...
    //Get the JNDI Initial Context to do JNDI lookups
    InitialContext initCtx = new InitialContext();

    //Get the QueueConnectionFactory by JNDI name
    QueueConnectionFactory qcf = (QueueConnectionFactory)
        initCtx.lookup("java:comp/env/jms/ItsoMDBConnectionFactoryRef");

    //Create a connection
    QueueConnection conn = qcf.createQueueConnection();

    //create a JMS session
    QueueSession session = conn.createQueueSession(false,
        Session.AUTO_ACKNOWLEDGE);

    //get the queue used to send the message by JNDI name
    Queue queue = (Queue) lookup("java:comp/env/jms/ITSOMdbQueueRef");

    //send a message
    QueueSender sender = session.createSender(queue);
    TextMessage msg = new TextMessage("Test Message");
    sender.send(msg);

    sender.close();
    session.close();
    conn.close();

...
```

Figure 6-2   Simple JMS message producer

Several other JMS objects are introduced in this example that are described as follows:

► **QueueConnection**—Used to create a live connection to the JMS messaging service, and are used to create `QueueSessions`. Is analogous to the connection object in JDBC. In a pub/sub model, a `TopicConnection` would be used.

► **QueueSession**—Used to create sender objects and messages. Can only be used by one thread at a time. In a pub/sub model, a `TopicSession` would be used.

► **QueueSender**—Used to send the message on the queue. In pub/sub, this would be a `TopicPublisher`.

► **TextMessage**—A simple text message type. Other types are `ObjectMessage`, `BytesMessage`, `StreamMessage`, and `MapMessage`. Each message type extends the `Message` superclass.

In this example, a simple text message is sent on a queue. A good practice to employ is to close these objects when you are done using them, as you would for JDBC type objects.

JMS message listener

The example in Figure 6-2 shows a JMS client. A simple JMS queue message consumer example is shown in Figure 6-3 to introduce a few additional important JMS objects.

```java
import javax.jms.*;
public class AListener implements MessageListener {

    public void onMessage(Message aMsg) {
        try {
           TextMessage msg = (TextMessage) aMsg;
           System.out.println("Got Message: " + msg.getText());
        } catch (Exception e) {
            e.printStackTrace();
        }
    }
    // a method that sets up the listener..
    public void runIt() {
        // Lookup connection factories, queue, session, same as in producer
        ...
        QueueReceiver rec = session.createReceiver(queue);
        rec.setMessageListener(this);
        rec.close();
        ...
    }
...
}
```

Figure 6-3   Simple JMS message consumer

All standard message listeners (our MDBs included) must implement the `javax.jms.MessageListener` interface, so that the object can be registered as a JMS listener. In this example, we register ourselves as a listener. For an MDB, the container would register the bean as a listener. When a JMS message is received, the container (ourselves in this example) triggers the `onMessage` method, which is required by the `MessageListener` interface.

Several other JMS objects are introduced in this example::

▶ **QueueReceiver**—The object used to get messages from a queue. In pub/sub, this would be a `TopicSubscriber`.

▶ **MessageListener**—Interface that declares the `onMessage` method.

The example in Figure 6-3 shows the requirements for having a distinct `MessageListener` object. There is another way to receive a message from a queue, rather than registering as a `MessageListener`. Receiving objects may be done by just creating a reference to a `QueueReceiver` object directly, and blocking until a message is received (Figure 6-4).

```
...
    QueueReceiver rec = session.createReceiver(queue, selector);
    TextMessage inMessage = rec.receive(15000);
    rec.close();
...
```

Figure 6-4   QueueReceiver instead of MessageListener

In this example, the `receive(timeout)` method is called. It listens on the queue for the message until the timeout has elapsed. The selector is used to qualify which message is to be received. With no selector, the next message received in the queue is the one processed.

Message

What we send as messages is really the heart of the messaging system. We hope that the message has some meaningful data with which the receiving message can perform its work. The message is really the contract between the message producer and the message consumer, and is generally agreed upon in advance, in the same way that method parameters are the contract between collaborating classes. Therefore, messaging-based systems are not completely decoupled processes, in that they must still have a fundamental understanding, and agreement of, what is to be sent.

A message is generally defined in terms of three things: header, properties, and payload:

▶ The header of a message defines the metadata describing the message, such as the routing information and correlationIDs of the message.

▶ The properties define some additional data about the message that may be manipulated.

▶ The payload, or message body, contains the actual business-specific data that the message consumer is interested in.

In JMS, messages are defined according to the type of payload that they are able to transport. There are six message payload types in JMS:

► **Message**—This is a message that has no payload, just a header (and other properties).

► **TextMessage**—This is usually a Java string or other simple text type, such as XML. This type of message provides a looser coupling between the technologies of the message producer and consumer. The consumer is responsible for constructing something meaningful from the text of the message.

► **ObjectMessage**—A serialized Java object. This is an easy model to use, because you can rely on your existing object models, and is often used when MDBs are used for intra-application communication. The message producer and consumer are now tightly coupled to both the technology and version of the message, so use caution when choosing object messages.

► **MapMessage**—Like a hash map, this is a set of name-value pairs. This is easier than either text or object messages, because built-in setters/getters can be used to manipulate the data.

► **BytesMessage**—Stream of raw data bytes. This can be used to transfer more complex structures.

► **StreamMessage**—Stream of primitive Java types.

Message-driven bean concepts

You should now have a good understanding of the various JMS objects and how they interact for sending and receiving messages. This section provides some detail on the structure of message-driven beans.

Extending the JMS model to MDBs

As mentioned above, message-driven beans sit on the backbone of JMS. The example in "Example JMS interaction" on page 227 shows a JMS client (message producer) interacting with the JMS message service. Each of the JMS objects must be interacted with in order for the message to be sent, and managed by the client.

MDBs on the other hand are not nearly as difficult to build as a standard JMS client above. MDBs must implement the `MessageListener` interface, and the corresponding `onMessage` method, but the container actually performs the other interactions above for the JMS listener for MDBs on behalf of the bean.

Therefore, MDBs normally do not have to interact with `QueueConnectionFactory`, `QueueConnection`, `Queue`, and `QueueReceiver` objects directly. An exception to this is when the MDB is also a message producer, as in the case of pseudo-synchronous messaging where the MDB sends back a reply. This scenario, among others, is described later in this chapter. The MDB would have to have knowledge of the JMS message type, however, in order to properly handle the message.

Although for a simple MDB the client is not programmatically managing these objects, they are still being used, albeit by the container. The association of the bean with properties is done by a combination of deployment descriptor entries and other WebSphere administration deployment tasks that essentially bind the bean with the appropriate `QueueConnectionFactory` and `Queue`.

Like the example above, when a message is received, the container knows how to invoke the appropriate MDB instance, and it calls the `onMessage` method of the bean. It is possible that multiple instances of MDBs are executing the `onMessage` at any given time, but for queue-based processing (point-to-point), we are guaranteed that a message is only processed by a single bean.

Message-driven beans structure

Recall that message-driven beans implement the `javax.ejb.MessageDrivenBean` interface. Message-driven beans must also implement the `javax.jms.MessageListener` interface. This hierarchy is shown in Figure 6-5.

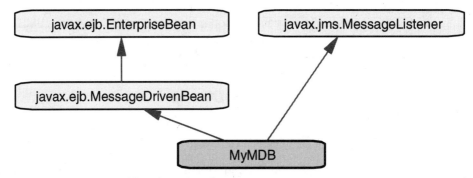

Figure 6-5   Message-driven bean interfaces

No home or component interfaces

MDBs do not require home or component interfaces since there is no direct client interaction with MDBs. Recall that home methods are used to locate the beans, and the only entity that does this is the container, and the container already has sufficient knowledge to locate the MDB. Recall that component interfaces are intended to expose business logic to clients. Although the MDB might implement business knowledge when the `onMessage` method is called, the bean itself does not expose this in any way to external clients.

Callback methods

Given that there are no home or component interfaces, the callback and container-managed mechanism of the beans is greatly simplified. Figure 6-6 shows the callback methods that message-driven bean classes must implement because they implement the `javax.ejb.MessageDrivenBean` interface:

```
public interface MessageDrivenBean extends javax.ejb.EnterpriseBean {
    public void setMessageDrivenContext(MessageDrivenContext ctx);
    public void ejbRemove();
}
```

Figure 6-6   Message-driven bean callback methods

Although not truly container callback methods, the message bean must also implement the `ejbCreate` method. This is so the container can actually create the bean instance.

Application Developer also generates a `getMessageDrivenContext` method. Normally the `ejbCreate` would be required through an association with a home interface, but in the case of MDBs, the object creation is implied by the container, so no home is required.

Figure 6-7 shows the additional methods of a message-driven bean.

```
...
    public MessageDrivenContext getMessageDrivenContext()...
    public void ejbCreate()...
}
```

Figure 6-7   Additional message-driven bean methods

Bean-container contract

To understand what you as a bean developer would have to do to develop a meaningful message-driven bean means understanding the callback and life-cycle methods of the bean, and how this bean-container contract is enforced.

States of a MDB

There are two states of an MDB (Figure 6-8). It either does not exist (no state), or it is in the method-ready pool state. The method-ready pool of message-driven beans is similar to that of the instance pool of stateless session beans.

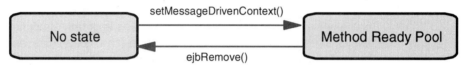

Figure 6-8   States of a message-driven bean

Pooling is a service of the container that allows the container to reuse bean instances, as opposed to creating new ones every time a request for a bean is made. This is a performance optimization that is done by the container. This allows for a scalable environment, because this pool size can be increased as needed, by either adding more memory, or more machines, based on the message load that might be expected.

Essentially, if the bean instance has not been created, then it is in *no state*. Once the container decides it needs an MDB, it moves to the *method ready pooled* state. The bean will remain in this method ready state until the container decides it no longer needs it.

These state transitions are important, because each state change will trigger the container to invoke a callback method appropriate to that state change. As a developer you have to understand these transitions to know if you should apply appropriate logic in these callback methods for your bean.

The following are the purposes of each callback method:

▶ **setMessageDrivenContext**—Called by the container when the bean is first added to the pool, it should be used to capture a reference to the MessageDrivenContext for the bean. Used most often for one-time initialization with the benefit of MessageDrivenContext. Figure 6-9 shows the most common form of this method.

```
public void setMessageDrivenContext(javax.ejb.MessageDrivenContext ctx){
   myMessageDrivenCtx = ctx;
}
```

Figure 6-9   Message-driven bean setMessageDrivenContext method

▸ **ejbRemove**—Called when the container moves the bean from the method
ready pool back to the no state. Any cleanup operations could be performed
in this method.

Additional life cycle of a message-driven bean

Since there is no direct client interaction with an MDB, as there is in the case of
the other enterprise beans, the life cycle of the bean is not dictated by the finding
or locating required by a client. Its life cycle is dictated completely by the
interaction with the container. There are, however, some important other
activities that occur besides the calling of the callback methods described above,
when transitioning between states (Figure 6-10).

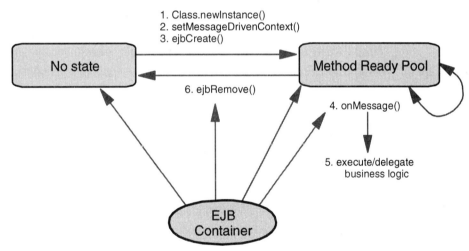

Figure 6-10   Life cycle of a message-driven bean

Let us describe the life-cycle sequence for message-driven beans:

1. **Class.newInstance**—The container decides to move some beans to the
   pool, but must first create an instance of the class. WebSphere sets the
   minimum pool count for MDBs to be 1; therefore, this action will occur as the
   server starts up, and as new beans are required to process the incoming
   messages.

2. **setMessageDrivenContext**—The MessageDrivenContext is now available.

3. **ejbCreate**—Although there is no home interface, an `ejbCreate` is still called that will allow the bean to perform a one-time initialization. The bean will have access to the `MessageDrivenContext` if required.

4. **onMessage**—When a message is received by the container, it delegates the processing to an instance in the method ready pool and executes the `onMessage` method. An MDB instance can only execute against one message at a time. Although this bean is still technically in the pool, a bean that is in the middle of executing its `onMessage` method is unavailable to process other messages until it is complete.

5. **execute/delegate business logic**—The message-driven bean must perform some business logic. Typically, it is not recommended that the business logic itself be implemented in the `onMessage` method of the bean, or any other method of the bean. A best practice is that the MDB behave just as a pass-through to another stateless session bean that actually implements the business logic.

6. **ejbRemove**—When the container decides that it no longer requires the bean, it will execute the `ejbRemove` method and move it to a no state.

Developing a message-driven bean

Tools such as Application Developer provide powerful tooling to assist with the development of MDBs. Developing within Application Developer will be discussed in great detail in Chapter 16, "Message-driven bean development" on page 563.

This section will bring together all the concepts discussed in this chapter, and show how the actual beans could be constructed. We continue with the application that has been presented so far, and extend the transfer activity to be that which is invoked asynchronously.

Building message-driven beans

When we build a message-driven bean, we are concerned with building only the bean class and the deployment descriptor.

► **Bean class**—The bean class must contain the callback methods as well as an implementation of the `onMessage` method.

► **Deployment descriptor**—The XML deployment descriptor for the bean.

What about the business logic? As described above, burdening the bean class with the business logic is not recommended. A better practice is to delegate this to another class, preferably a stateless session bean. In this way, the stateless session bean will have the responsibility of providing the actual implementation of the business logic, and the MDB's responsibility will be to simply act as a delegator for this business logic.

Therefore, we will require the following to be built as a part of the complete MDB bean development cycle:

► **Stateless session business logic bean**—The bean that the MDB delegates to that implements the actual business logic. This is more of a guideline than a rule.

Expanded online banking requirements

We continue to expand the banking example used thus far to introduce an example of MDBs.

Recall that in our banking example, we built a stateless session enterprise bean called Banking that performs the core business functions of our online banking system, such as deposit, withdrawal, and transfer, among others. This Banking bean provides a facade layer of our system, and hides the details of the entity bean interactions from the EJB clients (Figure 6-11).

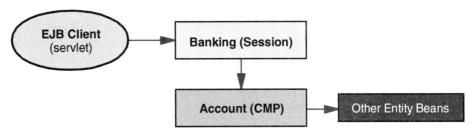

Figure 6-11   Banking application example

The transfer method of the Banking bean is currently called synchronously by the EJB client, in this case a servlet, which transfers funds for a customer between accounts. For some reason, we decide that we want this function to be provided asynchronously (this is contrived, but stick with us) over JMS as opposed to invoking the Banking.transfer method directly.

Actually, exposing existing business logic to another invocation mechanism is a common function of MDBs. This can often provide the basis for service-oriented architectures, where the session beans are pure representations of business services, but can be invoked by anything that can put messages onto a queue (or topic), such as non-Java based systems.

We expand the online banking example and introduce a new Transfer MDB (Figure 6-12).

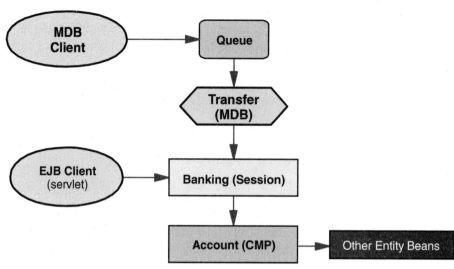

Figure 6-12   Banking application example with MDB

We can see that now our Banking EJB can be invoked synchronously and asynchronously.

Designing the message payload

We introduced a new interaction pattern for our Banking bean through the use of the message-driven bean construct, but we are not actually changing the structure of the transfer method. Therefore, we have to ensure that the information required to execute this transaction is part of the message payload. We have to determine exactly what our message payload, or structure, has to look like. At a minimum, we have to be able to pass the accounts for which we need to perform the transfer, and the amount of the transfer.

We have a choice of six different message payloads to choose from. In this example, we choose to use the ObjectMessage structure more for simplicity than anything else. We design a special TransferDataObject to be used as the actual object payload for our message that contains three fields: fromAccount, toAccount, and amount.

Perhaps a more extensible service-oriented design might lead us to design an XML-based message, and use the TextMessage construct. This would require us to parse this message on the consumer side. Alternatively, using the MapMessage might also have been an option, because we could easily map these three fields into name/value pairs of primitive types. And finally, the StreamMessage could have been chosen if we could guarantee the order of the primitives that were passed. In the end, the ObjectMessage was chosen for its simplicity only.

What about a reply?

Asynchronous messaging is generally a fire-and-forget type activity, where no reply to the consumer is required or expected. However, pseudo-synchronous request/reply type semantics are common and can be incorporated into a messaging interaction if required, although this is not an appropriate choice for long-running transaction cycles. In this way, the message-consumer MDB can process the message, and then leverage messaging itself as a JMS message producer to send back a reply. The original message producer must listen for a message request that is being sent back from the consumer, so is now also a JMS message consumer. It is most likely the case that one queue is used for the send, and another queue is used for the reply. Different interaction scenarios and patterns are discussed later in this chapter, as alternatives to those mentioned so far.

In our case, we want to know the status of the transfer. We extend our scenario to include the reply as part of the interaction (Figure 6-13).

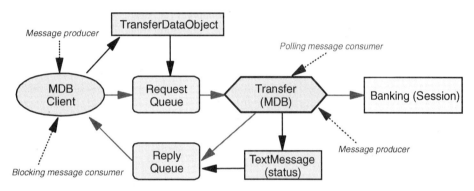

Figure 6-13   MDB request/reply semantics

Even though the MDB client and the `Transfer` MDB are both message consumers, their behavior is different. The MDB is a polling consumer, that is, it is actively, and repeatedly, listening for messages that it can work on. The MDB client in this example is a blocking consumer, essentially blocking for a message, that is, it is asking for a particular message to be received on the reply queue.

Building the MDB bean class

The MDB is perhaps the simplest bean to actually build, particularly if you delegate the processing to another business logic bean, as is the case with our banking example. The bulk of the work is deciding what behavior to implement in the `onMessage` method, and how to recover from errors. Because we also require a reply in our scenario, we are putting the reply logic in the MDB itself. Therefore, the MDB is primarily concerned with the extraction of the message, forwarding to the stateless session bean, handling the request and reply, and any error handling. The skeleton of our `Transfer` MDB is shown in Figure 6-14.

```
import javax.ejb.*;
import javax.jms.*;
public class Transfer implements MessageDrivenBean, MessageListener {
    private MessageDrivenContext msgCtx;
    public void ejbCreate() {
        //initialize the bean to find the BankingHome, not shown here...
    }
    public void setMessageDrivenContext(MessageDrivenContext ctx) {
        msgCtx = ctx;
    }
    public void ejbRemove() {
    }
    public void onMessage(javax.jms.Message msg){
     try {
        String selector = msg.getJMSCorrelationID();
        ObjectMessage objectMsg = (ObjectMessage) msg;
        TransferDataObject transferMsg =
                (TransferDataObject) objectMsg.getObject();
        String fromAccount = transferMsg.getFromAccount();
        String toAccount = transferMsg.getToAccount();
        BigDecimal amount = transferMsg.getAmount();
        Banking bank = bankingHome.create();
        BigDecimal balance = bank.transfer(fromAccount, toAccount, amount);
        sendResponseMessage(selector, response);
     } catch (Exception e) {
        e.printStackTrace();
        sendResponseMessage(selector, "ERROR: " + e.getMessage());
     }
    }

    private sendResponseMessage(String selector, String text) {
        //this will connect to the reply queue, and send the message.
        //not shown here in detail - will be described in development chapter
    }
}
```

Figure 6-14   Message-driven bean skeleton coding

We have left out some details, such as the actual lookup to the JNDI for the `Banking` EJB and the reply queue. These are discussed in detail in Chapter 16, "Message-driven bean development" on page 563.

Deployment descriptor

Figure 6-15 shows the deployment descriptor entries for the `Transfer` MDB.

```
<message-driven>
    <ejb-name>Transfer</ejb-name>
    <ejb-class>itso.bank5.mdb.TransferMDB</ejb-class>
    <transaction-type>Bean|Container</transaction-type>
    <message-driven-destination>
        <destination-type>javax.jms.Queue</destination-type>
    </message-driven-destination>
</message-driven>
```

Figure 6-15   Deployment descriptor for a message-driven bean

If we want this EJB to have references to the `Banking` session EJB (`<ejb-ref>`), and reply resource destination (`<resource-ref>`), then we could optionally define these entries here as well, so that we would not have to hardcode these values. This is not shown here for brevity.

Transaction type

The transaction type can be set as `Bean` or `Container`:

► With the `Bean` transaction type, the MDB itself can start and commit (or roll back) transactions. The bean can also not implement transactional behavior and leave transaction management to the session bean that is called.

► With the `Container` transaction type, the container manages transactions and by default starts a transaction when the `onMessage` method is invoked.

When an MDB participates in a transaction, the consequence is that the JMS input message is part of the transaction and is committed (removed) or recovered. In case of an abend (for example, an exception in the back end) the input message is recovered and placed back on the queue again. This can lead to a loop because the same message is processed again.

The listener port can be defined with a retry count that will stop the same message from being delivered indefinitely. The MDB itself can query the retries using the method call:

```
message.getStringProperty("JMSXDeliveryCount")
```

Using these techniques, an MDB can be prevented from processing the same message forever. See also "Be aware of poison messages" on page 247.

MDB client programming

There is no MDB client programming, per se, as clients may not interact directly with the MDB. However, the MDB client is really just a JMS message producer whose ultimate destination is the MDB. We have already seen an example of a simple JMS message producer (sender) in the JMS concepts section.

An MDB client that operates in a pseudo-synchronous request/reply mode, however, must also implement QueueReceiver logic in order to receive the reply, and also some message selection to ensure that the appropriate reply is being received. MDBs are designed to execute in a multi-threaded manner; therefore, multiple reply messages can be produced at the same time. There is nothing to guarantee the affinity or order of reply messages to the MDB client example that we described above. Therefore, it is our responsibility to ensure that we get the proper reply back for the message that we sent.

Correlation ID

In our example, we leverage the JMS message correlation ID for this reason. The correlation ID is guaranteed not be changed by a JMS provider, since a message is actually sent, and therefore, we can use this field to correlate two distinct, but related, JMS messages to each other. We use this to correlate the request message with the reply message, such that the MDB client knows how to select the appropriate reply message from the reply queue. There are several techniques for setting the correlation ID. In our example, we let the client set it based on some random number, and then use the same ID to select the reply message. This client snippet is shown in Figure 6-16.

```
selector = "CORR:TF"+ (new java.util.Random()).nextInt(999999);
outMessage.setJMSCorrelationID(selector);
```

Figure 6-16   Setting a correlation ID

Message type

An MDB could be an asynchronous front-end for many methods of the same session bean. For example, an MDB could not only front-end the transfer method, but also deposit and withdraw.

One way to pass information from a client to an MDB is by setting a property (Figure 6-17). Based on the property value, the MBD can extract different payload objects and invoke the correct method of the session bean.

```
outMessage.setStringProperty("BUSINESSMETHOD", "transfer");
```

Figure 6-17   Setting a message property

Timeout

Another implication of doing this type of request/reply is that there is no guarantee that the reply message will be received back in a reasonable amount of time. This is not to say that there is no guaranteed delivery, just that the time of delivery cannot be guaranteed. It is the client's responsibility to set an appropriate timeout for the application, but too long of a timeout might have a negative impact on an application's performance, because the client essentially blocks until the message is received. If the timeout is too long, then an alternative messaging interaction pattern might have to be used.

Message-driven bean interaction patterns

This section describes some common interaction patterns for message-driven beans. We have already introduced two: asynchronous fire-and-forget, and pseudo-synchronous request/reply in the examples above.

We expand on these, and discuss some variations of these themes that may help you to choose an appropriate pattern for your messaging application. We then describe some common best practices as well as some pitfalls to avoid when designing MDBs.

Message interactions

In this section, we list some common messaging system interactions. We are sure that this is not a complete list, and that many more interaction patterns can be discovered based on your own interaction requirements.

Fire-and-forget

This is a scenario in which a message producer sends (or publishes) a message, but does not wait for, or ever get back, a reply. This pattern might be best used for such systems as remote logging, where we do not require a response to be sent back, or broadcast-type messages. This is not to say that the message producer does not care what happens to the message, or that there is not some quality-of-service associated with this message, just that in this case the MDB client trusts the MDB receiver to handle it or compensate in some way if it cannot be handled.

Fire-and-forward

This is a variation on the fire-and-forget scenario above, in that the client does not require a response. However, the message consumer is responsible for processing the message, and then forwarding this message onto some other process. This could be to another queue, or another system. This is a common scenario that one might find in workflow-based systems, or other hub-based systems, and is a feature of the WebSphere MQ Integrator Broker and IBM WebSphere MQ Workflow products.

Pseudo-synchronous request/reply

This is the variation that we have used in our example. The idea is that the request and reply of the message are intended to be processed within a single interaction cycle. This interaction says that the message producer sends a message, then blocks the reply. From a message producer's perspective, the implication is that the reply might not be received back in a reasonable time frame, and it must have a means in which to ensure that the appropriate reply is received (through message correlation).

There are some creative alternatives to this that could be implemented by the consumer so that message receipt blocking is not required, such as having a dedicated message listener that polls for the message and triggers an event back to the waiting client. Regardless of how efficient the underlying implementation of this waiting can be made, the client is still waiting for a message, and will time out if it is not received in a reasonable time frame.

Asynchronous request/reply

Often replies are still required, just not as part of this particular interaction. In this way, the client can fire the request, but does not forget about it. As in the pseudo-synchronous example above, the client ultimately receives some reply back, but it does not happen within the particular interaction.

Later, the client may go back to see if a reply has been received, or alternately, the reply may be sent by means of some notification. This is common in workflow-based systems, as well as long-running activities where the client cannot wait for the reply in real time. An example is where a client submits a request to produce a report that takes a long time to produce. When the report is completed, a message is sent back to the originator.

In this scenario, the reply message must somehow still be correlated with the original request message, so the client knows which report request is complete. Given that the request and reply are part of two different interactions, the correlation must be maintained somewhere else, maybe in an HTTP session or a database, such that the correct reply can be queried later.

Publish and subscribe patterns

In this chapter, we have focused primarily on point-to-point based messaging interactions and patterns. Recall that pub/sub allows for the publishing of a message to a topic by a message producer, of which multiple consumers may have subscribed to that topic. Therefore, there may be many consumers of a message.

It is not fair to classify pub/sub as a completely different domain of interaction patterns. However, it is important to understand that there are multiple message consumers that vary from the original interaction patterns in some way.

Any, or all, of these messaging consumers for pub/sub could participate in fire-and-forget or fire-and-forward based interactions as above, because what happens after the message is sent is not the concern of the message producer.

Pseudo-synchronous request/reply is a little bit more difficult with pub/sub, because pseudo-synchronous assumes a single reply from a single consumer, but it is possible that even though there are multiple message consumers, a single reply is always sent back through some sort of back-end orchestration.

Asynchronous request/reply could be more common in the pub/sub model. In this case, the single request could be broadcast to the multiple message consumers, each constructing part of a whole reply message. The individual replies could be sent back, or some other back-end orchestration could be used to send a single reply back. The idea that this does not happen at the same time as the original message publish still holds true.

Message-driven bean best practices

We have seen throughout this book some guidelines and best practices for entity and session bean development. We continue this theme with an overview of some of the message-driven bean best practices, as well as some common mistakes to avoid, in the form of *do* or *do not*.

▶ **Do delegate business logic to another handler**—In our example, we show that the MDB's responsibility is to receive the message, but the handling of it is delegated to another process, in our case a stateful session bean. This best practice holds true in any interaction pattern mentioned above.

▶ **Do consider making the MDB a request/reply controller**—We could have taken this delegation a step further, and delegated the reply handling to another component to do as well, to make the system a bit more object-oriented. Particularly when considering request/reply as an interaction pattern, consider incorporating request/reply messaging semantics in your model (similar to what is commonly done in servlets/JSPs), and make the MDB more of the controller of the interaction.

▶ **Do not attempt to maintain state with MDBs**—MDBs do not have the notion of client state, and are designed to be stateless processes. We recommend not attempting to do multiple MDB interactions that are somehow dependent on a conversational state with the MDB client in an asynchronous way, such that the MDB is responsible for managing the state.

Definitely do not attempt to use stateful session beans from within the MDBs. If multiple MDB interactions must be coordinated, then it should be up to the client to coordinate these interactions, and not rely on the MDB to use some state system to do so. MDBs are pooled instances, so there is no guarantee that the same MDB instance will execute the next message that you send, so no affinity to a stateful session could be properly maintained.

▶ **Do not have a message process depend on another message being processed**—Queuing, by definition, implies a first-in/first-out (FIFO) processing model. Although a message sent before another message is guaranteed by this model to be consumed in a FIFO order, there is no guarantee that the processing of the message finishes in any particular order. Therefore, if there is some dependency on the message order, the client must handle this through some other means, such as request/reply, where the second message is not sent until the first one has successfully completed. This responsibility could be offloaded to the message consumers to check and wait, but this creates an dependency within the consumer that is difficult to manage.

▶ **Do watch the size of the message payload**—It is possible to overburden your messaging system with messages that are just too big for it to handle efficiently. The messaging server (whether internal or external) is another system resource that now must be monitored as another application resource. Appropriate consideration of the size of the message will influence your choice of whether to incorporate messaging in the system.

▶ **Do consider using XML-based messages for inter-application integration**—XML is commonly used as a messaging structure that allows for a more portable inter-application integration model. Although it does add some overhead to the message payload size, and does most likely require both the MDB clients and MDBs to now deal with XML parsers, it is fast becoming a standard for interoperability. The SOAP-based model of messaging used in Web services is available for JMS and WebSphere MQ (SupportPac MA0R for WebSphere MQ 5.3, February 2003).

- **Do not use for real long-running transactions**—Although we indicated that asynchronous request/reply might be appropriate when the request is too long running for the MDB client to wait for, we are not saying the MDBs themselves should be used for long-running transactions. This might be better left to a batch cycle, or some other activity that breaks the work into smaller executable components. The MDB can be the launching point for coordinating the activities of the complete long-running transaction.

- **Be aware of poison messages**—Because MDBs are EJBs, they have many of the capabilities available to enterprise beans, such as transactional support. Although we have not yet discussed transactions, we have seen that the deployment descriptor setting for the MDB can denote a transaction type of container. What this means is that if the MDB has a problem processing the message (the onMessage method throws an exception), the container will attempt to roll back the transaction automatically. Rollback in JMS means to put the message back on the queue. Of course, the container will now see this message on the queue, and will deliver it to the MDB again, which could cause it to fail again. If this message is somehow fundamentally unprocessable, this poison message might continually be delivered and rolled back indefinitely unless you handle it.

  If you are leveraging WebSphere MQ, a redeliver count can be set on a message to prevent this for being redelivered after a number of attempts, at which point it can go to a dead-letter queue. Otherwise, you may have to handle the problems with this message by manually putting it onto your own dead letter queue or log, to avoid this recursive problem.

See "Transactions and message-driven beans" on page 298 for more information on transaction handling with MDBs.

Summary

In this chapter, we explored MDBs from a conceptual view and also provided guidelines for their usage.

7

EJB clients

In this chapter, we describe EJB clients. We provide a list a client types and programming techniques, including the use of relationships, inheritance, and finder methods.

We then provide guidelines for client design through the use of the model-view-controller pattern, access beans, and the session facade pattern.

Finally, we compare the different design techniques.

© Copyright IBM Corp. 2003. All rights reserved.

Client types

There are several different types of clients that access EJBs in a WebSphere Application Server Version 5 and the J2EE programming environment.

Session beans

A session bean can be looked at as being a client of the entity beans it accesses. In most cases these beans run in the same EJB container and can use local interfaces.

Servlets

Servlets can interact with EJBs through remote or local interfaces. A suggested approach is that servlets only interact with session beans, and the session beans interact with entity beans. To access session beans, the servlet can use either remote or local interfaces; for portability, remote interfaces are suggested.

The servlet is a typical thin-client implementation where the user front end is in HTML and JSPs, which invoke the servlets.

Model-view-controller

The programming model that is used with HTML pages, servlets, and JSPs is the model-view-controller (MVC). MVC is a programming paradigm that was first introduced by Smalltalk. It is a design pattern that aims at separating the business logic from interaction and presentation logic.

In a typical Web application, a user interacts with a Web site using a browser. The user makes a request by following a link or submitting a form. The application, after processing the request, returns a response to the user. The response is presented to the user in HTML. A typical example is when a user tries to get product or account information by using the product or account ID respectively.

The MVC model enforces the application to be split into three main parts: the *model*, the *view*, and the *controller* (Figure 7-1).

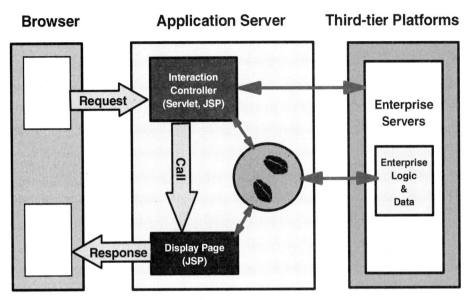

Browser **Application Server** **Third-tier Platforms**

Interaction Controller (Servlet, JSP)

Request

Call

Enterprise Servers

Enterprise Logic & Data

Display Page (JSP)

Response

Figure 7-1   MVC programming paradigm

Model   The model encapsulates all the business logic and rules and does the business processing. It is usually implemented by JavaBeans or EJBs.

View   The view uses the result of the business processing and constructs the response that is presented to the user. It is usually implemented by JSPs.

Controller The controller manages and controls all the interaction between the user and the application. Usually, it is a servlet that receives the user request and passes all the input parameters to the model that does the actual work. Finally, a JSP is called to return the output.

This approach gives us many advantages, for example:

► It provides clear separation of the business logic from presentation and interaction logic.

► It allows the use of three-tier architectures where business logic and presentation logic are placed on different servers with different security models applied.

► It enables role separation in a development team, where the work of a page designer smoothly integrates with the work of a business developer.

When applying this programming model in Web applications, the vehicle that is used for carrying data or objects from the servlet to the JSP is often the `HttpServletRequest` or `HttpSession`. The request object contains all the information that a Web browser sends to a Web server when a user requests a resource (URL) on the server.

Application clients

With WebSphere Application Server Version 5, application clients now consist of the following models:

▶ **ActiveX application client**—The ActiveX application client model uses the Java Native Interface (JNI) architecture to programmatically access the Java Virtual Machine (JVM). Therefore the JVM exists in the same process space as the ActiveX application (Visual Basic, VBScript, or ASP) and remains attached to the process until that process terminates.

▶ **Applet application client**—In the applet application client model, a Java applet is embedded in an HTML document residing on a remote client machine from the WebSphere Application Server. With this type of client, the user accesses an enterprise bean in the WebSphere Application Server through the Java applet in the HTML document.

▶ **J2EE application client**—The J2EE application client is a Java application program that accesses enterprise beans, JDBC databases, and Java Message Service message queues. The J2EE application client program runs on client machines. This program follows the same Java programming model as other Java programs; however, the J2EE application client depends on the application client runtime to configure its execution environment, and uses the Java Naming and Directory Interface (JNDI) name space to access resources.

▶ **Pluggable application client** and **thin application client** —The pluggable and thin application clients provide a lightweight Java client programming model. These clients are best suited to situations where a Java client application exists but the application needs enhancements to use enterprise beans, or where the client application requires a thinner, more lightweight environment than the one offered by the J2EE application client. The difference between the thin application client and the pluggable application client is that the thin application client includes a Java Virtual Machine (JVM), and the pluggable application client requires a JVM be provided by the user.

The J2EE application client programming model provides the benefits of the J2EE platform for the Java client application. The J2EE application client offers the ability to seamlessly develop, assemble, deploy and launch a client application. The tooling provided with the WebSphere platform supports the seamless integration of these stages to help the developer create a client application from start to finish.

When you develop a client application using and adhering to the J2EE platform, you can move the client application code from one J2EE platform implementation to another. The client application package can require redeployment using each J2EE platform deployment tool, but the code that comprises the client application does not change.

The application client runtime supplies a container that provides access to system services for the client application code. The client application code must contain a main method. The application client runtime invokes this `main` method after the environment initializes and runs until the Java Virtual Machine code terminates.

The J2EE platform allows the application client to use nicknames or short names, defined within the client application deployment descriptor. These deployment descriptors identify enterprise beans or local resources (JDBC, JMS, Java Mail and URL APIs) for simplified resolution through the use of JNDI. This simplified resolution to the enterprise bean reference and local resource reference also eliminates changes to the client application code, when the underlying object or resource either changes or moves to a different server. When these changes occur, the application client can require redeployment (for details see Chapter 17, "Client development" on page 587).

The application client also provides initialization of the runtime environment for the client application. The deployment descriptor defines this unique initialization for each client application. The application client runtime also provides support for security authentication to the enterprise beans and local resources.

The application client uses the RMI-IIOP protocol. Using this protocol enables the client application to access enterprise bean references and to use CORBA services provided by the J2EE platform implementation. Use of the RMI-IIOP protocol and the accessibility of CORBA services assist users in developing a client application that requires access to both enterprise bean references and CORBA object references.

When you combine the J2EE and CORBA environments or programming models in one client application, you must understand the differences between the two programming models to use and manage each appropriately.

How to access EJBs

The basic steps for accessing EJBs from any type of client are:

- ▶ Retrieve the home interface
- ▶ Find or create an EJB instance
- ▶ Invoke the methods of the EJB instance

Home interface

There are basically two ways to retrieve a home interface:

- ▶ **Access with fully qualified bean home name**—You access a bean using its JNDI name. This is only possible for a remote home interface and should only be used for thin clients where no J2EE container is available. The JNDI name is stored in an extension of the deployment descriptor (`ibm-ejb-jar-bnd.xmi`).

- ▶ **Access with an EJB reference**—You access a bean using an EJB reference that is defined in the deployment descriptor and that points to the EJB. The container is responsible for translating this reference to the real JNDI name of the component at runtime.

  EJB references decouple the application from the JNDI settings in the deployment descriptor. EJB references require a J2EE container and are the only way to access local home interfaces, but references are also the suggested way for remote home interfaces. An EJB reference is either a remote or a local reference; one name cannot be both.

JNDI names must be assigned by the deployer latest when an enterprise application is installed into an application server.

Note that by using access beans the retrieval of the home interface can be generated into the factory access bean and is transparent to the client.

Basics programming principles

We will first see how we can write a simple EJB client that can find and use enterprise beans in an EJB container.

There are certain steps a client has to follow before accessing enterprise beans on an EJB server. These steps are presented here.

Obtain an initial naming context

When you are writing an EJB client, you are responsible for creating a JNDI `InitialContext` that will be hooked to the naming service running in the application server.

In the simplest form we get the initial context using its constructor:

```
javax.naming.InitialContext initialContext =
                    new javax.naming.InitialContext();
```

This simple form is appropriate when running in the same JVM or in the same machine as the EJBs and the target is a WebSphere Application Server.

When constructing an initial context, you can pass two parameters:

▶ The location, host name, and port of the naming service (PROVIDER_URL)

▶ The name of the initial context factory (INITIAL_CONTEXT_FACTORY)

This information is provided to the constructor of the InitialContext as a java.util.Properties. Here is an example:

```
java.util.Properties properties = new java.util.Properties();
properties.put(javax.naming.Context.PROVIDER_URL, "iiop:///");
properties.put(javax.naming.Context.INITIAL_CONTEXT_FACTORY,
                    "com.ibm.websphere.naming.WsnInitialContextFactory");
javax.naming.InitialContext initialContext =
                    new javax.naming.InitialContext(properties);
```

Notice that we use the string iiop:/// for the PROVIDER_URL property. This string indicates to the runtime environment to find the naming service at the standard port on the local machine. The general form of the PROVIDER_URL string is iiop://hostname:port/.

The value of the second property, INITIAL_CONTEXT_FACTORY, is the class name of the naming service factory. For WebSphere Application Server Version 5, use com.ibm.websphere.naming.WsnInitialContextFactory.

Looking up an EJB home from the initial context

Using the initial naming context, we can retrieve the EJB home of the entity bean we want to access, for example, the Customer entity bean.

For a remote home interface we can use the global JNDI name or an EJB reference. For a local home interface we must use a local reference.

Using a global JNDI name
The coding sequence for a remote home interface using a global JNDI name is:

```
Object objHome = initialContext.lookup("ejb/itsobank/Customer");
CustomerHome customerHome = (CustomerHome)
        javax.rmi.PortableRemoteObject.narrow(objHome,CustomerHome.class) ;
```

Notice the JNDI name of the customer entity bean, `ejb/itsobank/Customer`. This is the name we define in the deployment descriptor when we created the `Customer` bean.

In the second line we use the utility class `PortableRemoteObject` to narrow the reference that was obtained from the `InitialContext`. This can be seen as equivalent to casting; it takes a generic RMI-IIOP reference and returns an instance of the proper class.

Using an EJB reference

The coding sequence for a remote home interface using an EJB reference is:

```
Object objHome = initialContext.lookup("java:comp/env/ejb/CustomerR");
CustomerHome customerHome = (CustomerHome)
        javax.rmi.PortableRemoteObject.narrow(objHome,CustomerHome.class);
```

The coding sequence for a local home interface using an EJB reference is:

```
Object objHome = initialContext.lookup("java:comp/env/ejb/CustomerL");
CustomerLocalHome customerLocalHome = (CustomerLocalHome)objHome;
```

When looking for a reference you use the prefix `java:comp/env/`. The reference name (`ejb/CustomerL`) is defined by tooling, such as Application Developer in the deployment descriptor editor and stored in an extension file. EJB references are automatically defined when you use container-managed relationships in Application Developer. Other references, for example from a session EJB to an entity EJB, are defined manually.

Note that with local references simple class casting can be used to convert the lookup result object into a local home interface.

Using the EJB home

With the EJB home, we can create new instances, find, and remove entity beans. Note that most methods can throw a `FinderException` and a `RemoteException`; these have to be handled in a `try/catch` block.

▶ Creating a new customer bean:

```
Customer customer = customerHome.create(customerID);
customer.setTitle("Mr.");
customer.setFirstName("Ueli");
......
```

Here we use one of the available constructors of the `Customer` bean that only takes the `customerID`. Other properties are set using setter methods.

▶ Finding a customer bean:

```
Customer customer = customerHome.findByPrimaryKey(new CustomerKey(id));
```

The `findByPrimaryKey` method takes a parameter of type `CustomerKey` that we initialize with the an ID entered by the user as an input parameter.

Custom finder methods are also invoked from the home:

```
java.util.Collection specialCustomers = customerHome.findHighInterest(x);
```

▶ Removing a customer bean:

```
customerHome.remove(customer);
```

You can also use the `javax.ejb.Handle` of the customer as a parameter. This method results to the deletion of the corresponding row in the customer table.

> **Note:** The `remove` method is not defined in the home interface. It is inherited from the `EJBHome` superclass.

Manipulating EJB references

After acquiring the customer bean object, we can invoke any of the methods available in the component interface, for example, we can get or set the customer properties. We can also invoke the `remove` method on the EJB object.

```
customer.getName();
customer.setLastName("Newname");
customer.remove();
```

Following relationships

With container-managed relationships, you can invoke methods in an entity bean that retrieve one or multiple instances of a related entity bean.

Multiplicity one

If you traverse a 1:1 or 1:m relationship to the *one* side, then the result is a single object. For single object retrieval, coding is very simple. For example, to retrieve the account object from a transaction record:

```
Account account = transrecord.getTheAccount();
```

Multiplicity many

If you traverse a 1:m or m:m relationship to the *many* side then the result is a `Collection` or a `Set`. You have to iterate through the collection (or set) result to get the related entity bean instances. For example, to list all the transaction records of an account:

```
Account account = accountHome.findByPrimaryKey("101-1001");
Collection coll = account.getTransrecords();
Iterator collit = coll.iterator();
```

```
while ( collit.hasNext() ) {
    TransRecordLocal tr = (TransRecordLocal)collit.next();
    System.out.println ( ((java.sql.Timestamp)tr.getPrimaryKey()).toString()
        +" "+tr.getTransType()+" "+tr.getTransAmount().toString() );
}
```

Note that an `Iterator` is only one way to access the members of a collection; the `Collection` and `Set` classes provide a number of methods.

> **Important:** A collection result of a relationship retrieval must be accessed within one transaction. You cannot retrieve instances at a time using different transactions. Therefore it is good practice to provide a session bean method that iterates through a relationship and collects the information into a result JavaBean.

Finder methods

Finder methods return either single objects or values or collections of objects or values. To retrieve all the results of a multi-object finder methods uses coding similar to relationships:

```
Collection coll = accountHome.findGoldAccounts(aBalance);
Iterator collit = coll.iterator();
while ( collit.hasNext() ) {
    AccountLocal account = (AccountLocal)collit1.next();
    //..... process the account
}
```

The same transactional principles apply to finder methods as for relationships.

Inheritance

Inheritance of entity beans touches the coding in two ways:

► Subclass entity beans inherit the methods of the superclass. From a `Checking` bean (subclass of `Account`), you can follow all the relationships defined for the account. There is no special coding required:

```
Checking checking = checkingHome.findByPrimaryKey("xxx-xxxx");
Collection coll = checking.getTransrecords();
Iterator collit = coll.iterator();
while ( collit.hasNext() ) {
    TransRecordLocal tr = (TransRecordLocal)collit.next();
    // process transaction record
}
```

- When following relationships from another entity bean to the superclass or when using a custom finder method on the superclass, the result collection contains instances of any of the subclasses.

  For example, when retrieving accounts for a customer when using the findGoldAccounts custom finder, the result contains Checking and Savings instances. You can check the type of instance using this code sequence:

```
Collection coll = accountHome.findGoldAccounts(currentBalance);
Iterator collit = coll1.iterator();
while ( collit.hasNext() ) {
    AccountLocal account = (AccountLocal)collit.next();
    BigDecimal balance = account.getBalance(); // shared attribute
    if (account instanceof CheckingLocal) {
        CheckingLocal checking = (CheckingLocal)account;
        // process checking instance
        BigDecimal over = checking.getOverdraft();
    } else if (account instanceof SavingsLocal) {
        SavingsLocal savings = (SavingsLocal)account;
        // process savings instance
        BigDecimal minimum = savings.getMinAmount();
    } else {
        // process generic account instance
    }
}
```

Simple EJB client application

Figure 7-2 shows a simple main application that uses the basic code to find the home, create, and retrieve Customer entity beans, and delete a bean.

It also follows a relationship to list the related accounts. The getAccountNumbers method is a method on the remote interface that uses the container-managed relationship to get the account numbers.

> **Note:** Because we did not define a remote interface for the Account bean, we cannot explore the account attributes in a remote client.

In a remote client, we can use the UserTransaction to execute multiple remote calls within one transaction. A transaction object is retrieved from the initial context using the JNDI name of jta/usertransaction:

```
UserTransaction tx = (UserTransaction)initialContext.
                                    lookup("jta/usertransaction");
tx.begin();          // starts a transaction
......
tx.commit();         // ends a transaction
```

```
package itso.bank5.simpleapp;
import itso.bank5.cmp.*;
import javax.transaction.UserTransaction;

public class SimpleApp {
    public static void main(java.lang.String[] args) {
    UserTransaction tx = null;
    try {
        javax.naming.InitialContext initialContext =
                     new javax.naming.InitialContext();
        tx = (UserTransaction)initialContext.lookup("jta/usertransaction");
        Object objHome = initialContext.lookup("ejb/itsobank/Customer");
        CustomerHome customerHome = (CustomerHome)
            javax.rmi.PortableRemoteObject.narrow(objHome,CustomerHome.class);
        tx.begin();
        Customer cust2 = customerHome.create(201);
        System.out.println("Customer 201 created");
        cust2.setFirstName("John");
        cust2.setLastName("Smith");
        System.out.println("Customer 201: name="+cust2.getName());
        cust2.setLastName("Keller");
        System.out.println("Customer 201: name="+cust2.getName());
        tx.commit();
        tx.begin();
        Customer cust1 = customerHome.findByPrimaryKey(new CustomerKey(101));
        System.out.println("Customer 101: name="+cust1.getName());
        String[] accounts = cust1.getAccountNumbers();
        if (accounts != null) {
            for (int i=0; i< accounts.length; i++ ) {
                System.out.println(" - Account: " + accounts[i]);
            }
        }
        cust2.remove();
        tx.commit();
        System.out.println("Customer 201 removed");
    } catch(Exception ex) {
        ex.printStackTrace();
        try { tx.rollback(); } catch(Exception e) {}
    }
    }
}
```

Figure 7-2   Simple EJB client application

Programming restriction

> **Important:** The EJB specification restricts a session bean to declare static variables. The reason is that static variables (class variables) are maintained within the current JVM. If another EJB of the same type uses the same static field inside another container running in a different machine, then the value of the static variable will be different. Therefore, we are forced to use instance variables for caching the home object.
>
> When using an external JavaBean as a utility class, we can then cache the home in a static variable. Therefore, the home is retrieved by the utility bean only once in each JVM and all the facade bean instances use the same reference. In our example, each bean instance has to retrieve a separate reference the first time the client invokes a method.

Using access beans

Access beans are an IBM extension to the EJB programming model to make client programming simpler and to improve performance:

- ► The code to access the home interface can be generated into a factory class. The home interface is retrieved automatically as soon as a client creates or finds a bean instance.

- ► A data class can cache the attributes of an entity bean for fast access within a client. All or a subset of entity bean attributes are retrieved and cached at the client when the access bean is created or at the first attribute access. The client decides when data that has been changed is synchronized with the EJB container. This technique simplifies transaction management by the client.

The data class access bean is a data transfer object that is moved between the client and the EJB container. The factory and data class are generated by Application Developer.

There is also an older style of an access bean called *copy helper* that is generated by IBM VisualAge for Java (and optionally by Application Developer). Copy helper functions are similar to the combination of data classes and factory.

> **Important:** We do not cover the details of access beans in this chapter. Refer to Chapter 15, "EJB access beans" on page 551 for conceptual details about the different access beans and how to create access beans in Application Developer. Refer to "GUI client using access beans" on page 634 for an example of a client that uses an access bean.

Using a session facade to entity beans

We have seen how clients can access enterprise beans directly or by using access beans. We saw that using access beans simplifies the client code and accelerates its execution.

The trade-off of simplicity and speed is freedom. Using access beans limits the flexibility of the design and restricts the developer from using other techniques. In this section, we show how EJB client applications can use session beans instead.

Facade session beans

A common approach when designing EJB applications with entity and session beans is to use a facade in front of entity beans that protects the persistent data layer and controls all the client access. Such a facade can be built using a stateless session bean that provides:

- Home interface—create method of the session bean
- Component interface—Business methods for the client
  - Business methods of entity beans, for example the deposit method of the Account bean is made available as a deposit method of the session bean.
  - New business methods that combine entity bean methods, for example a transfer method in the session bean that invokes withdraw and deposit methods in two entity beans.
  - New business methods that wrap entity bean finder methods and format the retrieved entity beans into usable data for the client.

The advantages of using facade session beans are:

- The persistence model is hidden from the client. Entity beans are viewed as general-purpose data sources and are not visible to client applications.
- Session beans can tie together multiple data sources and act as the single point of entry to the business data layer.
- Centralized control of transactions and security is delegated to the session facade layer and managed more efficiently for the application.

Figure 7-3 illustrates how session beans can act as a facade layer to entity beans in front of clients.

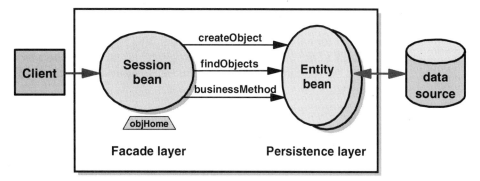

Figure 7-3   Session facade to entity beans

Facade session design

The facade session bean can be easily built using the EJB development tools in Application Developer. We recommend that stateless session beans be used, because they are lightweight and provide better performance.

For a session bean to serve as a facade to entity beans, it should have these kind of members:

▶ **objHome**—These are `private` fields that cache the home of the entity bean(s) that the session bean will serve (instance variable). Caching the home object reference improves the performance. The session bean should also have a `getObjHome` method that performs a lazy initialization and returns the home object.

Entity data is not cached; stateless session beans do not carry any volatile data and any instance can serve a client for a given request.

▶ **createObject**—This is a `public` method that calls a create method on the home of the entity bean, such as `objHome.create(...)`. Such methods make entity bean creation available to the client. However, in many applications creation of entity beans is inside the business methods of the session bean.

▶ **findObjects**—This is a `public` method that calls a finder method of the entity bean. The resulting entity objects are packaged into a data transfer object to be returned to the client. The client should never see the entity bean itself. In many applications, entity bean finders are used inside the business methods of the session bean.

▶ **businessMethod**—This is a `public` method that provides the real application function to the client. The business methods use create and finder methods to retrieve entity bean instances, and getter and setter methods to manipulate entity bean data.

Using an access bean for the session facade

We can combine the session facade model with access beans by using a Java wrapper for the session bean. However, this approach is questionable and there is hardly a reason to wrap a session bean into an access bean. Stateless session beans do not carry any data and therefore there is nothing to cache in a data class.

Client comparison

After presenting the different ways of accessing enterprise beans from a client application (a servlet in our examples), let's now see the advantages and disadvantages of using them.

Direct access

This is the straightforward way for a client to access an enterprise bean. The home of the bean should be cached in a `static` variable and be initialized in the `init` method of the servlet. This gives good performance. However, the result of each method invocation performed by the client is a remote call. Even if the client is a servlet running in the same application server as the EJB container (same JVM), all the method calls are routed through the TCP/IP stack. Of course, this has an impact on the performance of the application.

Pros and cons

The advantages of using this approach are:

► Fast to code
► No need to create extra components
► No extra load generated on the client or server side
► The enterprise bean implementation is not modified

The disadvantages are:

► Poor performance
► Requires EJB programming in the client code
► The client developer has to know how to use EJBs

Access beans

This is a better way to access enterprise beans. The home is cached in the access bean, and for data classes the properties of the bean are cached as well. This improves the performance by eliminating many remote calls. However, the developer should always be careful when using the local cache of the bean properties, because the bean's data may have been updated in the meantime by another application.

The number of the remote method calls over the network is decreased greatly, as the access beans perform all the get or set methods in a single call. For example, if we assume that a customer bean has 10 properties, retrieving them generates only one remote method call instead of 10. However, this requires the modification of the enterprise bean implementation, because getter/setter methods for the data class are added to the bean.

Pros and cons

The advantages of using access beans are:

- ► Very good performance
- ► Simple to use
- ► The client developer uses EJBs in the same manner as JavaBeans

The disadvantages are:

- ► Extra components have to be created
- ► The enterprise bean implementation is modified
- ► Restrictive design that does not allow use of other models
- ► You have to use access beans for all the beans in an application

Facade beans

Facade beans are an alternative approach to access beans. It is applicable when accessing entity beans. The entity bean is accessed via a stateless session bean that caches the home and provides access to all the properties of the bean in a single method. This also does not require the modification of the bean class, as required when using access beans.

The performance is also very good here, since the number of the remote method calls is limited. Actually, all the method calls between the facade bean and the entity bean are made locally (through the local pipes), since both of them are in the same container.

However, the facade approach requires the creation of a session bean for each set of entity beans we access in one application. This requires more development time and system resources on the application server, because more beans are running in the container. Additionally, the client code is not as simple as when using access beans, because a session bean instance must be used for each method call.

However, the code here can be simplified by using an external Java class (a JavaBean) that retrieves and caches the home interface in a class variable instead. This increases the performance and enables code reuse, simplifying the development of all the facade beans that are needed for the entity beans.

Pros and cons

The advantages of using facade beans are:

- ▸ Very good performance
- ▸ Open design to other models
- ▸ The enterprise bean implementation is not modified

The disadvantages are:

- ▸ Extra development time
- ▸ More load in the EJB container
- ▸ Requires EJB programming in the client code

We believe that using facade session beans to entity beans is a better architecture approach than using access beans. This way we have better control over the persistence data layer and we manage all the security and the transaction issues in a more efficient and organized manner.

Recapitulation of approaches

Figure 7-4 demonstrates client access to entity beans:

- ▸ Directly
- ▸ Through an access bean
- ▸ Through a session facade bean

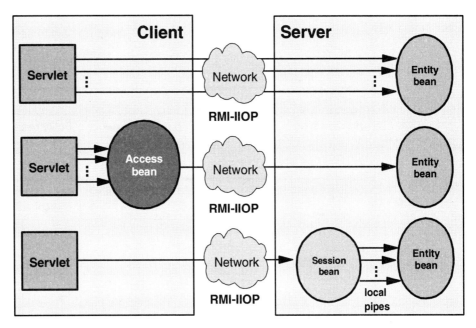

Figure 7-4   Client comparison

The client side in the figure represents the application server where the servlet engine resides. On the other hand, the server side represents the application server where the EJB container resides. Although these two components should be in the same application server for performance reasons, here we assume a more general case that can occur when, for example, a firewall is placed between the presentation and business logic for security reasons.

Notes:

► This comparison applies also when the servlet engine resides in the same application server with the EJB container. As we mentioned before, all method calls between a servlet and an EJB are routed through TCP/IP.

► The access bean shown in Figure 7-4 is a copy helper bean that encapsulates the RMI-IIOP access. When using a data class, the access bean itself is shipped between client and EJB container.

► Although the client is shown as a servlet, it could also be a stand-alone client, for example running in a J2EE client container.

What client type to chose?

Use the guidelines given in Table 7-1 when deciding how to design your client application.

Table 7-1   What client type to choose

Client type	Yes, when	No, when
Direct access	Simple EJB model is used	Entity bean contains many properties
	Performance is not critical	
Access beans	Simple and fast development is desirable	More complex design model is required
	The application server has limited system resources	Clustered environment with many application servers is used
	Java wrapper is used for accessing session beans	
Facade beans	Scalability is critical	Client has to access session beans
	Open design is applied	Development time is critical
	Better overall performance is required	

Home factory pattern

In the EJB programming mode, clients require access to the home interface of EJBs before accessing the EJBs. Therefore, every client is faced with coding the retrieval of home interfaces through the naming service.

The idea of the home factory is to centralize this code and write it only once. EJB clients then use the home factory to access the home of any EJB.

Benefits

The home factory pattern provides the following benefits:

► Insulate EJB clients from naming service complexity.

► Cache naming context creation and EJB home lookup to achieve better performance.

- ▶ Provide an interface for creating remote and local EJB homes without specifying the method used to retrieve the concrete class at runtime.

This pattern is also known as home factory or home caching.

Motivation

Before invoking an EJB's business method, a client must create or find an EJB object for that bean. To create or find an instance of a bean's EJB object, the client must:

- ▶ Locate and create an EJB home object for that bean.
- ▶ Use the EJB home object to create or find an instance of the bean's EJB object.

JNDI is used to find the EJB home object by name. We already described the basic programming techniques for creating an initial context (see "Obtain an initial naming context" on page 254) and retrieving the home (see "Looking up an EJB home from the initial context" on page 255).

Getting access to EJB homes is complex, requires inter-process communication, and is different for remote and local homes. Implementing a home factory simplifies the process.

Applicability

Use the home factory pattern when:

- ▶ The result of EJB homes lookups should be cached for performance reasons.
- ▶ A client should be configurable to access different sets of classes, implementing an EJB with the same EJB home JNDI name.
- ▶ The client should be independent of how the EJB homes are retrieved (narrow method or cast).

The first bullet has proven to be a mandatory requirement in any real-life application.

Structure

The structure of the home factory pattern is shown in Figure 7-5:

- ▶ A single instance of `HomeFactory` is created at runtime. This `HomeFactory` creates EJB homes as defined in an externalized manner, for example, by means of resource bundles or XML files.
- ▶ `HomeFactory` uses the metadata stored in this externalized manner for instantiating and returning the appropriate EJB home class.

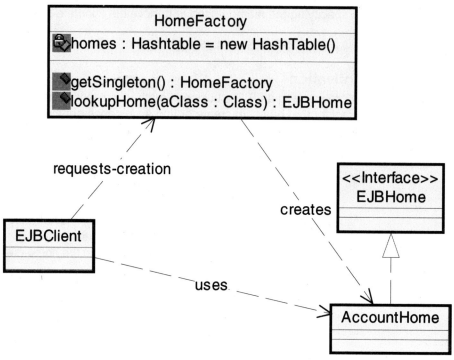

Figure 7-5   Home factory pattern structure

Consequences

The home factory pattern has the following benefits:

- ► *It promotes consistency among clients*—When naming context and EJB homes are accessed in the same way, it is easy to modify and/or enhance the level of service provided by the factory.

- ► *The support of new kinds of EJB homes is transparent*—If specified externally, EJB homes and their concrete classes can be added and made available without effort.

- ► *It isolates the EJB home actual classes*—The factory encapsulates and as such isolates clients from actual EJB home concrete classes, as long as those concrete classes are not needed for usage (that is, none of their specific methods are called).

Implementation

A pure implementation of the home factory with externalized metadata in an XML file is quite complex.

Singleton factory

A singleton factory instance ensures that only one instance of the factory class is created, and that this one instance is accessible to all clients. Clients get access to this instance by calling the static `getSingleton` method, rather than by constructing the instance themselves. Therefore, the constructors are `private` (be sure to declare at least one private constructor; otherwise, a default public constructor is automatically generated).

The skeleton code of the `HomeFactory` class is shown in Figure 7-6.

```
public class HomeFactory {
    private static HomeFactory singleton = null;
    private HomeFactory() {
        super();
    }
    public static HomeFactory getSingleton() {
        if (singleton == null) singleton = new HomeFactory();
        return singleton;
    }
    ...
}
```

Figure 7-6   Factory as singleton

XML configuration data

Figure 7-7 shows the structure of an XML file that holds configuration data of EJB homes. Alternatives to XML are environment properties, resource bundles, and property files.

```
<configuration>
    <jndi-property>java.naming.factory.initial=
                    com.ibm.websphere.naming.WsnInitialContextFactory
    </jndi-property>
    <jndi-property>java.naming.provider.url=iiop://NameServer:900
    </jndi-property>
    <enterprise-beans>
        <entity>
            <jndi-name>ejb/itsobank/Banking</jndi-name>
            <home>itso.bank5.session.BankingHome</home>
            <helper-class>javax.rmi.PortableRemoteObject.narrow</helper-class>
        </entity>
    </enterprise-beans>
</configuration>
```

Figure 7-7   Information in XML format

Externalize information

The properties that an EJB client uses to initialize JNDI and find an EJB home object may vary across EJB server implementations. To make an enterprise bean more portable between EJB server implementations, we have to externalize these properties in environment variables, XML files, properties files, or resource bundles, rather than hardcode them into the EJB client code.

One of the issues we face is the EJB home fully qualified class name to be used for narrowing the result of the lookup. Figure 7-8 shows how to read XML configuration data.

```
private static ConfigurationData configuration = null;

public static ConfigurationData getConfigurationData() {
    if (configuration != null) return configuration;
    configuration = new ConfigurationData();
    // obtaining an input stream and a DOM parser
    ......
    Document document = parser.readStream(inputStream);
    NodeList nodeList = document.getElementsByTagName("entity-bean");
    int length = nodeList.getLength();
    for (int i = 0; i < length; i++) {
        EnterpriseBeanMetaData enterpriseBeanMetaData =
            new EnterpriseBeanMetaData();
        enterpriseBeanMetaData.readElement((Element) nodeList.item(i));
        Class homeClass = enterpriseBeanMetaData.getHomeClass();
        ConfigurationData.setEnterpriseBeanMetaData(homeClass,
            enterpriseBeanMetaData);
    }
    return configuration;
}
```

Figure 7-8   Loading externalized information (extract)

Caching of initial context and EJB homes

The initial context is a single object, whereas EJB homes are cached in a hash table with the JNDI names as keys. The point is that we can take advantage of the meta information stored in the XML file that specifies the EJB implementation classes for writing a full generic version of the lookupHome method.

Figure 7-9 shows the skeleton information of the caching in the lookupHome method.

```
private static Hashtable homeCache = new Hashtable();
private static InitialContext initialContext = null;
...
public static EJBHome lookupHome(Class aClass)
                                throws RemoteException {
try {
   EJBHome home = (EJBHome) homeCache.get(aClass);
   if (home != null) {
      return home;
   }
   ConfigurationData aConfigurationData = getConfigurationData();

   EnterpriseBeanMetaData enterpriseBeanMetaData =
      aConfigurationData.getEnterpriseBeanMetaData(aClass);

   if (initialContext == null) initialContext = new
            InitialContext(enterpriseBeanMetaData.getJndiProperties());

   String lookupString = enterpriseBeanMetaData.getJndiHomeName();
   Object anObject = initialContext.lookup(lookupString);

   Method narrowMethod = enterpriseBeanMetaData.getNarrowMethod();
   if (narrowMethod == null) {
      home = (EJBHome) anObject;
   } else {
      Object[] parameters = new Object[] {anObject, aClass};
      home = (EJBHome) narrowMethod.invoke(null, parameters);
   }
   if (home == null) {
      return null;
   }
   homeCache.put(aClass, home);
   return home;
} catch (Exception ex) {
   ex.printStackTrace();
   return null;
}
}
```

Figure 7-9   Naming context and EJB home caching

Concurrency

Multiple client threads may use the factory at the same time. We assume that it is better to let clients engage in looking up the same EJB home concurrently, and then update the same entry multiple times in the hash table (with the same value, as expected), rather than serializing access to a method or a resource other than the hash table synchronized `put` method.

Known uses

This work was based on the Freeside demo application (WebSphere Application Server sample application) and on the home factory developed for the ITSO banking application in the redbook *Enterprise JavaBeans Development Using VisualAge for Java*, SG24-5429.

Sample application: a modern home factory

For this redbook, we implemented a home factory without caching. Because the WebSphere Application Server provides caching of homes automatically, application-level caching is no longer required.

In addition, modern EJB programming techniques suggest the use of EJB references to look up home interfaces. The home factory could be expanded to support EJB references, but caching becomes inappropriate because multiple references can point to the same EJB.

Design

Based on the reasons stated, we decided to implement a modern home factory class that:

▶ Provides access through EJB references only

▶ Returns the local or remote home interface (EJBLocalHome or EJBHome)

▶ Caches the initial context but not EJB homes

Figure 7-10 shows an extract of the getHome method of the HomeFactory class of our sample application.

```
public Object getHome(String ejbRef) throws NamingException {
   Object nsObject = initialContext.lookup
           (new StringBuffer("java:comp/env/").append(ejbRef).toString());
   if (nsObject instanceof EJBLocalHome) {
      System.out.println("ejbRef " + ejbRef + " is a local reference.");
      return nsObject;
   } else {
      EJBHome ejbHome = (EJBHome) javax.rmi.PortableRemoteObject.narrow
                      ( (org.omg.CORBA.Object)nsObject, EJBHome.class );
      System.out.println("ejbRef " + ejbRef + " is a remote reference.");
      return ejbHome;
   }
}
```

Figure 7-10   Sample application home factory

Client usage

A client can use this code to access a remote home interface:

```
try {
    CustomerHome custRemoteHome = (CustomerHome)
                    HomeFactory.singleton().getHome("ejb/CustomerRemote");
} catch (NamingException ex) {
    ex.printStackTrace();
    throw new EJBException("Error looking up homes: "+ex.getMessage());
}
```

A client can use this code to access a local home interface:

```
try {
    AccountLocalHome accountHome = (AccountLocalHome)
                    HomeFactory.singleton().getHome("ejb/Account");
} catch (NamingException ex) {
    ex.printStackTrace();
    throw new EJBException("Error looking up homes: "+ex.getMessage());
}
```

Details

See "Implementing the home factory" on page 394 for details on the home factory developed for this redbook.

Summary

In this chapter, we presented the possible ways a client application can access and use enterprise beans. We described all the steps that have to be followed and included small programming examples.

We provided a short discussion on access beans and the session facade pattern, and we concluded with a description of the home factory pattern and an implementation of the pattern.

8

Additional concepts: transactions, exceptions, security

In this chapter, we wrap up our discussion of EJBs by introducing the important concepts of transactions, exception handling, and security.

All of these are vast topics In their own right, and could warrant their own chapters. However, we simply introduce you to the main areas here to round out your understanding of EJBs.

For more information, refer to the EJB specification as well as other Redbooks.

© Copyright IBM Corp. 2003. All rights reserved.

Introduction

In this chapter, we introduce the following topics:

- ▶ **Transactions**—We describe how transactions are defined in the context of J2EE and how transactions are managed around enterprise beans. We describe the transaction attributes for enterprise beans, and the effect they have on commit, rollback, concurrency, and locking. We then describe ways of starting and ending transactions by enterprise beans, the container ,and bean-managed transactions. Finally, we provide guidelines for transaction management.

- ▶ **Exception handling**—Exceptions are the customary way in Java to indicate to a calling method that an abnormal condition has occurred. When a method encounters an abnormal condition (an exception condition) that it cannot handle itself, it may throw an exception. Exceptions are thrown at many different levels in large applications. We introduce the customary wisdom in determining how to handle thrown exceptions in, and from, EJBs.

- ▶ **Security**—Distributed applications accessed through the Internet face the possibility of malicious attacks. This emphasizes security arrangements and the setting up of a security system. A security system gives us the power to determine who can and will access resources such as applications, servlets, EJBs, and Web pages. It also enables us to define the security policies to establish control of resources. In this chapter, we discuss securing EJBs and the procedures involved in it.

- ▶ **Additional deployment information**—We have already introduced deployment descriptor entries in this book. In this section, we present a final summary of deployment descriptor entries for the EJBs with resources, transaction assembly, and security assembly.

Transactions

A transaction is the execution of a set of activities as one *unit-of-work*. This unit-of-work is a set of activities that relate to each other and must be completed together. If any of these activities fail, the entire unit-of-work must be undone.

A transaction example: banking transfer

We extend our banking transfer example in the context of transactions. Let's say that we want to transfer money from one account to the other, as we do in the `transfer` method of the banking session bean. The activities that must be performed are:

▶ Withdraw the money from one account.
▶ Create a transaction record for that account.
▶ Deposit the money to another account.
▶ Create a transaction record for that account.

The transaction record is important because the balance of an account is verified based on all the recorded transactions. If there were a transaction that had not been recorded, then the account balance would not be consistent. It would be either higher or lower, depending on whether the transaction was a withdrawal or a deposit respectively.

Updating the balance for each account after withdrawing or depositing money is also important for the success of our operation. A money transfer from one account to another would not be complete if any of these activities failed.

Let us suppose that somehow a money transfer is done to the second account, without actually withdrawing the money from the first account. In that case, the first account would have the same balance and the second account an increased one. So, money would not have come out from an account, but would have been deposited to another account. The bank would lose money.

Therefore, all these activities have to be completed together. Only then is a money transfer considered successful. This action is known as *commit*. This is what makes the set of these activities a unit-of-work (Figure 8-1).

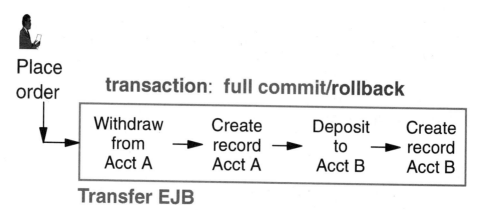

Figure 8-1   Transfer money transaction

But what happens if any of these activities do not succeed? This will cause all the other completed activities to be undone. This action is known as *rollback.*.

Problems like this are not unusual in real life. Systems that are running such business applications are usually pretty complex and distributed on several machines (multi-tier architecture). Because no system or network can reach 100% availability, it is likely that at some point a network connection or even a machine becomes unavailable. If this happens in the middle of a transaction, we would be in trouble.

Apart from availability, there is also a *concurrent data access* aspect. Such activities as reading or updating an account balance usually require access to an underlying database where all the account data is stored. In our implementation, the method that withdraws money from an account first checks to see if the balance is not exceeded by the amount to transfer. What would happen if, during the transfer transaction, another application would attempt to reduce the balance of the first account, after the withdraw method had already committed?

The transaction system itself saves us here, because it guarantees the four main properties of a transaction: *atomicity, consistency, isolation,* and *durability* (ACID).

ACID properties of a transaction

A transaction has the following four properties:

► **Atomic**—A transaction must execute completely or not at all. Every activity in a unit-of-work must execute successfully. If any activity fails, the entire transaction is aborted and all the data changes are rolled back. If all activities execute without an error, the transaction completes and all data changes are committed.

- ▶ **Consistent**—A transaction must not leave a system inconsistent after it completes. Consistency refers to the integrity of the underlying data store. For example, in our money transfer method, we should not have a negative balance in an account after the transfer is done. Notice that consistency should usually be enforced by the developer.

- ▶ **Isolated**—All transaction must be allowed to execute without interference from other processes or transactions. Any intermediate states are transparent to other transactions, allowing multiple transactions to execute serially.

- ▶ **Durable**—All data changes committed during a transaction must be written to a persistent data store and should survive hardware or software failures. If a failure occurs, the data can be recovered by using transactional logs.

Java Transaction Service (JTS)

Transactions in EJBs rely on the transaction APIs provided as part of the J2EE specification. JTS defines a low-level API that is meant to be used by the application server provider. JTS is the Java implementation of the OMG CORBA Object Transaction Service (OTS). This API is not meant to be used by EJB developers, because it is rather complex.

EJB developers should rather use the Java Transaction API (JTA). JTA provides a programming model that developers may leverage for explicit transaction demarcation.

Object Transaction Service

OTS is an optional CORBA service that provides transaction support involving one or more parties. It has a number of interfaces that the transaction manager, the resource manager, and the transactional objects use to collaborate.

One of the major advantages of OTS is that it has transaction context propagation built in. It allows propagating transaction contexts on multiple servers as long as they are using RMI-IIOP; this feature is what makes distributed transaction possible.

If there are concurrent transactions and one application acquires a lock of the data, all the other applications have to wait until the lock is released.

To improve performance, transactions use two main types of data locks: *read locks* and *write locks*. Read locks are non-exclusive. That is, any number of transactions can acquire the lock concurrently. Write locks are exclusive; only one transaction can hold a write lock at a time.

Transaction support in J2EE

A J2EE application server makes transactions very easy to use because it hides the complexity of distributed transactions from the developer. It is important to understand the basic terminology of the participants in transaction management:

- **Resource**—Any persistent store on which you can read or write. It could be a database, a JMS queue, or a JCA connector.

- **Resource manager**—Responsible for managing a resource. Typically, resource managers are a relational database or message provider product.

- **Transactional object**—Component involved in a transaction. In our example, the banking session bean is a transactional object.

- **Transaction manager**—Component or system responsible for managing the transactional operations of transactional components. WebSphere is a transaction manager. When an application uses more than one resource manager in one transaction, we need an *external* transaction manager, which WebSphere can be. A typical example is reading from a message queue and writing to a database in one transaction. This is a *distributed* or *global* transaction.

XA protocol

XA is the standard interface between a transaction manager and a resource manager. The transaction manager coordinates a distributed transaction. It typically uses the XA protocol to interact with the database back ends. The databases has to understand the XA protocol for distributed transactions.

There is a resource manager for each participant in the distributed transaction, and the resource manager is the communication point for the transaction manager. To support the XA protocol, a number of extra remote procedural calls must be sent to the database both before and after a given connection is used.

Two-phase commit

Resource managers that want to participate in a two-phase commit have to implement the XA protocol, which ensures that the result of a transaction is consistent across all resource managers participating in the transaction. It is used only in distributed transactions. The protocol operates in distinct phases to ultimately commit or abort a transaction:

- **Phase one**—evaluates the status of each resource manager. The transaction manager checks with each local resource manager whether they are ready to commit the transaction. Each resource manager responds that they are ready or not. A transaction can commit only when all participating resource managers agree during this phase one. This phase is called the *prepare* phase.

► **Phase two**—concludes the transaction. Based on the response from each resource manager, the transaction manager instructs all resource managers to commit the transaction if all agree or to roll back the transaction if at least one disagrees. This phase is called the *commit* phase.

Local versus global transactions in WebSphere

When an application uses only one resource during a transaction, for example when writing to two tables in the same database, then its resource manager can perform the role of transaction manager. This is called *local transaction optimization* and is transparent to the application. Transactions in this scenario engage in a one-phase-commit (1PC) transaction.

Global transaction is a transaction that uses an external resource manager. A distributed transaction is a transaction over a multi-tier deployment with several transaction participants—such as a database or JCA connection—within the same transaction. A global transaction manager is required to manage distributed transactions, and will coordinate the updates across multiple resources. This is called a two-phase-commit (2PC). The resource manager can only participate in a distributed transaction if it supports the XA protocol.

If you want your resources to be part of global 2PC transactions, then you have to ensure that the resources you define in WebSphere associate to XA-compliant drivers. For example:

DB2 UDB (JDBC):

► **COM.ibm.db2.jdbc.DB2ConnectionPoolDataSource**—1PC

► **COM.ibm.db2.jdbc.DB2XADataSource**—2PC

Refer to the development chapters in Part 2 for more information on configuring XA-compliant JMS and JDBC resources.

EJB transaction demarcation

Determining when a transaction begins and ends is called transaction demarcation. Bean providers can choose to either control when transactions begin and end programmatically, by using bean-managed transaction (BMT) demarcation, or can delegate this to the container through container-managed transaction demarcation (CMT).

Bean-managed transactions (BMT)

When a developer explicitly manages the bean demarcation levels in the code, they are said to be employing bean-managed transactions (BMT). Bean-managed transactions must declare when transactions start, what behavior is part of the transaction, and when they end. This is accomplished through the use of the javax.transaction.UserTransaction interface as defined in the Java Transaction API (JTA). This interface provides methods to explicitly begin, commit, and roll back transactions.

Figure 8-2 shows a simple interaction using the UserTransaction interface.

```
// desclare the user transaction
UserTransaction tran = null;
try {
    // get a user transaction using the initial context
    InitialContext ctx = new InitialContext();
    tran = ctx.lookup("java:comp/UserTransaction");
    // or using the EJBContext object - discussed later
    tran = getSessionContext().getUserTransaction();

    // begin the transaction
    tran.begin();

            Perform™ transactional work, such as db connection, execute.....

    // commit the transaction
    tran.commit();
} catch (Exception e) {
    if (tran != null) tran.rollback();
    ...
}
```

Figure 8-2   Bean-managed transaction example

Only beans that are declared to use bean-managed transactions may use the UserTransaction interface within their code. To do otherwise results in exceptions being thrown by the container.

To declare a bean as using bean-managed transactions means setting the <transaction-type> deployment descriptor attribute:

```
<transaction-type>Bean</transaction-type>
```

> **Note:** Bean-managed transactions are only available to session and message-driven beans; they are illegal for entity beans. Spanning a transaction across many methods is only allowed in stateful session beans (see "Conversational state" on page 185). Stateless session beans, and the `onMessage` method of message-driven beans, must end or roll back the transaction they start in the method call.

Container-managed transactions (CMT)

The bean provider must now be responsible for managing transactions in BMT. This can get complicated rather fast. A simpler and more elegant solution is to let the container manage the transactions for you. There is no need to write any transaction logic, because this is handled by the container at runtime. The code becomes cleaner, because transaction demarcation is not intertwined in the code. The developer simply has to declare the transactional behavior in the deployment descriptor. One of the most powerful features of EJBs is their ability to employ declarative transaction management.

To declare a bean as using container-managed transactions means setting the `<transaction-type>` deployment descriptor attribute:

```
<transaction-type>Container</transaction-type>
```

In addition, the developer or deployer can declare additional transactional attributes that govern the behavior of the beans in the transactions. The transactional attribute behavior of CMTs can be set at either the bean globally, or the individual methods within a bean. Depending on how the transaction attributes are defined, the container will either start, continue, suspend, ignore, stop, or throw an exception on a transaction when a bean method is executed.

The bean provider is not required to call explicit commit or rollbacks in the code. A transaction starts when a method is called that requires a transaction. The transaction boundary, or scope, is for the length of this method. If the method executes successfully, then the transaction is automatically committed when the method ends.

How does the container know when it should or should not commit? If the bean method (or any other bean method that it subsequently calls) calls the `setRollbackOnly` method (using the `EJBContext` object), then the transaction is marked for a rollback. The container guarantees that the transaction is rolled back when completed, but does not force an end of the transaction immediately. The bean developer can use the `getRollbackOnly` method to determine if a transaction has been marked for rollback, and not continue with the current code sequence if they choose.

> **Note:** Application exceptions do not automatically cause the container to roll back the transaction, so this must be handled explicitly by the developer if a rollback is desired, by use of the `setRollbackOnly` method.

CMT transaction attributes

The following are the transaction attributes that can be set for beans employing container-managed transactions. These attributes may be set at either the bean or individual method level. Although these attributes are most commonly set at the component interface level, they may also be declared on the home methods (such as `create`) for entity beans.

- **NotSupported**—This value means that the bean or a method cannot be involved in a transaction at all. If a client has started a transaction, it is ignored, and methods will always execute outside the transaction context. The initial transaction will be resumed after the end of those methods. Available for session, entity, and message-driven beans, although methods of entity beans with CMP are not supported.

- **Required**—This value means that the bean methods must always execute in a transaction context. If there is a transaction already running, the bean participates in that transaction. If there is no transaction, the EJB container starts a transaction on behalf of the bean. Available for session, entity, and message-driven beans. **This is the default in a WebSphere environment**.

- **Supports**—This value means that the bean participates in a running transaction but does not require it. So, if there is no transaction, the method executes without a transaction. Available for session and entity beans only, although methods of entity beans with CMP are not supported.

- **RequiresNew**—Here the bean requires that a new transaction is always started when a method is called. If there is a transaction running, it is suspended. The container will start a new transaction and at the end of the method execution, it will commit or abort it. After that, the container will resume the client transaction. Available for session and entity beans only.

- **Mandatory**—When this value is used, a transaction must already be running when the bean method is called. The object will participate in the existing transaction initiated by the caller. If no transaction context is present, the `javax.ejb.TransactionRequiredException` is thrown back to the caller. Available for session and entity beans only.

- **Never**—If this bean is called in an existing transaction, the container throws a `java.rmi.RemoteException`. Available for session and entity beans only, although methods of entity beans with CMP are not supported.

Transactional attribute summary

Table 8-1 summarizes how transactional attributes affect transactions from client-to-bean, or bean-to-bean method invocations:

Table 8-1   CMT transaction attribute summary

Transaction attribute	Client/Other bean transaction	Transaction associated with bean method
NotSupported	none	none
	T1	none
Required	none	T2
	T1	T1
Supports	none	none
	T1	T1
RequiresNew	none	T2
	T1	T2
Mandatory	none	error
	T1	T1
Never	none	none

How to read the table

- ► The first column contains the transaction attributes.

- ► The second column shows whether a transaction is already running in the client, or other EJB, when a bean method is called. If there is a transaction, it is named T1; otherwise it is marked as none. A client could be a session bean calling an entity bean.

- ► The third column shows what happens when the method is executed on the bean. If the bean participates in the existing transaction, this is marked as T1. If the bean starts a new transaction, then T2 is used. If the bean ignores the running transaction, it is marked as none. If the bean requires a transaction and none is running, it is marked as an error.

Transaction attribute method rules

There are some rules when setting the method-level transactional attributes based on bean types:

- ► **Session beans**—Can only define attributes for methods of the component interface.

- **Message-driven bean**—Can only define for the `onMessage` method.

- **Entity beans**—Can define for methods of the component interface, and methods defined in the bean's home interface.

Setting the transaction attributes

The transaction attribute settings are declared in the deployment descriptor for each bean in the `ejb-jar.xml` file. Figure 8-3 shows how this might look for the `Banking` session bean and `Account` entity bean.

```
<assembly-descriptor>
    <container-transaction>
        <method>
            <ejb-name>Banking</ejb-name>
            <method-intf>Remote</method-intf>
            <method-name>transfer</method-name>
            <method-params>
                <method-param>java.lang.String</method-param>
                <method-param>java.lang.String</method-param>
                <method-param>java.math.BigDecimal</method-param>
            </method-params>
        </method>
        <method>
            <ejb-name>Account</ejb-name>
            <method-intf>LocalHome</method-intf>
            <method-name>create</method-name>
        </method>
        <trans-attribute>Required</trans-attribute>
    </container-transaction>
</assembly-descriptor>
```

Figure 8-3   Transaction attributes in deployment descriptor

Activity sessions in WebSphere Enterprise Edition: The `ActivitySession` service provides an alternative unit-of-work (UOW) scope to that provided by global transaction contexts. An `ActivitySession` context can be longer-lived than a global transaction context and can encapsulate global transactions.

Managing access to data in transactions

Ultimately, transactions are about coordinating access to data accessible across a single or multiple resource managers. It either works, and we commit, or it fails, and we roll back.

The transaction attributes discussed previously help us to express the business rules of our application. Whether something should be included as part of a transaction is up to the rules of the application and any data integrity rules that are necessary to maintain.

But where might things go wrong? Rather than just crossing our fingers and hoping for the best with regard to transactions, it is important to understand where things could go wrong, and what can be done to circumvent problems. This goes beyond simple transaction demarcation guidelines. Understanding how and when the underlying data is accessed is a key to this equation.

In this section, we discuss some common problems when accessing transactional data concurrently, that address isolation conditions, database locking, and transactional isolation levels. An isolation level describes the degree to which the access to a resource manager by a transaction is isolated from the access to the resource manager by other concurrently executing transactions, and locking strategies and transaction isolation are techniques that can help with setting appropriate isolation conditions. Because this discussion is geared toward the access of data, it applies mostly to the use of entity beans within transactions.

Problems of concurrent transactions

Data that can possibly be accessed across concurrent transactions can be subject to the following problems that are sometimes also referred to as *isolation problems*:

▶ **Dirty read**—Occurs when an application reads data from a database that has not been committed to permanent storage:

- User A modifies a row. User B reads the same row before user A commits. User A performs a rollback. User B has read data that has never existed.

▶ **Nonrepeatable read**—Occurs when data has been changed between two consecutive reads of the same data:

- User A reads a row but does not commit. User B modifies or deletes the same row and then commits. User A rereads the row and finds it has changed (or it has been deleted).

▶ **Phantom read**—Occurs when new data is inserted into a table between two read operations:

- User A uses a search condition to read a set of rows but does not commit. User B inserts one or more rows that satisfy this search condition, then commits. User A rereads the rows using the search condition and discovers rows that were not present before.

Database locking strategies

Relational databases typically use different locking schemes to help isolate access to data. The following are the four types of locks:

- ▶ **Read locks**—Prevent transactions from changing data read during a transaction until the transaction ends, thus preventing nonrepeatable reads.

- ▶ **Write locks**—Used for updates, prevents other transactions from changing the data until the current transaction is complete, but allows dirty reads.

- ▶ **Exclusive write locks**—Used for updates, prevents other transactions from reading or changing the data until the current transaction is complete. Prevents dirty reads.

- ▶ **Snapshots**—Some databases provide snapshots of a frozen view of data. Can prevent dirty reads, nonrepeatable reads, and phantom reads, but can be problematic because they are not actual data.

Deadlocks

Deadlocks occur when two concurrent transactions place a shared lock on the same resource (table or row) when they read it—then attempt to update the information and commit. This can happen when the same enterprise bean is accessed and updated by two or more clients at the same time. When using DB2, a deadlock results in one of the clients getting a rollback exception.

Note: In WebSphere, you can verify when this happens by activating an application server trace on the `com.ibm.ejs.cm.portability` component.

Isolation levels

An isolation level represents a particular locking strategy employed in the database system to improve data consistency with regard to the problems of dirty, nonrepeatable, and phantom reads. Isolation levels are specified for Enterprise JavaBeans similar to transaction attributes. We will see that isolation levels are part of the access-intent strategy for enterprise beans.

Understanding what an isolation level is, and what it means when data is accessed concurrently, is discussed here. Because this applies only to databases, it is applicable only to enterprise beans using JDBC (either CMP or BMP) to access a database resource.

We can either specify a strict isolation or a relaxed isolation. It is a trade-off between concurrency control and performance. That is, a strict isolation level can only be achieved at the expense of performance. The isolation level can be set for a bean, or for individual methods.

New in J2EE 1.3: The EJB specification does not govern how isolation levels or locking mechanisms are declared, because the APIs for the managing of isolation levels is generally resource-manager specific. Therefore, defining specific transaction isolation levels, and managing this through deployment, is a WebSphere-specific discussion.

In a J2EE 1.2 module, you can specify the isolation level at an enterprise bean method level, bean level, or module level. This capability has been removed from the J2EE 1.3 module. WebSphere Application Server Version 5.0 is compliant with the J2EE 1.3 specification; therefore you cannot specify isolation level on the EJB method level or bean level. Managing the isolation levels is still important; it is now explicitly part of the specification.

There are four isolation levels:

▶ **Read uncommitted**—This is the weakest isolation level. When this isolation level is used, all the above-mentioned isolation problems can occur, regardless of the isolation levels of other transactions. Therefore, this isolation level should not be used for mission-critical applications. This level is more suitable if we know that only one application will be running at a given time and there are no other concurrent transactions. The advantage of this isolation level is good performance.

▶ **Read committed**—This level is very similar to read uncommitted. The only difference is that this isolation level addresses *dirty read*. With read committed transactions will read committed data only. However, this isolation level does not address nonrepeatable reads and phantom reads. This level guarantees that the data we read is always consistent. This mode is useful for report-generating programs that use the current state of the database at the time of report generation.

▶ **Repeatable read**—This mode guarantees that repeated reads of the database result with the same data values. Therefore, it addresses both *dirty read* as well *nonrepeatable read*. This mode is useful, when we have to update the database records often. This prevents data from being modified by other concurrent transactions. However, phantom reads may occur.

▶ **Serializable**—This is the strictest isolation level. This mode enforces all the ACID properties and guarantees fully independent transactions. This is useful for mission critical applications. It ensures that no intermediate transaction results can appear. Therefore, even if transactions occur concurrently, users will view their effects only successively. However, database access performance may suffer when this isolation level is used.

Limits

Because locking physically prevents other concurrent transactions from accessing the data, major performance problems may arise. In addition, deadlock of transactions can also occur, which may cause stability concerns to the applications. An example of deadlock is when two concurrent transactions are waiting for each other to release a lock. This should be considered when employing an appropriate isolation strategy for your application.

Isolation levels in JDBC

JDBC in particular also deals with transaction and supports its own set of isolation levels. They correspond exactly to the isolation levels supported by enterprise beans. The only exception is the `TRANSACTION_NONE` isolation level in JDBC, which is not supported by enterprise beans. The equivalent of this isolation level can be achieved by specifying the bean transaction attribute as *Never*.

Mapping JDBC isolation levels to DB2

DB2 accepts a set of isolation levels when you bind an application. The DB2 specification is a little different from the JDBC specification, but there is a close match between the two sets (Table 8-2).

Table 8-2   DB2 isolation levels

Isolation level in JDBC	Isolation level in DB2	Abbreviation
`TRANSACTION_SERIALIZABLE`	Repeatable read	RR
`TRANSACTION_REPEATABLE_READ`	Read stability	RS
`TRANSACTION_READ_COMMITTED`	Cursor stability	CS
`TRANSACTION_READ_UNCOMMITTED`	Uncommitted read	UR
`TRANSACTION_NONE`	Not supported in DB2	

Important: Database system such as DB2 do not allow changing the isolation level during a transaction. Assigning different isolation levels to individual methods must be carefully designed so that no change of isolation level occurs during the processing of one transaction.

How isolation levels solve a problem

A summary of the isolation levels is shown in Table 8-3. The value *NO* indicates that the problem does not occur; *YES* indicates that the problem may occur.

Table 8-3   Isolation levels and possible problems

Isolation level	Dirty read	Nonrepeatable read	Phantom read
Serializable	NO	NO	NO
Repeatable read	NO	NO	YES
Read committed	NO	YES	YES
Read uncommitted	YES	YES	YES

Resource access intent

New WebSphere Version 5: The *isolation level* and *read only* method level modifiers that could be defined for EJB1.1 are now part of the access intent mechanism of WebSphere. Isolation levels were specific to JDBC, but because the persistence mechanism is now based on J2C resources, a more abstract mechanism was needed. If the underlying resource is a JDBC resource, then the access intent hints will still be translated to JDBC isolation levels under the covers. If the resource is not a relational database, then the access intent will be translated to the mechanism appropriate to that resource.

An access intent policy is a named set of properties (access intents) that governs data access for EJB persistence. You can assign a policy to individual methods on an entity bean's home, remote, or local interfaces during assembly. Access intents are available only within EJB 2.x-compliant modules for entity beans with CMP 2.x and for BMPs.

Access intent enables developers to configure applications so that the EJB container and its agents can make performance optimizations for entity bean access. Entity bean methods are configured with access intent policies at the module level. A policy is acted upon by either the combination of the WebSphere EJB container and persistence manager (for CMP entities) or by BMP entities directly. Note that access intent policies apply to entity beans only.

The intent of the access intent mechanism in WebSphere Version 5 is to allow developers to supply the container with optimization hints. The container will use these hints to make decisions about isolation levels, cursor managements, and so forth. The hints are organized into groups called *policies*. The policies are defined at the module level and applied to individual methods on the bean's interface (local or remote).

Concurrency control

Concurrency control is the management of contention for data resources. A concurrency control scheme is considered *pessimistic* when it locks a given resource early in the data-access transaction and does not release it until the transaction is closed. A concurrency control scheme is considered *optimistic* when locks are acquired and released over a very short period of time at the end of a transaction.

Read-ahead hints

Read-ahead schemes enable applications to minimize the number of database roundtrips by retrieving a working set of CMP beans for the transaction within one query. Read-ahead involves activating the requested CMP beans and caching the data of related beans (relationships), which ensures that data is present for the beans that are most likely to be needed next by an application. A *read-ahead hint* is a canonical representation of the related beans that are to be read. It is associated with a finder method for the requested bean type, which must be an EJB 2.x-compliant CMP entity bean.

Specifying access intent in WebSphere

WebSphere 5 has several predefined access intent policies that are useful combinations of the five available *access intent attributes*:

► Access type
► Collection scope
► Collection increment
► Resource adapter prefetch increment
► Read-ahead hint

The *access type* hint is relevant for transactions because it has to do with concurrency and update intent. For a more detailed explanation of the access intent policies, please refer to the Application Developer help.

Table 8-4 describes the access intent settings, and how this might affect the underlying isolation levels.

Table 8-4   Access intent settings

Access intent profile name	Concurrency control, access type	Transaction isolation
wsPessimisticRead	Pessimistic/Read (lock held for duration of transaction)	Repeatable read
wsPessimisticUpdate	Pessimistic/Update (generates SELECT FOR UPDATE and grabs locks at beginning of transaction)	Repeatable read

Access intent profile name	Concurrency control, access type	Transaction isolation
wsPessimisticUpdate-Exclusive	Pessimistic/Update (lock held for duration of transaction)	Serializable
wsPessimisticUpdate-NoCollision	Pessimistic/Update (no locks are held, updates permitted, locks escalated on update)	Read committed
wsPessimisticUpdate-WeakestLockAtLoad (**default**)	Pessimistic/Update (no locks are held, updates permitted, locks escalated on update)	Repeatable read
wsOptimisticRead	Optimistic/Read (read-only access)	Read committed
wsOptimisticUpdate	Optimistic/Update (generates overqualified SQL UPDATE statements and forces compare before update)	Read committed

Pessimistic read

Locks will not be acquired during ejbLoad; therefore, in order to assure data integrity, updates will not be permitted.

Pessimistic update

To assure data integrity, locks will be held during the scope of the transaction under which ejbLoad was invoked. This access type can be further qualified with the following update hints:

- ► **Exclusive**—This is a hint that the normal isolation value used for pessimistic update may not be sufficient.

- ► **No collision**—This hint indicates that the application will have no row collisions by design and a lesser isolation level may be chosen by the runtime. WebSphere can, of course, make no assurances guaranteeing the data integrity; in fact, row collisions do occur when the no collision hint is specified, and concurrent transactions can overwrite each other's updates. Use this policy if only one transaction updates at any given time.

- ► **Weakest lock**—Same as no collision, but with repeatable read isolation level. Deadlocks can occur when updating of one entity bean by two transactions is attempted. This is the default type that will be used if no type has been explicitly assigned.

Optimistic read

This type is equivalent to pessimistic read, but with a different isolation level.

Optimistic update

Locks will not be acquired during ejbLoad; instead, *overqualified updates* will be used in order to assure data integrity. For a JDBC resource, an overqualified update will use the WHERE part of the UPDATE statement to compare every field of the record to its old value as in:

```
UPDATE Customer SET field1=newvalue1, field2=newvalue2
WHERE field1=oldvalue1 AND field2=oldvalue2
```

Note that, for records with a large number of fields, this type of comparison can become a rather expensive operation.

So with optimistic update, instead of locking everything, you hope that nobody else will change the data, or only a few columns are changed. This could be the case for your application if changes are highly unlikely and always locking the data would affect scalability. When a conflict does occur, an exception is thrown.

It is important to note that nullable columns are not supported by optimistic concurrency in WebSphere 5.0. Nullable columns are excluded from overqualified updates so that changes to nullable columns are not detected.

Optimistic concurrency always faces the possibility of getting locked out by another transaction using a stronger locking strategy. However, optimistic concurrency does not suffer from the pessimistic restriction that an entity loaded under read intent cannot be updated.

Important:

► Optimistic locking here refers to locking within one transaction.

► The isolation level that is applied by the persistence manager depends on the particular database. Therefore, the behavior of these access intents may vary depending on the implementation of the underlying resource manager. For example, pessimistic read and pessimistic update on Oracle will result in read committed. Refer to the Access intent isolation levels topic in the WebSphere InfoCenter documentation for more information.

Dynamic access intent

The standard access intent allows us to declare at deployment time how we expect an enterprise bean to be used. The problem is that we make these access declarations for an EJB and its methods for *all instances* of the EJB and we must do it for the worst case. That is, if we think the enterprise bean might be updated, then we must declare it as updatable even though in most cases the usage may be read only.

The *dynamic access intent* facility provides a way to declare this information for each EJB and method *per application*, so that this information can be accessed at runtime by either the container (for CMP) or developer (for BMP).

> **Restriction:** Dynamic access intent is only available in WebSphere Application Server Enterprise Edition.

Transactional programming considerations

This section addresses the various programming considerations of transaction management that a bean developer has to consider.

Client-managed transaction

Client-managed transaction refers to the situation in which a client of an EJB manages the transaction demarcation. The client could be a servlet, or another EJB, such as a session bean calling entity beans. For example, this can be a Java servlet that updates records in a database and starts, ends, or rolls back a transaction based on some external criteria.

As with bean-managed transactions, we use the UserTransaction interface. Here it can be obtained by a JNDI lookup of java:comp/UserTransaction. Figure 8-4 shows an example where a client manages the transaction.

```
// Use JNDI to locate the UserTransaction object
   Context context = new InitialContext();
   UserTransaction userTransaction= (UserTransaction) /
      context.lookup("java:comp/UserTransaction");

// Begin the transaction
   userTransaction.begin();

         Perform transactional work.....

// Commit the transaction
   userTransaction.commit();
```

Figure 8-4   Client-managed transaction

> **New J2EE 1.3:** Obtaining a lookup to a user transaction object in previous releases was accomplished using the JNDI context of jta/usertransaction. This is now changed to java:comp/UserTransaction.

When the client is demarcating a transaction, it is recommended that the bean methods that the client calls be enabled for container-managed transaction. This simplifies the application and protects the developer from many problems.

If the client that starts a transaction is another EJB (essentially, a bean with BMT), then it will look up the transactional context as shown in Figure 8-5.

```
//For session beans
UserTransaction tran = getSessionContext().getUserTransaction();

// For message-driven beans
UserTransaction tran = getMessageDrivenContext().getUserTransaction();
```

Figure 8-5   Getting a user transaction from the EJB context

Transactions and message-driven beans

The general rules governing transactional management for EJBs has not changed too dramatically between EJB 1.1 and EJB 2.0, as it relates to session and entity beans. Because message-driven beans are new to EJB 2.0, we will spend a little time here discussing how transactional semantics influence message-driven bean implementations.

Message-driven bean transactions scope

Recall that message-driven beans do not have a traditional client, as is the case with session and entity beans. Their client exists as a completely disconnected process separated by the JMS provider.

Because MDBs do not have a client per se, a message-driven bean cannot participate in a transaction that already exists at the client side. This is not to say that MDBs cannot be transactional, because they can be, but only on the server side in the context under which they execute. Rather, this client restriction implies that the invocation of the MDB cannot be part of a transaction that may have been started on the client side.

But clients do not invoke the MDBs directly. They do so by sending a message to a JMS destination, either queue or topic. If the client is utilizing transactions, then the JMS send may be part of the transaction, but not the actual MDB execution itself. This is because the message is only sent when the transaction commits on the client side. Therefore, the MDB would never execute until after the client transaction has actually ended.

Because there is never any chance of an MDB executing within a client transactional context, the transactional attributes of Supports, RequiresNew, Mandatory, and None do not have any meaning. These attributes imply transactional propagation from a client to set the appropriate transactional context of the bean. Therefore, the NotSupported and Required transaction attributes are the only valid attributes for message-driven beans.

BMT versus CMT for message-driven beans

A message-driven bean may participate in either bean-managed or container-managed transactions. The onMessage method is the only MDB method that can participate in a transaction. In this way, the bean is functioning as a transaction coordinator for the accessing of resources that the bean is using.

Bean-managed transactions

If the MDB uses bean-managed transaction demarcation, then it is allowed to begin and end transactions within the scope of the onMessage method. The problem with this, however, is that the receipt of the message itself cannot be part of the transaction, and any handling of this would have to be manually done.

Container-managed transactions

The CMT attributes of Required or NotSupported are the only declarative transaction settings that may be set. A declarative transaction demarcation of Required lets the container start a transaction when a message is received. Therefore, the receipt of the message itself can be part of a transaction, such that this message receive can be committed, or rolled back, at the end of the transaction. If using NotSupported, then the message is not part of the transaction.

Handling a rollback

When a transaction in this context is marked for rollback, either through explicitly setting the setRollbackOnly method, or by throwing a system exception in the onMessage method, a rollback will occur, which means the message is put back onto the queue.

However, the listener will simply attempt to redeliver the message to the MDB again. This can result in a poison message loop situation as discussed in "Message-driven bean best practices" on page 245, because there is no guarantee that the MDB can handle it any better the second time around. In WebSphere, the listener will attempt to deliver the message to an MDB up to the *Max retries* configuration option of the listener port. This maximum retries setting represents the maximum number of times the listener attempts to read a message from a destination and deliver it to an MDB before the listener stops.

So although an infinite loop is avoided, having the message listener just stop delivering messages also has its obvious drawbacks. The application, essentially, has just stopped, and messages will continue to queue up, all because of one poison message.

WebSphere MQ message retry count

Luckily, using a full-fledged WebSphere MQ implementation for the JMS provider can help in this situation. This is because MQ can be configured to not attempt redelivery of a message after a certain number of retries of the message within MQ itself, and can put these messages on a special queue destination for temporary holding until a problem can be resolved.

For example, WebSphere MQ will attempt to keep a re-delivery count per message, and when the message reaches a pre-determined maximum redelivery count, say 2, it will put the message on a temporary error queue instead. This would solve the problems of the listener just stopping, the messages queueing up and flooding the queue, or the application becoming unavailable.

Of course, a problem still exists that would have to be investigated, but the application continues function for good messages.

Session synchronization interface

Stateful session beans may optionally implement a session synchronization interface if these beans are transactional, and the beans have to control the behavior based on these transactions. The javax.ejb.SessionSynchronization interface allows the session bean to receive additional notification of the session bean's involvement in transactions.

When a method is called that starts a transaction in a session bean that implements this interface, the following events occur:

- ▶ The bean is moved to a transaction read state.
- ▶ A transaction is started.
- ▶ The afterBegin method is called. This allows the bean to set up any state that is required to execute the logic.
- ▶ Business methods are executed.
- ▶ The transaction comes to an end, either by commit or rollback.
- ▶ If committed, the beforeCompletion method is called to allow the bean to write any final cached updates.
- ▶ If the transaction is rolled back, the beforeCompletion method is not invoked.

- With either commit or rollback, the `afterCompletion(boolean)` method is invoked. After a commit, the argument is `true`, after a rollback `false`. This allows the bean to reset the state after completion of the transaction.

Guidelines for using transactions

Here are some guidelines for transaction demarcation and transaction attributes:

- Use long-running read-only transactions to cache static data only.
- Avoid referring to dynamic data in long-running read-only transactions, because the repeatable-read transaction isolation prevents detecting changes committed by other transactions.
- Properly demarcate transaction boundaries and complete transactions quickly.
- The recommended way to manage transactions in EJB is through container-managed demarcation.
- Entity beans must always use container-managed transaction demarcation. Session and message-driven beans can use either container-managed or bean-managed transaction demarcation.
- Bean-managed transaction demarcation should be used when it is the only way to address a problem.
- Stateless session beans must always either commit or roll back a transaction before the business method returns.
- Implement short commit cycles. A commit cycle should not span user think time. A session facade supports this strategy because a method invocation is processed within a single unit of work. Set the transaction demarcation in session beans implicitly through the container (CMT) or as part of the method implementation (BMT).
- The default choice for a transaction attribute is `Required`. Enterprise beans with the `Required` transaction attribute can be easily composed to perform work under the scope of a single JTA transaction.
- The `RequiresNew` transaction attribute is useful when the bean method has to commit its results independent of other transactions, enabling normal transactions to be isolated from critical transactions.
- Session beans that implement the interface `SessionSynchronization` must have either the `Required`, `RequiresNew`, or `Mandatory` transaction attribute.
- Message-driven beans may only have a transactional attribute of `Required` or `NotSupported`.
- The transaction attributes `Mandatory` and `Never` reduce composition of a component by putting constraints on the calling client's transaction context.

These attributes can be used when it is necessary to verify the transaction association of the calling client.

► The transaction attribute Supports is not recommended. It has transactional behavior depending on the client association with a transactional context, which is a violation of ACID properties.

► If the message receipt of a message-driven bean is to be part of the transaction, then the MDB must use the Required transactional attribute.

► Try to avoid using Supports and NotSupported, because if the application accesses multiple entities with container-managed persistence in a single high-level business operation, such as a servlet invocation, you may experience unexpected results.

The bean methods for these cases are run under an *unspecified transaction context*, where the container determines the semantics. In the absence of a transaction, the current implementation of the container executes the database accesses in a local transaction. If such a local transaction uses a different connection to the same database, deadlocks can occur. This is true regardless of whether there is a single or multiple application servers, and whether JTA is enabled.

Guidelines for application transaction programming

Here are some guidelines for application programming of transactions:

► Although not required, application beans should explicitly make the decision to cause a rollback and not leave it to the container. They can do this by calling the EJBContext.setRollbackOnly method. Remember, application exceptions result in a commit unless you explicitly call the setRollbackOnly method.

Note that setRollbackOnly is only available for container-managed transactions; bean-managed transactions must use the rollback method of the UserTransaction object.

► When calls are returned from downstream EJBs, application beans should check if their transaction has been marked for rollback using the EJBContext.getRollbackOnly method, and act accordingly. They should not just rely on getting this notification as a result of a rollback exception.

Note that getRollbackOnly is only available for container-managed transactions; bean-managed transactions must call the getStatus method of the UserTransaction object.

► An application can invoke setRollbackonly without necessarily throwing an exception, although this should be avoided.

- When a call to a bean results in a `RemoteException`, you cannot know that the target bean rolled back, or was even called. In this case (unless you really know what you are doing), you should call `EJBContext.setRollbackOnly` and throw an appropriate application or `RemoteException` and cause the entire transaction to roll back. Leave it to the next level up to retry the transaction if desired.

- If an application bean wants to ensure that its work is committed regardless of the outcome of calls to other downstream beans, the downstream bean's transaction attribute should be marked as `RequiresNew` or `NotSupported`, or the calling bean should manage its own transaction. This will cause the caller's transaction to be suspended when the downstream bean is called.

- Note that a transactional attribute of `RequiresNew` can set the stage for a deadlock, if the new and the suspended transactions try to use the same resources, depending on their transaction isolation levels.

- It is generally stated in EJB books and articles that bean-demarcated transaction management should be avoided. While this is true in most cases, it should not be dismissed as a bad thing.

  In the case where a session bean is coordinating a complex process or set of activities, it may be more practical to use bean-demarcated transactions. This will allow you to split the processing into multiple transactions, recover from downstream beans that cause rollback, and explicitly ensure that a downstream bean will not affect your processing.

  If you find yourself fighting transaction problems, consider using bean-demarcated transactions in your main session bean. Alternatively, instead of a session bean, you can resort to a non-EJB caller that will demarcate transactions explicitly, but that requires writing even more code.

EJB exception handling

This section describes the basic concepts of exception handling for EJBs. The bean developer must be aware of how different exceptions affect the life cycle of a bean, and when necessary, account for this within the code.

Exceptions allow us to separate error handling code from normal code. We can wrap the code that we expect to execute most of the time with a `try` block, and then place error handling code in `catch` clauses. That is the code that we do not expect to get executed often, if ever.

> ***New EJB 2.0 - Local exceptions:** The exception handling semantics of EJB 2.0 have not changed much since EJB 1.1. The biggest difference in EJB 2.0 exception handling is the introduction of local exceptions for the local component interfaces, which are new to EJB 2.0. From a container perspective, these local exceptions behave similarly to the remote exceptions in EJB 1.1 as far as the life-cycle management of the beans. We discuss these new exception types in the context of component interface interaction throughout this document.

Checked and unchecked exceptions

There are two kinds of exceptions in Java, checked and unchecked (Figure 8-6). Only checked exceptions have to appear as part of the signature of the method through a `throws` clause. Checked exceptions that may be thrown in a method must either be caught or declared in the `throws` clause.

If we feel that a method does not know how to handle a particular error, we can throw an exception from the method and let the caller of the method deal with it. If we throw a checked exception, we utilize the help of the Java compiler to force client programmers to deal with the potential exception, either by catching it or declaring it in the `throws` clause of their methods. The fact that Java compilers make sure checked exceptions are handled helps make Java programs more robust. The exception essentially becomes part of the interaction contract between users of classes.

The difference between checked and unchecked exceptions is that checked exceptions signal abnormal conditions that the client programmers can deal with. Most unchecked exceptions are problems that will be detected by the Java Virtual Machine at runtime; they are subclasses of `Error` and `RuntimeException`.

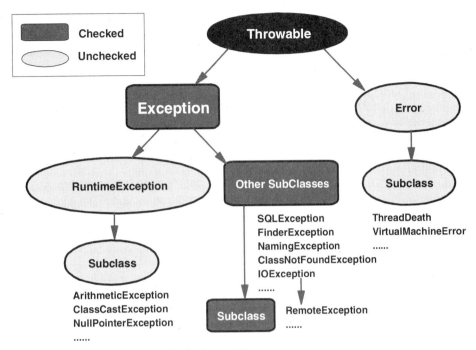

Figure 8-6   Checked and unchecked exceptions

Exceptions and EJBs

The EJB specification groups exceptions into two categories to enable bean developers, client developers, and container providers to handle exceptions and transactions more effectively. These can be either application or system exceptions (although the concept of this separation is not unique to EJBS, J2EE, or Java for that matter). Each type of exception is handled differently by the container, and may affect the life cycle of the bean. These exceptions are propagated to the client across remote or local invocations, so that the client is able to deal with the exceptions if necessary.

We describe the difference between application and system exceptions in more detail below.

Application exceptions

An application exception is one that is defined in the throws clause of a method of an enterprise beans home or remote interface and that does not extend RuntimeException or RemoteException. Because they are specified in the throws clause, they are (must be) checked exceptions.

Application exceptions represent errors in business logic or abnormal application-level conditions specific to a use case or business service provided by your EJBs, for example, `InSufficientFundException` in a banking application. Clients typically can recover normally from application exceptions. Therefore, application exceptions are not intended for reporting system-level problems.

Goals of EJB application-level exception handling

The goals of an application exception are as follows:

▶ **Precision**—The exception is propagated to the client layer as it is thrown, so the original intent and meaning of the exception is maintained.

▶ **Recovery**—When a bean instance throws an exception, it should not automatically roll back a client's transaction. This gives the client the ability to recover from a transaction in any way that it deems fit.

▶ **Cleanup**—The bean instance is not destroyed with an application exception. Therefore, it gives the developer the opportunity to clean up the underlying persistent state in a safe manner.

Custom application exceptions

A bean developer is free to develop custom application exceptions that meet the requirements of their application that represent business conditions that have nothing to do with whether it is an EJB or not. In our example, `InsufficientFundException` is a custom application exception. These must be checked exceptions represented in the `throws` clause of the bean methods.

EJB standard application exceptions

The EJB specification itself defines some basic application exceptions, which are referred to as *standard* application exceptions.

Figure 8-7 is a summary of the types of application exceptions available to EJBs.

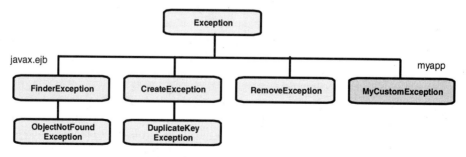

Figure 8-7   EJB application exceptions

These exceptions may be thrown by the beans themselves. These exceptions only apply to entity beans, and are typically used only in the methods of the home interfaces. However, the exception could be propagated through a session bean facade business method that called an entity bean. In the case of container-managed persistence (CMP), the container can also throw any of these exceptions while handling the ejbCreate, ejbFind, and ejbRemove methods.

A bean developer can always choose to throw a standard EJB application exception, or one of their own, from the appropriate method regardless of how persistence is managed. They are always delivered directly to the client, without being repackaged as RemoteException or EJBException. Furthermore, these exceptions do not cause a transaction to roll back, giving the client the opportunity to retry the operation if they want. (We will see that this behavior is in contrast to how system exceptions are handled.)

Business methods defined in the component interface can throw any kind of custom application exception. Let's explain the standard application exceptions in detail.

CreateException

The CreateException is thrown by the create method in the home interface, propagated from the ejbCreate or ejbCreateXXXX methods.

This exception indicates that an application error has occurred (for example, invalid arguments) while the bean was being created. Bean developers should roll back the transaction (setTransactionRollback) before throwing this exception only if data integrity is a concern (for example, if other instances have been created or modified).

DuplicateKeyException

The DuplicateKeyException is a subclass of the CreateException. It can be thrown by the create method in the home interface. This exception indicates that the primary key already exists in the database.

FinderException

The FinderException is thrown by the finder methods in the home interface. This exception indicates that an application error occurred, for example invalid arguments, while the container attempted to find the beans.

> **Note:** Multiple-entity finder methods return an empty collection if no entities are found; single-entity finder methods throw an ObjectNotFoundException to indicate that no object was found.

ObjectNotFoundException

A `FinderException` by itself may not necessarily indicate an entity object not found. An `ObjectNotFoundException` is thrown from a single-entity finder method, for example, `findByPrimaryKey`, to indicate that the container could not find the requested entity. This exception should not be thrown to indicate a business logic error (for example, invalid arguments). This is a type of finder exception.

RemoveException

The `RemoveException` can be thrown by the `remove` methods in the component and home interfaces. This exception indicates that an application error has occurred while the bean was removed.

Bean handling of application exceptions

There are a couple of responsibilities and guidelines for handling of application exceptions that the bean developer should consider.

► The bean developer has to ensure that the use of application exceptions is for the handling of business logic-only conditions. More serious conditions should be handled by system exceptions (below).

► The container does not automatically roll back a transaction when an application level exception is thrown. Therefore, for entity beans in particular, the bean must either mark the transaction for rollback before the exception is thrown (so it does not commit), or ensure that the instance is in a state such that an attempt to continue or commit the transaction does not result in loss of data integrity.

► Application-level exceptions only make sense for beans in which the context of the exception can be passed back to a client. Therefore, message-driven beans, which do not have a direct client, cannot throw application exceptions in container-managed methods (`onMessage` or `create`).

► Any container-invoked callback method should not throw an application exception, because there may not be a client to intercept it. This includes such methods as `ejbActivate`, `ejbLoad`, and `setSessionContext`.

Enhancing standard EJB application exceptions

Standard EJB application exceptions can be extended, if necessary, to show the client that a specific error occurred. For example, we can subclass `CreateException` to indicate more specifically that the parameters passed into `ejbCreate` are incorrect.

Subclassing standard EJB exceptions can be effective for other reasons, such as providing a better description for root errors.

System exceptions

System exceptions represent more serious unexpected conditions within the system that are not business related, and that prevent the bean method from successfully completing.

System exceptions include unexpected `RuntimeException`, `RemoteException`, `EJBException`, and all exceptions that inherit from them. Therefore, it may include both checked and unchecked exceptions. System exceptions in EJBs cause the container to automatically do some cleanup of the bean that affects its life cycle, such as rolling back the transaction, and possibly discarding of the bean. This is different from application exceptions, which are passed to the client for further handling.

The container plays a much bigger role in the handling of system exceptions for container-managed transactions (CMT). Any runtime exception (system exception) that is not caught by a bean will be caught by the container. The container will intercept the exception, and then will throw back to the client either a `java.rmi.RemoteException`, which is the case when using a remote component interface, or a `javax.ejb.EJBException`, when using a local component interface. The container now will roll back any existing transaction that the method was involved in, and discard the bean. Any cleanup or special rollback logic that a bean developer may have done for an application exception is now done by the container.

Goals of EJB system level exception handling

The goals of EJB system exceptions are:

- **Wrapping**—The original exception may be wrapped as a `RemoteException` or `EJBException`.

- **Rollback**—When a bean instance throws an exception, the container should automatically roll back the transaction (for CMT only).

- **Cleanup**—The bean instance is made unavailable for further invocation, which most likely means it is destroyed.

RemoteException versus EJBException

In EJB 1.1, all bean instances were accessed through a remote component interface only (RMI-IIOP). RMI is used to distribute both the remote and home interfaces. All RMI remote methods must throw a `java.rmi.RemoteException`, which indicate a system-level failure that originates in the communication layer between the client and the server (bean).

`RemoteException` is actually what the container throws when it encounters a system exception. There are specific subclasses of this exception, such as

`NoSuchObjectException`, that indicate specific conditions detected by the container itself. This exception is actually not a runtime exception, so it would have to be caught by the client.

However, EJB 2.0 introduced the concept of local component interfaces, and as such, the `RemoteException` no longer applies to local instances. Therefore, when the container encounters a runtime system exception with a local bean instance, it throws an `EJBException` instead. There are specific subclasses of this exception, such as `NoSuchObjectLocalException`, that indicate specific conditions detected by the container itself. `EJBException` is a runtime (unchecked) exception, and therefore, the client is not required to explicitly catch this, although all the other rules about rollback and life cycle destroy still apply. We will see below that a client may have to take additional actions to catch an `EJBException` and perform the appropriate behavior.

Remote exceptions

The following are some specific RMI system exceptions that may be thrown by an EJB container:

- `java.rmi.RemoteException`
- `javax.rmi.NoSuchObjectException`
- `javax.transaction.TransactionRequiredException`
- `javax.transaction.TransactionRolledBackException`
- `javax.transaction.InvalidTransactionException`

Local exceptions

The following are some EJB system exceptions that may be thrown by an EJB container:

- `javax.ejb.EJBException`
- `javax.ejb.NoSuchEntityException`
- `javax.ejb.AccessLocalException`
- `javax.ejb.NoSuchObjectLocalException`
- `javax.ejb.TransactionRequiredLocalException`
- `javax.ejb.TransactionRolledBackLocalException`

EJB system exceptions explained

Figure 8-8 is a summary of the types of application exceptions available to EJBs.

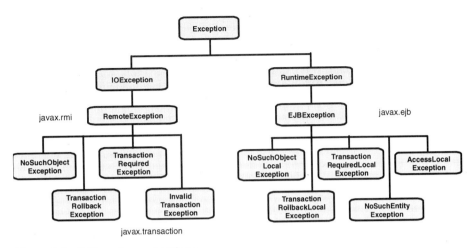

Figure 8-8 EJB system exceptions

Let's explain the meaning and behavior of some of these system exceptions in more detail.

NoSuchEntityException (local)

The NoSuchEntityException is a subclass of EJBException. It should be thrown by the entity bean methods to inform the clients that the required entity bean instance has been removed from the database. This method is typically thrown from ejbLoad and ejbStore methods. The container may rethrow this as a NoSuchObjectException (remote) or NoSuchObjectLocalException (local).

AccessLocalException (local)

An AccessLocalException is thrown to indicate that the caller does not have permission to call the method. This exception is thrown to local clients.

NoSuchObjectException (remote) and NoSuchObjectLocalException (local)

These exceptions are thrown if an attempt is made to invoke a method on an object that no longer exists. This is what might be returned with a call to an entity bean (NoSuchEntityException) when the database record has been deleted. These exceptions will be called if a stateless session bean that is called has been removed.

EJB transaction exceptions

The system exceptions that are thrown as the result of (or lack of) transaction processing require additional explanation.

We discussed that the container will roll back a transaction in a method that throws a system exception if it started the transaction. Essentially, if the method in which the exception occurred has started a transaction, the transaction is rolled back. If the transaction started from a client that invoked the method, the client transaction is marked for rollback and cannot be committed.

However, there are some additional points to consider if the client started the transaction. The server rolls back a transaction and throws an exception to the client only if one of the following conditions is true:

▶ The exception occurred in a container-managed transaction context.

▶ The exception occurred in a container-managed transaction nested in a client-managed transaction (in this case the outer transaction is marked for rollback).

To mark a transaction for rollback manually:

▶ Use the `setRollbackOnly` method on the `EJBContext` for container-managed transactions.

▶ Use the `setRollbackOnly` method on the `UserTransaction` for bean-managed transactions.

This ensures that the transaction is never committed after your code throws an exception. Additionally, if a transaction has been marked for rollback, either by the container or by the bean itself, the client should not continue trying to commit the transaction. The client can be aware of this by catching one of the system exceptions below, or by checking using `getRollbackOnly` or `getStatus` of the transaction for an application exception.

TransactionRolledBackException (remote)
TransactionRolledBackLocalException (local)

Clients that use explicit transactions must be prepared to handle both the `RemoteException` and `TransactionRolledBackException` for remote beans, and the `EJBException` and `TransactionRolledBackLocalException` for local beans. If a client program receives the `TransactionRolledBackException` or `TransactionRolledBackLocalException`, the client should roll back the transaction, because it will not be able to commit.

TransactionRequiredException (remote)
TransactionRequiredLocalException (local)

These exceptions occur when a client invokes a bean method that is marked as `Mandatory` without first starting a transaction.

Bean handling of system exceptions

The following are some guidelines for bean developers in implementing exception handling within their EJBs:

- **Propagation of runtime exceptions**—Typically, it is desirable to just propagate the runtime exception to the container, which will then throw an appropriate `RemoteException` or `EJBException`.

- **Checked subsystem exceptions**—Checked subsystem exceptions are exceptions thrown from various components of a J2EE server, including JNDI, JDBC, and JMS. Typically, the approach is to look for checked exceptions from J2EE subsystems and nest them in an `EJBException`. Then throw the `EJBException` to indicate to the container that it should mark the current transaction for rollback. Naming and SQL exceptions are examples of the checked subsystem exceptions.

- **Checked application exceptions**—If an application exception is caught in a bean, and the bean cannot recover, it is recommended that it also be wrapped in an `EJBException` and rethrown. If the bean can recover, then no exception at all would be thrown. If the business meaning of this exception would have to be sent back to the client (such as `CreateException`), then this application exception should just be rethrown or propagated to the client.

- **Other unexpected conditions**—Also should just be thrown as an `EJBException`.

Discarding the bean

The impact of discarding a bean instance depends on the bean type. In the case of stateless session beans and entity beans, the client does not notice that the instance was discarded. With stateful session beans, however, the impact on the client is severe. Discarding a stateful bean instance destroys the instance conversational state and invalidates the client reference to the bean.

Client view of exceptions

We have already seen that the client's view of the EJB exception may influence the client's behavior. We will expand on this here.

The client can continue working with the enterprise bean even after receiving an application exception. Similarly, the client can continue the transaction with which it is associated. The container does not automatically roll back the transaction for an application exception. But the transaction might have been marked for rollback by the bean itself before an application exception is thrown. It can be checked in one of the following ways:

- We can check in the documentation of the bean. The bean provider may have specified the application exceptions for which transaction rollbacks occur.
- If the client is an EJB with container-managed transaction, it can use the `getRollbackOnly` method of `EJBContext` to learn whether the current transaction is marked for rollback or not.
- Clients that are not using container-managed transaction can use the `getStatus` method on the `UserTransaction` to obtain the transaction status.

RMI limitations (remote)

The exception model for remote components uses the CORBA/RMI style of forcing code to catch and handle exceptions. We can easily end up with big try/catch blocks for every remote method invocation.

It is very hard to make the code clear, simple, and easy to understand when the few lines that actually do something are wrapped with many more lines of nested exception handling.

A small but annoying feature of many Java exception hierarchies is the lack of subsystem-specific clustering. For example, consider the EJB and transaction exception hierarchy shown in Figure 8-8 on page 311.

- If we consider the transaction-based exceptions, they just extend from a `RemoteException`. Therefore, when we try to catch only transaction exceptions, either we have to write a catch block for each transaction exception or we have to catch a `RemoteException` as a whole.
- A better approach is to subclass all transaction based exceptions from a common base class, say, for example `TransactionException`. This gives more clarity.

Message-bean exception handling

We have already discussed the main reason why application exceptions are not thrown by message-driven beans: there is no client to intercept them.

Because message-driven beans may not throw application exceptions while processing messages, this means that the only exceptions that may be thrown by a message-driven bean are runtime exceptions indicating a system-level error.

Message-driven beans may encounter unexpected errors in the processing of a message. Therefore, when runtime exceptions are encountered, the container must handle them, as in the case or normal session or entity beans.

There are some considerations regarding if the message bean is in a transaction or not. If the message-driven bean is running in the transactional context of the container (CMT), then the container will discard the bean instance and roll back the transaction. If the CMT attribute is `NotSupported`, then it will just discard the bean. If the container is running in a BMT, it marks the transaction for rollback, which must then be rolled back, and then it discards the bean.

Additional exception handling in MDBs

We will discuss a few additional points of the exception handling for MDBs that you may have to consider.

MDB system exception

System exceptions that are handled in the MDBs are generally put back onto the queue given a specific retry count (see "Transactions and message-driven beans" on page 298). They may end up on an error queue for further investigation. The idea is that once the original serious problem is investigated and fixed, the messages could possibly be redelivered.

Propagation of application exceptions in MDBs

It may or may not make sense for application exceptions in MDBs to cause a rollback and put the message back onto the error queue, because the business reason why they could not be processed is most likely still valid, and redelivering the message in the future does not change their handling. For example, an `InsufficientFunds` application exception will still exist after the message is processed.

Application exceptions still have some business meaning in the context of a message-driven bean. Our problem is that there is really no easy way to propagate this context back to the original client. This must be taken into consideration when determining what to do if application exceptions are encountered. Should the exception be logged somewhere to fix later? Should some other notification be sent? These are all really up to the application to determine the best strategy for this situation.

In general, the asynchronous paradigm does not factor in a blocking reply on the client side to know if the MDB did process the request. If this application exception state is important to communicate back to a client, then it might be necessary to consider a pseudo-synchronous request reply scenario for MDB invocations, where the reply could also include any error context if necessary, or possibly some other notification mechanism that the client can act on at some later point in time. In our `Transfer` MDB example, we send a flag back determining that this application error state occurred as a way to propagate the application error context back to the original client. In a real-world scenario, there might be many different types of error contexts that could be sent back, and a standard format to communicate these may have to be pursued.

Security

Distributed applications accessed through the Internet face the possibility of malicious attacks. This necessitates security arrangements and the setting up of a security system. A security system gives us the power to determine who can and should access resources, such as application modules, servlets, EJBs, and Web pages. It also enables us to define the security policies to establish control of resources.

Before getting access to any service in the application server, a client has to pass two checks: authentication and authorization:

▶ **Authentication**—Is the process of determining whether you are who you say you are.

▶ **Authorization** —Decides if you are allowed to perform the operation you have requested.

In this section, we discuss the concepts of security in the context of securing EJBs, and some procedures involved in doing so. Because security itself is a very complex (and vast) topic, it is really beyond the scope of this book to cover it in detail. Therefore, for a more in-depth discussion on security in WebSphere and EJBs, refer to the redbook *IBM WebSphere V5.0 Security: WebSphere Handbook Series*, SG24-6573.

Goals of EJB security

We have seen that EJBs follow a strong declarative model, where the attributes and behavior of transactions and persistence can be declared independent of the programming, through the deployment descriptor.

Security in EJBs is the same way. Security attributes are defined in the deployment descriptor, and can be declared and modified independent of the code in the application.

Overall, the EJB specification on security management architecture has identified the following high-level goals:

▶ Lessen the burden on the application developer or bean provider. The other roles involved, namely the container, provide the infrastructure, and the deployer and administrator define the policies.

▶ Allow the security policies to be set by the application deployer and assembler (in the deployment descriptor) rather than being hardcoded.

▶ Allow for the beans to be portable, where a consistent security management policy should work across EJB servers with underlying different security management implementations.

Security architecture overview

This section provides a brief overview of the infrastructure aspects of security architecture that sets the foundation for an EJB-specific security architecture discussion.

WebSphere security layers

The EJB security model is based on the idea that the container provides the tools to enforce, manage, and deploy security policies at runtime. It does so by creating an association between the logical roles defining the security policies of the EJBs (which are abstract) and the actual security group in the security management domain (which could be the operating system or other security providers). The specification does not dictate to the container or server how this is actually to be carried out.

WebSphere Version 5 provides a security infrastructure for securing J2EE resources that is based on industry standards, which are based on the concept of layers. The product provides a unified, policy-based, and permission-based model for securing Web resources and enterprise Java according to J2EE specifications. Specifically, Version 5 complies with J2EE specification 1.3.1 and has passed the J2EE compatibility test suite. Product security is a layered architecture built on top of the operating system platform, JVM, and Java 2 security.

Figure 8-9 shows the security layers of the WebSphere environment.

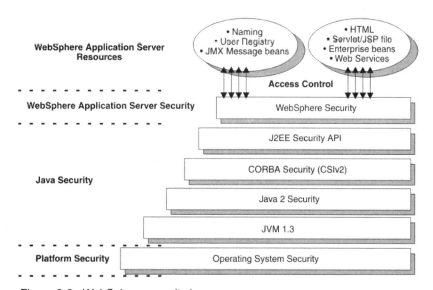

Figure 8-9   WebSphere security layers

- **Operating system security**—The security infrastructure of the underlying operating system provides certain security services to the WebSphere security application. This includes the file system security support to secure sensitive files in WebSphere product installation. The WebSphere system administrator can configure the product to obtain authentication information directly from the operating system user registry, for example the Windows NT system Security Access Manager (SAM).

- **JVM 1.3.1**—The JVM security model provides a layer of security above the operating system layer.

- **Java 2 security**—The Java 2 security model offers fine-grained access control to system resources including file system, system property, socket connection, threading, and class loading. Application code must explicitly grant the required permission to access a protected resource.

- **CORBA security/CSIv2**—Any calls made among secure ORBs are invoked over the Common Security Interoperability Version 2 (CSIv2) security protocol that sets up the security context and the necessary quality of protection. After the session is established, the call is passed up to the enterprise bean layer. WebSphere Application Server continues to support the secure association service (SAS) security protocol that was used in prior releases of WebSphere Application Server and other IBM products for backward compatibility.

- **J2EE security**—The security collaborator enforces J2EE-based security policies and supports J2EE security APIs.

- **WebSphere security**—WebSphere security enforces security policies and services in a unified manner for access to Web resources, enterprise beans, and JMX administrative resources. It consists of WebSphere security technologies and features to support the needs of a secure enterprise environment.

The security server contains an *authentication* mechanism and a role-based *authorization* engine, and collaborates with a *user registry* to perform authentication and authorization. The authentication mechanism and the user registry that the security server works with are configurable items.

Authentication

Authentication is the process of verifying the principal's identity: it checks if you are who you say you are. The *principal* is either a user or a computer process. Authentication takes place when a principal, such as a user, tries to access an application. The user would typically enter a user ID and password, whereas a computer process would present an encrypted key (programmatic authentication). If the authentication is successful, the principal will receive a token.

Authentication is now part of the J2EE 1.3 specification in the form of the Java Authentication and Authorization Service (JAAS).

Java Authentication and Authorization Services

JAAS 1.0 provides us with pluggable authentication that makes applications independent from the underlying authentication services. With WebSphere 5.0 you can use different user registries, which can be the operating system, an LDAP directory, or any other mechanism such as a list in a database (through the custom user registry). However, only one can be configured to be active.

Authentication modules can also be stacked (in which case you get two-phase login in the same way you have two-phase commit with databases).

► JAAS also adds user-based authorization to the Java security model.

► Single sign-on: ability to log in once and access multiple systems.

Authentication types

WebSphere provides two authentication mechanisms: Simple WebSphere Authentication Mechanism (SWAM) and Lightweight Third Party Authentication (LTPA). These two authentication mechanisms differ primarily in the distributed security features each supports (Table 8-5):

► SWAM does not allow single sign-on but does allow you to use the local operating system user registry. The SWAM authentication mechanism is suitable for simple environments, software development environments, or other environments that do not require a distributed security solution.

► LTPA does allow single sign-on but no local operating system user registry.

With both, you can use a custom user registry. Only a single authentication mechanism can be active at once.

Table 8-5   Summary of authentication mechanism capabilities

Type	Forwardable credentials	SSO	User registry		
			Local OS	LDAP	Custom
SWAM	No	No	Yes	Yes	Yes
LTPA	Yes	Yes	No	Yes	Yes

Authorization

Successful authentication is necessary, but not sufficient, for gaining access to protected resources. The authenticated user should also be authorized to use the resource. Authorization is the process by which the application server grants or denies permission to invoke the methods of an enterprise bean.

Java 2 security

With JAAS, we defined permissions based on *who* was running the code (user centric). Java 2 security provides fine-grained protection based on the *location* and *signer(s)* of the code (code centric). The following types of system resources can be protected:

► File system (files)
► Network connections (sockets)
► Java system properties
► Java Virtual Machine runtime operation (System.exitVM, class loaders, etc.)

The base Java2 security permissions are defined in the java.policy file, which can be found in the jre\lib\security subdirectory. For Application Developer, you find this file in <install-dir>\runtimes\base_v5\java\jre\lib\security.

WebSphere Version 5 also allows us to define permissions based on *resource types*, rather than code location or signer(s). These types can be:

► All
► Utility JARs
► EJB resources (JAR file)
► Web resources (WAR file)
► Connector resources

The granularity of these permissions is shown in Table 8-6.

Table 8-6   Overview of policy files

File	Defines permissions for	Path to file under <was-home>
java.policy	Everything running with this JRE	java/jre/lib/security/java.policy
spi.policy	JDBC, Java Mail and JMS	config/cells/<cellname>/nodes/<nodename>
library.policy	Shared libraries	config/cells/<cellname>/nodes/<nodename>
app.policy	All enterprise applications and resource adapters on a node level	config/cells/<cellname>/nodes/<nodename>
was.policy	One specific enterprise application	/META-INF of EAR file
ra.xml	One specific resource adapter	/META-INF/was.policy.RAR of RAR (resource adapter archive) file

The best way to edit the policy files is with the Java policy tool, which you can find in <WAS_HOME>/java/jre/bin/policytool.exe.

More detailed information on these settings can be found at:

http://java.sun.com/j2se/1.3/docs/guide/security/permissions.html

J2EE roles

In the life cycle of an application, different people perform different roles. From a security point of view, we can say that:

► The application provider can use programmatic security (as in Figure 8-10).

► The application assembler will use declarative security to set permissions on methods of beans.

► The application deployer links users and groups to roles.

► The system administrator tells the application server where to find the users (for example in an LDAP directory).

```
if ( isUserInRole("manager") ) {
    showAllCustomers();
} else {
    showCurrentCustomer();
}
```

Figure 8-10   Example of programmatic security

Important: Security is not enabled by default. To enable it open the WebSphere Administrative Console, select *Security Center -> Global Security* and check the *enabled* check box. Now click *Apply* and then *Save*.

EJB security details

This section describes the details of how security can be declared and managed for EJBs.

J2EE declarative security management

Declarative security externalizes the security constraints so that they do not reside in the code. This makes it much easier to manage the security policy for the application. Declarative security is role-based. The deployer of the application will give certain roles access to certain methods on the home and component interface of the beans. Methods can also further be secured, or put on the *exclude list* so that they become uncallable by anyone.

While declarative security, like declarative transaction management, is a nice ideal, there are some problem areas with declarative security:

▶ A user has a certain role or does not. There is no way to fine tune this by adding/removing one or more specific permissions.

▶ A user gets a particular role for *all* data elements. For a *salesperson* role, we might want to give the user full access to his own customers (with all purchase details), but only give limited access (summary) to other customers.

These situations cannot be handled within the declarative model but can be overcome by using programmatic security. Therefore, the J2EE declarative security model also provides a way to do programmatic bean-based security, similar to the way that bean-managed transactions allow specialization in handling of transactions.

Security roles

A security role is a semantic grouping of permissions that a user must have to use a particular part of an application. The assembler can then assign groups of methods (from home and component interfaces) to this security role. The assembler is only responsible for defining and naming the roles and can thus leave this work for the deployer. A best practice during deployment is to assign groups, rather than individual users, to roles for more flexibility.

These roles are logical associations that will map to a group (or user) name in a user registry. The EJB security roles are defined for all the EJBs in a JAR, and are defined using the `<security-role>` element (Figure 8-11).

```
......
<assembly-descriptor>
      <security-role>
          <description>A sample role</description>
          <role-name>myRole</role-name>               <== role used at runtime
      </security-role>
</assembly-descriptor>
```

Figure 8-11   User roles in EJB deployment descriptor

J2EE programmatic security management

If you really need more control inside of your components you can use programmatic security. This could be useful, for example, when you want one method to return different results depending on the role of the current user.

This could be the case when creating a navigation interface for an application where you only want to show those menu items that the user is allowed to access. This gives you the ability to fine tune your security policies.

EJB programmatic security management

The `EJBContext` interface defines the `isCallerInRole` method that allows us to identify the role with which the current method was called. The `EJBContext` can be either the `SessionContext` for session beans or the `EntityContext` for entity beans:

```
boolean authorized = context.isCallerInRole("SuperUser")
```

Another method is `getCallerPrincipal`, which returns the principal name of the caller of the method. The actual object returned with this method call is the `java.security.Principal` object. The `Principal` acts as a representative for the user or group that is attempting to access the system. The current principal's name can be determined through the `getName` method of the `Principal` object.

Table 8-7 shows the methods that are available for EJBs and servlets to access the security role and the principal.

Table 8-7   Accessing the security role and principal

EJB (EJBContext)	Servlets (HttpServletRequest)
isCallerInRole	isUserInRole
getCallerPrincipal	getUserPrincipal
	getRemoteUser

We mention the programmatic model for servlets as well, because servlets are typically the client of the EJBs. For servlets, three other methods are available:

▶ `isUserInRole`—Determines if a remote user is in a specified security role.

▶ `getUserPrincipal`—Determines the principal name of the current user and returns a `java.security.Principal` object.

▶ `getRemoteUser`—Returns the user name the client used for authentication.

Security role references

The role names you use in the EJB code may not be the role names that will be used when the EJB application is deployed. In the deployment descriptor, the application role is defined as a role reference that points to the actual role used in the runtime environment (Figure 8-12). This is similar to the local JNDI resource references.

```
...
<enterprise-beans>
   <entity>
      <ejb-name>Account</ejb-name>
      ...
      <security-role-ref>
         <description>A sample role</description>
         <role-name>myRoleRef</role-name>         <=== used in Account bean
         <role-link>myRole</role-link>            <=== used at runtime
      </security-role-ref>
   </entity>
</enterprise-beans>
```

Figure 8-12   Security role references

Assigning method-level permissions

Once security roles have been defined in the `ejb-jar` file, these roles can be assigned permissions to methods of the bean. Method-level permissions are defined using the `<method-permission>` element of the deployment descriptor (Figure 8-13).

```
......
<assembly-descriptor>
   <security-role>
      <description>A sample role</description>
      <role-name>myRole</role-name>              <=== this runtime role
   </security-role>
   <method-permission>
      <role-name>myRole</role-name>
      <method>
         <ejb-name>Account</ejb-name>            <=== for Account bean
         <method-intf>Local</method-intf>
         <method-name>transfer</method-name>     <=== can run this method
         <method-params>
            <method-param>java.lang.String</method-param>
            ......
         </method-params>
      </method>
   </method-permission></assembly-descriptor>
</assembly-descriptor>
```

Figure 8-13   Method permissions in the deployment descriptor

A method permission is a permission to invoke a specified group of methods of the enterprise bean's home and component interfaces.

There are variations on this model. For example, using the wildcard format `<method-name>*</method-name>` will apply this policy to every method of the bean, and not including a `<method-intf>` extends this to every method on the home and component interface. Additionally, if methods are overloaded, then the `<method-params>` option can be used to distinguish method permissions for overloaded methods.

Unchecked methods

Some methods of a bean can be defined as *unchecked*, that is, security permissions are not checked before the method is invoked. This is useful if all the methods of a bean were applied a security policy using the wildcard format, but a smaller number of methods were to go unchecked.

Security identity

In addition to specifying the security roles (or principals) that have access to an enterprise bean, the deployer can also specify the *run-as* role for the entire enterprise bean.

> **Note:** In WebSphere Version 5, you can also assign a run-as identity at the method level.

Run-as defines the identity that a bean runs with when it calls other beans. This does not change the identity of the caller of the bean (as retrieved with `getCallerIdentity`). There are three possible configurations:

- ► Run-as the identity of the caller (client identity); available at method level only.
- ► Run-as the identity of the EJB server (system identity).
- ► Run-as the identity assigned to a specific role name (specified identity).

The identity is configured using the `<security-identity>` element in the deployment descriptor (Figure 8-14). Because this is a per-bean setting, it must be declared for every EJB.

If the other beans that a bean calls should execute with the same identity, the `<use-caller-identity>` can be used. However, this requires the calling bean to account for all identities of client principals, as well as other beans. This could become difficult to manage if the number of roles is very large. If this were the case, it might just be easier to specify a single `<run-as>` role, to simplify the declarations. This might be useful for entity beans that are always called behind a session bean facade, and the session bean is essentially a trusted agent. Only the session bean would have to manage and maintain the larger list of user roles. A servlet can also pass the identity to EJBs, and if there are no other clients, then the security identity for all EJBs can be specified as `<use-caller-identity>`.

```
<enterprise-beans>
   ......
   <entity>
      <ejb-name>Account</ejb-name>                    <=== for this bean
         ......
         <security-identity>
            <description>security description</description>
            <run-as>
               <description>role description</description>
               <role-name>myRole</role-name>          <=== run as role
            </run-as>
         </security-identity>
   </entity>
   <entity>
      <ejb-name>Customer</ejb-name>                    <=== for this bean
         ......
      <security-identity>
         <use-caller-identity/>                        <=== use as caller
      </security-identity>
   </entity>
```

Figure 8-14   Caller identity examples in deployment descriptor

Best practice: authorization policy matrix

If the application has many methods and roles, the management of these associations can quickly become difficult. To keep an overview of your security policy it could prove beneficial to create overview tables such as Table 8-8 (for methods and roles) and Table 8-9 (for users and groups).

Table 8-8   Authorization policy: linking methods to roles

		Granted Methods		
		/finance /account GET	/finance /account POST	Banking transfer
Roles	Teller	yes		
	Cashier			yes
	Supervisor	yes	yes	yes

Table 8-9   Protection matrix: linking roles to subjects

		Roles		
		Teller	Cashier	SuperVisor
Subjects	TellerGroup	1		
	CashierGroup		1	
	Supervisor			1
	Ueli	1	1	

Tieing it all together

We have discussed the relationship between security roles and methods, as well as the identities that can be set when beans propagate security context when calling other EJBs.

Figure 8-15 shows how security is defined using roles and permissions, and how the security identity is used when a client (for example, a servlet) calls an EJB method, and that method calls another EJB.

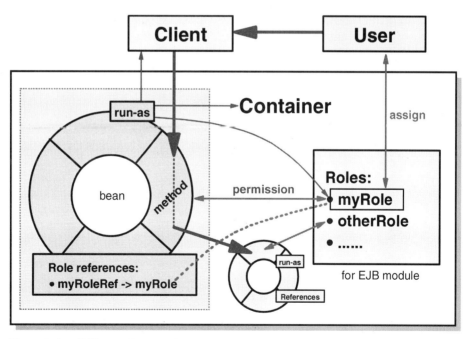

Figure 8-15   EJB security recapitulation

- Roles are defined for an EJB module.
- For an individual bean, we define the security identity that should be used. This can be the caller (client), the EJB server (container), or a specified role.
- In the EJB method code, we use local role names that are defined as role references, pointing to the roles defined for the module.
- Real users are assigned to roles in the WebSphere configuration.

Summary

In this chapter, we expanded the EJB discussion to advanced topics, such as transaction management, exception management, and security management.

For transaction management, we described container- and bean-managed transactions, and the link between transactions and the underlying resource managers, specifically relational database systems.

For exception management, we classified the exceptions into application and system exceptions and described how exceptions should be handled by EJBs and clients.

For security, we described the basic security schema used by WebSphere Application Server and specifically how it applies to EJBs.

Developing and testing EJBs with Application Developer

In Part 2, we describe the development and deployment of EJBs using WebSphere Studio Application Developer.

We introduce the Application Developer and the sample banking scenario. Then we develop entity beans, session beans, access beans, message-driven beans, and EJB clients. Finally, we deploy the sample applications to WebSphere Application Server.

© Copyright IBM Corp. 2003. All rights reserved.   **329**

9

WebSphere Studio Application Developer

This chapter provides an overview of WebSphere Studio Application Developer (abbreviated as Application Developer), which we use to develop the sample application. We provide a tour of the integrated development environment (IDE) in which we discuss:

► WebSphere Studio Workbench open tooling platform

► The different types of projects within Application Developer, such as the Java, EAR, Web, EJB and server projects

► The different perspectives available in Application Developer, such as the Web, Java, J2EE, Data, XML, Server, and Debug perspectives

© Copyright IBM Corp. 2003. All rights reserved.   **331**

WebSphere Studio Application Developer

Application Developer brings together most of the functionality offered by VisualAge for Java and WebSphere Studio *classic edition*. Besides the functionality of these two products, new features were added, as shown in Figure 9-1.

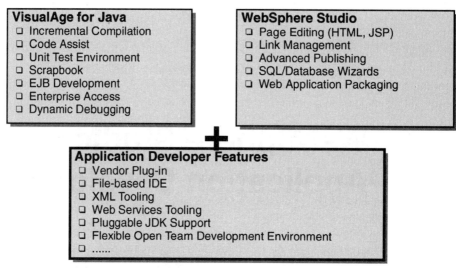

VisualAge for Java
- ❑ Incremental Compilation
- ❑ Code Assist
- ❑ Unit Test Environment
- ❑ Scrapbook
- ❑ EJB Development
- ❑ Enterprise Access
- ❑ Dynamic Debugging

WebSphere Studio
- ❑ Page Editing (HTML, JSP)
- ❑ Link Management
- ❑ Advanced Publishing
- ❑ SQL/Database Wizards
- ❑ Web Application Packaging

Application Developer Features
- ❑ Vendor Plug-in
- ❑ File-based IDE
- ❑ XML Tooling
- ❑ Web Services Tooling
- ❑ Pluggable JDK Support
- ❑ Flexible Open Team Development Environment
- ❑ ......

Figure 9-1   Application Developer features

WebSphere Studio Workbench

WebSphere Studio Workbench is the brand name for the new open, portable universal tooling platform and integration technology from IBM. It forms the base for the new WebSphere Studio suite (WebSphere Studio Site Developer, WebSphere Studio Application Developer, WebSphere Studio Application Developer Integration Edition, and WebSphere Studio Enterprise Developer).

The Workbench is for customers and for tool builders who want to plug their tools into the WebSphere Studio product set. The Eclipse open source project (http://www.eclipse.org) enables other tool vendors to develop plug-ins for the WebSphere Studio Workbench. The tool providers write their tools as plug-ins for the Workbench, which operates on files in the workspace.

When the Workbench is launched, the user sees the integrated development environment composed of the different plug-ins. WebSphere Studio Workbench provides APIs, building blocks, and frameworks to facilitate the development of new plug-ins. There can be interconnections between plug-ins by means of extension points. Each plug-in can define extension points that can be used by other plug-ins to add function. For example, the Workbench plug-in defines an extension point for user preferences. When a tool plug-in wants to add items in that preferences list, it just uses that extension point and extends it.

Workspace

The resources you work with are stored in the workspace. By default, the workspace is a directory called *workspace* inside the product installation directory.

It is possible and suggested to place the workspace directory anywhere on the file system by starting the Application Developer with a flag:

```
wsappdev.exe -data d:\WSAD5sg246819
```

We will store our projects in the workspace named `WSAD5sg246819`.

User interface

The Workbench user interface (UI) is implemented using two toolkits:

► Standard widget toolkit (SWT)—A widget set and graphical library integrated with the native Windows operating system but with an operating system-independent API.

► JFace—A UI toolkit implemented using SWT.

The whole Workbench architecture is shown in Figure 9-2.

Here are some explanations of the acronyms:

Concurrent Versions System (CVS)
CVS is the open standard for version control systems. More information on CVS can be found at `http://www.cvshome.org`.

ClearCase (CC and CCLT)
ClearCase LT is from Rational and is shipped with the Application Developer. ClearCase full function can be purchased separately from Rational. More information can be found at `http://www.rational.com`.

Other versioning systems will be supported in future versions of the Application Developer product or by code shipped by other vendors (Merant, for example).

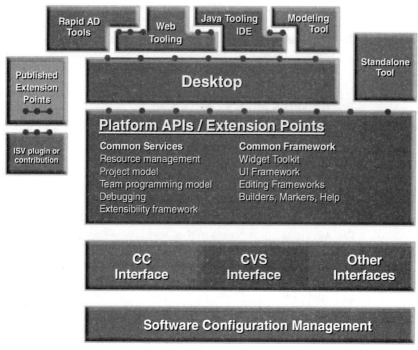

Figure 9-2   The Workbench architecture

Workbench window

In this redbook, we refer to the interface of Application Developer as the Workbench. It is an integrated development environment that promotes role-based development. For each role in the development of your e-business application, there is a different and customizable perspective.

A perspective is the initial set and layout of the views in the Workbench. Each perspective is related to a development task or role. For example, if you want to develop Java applications, you first create a Java project. When you work in a Java project, you probably use the Java perspective because that is the most useful perspective to do Java developing. We give an overview of the different perspectives and projects in the next sections.

Note: The screens shown were captured at the end of the redbook writing project. No projects are visible when you start the product for the first time.

Perspectives and views

Perspectives are a way to look through different glasses at a project. Depending on the role you have (Web developer, Java developer, EJB developer) and/or the task you have to do (developing, debugging, deploying), you open a different perspective. The Workbench window can have several perspectives opened, and each can have its own window on the desktop if desired (select *Window ->* *Preferences -> Workbench -> Perspectives* to set the option for multiple windows).

Perspective basics

Figure 9-3 shows the Web perspective. You can switch easily between perspectives by clicking the different icons in the perspective tool bar.

- You can open a new perspective by clicking the icon in the perspective toolbar. Alternatively you can select *Window -> Open Perspective* and then select the desired perspective from the list (in some cases you have to select *Other* to get a list of all perspectives).

- Each perspective has its own views and editors that are arranged for presentation on the screen (some may be hidden at any given moment). Several different types of views and editors can be open at the same time within a perspective.

- There are several perspectives predefined (Resource, Java, Web, J2EE, EGL, Data, XML, Server, Debug) in the Workbench. You can customize them easily by adding, deleting, or moving the different views.

- You can also compose your own perspective by defining the views it should contain.

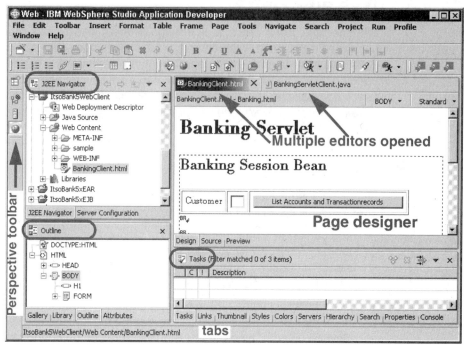

Figure 9-3   Web perspective

Views and editors

We first discuss the different views that appear in most perspectives and then take a closer look at some of the most used perspectives. Some of the views appear in most of the perspectives.

Navigator view

The Navigator view shows you how your resources are structured into folders. The Navigator view is available in most perspectives and it always displays all the folders and files of all projects. There are three kinds of resources:

Projects   You use projects to organize all your resources and for version management. When you create a new project, a folder with the name of the project is created in the workspace.

Folders   Folders are like directories in the file system. They can contain files as well as other folders. Folders are usually stored in the project directory, but they can also be outside of the workspace.

Files   Files correspond to files in the file system and reside in folders.

Editors

By double-clicking a resource, the associated editor opens and allows you to modify it. In Figure 9-3, the active editor is the page designer, associated with JSP and HTML files. If no editor is currently associated with a particular file extension, the Workbench checks if there is one associated in the operating system and uses that editor to edit the file. You can also open OLE document editors such as Word, which is associated with the *.doc* extension.

You can change or add editors associated with a file extensions:

► From the menu bar, select *Window -> Preferences*.

► In the left pane, select *File editors* under the *Workbench* hierarchy.

► You can then select a file extension and associate an internal or external editors for it.

When you double-click another resource, a different editor shows up. You can easily switch between the different opened resources by selecting them on the top bar above the editor area. If the tab of your editor contains an asterisk (*), it means that it contains unsaved changes.

Outline view

The Outline view is always associated with the active editor.

The Outline view gives you an overview of the key elements that make up the resource that is being edited. It allows quick and easy navigation through your resource. By selecting one of the elements in the Outline view, the line in the editor view that contains the selected element gets highlighted and the editor pane is adjusted to make the element visible.

Properties view

When you click a resource in the Navigator view and then open the Properties view, you can view the different properties of that resource. The Properties view contains general things such as the full path of the file system, the date when it was last modified, and the size, as shown in Figure 9-4.

Property	Value
⊟ Info	
editable	true
last modified	12/16/02 5:53 PM
name	BankingClient.html
path	/ItsoBank5WebClient/Web Content/BankingClient.html
size	1667

Figure 9-4   Properties view

Tasks view

The Tasks view contains a list of two types of elements:

Problems   Problems are tool-determined issues that have to be resolved. Example problems are Java compile errors or broken links for HTML/JSP files. They are automatically added to the Tasks view when working with the tool. When you double-click a problem, the editor for the file containing the problem opens and the cursor is pointed at the location of the problem.

Tasks   You can manually add tasks yourself. For example, you can add a task that reminds you that you have to implement a Java method. Place the cursor in the method's implementation, right-click and select *Add -> Task*. When you double-click, the file opens and the cursor is located in the method. You can also add general tasks that do not refer to a specific file.

You can set up several filters to show only the tasks you really want to see. For example, by clicking the filter icon ![filter icon], you can specify that you want to show only the Java compile errors from a particular Java class or for the particular project. An example of the Tasks view with a Java code error is shown in Figure 9-5.

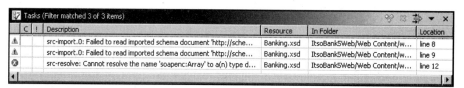

Figure 9-5   Tasks view

Double-clicking an error opens the file with the error at the point of the error.

Console view

The Console view displays console output of Java programs that you run or messages of servers that you start.

Other views

There are many other views in the different perspectives, tailored for certain user tasks. Some of the other views will be explained when we discuss other perspectives.

Customizing perspectives

You can highly customize the different perspectives by:

► Closing or opening views.

► Maximizing the view by double-clicking the title bar. You do this when you need a large pane for code editing. Double-click again to restore the layout.

► Moving views to other panes or stacking them behind other views. To move a view:

— Select the view's title bar and start dragging the view.

— While you drag the view, the mouse cursor changes into a drop cursor. The drop cursor indicates what will happen when you release the view you are dragging:

The floating view appears below the view underneath the cursor.

The floating view appears to the left of the view underneath the cursor.

The floating view appears to the right of the view underneath the cursor.

The floating view appears above the view underneath the cursor.

The floating view appears as a tab in the same pane as the view underneath the cursor. You can also drop the view on the perspective toolbar to make it a fast view.

You cannot dock the floating view at this point.

► Adding views and icons. You can add a view or a set of icons as follows:

— Select *Window -> Customize Perspective* from the main menu bar.

— Select the views you want to add and the icons (*Other*) you want to add and click *OK*.

— Select *Window -> Show View* and select the view you just added.

Once you have configured the perspective to your liking, you can also save it as your own perspective by selecting *Window -> Save Perspective As*.

When you want to reset a perspective to its original state, select *Window -> Reset Perspective* from the main menu.

New icon

The 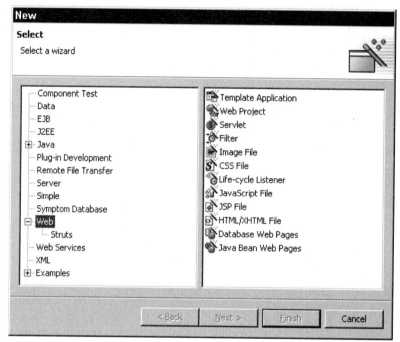 icon (*New*) opens a window where you can create any type of resource from a selection list. This window is also opened when selecting *File -> New -> Other* from the main tool bar (Figure 9-6).

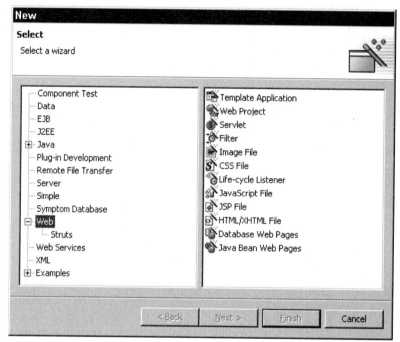

Figure 9-6   New wizard

You can also select the drop-down menu next to the New icon. This action displays a list of most used resources that you may want to create in the current perspective. If the desired resource is not in the list, select *Other* to open the New window.

Web perspective

In Figure 9-3 on page 336 you see the Workbench opened in the Web perspective. You use the Web perspective when you want to develop Web applications. The Web perspective is the best perspective for adding and organizing static content (HTML, images) and dynamic content (servlets and JSPs) to a Web application.

On top of the perspective, you see the Workbench toolbar. The contents of the toolbar change based on the active editor for a particular resource. The current editor is the page designer for editing our JSP page. The toolbar now reflects JSP development and contains icons to add JSP tags and a JSP menu item.

The Outline view shows the outline of a JSP page. It contains all the tags from which the JSP page is constructed. When you switch to the source tab of the page designer and you select a tag in the Outline view, the matching line in the Source view is highlighted.

We use the Web perspective in the chapters that follow, where we develop the sample Web application and the Web services.

Web Structure view

The Web Structure view (Figure 9-7) shows the logical layout of a Web application with Web pages and actions. This is most useful in a Struts-based Web application:

▶ Web pages are shown with referenced files and Struts actions.

▶ Struts actions are shown with forms and action mappings.

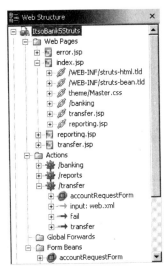

Figure 9-7   Web Structure view

Java perspective

When you want to develop Java applications, you use the Java perspective. The Java perspective is shown in Figure 9-8. It contains a lot of useful editors and views which help you in your Java development.

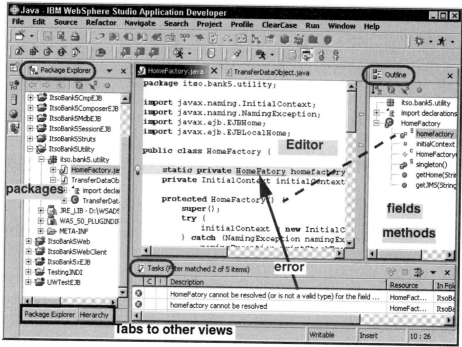

Figure 9-8   Java perspective

You navigate in the Java perspective through the **Package Explorer** view, which enables you to define and manage Java packages and the Java classes defined in the packages.

When you select a Java class in the Packages view and select *Navigate -> Open Type Hierarchy*, the **Hierarchy** view for that Java class opens. The Hierarchy view allows you to see the full hierarchy of a Java class. In Figure 9-8, the Hierarchy view is currently hidden by the Package Explorer view.

When you double-click a Java file, the Java editor opens. You can open multiple Java files at the same time. The Java editor features syntax highlighting and a code assistant by pressing *Ctrl+spacebar*.

The Outline view in the Java perspective gives an overview of all the methods and fields for the Java file that is currently opened. When you click a method in the Outline view, the cursor is positioned in the method signature in the Java editor. The tool bar at the top contains filters to include or exclude static methods or fields, and to sort the Outline view.

In the Java perspective, the Workbench toolbar contains several icons to add new packages, new Java classes, and new Java interfaces, or to create a new Scrapbook page.

Search

Clicking the search icon 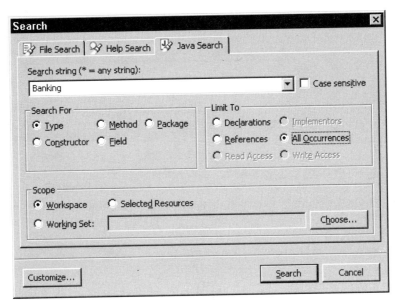 invokes the search window shown in Figure 9-9. Now you can either do a full text search or a more intelligent Java search to look, for example, for a particular type declaration or references to it.

Figure 9-9   Search window

The **Search** view (Figure 9-10) shows the results of a search action. From the Search view you can double-click any of the result lines to open the class that contains the declaration or reference.

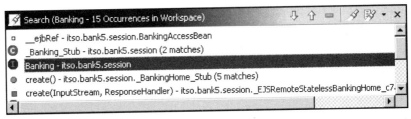

Figure 9-10   Search results

J2EE perspective

The J2EE perspective (Figure 9-11) provides useful views for the J2EE or EJB developer. The **J2EE Hierarchy** view shows you a list of all the different modules such as Web modules, EJB modules or server configurations that make up your enterprise application. You can expand the module you want to explore and you can edit the associated deployment descriptors for that module by double-clicking.

In Figure 9-11, the EJB deployment descriptor (`ejb-jar.xml`) is currently opened in the EJB deployment descriptor editor.

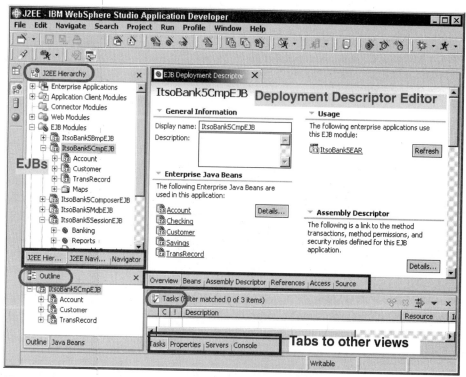

Figure 9-11   J2EE perspective

The **J2EE Navigator** view, hidden by the J2EE Hierarchy view in Figure 9-11, shows a hierarchical view of all the resources in the workspace. When you double-click a resource, the registered editor for that file extension opens and the Outline view shows the outline for the file you are editing.

Data perspective

You use the Data perspective (Figure 9-12) for relational database design for your application. You can either create a relational database schema yourself, or import it from an existing database. Afterwards, you can browse, query or modify it. The Data perspective provides the views to manage and work with database definitions.

In the **DB Servers** view, you can create a connection to an existing database and browse its schema. When you want to modify or extend the schema, you have to import it into the Data Definition view.

The **Data Definition** view allows you to define new tables, or to modify existing tables. If you double-click a table in the Data Definition view, the table editor opens and you can add or change columns and primary or foreign keys.

The Navigator view shows all the resources in the folder structure.

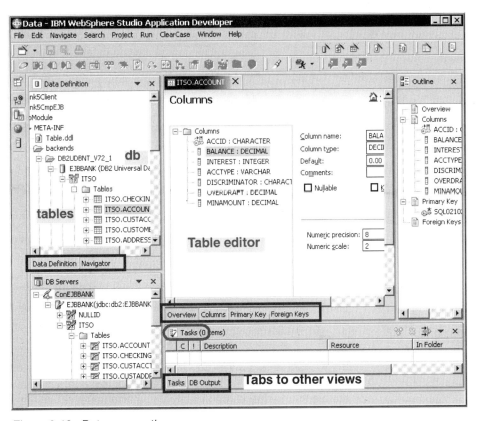

Figure 9-12   Data perspective

XML perspective

The XML perspective (Figure 9-13) is the perspective for XML development. The XML perspective contains several editors and views that help you in building XML, XML schemas, XSD, DTD, and integration between relational data and XML.

In Figure 9-13, the XML editor is opened on a Struts configuration file. You can switch between the Design and Source tabs of the editor to develop your XML file. The Outline view contains all the XML tags that make up the XML document that is currently opened in the XML editor.

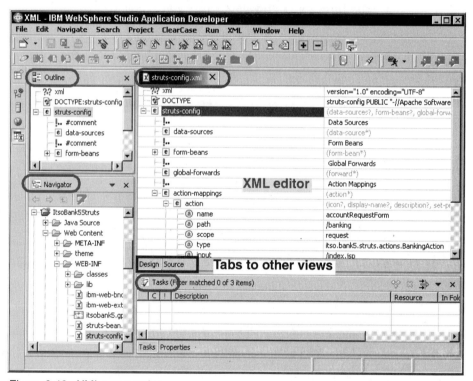

Figure 9-13   XML perspective

Server perspective

When you want to test a Web application or EJB module you use the Server perspective (Figure 9-14). The Server perspective contains views and editors that enable you to define, configure, and manage server instances and configurations.

The **Server Configuration** view (left bottom) enables you to define or modify server configurations, and bind them to a project. When you double-click the server configuration file in the Server Configuration view, the Server Configuration editor opens.

The **Servers** view (right bottom) lists all the currently defined servers. Here you can start or stop their execution, restart projects, and start the administrative console or the universal test client.

The **Console** view (currently hidden by the Servers view) shows all the output listed by a running server.

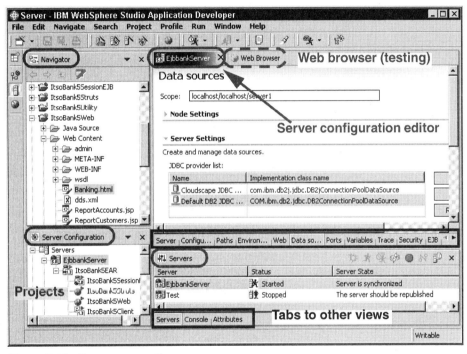

Figure 9-14   Server perspective

Debug perspective

Use the Debug perspective (Figure 9-15) when you want to debug your code. The Debug perspective automatically opens when you click the Debug icon 🔅 in the Java perspective to run an application in debug mode. It allows you to step through your code, inspect the values of variables, modify your code and resume execution.

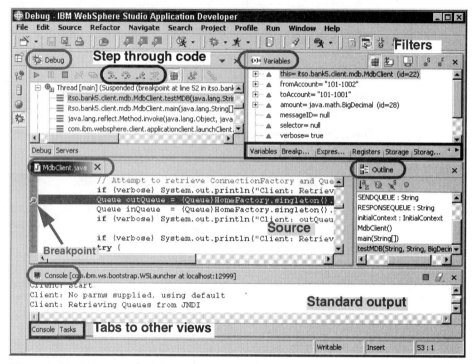

Figure 9-15 Debug perspective

The Debug perspective is built from the following views:

▶ The **Debug view** lists all threads within the different processes and shows you where the execution is halted when reaching a breakpoint.

▶ Beneath the Debug view there is a Java editor that shows the source of the code you are stepping into.

▶ The **Breakpoint view** lists all currently defined breakpoints. The *Exception* icon ![icon] on top of the Breakpoint view allows you to define exceptions that will halt execution when thrown.

▶ The **Variables view** lists all variables defined currently in the running thread. You can view and modify their values and set up filters to exclude, for example, static fields.

▶ In the **Expressions view** you can enter Java code and execute it using all the variables that are visible at the current breakpoint.

▶ The **Console view** (bottom) shows the output of your application.

CVS Repository Exploring perspective

The CVS Repository Exploring perspective provides an interface to the Concurrent Versions System (CVS), which is one of the supported products for team development (Figure 9-16).

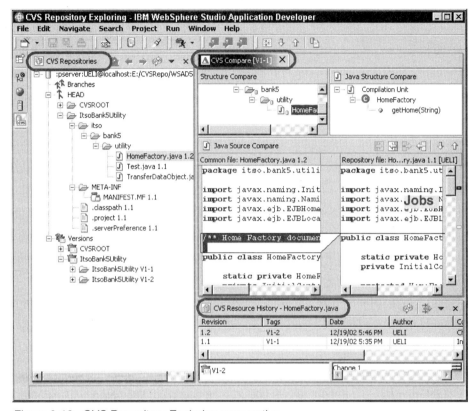

Figure 9-16   CVS Repository Exploring perspective

The **CVS Repositories** view displays connections to repositories, the projects that have been shared with team members, either as a branch (current code) or as versions (frozen code).

The **CVS Resource History** view shows the revisions that have been performed on a file.

Revisions of files can be compared and the differences are shown in the **Compare** view.

We describe simple usage procedures for CVS in Chapter 19, "Application Developer team development environment" on page 669.

Help

The Application Developer provides help in a separate window that you can open using *Help -> Help Contents* (Figure 9-17).

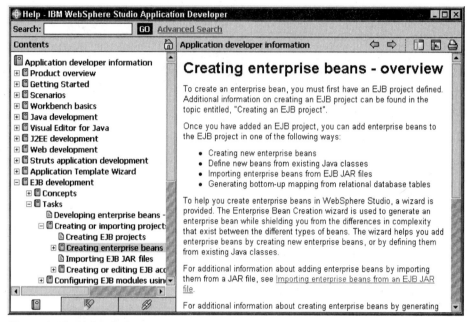

Figure 9-17   Help window

The Help window contains a lot of useful information about the Workbench. It provides information about the different concepts used by the Workbench, the different tasks you can do within the Workbench and some useful samples. The Search field allows you to do a search in the help.

Memory considerations

After working with Application Developer for some time, you will have opened several perspectives. You might have the impression that Application Developer is working slower. It is good practice to close down the perspectives you have not been using for a while, because they can consume a lot of memory, and hence, slow down the overall performance.

Projects

A project is the top-level construct for organizing the different resources. It contains files as well as folders. In the Workbench you can create different kinds of projects, and they will have a different structure. A Web project, for example, has a different nature from a Java project; therefore it will have a different folder structure.

We now briefly discuss the types of projects referred to in this document:

- Java project
- EAR project
- Web project
- EJB project
- Server project

Java project

When you want to create a Java application, you first have to create a Java project to contain the Java files. Each Java project has a Java builder and builder path associated with it, which are used to compile the Java source files.

Creating a Java project

Here are the steps to create a Java project:

- Select *File -> New -> Project*.

- In the New window, select *Java* in the left panel and *Java Project* in the right panel. Click *Next*.

- Specify a name for the project and the location of the project contents. By default the content is stored in the workspace. Click *Next*.

- The *Java build settings* panel (Figure 9-18) contains four tabs to specify the folders, projects, and libraries used for compilation.

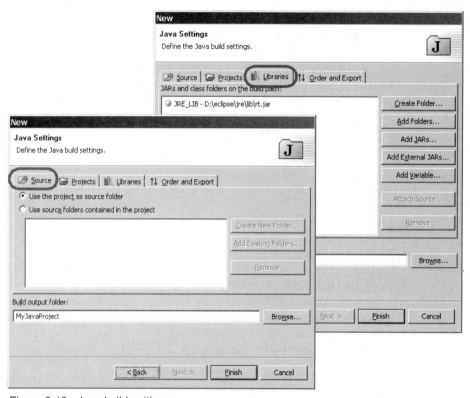

Figure 9-18 Java build settings

Source   In the *Source* tab you specify where the source files should be
                stored, either within the normal project folders or in folders
                designated by you.

Projects   In the *Projects* tab you specify whether other projects are
                required in the build path. For example, a Web project may
                require an EJB project.

Libraries   In the *Libraries* tab you can add internal and external JAR files to
                the build path:

> ► An internal JAR is contained in the Workbench. The
>   advantage of an internal JAR is that it can be treated as a
>   normal resource within the Workbench, which allows
>   version management.

> ► External JARs are referenced with absolute paths in the
>   file system. This may make it difficult to share them in a
>   team environment. Variables can be used to alleviate the
>   issue introduced by absolute paths. An example of an

external JAR file would be the `db2java.zip` file used for JDBC access to DB2.

Order/Export The *Order and Export* tab enables you to specify the order in which the different items in the build path are accessed, when loading Java classes. You can also select which directories and files are exported with the project.

> **Tip:** Use the predefined variables instead of adding external JARs with absolute paths to your build path whenever possible. The Workbench contains various predefined variables, such as the DB2JAVA variable, which defines the `db2java.zip` file. You can add variables for other JAR files through the *Window -> Preferences -> Java -> Classpath Variables* window.

You can modify the Java build path after you have created a project through the *Properties* context menu of the project.

When you are finished creating the Java project, the Workbench switches automatically to the Java perspective.

Creating a package and a class

To create a Java package, select *File -> New -> Java Package* or click the *New Package* icon in the toolbar. Enter the package name and click *Finish*. The package appears in the Packages view.

To create a class in the new package, select the package and select *File -> New -> Java Class* or select the *New Class* icon in the toolbar. In the SmartGuide, check the package name and enter the desired class name and superclass. If you want a *main* method in your class, select the *main* method under *Which method stubs would you like to create*. Click *Finish*. The class appears under the package and a Java editor opens and you can start coding.

Java editing

The following useful features are available when you edit Java code:

- ▶ Double-clicking in the title bar of the Java editor maximizes the editor so that it occupies the whole perspective. Double-click again to restore its original size.

- ▶ Press *Ctrl-spacebar* to launch the code assist in the Java editor when coding.

- ▶ If you select the edited Java source and you click the *Show Source of Selected Element Only* icon in the toolbar then only the source of the selected element in the Outline view is displayed in the editor.

- ▶ If you place the cursor in the Java editor on a variable, then the full package name of that variable displays in the hover help (a small pop-up that opens at the cursor location over the text). Hide the hover help by clicking the *Text Hover* icon in the toolbar ▣ .

▶ If you select a method in the Outline view and then select *Replace from Local History* from the context menu, a window opens and shows all the states of the method that you saved. You can replace the method with an older version. The same can be done for the class itself from the Navigator view.

EAR project

To develop a J2EE enterprise application you have to create an enterprise application project (EAR project). An EAR project usually consists of one or more EJB modules, one or more Web modules (Web applications), and one or more application client modules.

Creating an EAR project

To create an EAR project, do the following:

▶ Select *File -> New Project*.

▶ Select *J2EE* in the left pane and *Enterprise Application Project* in the right pane, and click *Next*.

▶ Specify a *Name* for the EAR project.

▶ Specify contained modules (client, EJB, and Web projects) that you want to include in the EAR project, and click *Finish*.

▶ We recommend that you follow a naming standard for your projects.

EAR deployment descriptor (application.xml)

When you create an EAR project, a deployment descriptor (`application.xml`) is created in the `/META-INF` folder. The EAR deployment descriptor defines all modules in the EAR file.

To open the EAR deployment descriptor, do the following:

▶ Open the J2EE perspective and J2EE Hierarchy view.

▶ Expand *Enterprise Applications* and double-click the EAR project. Alternatively double-click the `application.xml` file in the Navigator view.

J2EE packaging

An EAR project can be packaged as an enterprise archive file (EAR file). An enterprise application consists of the following modules:

▶ Web applications, which are packaged in `.WAR` files. The WAR file contains the resources that compose the Web application and a deployment descriptor (`web.xml`). A Web application is contained in a Web project, which we discuss in "Web project" on page 356.

► EJB modules, which are packaged in `.JAR` files. The EJB JAR file contains all the EJBs and a deployment descriptor (`ejb-jar.xml`). EJBs are contained in an EJB project, which we discuss in "EJB project" on page 359.

► Optionally we can have stand-alone client applications that use EJBs, for example. An application client is also packaged in a JAR file. The application client JAR contains all the Java classes of the application client and a deployment descriptor (`application-client.xml`).

Figure 9-19 shows how WAR files and JAR files together constitute the EAR file, which also contains the application deployment descriptor (`application.xml`).

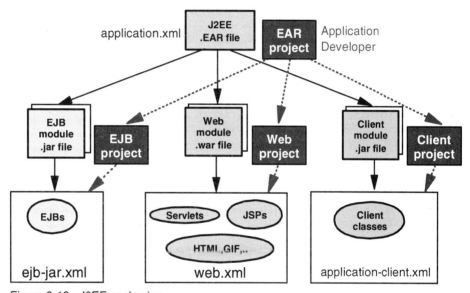

Figure 9-19   J2EE packaging

EAR deployment

Exporting an EAR project into an EAR file assembles all the components (EJB, Web, and client projects) into one file that can be deployed into a J2EE conforming application server, such as WebSphere Application Server.

Web project

You use a Web project when you want to create and maintain resources that compose a Web application. A Web project contains the structure of folders to contain all files that are needed to build a Web application. Typically, a Web application consists of HTML pages, images, XML, servlets, JSPs, and JavaBeans. How to build a Web application is described in "Developing a servlet client" on page 590.

Creating a Web project

To create a Web project do the following:

► Select *File -> New -> Project*.

► Select *Web* in the left pane, *Web Project* in the right pane, and click *Next* to start the wizard.

► Specify the Project name and the workspace location for the project. Choose between a *J2EE Web project* (with servlets, JSPs, and EJBs) and a *Static Web project* (HTML only). For this document, we always create J2EE Web project. Optionally, select *Create a CSS file* (HTML style sheet).

Here is also where you specify if you want Struts support in the J2EE Web project. See "Developing a Struts-based Web client" on page 609 for information on Struts.

► On the J2EE Settings page, you specify the EAR project, either an existing one or a new one. Specify the *Context root*, the alias that will be used in URLs to access project resources. Select the J2EE level, 1.3 or 1.2. Note that you can run a 1.3 project only in a WebSphere Version 5 server, but you can run a 1.2 project in either WebSphere Version 4 or Version 5.

► On the Module Dependencies page, you can specify JAR files required by the Web application, for example EJB modules within the same EAR project.

► On the Struts Settings page, you specify if and where the Struts resource bundle should be created. The resource bundle holds text constants that can be used in Web pages.

► Click *Finish*. Your Web project is automatically opened in the Web perspective.

When you create a new Web project, a default directory structure is created that reflects the J2EE view of a Web application. A Web deployment descriptor `web.xml` is generated in the `/webApplication/WEB-INF` folder.

Web application archive files (WAR files)

As defined in the J2EE specification, a WAR file is an archive format for Web applications. The WAR file is a packaged format of your Web application that contains all the resources (HTML, servlets, JavaBeans, JSPs, XML, XML schemas) that compose your Web application.

You can deploy a Web application by itself to an application server by creating a WAR file. Select *File -> Export -> WAR* and specify the output file and directory.

In general, however, it is easier to have the Workbench create the EAR file that contains the WAR file and deploy the EAR to an application server.

Struts

A difficult aspect of building a Web application is connecting components that comprise disparate technologies (for example, building the controller, in MVC terms).

Application Developer leverages Struts, an emerging open standard for constructing MVC-based Web applications. Struts provides (among other things) an action servlet that manages the runtime relationship between JSPs and actions. The use of Struts helps to ensure an effective separation of code responsibilities and developer roles (see "Developing a Struts-based Web client" on page 609 for a more detailed description of Struts).

Application Developer provides a powerful visual component assembly environment, the Struts application diagram editor, for Struts-based Web applications (Figure 9-20).

The diagram editor is used to define the basic flow of the Web application graphically, connecting JSPs with component services (or actions) as desired. This approach simplifies the creation of an MVC application by masking the complexity of the disparate technologies involved.

The diagram editor is used initially as part of the design process, helping a development team quickly lay out view (JSP) and model (action) components without having to consider the technical issues of combining disparate technologies that have yet to be created or harvested from existing capability. Throughout the development process, the diagram editor can be used to extend and test a Web application's capability.

The actions defined in the visual assembly environment can be implemented in different technologies, for example, JavaBeans or EJBs.

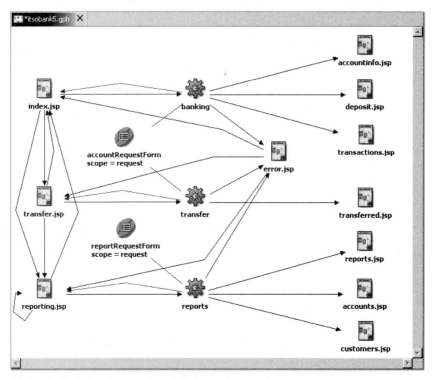

Figure 9-20   Visual assembly of Web application flow

The Application Developer also provides a number of wizards to define Struts components, such as action classes, action forms, and JSPs.

Struts project

A Struts project is a special case of a Web project that includes:

▶ Struts taglibs and Struts configuration file (`struts-config.xml`) in the `WEB-INF` folder

▶ Struts runtime JAR file (`struts.jar`) in the `WEB_INF/lib` directory

▶ Struts resource bundle (`ApplicationResources.properties`) for the externalized user interface resources

A Struts project is defined as a Web project. The Struts support is added to the Web project during the creation of the project through the new Web project wizard.

EJB project

If you want to develop Enterprise JavaBeans (EJBs), you have to create an EJB project first. An EJB project is a logical group for organizing the EJBs. To create an EJB project:

► Select *File -> New -> Project*.

► Select *EJB* in the left pane and *EJB project* in the right pane and click *Next*.

► Specify the *Name* of the EJB project and the workspace location. You also have to specify an EAR project name that will contain your EJB project. You can select an existing EAR project or create a new one. Click *Next*.

► On the *Module Dependencies* page you can specify JAR files required by the EJB application, for example other EJB modules within the same EAR project.

► When you click *Finish*, the EJB project opens in the J2EE perspective. The deployment descriptor for the EJB module (`ejb-jar.xml`) is created in the `/YourProject/ejb-module/META-INF` folder.

EJB deployment descriptor (ejb-jar.xml)

An EJB module requires a deployment descriptor (`ejb-jar.xml`) in the same way a Web application requires a deployment descriptor (`web.xml`).

In addition to the standard deployment descriptor, the Workbench also defines EJB bindings and extensions. Both binding and extension descriptors are stored in XMI files, `ibm-ejb-jar-bnd.xmi` and `ibm-ejb-jar-ext.xmi`, respectively.

EJB deployment descriptor editor

To edit the deployment descriptor for the EJB module:

► In the *J2EE* view of the J2EE perspective, expand EJB Modules.

► Right-click the EJB module and select *Open With -> EJB Editor,* or just double-click the module.

► The `ejb-jar.xml` deployment descriptor opens in the EJB deployment descriptor editor. Figure 9-21 shows the Beans page of the editor. The Overview page was shown in Figure 9-11 on page 344.

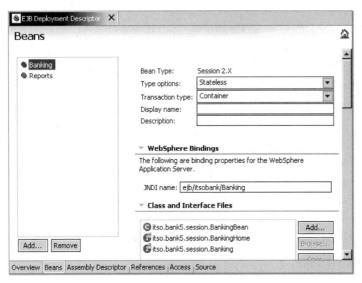

Figure 9-21   EJB deployment descriptor editor

The `ejb-jar.xml` is presented in several sections defined by the tabs at the bottom of the editor.

Server project

To test an EJB or Web project, you have to define a server with a server configuration to publish and run the code. Servers and server configurations are defined in server projects.

Creating a server project

To create a new server project:

▶ Select *File -> New -> Project*.

▶ Select *Server* in the left pane and *Server project* in the right pane.

▶ Specify a *Name* for your project and click *Finish*. We will use `ItsoServers` as our project name.

After creating a project, the Server perspective opens and you can now add a server and a server configuration.

Servers

A server identifies the server used to test your application. Unlike VisualAge for Java, Application Developer has the option to deploy to and test with both local and remote instances of the WebSphere application server, and additionally Apache Tomcat. Here is a brief explanation of each of the servers.

WebSphere Version 5.0

This enables the developer to work with an integrated version of WebSphere Application Server Version 5, which supports the entire J2EE 1.3 and 1.2 programming model. This is the best option for testing EJB-based applications. Three options are provided:

- ▶ **Test Environment**—Built-in server inside the Application Developer. Application Developer configures the server to run the projects from the workspace and starts the server in a separate process.

- ▶ **Remote Server**—Stand-alone server on the same or other machine. When the application is executed, Application Developer publishes the code to the external server and attempts to start the server using the IBM Agent Controller service, which is supplied with Application Developer. This feature provides a very efficient approach to remotely deploying an application.

- ▶ **Remote Server Attach**—A server instance that will attach to a WebSphere Version 5 server that is already started.

WebSphere Version 4.0

This enables the developer to work with an integrated version of WebSphere Application Server Advanced Edition Single Server Version 4.0.1, which supports the entire J2EE 1.2 programming model. The same three options as for Version 5.0 are provided.

Apache Tomcat Version 4.0 and 4.1

Tomcat Version 4 has been developed by the Apache group on a completely separate code base from the Version 3.2 release, and is the reference implementation for the Servlet 2.3 and JSP 1.2 specifications.

For more information on Tomcat and the Apache Jakarta project, see `http://jakarta.apache.org`. Application Developer does not ship with the Tomcat binaries, but only a toolkit to support its execution. You must already have a working Tomcat instance installed in order for this to work. Two options are provided:

- ▶ **Test Environment**—Application Developer configures Tomcat to run the projects from the workspace and starts the server in a separate process.

▶ **Local Server**—Stand-alone Tomcat server on the same machine. Permits publishing and execution of the Web application to an external version of Tomcat 4.0. Unlike the WebSphere Remote Server option, this is only supported for a local instance on the same machine.

Apache Tomcat Version 3.2

This release supports the servlet 2.2 and JSP 1.1 specifications. The same two options as for Version 4 are provided.

Publishing Server

The publishing server supports the publishing of static Web projects, as well as J2EE projects such as EAR projects, Web projects, and EJB projects.

Static Web Server

A static Web server is a Web server that runs static Web projects. Use the static Web server for the testing of HTML and Java script files. JSPs and EJBs are not supported.

Remote Application Server Attach

This is a server that will attach to a generic application server that is already started.

TCP/IP Monitoring Server

This is a simple server that forwards requests and responses, and monitors test activity. This runtime environment can only be run locally, and it only supports Web projects. You cannot deploy projects to the TCP/IP Monitoring Server.

Because Tomcat does not have EJB support, you cannot deploy EAR files to it, but only WAR files containing servlets and JSPs.

> **Important:** Before you can do a remote unit test you have to install and run the IBM Agent Controller, which comes with Application Developer, on the remote machine. IBM Agent Controller is a process that runs on the remote machine and which enables client applications to start new host processes.

Server configuration

A server configuration contains the information about the server.

The Server Configuration view of the Server perspective shows the servers and the projects that are assigned to a configuration. The Servers view shows the servers for start and stop operations (Figure 9-22).

Figure 9-22   Server configuration and servers

A server configuration is stored in XML files in the server project. The properties can be set by opening (double-clicking) the configuration in an editor.

A server configuration defines:

▶ Port numbers for the different processes such as the naming service
▶ Mime types
▶ JDBC drivers
▶ Data sources
▶ Security enablement
▶ EJB test client and administrative console enablement
▶ Message listener, queue managers, and queue definitions

Each project has a preferred server configuration that is used when the project is run by selecting *Run on Server* from its context menu (this can be set in the project *Properties -> Server Preference*).

Creating a server and a configuration

In the server perspective, select *New -> Server -> Server and server configuration* and complete the window as shown in Figure 9-23.

In the next window, set the port (default is 8080) and click *Finish*.

The new server appears in the Server perspective and you can assign EAR projects to the server. Those projects will be loaded when the server is started. To assign a project to a server, select the server and *Add -> Project* (context).

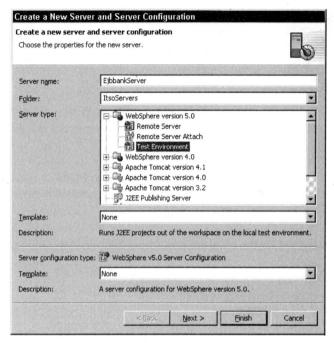

Figure 9-23   Creating a server and server configuration

Server templates

When you have to create several similar servers or configurations, you can create them from a template to save time. You could also share a template across a team so that team members can start personalizing their server configuration or instance starting from a template. To create a template:

▶ Select *Window -> Preferences*.

▶ Expand *Server* on the left pane and select *Templates*.

▶ Click *Add* and specify the server to be stored as a template.

Starting and stopping a server

A server can be started from the Servers view in normal or debug mode. To debug servlets or JSPs at the source level, you must start the server in debug mode. Note that startup and execution is slower in debug mode.

A server can be started explicitly from the Servers view by clicking the *Start* icon. A server can be started implicitly by selecting a Web resource (for example an HTML file) and *Run on Server* or *Debug on Server* (context).

The first time you select *Run on Server* in a Web project, you are prompted to select a server (Figure 9-24). You can bypass this window in the future by selecting *Do not show this dialog the next time*. From then on, the server associated with the Web project is started automatically.

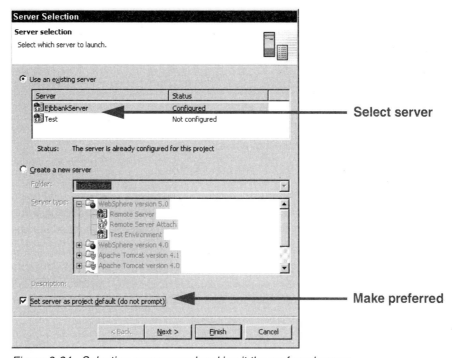

Figure 9-24   Selecting a server and making it the preferred server

Before a server is started, the associated projects are published.

When you are done with testing, you stop the server explicitly from the Servers view. When certain resources are modified (for example EJB definitions), a server must be restarted.

Publishing

Publishing means copying all the resources that are required to test a project to the right place so that the server can find them. In cases when you are testing within the Workbench, the resources might already be at the right place. However, when you are testing with WebSphere Application Server on a local or remote machine, or with Tomcat on a local machine, publishing means to copy the resources outside of the Workbench.

By default, the *Automatically publish before starting server* option is turned on. This option can be found by selecting *Window -> Preferences -> Server*. When this option is turned on, all files and folders on the server are synchronized with the Workbench whenever starting or restarting that server.

You can manually publish by selecting the server in the Servers view of the Server perspective and selecting *Publish* from the context menu.

Remote server

For a remote WebSphere Application Server, you must configure how the files are transferred to the server. The Create a Server window prompts you for:

► The installation directory where the server is installed, for example `C:\WebSphere\AppServer`.

► The platform (*Windows* or *Other*).

► One of two possible transfer mechanisms:

 – Copy file transfer mechanism—You must specify the remote target directory (as seen from the local machine on a LAN drive), for example `X:\WebSphere\AppServer`.

 – FTP file transfer mechanism—You must specify the remote target directory (on the remote machine), the host name, login user ID and password, connection timeout, and optionally firewall settings.

Agent Controller

The IBM Agent Controller is a service that must be installed on the remote machine. The Agent Controller code is provided with the Application Developer for all platforms supported by WebSphere Application Server.

EJB development environment

Application Developer provides a full EJB development environment. We can define EJBs of all types, map container-managed entity EJBs to relational database tables, implement queries using EJB QL, generate deployed code, and test EJBs in a built-in WebSphere Application Server.

The basic sequence of operations when defining and testing EJBs in Application Developer is as follows:

- ► Set up an EJB project
- ► Define EJBs
- ► Add business logic
- ► Optionally define relationships and inheritance
- ► Define finder methods
- ► Map entity beans to relational tables
- ► Generate the deployed code
- ► Test the EJBs in the built-in server using the universal test client
- ► Create client applications

In the chapters that follow, we describe and implement a banking sample application. We will use all the features of the EJB development environment. We develop the sample step-by-step, and at each step generate deployed code and test the EJBs in the server.

- ► Describe the sample application and set up the enterprise application and the server for testing in Application Developer.

- ► Develop container-managed persistence entity beans, including relationships and inheritance.

- ► Develop finder methods using EJB query language.

- ► Describe different mapping approaches for container-managed EJBs.

- ► Develop a bean-managed persistence entity bean.

- ► Develop a stateless and a stateful session bean. Generate a Web service from a session bean.

- ► Describe and generate access beans.

- ► Develop a message-driven bean and a test client.

- ► Develop client applications that use the EJBs. Sample clients include servlets, a Struts application, J2EE clients, and a Web service client.

10

Introducing and preparing for the sample application

In this chapter, we describe the model and database for a banking application. In subsequent chapters, we implement parts of the model as enterprise beans, and parts of the business logic as session beans.

In addition, we prepare Application Developer projects and a server to implement and test the sample application.

© Copyright IBM Corp. 2003. All rights reserved.

Bank model

The ITSO bank model consists of a few entities and relationships (Figure 10-1).

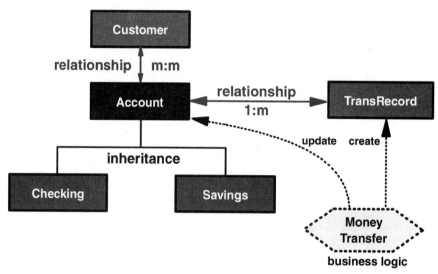

Figure 10-1   Bank model

The entities and relationships in the model are:

Customer   A customer of the bank.

Account   A generic bank account. A customer may have multiple bank accounts and an account may be owned by multiple customers. A bank account is either a checking or a savings account.

Checking   A subclass of the generic bank account.

Savings   A subclass of the generic bank account.

TransRecord A transaction record that is generated for each banking transaction, such as a deposit, withdrawal, or transfer of money between two accounts. A bank account may have many transaction records.

We will implement the entities as enterprise beans. For illustration purposes, we will use container-managed and bean-managed entity beans.

We will also use the advanced features of the IBM EJB product set to implement the inheritance of the bank accounts.

We will implement a money transfer between two accounts as a session bean.

Bank database

The bank model is based on an underlying relational database. The EJBBANK database consists of the tables shown in Figure 10-2.

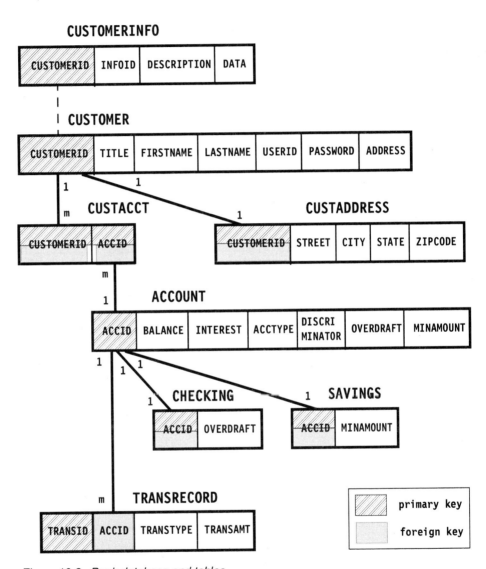

Figure 10-2 Bank database and tables

Tables

All the tables have a primary key. Some tables have a foreign key that relates the table to another table. The data types used in the tables are for illustration and do not represent a real banking system.

Customer table

The CUSTOMER table includes all the information recorded for a bank customer (Table 10-1).

Table 10-1   Customer table

Column name	Type	Length	Key	Nulls	Description
CUSTOMERID	INTEGER		PK	No	Customer ID
TITLE	CHAR	3	No	No	Title
FIRSTNAME	VARCHAR	30	No	No	First name
LASTNAME	VARCHAR	30	No	No	Last name
USERID	CHAR	8	No	Yes	User ID
PASSWORD	CHAR	8	No	Yes	Password
ADDRESS	BLOB	2000	NO	YES	Address object

The address information can be stored either as a BLOB in the CUSTOMER table, or as individual fields in the ADDRESS table. We will explore the mapping of customer entity beans into one table and into two tables.

Customer address table

CUSTADDRESS is a dependent table of CUSTOMER. The CUSTADDRESS table includes the detailed address fields when customer information is mapped into two tables (Table 10-2).

Table 10-2   Customer address table

Column name	Type	Length	Key	Nulls	Description
CUSTOMERID	INTEGER		PK, FK	No	Customer ID
STREET	CHAR	20	No	Yes	Street name, number
CITY	CHAR	12	No	Yes	City
STATE	CHAR	12	No	Yes	State or country
ZIPCODE	CHAR	10	No	Yes	Postal code

The customer address table includes the customer ID as a foreign key, which also serves as the primary key. Therefore, only one entry in the customer address table can point to a matching entry in the customer table.

Account table

Information about bank accounts is spread over three tables. This design enables us to implement an inheritance model with two types of bank accounts, checking and savings.

The ACCOUNT table includes all the information common to both checking and savings accounts (Table 10-3).

Table 10-3   Account table

Column name	Type	Length	Key	Nulls	Description
ACCID	CHAR	8	PK	No	Account ID
BALANCE	DEC	(8, 2)	No	No	Balance
INTEREST	SMALLINT		No	No	Interest rate in percent
ACCTYPE	VARCHAR	8	No	No	Account type (ACCOUNT, CHECKING, SAVINGS)
DISCRIMINATOR	CHAR	1	No	No	Account type (A,C,S)
OVERDRAFT	DEC	(8, 2)	No	Yes	Overdraft amount
MINAMOUNT	DEC	(8, 2)	No	Yes	Minimum amount

The account type (ACCTYPE) column serves as an indicator to the type of account. The DISCRIMINATOR column serves the same purpose and is used in the EJB inheritance model. We use two columns so that the ACCTYPE can be used as an EJB attribute, whereas the DISCRIMINATOR is used to distinguish the EJB types. (The code value A would be a generic account.) We use a trigger to make sure that the two columns are synchronized.

OVERDRAFT and MINAMOUNT are the details of checking and savings accounts and are used if we use only one table (ACCOUNT) for both types of accounts. Alternatively, we can use separate tables for checking and savings accounts.

CHECKING and SAVINGS are dependent tables. Each account is either a checking or a savings account and, therefore, is implemented with a row in the ACCOUNT table and a row in either the CHECKING or SAVINGS table.

Checking table

The CHECKING table contains the fields that are specific to checking accounts, in our case an overdraft limit (Table 10-4). The balance of the account may be negative up to this limit. The ACCID column is a foreign key that points to the row in the ACCOUNT table.

Table 10-4   Checking table

Column name	Type	Length	Key	Nulls	Description
ACCID	CHAR	8	PK, FK	No	Account ID
OVERDRAFT	DEC	(8, 2)		No	Yes	Overdraft amount

Savings table

The SAVINGS table contains the fields that are specific to savings accounts, in our case a minimum balance amount (Table 10-5). The balance of the account must be at least the minimum amount. The ACCID column is a foreign key that points to the row in the ACCOUNT table.

Table 10-5   Savings table

Column name	Type	Length	Key	Nulls	Description
ACCID	CHAR	8	PK, FK	No	Account ID
MINAMOUNT	DEC	(8, 2)		No	Yes	Minimum amount

Transaction records table

The TRANSRECORD table includes the information recorded for successful banking transactions (Table 10-6).

Table 10-6   Transaction records table

Column name	Type	Length	Key	Nulls	Description
TRANSID	TIMESTAMP	26	Yes	No	Transaction ID
ACCID	CHAR	8	FK	Yes	Account ID
TRANSTYPE	CHAR	1	No	No	Transaction type (D = Debit C = Credit)
TRANSAMT	DEC	(8, 2)	No	No	Transaction amount

A deposit transaction generates a record with transaction type D (debit), a withdrawal generates transaction type C (credit), and a money transfer generates a record for each account involved, one with transaction type D (to account) and one with transaction type C (from account).

Important: The foreign key must be defined with NULLS for now, because the EJB 2.0 implementation does not allow for non-nullable keys in 1:m relationships.

Customer-Account table

The CUSTACCT table (Table 10-7) defines the many-to-many relationship between customers and accounts, that is, a customer can own many accounts (for example, a checking and a savings account), and an account can be owned by many customers (for example, husband and wife).

Table 10-7 Customer - account relationship table

Column name	Type	Length	Key	Nulls	Description
CUSTOMERID	INTEGER		PK, FK	No	Customer ID
ACCID	CHAR	8	PK, FK	No	Account ID

Each column is a foreign key pointing to either the customer or the account table. Both columns together form the primary key.

Customer information table

The CUSTOMERINFO table holds additional information about the customer, such as pictures. We will use this table to illustrate a bean-managed persistence entity typo.

Table 10-8 shows the layout of the CUSTOMERINFO table. This table is not linked to the customer table by a foreign key (although it could be).

Table 10-8 Customer information table

Column name	Type	Length	Key	Nulls	Description
CUSTOMERID	INTEGER		PK	No	Customer ID
INFOID	INTEGER		PK	No	Information ID (1,2,...)
DESCRIPTION	VARCHAR	50	No	Yes	Description of information
DATA	BLOB	10000	No	Yes	Binary data

This design allows for one entry of each kind of information. We map the BLOB data to a byte array in Java.

Triggers

To keep the two columns ACCTYPE and DISCRIMINATOR synchronized, we use a set of triggers. These triggers are fired after inserts and updates and set the ACCTYPE column to the correct value based on the DISCRIMINATOR column.

The triggers are shown below:

```
CREATE TRIGGER ITSO.INSERTACCOUNT NO CASCADE BEFORE INSERT
    ON ITSO.ACCOUNT referencing new as ACCT for each row mode db2sql
    BEGIN ATOMIC
      SET ACCT.acctype =
        CASE
          WHEN ACCT.discriminator = 'C' THEN 'CHECKING'
          WHEN ACCT.discriminator = 'S' THEN 'SAVINGS'
          WHEN ACCT.discriminator = 'A' THEN 'ACCOUNT'
        END;
    END


CREATE TRIGGER ITSO.UPDATEACCOUNT NO CASCADE BEFORE UPDATE
  ON ITSO.ACCOUNT referencing new as ACCT for each row mode db2sql
    BEGIN ATOMIC
      SET ACCT.acctype =
        CASE
          WHEN ACCT.discriminator = 'C' THEN 'CHECKING'
          WHEN ACCT.discriminator = 'S' THEN 'SAVINGS'
          WHEN ACCT.discriminator = 'A' THEN 'ACCOUNT'
        END;
    END
```

Database definition DDL

The database objects can be created using the DDL shown in Example 10-1.

Example 10-1   Bank database DDL

```
echo --- create the EJBBANK database ---
CREATE DATABASE EJBBANK

echo --- connect to EJBBANK database ---
CONNECT TO EJBBANK

echo --- drop tables and triggers ---
DROP TABLE ITSO.TRANSRECORD
DROP TABLE ITSO.CUSTACCT
DROP TABLE ITSO.CUSTADDRESS
DROP TABLE ITSO.CHECKING
DROP TABLE ITSO.SAVINGS
DROP TABLE ITSO.ACCOUNT
```

```
DROP TABLE ITSO.CUSTOMER
DROP TABLE ITSO.CUSTOMERINFO
DROP TRIGGER ITSO.INSERTACCOUNT
DROP TRIGGER ITSO.UPDATEACCOUNT

echo --- create tables ---
CREATE TABLE ITSO.CUSTOMER (                                       \
    customerid   INTEGER      NOT NULL,                            \
    title        CHAR(3)      NOT NULL,                            \
    firstName    VARCHAR(30)  NOT NULL,                            \
    lastName     VARCHAR(30)  NOT NULL,                            \
    userID       CHAR(8),                                          \
    password     CHAR(8),                                          \
    address      BLOB(2000),                                       \
                              PRIMARY KEY (CUSTOMERID)             \
)

CREATE TABLE ITSO.CUSTADDRESS (                                    \
    customerid   INTEGER      NOT NULL,                            \
    street       CHAR(20),                                         \
    city         CHAR(12),                                         \
    state        CHAR(12),                                         \
    zipcode      CHAR(10),                                         \
                              PRIMARY KEY (CUSTOMERID)             \
)

CREATE TABLE ITSO.CUSTACCT (                                       \
    customerid   INTEGER      NOT NULL,                            \
    accID        CHAR(8)      NOT NULL,                            \
                              PRIMARY KEY (CUSTOMERID,ACCID)       \
)

CREATE TABLE ITSO.ACCOUNT (                                        \
    accid         CHAR(8)     NOT NULL,                            \
    balance       DEC(8,2)    NOT NULL DEFAULT 0.00,               \
    interest      INTEGER     NOT NULL DEFAULT 5,                  \
    acctype       VARCHAR(8)  NOT NULL DEFAULT 'ACCOUNT',          \
    discriminator CHAR(1)     NOT NULL DEFAULT 'A',                \
    overdraft     DEC(8,2),                                        \
    minamount     DEC(8,2),                                        \
                              PRIMARY KEY (ACCID)                  \
)

CREATE TABLE ITSO.CHECKING (                                       \
    accid         CHAR(8)     NOT NULL,                            \
    overdraft     DEC(8,2)    NOT NULL DEFAULT 200.00,             \
                              PRIMARY KEY (ACCID)                  \
)
```

```
CREATE TABLE ITSO.SAVINGS (                                       \
    accid        CHAR(8)      NOT NULL,                            \
    minamount    DEC(8,2)     NOT NULL DEFAULT 100.00,             \
                              PRIMARY KEY (ACCID)                  \
)

CREATE TABLE ITSO.TRANSRECORD (                                   \
    transid      TIMESTAMP    NOT NULL,                           \
    accid        CHAR(8)             ,                            \
    transtype    CHAR(1)      NOT NULL,                           \
    transamt     DEC(8,2)     NOT NULL,                           \
                              PRIMARY KEY (TRANSID)               \
)

CREATE TABLE ITSO.CUSTOMERINFO (                                  \
    customerid   INTEGER      NOT NULL,                           \
    infoid       INTEGER      NOT NULL,                           \
    description  VARCHAR(50),                                     \
    data         BLOB(10K),                                       \
                              PRIMARY KEY (CUSTOMERID, INFOID)    \
)

echo --- referential integrity ---
ALTER TABLE ITSO.TRANSRECORD                                      \
    ADD CONSTRAINT "AccountTransrecord" FOREIGN KEY (ACCID)       \
    REFERENCES ITSO.ACCOUNT ON DELETE RESTRICT

ALTER TABLE ITSO.CUSTACCT                                         \
    ADD CONSTRAINT "CAtoCustomer"  FOREIGN KEY (CUSTOMERID)       \
    REFERENCES ITSO.CUSTOMER ON DELETE RESTRICT

ALTER TABLE ITSO.CUSTACCT                                         \
    ADD CONSTRAINT "CAtoAccount"  FOREIGN KEY (ACCID)             \
    REFERENCES ITSO.ACCOUNT ON DELETE RESTRICT

ALTER TABLE ITSO.ADDRESS                                          \
    ADD CONSTRAINT "CustAddress"  FOREIGN KEY (CUSTOMERID)        \
    REFERENCES ITSO.CUSTOMER ON DELETE RESTRICT

ALTER TABLE ITSO.CHECKING                                         \
    ADD CONSTRAINT "CheckingAccount"  FOREIGN KEY (ACCID)         \
    REFERENCES ITSO.ACCOUNT ON DELETE RESTRICT

ALTER TABLE ITSO.SAVINGS                                          \
    ADD CONSTRAINT "SavingsAccount"  FOREIGN KEY (ACCID)          \
    REFERENCES ITSO.ACCOUNT ON DELETE RESTRICT

echo --- triggers -------------------
CREATE TRIGGER ITSO.INSERTACCOUNT NO CASCADE BEFORE INSERT                \
```

```
      ON ITSO.ACCOUNT referencing new as ACCT for each row mode db2sql  \
      BEGIN ATOMIC                                                       \
        SET ACCT.acctype =                                              \
          CASE                                                          \
            WHEN ACCT.discriminator = 'C' THEN 'CHECKING'              \
            WHEN ACCT.discriminator = 'S' THEN 'SAVINGS'               \
            WHEN ACCT.discriminator = 'A' THEN 'ACCOUNT'               \
          END;                                                          \
      END

CREATE TRIGGER ITSO.UPDATEACCOUNT NO CASCADE BEFORE UPDATE             \
      ON ITSO.ACCOUNT referencing new as ACCT for each row mode db2sql  \
      BEGIN ATOMIC                                                       \
        SET ACCT.acctype =                                              \
          CASE                                                          \
            WHEN ACCT.discriminator = 'C' THEN 'CHECKING'              \
            WHEN ACCT.discriminator = 'S' THEN 'SAVINGS'               \
            WHEN ACCT.discriminator = 'A' THEN 'ACCOUNT'               \
          END;                                                          \
      END

echo --- execute GRANT statements ---
GRANT CONNECT ON DATABASE          TO PUBLIC
GRANT ALL     ON ITSO.CUSTOMER     TO PUBLIC
GRANT ALL     ON ITSO.ACCOUNT      TO PUBLIC
GRANT ALL     ON ITSO.CHECKING     TO PUBLIC
GRANT ALL     ON ITSO.SAVINGS      TO PUBLIC
GRANT ALL     ON ITSO.TRANSRECORD  TO PUBLIC
GRANT ALL     ON ITSO.CUSTACCT     TO PUBLIC
GRANT ALL     ON ITSO.CUSTADDRESS  TO PUBLIC
GRANT ALL     ON ITSO.CUSTOMERINFO TO PUBLIC

echo --- connect reset ---
CONNECT RESET
```

Database content

The database can be filled with sample data, as shown in Example 10-2.

Example 10-2   Bank sample data

```
echo --- load the EJBBANK database ---

echo --- connect to EJBBANK database ---
CONNECT TO EJBBANK

DELETE FROM ITSO.TRANSRECORD
DELETE FROM ITSO.SAVINGS
```

```
DELETE FROM ITSO.CHECKING
DELETE FROM ITSO.CUSTACCT
DELETE FROM ITSO.ACCOUNT
DELETE FROM ITSO.CUSTADDRESS
DELETE FROM ITSO.CUSTOMER
DELETE FROM ITSO.CUSTOMERINFO

echo --- insert into CUSTOMER tables ---
INSERT INTO ITSO.CUSTOMER                                              \
   (customerid, title, firstname, lastname, userid, password) VALUES  \
   (101, 'Mr', 'Martin',  'Weiss',   'cust101', 'MW'),                \
   (102, 'Mr', 'Lars',    'Schunk',  'cust102', 'LS'),                \
   (103, 'Mr', 'Wouter',  'Denayer', 'cust103', 'WD'),                \
   (104, 'Ms', 'Deborah', 'Shaddon', 'cust104', 'DS'),                \
   (105, 'Ms', 'Unknown', 'Lady',    null,      null),                \
   (106, 'Mr', 'Ueli',    'Wahli',   'cust106', 'UW')

INSERT INTO ITSO.CUSTADDRESS                                    \
   (customerid, street, city, state, zipcode) VALUES           \
   (101, 'A St', 'A Village', 'Switzerland', '11111'),         \
   (102, 'B Bl', 'B City',    'Germany',     '22222'),         \
   (103, 'C Rd', 'C City',    'Belgium',     '33333'),         \
   (104, 'D Ln', 'D Metro',   'Michigan',    '44444'),         \
   (105, 'E Ct', 'E Farm',    'Hawaii',      '55555'),         \
   (106, 'F Av', 'F Town',    'California',  '66666')

echo --- insert into ACCOUNT tables ---
INSERT INTO ITSO.ACCOUNT                                              \
   (accid, balance, interest, acctype, discriminator) VALUES         \
   ('101-1001',   80.00, 4, 'CHECKING', 'C'),                        \
   ('101-1002',  375.26, 5, 'SAVINGS',  'S'),                        \
   ('102-2001', 9375.26, 5, 'SAVINGS',  'S'),                        \
   ('102-2002',   75.50, 3, 'CHECKING', 'C'),                        \
   ('103-3001',  100.00, 6, 'SAVINGS',  'S'),                        \
   ('104-4001',  888.88, 4, 'SAVINGS',  'S'),                        \
   ('104-4002',   88.88, 4, 'CHECKING', 'C'),                        \
   ('105-5001',    0.00, 2, 'CHECKING', 'C'),                        \
   ('106-6001', 1000.00, 3, 'CHECKING', 'C'),                        \
   ('106-6002', 2000.00, 4, 'SAVINGS',  'S'),                        \
   ('106-6003', 3000.00, 6, 'SAVINGS',  'S')

INSERT INTO ITSO.CHECKING     \
   (accid, overdraft) VALUES  \
   ('101-1001',200.00),       \
   ('102-2002',200.00),       \
   ('104-4002',250.00),       \
   ('105-5001',200.00),       \
   ('106-6001',300.00)
```

```
INSERT INTO ITSO.SAVINGS        \
   (accid, minamount) VALUES    \
   ('101-1002',100.00),         \
   ('102-2001',100.00),         \
   ('103-3001',150.00),         \
   ('104-4001',200.00),         \
   ('106-6002',100.00),         \
   ('106-6003',250.00)

echo --- insert into CUSTACCT table ---
INSERT INTO ITSO.CUSTACCT                                   \
   (customerid, accid) VALUES                               \
   (101,'101-1001'), (101,'101-1002'),                      \
   (102,'102-2001'), (102,'102-2002'),                      \
   (103,'103-3001'),                                        \
   (104,'104-4001'), (104,'104-4002'),                      \
   (105,'105-5001'),                                        \
   (106,'106-6001'), (106,'106-6002'), (106,'106-6003'), (106,'105-5001')

echo --- insert into TRANSRECORD table ---
INSERT INTO ITSO.TRANSRECORD                                        \
   (transid,        accid,        transtype, transamt) VALUES \
   (CURRENT TIMESTAMP, '101-1001', 'C',        80.00 )
INSERT INTO ITSO.TRANSRECORD                                VALUES \
   (CURRENT TIMESTAMP, '101-1002', 'D',       200.00 )
INSERT INTO ITSO.TRANSRECORD                                VALUES \
   (CURRENT TIMESTAMP, '102-2001', 'C',      1000.00 )
INSERT INTO ITSO.TRANSRECORD                                VALUES \
   (CURRENT TIMESTAMP, '102-2002', 'D',        70.00 )
INSERT INTO ITSO.TRANSRECORD                                VALUES \
   (CURRENT TIMESTAMP, '103-3001', 'C',       100.00 )
INSERT INTO ITSO.TRANSRECORD                                VALUES \
   (CURRENT TIMESTAMP, '104-4001', 'C',        88.00 )
INSERT INTO ITSO.TRANSRECORD                                VALUES \
   (CURRENT TIMESTAMP, '104-4002', 'C',        88.88 )
INSERT INTO ITSO.TRANSRECORD                                VALUES \
   (CURRENT TIMESTAMP, '106-6001', 'D',        66.66 )
INSERT INTO ITSO.TRANSRECORD                                VALUES \
   (CURRENT TIMESTAMP, '106-6001', 'C',        10.00 )
INSERT INTO ITSO.TRANSRECORD                                VALUES \
   (CURRENT TIMESTAMP, '106-6002', 'C',        66.66 )
INSERT INTO ITSO.TRANSRECORD                                VALUES \
   (CURRENT TIMESTAMP, '106-6003', 'C',      3000.00 )

echo --- insert into CUSTOMERINFO table ---
INSERT INTO ITSO.CUSTOMERINFO                       \
   (customerid, infoid, description,data) VALUES    \
   (101, 1, 'Picture', blob('xxxxxxxxxx')),         \
   (101, 2, 'Scanned image', blob('yyyyyy'))
```

```
echo --- connect reset ---
CONNECT RESET
```

Creating the EJBBANK database and tables

The DDL and SQL statements are provided in the additional material that accompanies this redbook as files ejbbank.ddl and ejbbank.sql. See "Setting up the EJBBANK database" on page 697 for instructions. You can always rerun the commands to restore the database to its initial state..

Preparing Application Developer

To implement the sample banking application, we prepare the environment in Application Developer.

Workspace

We use a separate workspace to implement the sample: d:\WSAD5sg246819, where d is any disk drive on the machine.

To start Application Developer with this workspace, create a copy of the Application Developer icon and add the directory to the target executable using the -data flag:

```
d:\<WSAD-HOME>\wsappdev.exe -data d:\WSAD5sg246819
```

Preparing a J2EE 1.3 enterprise application

Before we start developing EJBs, we prepare a J2EE 1.3 enterprise application with an EJB and a Web project (Figure 10-3).

We start with one EJB module and one Web module. We will add more modules while developing our EJBs and client applications.

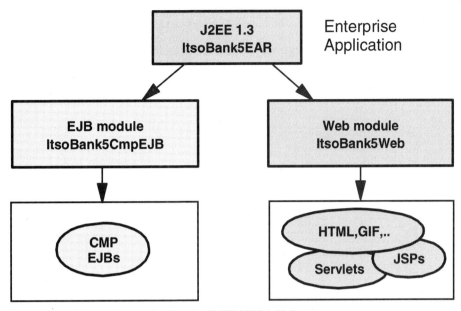

Figure 10-3 Enterprise application for EJBBANK: initial state

Naming convention

We use a naming convention throughout this document:

- ► ItsoBank5EAR—Enterprise application
- ► ItsoBank5XxxxEJB—EJB projects for different types and implementations, where Xxxx stands for Cmp, Bmp, Session, Mdb, and so forth
- ► ItsoBank5Web—Web project for Web-based client applications
- ► ItsoBank5Util—Utility project
- ► ItsoBank5Struts—Web project for a Struts-based Web client
- ► ItsoBank5Client—J2EE application client project
- ► itso.bank5.xxxx—Convention for package names, for example, itso.bank5.cmp for container-managed persistence

Creating the enterprise application

Start the Application Developer with the workspace for this redbook and open the J2EE perspective. All EJB development is done in the J2EE perspective.

Select *File -> New -> Project* (or use the *New* icon). Select *J2EE* in the left pane and *Enterprise Application Project* in the right pane, and click *Next*.

In the J2EE Specification version window, select *Create J2EE 1.3 Enterprise Application project* (Figure 10-4). EJB 2.0 requires the J2EE 1.3 level. Click *Next*.

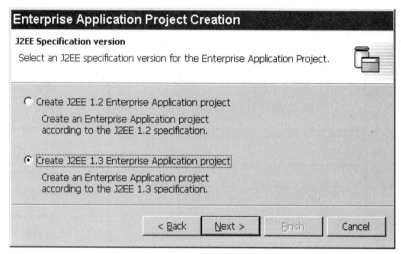

Enterprise Application Project Creation

J2EE Specification version

Select an J2EE specification version for the Enterprise Application Project.

○ Create J2EE 1.2 Enterprise Application project

Create an Enterprise Application project according to the J2EE 1.2 specification.

◉ Create J2EE 1.3 Enterprise Application project

Create an Enterprise Application project according to the J2EE 1.3 specification.

< Back   Next >   Finish   Cancel

Figure 10-4   Selecting the J2EE level

In the Enterprise Application Project window (Figure 10-5):

► Enter ItsoBank5EAR for the enterprise application name.

► Deselect *Application client module*. For now, we do not create stand-alone clients.

► Select *EJB module* and overtype the name with ItsoBank5CmpEJB.

► Select *Web module* and overtype the name with ItsoBank5Web.

► Use the default location for all the modules.

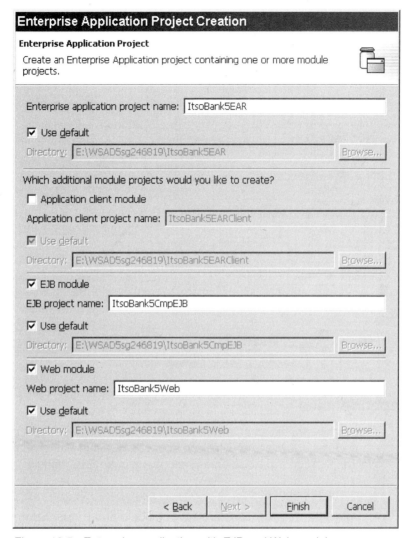

Figure 10-5   Enterprise application with EJB and Web modules

▶ Click *Finish* and the three projects are created.

For details about Application Developer projects, see "Projects" on page 351.

Figure 10-6 shows the J2EE Hierarchy and Navigator views after the creation of the projects.

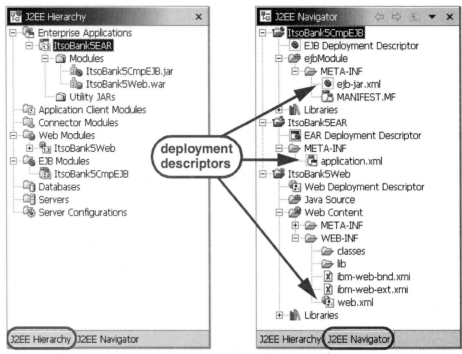

Figure 10-6   Enterprise application views

Module dependencies

The modules within an enterprise application can be dependent on each other. In many cases, the Web modules are dependent on the EJB modules, that is, a Web application accesses enterprise beans in an EJB module.

To set the dependency:

► Select the ItsoBank5Web project or module and *Properties* (from the context menu).

► Select *Java JAR Dependencies* and select the ItsoBank5CmpEJB.jar file. Click *Apply*.

► Select *Java Build Path* and you can see that the ItsoBank5CmpEJB project is selected on the Projects page.

► Close the Properties window.

Preparing the WebSphere test environment

To test the sample application we prepare a WebSphere server within Application Developer.

Server project

Definitions of servers are stored in a server project. To define such a project:

► Select *File -> New -> Project* (or use the *New* icon), *Server* in the left pane and *Server Project* in the right pane, and click *Next*.

► Enter ItsoServers as project name and click *Finish* (Figure 10-7).

► The Server perspective opens.

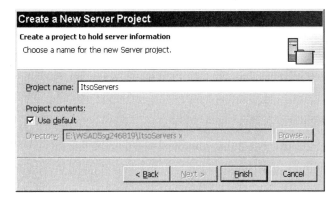

Figure 10-7   Creating a server project

Server

Now we define a WebSphere server for testing of the sample. Because we will use EJB 2.0 beans we must use a Version 5 server for testing:

► Select *File -> New -> Server and Server Configuration* (or use the *New* icon and *Server* in the left pane and *Server and Server Configuration* in the right pane, and click *Next*).

► Enter EjbbankServer as the name. The ItsoServers project is preselected. Expand *WebSphere version 5.0* and select *Test Environment* (Figure 10-8).

► Click *Next*. Check that the port is set to 9080.

► Click *Finish*.

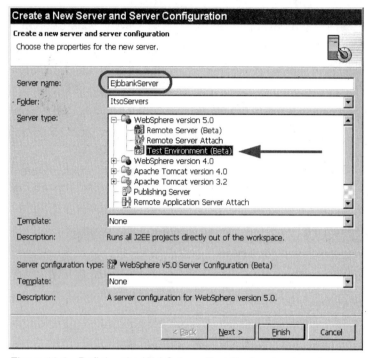

Figure 10-8   Defining the WebSphere Test Environment

Adding the enterprise application to the server

To test the enterprise application we add it to the server:

► In the Server Configuration view, select the EjbbankServer and *Add ->
   ItsoBank5EAR*. The enterprise application and its modules are added to the
   server (Figure 10-9).

Figure 10-9   Adding an enterprise application to a server

Configuring the server with a data source

We will use the `EjbbankServer` to access the `EJBBANK` database using EJBs. We have to configure a data source for this access:

▶ Open the server configuration by double-clicking `EjbbankServer`.

▶ Look through the different pages of configuration information.

▶ Go to the Security page to define a user ID and password for the data source. Click *Add* for JAAS Authentication Entries. Complete the window as shown in Figure 10-10 and click *OK*.

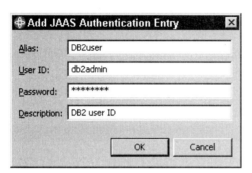

A JAAS alias is required if the container does the authentication of the user ID.

Figure 10-10   Defining a user ID for a data source

▶ The entry appears in the list on the Security page (Figure 10-11).

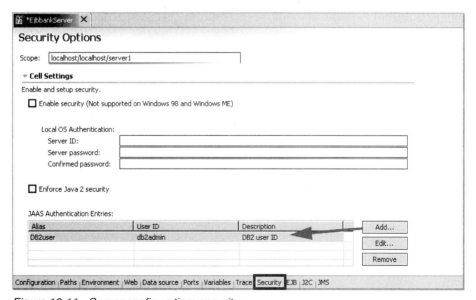

Figure 10-11   Server configuration: security

► Next, go to the Data source page. Note that there are Node Settings and Server Settings. In the test environment we only run one server on one node. Therefore, it does not matter where we define the data source for the EJBBANK database.

► Scroll down to Server Settings and select the *Default DB2 JDBC Provider* entry.

> **Tip:** We could also use an XA-compliant DB2 JDBC driver. This would be required if an application has other resources to be synchronized with the database updates. See "Transaction types" on page 584 for a discussion.

► Click *Add* next to the data source list.

► In the Create a Data Source window, select *Version 5.0 data source* for the type of data source and click *Next*.

► Complete the Modify Data Source window (Figure 10-12).

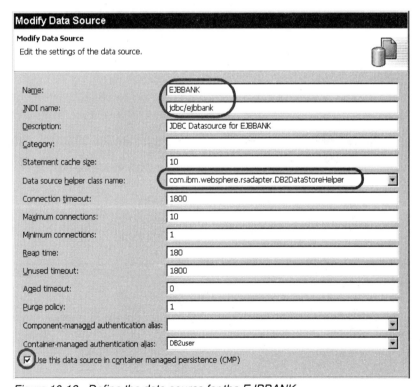

Figure 10-12 Define the data source for the EJBBANK

– Enter EJBBANK as the name to be displayed in the list of data sources.

- Enter `jdbc/ejbbank` as the JNDI name (this is what we will specify in the EJB deployment descriptor to access the database).

- Optionally enter a description.

- Verify the Data store helper class name (`DB2DataStoreHelper`).

- Select the `DB2user` for container-managed authentication alias.

- Check that *Use this data source in container-managed persistence (CMP)* is selected. This is required for EJB access to the database.

- Note that we do not specify the database name anywhere!

- Click *Next*.

► In the Modify Resource Properties window, select the *databaseName* property and change the value to `EJBBANK` (Figure 10-13).

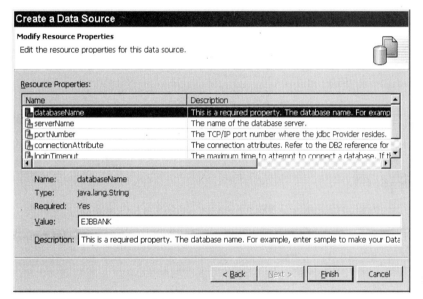

Figure 10-13   Setting the database name

► Click *Finish*.

► The data source is added to the list and displayed in the server configuration (Figure 10-14).

► Save the server configuration and close the editor.

Important: The `db2java.zip` file must be in the system class path. This is done automatically when you install DB2.

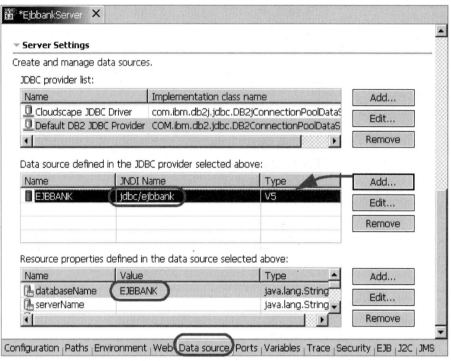

Figure 10-14   Server configuration with data source

Utility project

Utility projects are Java projects containing code that should be available to multiple modules of an enterprise application.

J2EE 1.3 provides support for utility JAR files at the enterprise application level. Such JAR files are then made available to Web and EJB modules as JAR file dependencies.

When we implement session beans with remote interfaces, we will use the home factory pattern described in "Home factory pattern" on page 268. We will implement the HomeFactory class in this utility project in a moment.

Creating a utility project

The utility project is a simple Java project:

► In the Java perspective, select *New -> Project -> Java -> Java Project*. Click *Next*.

► Enter ItsoBank5Utility as the project name and click *Next*.

- ▶ For Java build settings, select *Use source folders contained in the project*. Click *Create new folder*, enter `source` as the name and click *OK*.

- ▶ Click *Yes* in the prompt to update the output folder to `bin`.

- ▶ Select the *Libraries* tab and click *Add variable*. Select the `WAS_50_PLUGINDIR` variable and click *Extend*. Expand the `lib` folder and select the `j2ee.jar` file. Click *OK*.

- ▶ Click *Finish* to create the project.

Adding a utility project to an enterprise application

Java projects such as the `ItsoBank5Utility` project can be added to enterprise applications so that their code is available to the Web and EJB modules:

- ▶ In the J2EE Hierarchy view, open (double-click) the `ItsoBank5EAR` project.

- ▶ In the application deployment descriptor editor, go to the Modules page.

- ▶ Click *Add* under Project Utility JARs.

- ▶ In the Add Utility JAR window, select the `ItsoBank5Utility` project and click *Finish*.

- ▶ Figure 10-15 shows the deployment descriptor with the utility JAR.

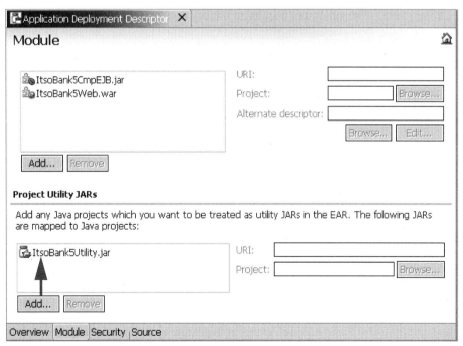

Figure 10-15   Adding a utility JAR to an enterprise application

- ► Save the application deployment desrciptor.
- ► You are prompted that the `EjbbankServer` server configuration must be repaired (Figure 10-16).

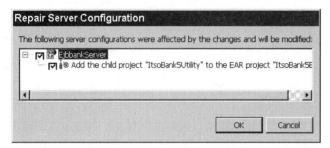

Figure 10-16 Repairing a server configuration

- ► Click *OK* and the utility project is added in the Server Configuration view.
- ► The utility JAR file is now part of the enterprise application and can be made available to the modules.

Implementing the home factory

We implement the home factory in the `ItsoBank5Utility` project:

- ► Select the `source` folder and *New -> Package* (context). Enter *itso.bank5.utility* as the package name and click *Finish*.
- ► Select the new package and *New -> Class* (context). Enter `HomeFactory` as the name, select *Constructors from superclass*, and click *Finish*.
- ► Complete the class with the code shown in Figure 10-17.

This `HomeFactory` class provides access to remote and local EJB homes using EJB references only. It does not provide any caching, as described in "Home factory pattern" on page 268.

A client can use this code to access a remote or local home:

```
try {
    CustomerHome custRemoteHome = (CustomerHome)
                    HomeFactory.singleton().getHome("ejb/CustomerRemote");
    AccountLocalHome accountHome = (AccountLocalHome)
                        HomeFactory.singleton().getHome("ejb/Account");
} catch (NamingException ex) {
    ex.printStackTrace();
    throw new EJBException("Error looking up homes: "+ex.getMessage());
}
```

```
package itso.bank5.utility;
import javax.naming.InitialContext;
import javax.naming.NamingException;
import javax.ejb.EJBHome;
import javax.ejb.EJBLocalHome;

public class HomeFactory {

    static private HomeFactory homefactory = new HomeFactory();
    private InitialContext initialContext = null;

    protected HomeFactory() {
        super();
        try {
            initialContext = new InitialContext();
        } catch (NamingException namingException) {
            namingException.printStackTrace();
        }
    }

    static public HomeFactory singleton() {
        return homefactory;
    }

    public Object getHome(String ejbRef) throws NamingException {
        if (initialContext != null) {
            Object nsObject =
                initialContext.lookup(
                    new StringBuffer("java:comp/env/")
                        .append(ejbRef).toString());
            System.out.println("class=" + nsObject.getClass());
            if (nsObject instanceof EJBLocalHome) {
                System.out.println("ejbRef " + ejbRef + " is a local ref.");
                return nsObject;
            } else {
                EJBHome ejbHome = (EJBHome) javax.rmi.PortableRemoteObject
                    .narrow( (org.omg.CORBA.Object)nsObject, EJBHome.class );
                System.out.println("ejbRef " + ejbRef + " is a remote ref.");
                return ejbHome;
            }
        } else {
            throw new NamingException("HomeFactory: no InitialContext");
        }
    }
}
```

Figure 10-17   Home factory implementation

Module dependency

The `ItsoBank5Web` project will depend on the `ItsoBank5Utility` project to have access to the home factory. To set the dependency:

- ▶ Select the `ItsoBank5Web` project or module and *Properties* (from the context menu).
- ▶ Select *Java JAR Dependencies* and select the `ItsoBank5Utility.jar` file (in addition to the `ItsoBank5CmpEJB.jar` file). Click *OK* to close the Properties window.

Summary

In this chapter, we described the banking scenario that will be implemented in the chapters that follow.

We also prepared Application Developer with the basic project structure for implementing and testing the sample application.

11

Container-managed entity bean development

In this chapter, we discuss the development of container-managed entity beans to implement the sample application presented in Chapter 10, "Introducing and preparing for the sample application" on page 369.

The implementation of the sample model is in three stages:

1. We implement a single CMP to illustrate the development process in detail, then we implement the other CMPs.

2. We implement the relationships as container-managed relationships.

3. We implement the inheritance structure for the account subclasses.

If you want to follow the description provided in this chapter, you must have installed the ITSOBANK database (see "Creating the EJBBANK database and tables" on page 382) and prepared the projects and the server in Application Developer (see "Preparing Application Developer" on page 382).

© Copyright IBM Corp. 2003. All rights reserved.

Developing the account CMP entity bean

We can add a container-managed persistence entity bean to an EJB project in different ways:

► Creating beans with the EJB creation wizard (this is what we will do now).

► Importing a bean from an EJB JAR file. Two typical scenarios where we have to import beans are:

  – We create a relationship with a CMP 2.0 that was developed in another EJB project. Related entity beans have to be part of the same EJB module. See "Developing relationships" on page 435 for details.

  – We derive a bean from a CMP 2.0 that was developed in another EJB project. Parent and child entity beans must be in the same EJB module. See "Developing inheritance structures" on page 447 for details.

► Generating the bean with the EJB-to-RDB mapping tool (bottom-up approach). For a detailed description, see "Bottom-up" on page 470.

CMP development with the Enterprise Bean Creation wizard

The Enterprise Bean Creation wizard shortens the development cycle of EJBs by generating code templates based on our input in the wizard panels.

The development of an EJB includes three steps:

1. We create an EJB with the wizard.

2. The wizard generates the bean class and the component and home interfaces. We describe the output of the wizard in "Generated classes" on page 404.

3. We customize the code and add business logic methods as described in "Adding business logic to the enterprise bean" on page 412.

Creating a CMP entity bean

In this section, we develop the Account CMP 2.0 entity bean of the sample model. We do not describe the development of CMP 1.1 entity beans in this redbook.

Creating a package
We store all the Java code of the CMPs in the itso.bank5.cmp package. To create the Java package, expand the ItsoBank5CmpEJB project in the J2EE Navigator view (in the J2EE perspective), select the ejbModule folder and *New -> Package* (context).

Enter `itso.bank5.cmp` as the name and click *Finish* (Figure 11-1).

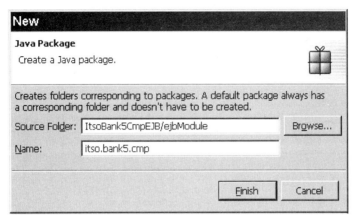

Figure 11-1   Java package creation

Create a CMP 2.0

In the J2EE Hierarchy view, select the `ItsoBank5CmpEJB` project and *New ->*
Enterprise Bean (context). In the first panel, make sure that the project is
preselected. Click *Next* and the Create an Enterprise Bean wizard starts
(Figure 11-2).

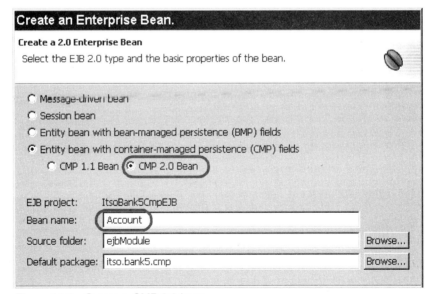

Figure 11-2   Create a CMP 2.0 bean

- ▸ Select *Entity bean with container-managed persistence (CMP) fields* and *CMP 2.0 Bean*.

- ▸ In the Bean name field, enter `Account`.

- ▸ The Source folder field is set to `ejbModule`; otherwise, click the *Browse* button to select the source folder.

- ▸ The Default package is set to `itso.bank5.cmp`; otherwise, click the *Browse* button to select the default package.

- ▸ Click *Next* to display the Enterprise Bean Details panel (Figure 11-3).

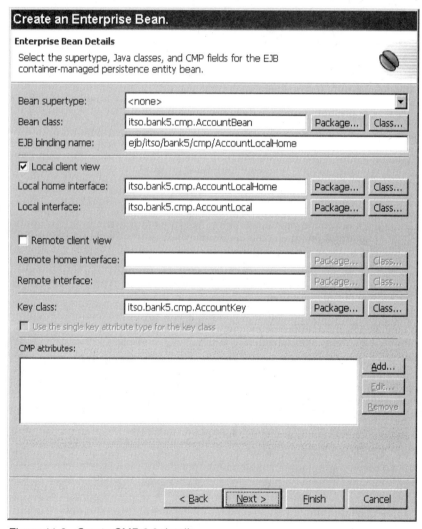

Figure 11-3   Create CMP 2.0 details

- In the Bean supertype drop-down list, accept <none>, because the `Account` entity does not derive from another CMP 2.0 in the same EJB project. CMP 2.0 inheritance is an EJB extension to the specification.

- Accept the names given for the Bean class, EJB binding name, and Key class.

- Accept the selected *Local client view* check box and the names for Local home interface and Local interface.

- Do not select the *Remote client view* check box. For this bean, we do not use the remote capabilities at the entity level (see design considerations in "Using a session facade to entity beans" on page 262).

> **Important:** CMP 2.0 entities in combination with local interfaces yield big performance improvements compared to CMP 1.1. For a detailed discussion, see "Local versus remote interfaces" on page 43.

Create attributes

In the next step, we capture the CMP fields for the `Account` bean. Click *Add* next to the CMP attributes list box and the Create CMP Attribute panel appears (Figure 11-4).

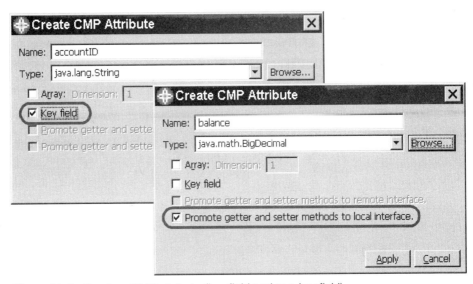

Figure 11-4   Create a CMP attribute (key field and non-key field)

- Define each field as shown in Table 11-1. Enter the field name and the field type. For types that are not in the drop-down list, click *Browse* and enter the first characters of the type, for example, `bigdec` (for `java.math.BigDecimal`).

Table 11-1   List of CMP fields for the account bean

Attribute	Type	Key field	Promote getter and setter to local interface	Promote getter and setter to remote interface
`accountID`	`java.lang.String`	Yes	---	---
`balance`	`java.math.BigDecimal`	No	Yes	---
`interest`	`int`	No	Yes	---
`accountType`	`java.lang.String`	No	yes	---

► Select the *Key field* check box, if the field represents the primary key (or part of it), `accountID` in our sample. For the key field, you cannot select other options. A bean can have more than one key field (*compound key*).

► For non-key fields, select *Promote getter and setter methods to local interface*, if the methods should be exposed to the component interface.

► Click *Apply* and repeat the steps above for all attributes.

► Click *Cancel,* when finished.

Notes:

► The attribute name must begin with a lowercase letter (EJB specification).

► CMP attributes can be Java primitive types, for example, `int`.

► CMP attributes can be primitive wrappers (`Integer`, `Long`, `Double`).

► CMP attributes can be serializable classes that map naturally to fields in relational database (`java.lang.String`, `java.sql.Timestamp`, `java.util.Date`).

► We can also define our own serializable JavaBean and use them as complex fields (dependent value class). In "Implementing a JavaBean for the address information" on page 429, we define the customer address as a JavaBean and assign it to a CMP attribute. Dependent value classes are not exposed by the deployment descriptor and can be mapped to a single database field in a compressed form (BLOB) or to individual columns in a table.

If the key field type is a Java class, for example, `java.lang.String`, select *Use the single key attribute type for the key class*. Such a selection prevents the Application Developer from generating a key wrapper class.

A compound key or a Java primitive (`int`) always requires a wrapper class.

Figure 11-5 shows the CMP attribute list with all the attributes defined and the single key attribute type as key class.

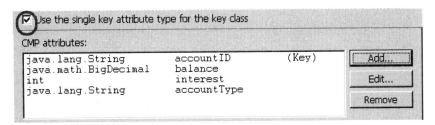

Figure 11-5 CMP attributes list

Click *Next* to open the EJB Java Class Details panel (Figure 11-6).

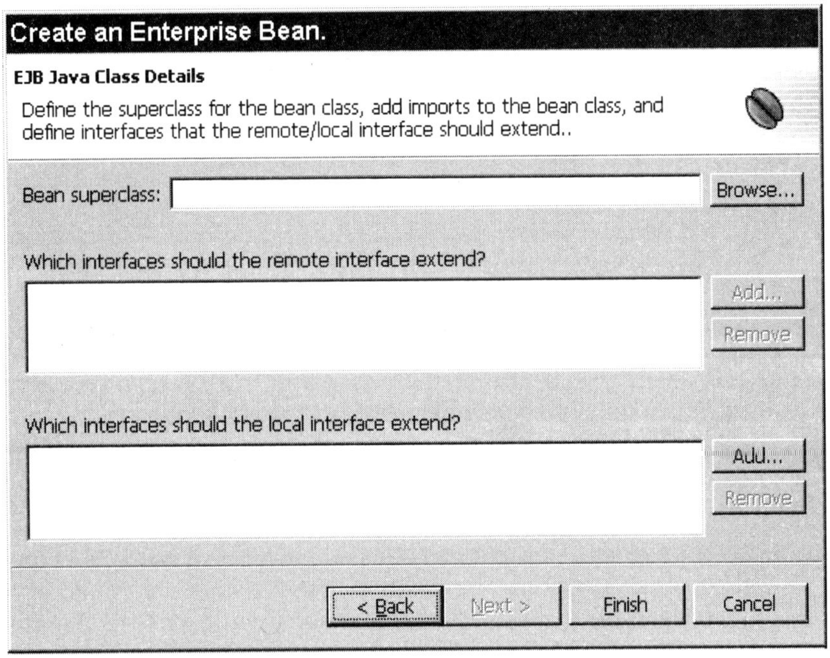

Create an Enterprise Bean.

EJB Java Class Details

Define the superclass for the bean class, add imports to the bean class, and define interfaces that the remote/local interface should extend..

Bean superclass: [   ] Browse...

Which interfaces should the remote interface extend?

[   ] Add...
                                                              Remove

Which interfaces should the local interface extend?

[   ] Add...
                                                              Remove

[< Back] [Next >] [Finish] [Cancel]

Figure 11-6 CMP class details

In our case, no further information is required (no superclass for the bean, no extensions to the component interface).

Click *Finish* to generate the bean class and interfaces.

Generated classes

As a result of the creation process, the Application Developer generates three classes for the account bean:

▶ `AccountBean`—Abstract class that defines the attributes of the bean

▶ `AccountLocalHome`—Home interface with create and find methods

▶ `AccountLocal`—Component interface with methods available to a client

Account bean

The account bean (`AccountBean` class) is an abstract class with default implementations of the `javax.ejb.EntityBean` callback methods and a pair of getter/setter methods for each CMP attribute.

The first part are the callback methods, mostly in the form of empty method bodies. The only interesting method is the `ejbCreate` method, which initializes the attributes of a new entity bean.

The second part are the getter and setter methods:

▶ The getter/setter methods are `public abstract`.

▶ The method names are derived from the attribute name, with the first letter in uppercase and a *get* or *set* prefix:

```
balance ==> getBalance and setBalance
```

Notes:

▶ In contrast to CMP 1.1, the container-managed persistent fields are not defined in the entity bean class. They are *virtual* fields only, and are accessed through get and set methods. The real field definitions are part of the concrete bean class, which will be generated during deployment.

▶ The EJB architecture for container-managed persistence enables a separation between the abstract bean class, which is defined by the bean provider, and its persistent representation, which is part of the deployment process. This allows an entity bean to be redeployed across different containers and different persistent data stores, without requiring the redefinition or recompilation of the entity bean class.

Figure 11-7 shows an extract of the generated code of the bean class. Comments have been removed to fit the code into the figure.

```
package itso.bank5.cmp;

public abstract class AccountBean implements javax.ejb.EntityBean {
    private javax.ejb.EntityContext myEntityCtx;

    public void setEntityContext(javax.ejb.EntityContext ctx) {
        myEntityCtx = ctx;
    }
    public javax.ejb.EntityContext getEntityContext() {
        return myEntityCtx;
    }
    public void unsetEntityContext() {
        myEntityCtx = null;
    }
    public void ejbActivate() {
    }
    public java.lang.String ejbCreate(java.lang.String accountID)
        throws javax.ejb.CreateException {
        setAccountID(accountID);
        return null;
    }
    public void ejbLoad() {
    }
    public void ejbPassivate() {
    }
    public void ejbPostCreate(java.lang.String accountID)
        throws javax.ejb.CreateException {
    public void ejbRemove() throws javax.ejb.RemoveException {
    }
    public void ejbStore() {
    }
// getter and setter methods

    public abstract java.lang.String getAccountID();
    public abstract void setAccountID(java.lang.String newAccountID);

    public abstract java.math.BigDecimal getBalance();
    public abstract void setBalance(java.math.BigDecimal newBalance);

    public abstract int getInterest();
    public abstract void setInterest(int newInterest);

    public abstract java.lang.String getAccountType();
    public abstract void setAccountType(java.lang.String newAccountType);
}
```

Figure 11-7   Generated bean class for a CMP 2.0 (comments removed)

Home interface

Application Developer generates the home interface(s), local and/or remote, depending on the creation settings (see Figure 11-3 on page 400).

Figure 11-8 shows the home interface of the account bean (AccountLocalHome).

```
package itso.bank5.cmp;
/**
 * Local Home interface for Enterprise Bean: Account
 */
public interface AccountLocalHome extends javax.ejb.EJBLocalHome {
    /** Creates an instance from a key for Entity Bean: Account */
    public itso.bank5.cmp.AccountLocal create(java.lang.String accountID)
        throws javax.ejb.CreateException;
    /** Finds an instance using a key for Entity Bean: Account */
    public itso.bank5.cmp.AccountLocal findByPrimaryKey(
        java.lang.String primaryKey)
        throws javax.ejb.FinderException;
}
```

Figure 11-8   Generated local home interface

Component interface

Application Developer generates the component interface(s), local and/or remote, depending on the creation settings (Figure 11-9).

```
package itso.bank5.cmp;
/**
 * Local interface for Enterprise Bean: Account
 */
public interface AccountLocal extends javax.ejb.EJBLocalObject {
    /** Get accessor for persistent attribute: balance */
    public java.math.BigDecimal getBalance();
    /** Set accessor for persistent attribute: balance */
    public void setBalance(java.math.BigDecimal newBalance);

    public int getInterest();
    public void setInterest(int newInterest);

    public java.lang.String getAccountType();
    public void setAccountType(java.lang.String newAccountType);
}
```

Figure 11-9   Generated local component interface

The tool generates getter and setter method pair for CMP attributes where we selected *Promote getter and setter methods to interface* (Figure 11-4 on page 401).

> **Note:** Getter and setter methods, which are exposed in the component interfaces, tightly couple EJB clients with the underlying persistence layer. Defining the interface independently of the persistence model allows the persistence layer to change over time without EJB client implications. To support this independency we could consider not promoting the accessor methods in the interface and implementing our own business logic oriented getter and setter methods.

Primary key class

We do not get a wrapper key class, because we selected *Use the single key attribute type for the key class*. WIthout this selection, Application Developer would generated an `AccountKey` class that wraps the key field(s).

Generated deployment descriptor

Application Developer generates an `<entity>` element into the deployment descriptor (`ejb-jar.xml`). To open the deployment descriptor, double-click the EJB module in the J2EE Hierarchy view or double-click the `ejb-jar.xml` file in the J2EE Navigator view.

The EJB deployment descriptor editor consists of a number of pages:

► The Overview page acts like a summary (Figure 11-10).
► The Beans page lists all EJBs with their attributes, WebSphere bindings (the JNDI name), and the generated classes (Figure 11-11).
► For now we skip the Assembly Descriptor, References, and Access pages.
► The Source page shows the XML source (Figure 11-12).

> **Note:** The type of a container-managed persistent field is not part of the deployment descriptor source. During the deployment process, Application Developer generates the concrete bean class and inspects the accessor methods of the abstract class to determine the types of the instance variables.

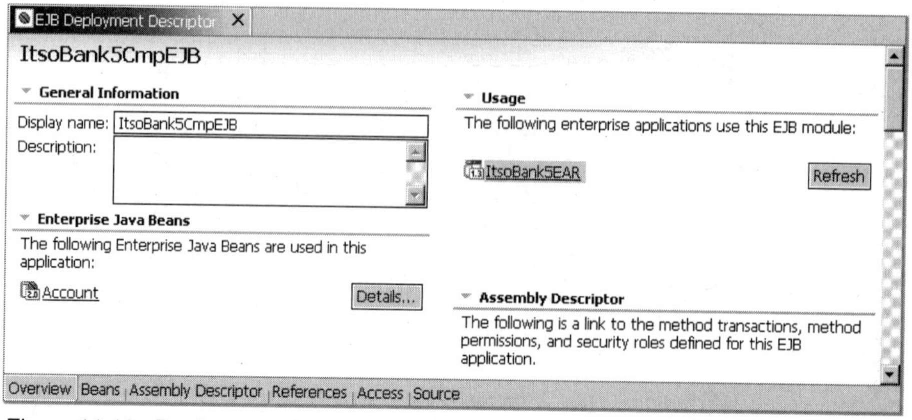

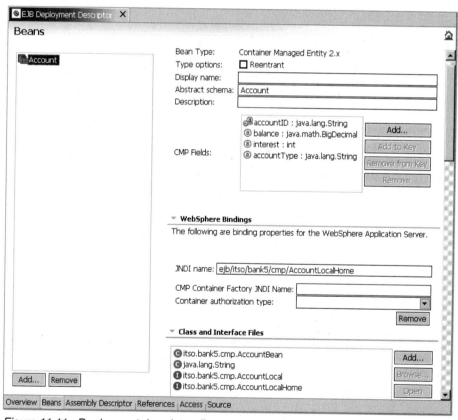

Figure 11-10   Deployment descriptor: Overview

Figure 11-11   Deployment descriptor: Beans

```
<?xml version="1.0" encoding="UTF-8"?>
<!DOCTYPE ejb-jar PUBLIC "-//Sun Microsystems, Inc.//DTD Enterprise
JavaBeans 2.0//EN" "http://java.sun.com/dtd/ejb-jar_2_0.dtd">
<ejb-jar id="ejb-jar_ID">
   <display-name>ItsoBank5CmpEJB</display-name>
   <enterprise-beans>
      <entity id="Account">
         <ejb-name>Account</ejb-name>
         <local-home>itso.bank5.cmp.AccountLocalHome</local-home>
         <local>itso.bank5.cmp.AccountLocal</local>
         <ejb-class>itso.bank5.cmp.AccountBean</ejb-class>
         <persistence-type>Container</persistence-type>
         <prim-key-class>java.lang.String</prim-key-class>
         <reentrant>False</reentrant>
         <cmp-version>2.x</cmp-version>
         <abstract-schema-name>Account</abstract-schema-name>
         <cmp-field>
            <field-name>accountID</field-name>
         </cmp-field>
         <cmp-field>
            <field-name>balance</field-name>
         </cmp-field>
         <cmp-field>
            <field-name>interest</field-name>
         </cmp-field>
         <cmp-field>
            <field-name>accountType</field-name>
         </cmp-field>
         <primkey-field>accountID</primkey-field>
      </entity>
   </enterprise-beans>
</ejb-jar>
```

Figure 11-12 Deployment descriptor: Source

In addition to the `ejb-jar.xml` file, there is also an `ibm-ejb-jar-bnd.xmi` file. This file contains the WebSphere binding information:

```
<?xml version="1.0" encoding="UTF-8"?>
<ejbbnd:EJBJarBinding xmi:version="2.0" xmlns:xmi="http://www.omg.org/XMI"
                                                             ......>
   <ejbJar href="META-INF/ejb-jar.xml#ejb-jar_ID"/>
   <ejbBindings xmi:id="Account_Bnd"
               jndiName="ejb/itso/bank5/cmp/AccountLocalHome">
      <enterpriseBean xmi:type="ejb:ContainerManagedEntity"
                 href="META-INF/ejb-jar.xml#Account"/>
   </ejbBindings>
</ejbbnd:EJBJarBinding>
```

Tailoring the create method

When creating a new bean by calling the `create` method of the home interface, the `ejbCreate` method and the `ejbPostCreate` method with the same method signature are invoked on the bean. The generated `ejbCreate` method of an entity bean only sets the key field:

```
public java.lang.String ejbCreate(java.lang.String accountID)
    throws javax.ejb.CreateException {
    setAccountID(accountID);
    return null;
}
```

Setting only the key field may not satisfy the database requirement for the columns that have a NOT NULL specification and no default value. There are a number of ways to solve the problem:

▶ Set all the attributes to a default value in the `ejbCreate` method. The client or session facade can then use the setter methods to change the default values to good values. The drawback of this approach is that two database calls are issued, an insert (done at `ejbPostCreate`) and an update. The EJB container of WebSphere creates the entity bean when `ejbPostCreate` returns.

▶ Change the `ejbCreate` method to have a parameter for each attribute. However, this practice has a major disadvantage: when adding or removing an attribute, we have to change `ejbCreate`, `ejbPostCreate` and the home interface. And the client code has to be changed as well.

▶ Use a transfer object that carries all the attributes as the single parameter in the `ejbCreate` call. With this solution, we have only one database access (insert). However, we have a dependency between the transport layer and the domain layer.

In this section, we discuss how to modify the `ejbCreate` method to set the rest of the attributes and how to add another create method with more parameters.

Changing the ejbCreate method

The `ejbCreate` method should always be changed to set all the fields. In our case we change the code to:

```
public java.lang.String ejbCreate(java.lang.String accountID)
    throws javax.ejb.CreateException {
    setAccountID(accountID);
    setBalance( new java.math.BigDecimal(0.00) );
    setInterest(0);
    setAccountType("ACCOUNT");
    return null;
}
```

Adding an ejbCreate method

An entity bean can have multiple `ejbCreate` methods with different signatures. For each `ejbCreate` method, matching `ejbPostCreate` methods must be defined.

We enhance the account bean with these methods:

```
public java.lang.String ejbCreate(java.lang.String accountID,
                        java.math.BigDecimal balance, int interest)
    throws javax.ejb.CreateException {
    setAccountID(accountID);
    setBalance(balance);
    setInterest(interest);
    setAccountType("ACCOUNT");
    return null;
}
public void ejbPostCreate(java.lang.String accountID,
                        java.math.BigDecimal balance, int interest)
    throws javax.ejb.CreateException {
}
```

Promoting the new ejbCreate method to the home interface

The new `ejbCreate` method must be promoted to the home interface as a `create` method:

▶ Select `ejbCreate(int,BigDecimal,int)` in the Outline view of `AccountBean` and *Enterprise Bean -> Promote to Local Home Interface* (context).

▶ A matching `create` method is added to `AccountLocalHome`.

> **Important:** If you have an editor open on the class (`AccountLocalHome`), you have to explicitly save the updated interface.

Here are a few points to remember:

▶ If you decide to update the existing `ejbCreate` method with parameters, instead of creating a new method, then you have to promote the changed method to the home interface and explicitly delete the old `create` method from the home interface.

▶ If you choose to have local and remote interfaces, then you have to keep both the local and the remote home interface synchronized with the bean, that is, you have to promote any new or changed `ejbCreate` method to both interfaces.

Adding business logic to the enterprise bean

All the business methods for an enterprise bean are created first in the bean class and then promoted to the component interface in a second step. For our example, we want to add the following methods:

- `deposit`, to add funds to the account balance
- `withdraw`, to remove funds from the account balance

The `withdraw` method will signal an exception if not enough funds are available.

Creating an exception class

First we create the `InsufficientFundException` class that is used to signal a failed withdrawal:

- In the J2EE Navigator view, select the `ejbModule` folder and *New -> Class*.
- Enter `itso.bank5.exception` as package and `InsufficientFundException` as class name.
- For the superclass, click *Browse* and locate `Exception` (in `java.lang`).
- Select *Constructors from superclass* and click *Finish* (Figure 11-13).

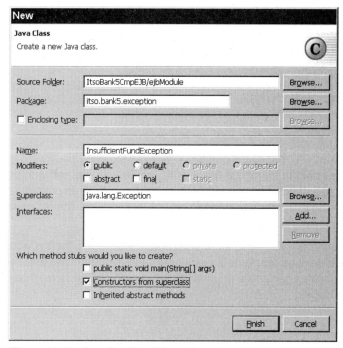

Figure 11-13   InsuffientFundException

Creating business logic methods

Next, we update the bean class (`AccountBean`) with the business methods:

```
// business methods
    /**
     * deposit funds
     */
    public java.math.BigDecimal deposit(java.math.BigDecimal amount) {
        setBalance( getBalance().add(amount) );
        return getBalance();
    }
    /**
     * withdraw funds
     */
    public java.math.BigDecimal withdraw(java.math.BigDecimal amount)
                    throws itso.bank5.exception.InsufficientFundException {
        if ( getBalance().compareTo(amount) == -1)
            throw new itso.bank5.exception.InsufficientFundException
                                            ("Not enough funds");
        else
            setBalance( getBalance().subtract(amount) );
        return getBalance();
    }
```

> **Important:** We use the abstract getter and setter methods to access the value of the persistent balance field.

► Save the changed code (press *Ctrl+S* or click *Save* in the context menu).

Adding methods to the component interface

After the business methods of an enterprise bean are created in the bean class, they can be added to the component interface (local and/or remote).

The generated get and set methods for the CMP fields of the `AccountBean` are already in the local component interface (`AccountLocal`).

For new business methods:

► Select the `deposit` and `withdraw` methods in the Outline view and *Enterprise Bean -> Promote to Local Interface*.

► Application Developer adds the methods to the local component interface.

Note that the *Promote to Remote Interface* selection is disabled because we did not specify to have a remote interface generated.

Deployment

The deployment of a CMP entity bean includes three steps:

▶ Map the CMP fields to a table in a relational database

▶ Generate the deployment code, that is, all the underlying classes that the container uses to instantiate the bean and home and to interact with the relational database

▶ Complete the deployment descriptor with WebSphere specific bindings

Mapping an entity bean to a table

Application Developer offers different mapping strategies, such as top-down, meet-in-the-middle, and bottom-up.

For now we will use the meet-in-the-middle strategy because we have an existing table for account data. For a detailed discussion of mapping, see "Mapping strategies" on page 468.

Meet-in-the-middle mapping

We want to map the AccountBean to the ACCOUNT table in the EJBBANK database:

▶ In the J2EE Hierarchy view, select the EJB project (ItsoBank5CmpEJB) and *Generate -> EJB to RDB Mapping*.

▶ In the EJB to RDB Mapping panel, select *Create a new backend folder* and click *Next*. Application Developer enables us to map an entity bean to multiple back-end stores, for example, different relational database systems (Figure 11-14).

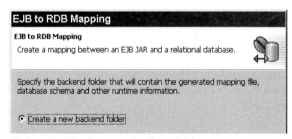

Figure 11-14   Create a back-end folder

▶ In the Create new EJB/RDB Mapping panel, select *Meet In the Middle* and click *Next*.

▶ The Database Connection panel opens (Figure 11-15).

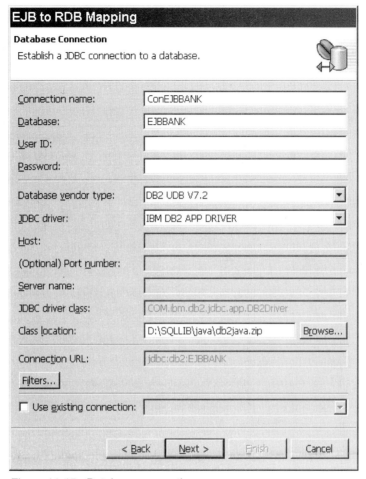

Figure 11-15 Database connection

- Enter any connection name (ConEJBBANK)

- Enter EJBBANK as database name.

- The user ID and password fields can be left empty if your user ID is authorized to the EJBBANK database and tables. Otherwise, use the user ID that was used to install DB2 and to define the EJBBANK database.

- For database vendor, select *DB2 UDB V7.2*.

- For JDBC driver, select *IBM DB2 APP DRIVER*.

- The class location is prefilled if DB2 is installed on your system. Make sure that the location points to the db2java.zip file.

– You can use the *Filters* button to limit the number of table definitions that are imported. In our case, we will use all the tables once we implement the complete model. Therefore, we do not use a filter.

▶ Click *Next* to open the Selective Database Import panel (Figure 11-16). Select the ITSO schema to import all the tables.

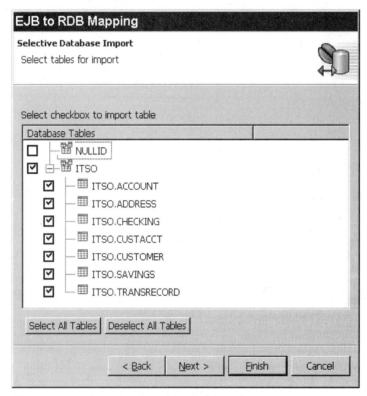

Figure 11-16   Selecting the tables for import

▶ Click *Next* and select *Match by Name* (Figure 11-17). This option should match entities and attributes to tables and columns with the same name.

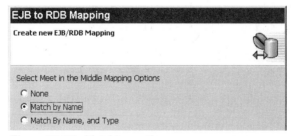

Figure 11-17   Matching options

► Click *Finish* to start the database schema import and to open the mapping editor (Figure 11-18).

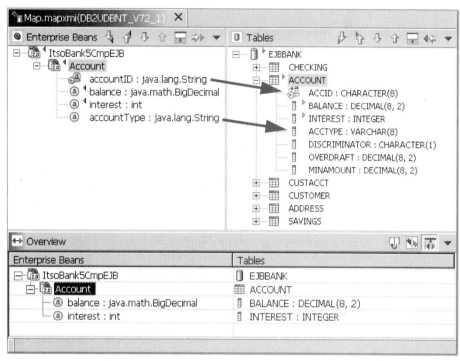

Figure 11-18   Mapping editor

- As you can see, matching by name has already mapped the `Account` bean to the `ACCOUNT` table and the `balance` and `interest` attributes to their respective columns. The mapped items carry a little triangle as an indicator and they are listed in the bottom pane.

- Mapping is performed by drag and drop. If we had not matched by name, we would drag the `Account` bean to the `ACCOUNT` table, and then drag the attributes to the columns. Drag and drop can be done left-to-right or right-to-left. A bean must be mapped to a table before you can map the attributes of the bean to the columns.

- You can also select an item in the left pane and in the right pane and *Create Mapping* (context). This is the same as drag and drop.

- For our example, we complete the mapping by dragging `accountID` to `ACCID` and `accountType` to `ACCTYPE`.

- Note the icons that enable you to navigate between items and to change the layout of the panes.

► The Outline view of the mapping editor summarizes our mapping activities (Figure 11-19).

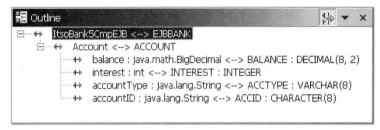

Figure 11-19 Outline view of the mapping editor

► Save the mapping (press *Ctrl+S*) and close the editor.

Back-end folder

Application Developer creates a back-end folder in the EJB project folder, `ejbModule\META-INF\backends\DB2UDBNT_V72_1` in our sample, with a number of files (Figure 11-20).

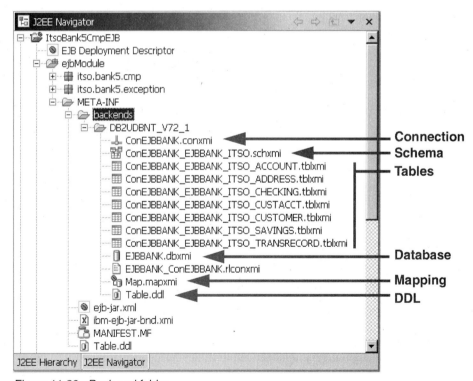

Figure 11-20 Back-end folder

Application Developer creates a separate XMI file for each imported table definition (.tblxmi), together with one for the schema (.schxmi) and one for the database (.dbxmi). The mapping information is stored in the Map.mapxmi file. The Table.ddl file includes the DDL for the table definitions.

Generating the deployed code

The last step is generating the deployed code for the container. This should only be done when all the definitions are complete:

▶ Create method(s) defined and promoted to the home interface

▶ Business logic methods defined and promoted to the component interface(s)

▶ Mapping completed

▶ Finder methods defined and added to the home interface

We will implement finder methods later when the model is complete, and then regenerate the deployed code (see "Developing custom finders" on page 455). For now we want to describe the generation process and then test the simple bean.

Code generation

To generate the deployed code, select the ItsoBank5Cmp project and *Generate -> Deployed and RMI Code*. In the generation window, select the Account bean and click *Finish*.

This option launches the command-line ejbdeploy tool to generate the deployed code. When generation is complete, expand the ejbModule folder to explore the generated code (Figure 11-21):

▶ In the EJB package (itso.bank5.cmp), you find:

    — ConcreteAccount_xxx, the concrete bean class, which extends our abstract AccountBean class. The concrete bean class provides an implementation of the abstract getters and setters.

    — EJSLocalCMPAccount__xxx, the local EJB object, which wraps the ConcreteAccountBean class and intercepts each method invocation to enable EJB container services for the bean. The class implements the itso.bank5.cmp.AccountLocal interface.

    — EJSCMPAccounHomeBean_xxx, the EJB home class, and EJSLocalCMPAccountHome_xxx, which wraps the home class and implements the itso.bank5.cmp.AccountLocalHome interface to act as a method interceptor to enable EJB container services for the home.

Figure 11-21　Deployed code of the account bean

▶ In addition, the deployment tool creates two packages with deployed code:

- itso.bank5.cmp.websphere_deploy—WebSphere internal interfaces
- itso.bank5.cmp.websphere_deploy.DB2UDBNT_V72_1—Data store specific helper classes that implement the WebSphere internal interfaces

Completing the deployment descriptor

Before we can test the entity bean, we have to update the deployment descriptor with WebSphere-specific binding information:

▶ In the J2EE Hierarchy view, double-click the ItsoBank5CmpEJB module (or select Open With -> Deployment Descriptor Editor (context).

▶ In the Overview pane of the deployment descriptor editor (Figure 11-22), we add two values for the CMP Factory Connection Binding:

- For the JNDI name, enter jdbc/ejbbank. This is the JNDI name we used for the data source definition during the setup of the WebSphere Test Environment (see "Preparing the WebSphere test environment" on page 387).

- For the Container authorization type, select *Per_Connection_Factory*.

▶ Check that the correct current Backend ID is selected (DB2UDBNT_V72_1).

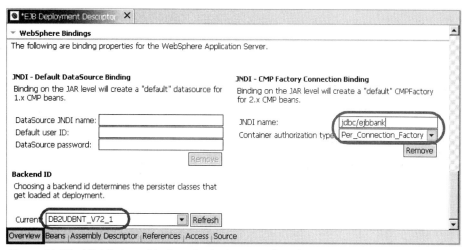

Figure 11-22   WebSphere bindings in deployment descriptor

For our first test activities, we do not have to change other properties of the deployment descriptor.

Testing the enterprise bean

In "Preparing the WebSphere test environment" on page 387 we discussed how to set up a server for testing.

Now we can start the WebSphere test environment and test the EJB:

▶ In the Servers view of the Server perspective, start the EjbbankServer and wait until the server is ready. The Console view opens and you should see that the data source is allocated, the Web and EJB modules are loaded, and the message *Server server1 open for e-business* is displayed.

▶ Select the ItsoBank5CmpEJB project and *Run on Server* (context).

▶ In the Server Selection window, make sure that the EjbbankServer is preselected as the existing server. Select *Do not show this dialog next time (set this server as the preferred server)* and click *Finish*.

▶ The universal test client launches and we can test the entity bean.

Universal test client

In this section, we describe some of the operations you can perform with the universal test client.

We will use the test client to find the `Account` EJB home, find and create instances of the `Account` bean, and perform methods on those instances.

Home page

Figure 11-23 shows the home page of the test client as it appears in a browser window after selecting an EJB project and *Run on Server*.

The test client can also be started from the Servers view by selecting a server and *Run universal test client* (context). The URL of the test client is:

```
http://localhost:9080/UTC/
```

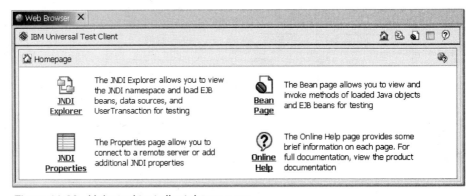

Figure 11-23   Universal test client: home page

The two main pages to work with are the JNDI Explorer and the Bean page. The JNDI Explorer is used to locate EJBs and the Bean Page is used to work with EJBs and JavaBeans.

JNDI Explorer

Click *JNDI Explorer* to display the JNDI Explorer page (Figure 11-24).

After expanding *[Local EJB beans]* and *jdbc* you can see:

▶ `AccountLocalHome`—The home interface of the `Account` EJB. The JNDI name `ejb/itso/bank5/cmp/AccountLocalHome` was assigned to the bean by Application Developer in the deployment descriptor (see Figure 11-11 on page 408).

▶ `jdbc/ejbbank`—The data source assigned to the `EJBBANK` database.

Figure 11-24   Universal test client: JNDI Explorer

To work with the `Account` EJB, we click `AccountLocalHome`, which brings us to the Beans page.

Beans page

The Beans page shows EJB References (homes and components), Object References (any objects that are used and saved during the session), Class References (classes that are loaded explicitly), and Utilities (various functions, such as load a class, cast an instance).

In the JNDI explorer, we selected the `AccountLocalHome`, and therefore it shows up under EJB References once we expand that section (Figure 11-25).

The `create` and `findByPrimaryKey` methods of the home interface are visible under the account home. In addition, the `remove` method is visible.

Click *Method Visibility* and you can see from which superclasses and interfaces the methods are inherited, and which ones are selected to be displayed for the account home.

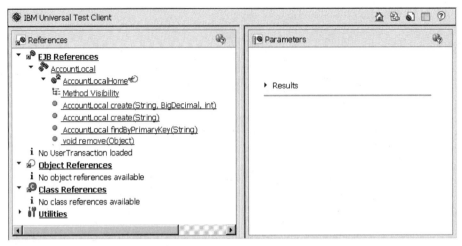

Figure 11-25   Universal test client: EJB home

To find an EJB instance, select the findByPrimaryKey method. Expand the
parameter, enter a valid account number (101-1001), and click *Invoke*.

The EJB is instantiated from the table data and shows up in the results section.
Click *Work with Object* to add the EJB instance under EJB References
(Figure 11-26).

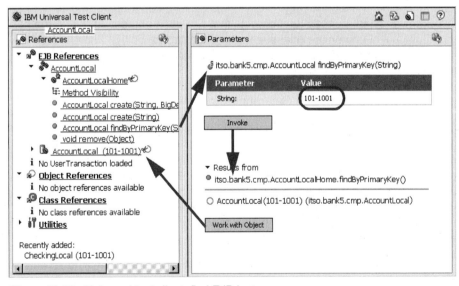

Figure 11-26   Universal test client: find EJB instance

Expand the AccountLocal instance, select the getBalance method, and click *Invoke*. The balance value is shown under results. Click *Work with Object* to save that BigDecimal object for later use (Figure 11-27).

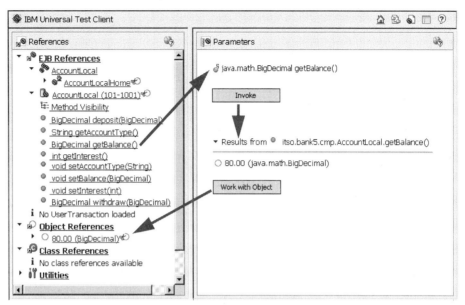

Figure 11-27   Universal test client: invoke a bean method

Next, select the deposit method, which requires a BigDecimal parameter (Figure 11-28).

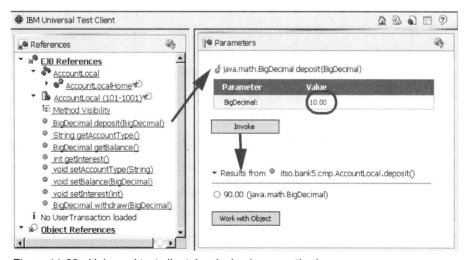

Figure 11-28   Universal test client: invoke business method

Try the `withdraw` method with a large value and you will receive the
`InsufficientFundException` (Figure 11-29).

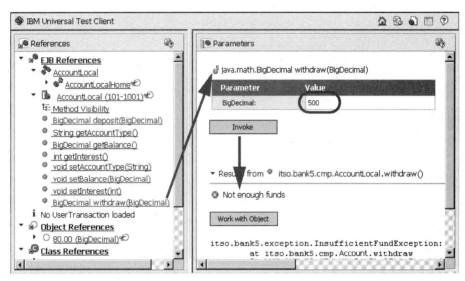

Figure 11-29   Universal test client: business method exception

Next, we create a new account. Select the `create(String)` method of the home.
Enter a new account number (`101-1111`) and click *Invoke*. The instance is created
and appears in the results section. Click *Work with Object* to add the instance to
the EJB References (Figure 11-30).

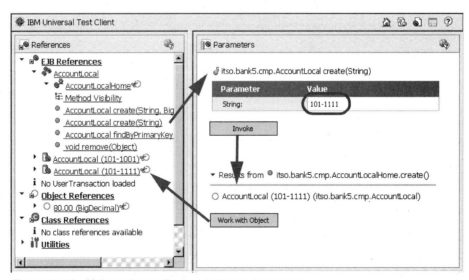

Figure 11-30   Universal test client: create a new account

Expand the new account bean and run some of the get methods. You can see that the balance is 0, the interest is 0, and the account type is ACCOUNT.

These are the default values that we added to the ejbCreate method (see "Changing the ejbCreate method" on page 410).

We can use the set methods to change the default values.

> **Important:** When you use the setAccountType method to change the account type and then retrieve it using getAccountType, you notice that the type is still ACCOUNT. This is because of the database trigger that makes sure that the account type is consistent with the DISCRIMINATOR column.
>
> We will be able to create other account types only when we implement the inheritance structure.

Next, select the tailored ejbCreate method with three parameters. Enter values for the accountID, balance, and interest and click *Invoke*. Click *Work with Object* to save the new account (Figure 11-31).

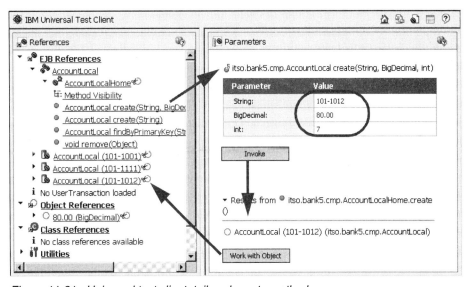

Figure 11-31   Universal test client: tailored create method

Use a DB2 command window to verify that the instances were added to the database. Enter these commands to list the ACCOUNT table:

```
db2 connect to ejbbank
db2 select * from itso.account
```

To remove the new account instances, expand the instance, select the remove method and click *Invoke*. This deletes the account EJB and also the row in the ACCOUNT table. The remove method is inherited from the EJBLocalObject interface.

To remove unwanted objects from the universal test client pane, click the scissor icon ✂ that is displayed next to the object name.

This concludes the tour of the universal test client. Close the browser and stop the EjbbankServer in the Servers view.

Developing the customer and transaction record EJBs

In this section, we develop the customer and transaction record CMP entity beans.

Customer EJB

Table 11-2 shows the attributes of the customer bean. To illustrate that an entity bean can have a local and a remote interface, we will implement both.

Table 11-2   List of CMP fields for the customer bean

Attribute	Type	Key field	Local interface	Remote interface
customerID	int	Yes	---	--
firstName	java.lang.String	No	Yes	Yes
lastName	java.lang.String	No	Yes	Yes
title	java.lang.String	No	Yes	Yes
userID	java.lang.String	No	Yes	Yes
password	java.lang.String	No	Yes	Yes
address	itso.bank5.beans.Address	No	Yes	Yes

Notice the address attribute; it refers to a JavaBean that holds the detailed address information. We will map this attribute to a BLOB column in the CUSTOMER table. In "Mapping a dependent value class" on page 479, we implement a mapping into a separate CUSTADDRESS table.

Implementing a JavaBean for the address information

Before we implement the customer EJB, we have to define the address bean with its properties `street`, `city`, `state`, and `zipcode`:

► In the `ItsoBank5CmpEJB` project, create a new `itso.bank5.beans` package under `ejbModule` (see "Creating a package" on page 398).

► In the new package, create a class named `Address`:

– Select the package and *New -> Class* (context).

– Enter `Address` as name.

– Click *Add* for Interfaces, enter `serial`, select `java.io.Serializable`, click *OK*.

– Select none of the method stubs.

– Click *Finish*.

► The editor opens the class. Add four fields:

```
private String street;
private String city;
private String state;
private String zipcode;
```

► Select the four fields in the Outline view and *Generate Getter and Setter* (context). Click *OK* to generate the getter/setter methods.

► Add a constructor with four parameters:

```
public Address(String aStreet,String aCity,String aState,String aZipcode) {
    street  = aStreet;
    city    = aCity;
    state   = aState;
    zipcode = aZipcode;
}
```

► Save the class and close the editor.

Implementing the customer EJB

Follow the process described in "Creating a CMP entity bean" on page 398 to create the customer CMP entity bean:

► Use the same `itso.bank5.cmp` package.

► The name of the bean is `Customer`.

► Select *Local client view* and *Remote client view*.

- Add the attributes of Table 11-2 on page 428. For the `address` attribute, select `itso.bank5.beans.Address` as type. Promote the attributes to the remote and local interfaces.

- Note that you cannot select *Use the single key attribute type for the key class.*

Generated classes

The generated classes are:

`CustomerBean`—the abstract bean
`CustomerHome`—remote home interface
`Customer`—remote component interface
`CustomerLocalHome`—local home interface
`CustomerLocal`—local component interface
`CustomerKey`—wrapper class for the key

Key wrapper class

The wrapper class for the key attributes contains the key value. The key class is required in the `findByPrimaryKey` method and to retrieve the key value of a bean:

```
Customer customer = home.findByPrimaryKey( new CustomerKey(101) );
int keyvalue = ( (CustomerKey)customer.getPrimaryKey() ).getCustomerID();
```

Create method

Update the generated `ejbCreate` method to initialize all the fields:

```
public itso.bank5.cmp.CustomerKey ejbCreate(int customerID)
    throws javax.ejb.CreateException {
    setCustomerID(customerID);
    setFirstName("");
    setLastName("");
    setTitle("");
    setUserID("");
    setPassword("");
    setAddress(null);
    return null;
}
```

We do not add a tailored `ejbCreate` method with parameters.

Business logic

We add a business logic method to the customer bean to retrieve the full name of a customer, such as *Mr. First Last*. Use this code:

```
public String getName() {
    return new StringBuffer( getTitle() ).append(" ")
                .append( getFirstName() ).append(" ")
                .append( getLastName() ).toString();      }
```

Promote the `getName` method to both the remote and local interface. Select the method in the Outline view and *Enterprise Bean -> Promote to ...* (context).

Transaction record EJB

Table 11-3 shows the attributes of the transaction record bean. We only implement the local interface for this EJB because the data will only be retrieved as part of an account through the relationship.

Table 11-3 List of CMP fields for the transaction record bean

Attribute	Type	Key field	Local interface	Remote interface
transID	java.sql.Timestamp	Yes	---	--
transType	java.lang.String	No	Yes	--
transAmount	java.math.BigDecimal	No	Yes	--

Notice that we do not define the foreign key (`accountID`) as an attribute. This field will be used when we define the relationship between account and transaction record.

Implementing the transaction record EJB

Follow the process described in "Creating a CMP entity bean" on page 398 to create the customer CMP entity bean:

► Use the same `itso.bank5.cmp` package.

► The name of the bean is `TransRecord`.

► Select *Local client view* only.

► Add the attributes of Table 11-3 on page 431. Promote the attributes to the local interface.

► Be sure to select *Use the single key attribute type for the key class*.

Generated classes

The generated classes are:

`TransRecordBean`—the abstract bean
`TransRecordLocalHome`—local home interface
`TransRecordLocal`—local component interface

Create method

The generated `ejbCreate` method takes a `Timestamp` as parameter. This is not useful in a client application because we want to have the actual time of the transaction inserted and the type and amount provided by the business logic. In addition, the `Timestamp` values must be unique for the primary key of the table.

Change the `ejbCreate` method to this code:

```
// new field in the TransRecordBean class
private java.util.Random random = new java.util.Random();

public java.sql.Timestamp ejbCreate(String type,
                                    java.math.BigDecimal amount)
            throws javax.ejb.CreateException {
    java.sql.Timestamp ts = new
                         java.sql.Timestamp(System.currentTimeMillis());
    ts.setNanos( ts.getNanos() + random.nextInt(999999) );
    setTransID(ts);
    setTransType(type);
    setTransAmount(amount);
    return null;
}
```

Be sure to update the signature of the matching `ejbPostCreate` method:

```
public void ejbPostCreate(String type, java.math.BigDecimal amount)
    throws javax.ejb.CreateException { }
```

Promote the `ejbCreate` method to the local home interface from the Outline view. Open the `TransRecordLocalHome` class and delete the old `create` method.

Mapping the customer and transaction record beans

We have to map the new entity beans to their matching tables. To open the mapping editor, select the `ItsoBank5CmpEJB` module and *Open With -> Mapping Editor -> DB2UDBNT_V72_1*.

Complete the mapping as shown in Figure 11-32:

▶ Drag the `Customer` bean to the `CUSTOMER` table.

▶ Drag the customer attributes to their columns.

▶ Drag the `TransRecord` bean to the `TRANSRECORD` table.

▶ Drag the transaction record attributes to their columns.

▶ Note that the `ACCID` column in `TRANSRECORD` is not mapped. This is the foreign key and we will take care of this through a relationship. The relationship also shows up as "AccountTransrecord" : ACCOUNT in the `TRANSRECORD` table.

▶ Save the mapping when done.

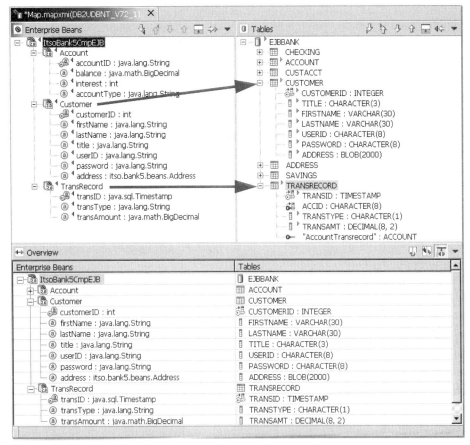

Figure 11-32 Mapping of customer and transaction record

Generate the deployed code

Select the `ItsoBank5CmpEJB` module and *Generate -> Deploy and RMIC Code*.
You can select all the beans or just the `Customer` and `TransRecord` beans (we did
not change the `Account` bean).

Testing the EJBs in the universal test client

Start the `EjbbankServer` and the universal test client to test the `Customer` and
`TransRecord` beans. Here are a few hints on how to proceed:

▶ In the JNDI explorer, you find the local homes by expanding *[Local EJB
beans] -> ejb -> itso -> bank5 -> cmp*.

- ▶ You find the remote home for the `Customer` bean by expanding *ejb -> itso -> bank5 -> cmp*.

- ▶ You can use local and remote homes to retrieve entity beans.

- ▶ To retrieve a customer, select the `findByPrimaryKey` method, then expand the `CustomerKey`, enter a key value (for example 101), and click *Invoke*. Click *Work with Object* to access the Customer object.

- ▶ Use the get methods to retrieve the customer data. For example, the `getName` method should format the `title`, `firstname`, and `lastname`.

- ▶ Note that all the `getAddress` method retrieves null values. The database does not have any data initialized in the `ADDRESS` column, which is a BLOB.

- ▶ To create a customer with an address stored in the `table`:
  - − Retrieve a `Customer` as described above, then click *Work with Object*.
  - − Expand the `Customer` object and select the `setAddress` method.
  - − For the parameter, expand the Address parameter, enter four string values for street, city, state, and zipcode, then click *Invoke*.
  - − The `Address` object is stored in the `ADDRESS` column. You can check this with this DB2 select statement in a DB2 command window:

    ```
    db2 select length(address) from itso.customer
    ```

- ▶ You can create a `TransRecord` bean. Exapnd the parameter, enter `C` as `transType`, 15.00 as the `transAmount`, and select `null` for the `AccountLocal`. Note that the foreign key (`ACCID` column) will be `NULL` and this transaction record will not belong to an account.

- ▶ Retrieving an existing `TransRecord` bean is almost impossible because our `ejbCreate` method adds a nanosecond value to the key to be unique. The full key value is not displayed in a DB2 command window.

- ▶ To see the properties of an `Address` object:
  - − Select and execute the `getAddress` method on a `Customer` object.
  - − Click *Work with Object* and the `Address` object is added under Object References.
  - − Expand the `Address` object and invoke the get methods to see the values of the properties.

Close the universal test client and stop the `EjbbankServer`.

Developing relationships

In this section, we add the two relationships of the bank model (Figure 11-33) as container-managed relationships (CMR) to the existing CMP entity model.

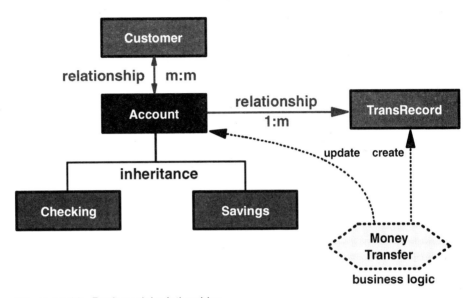

Figure 11-33   Bank model relationships

In "Developing inheritance structures" on page 447, we implement the inheritance hierarchy; for now we are implementing the relationships between the entity beans.

Support for relationships in Application Developer

Application Developer supports the creation of three types of relationships as CMR.

One-to-one (1:1) relationship

In such a case, usually one of the entity beans is the master and the other is a dependent of the master (although they could be equal in importance and independent as well).

In the database, such a relationship is implemented as a foreign key in one of the tables. To enforce that each foreign key points to another instance in the target table, a unique index must be defined on the foreign key.

Our model does not show a 1:1 relationship. However, we could implement the Address as a separate entity that is related by a 1:1 relationship from the Customer entity.

One-to-many (1:m) relationship

An entity instance of one type is related to many entity instances of a second type, but each of the instances of the second type is related to only one instance of the first type. In many real cases, this is a parent-child composition structure, that is, the second entity type is a subordinate and instances can only exist if they have a parent instance in the first type.

In the database, such a relationship is implemented as a foreign key in the table of the second type.

In our model, Account-TransRecord is a 1:m relationship. One account can have many transaction records.

Many-to-many (m:m) relationship

Two independent entity types are related, and an instance of each type can be related to many instances of the other type.

In the database, such a relationship is implemented as an intermediate table that contains two foreign keys, each pointing to the table of one of the related entities. The intermediate table does not contain any other data; otherwise the model should have an entity to map to that table.

In our model, Customer-Account is an m:m relationship. A customer can have many accounts and an account can belong to many customers. The intermediate table is called CUSTACCT in the EJBBANK database.

Relationship roles

A role is assigned to a relationship in each direction. These role names become the method names (with a *get* prefix) to traverse the relationship from one entity instance to another.

Navigation and CMR fields

Each direction of a relationship can be marked as *Navigable*. For a navigable relationship, a CMR field is generated into the bean.

The type of the CMR field is either the target entity bean type (in the :1 direction), or either a java.util.Collection or java.util.Set (in the :m direction). A Collection or Set holds all the target instances.

Deployment descriptor

Relationships are defined in the deployment descriptor using the deployment descriptor editor. Click *Add* for Relationships 2.0 in the Overview page (Figure 11-34).

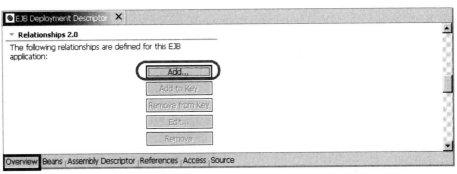

Figure 11-34   Adding relationships in the deployment descriptor editor

Alternatively there is also an *Add* button for relationships in the Beans page after selecting an entity bean.

From the deployment descriptor, the deployed code is generated.

Defining the account to transaction record relationship

Now let us define the 1:m relationship between accounts and transaction records:

► Click *Add* to open the Add Relationship window. In the first panel, select the two entity beans, Account and TransRecord, then click *Next* (Figure 11-35).

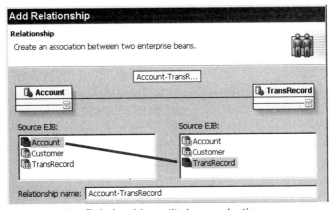

Figure 11-35   Relationship: entity bean selection

- ► In the Relationships Roles panel (Figure 11-36):
  - For the `Account` bean, set the role name to `transrecords` (to indicate many), leave multiplicity at *One* (one account), leave the CMR field the same as the role name, and set the CMR type to `Collection`.
  - For the `TransRecord` bean, set the role name to `theAccount` (to indicate one), set multiplicity to *Many* (many transaction records), and leave the CMR field the same as the role name.
  - Set both directions to *Navigable*.
  - Select *Cascade delete* to delete all transaction records when an account is deleted.
  - The *Foreign key* check box is selected and disabled. A 1:m relationship requires a foreign key in the table of the singled-value entity bean and no foreign key option setting is available. In a 1:1 relationship, you have to indicate on which side of the relationship the foreign key exists.
  - Click *Finish*.

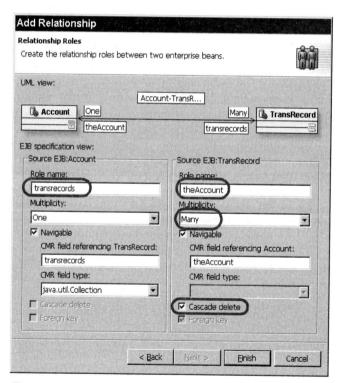

Figure 11-36   Relationship: roles for account transaction record

Deployment descriptor and generated methods

Save the deployment descriptor. You can select the Source page and scroll down to see the definition of the relationship as an <ejb-relation> element in the XML source.

For a detailed discussion of the relationship element, see "Declaring the relationship in the deployment descriptor" on page 125.

BankAccount methods

Open the AccountBean class and the AccountLocal interface and look at the methods generated for the relationship:

```
public java.util.Collection getTransrecords();
public void setTransrecords(java.util.Collection aTransrecords);
```

TransRecord methods

Similarly methods are generated into the TransRecordBean and the TransRecordLocal:

```
public itso.bank5.cmp.AccountLocal getTheAccount();
public void setTheAccount(itso.bank5.cmp.AccountLocal aTheAccount);
```

Code customization for transaction records

Our database model does allow that the foreign key (ACCID) in the TRANSRECORD table is NULL. This was set to enable the creation of TransRecord instances for testing. In reality, the foreign key should be set to NOT NULL because transaction records cannot exist without an account.

We have to set the relationship to the related account during the creation of a transaction record.

We modify the source code by adding the account local interface (AccountLocal) as a parameter in the ejbCreate and ejbPostCreate methods of the TransRecord bean, and modifying the create method of TransRecordLocalHome.

TransRecordBean

```
public java.sql.Timestamp ejbCreate(String type, java.math.BigDecimal
                                           amount, AccountLocal anAccount)
            throws javax.ejb.CreateException {
    ...... // no change to code
    return null;
}
```

```
public void ejbPostCreate(String type, java.math.BigDecimal amount,
                                              AccountLocal anAccount)
        throws javax.ejb.CreateException {
    setTheAccount(anAccount);
}
```

TransRecordLocalHome

```
public itso.bank5.cmp.TransRecordLocal create(
    String type, java.math.BigDecimal amount, AccountLocal anAccount)
    throws javax.ejb.CreateException;
```

> **Important:** To enable non-nullable foreign keys, the WebSphere Application Server v5.0 container defers the insert of CMP 2.0 entities in the data store until the `ejbPostCreate` method returns. According to the EJB specifications, relationship maintenance, including foreign key setting, are part of `ejbPostCreate`.
>
> WebSphere Application Server v4.x inserts container-managed entities after termination of `ejbCreate`.

To prevent the moving of transaction records from one account to another, we have to delete two generated setter methods from the local interfaces:

- ► `setTheAccount` in the `TransRecordLocal` interface
- ► `setTransrecords` in the `AccountLocal` interface

Instead of deleting the methods, we can comment out the methods in the code:

```
// public void setTheAccount(itso.bank5.cmp.AccountLocal aTheAccount);
// public void setTransrecords(java.util.Collection aTransrecords);
```

> **Important:** Invoking `setTransrecords` can lead to SQL exceptions if an account foreign key cannot be set to `null`.

Mapping and deployed code

We will wait with the mapping and code generation after we define the m:m relationship between customer and account.

Defining the customer to account relationship

Now let us define the m:m relationship between customer and accounts:

▶ In the Overview page of the deployment descriptor editor, click *Add* to open the Add Relationship window. In the first panel, select the two entity beans, Customer and Account, then click *Next*.

▶ In the Relationships Roles panel (Figure 11-37):

  – Set the role names to accounts and customers (to indicate many).

  – Set multiplicity to *Many* on both sides.

  – Accept the defaults in the rest of the fields.

  – Click *Finish*, then save the deployment descriptor.

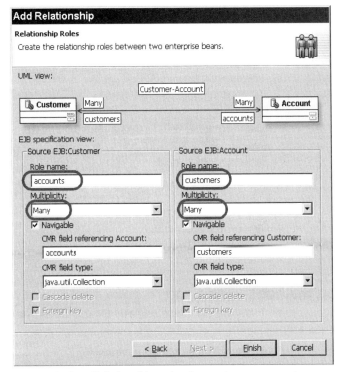

Figure 11-37   Relationship: roles for customer account

Deployment descriptor

Figure 11-38 shows the Overview page of the deployment descriptor with the two relationships.

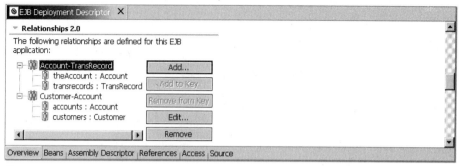

Figure 11-38   Deployment descriptor with relationships

Code customization for customer to account

We want to have tailored methods to add and remove an account to/from a customer and to add and remove a customer to/from an account. We remove the generated methods from the CustomerLocal and AccountLocal interfaces:

```
// public void setAccounts(java.util.Collection anAccounts);
// public void setCustomers(java.util.Collection aCustomers);
```

Customer methods to add and remove accounts

We add two relationship-specific methods in the CustomerBean class and then promote the methods to the local interface, CustomerLocal:

```
public void addAccount(AccountLocal anAccount) {
    getAccounts().add(anAccount);
}
public void removeAccount(AccountLocal anAccount) {
    getAccounts().remove(anAccount);
}
```

Account methods to add and remove customers

In the AccountBean class, we add two methods for customers and then promote the methods to the local interface, AccountLocal.

```
public void addCustomer(CustomerLocal aCustomer) {
    getCustomers().add(aCustomer);
}
public void removeCustomer(CustomerLocal aCustomer) {
    getCustomers().remove(aCustomer);
}
```

> **Note:** The methods generated for the relationships are not promoted to remote interfaces. Relationships are handled by local interfaces, `CustomerLocal` and `AccountLocal`.
>
> The `getCustomers` and `getAccounts` methods return collections of local EJB objects. To use such data in a remote method, the references would have to be converted.

Creating a remote method

The container-managed relationships generate methods using local interfaces only. To use such a relationship method in a remote interface, we have to code special methods. For example, to retrieve the account numbers for a customer for the remote interface, we can write a `getAccountNumbers` method and promote it to the remote interface:

```
// CustomerBean
public String[] getAccountNumbers() {
    java.util.Collection accounts = getAccounts();
    if ( accounts.size() == 0 ) return null;
    String[] result = new String[ accounts.size() ];
    java.util.Iterator it = accounts.iterator();
    for (int i=0; it.hasNext(); i++ ) {
        AccountLocal account = (AccountLocal)it.next();
        result[i] = (String)account.getPrimaryKey();
    }
    return result;
}
```

JNDI names and references

Open the deployment descriptor on the References page (Figure 11-39).

For every entity bean with a relationship, a reference to the related entity bean is inserted. You can see the name, which is the local JNDI name used in the deployed code, and the WebSphere binding, which is the global JNDI name.

For example, a customer entity bean finds the account home interface to access related accounts through the local name `ejb/Account`, which points to the global name `ejb/itso/bank5/cmp/AccountLocalHome`.

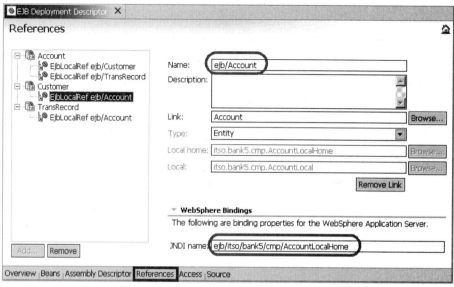

Figure 11-39   EJB references in the deployment descriptor

Changing JNDI names

Because we generated remote and local interfaces for the `Customer` bean, the global JNDI name for `Customer` is `ejb/itso/bank5/cmp/CustomerHome`.

JNDI names with many qualifications are not good for performance. Therefore, we change all the global JNDI names to a new naming convention:

```
ejb/itsobank/Account
ejb/itsobank/Customer
ejb/itsobank/TransRecord
```

► First, on the Beans page (Figure 11-40), select each entity bean and change the JNDI name under the WebSphere Bindings heading (three changes).

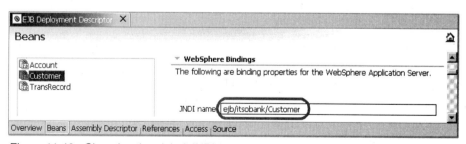

Figure 11-40   Changing the global JNDI name

▶ Second, on the References page (Figure 11-41), select each EJBLocalRef entry and change the JNDI name under the WebSphere Bindings heading (four changes).

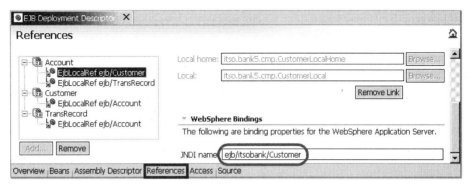

Figure 11-41   Changing the EJB references to the JNDI name

▶ Save and close the deployment descriptor when done.

Mapping the relationships

Open the mapping editor by selecting the `ItsoBank5CmpEJB` module and *Open With -> Mapping Editor -> DB2UDBNT_V72_1*.

Complete the mapping by dragging the CMR fields of the entity beans to the foreign key relationships in the tables (Figure 11-42):

▶ In the `Account` bean, drag the `customers:Customer` CMR field (left side) to "CAtoCustomer":`CUSTOMER` (right side). This maps the relationship from `Account` to `Customer`.

▶ In the `Customer` bean, drag the `accounts:Account` CMR field (left side) to "CAtoAccount":`ACCOUNT` (right side). This maps `Customer` to `Account`.

▶ In the `TransRecord` bean, drag the `theAccount:Account` CMR field (left side) to "AccountTransrecord":`ACCOUNT` (right side). This maps the relationship between `Account` and `TransRecord`.

Note that the `transrecords:TransRecord` CMR field under `Account` is now mapped as well. (You cannot drag the CMR field under `Account` to the foreign key—the mapping must be done in the direction of the foreign key.)

▶ Save the mapping when done.

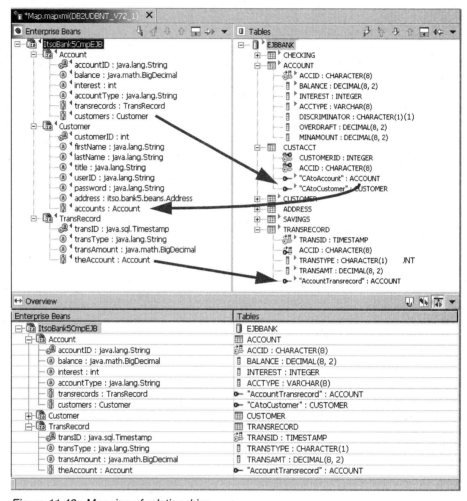

Figure 11-42   Mapping of relationships

Generating the deployed code for relationships

An update in the interfaces (relationship methods) and in the database mappings requires a regeneration of the deployed code:

► In the J2EE Hierarchy view, select the ItsoBank5CmpEJB project and *Generate -> Deploy and RMIC Code* (context).

► Select all the entity beans and click *Finish*.

> **Important:** Check the Tasks view after generation. If there are errors, it is sometimes necessary to delete all the deployed code and regenerate again.
>
> Select the entity beans and *Delete* (context). In the Delete window, deselect *Delete Bean Only* and *Delete Bean Classes*. Then deselect *Delete Access Bean*; **only select *Delete Deployed Code*.** Click *OK*.
>
> These are the packages and classes that should be deleted:
>
> ▶ The whole package `itso.bank5.cmp.websphere_deploy`
>
> ▶ The whole package `itso.bank5.cmp.websphere_deploy.DB2UDBNT_V72_1`
>
> ▶ In package `itso.bank5.cmp`, all classes starting with an underscore (*_Xxxxxxx*), ***Concrete*Xxxxxxx**, or *EJS*Xxxxxxx.

Testing relationships in the universal test client

The universal test client is not suited well to test the relationships. The result of the relationship calls are `Collection` objects that are invalidated as soon as the transaction ends. Each method call from the test client is a transaction, so when you want to explore a collection result, the data is already invalid and you get an `IllegalStateException`.

We will test the relationships using a session bean (see "Testing the business logic in the universal test client" on page 534).

Developing inheritance structures

To complete the banking model shown in Figure 11-33 on page 435, we now implement the two subclasses of `Account`, `Checking` and `Savings`.

Support for inheritance in Application Developer

The EJB 2.0 specification does not support inheritance. However, IBM products, such as VisualAge for Java, WebSphere Application Server, and the Application Developer, provide support for inheritance structures of entity EJBs.

Entity EJBs can inherit attributes and methods from the superclass entity bean, define additional attributes and methods, and overwrite inherited methods.

Defining the inheritance structure

Application Developer enables us to define entity beans as subclasses of existing entity beans in the Create an Enterprise Bean wizard.

Checking accounts

Let's define the `Checking` entity EJB as a subclass of `Account`:

▶ In the J2EE Hierarchy view, select the `ItsoBank5CmpEJB` module and *New -> Enterprise Bean* (context).

▶ The project is preselected, so click *Next*. Select *CMP 2.0 Bean*, enter `Checking` as bean name, make sure the `itso.bank5.cmp` package is selected, and click *Next*.

▶ Complete the Enterprise Bean Details panel (Figure 11-43) as follows:

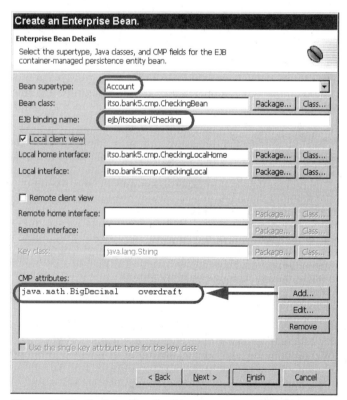

Figure 11-43   Defining the checking account entity bean

– Select `Account` as bean supertype.

- Set the EJB binding name to `ejb/itsobank/Checking` (to follow the convention we implemented in "Changing JNDI names" on page 444).

- Select *Local client view* (subclasses must have the same interfaces).

- Click *Add* for CMP attributes. Define one attribute with the name `overdraft`, `java.math.BigDecimal`, and promote getter/setter methods.

▶ Click *Finish* and the `Checking` entity bean appears under the `Account` bean in the J2EE Hierarchy view.

Savings accounts

Repeat the definition process for savings accounts:

▶ The bean name is `Savings`

▶ The superclass is `Account`

▶ The EJB binding name is `ejb/itsobank/Savings`

▶ Define one attribute: `minAmount`, `java.math.BigDecimal`

Generated classes and interfaces

The two subclasses `Checking` and `Savings` are now visible in the J2EE Hierarchy view, together with the bean class (`CheckingBean`, `SavingsBean`), the local home interfaces (`CheckingLocalHome`, `SavingsLocalHome`), and the local component interfaces (`CheckingLocal`, `SavingsLocal`).

The bean classes extend the `AccountBean` class and contain only the abstract getter and setter method for the attribute that was added to the subclass.

The home interfaces contain `create` and `findByPrimaryKey` methods. Note that the home interfaces do not extend the `AccountLocalHome` interface.

The component interfaces contain the getter and setter method for the attribute that was added to the subclass. The component interfaces do extend the `AccountLocal` interface and inherit all the methods of the `Account` bean.

Tailoring the generated code

Tailoring of the generated code involves the create methods and the business methods.

Create methods

In the create methods, we have to set the correct account type and initialize the extra attribute. Because the home interface does not inherit from the parent bean, we can design the create methods for each class individually.

Checking bean

We add an ejbCreate method with a parameter for the extra attribute (do not forget to have a matching ejbPostCreate method):

```
public java.lang.String ejbCreate(java.lang.String accountID,
                          java.math.BigDecimal balance, int interest,
                          java.math.BigDecimal overdraft)
    throws javax.ejb.CreateException {
    super.ejbCreate(accountID, balance, interest);
    setAccountType("CHECKING");
    setOverdraft(overdraft);
    return null;
}
public void ejbPostCreate(java.lang.String accountID,
                          java.math.BigDecimal balance, int interest,
                          java.math.BigDecimal overdraft)
    throws javax.ejb.CreateException {
}
```

Promote the ejbCreate method to the local home interface and it appears as a create method in CheckingLocalHome.

Delete the create(String) method from CheckingLocalHome. We only keep the method with parameters.

Savings bean

Make the same changes in the SavingsBean. Add an ejbCreate method:

```
public java.lang.String ejbCreate(java.lang.String accountID,
                          java.math.BigDecimal balance, int interest,
                          java.math.BigDecimal minAmount)
    throws javax.ejb.CreateException {
    super.ejbCreate(accountID, balance, interest);
    setAccountType("SAVINGS");
    setMinAmount(minAmount);
    return null;
}
public void ejbPostCreate(java.lang.String accountID,
                          java.math.BigDecimal balance, int interest,
                          java.math.BigDecimal minAmount)
    throws javax.ejb.CreateException {
}
```

Do not forget to promote the ejbCreate method to the local home interface and delete the create(String) method from SavingsLocalHome. We only keep the method with parameters.

Business methods

The business methods are `deposit` and `withdraw`. There is no change required for deposit; however, for `withdraw` we have to compare with the `overdraft` value for checking accounts and the `minAmount` value for savings accounts.

Overwrite the `withdraw` method in the `CheckingBean` and `SavingsBean` classes:

Checking bean

```
public java.math.BigDecimal withdraw(java.math.BigDecimal amount)
                throws itso.bank5.exception.InsufficientFundException {
    if ( getBalance().add( getOverdraft() ).compareTo(amount) == -1)
        throw new itso.bank5.exception.InsufficientFundException
                        ("Checking: Not enough funds - overdraft");
    ......
```

Savings bean

```
public java.math.BigDecimal withdraw(java.math.BigDecimal amount)
                throws itso.bank5.exception.InsufficientFundException {
    if ( getBalance().subtract( getMinAmount() ).compareTo(amount) == -1)
        throw new itso.bank5.exception.InsufficientFundException
                        ("Savings: Not enough funds - minAmount");
    ......
```

Note that we do not have to promote the `withdraw` method to the local interface because it is inherited and we did not change the signature of the method.

Relationships for inherited beans

The subclasses inherit the bean and component interface methods from the parent. Therefore we can use the generated methods (`getTransrecords`, `gctCustomers`) to follow relationships from `Checking` and `Savings` beans to related entities.

When traversing a relationship from a `Customer` or `TransRecord` to `Account` beans, the actual instance of a related account is either a `Checking` or a `Savings` object. The client code can examine the type of object and then cast the `Account` object to the correct subclass for further operations. This is illustrated in "List a customer with accounts and transaction records" on page 530.

Mapping approaches for inheritance

There are two approaches to map an inheritance structure:

► Map all entity beans into one table that contains columns for all the attributes. Attributes of subclasses must be mapped to nullable columns.

▶ Map the superclass entity type into a root table (parent) that contains the shared attributes. Map the subclass entity types into leaf tables (children) that contain a foreign key to the parent table and the attributes of the subclass.

Root/leaf mapping should not be used with deep inheritance structures, because many tables must be joined to retrieve a single entity bean.

In both approaches, the table of the top-level entity bean must include a special column called the *discriminator* column. The value of the discriminator column determines the type of the entity bean.

> **Important:** The discriminator column must not be used as an attribute of the top-level entity bean.

Mapping the account inheritance structure

In our sample model, we can use the ACCOUNT table for Account, Checking, and Savings entity beans, or we can use individual tables for all three beans. For now, we will map all three beans into one table. In Chapter 12, "Mapping strategies for CMPs" on page 467, we show root/leaf table mapping.

The ACCOUNT table includes a discriminator column named DISCRIMINATOR, which contains these values:

▶ **A**—A generic account that is not a checking or savings account
▶ **C**—A checking account
▶ **S**—A savings account

We also included an ACCTYPE column that contains the account type (ACCOUNT, CHECKING, or SAVINGS). This column is used as an attribute of Account.

The ACCTYPE column value is synchronized with the DISCRIMINATOR column value through triggers.

Mapping the inheritance beans

Open the Mapping editor by selecting the ItsoBank5CmpEJB module and *Open With -> Mapping Editor -> DB2UDBNT_V72_1* (Figure 11-44):

▶ Drag the Checking bean to the ACCOUNT table and the overdraft attribute to the OVERDRAFT column.

▶ Drag the Savings bean to the ACCOUNT table and the minAmount attribute to the MINAMOUNT column.

▶ The mapping of the subclasses appears indented under the superclass.

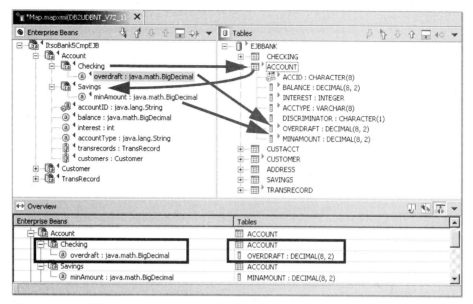

Figure 11-44   Mapping an inheritance structure

Mapping the discriminator column

Select the `Account` bean in the bottom pane of the editor. In the Properties view, select the `DISCRIMINATOR` column from the pull-down and enter the value `A` (Figure 11-45).

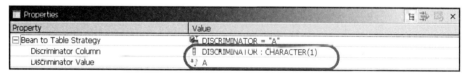

Figure 11-45   Selecting the discriminator column and its value

Select the `Checking` bean and set the discriminator value to `C` (Figure 11-46). Select the `Savings` bean and set the discriminator value to `S`.

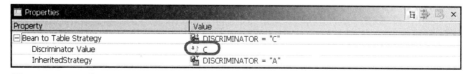

Figure 11-46   Setting the discriminator value for a subclass

Save the mapping and close the editor.

Generating the deployed code for inheritance

An update in the structure and in the database mappings requires a regeneration of the deployed code:

- ▶ In the J2EE Hierarchy view, select the ItsoBank5CmpEJB project and *Generate -> Deploy and RMIC Code* (context).
- ▶ Select the three account entity beans and click *Finish*. We did not touch the customer and transaction record beans.

> **Important:** Check the Tasks view after generation. If there are errors, it is sometimes necessary to delete all the deployed code and regenerate again. Select the bean and *Delete* (context). Then deselect the bean and the classes and only select *Delete Deployed Code*.

Testing inheritance in the universal test client

Start the EjbbankServer and the universal test client to test the inheritance. Here are a few hints on how to proceed:

- ▶ In the JNDI explorer, you find the local homes by expanding *[Local EJB beans] -> ejb -> itsobank*. Select the Account local home interface.
- ▶ Retrieve an account using the findByPrimaryKey method with an accountID of 101-1001. You will see that the result object is a CheckingLocal object.
- ▶ Click *Work with Object* and invoke the getOverdraft method to see the attribute value. Invoke other get methods as well.
- ▶ Do the same for accountID 101-1002 and a SavingsLocal is returned.
- ▶ In the JNDI explorer, select the Checking local home interface.
- ▶ Select the create method and enter parameter values of 101-1008, 99.00 (balance), 9 (interest), and 90.00 (overdraft). Click *Invoke* to create a new checking account.

Cleaning the model

To have a clean and complete model and implementation, we should:

- ▶ Remove the create methods from AccountLocalHome, because all accounts should be either checking or savings accounts.
- ▶ Remove the setAccountType method from the AccountLocal interface, because the type of an account cannot be changed.

- Remove the `setBalance` method from the `AccountLocal` interface, because the balance can only be changed through deposit and withdraw transactions.

This is not necessary for our sample, but should give you ideas for design issues you should think about in a real application.

Developing custom finders

In this section, we develop custom finders for the banking model with Application Developer. For the basics of finder methods, read "EJB custom query methods" on page 140.

Here is a short recapitulation:

- There are two kind of methods: finder methods in the home interface and select methods in the bean class.
- These methods can be mapped to EJB query language.
- EJB QL statements are specified in the deployment descriptor.
- SQL statements are generated from EJB QL into deployed classes.

The process of defining custom finder methods is very simple:

- Open the deployment descriptor editor and select an entity bean.
- Create a new finder method and specify the method name and signature (parameters), and select the local or remote interface.
- Specify the EJB QL statement.

When you generate the deployed code, the EJB QL statement is converted into an SQL statement in the deployed code.

Creating a simple custom finder method

We describe the development process in detail for the first finder method. The `findGoldAccounts` method retrieves accounts with a large balance:

- Open the deployment descriptor of the `ItsoBank5CmpEJB` project.
- On the Beans page, select the `Account` bean and scroll down to Queries.
- In the Add Finder Descriptor window (Figure 11-47):
  - Select *New* for method. (Selecting *Existing* would look into the home interface to find finder method definitions.)
  - Select *find method* and *Local* (*Remote* is not available because the `Account` bean does not have a remote interface).

- Enter `findGoldAccounts` as the method name.
- Select `java.util.Collection` as the return type (the other choice is a single object, `AccountLocal`).
- Click *Add* for parameters. In the Add Method Parameter window, enter `balance` as the name and *Browse* to `BigDecimal` (`java.math`) for the type.

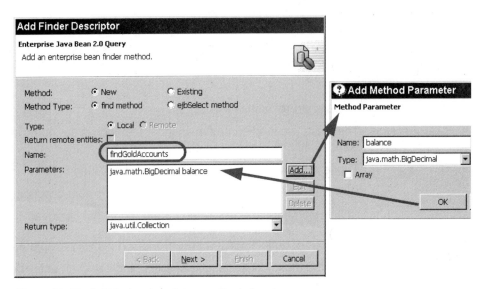

Figure 11-47   Add finder descriptor: method signature

▶ Click *Next*. In the second panel of the window, we enter a description (optional) and the EJB QL statement (Figure 11-48):

- You can add a description for the method. Keep in mind that an enterprise bean should be a reusable component. If you are creating complex finders for your core business objects of your enterprise and anyone else has to reuse this component in another project, this short description of the purpose and the parameters are really helpful. This description is also a part of the deployment descriptor.

- You can type the complete EJB QL statement yourself. Alternatively, select one of the sample query statements from the pull-down. Every selection puts a sample query into the query statement box and you can use it as a model. Explore the different options and you can see the model statements.

  The *Single Where Predicate* selection results in this statement:

  ```
  select object(o) from Account o where o.accountID is null
  ```

Modify the statement to read:

```
select object(o) from Account o where o.balance > ?1
```

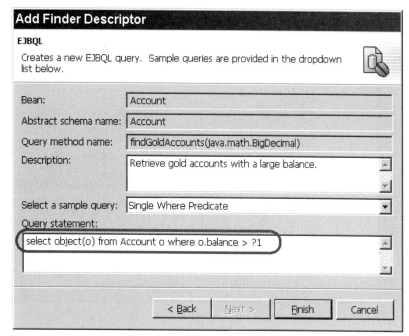

Figure 11-48   Add Finder Descriptor: EJB QL statement

► Click *Finish* and save the deployment descriptor.

Generated deployment descriptor

The query and finder method appears in the deployment descriptor (Figure 11-49).

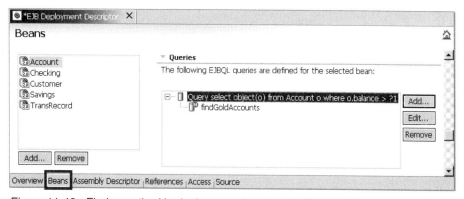

Figure 11-49   Finder method in deployment descriptor editor

Switching to the Source page reveals the `<query>` tag added under the entity bean (Figure 11-50).

```
<ejb-jar id="ejb-jar_ID">
<display-name>ItsoBank5CmpEJB</display-name>
<enterprise-beans>
   <entity id="Account">
      ......
      <query>
         <description>Retrieve gold accounts with a large balance.
         </description>
         <query-method>
            <method-name>findGoldAccounts</method-name>
            <method-params>
               <method-param>java.math.BigDecimal</method-param>
            </method-params>
         </query-method>
         <ejb-ql>select object(o) from Account o where o.balance &gt; ?1
         </ejb-ql>
      </query>
   </entity>
   ......
```

Figure 11-50   Finder method deployment descriptor

The finder is completely described in this tag including the EJB QL statement. You can change the definition in the source view of the deployment descriptor and save the changes.

Generate method in the home interface

The following method is generated into the home interface, either in the local home (our case) or in the remote home interface, depending on your selection.

Local home interface:

```
public java.util.Collection findGoldAccounts(java.math.BigDecimal balance)
               throws javax.ejb.FinderException;
```

Remote home interface (as it would be):

```
public java.util.Collection findGoldAccounts(java.math.BigDecimal balance)
               throws javax.ejb.FinderException, java.rmi.RemoteException;
```

Important: Note that the query statement and the finder method are handled separately:

- If you create a query statement and the corresponding method in the same step (as we did in our example by selecting *New*), the method itself and the mapping to this method are automatically created.

- You can create the signature of a finder method yourself in the home interface, then select *Existing* in the window to enter the EJB QL statement.

- If you delete the query statement, the tasks lists claims a missing mapping for the finder or select method to a query statement. You have to create a new query statement and map it to the method, or you have to delete the method manually to remove the error.

When you finish the window, the code and deployment descriptor are generated. Check the Tasks view. The EJB QL statement is analyzed and you may see error messages that point to the ejb-jar.xml file. By looking at the error message, you may be able to fix the statement directly in the Source view of the deployment descriptor.

When you generate the deployed code, more errors may be found in the EJB QL statement and you have to go back and fix the error:

- Select the statement in the deployment descriptor and click *Edit*. The same window is opened with the definition filled in and you can make corrections.

- Change the query statement directly in the Source view of the deployment descriptor and save it.

Creating finder methods using relationships and inheritance

Let's create a few more finders to experiment with relationships and inheritance. Follow the process outlined in "Creating a simple custom finder method" on page 455 to specify the method name and signature and the EJB QL statement.

Retrieve all accounts

Create a finder for the `Account` bean to retrieve all the accounts in the database:

```
Method: findAllAccounts(), returns Collection

EJB QL: select object(o) from Account o
```

Retrieve customers that have gold savings accounts

Create a finder for the `Customer` bean to retrieve customers that have savings accounts with large balances:

```
Method: findGoldCustomers(BigDecimal balance), local, returns Collection

EJB QL: select distinct object(c) from Customer c, in(c.accounts) a
            where a is of type (Savings) and a.balance > ?1
```

This custom finder uses inheritance to check for the account type.

Try to create the same finder (`findGoldCustomers`) for the remote interface; Application Developer does not allow it!

> **Restriction:** The specification says (last paragraph in 10.5.6): If home and local home interface have the same methods (name and signature are the same), then they have to be mapped to the same EJB QL statement. But this does not work in the Application Developer. It is possible by manually changing the source of the deployment descriptor, or by creating the remote interface after the local interface has been created with the finder and using the "copy methods from other home interface" option.

Retrieve customers with high interest accounts and a deposit

Create a finder for the `Customer` bean to retrieve customers that have accounts with a high interest rate and at least one deposit transaction in that account:

```
Method: findHighInterest(int interest), remote, returns Collection

EJB QL: select distinct object(c)
            from Customer c, in(c.accounts) a, in(a.transrecords) t
            where a.interest > ?1 and t.transType = 'C'
```

This custom finder traverses two relationships.

Retrieve accounts for a transfer

Create a finder for the `Account` bean to retrieve all other accounts of a customer for a transfer of funds:

```
Method: findTransferAccounts(int customerID, String accountID),
            returns Collection

EJB QL: select object(b)
            from Account a, in(a.customers) c, in(c.accounts) b
            where c.customerID = ?1 and a.accountID = ?2
            and a.accountID <> b.accountID
```

This custom finder traverses the same relationship back and forth.

Largest account of a customer

Create a finder for the `Account` bean to retrieve the account with the largest balance for a customer:

```
Method: findLargestAccount(int customerID), returns AccountLocal

EJB QL: select object(a) from Account a, in(a.customers) c
           where c.customerID = ?1
               and a.balance = ( select max(a1.balance) from in (c.accounts) a1
        )
```

Home interfaces

After saving the deployment descriptor, open the home interfaces of the `Customer` and `Account` beans and verify that the methods have been added:

AccountLocalHome:
```
java.util.Collection findGoldAccounts(java.math.BigDecimal balance)
java.util.Collection findAllAccounts()
java.util.Collection findTransferAccounts(int ..., String ...)
itso.bank5.cmp.AccountLocal findLargestAccount(int customerID)
```

CustomerLocalHome:
```
java.util.Collection findGoldCustomers(java.math.BigDecimal balance)
```

CustomerHome:
```
java.util.Collection findHighInterest(int interest)
```

Creating a select method in the bean class

The second type of finder methods are select methods that are implemented in the bean class. We implement two methods:

► Retrieve all customer names

► Retrieve the account numbers for a given customer name

Retrieve all customer names

We define a select method in the `Customer` bean to retrieve all the customer names. This can be useful to display a list of customers in a client application. We will implement a home method for that purpose (see "Developing a home method" on page 463).

The process of adding a select method is the same as for finder methods:

► In the deployment descriptor, select the `Customer` bean and click *Add* for queries.

► In the Add Finder Descriptor window (Figure 11-51), do as follows:

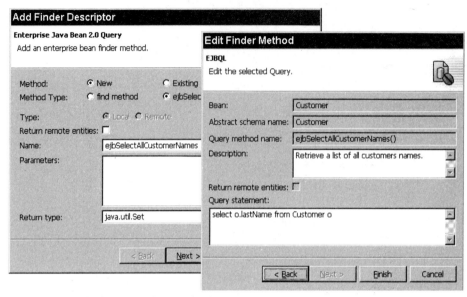

Figure 11-51 Defining a select method

- Select *New* and *ejbSelect* method.
- Enter `ejbSelectAllCustomerNames` as the name, no parameters, and `java.util.Set` as return type.
- Click *Next*.
- Enter a description and the EJB QL statement:

  `select o.lastName from Customer o`

- Click *Finish*.

► Save the deployment descriptor.

The `ejbSelect` method is created in the `CustomerBean` class:

```
public abstract java.util.Set ejbSelectAllCustomerNames()
                             throws javax.ejb.FinderException;
```

There is nothing more to do in the bean class. This method is not accessible over any interface. It is for use within the bean class only. Therefore, an `ejbSelect` method is sometimes called a private finder method. You can use it from now on in the bean class because of the abstract method declaration. The implementation is generated in the concrete bean class.

Retrieve the account numbers for a given customer name

Add another select method to the `Customer` bean in the same way:

- Name: `ejbSelectNumberOfAccounts`
- Parameter: *name* of type `java.lang.String`
- Return type: `java.util.Collection`
- EJB QL statement:

  ```
  select a.accountID from Customer o, in(o.accounts) a where o.lastName = ?1
  ```

Using select methods

One of the typical uses of an `ejbSelect` method is to invoke the method within a home method. If you want to test the `ejbSelect` method, you can create a simple home method that invokes the `ejbSelect` method. This enables you to test the method through the local or remote home interface.

Developing a home method

For an introduction to the home methods, see "EJB home methods" on page 24. Creating a home method is very simple. It does not make any difference whether the entity bean is container-managed or bean-managed.

There are no wizards or windows to create a home method. We have to code the method in the bean class and promote it to the home interface.

We create a home method called `ejbHomeGetAllCustomers` in the `CustomerBean` class. This method returns an array of strings with each element containing a customer name and the account numbers. This home method uses the two `ejbSelect` methods we created earlier.

```java
public String[] ejbHomeGetAllCustomers() throws javax.ejb.FinderException {
    Object[] objects = ejbSelectAllCustomerNames().toArray();
    String[] names = new String[objects.length];
    for (int i=0; i < objects.length; i++) {
        String custname = (String)objects[i];
        StringBuffer text = new StringBuffer(custname).append(" ");
        Object[] accounts = ejbSelectNumberOfAccounts(custname).toArray();
        for (int j=0; j < accounts.length; j++) {
            text.append( (String)accounts[j] ).append(" ");
        }
        names[i] = text.toString();
        System.out.println("Customer: " + names[i]);
    }
    return names;
}
```

The Tasks view shows an information message when we save the class. This reminds us that we have to promote the method to the home interface:

► Select the `ejbHomeGetAllCustomers` method in the Outline view and *Enterprise Bean -> Promote to Local Home Interface* (context). (We could also promote the method to the remote interface.)

► The method signature is added to the `CustomerLocalHome` interface:

```
public java.lang.String[] getAllCustomers()
    throws javax.ejb.FinderException;
```

The `getAllCustomer` method is now available to clients (for example, session beans) through the home interface.

Code generation for finder and select methods

When you generate the deployed code, EJB QL statement are converted into SQL. You can find the generated SQL statements for the `Account` bean in the package `itso.bank5.cmp.websphere_deploy.DB2UDBNT_V72_1` and class called `AccountFunctionSet`. Let's look at two examples.

Retrieve all accounts

The simple EJB QL statement `select object(o) from Account o` translates into:

```
select  q1.\"ACCID\",  q1.\"BALANCE\",  q1.\"INTEREST\",  q1.\"ACCTYPE\",
q1.\"DISCRIMINATOR\",  q1.\"MINAMOUNT\",  q1.\"OVERDRAFT\" from
ITSO.ACCOUNT q1 where  ( ( q1.\"DISCRIMINATOR\" = \'A\')  or  (
q1.\"DISCRIMINATOR\" = \'S\')  or  ( q1.\"DISCRIMINATOR\" = \'C\')  )
```

Find the largest account of a customer

The EJB QL statement is:

```
findlargestAccount(int customerID), returns AccountLocal
select object(a) from Account a, in(a.customers) c
 where c.customer = ?1
    and a.balance = ( select max(a1.balance) from in (c.accounts) a1  )
```

The SQL statement is:

```
select  q1.\"ACCID\",  q1.\"BALANCE\",  q1.\"INTEREST\",  q1.\"ACCTYPE\",
q1.\"DISCRIMINATOR\",  q1.\"MINAMOUNT\",  q1.\"OVERDRAFT\" from
ITSO.ACCOUNT q1, ITSO.CUSTOMER q2, ITSO.CUSTACCT q3 where  ( (
q1.\"DISCRIMINATOR\" = \'A\')  or  ( q1.\"DISCRIMINATOR\" = \'S\')  or  (
q1.\"DISCRIMINATOR\" = \'C\')  )  and  ( q2.\"CUSTOMERID\" = ?)  and  (
q1.\"BALANCE\" = ( select  max( q4.\"BALANCE\") from ITSO.ACCOUNT q4,
ITSO.CUSTACCT q5 where  ( ( q4.\"DISCRIMINATOR\" = \'A\')  or  (
```

```
q4.\"DISCRIMINATOR\" = \'S\') or ( q4.\"DISCRIMINATOR\" = \'C\') ) and
( q5.\"CUSTOMERID\" = q2.\"CUSTOMERID\") and ( q4.\"ACCID\" =
q5.\"ACCID\") ) ) and ( q3.\"ACCID\" = q1.\"ACCID\") and (
q2.\"CUSTOMERID\" = q3.\"CUSTOMERID\")
```

Inheritance with root/leaf mapping

Top-down mapping of the inheritance structure with root/leaf is covered in
"Top-down mapping of the bank model" on page 475 and "Mapping inheritance"
on page 478. Note that SQL statements get more complex with root/leaf mapping
of inheritance, because the tables for all subclasses must be joined.

SQL statements with errors

> **Important: SQL Errors.** The SQL code for some of the EJB QL statements is
> wrong when using root/leaf mapping for inheritance. When traversing the m:m
> relationship from `Customer` to `Account`, wrong join clauses are generated.
>
> **This error is documented in the release notes and will be fixed in 5.0.1.**
>
> For example: **findGoldCustomers** in `CustomerBeanFunctionSet`
> (DB2UDBNT_V72_2)
> **Generated**:
> ```
> select q1.\"CUSTOMERID\", q1.\"FIRSTNAME\", q1.\"LASTNAME\", q1.\"TITLE\",
> q1.\"USERID\", q1.\"PASSWORD\", q1.\"ADDRESS\" from ITSOTOP.CUSTOMER q1 left
> outer join ITSOTOP.ACCOUNT q2 on left outer join ITSOTOP.SAVINGS q3 on (
> q2.\"ACCOUNTID\" = q3.\"ACCOUNTID\") left outer join ITSOTOP.CHECKING q4 on (
> q2.\"ACCOUNTID\" = q4.\"ACCOUNTID\") left outer join ITSOTOP.Accounts_Customers
> q5 on ( q2.\"ACCOUNTID\" = q5.\"ACCOUNTS_ACCOUNTID\") where ( (
> q2.\"ACCOUNT_DISCRIM\" = \'Account\') or ( q2.\"ACCOUNT_DISCRIM\" = \'Savings\')
> or ( q2.\"ACCOUNT_DISCRIM\" = \'Checking\') ) and ( q2.\"ACCOUNT_DISCRIM\" =
> \'Savings\') and ( q2.\"BALANCE\" > ?) and ( q5.\"CUSTOMERS_CUSTOMERID\" =
> q1.\"CUSTOMERID\") order by q1.\"CUSTOMERID\" asc
> ```
> **Corrected (one possible way):**
> ```
> select q1.\"CUSTOMERID\", q1.\"FIRSTNAME\", q1.\"LASTNAME\", q1.\"TITLE\",
> q1.\"USERID\", q1.\"PASSWORD\", q1.\"ADDRESS\" from ITSOTOP.CUSTOMER q1      ,
>          ITSOTOP.ACCOUNT q2     left outer join ITSOTOP.SAVINGS q3 on (
> q2.\"ACCOUNTID\" = q3.\"ACCOUNTID\") left outer join ITSOTOP.CHECKING q4 on (
> q2.\"ACCOUNTID\" = q4.\"ACCOUNTID\") left outer join ITSOTOP.Accounts_Customers
> q5 on ( q2.\"ACCOUNTID\" = q5.\"ACCOUNTS_ACCOUNTID\") where ( (
> q2.\"ACCOUNT_DISCRIM\" = \'Account\') or ( q2.\"ACCOUNT_DISCRIM\" = \'Savings\')
> or ( q2.\"ACCOUNT_DISCRIM\" = \'Checking\') ) and ( q2.\"ACCOUNT_DISCRIM\" =
> \'Savings\') and ( q2.\"BALANCE\" > ?) and ( q5.\"CUSTOMERS_CUSTOMERID\" =
> q1.\"CUSTOMERID\") order by q1.\"CUSTOMERID\" asc
> ```
>
> **Bad SQL statements are also generated for:**
> ```
> findHighInterest (CustomerBeanFunctionSet)
> findTransferAccounts and ejbSelectNumberOfAccounts (AccountBeanFunctionSet).
> ```

12

Mapping strategies for CMPs

This chapter describes the mapping strategies for CMPs:

► Top-down
► Bottom-up
► Meet-in the-middle

In addition, we describe mapping strategies for relationships and inheritance, as well as special cases of dependent entities and writing composers and converters.

© Copyright IBM Corp. 2003. All rights reserved.

Mapping strategies

Application Developer supports three mapping strategies for entity beans and relationships:

- **Top-down**—From entity beans to new tables
- **Bottom-up**—From existing tables to new entity beans
- **Meet-in-the-middle**—Map entity beans to existing tables

Figure 12-1 summarizes the three approaches.

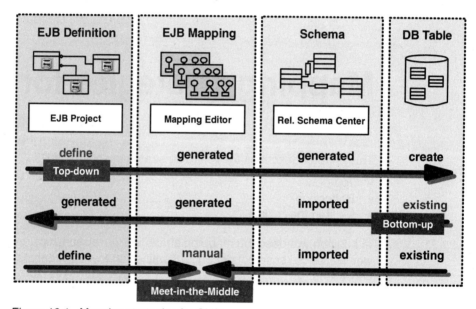

Figure 12-1   Mapping strategies for CMPs

In the sections that follow, we look at the three strategies in detail.

Top-down

The *top-down* approach is the easiest to handle, because no legacy database is imposed on you (Figure 12-2). You have full freedom to design the entity beans.

The top-down approach is also called *forward engineering*.

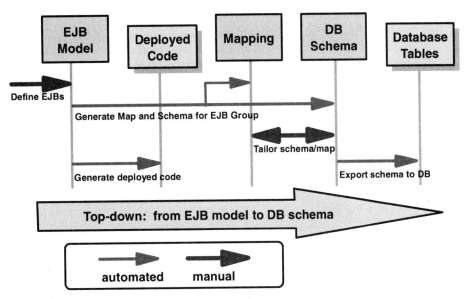

Figure 12-2   EJB mapping: top-down approach

Approach

The steps in the top-down approach are:

- ► Create an EJB project, add entity beans, and define the required relationships for the application.
- ► Once the entity model is complete, you can generate the mapping by selecting *Generate -> EJB to RDB Mapping* (context).
- ► Check the schema and map for errors. Typical errors are due to serialized objects (EJB handles, for example) being mapped to VARCHAR columns instead of BLOB. Fix them and you are done.
- ► Tailor the schema: table and column names, column characteristics (CHAR or VARCHAR, maximum length of strings, precision of DECIMAL columns).
- ► Save the schema and the mapping.
- ► Generate the DDL for the tables and run the DDL into a database.

Important: You should avoid designing object models that lead to unrealistic database design. Always have a database administrator check the resulting database design.

Bottom-up

The *bottom-up* approach is the exact opposite of the top-down approach. Basically, you create an EJB layer on top of an existing database design (Figure 12-3). This approach is also called *reverse engineering*.

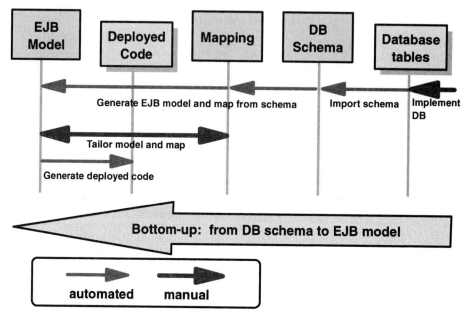

Figure 12-3   EJB mapping: bottom-up approach

Here your freedom of development is on top of the EJB layer. You have to add session beans to provide all the business logic that the entity beans do not provide.

Approach

The steps in the bottom-up approach are:

► Implement a database (or have an existing database).

► Import a schema from the database and generate the entity beans and the mapping.

► Tailor the model (Java types) and adjust the mapping if necessary. For example, m:m relationships are not imported (an intermediate entity is created), and inheritance is not recognized.

Meet-in-the-middle

Meet-in-the-middle is the most common approach used in the e-business projects. It combines an existing database and an entity model design (Figure 12-4).

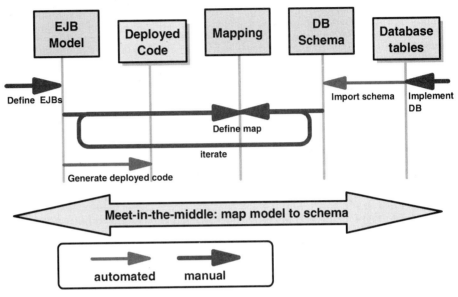

Figure 12-4   EJB mapping: meet-in-the-middle approach

The real difficulty is in finding a good balance between the design and the mapping. The entity model must match the database design with enough commonality so that a mapping is feasible.

The schema has a very limited role here, because it is imposed and cannot be changed. The development life cycle mainly will be a cycle between the EJB model and the mapping, where one has to accommodate changes to make the other viable.

Approach

The steps in the meet-in-the-middle approach are:

► Implement a database (or have an existing database).

► Create an EJB project, add entity beans, and define the required relationships for the application.

► Perform the mapping by importing a schema from the database and mapping the entities and relationships to the tables.

The real challenge is to make the design and the legacy tables match! Here you will have to deploy all your knowledge of composers, converters, as well as compromising skills to have the two coexist. It may happen that your design is impossible to map in its entirety and, therefore, redesign will have to be done.

In most cases, this is an iterative process that takes several cycles to result in a good entity bean design and also good performance.

Mapping examples

In Chapter 11, "Container-managed entity bean development" on page 397, we used an iterative process and meet-in-the-middle mapping between our entity model and the existing tables.

Now let us look at bottom-up and top-down mapping.

Bottom-up mapping from the EJBBANK database

To illustrate the bottom-up process, we create an entity model from the existing tables.

Restriction

Originally we had an `address` column in the `CUSTOMER` table and an `ADDRESS` table that was related to the `CUSTOMER` table. Bottom-up does not work for such a combination, because the `Customer` entity bean would have an `address` CMP attribute and an `address` CMR relationship.

We renamed the `ADDRESS` table to `CUSTADDRESS` to get around this problem.

Create a project

Create a new EJB project named `ItsoBank5xEJB`, attached to a new enterprise application named `ItsoBank5xEAR`.

Generate a bottom-up model

To generate the bottom-up EJB model, follow this process:

► Select the `ItsoBank5xEJB` project and *Generate -> EJB to RDB Mapping* (context).

► Select *Create a new backend folder* and click *Next*.

► Select *Bottom Up* and click *Next*.

- In the Database Connection window, enter `ConEJBBANKbot` as name and `EJBBANK` as database. Select the database vendor (DB2 Universal Database™ V7.2) and check that the class location is correct. Click *Next*.

- Select all the tables of the `ITSO` schema and click *Next*.

- Select *Generate 2.0 enterprise beans*. Enter `itso.bank5.bottom` as package. Click *Finish*.

- Wait.... it takes a while to generate the entities and relationships.

- When the process is finished, the mapping editor is opened and shows the mapping of the generated entity beans. Close the editor.

Analyze the generated model

The bottom-up process creates one entity bean for each table. It also creates these 1:m relationships:

- `Custaddress_To_Customer`
- `Custacct_To_Customer`
- `Custacct_To_Account`
- `Checking_To_Account`
- `Savings_To_Account`
- `Transrecord_To_Account`

Many-to-many relationship

The relationship between customer and account is not recognized as an m:m relationship, despite the fact that the `CUSTACCT` table has only foreign keys and no other attributes.

> **Restriction:** Bottom-up mapping does not recognize m:m relationships. It creates an intermediate entity bean and two 1:m relationships.

Change the model

To make the model usable for our application we change the entity model in the deployment descriptor:

- On the Beans page, select the `Custacct` entity (it has no data) and click *Remove*. This also removes the two relationships to the `Customer` and `Account` beans.

- On the Overview page, define an m:m relationship between `Customer` and `Account` with roles set as `accounts` and `customers`.

- Delete the relationships from `Checking` and `Savings` to `Account`.

- On the Beans page, delete the attributes `discriminator`, `overdraft`, and `minamount` from the `Account` bean (we will use root/leaf inheritance).

- ▸ Make `Checking` a subclass of `Account`:
  - – Use the Inheritance section on the Overview page.
  - – Select the `Checking` class and click *Edit*.
  - – Select *Inherits from supertype* and select the `Account` bean.
  - – Click *Finish*.
- ▸ Make `Savings` a subclass of `Account` in the same way.
- ▸ Delete the `Customerinfo` bean (we ignore this data for this example).
- ▸ Delete the `Custaddress` bean (we will map customer attributes to the `CUSTADDRESS` table).
- ▸ Select the `Customer` bean, delete the `address` attribute, add `street`, `city`, `state`, and `zipcode` attributes (all strings).
- ▸ Edit the relationship between `Transrecord` and `Account` and set the roles and the CMR field names to `theAccount` (under `Transrecord`) and `transrecords` (under `Account`).
- ▸ Save the deployment descriptor.

Fixing the code
Several errors in the code must be fixed:

- ▸ `CheckingBean` and `SavingsBean` refer to their own key class:
  - – Change all references to the key class to `AccountKey`, the shared class.
  - – Also the `setCheckingaccount_accid` and `setSavingsaccount_accid` method calls must be deleted from `ejbCreate` and `ejbPostCreate` methods.
- ▸ In the `AccountBean`, the `ejbCreate` methods refers to the three deleted fields:
  - – Remove the last three parameters from the method signature and the three set calls for `discriminator`, `overdraft`, and `minamount`.
  - – Change the `ejbPostCreate` method signature in the same way.
  - – Open the `AccountLocalHome` class and change the `create` method signature in the same way.

Adjust the mapping
We have to synchronize the mapping with the model. Open the mapping editor (select the project and *Open With -> Mapping Editor -> DB2UDBNT_V72_1*):

- ▸ Check the mapping of `Checking` and `Savings`. The single attribute should be mapper to the column.
- ▸ Map `Customer` to `CUSTADDRESS` (drag/drop), then map the four attributes to the columns of `CUSTADDRESS`.

- ▶ Map the inheritance discriminator:
  - – Select the `Account` bean in the mapped section (bottom pane of the editor) and set the discriminator in the Properties view to the `DISCRIMINATOR` column and the value A. (Expand the *Bean to Table Strategy*.)
  - – Select the `Checking` and `Savings` beans and set the discriminator values to C and S respectively.
- ▶ Map the `Customer - Account` relationship:
  - – Drag the `accounts` attribute of the `Customer` bean to the `CustAcct` table `CAtoAccount` foreign key.
  - – Drag the `customers` attribute of the `Account` bean to the `CustAcct` table `CAtoCustomer` foreign key.
- ▶ Save the mapping.

At this point, all errors have disappeared and the model and mapping is complete. We could generate the deployed code, but we do not implement this mapping approach.

Top-down mapping of the bank model

To illustrate the top-down approach, we take the CMP entity model of the `ItsoBank5CmpEJB` project and perform a top-down mapping:

- ▶ Select the `ItsoBank5CmpEJB` project and *Generate -> EJB to RDB Mapping*.
- ▶ Select *Create a new backend folder* (we do not want to overwrite the good implementation) and click *Next*.
- ▶ Select *Top Down* and click *Next*.
- ▶ Select *DB2 UDB V7.2* as target database, enter `EJBBANK` as database name, and `ITSOTOP` as schema (to differentiate from the existing ITSO schema). Select *Generate DDL*. Click *Next*.
- ▶ For advanced inheritance options, select the `Checking` and `Savings` beans to generate root/leaf tables. Click *Finish*.

A new back-end folder `DB2UDBNT_V72_2` is created with the tables and the mapping (Figure 12-5).

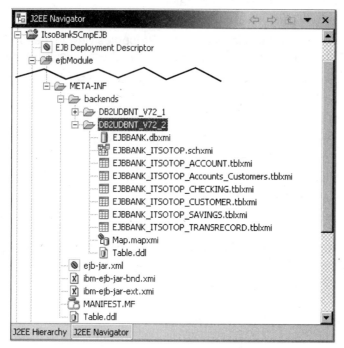

Figure 12-5   Top-down mapping back-end folder

Analyzing the generated table model

The DDL is generated into a file named `Table.ddl` (Example 12-1).

Example 12-1   Top-down table model

```
CREATE TABLE ITSOTOP.ACCOUNT
  (ACCOUNT_DISCRIM VARCHAR(32),
   ACCOUNTID VARCHAR(250) NOT NULL,
   BALANCE DECIMAL(10, 2),
   INTEREST INTEGER NOT NULL,
   ACCOUNTTYPE VARCHAR(250));

ALTER TABLE ITSOTOP.ACCOUNT
  ADD CONSTRAINT PK_ACCOUNT PRIMARY KEY (ACCOUNTID);

CREATE TABLE ITSOTOP.CHECKING
  (ACCOUNTID VARCHAR(250) NOT NULL,
   OVERDRAFT DECIMAL(10, 2));

ALTER TABLE ITSOTOP.CHECKING
  ADD CONSTRAINT PK_CHECKING PRIMARY KEY (ACCOUNTID);
```

```
CREATE TABLE ITSOTOP.SAVINGS
  (ACCOUNTID VARCHAR(250) NOT NULL,
   MINAMOUNT DECIMAL(10, 2));

ALTER TABLE ITSOTOP.SAVINGS
  ADD CONSTRAINT PK_SAVINGS PRIMARY KEY (ACCOUNTID);

CREATE TABLE ITSOTOP.Accounts_Customers
  (CUSTOMERS_CUSTOMERID INTEGER NOT NULL,
   ACCOUNTS_ACCOUNTID VARCHAR(250) NOT NULL);

ALTER TABLE ITSOTOP.Accounts_Customers
  ADD CONSTRAINT PK_Accounts_Custo1 PRIMARY KEY (CUSTOMERS_CUSTOMERID,
ACCOUNTS_ACCOUNTID);

CREATE TABLE ITSOTOP.CUSTOMER
  (CUSTOMERID INTEGER NOT NULL,
   FIRSTNAME VARCHAR(250),
   LASTNAME VARCHAR(250),
   TITLE VARCHAR(250),
   USERID VARCHAR(250),
   PASSWORD VARCHAR(250),
   ADDRESS VARCHAR(1000) FOR BIT DATA);

ALTER TABLE ITSOTOP.CUSTOMER
  ADD CONSTRAINT PK_CUSTOMER PRIMARY KEY (CUSTOMERID);

CREATE TABLE ITSOTOP.TRANSRECORD
  (TRANSID TIMESTAMP NOT NULL,
   TRANSTYPE VARCHAR(250),
   TRANSAMOUNT DECIMAL(10, 2),
   THEACCOUNT_ACCOUNTID VARCHAR(250));

ALTER TABLE ITSOTOP.TRANSRECORD
  ADD CONSTRAINT PK_TRANSRECORD PRIMARY KEY (TRANSID);
```

After studying the generated table model, you may want to tailor the tables:

► The discriminator column ACCOUNT_DISCRIM in the ACCOUNT table is VARCHAR(32). You may use a shorter VARCHAR or even a CHAR.

► All string attributes default to VARCHAR(250). You have to look at each string attribute and decide what the correct column size is and if VARCHAR or CHAR is more appropriate.

► All BigDecimal attributes default to DECIMAL(10,2). Is that the correct length and precision?

► The address column in the CUSTOMER table is VARCHAR(1000) FOR BIT DATA. You may want to change to a BLOB data type.

- You can change the column names as well. Do not delete the column and redefine it; that would invalidate the mapping.

- Study what columns were generated as NOT NULL (keys and integers). Decide which columns should be NOT NULL for a realistic design.

All these changes would not affect the mapping.

Changes that would affect the mapping:

- Changing the names of tables. You would have to define the new table, change the mapping, and delete the old table.

- Changing the m:m relationship table that was generated as Accounts_Customers with two key fields and two foreign key definitions.

Deploying a design

In the deployment descriptor of the ItsoBank5CmpEJB project, you can now select the back-end folder to be used when deploying the EJBs. Open the deployment descriptor editor and at the bottom of the Overview page you can select the back-end folder.

When you generate the deployed code, a package is generated for each back-end folder as itso.bank5.cmp.websphere_deploy.DB2UDBNT_V72_x.

Mapping a CMP to multiple tables

An entity, such as Customer, can be mapped to two (or more) tables that are in a 1:1 relationship. As shown in "Change the model" on page 473 (bottom-up mapping), we can map the combined attributes of the Customer attributes to two tables, CUSTOMER and CUSTADDRESS.

Mapping relationships

The mapping of relationships is straightforward. A 1:1 or 1:m relationship maps to the foreign key of the subordinate table. In an m:m relationship, the two CMR fields map to the foreign keys in the intermediate table.

Mapping inheritance

Inheritance between CMP entity beans can be mapped into one table or multiple tables (root/leaf).

In "Mapping approaches for inheritance" on page 451, we discussed the mapping of inheritance structures. We implemented a mapping into one table (ACCOUNT) that holds all the attributes of all account subclasses.

In "Top-down mapping of the bank model" on page 475, we generated a mapping of the account subclasses into individual leaf tables.

If the subclasses have few attributes, then mapping into one table is advisable. Mapping into root/leaf tables makes access slower, because SQL joins have to be generated. Also EJB QL queries get more complicated with root/leaf mapping.

For example, the `findGoldAccounts` query (see "Creating a simple custom finder method" on page 455) generates these SQL statements:

Single table mapping (meet-in-the-middle mapping):

```
"select  q1.\"ACCID\",  q1.\"BALANCE\",  q1.\"INTEREST\",
q1.\"ACCTYPE\",  q1.\"DISCRIMINATOR\",  q1.\"MINAMOUNT\",
q1.\"OVERDRAFT\" from ITSO.ACCOUNT q1 where  ( ( q1.\"DISCRIMINATOR\" =
\'A\')  or  ( q1.\"DISCRIMINATOR\" = \'S\')  or  ( q1.\"DISCRIMINATOR\"
= \'C\') )  and  ( q1.\"BALANCE\" > ?)");
```

Root/leaf table mapping (top-down mapping):

```
"select  q1.\"ACCID\",  q1.\"BALANCE\",  q1.\"INTEREST\",
q1.\"ACCTYPE\",  q1.\"DISCRIMINATOR\",  q2.\"MINAMOUNT\",
q3.\"OVERDRAFT\" from ITSO.ACCOUNT q1 left outer join ITSO.SAVINGS q2 on
( q1.\"ACCID\" = q2.\"ACCID\")  left outer join ITSO.CHECKING q3 on  (
q1.\"ACCID\" = q3.\"ACCID\")  where  ( ( q1.\"DISCRIMINATOR\" = \'A\')
or  ( q1.\"DISCRIMINATOR\" = \'S\')  or  ( q1.\"DISCRIMINATOR\" = \'C\')
)  and  ( q1.\"BALANCE\" > ?)");
```

Note: You find the SQL in the `AccountBeanFunctionSet_xxxx` class. The generated SQL for the top-down mapping uses its generated names, for example `ITSOTOP` (instead of `ITSO`), `ACCOUNTID` (for `ACCID`), `ACCOUNT_DISCRIM` (for `DISCRIMINATOR`), value `'Account'` for `'A'`, and so forth.

Some of the EJB QL queries currently generate bad SQL statements when root/leaf mapping is used (see "SQL statements with errors" on page 465).

Mapping a dependent value class

Any serializable Java class can be used as the type of a CMP field (not as an CMR field). The structure is not described in the deployment descriptor. The content is normally streamed into a single table column. For example, the `address` attribute of the `Customer` bean in Chapter 11, "Container-managed entity bean development" on page 397 is mapped to the `address` column of the `CUSTOMER` table.

We have to use a composer to map the `address` attribute into individual columns of a table. WebSphere Application Server Enterprise allows such a mapping by standard tooling without a composer.

Converters and composers

Converters and composers are used to perform the mapping operation between an entity attribute and one or more table columns:

► A **converter** maps one attribute to one column. Many converters are provided to convert SQL data into Java types, but you can write your own as well. A converter is specified in the mapping editor and is used for simple mapping.

► A **composer** maps one attribute (which can be a complex class) to multiple table columns. A composer is specified in the mapping editor and is used for complex mapping.

The mapping editor allows you to specify a "complex mapping" for a CMP field. When you use this option, you have to provide a composer class. You typically use this option for complex attributes, such as the `Address` object used in the `Customer` bean.

The coding for converters and composers is very similar; both must provide methods for both ways of the mapping—from an entity attribute to column(s) and from column(s) to an entity attribute.

Using composers

To illustrate the use of a composer, we develop a composer for the customer's `address` attribute:

► Create a new EJB project named `ItsoBank5ComposerEJB` attached to an enterprise application named `ItsoBank5ComposerEAR`.

► Copy the `itso.bank5.beans` package from the `ItsoBank5CmpEJB` project to the `ItsoBank5ComposerEJB` project so that we can reuse the `Address` class.

► Define a `CustomerComposer` CMP entity bean, with attributes `customerid` (int), `title`, `firstName`, `lastName` (all strings), and `address` (`Address` class).

Writing a composer

A composer is designed to split a complex attribute into multiple columns. We develop an `AttributeComposer` for the address attribute:

► Select the `ItsoBank5ComposerEJB` project and *New -> Other -> EJB -> Converter or Composer* and click *Next*.

► In the EJB Converter or Composer Wizard (Figure 12-6):

    – Select *Composer*.

    – The project (`ItsoBank5ComposerEJB`) is prefilled.

    – Enter `itso.bank5.beans.AddressComposer` as the name of the composer.

– Leave the supertype as `VapAttributeComposer`.

– For the target type, click *Browse* and locate the `Address` class (in `itso.bank5.beans` of the `ItsoBank5ComposerEJB` project).

– Select `java.lang.String` as the new composed field type and click *Add* four times. Change the field names to `street`, `city`, `state`, and `zipcode`.

– Select *Generate a composer stub class*.

– Click *Finish*.

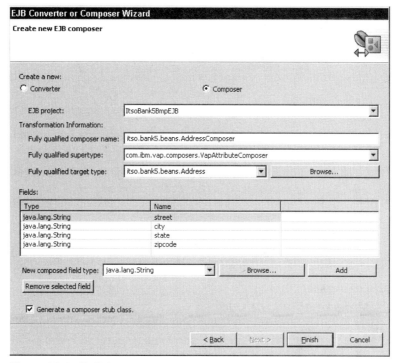

Figure 12-6   Defining a composer

► Open the generated class `itso.bank5.beans.AddressComposer`. You have to complete two methods, `dataFrom` and `objectFrom`. These are the two methods that convert between an object (`Address`) and an array of fields for the table mapping.

► Note the `getAttributeNames` method:

```
public static String[] getAttributeNames() {
    String[] attributes = { "zipcode", "state", "city", "street" };
    return attributes;
}
```

We have to code the `dataFrom` and `objectFrom` methods in the same sequence.

▶ The `getTargetClassName` method that returns `itso.bank5.beans.Address`, the type of the bean.

▶ The `dataFrom` method converts an `Address` object into four fields for the table. Change the code as shown here:

```
public Object[] dataFrom (Object anObject) {
    Object[] anArray = new Object[] {null, null, null, null};
    if (anObject != null) {
        Address address = (Address) anObject;
        anArray[0] = address.getZipcode();
        anArray[1] = address.getState();
        anArray[2] = address.getCity();
        anArray[3] = address.getStreet();
    }
    return anArray;
}
```

▶ The `objectFrom` method converts four table fields into an `Address` object. Change the code as shown here:

```
public Object objectFrom (Object[] anArray) {
    String name, street, city, state, zipcode;
    zipcode = (String) anArray[0];
    state   = (String) anArray[1];
    city    = (String) anArray[2];
    street  = (String) anArray[3];
    return new Address(street, city, state, zipcode);
}
```

Remarks about the code
The `singleton` method is using lazy-initialization on the `singleton` variable. Make sure that the order of the attributes is identical in the `getAttributeNames`, `objectFrom`, and `dataFrom` methods.

Composer definition file
In the `META-INF` folder, you can find the composer definition file, `UserDefinedComposers.xmi`. This file can be copied to other projects to make the composer available.

```
<?xml version="1.0" encoding="UTF-8"?>
<ejbrdbmapping:EJBComposer xmi:version="2.0"
xmlns:xmi="http://www.omg.org/XMI" xmlns:ejbrdbmapping="ejbrdbmapping.xmi"
xmlns:java="java.xmi" xmlns:ecore="ecore.xmi"
xmi:id="EJBComposer_1037077493820">
    <targetClass href="java:/itso.bank5.beans#Address"/>
    <transformerClass href="java:/itso.bank5.beans#AddressComposer"/>
```

```
        <attributes xmi:id="EAttribute_1037077493820" name="zipcode"/>
        <attributes xmi:id="EAttribute_1037077493821" name="state"/>
        <attributes xmi:id="EAttribute_1037077493822" name="city"/>
        <attributes xmi:id="EAttribute_1037077493823" name="street"/>
</ejbrdbmapping:EJBComposer>
```

Mapping with a composer

To create the mapping of the `CustomerComposer` bean:

► Select the `ItsoBank5ComposerEJB` project and *Generate -> EJB to RDB Mapping*.

► Select *Create a new backend folder* and click *Next*.

► Select *Meet In The Middle* and click *Next*.

► Enter connection information (`ConEJBBANKcomposer`, `EJBBANK` database) and click *Next*.

► Select the `ITSO` tables and click *Finish*.

► In the mapping editor:

– Drag the `CustomerComposer` bean to the `CUSTOMER` and to the `CUSTADDRESS` tables.

– Drag the `customerid`, `title`, `firstName` and `lastName` attributes to the columns of the `CUSTOMER` table.

– Select the `address` attribute (left side) and the four columns (`street`, `city`, `state`, `zipcode`) of the `CUSTADDRESS` table (right side) and *Create Mapping* (context).

– In the EJB Composer Wizard, select the `AddressComposer` and map the four attributes to the matching columns (Figure 12-7).

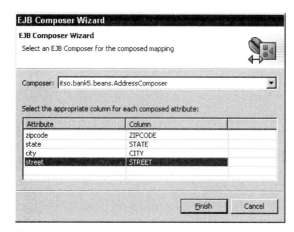

Figure 12-7   Selecting the composer

     – Click *Finish* and save the mapping.

The mapping is shown in Figure 12-8.

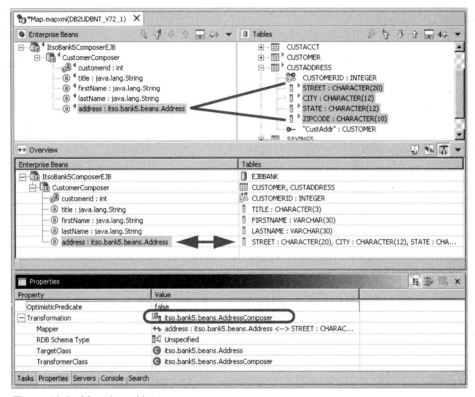

Figure 12-8   Mapping with a composer

Generate the deployed code

Before generating the deployed code, open the deployment descriptor on the Overview page and set the JNDI - CMP Factory Connection Binding name to jdbc/ejbbank and the container authorization type to *Per_Connection_Factory*. Set the back-end folder to DB2UDBNT_V72_1.

Generate the deployed code.

Testing the composer

To test the composer, you have to attach the ItsoBank5ComposerEAR project to the EjbbankServer:

► Select the server and add the EAR project.

- ▶ Start the server and the universal test client. In the JNDI Explorer, select the `CustomerComposer` bean under *[Local EJB beans]* -> *ejb* -> *itso* -> *bank5* -> *composer* -> *CustomerComposerLocalHome* (we used the default name generated by the tool).

- ▶ Expand the home interface, select the `findByPrimaryKey` method, expand the key, enter a value (101), and click *Invoke*.

- ▶ Click *Work with Object*. Expand the `CustomerComposerLocal` reference, select and invoke the `getAddress` method.

- ▶ Click *Work with Object* to access the fields of the `Address` object.

- ▶ Invoke *get* methods of the `Address` object to view the field values.

- ▶ Invoke *set* methods of the `Address` object to change the data.

- ▶ Select the `setAddress` method of the `CustomerComposerLocal` reference. In the Objects pull-down, select the `Address` object and click *Invoke*. This updates the address data in the `CUSTADDRESS` table. You can verify the update in a DB2 command window:

```
db2 connect to ejbbank
db2 select * from itso.custaddress
```

This sequence verifies that the composer is working properly. Close the browser and stop the server when done.

Using converters

A *converter* is always associated with a column definition. The converter has the responsibility to convert a Java type to an SQL type, and vice versa.

We could, for example, use a converter to map the address attribute to some string representation that is stored as a `VARCHAR` in the table.

Another example would be to map a bean that contains a collection of strings. If you let the default mapping handle it, the collection is serialized in a BLOB. The solution is to write a simple converter that reads the collection and stores it in `VARCHAR` or `CLOB` column as an XML stream. Of course, the converter must be able to handle the conversion in the other direction also, reading the XML and parsing it to recreate the collection.

We do not provide an example of a converter. The coding is similar to that of a composer. You would create a subclass of `VapAbstractConverter` and implement the same methods as for a composer, except that you deal with one object instead of an array.

The best approach for building your own converter would be to study the implementation of the converters provided with Application Developer.

13

Bean-managed entity bean development

This chapter discusses how to write bean-managed persistence (BMP) entity beans. We describe in detail how to build a bean-managed entity bean, what methods have to be implemented, and how the SQL statements must be coded.

We also discuss advantages and disadvantages of BMP beans versus CMP beans.

© Copyright IBM Corp. 2003. All rights reserved.

Bean-managed persistence (BMP)

Bean-managed persistence (BMP) enables you to manage the persistence of your bean instead of delegating it to the container. In order to achieve this, you have to write a number of methods that are usually handled by the CMP layer of the container.

This bean has to implement the same interfaces as a CMP entity bean:

► The bean class has to implement the `javax.ejb.EntityBean` interface. All callback methods in this interface have to be implemented.

► The component interface has to extend either the `javax.ejb.EJBObject` or the `javax.ejb.EJBLocalObject`, depending on whether it is a local or a remote component interface. In this interface, you will mainly find business methods as well as accessor methods.

► The home interface has to extend the `javax.ejb.EJBHome` or the `javax.ejb.EJBLocalHome`, depending on whether it is a local or a remote interface. This interface may contain create, finder, and home methods.

Why BMP?

So why would you need BMP? In some cases, there are some reasons why you cannot rely on CMP to do the work. Most of them concern legacy:

► The database schema is impossible to map to the EJBs.

► You have a relational database for entity beans that is not currently supported for CMP or does not have JDBC 2.0 level drivers and, therefore, you will have to use SQLJ, stored procedures, or some other tooling to access it.

► You have a relational database that requires a nonstandard way of handling specific data types such as BLOB or CLOB.

► You require non-relational persistence method, for example, WebSphere MQ, CICS with VSAM files, or IMS.

Recommendations

Use BMP only if there is no way to handle persistence with CMP. There are many reasons to use CMP, such as performance or portability over different types of databases.

If you have to use BMP, then implement the bean by subclassing a CMP 2.0 bean. We are following this recommendation and we use this approach in developing the BMP sample in this chapter.

BMP as subclass of a CMP

How does this approach work?

► Create a CMP entity bean as if you were going to implement persistence using CMP.

► Do not create any interfaces and do not generate deployed code. The only part we are going to use is the abstract bean class.

► Code the business methods in the bean class using the abstract getter and setter methods.

► The BMP bean extends the CMP bean. You can consider the BMP as just an alternative implementation of the abstract CMP class.

  During deployment the container would create a concrete subclass of the CMP bean with persistence functionality. This is exactly what we are doing by subclassing the abstract bean class. We are not delegating the persistence job to the container; we are implementing it ourselves.

► The EJB client accesses the BMP type over its bean home name in the normal manner. The EJB client does not know anything about out CMP type.

The advantages of implementing a BMP in this manner are:

► You can create the CMP attributes with the tool.

► You can easily switch to the CMP type later if the EJB container is able to handle this particular job with CMP. The abstract bean class will stay the same. In the EJB client, you only have to change the type you are accessing.

► You automatically separate the business logic from the implementation code by using different classes.

► You do not have to code the getters and setters manually.

► You can use the primary key class from the CMP, that is, you do not have to implement the key class yourself.

► You get the signatures of the `ejbCreate` and `ejbPostCreate` methods.

Developing a BMP entity bean

In this section, we develop a `CustomerInfoBmp` bean to illustrate the use of BMP.

The `CustomerInfoBmp` bean represents additional information for a customer of the bank. For each kind of additional information ,we create a row in a `CUSTOMERINFO` table. Additional information could be a photo for printing on the credit card or a scanned image for the identification card.

Underlying table for customer information

Table 13-1 shows the layout of the `CUSTOMERINFO` table.

Table 13-1   Customer information table

Column name	Type	Length	Key	Nulls	Description
CUSTOMERID	INTEGER		PK	No	Customer ID
INFOID	INTEGER		PK	No	Information ID (1,2,...)
DESCRIPTION	VARCHAR	50	No	Yes	Description of information
DATA	BLOB	10000	No	Yes	Binary data

This design allows for one entry of each kind of information. We map the BLOB data to a byte array in Java.

Create an EJB project for the BMP entity bean

We use a new EJB project named `ITSOBank5BmpEJB` for the BMP implementation:

► Select *File -> New -> Project, EJB -> EJB Project*.

► Select *Create 2.0 EJB Project*.

► Enter as `ITSOBank5BmpEJB` name, and select the existing enterprise application project `ItsoBank5EAR`. Click *Finish*.

► Create a package name `itso.bank5.bmp` in the new project.

Creating the superclass CMP entity bean

> **Note:** To create a BMP, we are following the recommendation described above by subclassing a CMP 2.0 class. If you do not want to use this approach, you can skip this step.

We create the superclass CMP entity bean with the name `CustomerInfoCmp`. This process is described in detail in "Create a CMP 2.0" on page 399:

- Create a CMP 2.0 with the name `CustomerInfoCmp` in the `itso.bank5.bmp` package.
- Set the EJB binding name to `ejb/itsobank/CustomerInfoCmp`.
- Select the remote interface only.
- Set the key class name to `itso.bank5.bmp.CustomerInfoKey`.
- Add the CMP fields shown in Table 13-2.

Table 13-2 Fields of the CMP supertype

Type	Name	key	Note
`int`	`cutomerID`	Primary key	
`int`	`infoID`	Primary key	Composed primary key
`java.lang.String`	`description`		
`byte[]`	`data`		Select `byte` as type and select *Array* of dimension 1

- Click *Finish*.

The key class

The most important part of what we get by defining the CMP entity bean is the key class. A key class is required for the BMP entity bean and instead of coding it ourselves, we can get it generated.

The main methods of the key class are:

- The constructor that creates a key from the two key fields
- The get and set methods to set the key fields

The `CustomerInfoKey` class is shown in Figure 13-1.

```
package itso.bank5.bmp;
/**
 * Key class for Entity Bean: CustomerInfoCmp
 */
public class CustomerInfoKey implements java.io.Serializable {
    static final long serialVersionUID = 3206093459760846163L;

    public int customerID;
    public int infoID;

    public CustomerInfoKey() {
    }
    public CustomerInfoKey(int customerID, int infoID) {
        this.customerID = customerID;
        this.infoID = infoID;
    }
    public boolean equals(java.lang.Object otherKey) {
        if (otherKey instanceof itso.bank5.bmp.CustomerInfoKey) {
            itso.bank5.bmp.CustomerInfoKey o =
                (itso.bank5.bmp.CustomerInfoKey) otherKey;
            return (
                (this.customerID == o.customerID) &&
                    (this.infoID == o.infoID));
        }
        return false;
    }
    public int hashCode() {
        return (
            (new java.lang.Integer(customerID).hashCode())
                + (new java.lang.Integer(infoID).hashCode()));
    }
    public int getCustomerID() {
        return customerID;
    }
    public void setCustomerID(int newCustomerID) {
        customerID = newCustomerID;
    }
    public int getInfoID() {
        return infoID;
    }
    public void setInfoID(int newInfoID) {
        infoID = newInfoID;
    }
}
```

Figure 13-1   Key class for BMP entity bean

Creating the BMP entity bean

To create the BMP entity bean, follow these steps:

► Create a new enterprise bean by selecting *New -> Enterprise Bean* from the context menu of the EJB project.

► Click *Next* on the project window.

► In the Create a 2.0 Enterprise bean panel (Figure 13-2):

  – Select *Entity bean with bean-managed persistence (BMP) fields.*

  – Enter `CustomerInfoBmp` as the bean name and make sure that the `itso.bank5.bmp` package is selected.

> **Note:** We are using the suffix `Bmp` to mark it as a technical subtype of the CMP type. Normally it makes no sense to point to the type of the bean in its name. If you do not use a supertype, you should use `CustomerInfo` as the bean name.

  – Click *Next.*

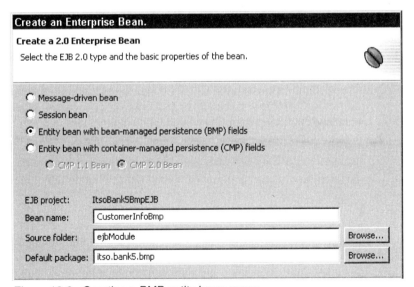

Figure 13-2   Creating a BMP entity bean: name

► In the Enterprise Bean Details panel (Figure 13-3), do as follows:

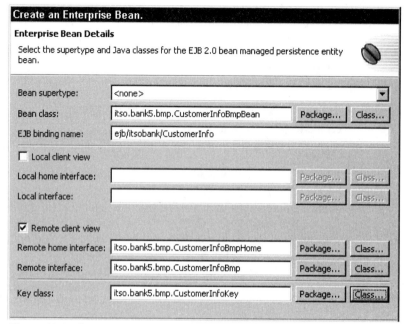

Figure 13-3 Creating a BMP entity bean: details

▶ Set the EJB binding name to `ejb/itsobank/CustomerInfo`.

▶ Select only *Remote client view*.

▶ If you are subclassing the CMP 2.0 bean, you can use the primary key class from the CMP type. Click *Class* and enter `cust` to locate and select the `CustomerInfoKey` class.

▶ You cannot change the bean supertype in this window. The supertype only applies to CMP inheritance (see "Defining the inheritance structure" on page 448).

▶ Click *Next*.

▶ In the EJB Java Class Details panel (Figure 13-4), if you want to subclass the CMP 2.0 bean class, click *Browse* for the Bean superclass and locate the `CustomerInfoCmpBean` class.

▶ Click *Finish*.

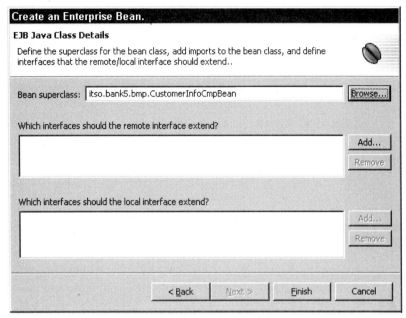

Figure 13-4   Creating a BMP entity bean: superclass

The BMP entity bean is added to the project as shown in Figure 13-5.

Figure 13-5   J2EE hierarchy of the ItsoBank5BmpEJB project

Table 13-3 shows the types that were generated for the BMP entity bean.

Table 13-3   Generated types

Type	Description
CustomerInfoBmpHome	The home interface of the bean with a `create` and a `findByPrimaryKey` method.
CustomerInfoBmp	The component interface of the bean. No methods have been generated into this interface.
CustomerInfoBmpBean	The bean itself, which will contain the actual implementation. Note that this class is concrete. Only the CMP bean classes are abstract. This bean shows many errors in the Tasks view because we have not yet provided the implementation of the abstract methods of the superclass.
CustomerInfoKey	The primary key class, which holds all the attributes used to compose the primary key of the bean. Note that this is the class from the CMP 2.0 type and we do not have to implement this key class. If you do not use inheritance from a CMP 2.0 type, then you have to implement the key class yourself, with code that matches this generated class.

Abstract methods

Application Developer provides a simple window to create skeleton implementations of abstract methods and to overwrite superclass methods:

► Open the CustomerInfoBmpBean class.

► In the Outline view, select the CustomerInfoBmpBean class and *Override Methods* (context).

► In the Override Methods window, the abstract methods are preselected (Figure 13-6).

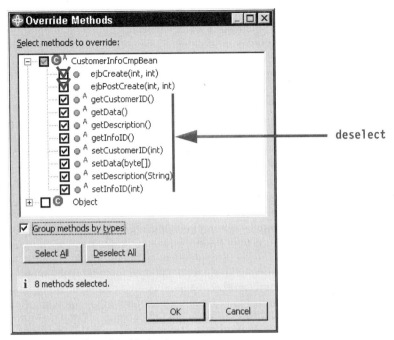

Figure 13-6   Override Methods

▶ You could create skeletons for these methods, but then you would have to write the implementation code for each method.

▶ It is easier to define the persistent fields and create getter and setter methods.

▶ Select only the `ejbCreate(int,int)` and `ejbPostCreate(int,int)` methods. We want to overwrite these methods in the BMP bean. The `ejbCreate` method that was generated has no parameters.

▶ Click *OK*.

Defining the persistent fields

The BMP entity bean does not have any persistent fields. We have to define fields that match the CMP bean:

```
// the BMP fields
private int customerID = 0;
private int infoID = 0;
private String description = null;
private byte[] data = null;
```

Select the four fields in the Outline view and *Generate Getter and Setter* (context). This operation creates the getter and setter methods that implement the abstract methods of the `CustomerInfoCmpBean` superclass.

Create method with parameters

The `CustomerInfoBmpBean` now has two `ejbCreate` methods:

▶ Delete the `ejbCreate` and `ejbPostCreate` methods with no parameters.

▶ Select the `ejbCreate(int,int)` method and *Enterprise Bean -> Promote to Home Interface* (context).

▶ Open the `CustomerInfoBmpHome` interface and delete the `create` method without parameters. We keep only the `create` method with two parameters.

Now we have to implement the code that is responsible for the persistence handling. Let's take a look on the methods in the bean class first.

A first look at the bean methods

After the bean has been created, we can examine the methods of the bean. There are two types of methods: the required callback methods for which we have to provide an implementation, and some utility methods that help us to reuse some code and also reduce the complexity of the required methods.

Callback methods

A number of callback methods have to be implemented in order to support the bean-managed persistence.

> **Note:** All these methods have been generated by Application Developer. Some of them are just a skeleton, while others must have a usable implementation.

Table 13-4 shows the callback methods:

▶ The first five methods (`ejbLoad`, `ejbStore`, `ejbFindByPrimaryKey`, `ejbCreate`, and `ejbRemove`) invoke SQL statement to synchronize the bean data with the database table.

▶ The `setEntityContext` and `unsetEntityContext` are used to allocate and free resources, such as the data source used to interact with the database.

▶ We will not touch the `ejbActivate` and `ejbPassivate` methods.

Table 13-4 Callback methods that must be implemented

Method	Description
ejbLoad	This method has to ensure that the bean data is consistent with the data in the persistent store. We will retrieve the data using an SQL select statement.
ejbStore	The container invokes this method to allow the bean to update the persistent store with its own data. It is up to the bean to determine if such update is relevant or not. We will use an SQL update statement.
ejbFindByPrimaryKey	This method has to be implemented to retrieve the bean using the primary key. A FinderException or ObjectNotFoundException can be thrown. We will use an SQL select statement.
ejbCreate	This method has to be updated with the correct number of parameters and it has to be implemented. It is used to create a new bean in the persistent store. Please note that a CreateException can be thrown if something goes wrong during creation. We will use an SQL insert statement.
ejbRemove	When a client is calling the remove method on a remote interface or is calling the remove(key) method on the home interface, it results in the container invoking the ejbRemove method to delete the matching data in the persistent store and to release held resources. We will use an SQL delete statement.
setEntityContext	This method is called when a bean instance is created in the pool but is not yet associated with an EJBObject. The data received is stored inside an instance variable. We will allocate resources in this method.
unsetEntityContex	When this method is called, the bean is about to be removed from the pool and destroyed. We will free resources in this method.
ejbActivate	This method is invoked when a client calls a method on a EJBObject with no associated bean instance. The container then takes an instance from the pool and invokes ejbActivate to allow the instance to acquire whatever resources it needs in order to be in the ready state.
ejbPassivate	When a particular bean instance is not used anymore, the container is passivating it. The result of that operation is a callback to ejbPassivate to allow the bean to release the resources acquired during the activation.

Implementing the bean methods

Instead of implementing the JDBC access in the BMP entity bean we create a persister bean named `CustomerInfoBmpPersister`.

There are five main tasks for the persistence:

- ▶ Load a state
- ▶ Sore a state
- ▶ Find a state
- ▶ Create a state
- ▶ Delete a state

For each task, we create a method in the persister class (Table 13-5):

Table 13-5   Methods of the JDBC persister class

Purpose	Method	Description
Load a state	`loadState`	Load all values from the database for the row with the given key by invoking an SQL `select` and reading all values from the result set.
Store a state	`storeState`	Stores all values of the given bean in the database by invoking an SQL `update`.
Find a state	`findPrimaryKey`	Checks if there is a row with the given key using an SQL `select`. Returns the key if found.
Create a state	`createState`	Create a row in the database by executing an SQL `insert`.
Delete a state	`deleteState`	Delete a database row for the given key by invoking an SQL `delete`.

How we implement the JDBC persister is described in "Implementing the persister class" on page 507. The interesting point is which persister action to call in which callback method.

We implement the callback methods by delegating to the persister class. Technical exceptions are caught and wrapped in an appropriate exception.

ejbFindByPrimaryKey method

We start with implementing the `ejbFindByPrimaryKey` method. We have to search for the key and return it if found by the persister class. If an SQL exception occurs, we wrap it in a `FinderException` (Figure 13-7).

```
public itso.bank5.bmp.CustomerInfoKey ejbFindByPrimaryKey(
                    itso.bank5.bmp.CustomerInfoKey primaryKey)
                    throws javax.ejb.FinderException {
    boolean found = false;
    try {
        found = persister.findPrimaryKey(primaryKey);
    }
    catch (SQLException e) {
        e.printStackTrace();
        throw new FinderException(e.getMessage());
    }
    if (found)
        return primaryKey;
    else
        throw new ObjectNotFoundException();
}
```

Figure 13-7   Implementing ejbFindByPrimaryKey

ejbCreate method

The implementation of the ejbCreate method creates a new instance of the bean key class and passes this instance to the persister class. SQL exceptions are caught and wrapped in a CreateException. The DuplicateKeyException is a subtype of the SQLException (Figure 13-8).

```
public CustomerInfoKey ejbCreate(int customerID, int infoID)
    throws CreateException {
    CustomerInfoKey key = new CustomerInfoKey(customerID, infoID);
    try {
        persister.createState(key);
        return key;
    }
    catch (SQLException e) {
        e.printStackTrace();
        throw new CreateException(e.getMessage());
    }
}
```

Figure 13-8   Implementing ejbCreate

ejbLoad method

The implementation of the ejbLoad method is shown in Figure 13-9. SQL exceptions are caught. We are delegating to the persister class, which loads the state from the database and copies the values to the bean attributes by invoking the setters of the bean class. An EJBException is thrown to cause a rollback if SQL errors occur.

```
public void ejbLoad() {
    try {
        persister.loadState(this);
    } catch (SQLException e) {
        e.printStackTrace();
        throw new EJBException(e.getSQLState()+" code: "+e.getErrorCode());
    }
}
```

Figure 13-9   Implementing ejbLoad

ejbStore method

The implementation of the ejbStore method in Figure 13-10 is very similar. It delegates to the persister class, which reads all the attribute values by invoking the getters of the bean class and writes them to the database. An EJBException is thrown to cause a rollback if SQL errors occur.

```
public void ejbStore() {
    try {
        persister.storeState(this);
    }
    catch (SQLException e) {
        e.printStackTrace();
        throw new EJBException(e.getSQLState()+" code: "+e.getErrorCode());
    }
}
```

Figure 13-10   Implementing ejbStore

ejbRemove method

The implementation of the ejbRemove method just delegates to the persister and throws a RemoveException either if the return value is false or if any other SQL exceptions are thrown (Figure 13-11).

```
public void ejbRemove() throws javax.ejb.RemoveException {
    try {
        boolean success = persister.deleteState(this);
        if (!success)
            throw new RemoveException("Not able to delete state");
    } catch (SQLException e) {
        throw new RemoveException(e.getMessage());
    }
}
```

Figure 13-11   Implementing ejbRemove

Completing the BMP entity bean

We have to add these import statements for the exceptions and the persister class used in the code:

```
import javax.ejb.*;
import java.sql.SQLException;
import itso.bank5.bmp.persister.CustomerInfoBmpPersister;
```

We have to allocate an instance of the persister class and initialize it for subsequent method calls.

► Create a field for the persister class:

```
// persister class
private CustomerInfoBmpPersister persister = null;
```

► Initialize the persister instance in the setEntityContext method:

```
public void setEntityContext(javax.ejb.EntityContext ctx) {
    myEntityCtx = ctx;
    if (persister == null) persister = new CustomerInfoBmpPersister();
}
```

► Free the resources in the unsetEntityContext method:

```
public void unsetEntityContext() {
    if (persister != null) persister.freeResources();
    persister = null;
    myEntityCtx = null;
}
```

Promoting the business methods

We have to make the business methods available to clients. In the Outline view, select all the getter methods (getCustomerID, getData, getDescription, getInfoID) and two setter methods (setData, setDescription) and *Enterprise Bean -> Promote to Remote Interface* (context).

Note that we do not promote setCustomerID and setInfoID, because key attributes of a bean cannot be changed.

The promoted methods are visible in the CustomerInfoBmp interface.

Completing the deployment descriptor

We have to set up the deployment descriptor with control information for the database access.

Open the deployment descriptor of the ItsoBank5BmpEJB project.

WebSphere bindings

On the Overview page, scroll down to set these properties:

► Set the JNDI name under JNDI - CMP Factory Connection Binding to jdbc/ejbbank.

► Set the Container authorization type to Per_Connection_Factory.

► Set the Backend ID to DB2UDNNT_V72_1.

This is the same as for the CMP project (see Figure 11-22 on page 421).

Environment variable for the data source

The persister class uses a data source for connection management. This is the desired approach with JDBC 2.0 so that connections can be shared between CMP and BMP entity beans.

Instead of hard-coding the data source name in the persister class, we define the name as an environment variable of the BMP entity bean.

On the Beans page, select the CustomerInfoBmp bean and scroll down to Environment Variables. Click *Add* to define a variable and complete the window as shown in Figure 13-12.

Note that we define a local JNDI name (java:comp/env/....). That means we have to define a reference that matches this name to a global JNDI name.

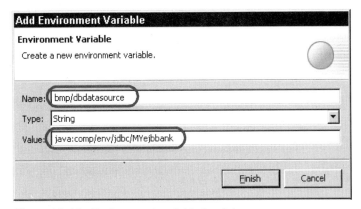

Figure 13-12   Environment variable for data source

We use the bmp/dbdatasource variable in the persister class to retrieve the JNDI name of the data source.

> **Note:** We could define more environment variables, such as the provider URL or the context factory class. The data source environment variable illustrates the concept of passing values from the deployment descriptor to the persister class.

JNDI reference for the data source

The persister class gets the name of the data source through the bmp/dbdatasource environment variable. The persister then invokes a JNDI lookup to get the data source object.

We associate the data source name used in the persister class with a real JNDI name through a reference.

On the References page, select the CustomerInfoBmp bean and click *Add*. In the Add Reference window:

- Select EJB resource reference and click *Next*.
- Complete the window as shown in Figure 13-13:
  - Enter jdbc/MYejbbank as the local name
  - Select javax.sql.DataSource as type
  - Select *Container* for authentication
  - Select *Shareable* for sharing scope
  - Click *Finish*.

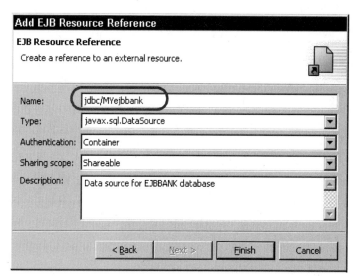

Figure 13-13   Defining a data source reference

The reference appears in the list of references. For WebSphere bindings, enter
jdbc/ejbbank as the JNDI name (Figure 13-14). Save the file when done.

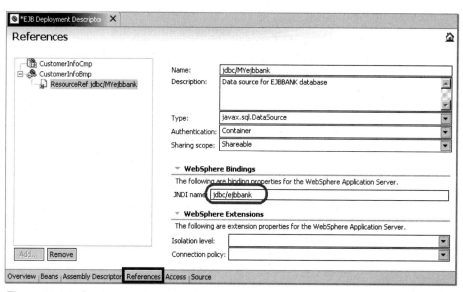

Figure 13-14   Deployment descriptor: references

Implementing the persister class

The persister class, CustomerInfoBmpPersister, implements the JDBC access for the BMP entity bean.

Create the CustomerInfoBmpPersister class in a new itso.bank5.bmp.persister package and complete the code as detailed in this section.

One of the important issues in the persister class is to always close the SQL objects, such as ResultSet, PreparedStatement, and Connection. This is accomplished by using a try/catch block with a finally clause.

Import statements

Add these import statements for SQL access, JNDI access, and exceptions:

```
import itso.bank5.bmp.CustomerInfoBmpBean;
import itso.bank5.bmp.CustomerInfoKey;
import java.sql.Connection;
import java.sql.PreparedStatement;
import java.sql.ResultSet;
import java.sql.SQLException;
import javax.sql.DataSource;
import javax.naming.InitialContext;
import javax.naming.NamingException;
```

Constants and variables

The persister class keeps the data source cached. To create the data source, the environment variable defined in the deployment descriptor is used. For database access, the SQL statements are defined.

```
// sql datasource and connection
private DataSource ds = null;

// environment variable key and value - must exist in bean environment
final String DB_DATASOURCE_KEY = "bmp/dbdatasource";

// SQL statements
final String SELECT_SQL = "SELECT T1.CUSTOMERID, T1.INFOID, T1.DESCRIPTION,
                          T1.DATA FROM ITSO.CUSTOMERINFO T1
                          WHERE T1.CUSTOMERID = ? AND T1.INFOID = ?";
final String INSERT_SQL = "INSERT INTO ITSO.CUSTOMERINFO (CUSTOMERID,
                          INFOID, DESCRIPTION) VALUES (?, ?, ?)";
final String UPDATE_SQL = "UPDATE ITSO.CUSTOMERINFO  SET DESCRIPTION = ?,
                          DATA = ? WHERE CUSTOMERID = ? AND INFOID = ?";
final String DELETE_SQL = "DELETE FROM ITSO.CUSTOMERINFO
                          WHERE CUSTOMERID = ? AND INFOID = ?";
```

Initialization

When the persister instance is created it gets the JNDI name of the data source from the environment variable and then retrieves the data source itself.

```
public CustomerInfoBmpPersister() {
    initializeResources();
}
public void initializeResources() {
    try {
        InitialContext ctx = new InitialContext();
        String dbDatasource = (String)
                        ctx.lookup("java:comp/env/"+DB_DATASOURCE_KEY);
        ds = (DataSource)ctx.lookup(dbDatasource);
        System.out.println("BMP persister datasource: "+dbDatasource);
    } catch (Exception e) { e.printStackTrace(); }
}
```

Returning the data source

The data source is returned to callback methods to get a connection.

```
private DataSource getDatasource() throws SQLException {
    if (ds == null ) throw new SQLException("Data source is null");
    else return ds;
}
```

The callback methods can get a connection using:

```
Connection con = getDatasource().getConnection();
```

Freeing resources

When the BMP entity bean is removed, this method is called to free the resources.

```
public void freeResources() {
    System.out.println("BMP persister free resources");
    ds = null;
}
```

Create state

The createState method is called by the ejbCreate method of the bean when a new instance is created.

```
public void createState(CustomerInfoKey key) throws SQLException {
    System.out.println("BMP persister createState");
    Connection        con = null;
    PreparedStatement ps  = null;
    try {
        con = getDatasource().getConnection();
        ps = con.prepareStatement(INSERT_SQL);
        ps.setInt(1, key.customerID);
```

```
            ps.setInt(2, key.infoID);
            ps.setString(3, "");  // description
            // data is left as null
            int result = ps.executeUpdate();
        } catch (SQLException e) { throw e; }
        finally {
            if (ps  != null) ps.close();
            if (con != null) con.close();
        }
    }
```

Find by primary key

The findPrimaryKey method is called by the ejbFindByPrimaryKey method of the bean when an existing bean is located.

```
public boolean findPrimaryKey(CustomerInfoKey key) throws SQLException {
    System.out.println("BMP persister findByPrimaryKey");
    Connection        con = null;
    PreparedStatement ps  = null;
    ResultSet         rs  = null;
    boolean result = false;
    try {
        con = getDatasource().getConnection();
        ps = con.prepareStatement(SELECT_SQL);
        ps.setInt(1, key.customerID);
        ps.setInt(2, key.infoID);
        rs = ps.executeQuery();
        result = rs.next();
    } catch (SQLException e) { throw e; }
    finally {
        if (rs  != null) rs.close();
        if (ps  != null) ps.close();
        if (con != null) con.close();
    }
    return result;
}
```

Load state

The loadState method is called by the ejbLoad method of the bean whenever the bean's data has to be retrieved from the database.

```
public void loadState(CustomerInfoBmpBean bean) throws SQLException {
    System.out.println("BMP persister loadState");
    CustomerInfoKey key = (CustomerInfoKey)
                            bean.getEntityContext().getPrimaryKey();
    Connection        con = null;
    PreparedStatement ps  = null;
    ResultSet         rs  = null;
    try {
```

```
            con = getDatasource().getConnection();
            ps = con.prepareStatement(SELECT_SQL);
            ps.setInt(1, key.customerID);
            ps.setInt(2, key.infoID);
            rs = ps.executeQuery();
            rs.next();
            bean.setCustomerID( rs.getInt(1) );
            bean.setInfoID( rs.getInt(2) );
            bean.setDescription( rs.getString(3) );
            bean.setData( rs.getBytes(4) );
        } catch (SQLException e) { throw e; }
        finally {
            if (rs  != null) rs.close();
            if (ps  != null) ps.close();
            if (con != null) con.close();
        }
    }
```

Store state

The storeState method is called by the ejbStore method of the bean whenever the bean's data must be saved to the database.

```
public void storeState(CustomerInfoBmpBean bean) throws SQLException {
    System.out.println("BMP persister storeState");
    Connection        con = null;
    PreparedStatement ps  = null;
    try {
        con = getDatasource().getConnection();
        ps = con.prepareStatement(UPDATE_SQL);
        ps.setString(1, bean.getDescription());
        ps.setBytes(2, bean.getData());
        ps.setInt(3, bean.getCustomerID());
        ps.setInt(4, bean.getInfoID());
        ps.executeUpdate();
    } catch (SQLException e) { throw e; }
    finally {
        if (ps  != null) ps.close();
        if (con != null) con.close();
    }
}
```

Delete state

The deleteState method is called from the ejbRemove method of the bean when an instance is deleted.

```
public boolean deleteState(CustomerInfoBmpBean bean) throws SQLException {
    System.out.println("BMP persister deleteState");
    CustomerInfoKey key = (CustomerInfoKey)
                        bean.getEntityContext().getPrimaryKey();
```

```
        Connection        con = null;
        PreparedStatement ps  = null;
        int result;
        try {
           con = getDatasource().getConnection();
           ps = con.prepareStatement(DELETE_SQL);
           ps.setInt(1, key.customerID);
           ps.setInt(2, key.infoID);
           result = ps.executeUpdate();  // is 0 for successful delete
        } catch (SQLException e) { throw e; }
        finally {
           if (ps  != null) ps.close();
           if (con != null) con.close();
        }
        return (result != 0);
    }
```

> **Note:** Note that the `createState` method only adds a table row with the `customerID` and `infoID`. The `description` is set to an empty string and the `data` column is left null (it is not set in the SQL insert statement).

Generating the deployed code

The BMP entity bean and its persistent implementation is complete and we can generate the deployed code. Select the `ItsoBank5BmpEJB` project and *Generate -> Deploy and RMIC Code* (context).

This action generates the deployed code for both the CMP and the BMP entity bean. For the CMP entity bean, a default top-down mapping to a table is generated. We can use these definitions to create the CUSTOMERINFO table.

Creating the database table

You can use the Data perspective to define databases, schemas, and tables. We could define the CUSTOMERINFO table from scratch. However, it is easier to use the skeleton definitions that the deployment step generated.

Open the Data perspective and expand the `ItsoBank5BmpEJB` project in the Data Definition view (Figure 13-15).

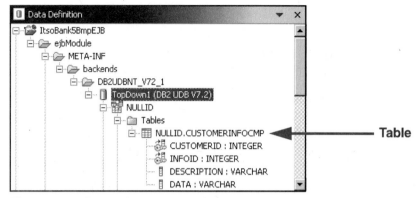

Figure 13-15 Data definition created by top-down mapping

Open the `NULLID.CUSTOMERINFOCMP` table. On the Columns page:

▶ Change the length of the `DESCRIPTION` column to `50`
▶ Change the data type of the `DATA` column to *BLOB*
▶ Change the length of the `DATA` column to `10` (leave the LOB multiplier as K, so the actual length is `10000`)

Save the table definition. Note that you cannot change the table name.

Generate the DDL

Select the `NULLID.CUSTOMERINFOCMP` table and Generate DDL (context). In the Generate SQL DDL window (Figure 13-16):

▶ Select *Generate associated drop statements* (so that we can rerun the DDL).

▶ Select *Open SQL DDL file for editing when done*.

▶ Click *Finish*.

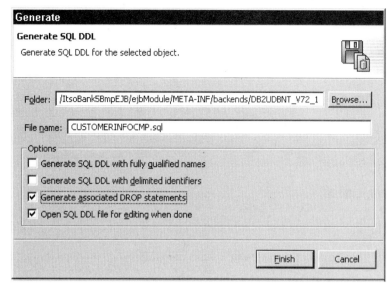

Figure 13-16   Generating the DDL for the table

The generated DDL for the table can be modified to suit our requirement
(Figure 13-17).

```
DROP TABLE CUSTOMERINFOCMP;                              ==> ITSO.CUSTOMERINFO

CREATE TABLE CUSTOMERINFOCMP                             ==> ITSO.CUSTOMERINFO
  (CUSTOMERID INTEGER NOT NULL,
   INFOID INTEGER NOT NULL,
   DESCRIPTION VARCHAR(50),
   DATA BLOB(10K));

ALTER TABLE CUSTOMERINFOCMP                              ==> ITSO.CUSTOMERINFO
  ADD CONSTRAINT PK_CUSTOMERINFOCMP PRIMARY KEY (CUSTOMERID, INFOID);
```

Figure 13-17   Generated DDL and modifications

Run the DDL

Select the CUSTOMERINFOCMP.sql file and *Run on Database Server* (context). This
starts the Run Script window:

▶ Select the statements to run (create and alter), and click *Next*.

▶ Select *Commit changes only upon success*, and click *Next*.

- In the Database Connection panel, leave the connection name as is, but set the database name to EJBBANK. Click *Finish*.

This action executes the DDL and the CUSTOMERINFO table is defined in the EJBBANK database.

> **Note:** The DDL (Example 10-1) and SQL (Example 10-2) jobs listed in Chapter 10, "Introducing and preparing for the sample application" on page 369 define and load the CUSTOMERINFO table. This section illustrates how a new table could be defined from Application Developer.

Load sample data

You can use a few SQL statements in a DB2 command window to load sample data:

```
db2 connect to ejbbank
db2 insert into itso.customerinfo (customerid, infoid, description, data)
        values (101, 1, 'Picture', blob('xxxxxxxxxx')
db2 insert into itso.customerinfo (customerid, infoid, description, data)
        values (101, 2, 'Scanned data', blob('yyyyyy')
db2 select customerid, infoid, description, substr(data,1,10)
        from itso.customerinfo
```

Testing the BMP entity bean

The ItsoBank5BmpEJB project is part of the ItsoBank5EAR enterprise application and attached to the EjbbankServer. Start the server and wait for the ready message.

Testing the BMP with the universal test client

When the server is ready, select the server in the Servers view and *Run universal test client* (context).

Here is a small test scenario:

- Select the JNDI Explorer.
- Expand *ejb -> itsobank* and select the *CustomerInfo* bean (this is the BMP entity bean).
- Expand the home and select the findByPrimaryKey method.
- Select the parameter and enter 1 and 101 as key values for infoID and customerID. Click *Invoke*.

▶ The BMP instance is retrieved and you can click *Work with Object* to add the result to the References (Figure 13-18).

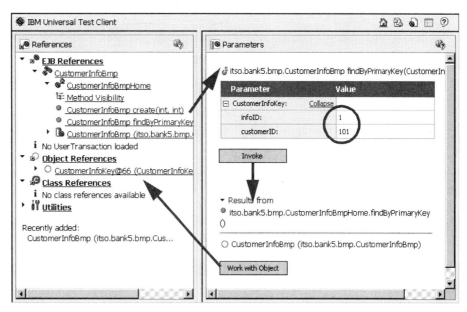

Figure 13-18   Testing a BMP in the test client

▶ Expand the instance, then run some of the getter methods to see the data.

▶ In the home reference, select the `create` method:

  – Enter values for the key fields, for example, `102` and `1`. Click *Invoke*.

  – A new instance is created.

  – Click *Work with Object*.

▶ Expand the new instance reference:

  – Invoke the `getDescription` and `getData` methods.

  – The description field is an empty string and the data field is null.

▶ Select the `setData` method:

  – Expand the parameter.

  – Click *Add* twice to add individual bytes.

  – Enter some values (numeric 0-127)

  – Click *Invoke* (Figure 13-19).

▶ Run the `setDescription` method to add a description text.

▶ Close the browser window and stop the server.

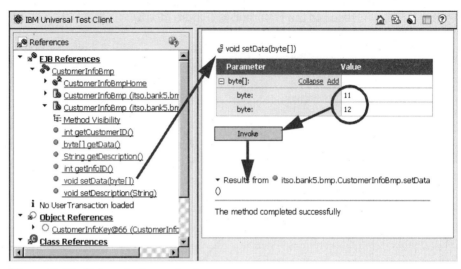

Figure 13-19   Using a setter method

Read-only methods

If you check the Console view, you can see test messages from the persister class. From this output you can see that even a get method invokes both the `loadState` and the `storeState` method of the persister class, and therefore the table is updated for every method.

For CMP entity beans, the container is smart enough to update the table only when the data has been modified.

For BMP entity beans, we have to implement this ourselves.

Making the BMP entity bean smarter

Because we implement the persistent logic, we have to add the code to make the BMP entity bean smarter and not update the table unnecessarily.

We add a *dirty* field that is set whenever the bean data is updated. In the `ejbStore` method, we then check the *dirty* flag to see if a table update is required.

Open the `CustomerInfoBmpBean` class:

► Define a field:

```
// dirty flag
boolean dirty = true;
```

► Change the `ejbLoad` method to reset the dirty flag:

```
persister.loadState(this);
dirty = false;
```

► Change the `ejbStore` method to test and reset the dirty flag:

```
if (dirty) persister.storeState(this);
dirty = false;
```

► Change the `ejbCreate` method to reset the dirty flag:

```
persister.createState(key);
dirty = false;
return key;
```

► Change the four set methods to set the dirty flag:

```
public void setXxxxxx(.....) {
    this.xxxxxxxxxx = ......;
    dirty = true;
}
```

If you rerun the test with the universal test client, you can see that the `storeState` method is not invoked for getters.

Summary

As we mentioned in the introduction:

► Try to use CMP whenever you can.

► However, there are still situations where developers will be forced to develop BMP entity beans. Because the only meaningful difference between BMP and CMP components is who provides the persistence logic, BMPs offer quite a good deal of flexibility in developing components within the J2EE architecture, when functionality is not covered by CMP.

► BMP are quite difficult and long to write. With abstractions and helper classes that we introduced in the code (environment variables from the deployment descriptor, separating the JDBC code in a persister helper class, subclassing a CMP 2.0 bean class), it is not too difficult.

Pros and cons of BMP entity beans

After seeing how BMPs are built, here are some points that could help you make a decision.

Advantages

► Basically, you have access to any persistent store.

- Optimization can be done for each access.

Disadvantages

- You have to write a lot of code.

- Data source dependency: It is difficult to isolate the bean from a specific data source (unlike CMP, which allows you to switch from one DB to another and eventually from vendor to vendor).

Access intent

Access intent can be specified for CMPs to optimize the access in the EJB container. For BMPs, access intent can also be specified. However, it is up to the bean developer to make use of the access intent specification.

> **Note:** From the documentation of access intent:
>
> - However, there are still situations where developers will be forced to develop BMP entity beans. Because the only meaningful difference between BMP and CMP components is who provides the persistence logic, BMPs should be able to leverage access intent hints just the same as the WebSphere Application Server does on behalf of CMPs. BMPs that use the access intent mechanism will participate in application profiling; that is, the value of the access intent attributes may differ from request to request, allowing the BMP to seamlessly modify its persistence strategy.
>
> - Developers may therefore apply access intent policies to BMP methods as well as CMP methods. There is, of course, no obligation for a BMP to exploit access intent hints, as they are not contractual in nature. It is in fact expected that BMP developers will not use every access intent attribute, but only the ones that are important to a particular BMP.
>
> - The current access intent policy is bound into the `java:comp` namespace for each particular BMP. That policy is current only for the duration of the method call during which the access intent policy was retrieved. The developer will most likely cache the access type during ejbLoad so that the appropriate actions can be taken during ejbStore.

14

Session bean development

In this chapter, we describe how to develop session beans using Application Developer.

We develop both a stateless and a stateful session for the banking scenario. Both session beans use the CMP entity beans that we developed earlier to update the database.

Finally, we develop a Web service from a session bean. This Web service can be used in SOAP clients to perform the logic of the session bean.

© Copyright IBM Corp. 2003. All rights reserved.

Design

We develop a stateless session bean (Banking) to serve as session facade for the ITSO bank business logic. This bean exposes several methods that allow a client to perform banking transactions, such as asking for the balance, depositing and withdrawing funds, transfering funds from one account to another, and listing the transaction records.

We also develop a stateful session bean (Reports) for reporting purposes. This bean enables a client to run multiple reports without losing the context, that is the customer and account numbers. This bean uses EQB-QL queries to retrieve customer and account information.

Throughout the book, several clients will use these session beans:

- ▶ Servlet client—"Developing a servlet client" on page 590
- ▶ Struts client—"Developing a Struts-based Web client" on page 609
- ▶ Message-driven bean—"Developing a message-driven bean client" on page 624
- ▶ GUI client—"GUI client using access beans" on page 634
- ▶ Web service client—"Client using a Web service" on page 639

Another possible client is a Java applet but we do not elaborate on this

The session bean methods will only be exposed in the *remote* interface of the session beans. They are, after all, our gateway for outside clients. Adding a local interface could be useful if a message-driven bean is used as an access point and better performance is required.

Figure 14-1 shows the basic design of the session beans.

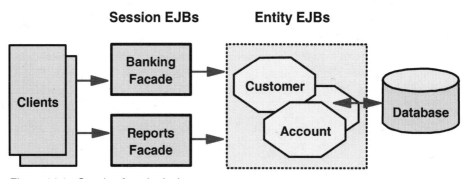

Figure 14-1   Session facade design

Home factory

Before starting this part, make sure you have completed the setup of the utility JAR file with the home factory class as described in "Utility project" on page 392. We will make use of the home factory in the session bean.

Session bean exceptions

There are a number of exceptions the session can possibly throw to its clients. One is the InsufficientFundException (see "Creating an exception class" on page 412) and the others are EJB exceptions, for example when an account is not found or a transaction record cannot be created.

Developing a stateless session bean

In this section, we develop the Banking session bean. The sequence of operations is:

- ▶ Create a project for session EJBs. We could use the same project as for the CMP entity beans, but using a separate project makes it easier to navigate the code in Application Developer.
- ▶ Create the session bean using the EJB wizard.
- ▶ Define EJB references to access the CMP entity beans.
- ▶ Implement the business logic.

Creating an EJB project for the session bean

We add the session bean to a new EJB module named ItsoBank5SessionEJB. To create the EJB module and link it to the existing ItsoBank5EAR enterprise application, do the following:

- ▶ Select File -> New -> Project -> EJB -> EJB Project. Click Next.
- ▶ Select Create 2.0 EJB Project, and click Next.
- ▶ Enter ItsoBank5SessionEJB as the project name, select Existing for the enterprise application, and click Browse to select ItsoBank5EAR. Click Next.
- ▶ For module dependencies, select the ItsoBank5CmpEJB.jar and the ItsoBank5Utility.jar files. The session bean requires access to the CMP entity beans and to the home factory.
- ▶ Click Finish.
- ▶ You get a pop-up message that the project is added to the EjbbankServer server configuration (see Figure 10-16 on page 394). Click OK.

► The project is created. You can verify the project dependencies by opening the project properties.

Creating the session bean for banking transactions

In the J2EE Hierarchy view (J2EE perspective), select the `ItsoBank5SessionEJB` project and *New -> Enterprise Bean* (context):

► The project is preselected, so click *Next*. Select *Session bean*, enter `Banking` as the name, and `itso.bank5.session` as the package (Figure 14-2). Click *Next*.

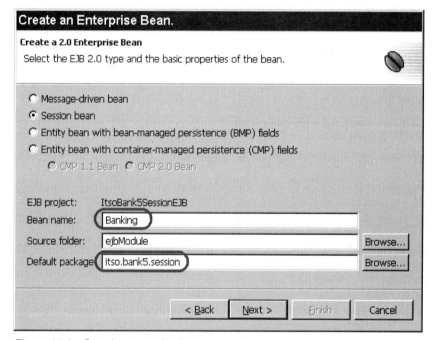

Figure 14-2   Creating a session bean

► In the details panel (Figure 14-3):
  – Change the EJB binding name to our convention: `ejb/itsobank/Banking`.
  – Select only *Remote client view* (we access the session bean from clients).
  – Click *Finish*.

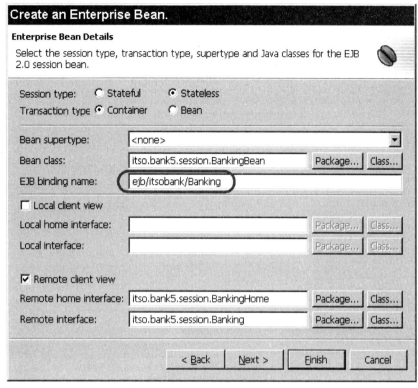

Figure 14-3 Details of the Banking session bean

Three classes are generated into the itso.bank5.session package:

- ► BankingBean—The abstract bean, with callback methods (ejbCreate, ...)
- ► BankingHome—The remote home interface with a create method
- ► Banking—The remote component interface, empty for now

Accessing CMP entity homes

The Banking session bean requires access to the CMP entity beans. In this regard, the session bean is a client of the entity beans. For performance reasons, the session bean uses the local interfaces to access the entity beans.

Session beans must acquire the local home interfaces of the entity beans using their JNDI names. There are a number of ways to implement this:

- ► JNDI access in the session bean code. The JNDI names of the entity beans can be hard-coded or stored in environment variables or property files.
- ► Access through a utility class, such as the home factory.

Since a J2EE 1.2 client should access EJBs using EJB references (local JNDI names), these EJB references are mapped in the deployment descriptor extensions to the global JNDI names used in the naming server.

Defining EJB references

The Banking session bean requires access to the Account and TransRecord CMP entity beans. The Account bean is used to run transactions, and the TransRecord bean is used to create new transaction records.

EJB references are defined in the deployment descriptor editor:

▶ Open the deployment descriptor of the ItsoBank5SessionEJB project.

▶ On the References page, select the Banking bean and click *Add*.

▶ In the Add Reference window, select *EJB local reference* and click *Next*.

▶ The Add EJB Local Reference window opens (Figure 14-4). The easiest way to fill in all the fields is to click *Browse* for Link. In the Link Selection window, select *Enterprise bean in different EJB project* and locate the Account bean. Click *OK*.

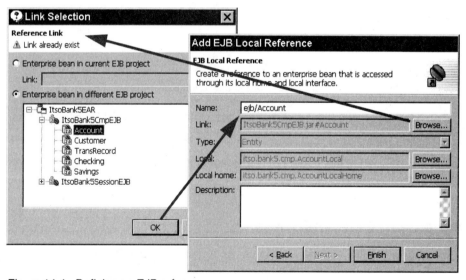

Figure 14-4   Defining an EJB reference

▶ Click *Finish* to add the reference to the Banking bean.

▶ Repeat this process to define references for the TransRecord and the Customer bean.

▶ Figure 14-5 shows the deployment descriptor with the EJB references.

Figure 14-5   EJB references in the deployment descriptor

▶ Save the deployment descriptor.

Using EJB references

Using the EJB references, the Banking session bean can access the CMP entity beans using this coding:

```
InitialContext initCtx = new InitialContext();
AccountLocalHome accthome =
        (AccountLocalHome)initCtx.lookup("java:comp/env/ejb/Account");
```

By using the home factory, the code can be written as:

```
import itso.bank5.utility.HomeFactory;
......
AccountLocalHome accthome =
        (AccountLocalHome)HomeFactory.singleton().getHome("ejb/Account");
```

Preparing methods for entity home access

Open the BankingBean class to define utility methods for entity home access:

▶ Define three fields for the local home interfaces:

```
// home fields
private AccountLocalHome     accountHome  = null;
private TransRecordLocalHome trecordHome  = null;
private CustomerLocalHome    customerHome = null;
```

► Define a method to retrieve the homes:

```
protected void getHomes() {
    try {
        // InitialContext initCtx = new InitialContext();
        // accountHome  = (AccountLocalHome)initCtx.lookup
        //                         ("java:comp/env/ejb/Account");
        // trecordHome  = (TransRecordLocalHome)initCtx.lookup
        //                         ("java:comp/env/ejb/TransRecord");
        // customerHome = (CustomerLocalHome)initCtx.lookup
        //                         ("java:comp/env/ejb/Customer");
        accountHome  = (AccountLocalHome)HomeFactory.singleton()
                                        .getHome("ejb/Account");
        trecordHome  = (TransRecordLocalHome)HomeFactory.singleton()
                                        .getHome("ejb/TransRecord");
        customerHome = (CustomerLocalHome)HomeFactory.singleton()
                                        .getHome("ejb/Customer");
    } catch (NamingException ex) {
        ex.printStackTrace();
        throw new EJBException("Error looking up Account home: "
                                    +ex.getMessage());
    }
}
```

Note that the method includes as comments the code to access the homes directly. However, the actual code relies on the home factory class.

► Invoke the getHomes method in the ejbCreate method:

```
public void ejbCreate() throws javax.ejb.CreateException {
    getHomes();
}
```

► Add these import statements:

```
import itso.bank5.cmp.*;                    // CMP entity beans
import itso.bank5.exception.*;              // Exception for withdraw failure
import javax.ejb.*;                         // EJB exceptions
import javax.naming.*;                      // JNDI access
import java.math.BigDecimal;                // Business logic parameters
import java.util.*;                         // Vector, Collection
import itso.bank5.utility.HomeFactory;      // Home factory
```

Now we are ready to implement the business logic methods.

Implementing the business logic

The `Banking` session bean is the facade to hide the CMP entity beans and the database from the client applications . In our design, clients should not access entity beans directly.

We implement a number of methods in the `Banking` bean so that clients can issue business transactions. The session bean also takes care of transaction management, because by default, each method invoked in a session bean starts and ends a transaction (in regard to EJBs and the database).

Here is the list of methods that we implement:

► `getBalance`—Retrieve the balance of an account.

► `deposit`—Deposit funds into an account, create a transaction record, return the balance.

► `withdraw`—Withdraw funds from an account, create a transaction record, return the balance.

► `transfer`—Transfer funds from one account to another, create two transaction records, return the balance of the from account.

► `getTransrecords`—Returns a vector of strings of transaction record information for an account:

`timestamp transactiontype transactionamount`

Transaction records carry a timestamp, a transaction type (`C` for credit or deposit, `D` for debit or withdraw), and the amount.

► `getCustomers`—Returns a vector of customers that can access an account:

`customerID customername`

► `listAccountsOfCustomer`—Returns a vector of information containing the customer name, the accounts that can be accesses, and the transaction records of each account.

This method returns a vector of an array[5] of strings (where <b> is blank):

```
C    customerid      customername    <b>       <b>
A    accountType     accountType     balance   Overdraft|MinAmount
T    Debit|Credit    timestamp       amount    <b>
```

There is one customer element (C), an account element (A) for each account followed by the transaction record elements (T) of that account. This information can be used in a client to format a report.

► `getAccountInfo`—Returns an array of strings with `accountID`, `accountType`, `balance`, and `interest`.

► `addCustAcct` and `removeCustAcct`—Add and remove account for a customer.

Retrieve the balance

```
public BigDecimal getBalance(String accountID) throws FinderException {
    try {
        AccountLocal account = accountHome.findByPrimaryKey(accountID);
        return account.getBalance();
    } catch (FinderException ex) {
        throw new FinderException("Account "+accountID+" not found");
    } catch (EJBException ex) {
        throw new EJBException("Account getBalance failed for "+accountID);
    }
}
```

Deposit funds

```
public BigDecimal deposit(String accountID, BigDecimal amount)
                        throws FinderException {
    try {
        AccountLocal account = accountHome.findByPrimaryKey(accountID);
        TransRecordLocal tr = trecordHome.create("C", amount, account);
        return account.deposit(amount);
    } catch (FinderException ex) {
        throw new FinderException("Account "+accountID+" not found");
    } catch (CreateException ex) {
        throw new EJBException
                    ("Account "+accountID+" create Transrecord failed");
    } catch (EJBException ex) {
        throw new EJBException("Account deposit failed for "+accountID);
    }
}
```

Withdraw funds

```
public BigDecimal withdraw(String accountID, BigDecimal amount)
                        throws FinderException, InsufficientFundException {
    try {
        AccountLocal account = accountHome.findByPrimaryKey(accountID);
        BigDecimal result = account.withdraw(amount);
        TransRecordLocal tr = trecordHome.create("D", amount, account);
        return result;
    } catch (InsufficientFundException ex) {
        getSessionContext().setRollbackOnly(); // force rollback
        throw new InsufficientFundException
                    ("Account "+accountID+": not enough funds");
    } catch (FinderException ex) {
        throw new FinderException("Account "+accountID+" not found");
    } catch (CreateException ex) {
        throw new EJBException
                    ("Account "+accountID+" create Transrecord failed");
    } catch (EJBException ex) {
        throw new EJBException("Account withdraw failed for "+accountID);
```

```
        }
    }
```

Transfer funds

```
public BigDecimal transfer(String accountID1, String accountID2,
    BigDecimal amount) throws FinderException, InsufficientFundException {
    AccountLocal account1 = null;
    AccountLocal account2 = null;
    try {
        account1 = accountHome.findByPrimaryKey(accountID1);
    } catch (FinderException ex) {
        throw new FinderException("Account "+accountID1+" not found");
    }
    try {
        account2 = accountHome.findByPrimaryKey(accountID2);
    } catch (FinderException ex) {
        throw new FinderException("Account "+accountID2+" not found");
    }
    try {
        account1.withdraw(amount);
        account2.deposit(amount);
        TransRecordLocal tr1 = trecordHome.create("D", amount, account1);
        TransRecordLocal tr2 = trecordHome.create("C", amount, account2);
        return account1.getBalance();
    } catch (InsufficientFundException ex) {
        getSessionContext().setRollbackOnly(); // force rollback
        throw new InsufficientFundException
                ("Account "+accountID1+": not enough funds");
    } catch (CreateException ex) {
        throw new EJBException("Account transfer create Transrecord failed");
    } catch (EJBException ex) {
        throw new EJBException
                ("Account transfer failed for "+accountID1+"/"+accountID2);
    }
}
```

List the transaction records

```
public java.util.Vector getTransrecords(String accountID)
                        throws FinderException {
    try {
        Vector result = new Vector();
        AccountLocal account = accountHome.findByPrimaryKey(accountID);
        Collection coll = account.getTransrecords();
        Iterator collit = coll.iterator();
        while ( collit.hasNext() ) {
            TransRecordLocal tr = (TransRecordLocal)collit.next();
            result.addElement (
                    ((java.sql.Timestamp)tr.getPrimaryKey()).toString()
```

```
                                    +" "+tr.getTransType()
                                    +" "+tr.getTransAmount().toString() );
            }
            return result;
        } catch (FinderException ex) {
            throw new FinderException("Account "+accountID+" not found");
        }
    }
```

List the customers

```
    public java.util.Vector getCustomers(String accountID)
                            throws FinderException {
        try {
            Vector result = new Vector();
            AccountLocal account = accountHome.findByPrimaryKey(accountID);
            Collection coll = account.getCustomers();
            Iterator collit = coll.iterator();
            while ( collit.hasNext() ) {
                CustomerLocal cust = (CustomerLocal)collit.next();
                result.addElement (
                        ((CustomerKey)cust.getPrimaryKey()).getCustomerID()
                            +" "+cust.getName() );
            }
            return result;
        } catch (FinderException ex) {
            throw new FinderException("Account "+accountID+" not found");
        }
    }
```

List a customer with accounts and transaction records

```
    public java.util.Vector listAccountsOfCustomer(int customerID)
                            throws FinderException {
        try {
            Vector result = new Vector();
            CustomerLocal cust = customerHome.findByPrimaryKey
                                    (new CustomerKey(customerID) );
            result.addElement( new String[]
                    { "C", String.valueOf(customerID), cust.getName(), "", "" } );
            Collection coll1 = cust.getAccounts();
            if ( coll1.isEmpty() ) {
                result.addElement( new String[]
                    { "A", "No accounts", "", "", "" } );
                return result;
            }
            Iterator collit1 = coll1.iterator();
            while ( collit1.hasNext() ) {
                AccountLocal account = (AccountLocal)collit1.next();
                if (account instanceof CheckingLocal) {
```

```
            CheckingLocal checking = (CheckingLocal)account;
            result.addElement ( new String[]
                { "A", account.getAccountType(),
                    (String)account.getPrimaryKey(),
                    account.getBalance().toString(),
                    "Overdraft: "+checking.getOverdraft().toString() } );
        } else if (account instanceof SavingsLocal) {
            SavingsLocal savings = (SavingsLocal)account;
            result.addElement ( new String[]
                { "A", account.getAccountType(),
                    (String)account.getPrimaryKey(),
                    account.getBalance().toString(),
                    "MinAmount: "+savings.getMinAmount().toString() } );
        } else {
            result.addElement ( new String[]
                { "A", account.getAccountType(),
                    (String)account.getPrimaryKey(),
                    account.getBalance().toString(), "" } );
        }
        Collection coll2 = account.getTransrecords();
        Iterator collit2 = coll2.iterator();
        while ( collit2.hasNext() ) {
            TransRecordLocal tr = (TransRecordLocal)collit2.next();
            if ( tr.getTransType().equals("C") )
                result.addElement( new String[]
                    {"T", "Credit",
                    ((java.sql.Timestamp)tr.getPrimaryKey()).toString(),
                    tr.getTransAmount().toString(), "" } );
            else
                result.addElement( new String[]
                    {"T", "Debit",
                    ((java.sql.Timestamp)tr.getPrimaryKey()).toString(),
                    tr.getTransAmount().toString(), "" } );
        }
    }
    return result;
} catch (FinderException ex) {
    throw new FinderException("Customer "+customerID+" not found");
}
}
```

Retrieve account information

```
public String[] getAccountInfo(String accountID) throws FinderException {
    try {
        String[] result = new String[4];
        AccountLocal account = accountHome.findByPrimaryKey(accountID);
        result[0] = accountID;
        result[1] = account.getAccountType();
        result[2] = account.getBalance().toString();
```

```
            result[3] = String.valueOf(account.getInterest());
            return result;
        } catch (FinderException ex) {
            throw new FinderException("Account "+accountID+" not found");
        }
    }
```

Add and remove an account for a customer

```
public void addCustAcct(int custid, String accid) {
    try {
        CustomerLocal cust = customerHome.findByPrimaryKey
                                        ( new CustomerKey(custid) );
        AccountLocal  acct = accountHome. findByPrimaryKey( accid );
        cust.addAccount(acct);
    } catch (Exception e) { e.printStackTrace(); }
}
public void removeCustAcct(int custid, String accid) {
    try {
        CustomerLocal cust = customerHome.findByPrimaryKey
                                        ( new CustomerKey(custid) );
        AccountLocal  acct = accountHome. findByPrimaryKey( accid );
        cust.removeAccount(acct);
    } catch (Exception e) { e.printStackTrace(); }
}
```

Promoting the methods

In the Outline view of the BankingBean class, select all the business logic methods and *Enterprise Bean -> Promote to Remote Interface* (context).

Now the business logic is available to client applications.

Setting deployment properties

We want each business logic method to run as a transaction (in regard to the database or other resources). This is the default behavior, but we want to illustrate here what settings are available.

Open the deployment descriptor of the ItsoBank5SessionEJB project:

► Go to the Assembly Descriptor page.

► Now click *Add* under *Container Transactions*.

► In the Add Container Transaction window, select the Banking bean and click *Next*.

► Select *Required* for Container transaction type.

A transaction is required; either a transaction is already started (when called from another EJB for example) or a new transaction is started.

Other selections are *Not supported*, *Supported*, *Requires New*, *Mandatory*, and *Never*.

▸ Expand the bean and select the business logic methods from the list, then click *Finish* (Figure 14-6).

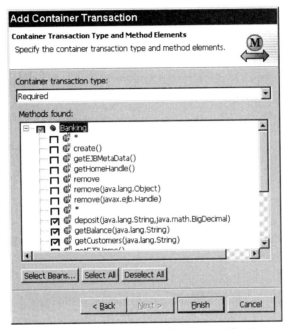

Figure 14-6   Setting the container transaction type

▸ The definitions appear in the deployment descriptor (Figure 14-7).

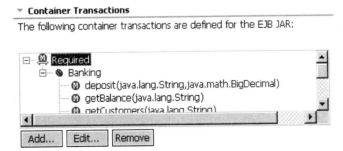

Figure 14-7   Deployment descriptor with container transactions

▶ Save the deployment descriptor, then go to the Source page to browse through the XML code and find the method definitions.

Generate the deployed code

All the definitions are complete and we can generate the deployed code:

▶ Select the `ItsoBank5SessionEJB` module and *Generate -> Deploy and RMIC Code* (context). Select the `Banking` bean and click *Finish*.

▶ The deployed code for the `Banking` session bean is generated into the `itso.bank5.session` package. In addition, some helper packages are generated into the project. However, no `itso.bank5.session.websphere` packages are generated for session beans.

Testing the business logic in the universal test client

Start the `EjbbankServer` and the universal test client to test the business logic of the session bean. Here are a few hints on how to proceed:

▶ In the JNDI explorer, you find the local homes by expanding *ejb -> itsobank -> Banking*. Select the `Banking` remote home interface.

▶ Expand the EJB References and select the `create` method of `BankingHome`. Click *Invoke*, then *Work with Object* for the result. An instance of `Banking` appears under EJB References.

▶ Expand the `Banking` bean, select the `getBalance` method, enter 101-1001 as account key, and click *Invoke*. The balance is displayed.

▶ Invoke the `deposit` and `withdraw` methods for the same account (Figure 14-8).

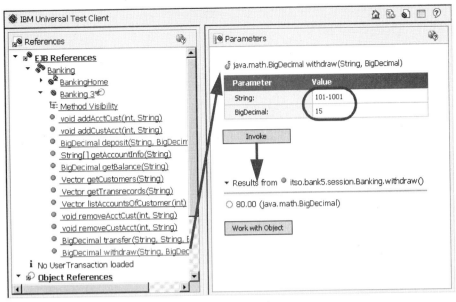

Figure 14-8   Running a banking withdraw transaction

► Invoke the `transfer` method and transfer `13.00` from account `101-1002` to account `101-1001` (Figure 14-9).

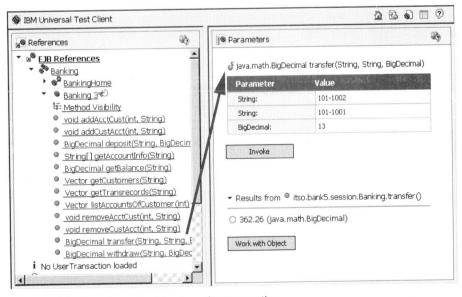

Figure 14-9   Running a banking transfer transaction

▶ Invoke the `getTransrecords` method for account 101-1001. Click *Work with Contained Objects* to see the content of the result vector (Figure 14-10).

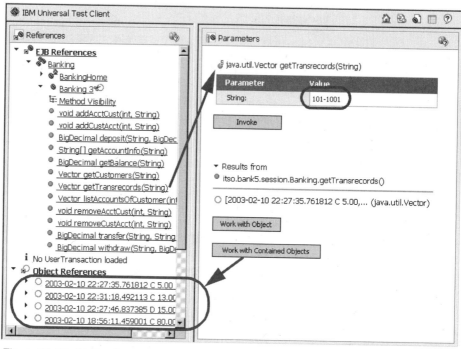

Figure 14-10   Listing the transaction records of an account

You should see a list of all the transactions that you invoked for that account, including the initial deposit of 80.00 that was loaded into the table.

▶ Invoke the `getCustomers` method for account 105-5001. This is the only account that has more than one customer attached. Click *Work with Contained Objects* to see the list of customers.

▶ If you click *Work with Object* for a result vector, you can invoke the methods of the `Vector` class.

For example, the `size` method returns the number of elements in the vector, the `firstElement` method returns the first string, and the `elementAt(x)` method returns the xth string (note that x starts at 0).

A fast way to see all the content is to invoke *Inspect Fields* for a result vector, and the content is listed by invoking `toString` on each element.

Close the universal test client when done and stop the `EjbbankServer`.

Developing a stateful session bean

In this section, we develop the stateful `Reports` session bean. This example may not be very real as a stateful session bean, but it illustrates some of the concepts.

Design issues

For a stateful session bean ,you have to decide what data should be persistent, that is, the data items that are carried from one interaction to the next. These data items have to be serializable so that they can be saved in case the session bean is passivated between invocations of methods. For passivation and activation, see "Activation and passivation" on page 186.

Note that home and EJB references are not serializable, so we cannot keep home references over passivation/activation.

Persistent state

We will keep these data items as the persistent state of the session bean:

► `Vector customerList`—List of customers retrieved using EJB QL

► `int currentCustomer`—Selected customer

► `String currentAccount` —Selected account

► `int currentInterest`—Selected interest rate

► `java.math.BigDecimal currentBalance`—Selected balance for queries

Home references

The session bean requires these home references:

► `AccountLocalHome`

► `CustomerLocalHome`

► `CustomerHome (remote home interface)`

Creating a stateful session bean

Define the `Reports` session bean using the same sequence as described for the `Banking` session bean in "Creating the session bean for banking transactions" on page 522:

► Use the `ItsoBank5SessionEJB` project

► Name the bean `Reports`

► Use the `itso.bank5.session` package

- ▶ Select *Stateful* for the session type (Figure 14-3 on page 523)
- ▶ Set the JNDI name to `ejb/itsobank/Reports`
- ▶ Select only the remote interface

EJB references

Define three references for the `Reports` session bean in the deployment descriptor editor (see "Defining EJB references" on page 524):

- ▶ Local reference for `Account`
- ▶ Local reference for `Customer`
- ▶ Remote reference for `Customer` (one of the EJB QL queries is only available in the remote interface). Select *EJB Reference* to define a remote reference.

The deployment descriptor editor with the references is shown in Figure 14-11.

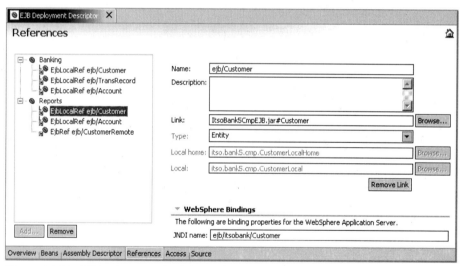

Figure 14-11   EJB references for Reports bean

Define the persistent fields

Open the `ReportsBean` file and add the persistent fields:

```
public class ReportsBean implements javax.ejb.SessionBean {
    // stateful fields
    private Vector    customerList   = null;
    private String    currentAccount = null;
    private int       currentCustomer = 0;
    private int       currentInterest = 0;
    private BigDecimal currentBalance = new BigDecimal(0.00);
```

Import statements

Add these import statements for the classes required in our code:

```
import itso.bank5.cmp.*;
import itso.bank5.exception.*;
import java.rmi.*;
import javax.rmi.*;
import javax.ejb.*;
import javax.naming.*;
import java.math.BigDecimal;
import java.util.*;
import itso.bank5.utility.HomeFactory;
```

Create methods

A default `ejbCreate` method without parameters is already defined. We want to have an additional method with a `customerID` and an `accountID` as parameters.

```
public void ejbCreateByAccount(int customerID, String accountID)
                                    throws javax.ejb.CreateException {
    setCurrentCustomer(customerID);
    setCurrentAccount(accountID);
}
```

Note that we define an `ejbCreateByAccount` method with a suffix, as allowed by EJB 2.0. Promote the method to the home interface.

Handling of home references

Home references cannot be kept in the persistent state of the session bean. If the session bean is passivated, we lose the home references and have to retrieve them again at activation time.

Define the home references

Define these fields for home references:

```
// home fields
private transient AccountLocalHome   accountHome   = null;
private transient CustomerLocalHome  customerHome  = null;
private transient CustomerHome       custRemoteHome = null;
```

By making the home references `transient`, they will not be serialized at passivation time. We will use the callback methods to establish the home references.

Retrieve the home references

We use a getHomes method to retrieve the home references:

```
protected void getHomes() {
    try {
        accountHome = (AccountLocalHome)
                    HomeFactory.singleton().getHome("ejb/Account");
        customerHome = (CustomerLocalHome)
                    HomeFactory.singleton().getHome("ejb/Customer");
        custRemoteHome = (CustomerHome)
                    HomeFactory.singleton().getHome("ejb/CustomerRemote");
    } catch (NamingException ex) {
        ex.printStackTrace();
        throw new EJBException("Error looking up homes: "+ex.getMessage());
    }
}
```

Managing the home references

We have to manage the home references so that they are available at creation and activation time. Add the following code to the callback methods:

```
public void ejbActivate() {
    getHomes();
}
public void ejbCreate() throws javax.ejb.CreateException {
    getHomes();
}
public void ejbCreateByAccount(int customerID, String accountID)
                                    throws javax.ejb.CreateException {
    getHomes();
    setCurrentCustomer(customerID);
    setCurrentAccount(accountID);
}
public void ejbPassivate() {
    accountHome    = null;
    customerHome   = null;
    custRemoteHome = null;
}
```

Implementing the business logic

The Reports session bean is the facade between the client applications and the EJB queries that we implemented using EJB QL.

We implement a number of methods in the Reports bean for reporting purposes:

► listCustomerNames—Retrieve and store the list of all customers

► getCustomerList—Return the customer list

- ► setCurrentCustomer—Set the current customer number for reporting
- ► setCurrentAccount—Set the current account number for reporting
- ► setCurrentBalance—Set current balance for gold customer/account reports
- ► setCurrentInterest—Set the interest rate for high interest report
- ► listGoldAccounts—Return accounts with high balances
- ► listTransferAccounts—Return customer's accounts valid for transfer
- ► listLargestAccount—Return the account with the highest balance
- ► listGoldCustomers—Return customers with high balances
- ► listHighInterest—Return customers with high interest rates
- ► listAllAccounts—Return a complete report of all accounts and their transaction records

Retrieve list of all customers

The list of customers is retrieved using the getAllCustomers finder method. Each entry contains an array of strings ,with the first item being the customer last name and the remaining items being the account numbers of that customer.

```
public java.util.Vector listCustomerNames() throws FinderException {
    try {
        customerList = customerHome.getAllCustomers();
        return customerList;
    } catch (FinderException ex) {
        throw new FinderException("List customer names find error
                                    "+ex.getMessage());
    }
}
```

Return customer list

```
public Vector getCustomerList() {
    return customerList;
}
```

Set current customer

```
public void setCurrentCustomer(int customerID) {
    currentCustomer = customerID;
}
```

Set current account

```
public void setCurrentAccount(String accountID) {
    currentAccount = accountID;
}
```

Set current balance

```
public void setCurrentBalance(java.math.BigDecimal balance) {
    currentBalance = balance;
}
```

Set current interest

```
public void setCurrentInterest(int interest) {
    currentInterest = interest;
}
```

Return list of gold accounts

The list of gold accounts is retrieved using the findGoldAccounts finder method. The result is a vector where each element is an array of strings. The array has three elements: account type, account number, and balance.

```
public java.util.Vector listGoldAccounts() throws FinderException {
    try {
        Vector result = new Vector();
        Collection coll1 = accountHome.findGoldAccounts(currentBalance);
        if (coll1 == null) {
            result.addElement( new String[] { "No gold accounts", "", "" } );
            return result;
        }
        Iterator collit1 = coll1.iterator();
        while ( collit1.hasNext() ) {
            AccountLocal account = (AccountLocal)collit1.next();
            if (account instanceof CheckingLocal) {
                CheckingLocal checking = (CheckingLocal)account;
                result.addElement ( new String[] { "Checking", (String)
                account.getPrimaryKey(), account.getBalance().toString() } );
            } else if (account instanceof SavingsLocal) {
                SavingsLocal savings = (SavingsLocal)account;
                result.addElement ( new String[] { "Savings", (String)
                account.getPrimaryKey(), account.getBalance().toString() } );
            } else {
                result.addElement ( new String[] { "Account",(String)
                account.getPrimaryKey(), account.getBalance().toString() } );
            }
        }
        return result;
    } catch (FinderException ex) {
        throw new FinderException("Gold accounts find error "
                                +ex.getMessage());
    }
}
```

Return list of transfer accounts

The list of transfer accounts is retrieved using the `findTransferAccounts` finder method, The result is a vector of an array of strings with two elements: account number and balance.

```
public java.util.Vector listTransferAccounts() throws FinderException {
    try {
        Vector result = new Vector();
        Collection coll1 = accountHome.findTransferAccounts
                                (currentCustomer, currentAccount);
        if ( coll1.isEmpty() ) {
            result.addElement( new String[] {"No transfer accounts", "", ""});
            return result;
        }
        Iterator collit1 = coll1.iterator();
        while ( collit1.hasNext() ) {
            AccountLocal account = (AccountLocal)collit1.next();
            result.addElement ( new String[] {
                (String)account.getPrimaryKey(), account.getAccountType(),
                account.getBalance().toString() } );
        }
        return result;
    } catch (FinderException ex) {
        throw new FinderException("Transfer accounts find error "
                                        +ex.getMessage());
    }
}
```

Return customer account with highest balance

The account with the highest balance is retrieved using the `findLargestAccount` finder method, The result is a string array with three elements: account number, account type, and balance.

```
public String[] listLargestAccount() throws FinderException {
    try {
        AccountLocal account =
                    accountHome.findLargestAccount(currentCustomer);
        if (account == null) {
            return new String[] { "No largest account", "", "" };
        } else {
            return new String[] { (String)account.getPrimaryKey(),
                account.getAccountType(), account.getBalance().toString() };
        }
    } catch (FinderException ex) {
        throw new FinderException("Largest account find error "
                                        +ex.getMessage());
    }
}
```

Return list of gold customers

The list of gold customers is retrieved using the `findGoldCustomers` finder method. The result is a vector where each element is an array of strings. The array has two elements: customer number and customer name.

```java
public java.util.Vector listGoldCustomers() throws FinderException {
    try {
        Vector result = new Vector();
        Collection coll1 = customerHome.findGoldCustomers(currentBalance);
        if ( coll1.isEmpty() ) {
            result.addElement( new String[] { "No gold customers", "" } );
            return result;
        }
        Iterator collit1 = coll1.iterator();
        while ( collit1.hasNext() ) {
            CustomerLocal cust = (CustomerLocal)collit1.next();
            result.addElement ( new String[] { String.valueOf(
                    ((CustomerKey)cust.getPrimaryKey()).getCustomerID() ),
                    cust.getName() } );
        }
        return result;
    } catch (FinderException ex) {
        throw new FinderException("Gold customers find error "
                                            +ex.getMessage());
    }
}
```

Return list of customers with high interest rate

The list of customers with a high interest rate is retrieved using the `findHighInterest` finder method. The result is a vector where each element is an array of strings. The array has three elements: customer number, customer name, and interest rate.

```java
public java.util.Vector listHighInterest() throws FinderException {
    try {
        Vector result = new Vector();
        Collection coll1 = custRemoteHome.findHighInterest(currentInterest);
        if ( coll1.isEmpty() ) {
            result.addElement( new String[] { "No high interest customers",
                                            "", "", "" } );
            return result;
        }
        Iterator collit1 = coll1.iterator();
        while ( collit1.hasNext() ) {
            Customer custRemote = (Customer)collit1.next();
            CustomerLocal cust   = customerHome.findByPrimaryKey(
                        (CustomerKey)custRemote.getPrimaryKey() );
            Collection coll2 = cust.getAccounts();
            Iterator collit2 = coll2.iterator();
```

```
                while ( collit2.hasNext() ) {
                    AccountLocal acct = (AccountLocal)collit2.next();
                    if ( acct.getInterest() > currentInterest )
                        result.addElement( new String[] {String.valueOf(
((CustomerKey)cust.getPrimaryKey()).getCustomerID() ), cust.getName(),
(String)acct.getPrimaryKey(), String.valueOf( acct.getInterest() ) } );
                }
            }
            return result;
        } catch (FinderException ex) {
            throw new FinderException("High interest customers find error "
                                        +ex.getMessage());
        } catch (java.rmi.RemoteException ex) {
            throw new FinderException("High interest customers remote error "
                                        +ex.getMessage());
        }
    }
```

Return list of all accounts with transaction records

The list of accounts is retrieved using the `findAllAccounts` finder method. Each
account is analyzed to find the account type in the inheritance hierarchy. The
transaction records are retrieved by following the `getAccounts` relationship. The
result is a vector where each element is an array of strings. The array has five
elements, and there are entries for accounts and transaction records:

► A for account, account type, number, balance, overdraft or minimum amount
► T for transaction record, debit or credit, timestamp, amount, blank

```
public java.util.Vector listAllAccounts() throws FinderException {
    try {
        Vector result = new Vector();
        Collection coll1 = accountHome.findAllAccounts();
        if (coll1 == null) {
            result.addElement( new String[] {"A", "No accounts", "", "", ""});
            return result;
        }
        Iterator collit1 = coll1.iterator();
        while ( collit1.hasNext() ) {
            AccountLocal account = (AccountLocal)collit1.next();
            if (account instanceof CheckingLocal) {
                CheckingLocal checking = (CheckingLocal)account;
                result.addElement ( new String[] { "A",
                    account.getAccountType(), (String)account.getPrimaryKey(),
                    account.getBalance().toString(),
                    "Overdraft: "+checking.getOverdraft().toString() } );
            } else if (account instanceof SavingsLocal) {
                SavingsLocal savings = (SavingsLocal)account;
                result.addElement ( new String[] { "A",
                    account.getAccountType(), (String)account.getPrimaryKey(),
```

```
                    account.getBalance().toString(),
                    "MinAmount: "+savings.getMinAmount().toString() } );
            } else {
                result.addElement ( new String[] { "A",
                    account.getAccountType(), (String)account.getPrimaryKey(),
                    account.getBalance().toString(), "" } );
            }
            Collection coll2 = account.getTransrecords();
            if (coll2 != null) {
                Iterator collit2 = coll2.iterator();
                while ( collit2.hasNext() ) {
                    TransRecordLocal tr = (TransRecordLocal)collit2.next();
                    if ( tr.getTransType().equals("C") )
                        result.addElement( new String[] {"T", "Credit",
                            ((java.sql.Timestamp)tr.getPrimaryKey()).toString(),
                            tr.getTransAmount().toString(), "" } );
                    else
                        result.addElement( new String[] {"T", "Debit",
                            ((java.sql.Timestamp)tr.getPrimaryKey()).toString(),
                            tr.getTransAmount().toString(), "" } );
                }
            }
        }
        return result;
    } catch (FinderException ex) {
        throw new FinderException("All accounts error "+ex.getMessage());
    }
}
```

Promote the business methods

Promote the public business methods to the remote interface.

Testing the stateful session bean

At this point, you are ready to generate the deployed code and test the stateful session bean. With a single container and one stateful session bean, you may not be successful in testing passivation and activation of the session bean. However, you can run multiple methods in sequence:

- ► Retrieve customer list
- ► Set current customer and current account
- ► Set balance for gold customers and accounts
- ► Set interest rate for high interest
- ► Run the business methods

Creating a Web Service from a session bean

Application Developer makes it very easy to deploy a session bean as a Web service and make its methods available to clients using SOAP. All the configuration is performed in Application Developer and the resulting Web service is installed in a Web application.

Creating the Web service

To create and install a Web service from a session bean, we run through the pages of a wizard:

► In the J2EE Hierarchy, select the `Banking` session bean and *New -> Other -> WebServices -> Web Service*.

► In the wizard (Figure 14-12):

– The Web service type is preselected as EJB Web service.

– We select to have a Java proxy generated and we want to test the Web service using the proxy.

– Click *Next*.

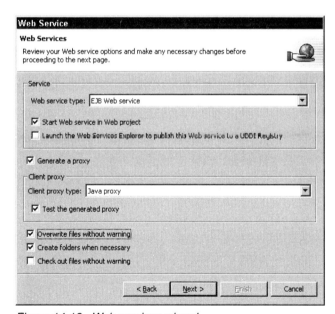

Figure 14-12   Web services wizard

► In the deployment settings panel, select *Choose server first* and select the `EjbbankServer`. For the Web project, the `ItsoBank5Web` project is preselected.

- In the EJB configuration panel, all the defaults are fine.

- In the JavaBean identity panel, enter `uri:Banking` as the Web service URI. All the defaults for the WSDL generation are fine.

- In the JavaBean methods panel, we can select which methods to turn into Web service; by default all methods are selected. Select *Show server type mappings*.

- In the Java to XML mappings panel, all encodings for parameters and results are fine.

- In the binding proxy generation panel, select *Generate proxy*. The proxy is generated into a Web project named `ItsoBank5WebClient`. Select *Show mappings*.

- In the XML to Java mappings panel, all mappings are fine.

- In the SOAP binding mapping configuration, all mappings are fine.

- In the Test panel, select *Test the generated proxy* and select *Web service sample JSPs*. Set the output folder as `sample/Banking`. Select *Run test on server*.

- Skip the publication panel (UDDI) and click *Finish*.

The Web service code is generated and the `EjbbankServer` is started or restarted. When the server is ready, the generated test client is started in a Web browser.

Testing the Web service with the generated test client

The generated test client can be used to execute the methods of the Web service through the generated proxy.

Figure 14-13 shows a sample run of the test client:

- Select the `deposit` method, enter an account number and an amount, click *Invoke*, and the resulting balance is displayed.

- Invoke some of the other methods and see the results of the call.

- Note that the result of the `listAccountsForCustomer` method is not formatted. The vector of an array of strings is not formatted by the simple test client.

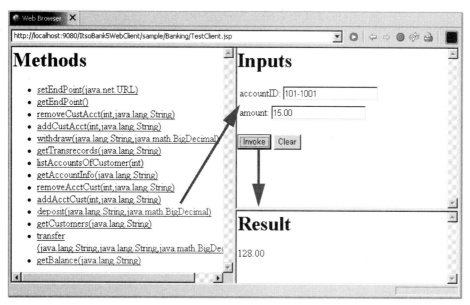

Figure 14-13　Web service test client run

Testing the Web service with the universal test client

Another way to test a Web service is to select the generated proxy class (`proxy.soap.BankingProxy` in the `ItsoBank5WebClient` project) and *Launch Universal Test Client* (context).

This starts the universal test client and instantiates a proxy object. Expand the proxy object, select one of its methods, enter suitable parameters, and click *Invoke*.

Analyzing the generated code

The Web service is installed in the `ItsoBank5Web` project:

▶ In the deployment descriptor, you find two servlets: `rpcrouter` and `messagerouter`.

▶ In `Web Content`, you find the Web service deployment descriptor (`dds.xml`) and the configuration file (`soap.xml`).

▶ In `Web Content\WEB-INF\isd`, you find the isd file, the deployment binding information that becomes part of `web.xml`.

▶ In `Web Content\WEB-INF\lib`, you find the SOAP runtime.

- In `Web Content\wsdl` you find the WSDL files and the XSD file. You may want to study the WSDL files:
  - `Banking.wsdl`—The interface definition
  - `BankingBinding.wsdl`—The SOAP binding (points to interface)
  - `BankingService.wsdl`—The service location (points to binding)
  - `BankingEJB.wsdl`—The EJB binding (can be used by the Web Services Invocation Framework)

  Note that the `Banking.xsd` file shows an error.

- In `Web Content\admin`, you find a small administrative application. Select the `index.html` file and *Run on Server*. You can list, start, and stop Web services.

The proxy and the test client are generated into the `ItsoBank5WebClient` project:

- You can find the `BankingProxy` proxy class in the `Java Source\proxy.soap` package.

- You can find the test client in `Web Content\sample\Banking`. Select the `TestClient.jsp` file and *Run on Server* to start the test client.

Summary

In this chapter, we developed two session beans that will be used as a facade between EJB clients and the entity beans.

We also showed how easy it is to turn a session bean into a Web service.

15

EJB access beans

In this chapter, we introduce access beans as a facility to simplify client programming when accessing enterprise beans.

Accessing an enterprise bean requires the use of the initial naming context and basic knowledge about the way the home and remote interfaces are used. The developer also has to provide important parameters, such as JNDI names and provider URL. The most important consideration, however, is probably the cost associated with the repeated calling of remote methods.

Considering all these, we need another way to write EJB clients, a way that enables developers with no EJB knowledge to write clients that can access enterprise beans and display their properties. Access beans are the solution.

© Copyright IBM Corp. 2003. All rights reserved.

What are access beans?

Access beans are Java components that adhere to the JavaBeans specification and are meant to simplify the development of EJB clients. An access bean adapts an enterprise bean to the JavaBean programming model by hiding the home and remote interfaces from the developer. They provide fast access to enterprise beans by letting you maintain a local cache of enterprise bean attributes. Access beans make it possible to use an enterprise bean in much the same way that you would use a JavaBean.

There are four types of access beans:

- EJB factory
- Data class (for an entity bean)
- JavaBean wrapper (for a session or entity bean)
- Copy helper (for an entity bean)

Important: if you are migrating from VisualAge for Java, you will notice that the Rowset access bean is no longer there. The copy helper and JavaBean wrapper are still supported but deprecated. For new projects, you are advised to use only the data class and the factory class that is generated along with it.

EJB factory

An EJB factory is an access bean that simplifies the creating or finding of an enterprise bean instance. It exposes the create and finder methods on the remote home interface. The factory is not available for local home interfaces.

The factory hides the lookup in the name service and the necessary `PortableRemoteObject.narrow`:

- It uses the JNDI name as defined in the Application Developer deployment descriptor editor, but this can be changed by calling the `setJNDIName` method.

- It performs the lookup in the default `InitialContext`, but this can be customized by calling the `setInitialContextFactoryName` and `setInitialContextProviderURL` methods.

EJB factories are generated when you create any of the other access beans. They cannot be generated separately.

Important: the created factory class uses the enterprise beans' global JNDI name to look up the bean. This means that the application deployer should not change the global JNDI name at deploy time or the access bean will not be able to find its bean anymore. The same remark is valid for the way home interfaces are looked up in copy helpers and JavaBean wrappers.

Data class

A data class access bean is an implementation of what is often referred to as a value object or data transfer object. It is a container that holds a local copy of selected entity bean attributes.

Each attribute has a getter and setter method. The data class keeps track of what attributes have changed by means of a dirty flag. When updating, only these dirty attributes will be written back to the entity bean.

Multiple data classes can be defined for an entity bean, each with a different set of cached properties. This can be useful to retrieve only those attributes that you are really going to use, especially if there are many of them.

The wizard creates three methods in the implementation class of the entity bean:

▶ To create a data class, call the **getXXXData** method on the entity bean, where XXXData is the name of the data class (the default name is the entity bean name with Data as suffix, for example, CustomerData).

▶ To update the entity bean with the data in the data class, invoke **syncXXXData**, which copies all changed attributes from the data class into the entity class. It also returns a new data class with the current state of the entity bean (and consequently with all dirty flags cleared).

▶ The **setXXXData** first performs the same as the syncXXXData method, but then throws a FieldChangedException if an entity bean field has been changed that was not changed in the data class.

When creating a data class, a factory is also created if the bean has a remote interface. This factory hides the lookup of the remote home interface and gives access to the create and finder methods.

The data class can be considered the improved version of the copy helper. Using copy helper for new projects is not recommended. Let us compare the usage of the data class (Figure 15-1) with that of the copy helper (Figure 15-2) by means of an example. We will change the firstname attribute of a customer.

```
CustomerFactory customerFactory = new CustomerFactory();
CustomerKey customerKey = new CustomerKey(999);
Customer customer = customerFactory.findByPrimaryKey(customerKey);
CustomerData customerData = customer.getCustomerData();
customerData.setFirstName("Elke");
customer.setCustomerData(customerData);
```

Figure 15-1   Sample code using a data class

```
CustomerKey customerKey = new CustomerKey(999);
CustomerAccessBean customerAccessBean =
                        new CustomerAccessBean(customerKey);
customerAccessBean.setFirstName("Elke");
customerAccessBean.commitCopyHelper();
```

Figure 15-2   Sample code using a copy helper

Note: After adding a data class access bean to an entity bean, you have to regenerate the deployed code, because of the changes made to the bean.

JavaBean wrapper

Important: The JavaBean access bean is here mainly for backward compatibility. If you are creating new code, consider using the data class access bean instead (see "Data class" on page 553).

The JavaBean wrapper is designed to allow either a session or entity bean to be used like a standard JavaBean, and it hides the enterprise bean home and component interfaces from the developer. Each JavaBean wrapper that you create extends either AbstractEntityAccessBean or AbstractSessionAccessBean.

A JavaBean wrapper access bean has the following characteristics:

► You can only have one JavaBean wrapper. The name of the wrapper class is the bean name with AccessBean as a suffix, for example CustomerAccessBean.

► It contains a no-argument constructor, which maps to either one of the create or one of the single object finder methods.

► The access bean contains one init_xxx property for each parameter of the create or finder method (for example, init_customerID for create or initKey_customerID for findByPrimaryKey).

- When a key class is used in the create and finder methods for a CMP entity bean, the key fields are used as the init_xxx properties instead of the key class. A key field is normally declared as a simple type. This makes it easier for visual construction tools to use an access bean.

- When the no-argument constructor is used, the init_xxx properties must be set before any other calls to the access bean. The actual create or finder method is invoked at the first method call to the access bean (lazy initialization).

- The access bean may contain several multiple-argument constructors, each corresponding to one of the create or finder methods defined in the bean home interface.

- A default JNDI name is generated into each access bean class. The code generator reads the deployment descriptor and passes the JNDI name to the access bean. You can change the JNDI name using the setInit_JNDIName method. It is not expected that you will have to change the JNDI name. However, in the event that an enterprise bean is deployed into a different home, the administrator may add a prefix to the JNDI name to indicate the different home.

Figure 15-3 shows sample code when the findByPrimaryKey method is mapped to the no-argument constructor.

```
CustomerAccessBean customerAccessBean = new CustomerAccessBean();
customerAccessBean.setInitKey_customerID(999);
customerAccessBean.setFirstName("Elke");          // this triggers the find
customerAccessBean.commitCopyHelper();
```

Figure 15-3   JavaBean wrapper with lazy initialization

Copy helper

Important: The copy helper access bean is here mainly for backward compatibility. If you are creating new code, consider using the Data class access bean instead (see "Data class" on page 553).

A copy helper access bean has all of the characteristics of a JavaBean wrapper, but it also maintains a local copy of attributes from a remote entity bean. A client program can retrieve the entity bean attributes from this local copy, which eliminates the need for accessing the attributes from the remote entity bean.

When you create a copy helper access bean, you can select all of the beans' attributes or only a subset. The selected attributes are saved in the access bean configuration file (`META-INF/ibm-ejb-access-bean.xmi`). These selections are re-displayed if you decide you want to change the access bean.

The remote interface of the entity bean is changed to extend the `CopyHelper` interface as well as the `EJBObject` interface. This interface defines two methods, `_copyFromEJB` and `_copyToEJB`. These methods are added to the bean implementation class to allow the access bean to move the bean attributes in and out of the entity bean. This is done by using a hash table that contains a name-value pair for each attribute.

The access bean has a get and set method for each entity bean attribute. These methods will `get` and `set` to the *local* copy of the data. In order to synchronize with the remote instance properties, you can use the following two methods:

▶ The `refreshCopyHelper` method refreshes the local copy data from the remote enterprise bean. It copies from the entity bean to the access bean.

▶ The `commitCopyHelper` method commits the changes in the local data to the remote enterprise bean. Notice that this method is smart enough to update only the modified attributes in the bean instance.

Note: After adding a copy helper access bean to an entity bean, you have to regenerate the deployed code, because of the changes made to the bean.

Access beans and relationships

Relationships are described in "EJB container-managed relationships (CMR)" on page 116. If you create an access bean (JavaBean wrapper or copy helper) for an enterprise bean involved in a relationship that has been made navigable, the navigation method of the access bean returns an access bean corresponding to the enterprise bean at the other side of the relationship.

Therefore, you have to generate access beans for all enterprise beans related through relationships. Otherwise, you encounter errors when following relationships through access bean methods.

Important: Data class access beans do not have relationship navigation methods generated; they only contain attributes.

Developing access beans

To illustrate access beans, we develop a data class for the `Customer` bean and a JavaBean wrapper for the `Banking` session bean.

Developing a data class

We develop a data class access bean for the `Customer` entity bean as follows:

► In the J2EE perspective, double-click the `ItsoBank5CmpEJB` project to open the EJB deployment descriptor editor.

► On the beans pane, select the `Customer` bean.

► We defined both remote and local interfaces for the `Customer` bean. We will make an access for the remote interface only.

► Scroll down to the Access Beans section and click *Add*. (You can also select *File -> New -> EJB -> Access Bean*.)

► In the Add an Access Bean window, select *Data class* and click *Next*.

► In the next panel, select the `Customer` bean of the `ItsoBank5CmpEJB` project and click *Next* (Figure 15-4).

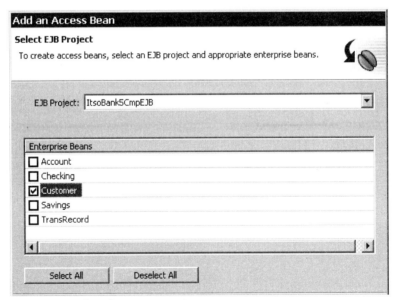

Figure 15-4   Creating an access bean

► In the Data Class Access Bean panel, select the *Remote* interface and enter `itso.bank5.access` as the package name for both the factory and the data class. Leave the default name of `CustomerData` for the access bean name, and leave all attributes selected (Figure 15-5).

▶ Click *Finish* and then save the EJB deployment descriptor editor.

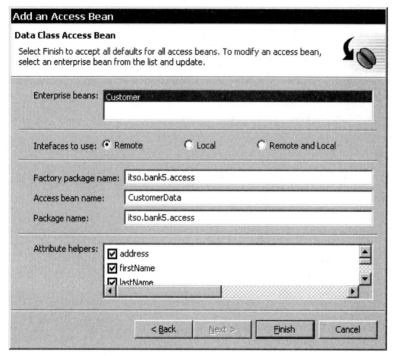

Figure 15-5   Specifying the package and the attributes of the access bean

Figure 15-6 shows the deployment descriptor after adding the data class access bean.

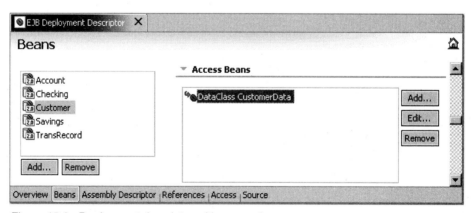

Figure 15-6   Deployment descriptor with access bean

Generated access bean

The Data Access Bean SmartGuide changes the existing `Customer` bean and creates two classes:

► Three method are added to the `CustomerBean` class:

`getCustomerData, setCustomerData, syncCustomerData`

Study the code, especially the `setCustomerData` method that checks if the bean was modified.

► The same three methods also appear in the remote component interface (`Customer`).

► The `itso.bank5.access` package contains the `CustomerFactory` (the factory) and the `CustomerData` (the access bean) classes.

Customer factory

The `CustomerFactory` class contains the JNDI name from the deployment descriptor (`ejb/itsobank/Customer`) in the `getDefaultJNDIName` method.

In addition, it contains the `create` method and the two finder methods (`findByPrimaryKey` and `findHighInterest`) of the remote home interface. These methods call the `_acquireCustomerHome` method that retrieves the home interface from the name server.

Customer data class

The `CustomerData` class contains copies of the attributes with a dirty flag each. The important internal methods are:

► `CustomerData(CustomerData.Store)`—The constructor that is called from the `getCustomerData` method in the `Customer` bean.

► `initialize`—Copies the attributes from the bean to the data class.

► `copyTo`—Copies the modified attributes from the data class to the bean (this method is called by `syncCustomerData` and `setCustomerData` in the `Customer` bean).

Generate deployed code

Because a data class access bean (and a copy helper as well) changes the component interface, we have to regenerate the deployed code of the bean.

In our case we have to regenerate the deployed code for the `Customer` bean.

Generating a JavaBean wrapper

To develop a JavaBean wrapper for the `Banking` session bean:

► Open the deployment descriptor of the `ItsoBank5SessionEJB` project.

► Select the `Banking` bean (on the Beans page), and click *Add* for Access Beans.

► In the window, select *Java bean wrapper* and click *Next*.

► Select the `Banking` bean and click *Next*.

► Select the create method and click *Finish*.

► Save the deployment descriptor.

Generated classes

The `BankingAccessBean` is generated into the `itso.bank5.session` package (you do not have a choice as with data classes). In addition, the `BankingFactory` class is also generated into the same package.

There is no need to regenerate the deployed code; a JavaBean wrapper does not modify the original bean or any of the interfaces.

Testing the access beans

We can test the `CustomerData` access bean with the universal test client:

► Start the `EjbbankServer`.

► Start the universal test client and select the EJB page (we do not need the JNDI Explorer).

► Expand the Utilities section and select *Load Class*.

► Enter `itso.bank5.access.CustomerFactory` as the name and click *Load*, then click *Work with Object*.

► Expand the `CustomerFactory` class (under Class References), select the `CustomerFactory` constructor method, and click *Invoke*, then *Work with Object*.

► Expand the `CustomerFactory` object (under Object References), select the `findByPrimaryKey` method, select the `CustomerKey(int)` constructor, expand the key, enter 101 as the value, and click *Invoke*. A `Customer` is returned; click *Work with Object*.

► Expand the `Customer` bean (under EJB References), select the `getCustomerData` method and click *Invoke*, then click *Work with Object*.

► Expand the `CustomerData` object (under Object References), and invoke a few get and set methods to change the data.

- Select the `syncCustomerData` method (of the `Customer` bean), select the `CustomerData` in the *Objects* pull-down, then click *Invoke*.

- Select the get methods of the `Customer` bean and verify that the data was changed in the EJB.

- Retrieve a new `CustomerData` access bean. Use a set method of the `Customer` bean to change the bean data. Then invoke the `setCustomerData` method with the access bean as the parameter (Objects pull-down). You should get a `FieldChangedException`, because the bean data was modified and the access bean was not modified.

To test the `BankingAccessBean` in the universal test client:

- Expand the Utilities section and select *Load Class*.

- Enter `itso.bank5.session.BankingAccessBean` as the name and click *Load*, then click *Work with Object*.

- Expand the `BankingAccessBean` class (under Class References), select the `BankingAccessBean` constructor method, and click *Invoke*, and then *Work with Object*.

- Expand the `BankingAccessBean` object (under Object References), and select the `getBalance` method. Enter a valid `accountID` as a parameter (for example, 101-1001) and click *Invoke*.

- At this point, an instance of the `Banking` session bean is created and the `getBalance` method is invoked (lazy initialization). The result is displayed.

- You can run other methods on the `BankingAccessBean`.

Stop the universal test client and the server.

Summary

In this chapter, we described the concept of access beans and the different types of access beans that can be generated with Application Developer.

Then we created an access bean for the `Customer` entity bean. We will use this access bean in a client GUI program (see "GUI client using access beans" on page 634).

Message-driven bean development

This chapter provides detailed instructions on how to create a message-driven bean (MDB) that acts as a front-end to the existing banking application.

We describe the design of the application, then implement the MDB, and also develop two clients, a servlet and a J2EE application client, that feed messages to the MDB.

We also describe the setup of the server with a JMS queue for the MDB so that we can test the MDB with the two clients.

© Copyright IBM Corp. 2003. All rights reserved.

Design

We will put a message-driven bean (MDB) called `Transfer` in front of the `Banking` session bean (facade) as an asynchronous entry point to the same business logic (Figure 16-1).

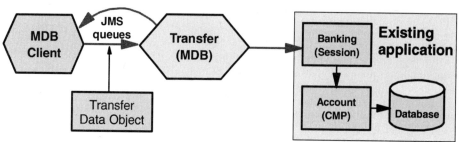

Figure 16-1   MDB design overview

▶ To let the `Transfer` distinguish between the different methods that it can process, we send a JMS string property along with the message.

▶ For our example, we implement only the `transfer` method. This method requires three parameters (`fromAccount`, `toAccount`, and `amount`) that we package into a `TransferDataObject`, which is a serializable JavaBean.

▶ We put the `TransferDataObject` into a JMS message and put the message on the queue that the `Transfer` MDB listens on. This technique illustrates that objects can be passed in a JMS message.

▶ The `Transfer` MDB invokes the `Banking` session bean to process the transfer.

▶ Once the processing is done, the `Transfer` MDB sends a reply on a second queue back to the client. This reply will be a string containing a description of the status, including any errors that may have occurred.

Naming convention

JMS queues require a connection factory, and the MDB requires a listener port. We will use the following names:

▶ `ItsoMdbListenerPort`—Listener port in the server
▶ `ItsoMdbConnectionFactory`—Factory for JMS queues
▶ `ItsoMdbQueue`—Queue for the message to the MDB
▶ `ItsoResponseQueue`—Queue for the response from the MDB

The JNDI names for the connection factory and the queues are `jms/Xxxx` (where `Xxxx` is the name) and we use references (`jms/XxxxRef`) in the application:

```
jms/ItsoMdbQueueRef ===points-to===> jms/ItsoMdbQueue
```

Developing a message-driven bean

Before starting this part, make sure you have completed the setup described in "Utility project" on page 392 with the home factory.

Creating the data transfer object

We will use this object to transport the `fromAccount`, `toAccount`, and `amount` parameters to the MDB. We would like all the interfaces that our facade exposes to be in the same project. This includes the `TransferDataObject` class.

For simplicity, we will use the utility project (`ItsoBank5Utility`) to store the `TransferDataObject`.

> **Remark:** Putting all exposed classes, exceptions and interfaces together in one project can help us later when we want to distribute them. If a third party wants to access the services exposed by our facade, we only have to give them the JAR file of this project. With this approach we do not have to give them the byte code of our facade, which they could decompile to gain insight into the implementation of our business logic. With Application Developer, we cannot separate the home and remote interfaces of our facade EJBs from the implementation. We can use an Ant script to accomplish this.

To create the `TransferDataObject`:

▶ In the `ItsoBank5Utility` project, select the `itso.bank5.utility` package and *New -> Class* (context).

▶ Enter `TransferDataObject` as the name. Add `java.io.Serializable` to the interfaces. Do not select a main method and a constructor. Click *Finish*.

▶ In the Java editor:

– Add three fields for the data (`fromAccount–string`, `toAccount–string`, `amount–BigDecimal`).

– Generate getter methods for the three fields (in the Outline view, select the fields and *Generate Getter and Setter*, and deselect the setter methods in the window).

– Create a constructor that initializes the three fields.

▶ The final code is shown in Figure 16-2.

```
package itso.bank5.utility;

import java.io.Serializable;
import java.math.BigDecimal;

public class TransferDataObject implements Serializable {
    // data variables
    private String fromAccount = null;
    private String toAccount   = null;
    private BigDecimal amount   = null;

    //constructor
    public TransferDataObject(String from, String to, BigDecimal amt) {
        fromAccount = from;
        toAccount = to;
        amount = amt;
    }

    public BigDecimal getAmount() {
        return amount;
    }
    public String getFromAccount() {
        return fromAccount;
    }
    public String getToAccount() {
        return toAccount;
    }
}
```

Figure 16-2   TransferDataObject for MDB

Creating the message-driven bean

We develop the MDB in a separate EJB project in the existing enterprise application.

Create an EJB project for the MDB

To create an EJB project in the existing enterprise application:

► Select *File -> New -> EJB Project*. Select *Create 2.0 EJB Project* in the wizard page, and click *Next*.

► Enter ItsoBank5MdbEJB as the project name.

► Select *Existing* for the enterprise application, click *Browse* and select the ItsoBank5EAR project. Click *OK* to return to the wizard page.

- Click *Next* to go to the *Module Dependencies* page. Select `ItsoBank5SessionEJB` and `ItsoBank5Utility` and click *Finish*.

- The wizard creates the new EJB project in the enterprise application.

Creating the MDB

To add a message-driven bean to the project:

- Select the `ItsoBank5MdbEJB` project and *New -> Enterprise Bean* (context).

- The project is preselected, and click *Next*.

- In the Create a 2.0 Enterprise Bean panel, select *Message-driven bean* as the EJB type, enter `Transfer` as the bean name and `itso.bank5.mdb` as the default package (Figure 16-3). Click *Next*.

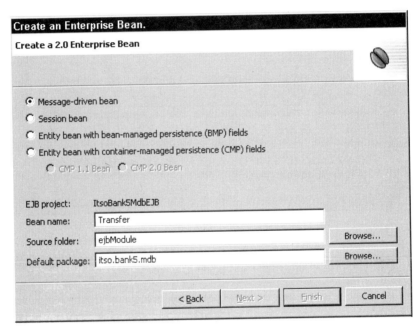

Figure 16-3   Creating an MDB

- On the Enterprise Bean Details panel, select *Bean* as the transaction type and *Queue* from the destination type pull-down, and enter `ItsoMdbListenerPort` as the listener port name (Figure 16-4). Click *Next*.

- There is no superclass, so click *Finish*.

Note: We discuss the Container transaction type in "Transaction types" on page 584.

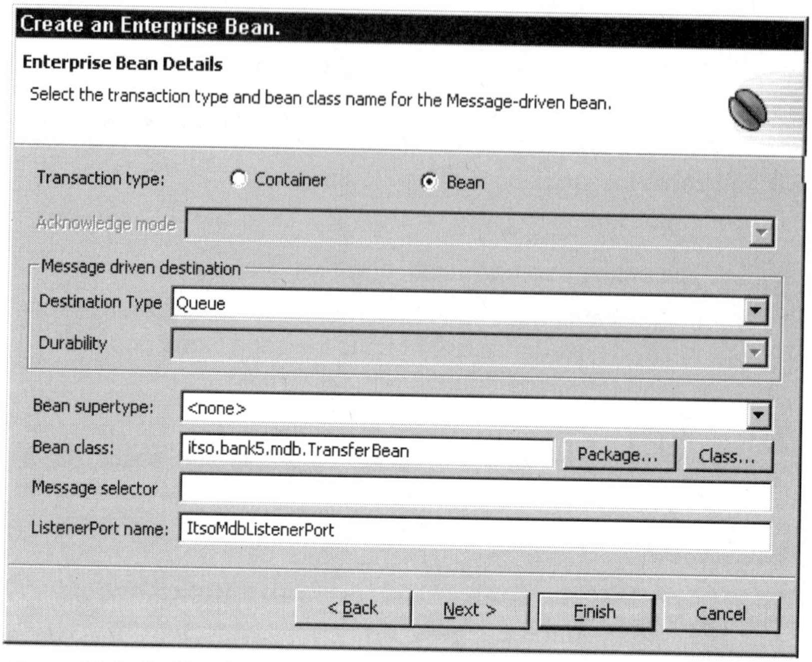

Figure 16-4   Setting the MDB detailed properties

The wizard creates the Transfer MDB. Figure 16-5 shows the entry that is added to the deployment descriptor.

```
<message-driven id="MessageDriven_1038863293603">
    <ejb-name>Transfer</ejb-name>
    <ejb-class>itso.bank5.mdb.TransferBean</ejb-class>
    <transaction-type>Bean</transaction-type>
    <message-driven-destination>
        <destination-type>javax.jms.Queue</destination-type>
    </message-driven-destination>
</message-driven>
```

Figure 16-5   Deployment descriptor of MDB

Note: Message-driven beans do not have home or remote interfaces and we do not have to generate deployed code for them.

Implementing the MDB

The wizard creates a skeleton `Transfer` MDB with some callback methods and the `onMessage` method the does the processing. We have to complete the coding.

The MDB receives the message from a client, processes the message by calling the existing `Banking` session bean, and returns a reply through a JMS queue.

> **Note:** The code includes a number of `System.out.println` statements. These should be commented out for a real application before deployment.

Import statements

The MDB requires access to JMS for the reply message, the session bean, and the utility package (for the home factory and the `TransferDataObject`).

```
import javax.jms.*;
import itso.bank5.session.*;
import itso.bank5.utility.*;
import java.math.BigDecimal;
```

Variables

To access the session bean and the JMS queues, we require a few variables:

```
private static final String QUEUECONNECTIONFACTORY =
                        "jms/ItsoMdbConnectionFactoryRef";
private static final String RESPONSEQUEUE        =
                        "jms/ItsoResponseQueueRef";
private BankingHome          bankingHome = null;
private QueueConnectionFactory qcf        = null;
private Queue                sendQueue   = null;
```

To access a JMS queue, we require a `QueueConnectionFactory` and a `Queue`. We use resource references for this purpose. These references will be defined in the deployment descriptor later.

Initialization

When the MDB is created, we initialize the home and JMS access:

```
public void ejbCreate() {
    initialize();
}
private void initialize() {
    try {
        System.out.println("MDB initialize");
        bankingHome = (BankingHome)HomeFactory.singleton()
                                    .getHome("ejb/Banking");
        System.out.println("MDB found session bean home");
```

```
        qcf = (QueueConnectionFactory)HomeFactory.singleton()
                                    .getJMS(QUEUECONNECTIONFACTORY);
        System.out.println("MDB found QueueConnectionFactory");
        sendQueue = (Queue)HomeFactory.singleton().getJMS(RESPONSEQUEUE);
        System.out.println("MDB found ResponseQueue");
    } catch (javax.naming.NamingException e) {
        System.out.println("MDB initialization failed: " + e.getMessage());
        e.printStackTrace();
    }
}
```

The getJMS method in the HomeFactory class is similar to the getHome method:

```
public Object getJMS(String jmsRef) throws NamingException {
    if (initialContext != null) {
        Object nsObject =
            initialContext.lookup(
            new StringBuffer("java:comp/env/").append(jmsRef).toString());
        System.out.println("class=" + nsObject.getClass());
        return nsObject;
    } else {
        throw new NamingException("HomeFactory: no InitialContext");
    }
}
```

Add the getJMS method to the HomeFactory class in the ItsoBank5Utility
project.

Implementing the onMessage method

The onMessage method is called by the container for each message received on
the queue that the MDB is assigned to.

The basic logic is quite simple:

- ► We extract the message type (we only accept transfer messages)
- ► We extract the TransferDataObject from the message
- ► We extract the parameters from the TransferDataObject
- ► We create a Banking session bean
- ► We invoke the transfer method of the session bean
- ► We create a response message and return it to the client through JMS using
  a helper method (sendResponseMessage)

Figure 16-6 shows the onMessage method implementation.

```
public void onMessage(javax.jms.Message msg) {
    String messageID = null;
    String selector  = null;
    System.out.println("MDB onMessage");
    try {
        messageID = msg.getJMSMessageID();
        selector  = msg.getJMSCorrelationID();
        ObjectMessage objectMessage = (ObjectMessage)msg;
        // JMS property for business method
        String businessMethod = msg.getStringProperty("BUSINESSMETHOD");
        if ( businessMethod.equalsIgnoreCase("transfer") ) {
            System.out.println("MDB got a transfer message: "+messageID);
            TransferDataObject transferMsg =
                        (TransferDataObject)objectMessage.getObject();
            String fromAccount = transferMsg.getFromAccount();
            String toAccount   = transferMsg.getToAccount();
            BigDecimal amount  = transferMsg.getAmount();
            System.out.println("MDB got parms: "+
                            fromAccount+"/"+toAccount+"/"+amount);
            Banking bank = bankingHome.create();
            System.out.println("MDB got session bean");
            BigDecimal balance = bank.transfer(fromAccount,toAccount,amount);
            System.out.println("MDB did the transfer: " + balance);
            String response = "Transfer OK: " + amount + " from/to " +
                    fromAccount + "/" + toAccount + " Balance=" + balance;
            sendResponseMessage(selector, response);
        } else {
            System.out.println("MDB got a wrong message: "+businessMethod);
        }
    } catch (Exception e) {
        System.out.println("MDB exception: " + e.getMessage());
        e.printStackTrace();
        if ( messageID != null ) {
            sendResponseMessage(selector, "ERROR: " + e.getMessage());
        }
    }
}
```

Figure 16-6   MDB onMessage method

The sendResponseMessage method sends a text message with the reply to the
response queue by creating a connection, a session, and a sender from the
QueueConnectionFactory.

A correlation ID is set up from the incoming message so that the client can
retrieve the correct message.

Figure 16-7 shows the `sendResponseMessage` implementation.

```java
private void sendResponseMessage(String corrid, String text) {
    System.out.println("MDB response " + corrid +": " + text);
    QueueConnection qc      = null;
    QueueSession    session = null;
    QueueSender     sender  = null;
    try {
        // Create a connection
        qc = qcf.createQueueConnection();
        qc.start();
        // Create a session.
        session = qc.createQueueSession(false, Session.AUTO_ACKNOWLEDGE);
        // Create a QueueSender
        System.out.println("MDB creating queue sender");
        sender = session.createSender(sendQueue);
        // Create a message to send to the queue...
        TextMessage message = session.createTextMessage(text);
        // Set CorrelationID from the input message and send
        System.out.println("MDB sending message to queue");
        message.setJMSCorrelationID(corrid);
        sender.send(message);
        // Close the connection (close calls will cascade to other objects)
        sender.close();
        session.close();
        qc.close();
        qc = null;
        System.out.println("MDB Send done");
    } catch (JMSException e) {
        System.out.println("MDB JMSException - send message failed with "+ e);
        Exception le = e.getLinkedException();
        if (le != null)
            System.out.println("MDB linked exception " + le);
    } catch (Exception e) {
        System.out.println("MDB exception: " + e);
    } finally { // Ensure that the Connection always gets closed
        if (qc != null) {
            try { qc.close(); } catch (JMSException e) {}
        }
    }
}
```

Figure 16-7   MDB sendResponseMessage method

Tip: WebSphere Enterprise Edition has *extended messaging* support, which allows you to use a *sender bean* that turns a method call into a JMS message. While message-driven beans make it easy to *receive* messages, the sender bean helps you to *send* messages.

Setting deployment information

Now we provide additional information to the deployment descriptor for this MDB:

► Double-click the `Transfer` bean in the J2EE Hierarchy to open the deployment descriptor editor (Figure 16-8).

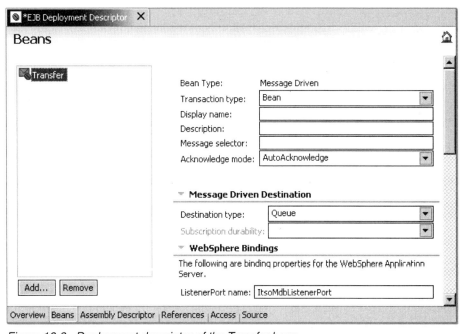

Figure 16-8 Deployment descriptor of the Transfer bean

► Set the transaction type to *Bean* and the acknowledge mode to *AutoAcknowledge*.

► The listener port should already be `ItsoMdbListenerPort`.

Adding references

The `Transfer` MDB accesses the `Banking` session bean and requires an EJB reference. In addition, the bean has to access the `QueueConnectionFactory` and the response `Queue`. This is done using a resource reference and resource environment references.

On the References page in the deployment descriptor:

- Select the `Transfer` bean and click *Add*.

- Select *EJB Reference* and click *Next*. Click the *Browse* button for the link field. Select *Enterprise bean in different EJB project*, select *ItsoBank5EAR -> ItsoBank5SessionEJB -> Banking*, and click *OK* and then *Finish* to leave the wizard.

- Click *Add* again. This time, select *EJB resource reference* and click *Next*. Enter `jms/ItsoMdbConnectionFactoryRef` as the name, and select `javax.jms.QueueConnectionFactory` for the type and *Container* for *Authentication*. Click *Finish*.

  Select the new entry and set the WebSphere bindings JNDI name to `jms/ItsoMdbConnectionFactory`.

- Click *Add*, select *Resource environment reference*. Enter `jms/ItsoResponseQueueRef` as the name and select `javax.jms.Queue` as the type. Click *Finish*.

  Select the new entry and set the WebSphere bindings JNDI name to `jms/ItsoResponseQueue`.

Figure 16-9 shows the deployment descriptor with the three references.

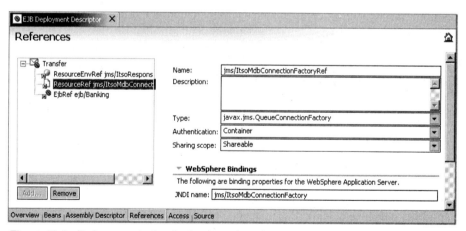

Figure 16-9   References in the deployment descriptor

- Save and close the deployment descriptor.

Setting up the server

To test the `Transfer` MDB, we have to configure the `EjbbankServer` and write a client. Let's start with preparing the server.

Server configuration

In the `EjbbankServer`, we have to configure a listener port, a connection factory, and the send and receive queues.

Open the server configuration in the Server perspective:

► On the EJB page, click *Add* for listener ports and complete the window as shown in Figure 16-10. Click *OK*.

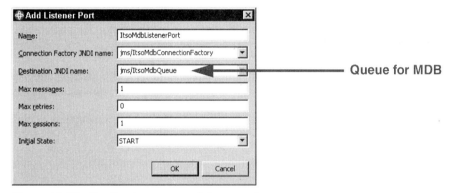

Figure 16-10   Configuring a server listener port

- The three names must match the names we defined in the EJB deployment descriptor for the MDB and in the references.
- Be sure to set the initial state as *START*.
- The Max retries field is set to 0.

  If we used container-managed transactions, we could limit the number of times the same message would be read after a rollback of the transaction because of errors.

► The port appears in the list of listener ports (Figure 16-11).

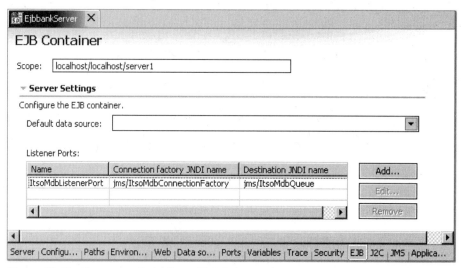

Figure 16-11   Server configuration with listener port

▶ On the JMS page, under Server Settings, click *Add* for JMS Connection
Factories (`WASQueueConnectionFactory` entries) and complete the window as
shown in Figure 16-12. Click *OK*.

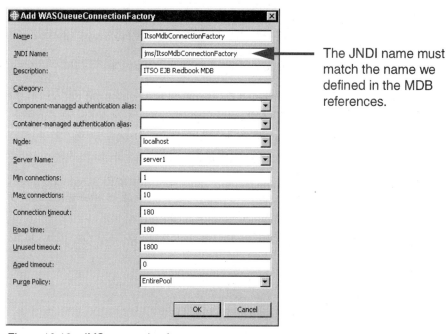

The JNDI name must
match the name we
defined in the MDB
references.

Figure 16-12   JMS connection factory

► Click *Add* for JMS Destinations (WASQueue entries) and complete the window as shown in Figure 16-13. Click *OK*.

This is the queue to which the listener port forwards the messages and the Transfer MDB gets the messages.

► Repeat the process to define the response queue (ItsoResponseQueue).

The MDB sends a reply to the response queue and the client can retrieve the response.

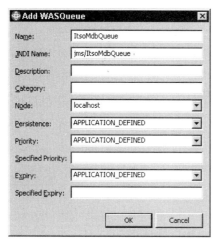

Figure 16-13   JMS destination queue

► The completed definitions are shown in Figure 16-14.

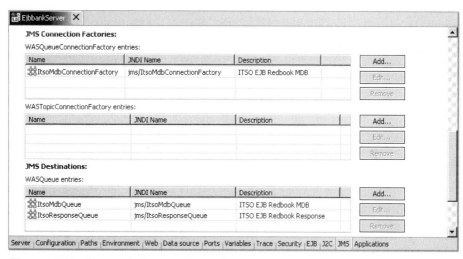

Figure 16-14   Server JMS connection factory and queues

- ► Scroll up to Server Settings.
- ► Click *Add* for queue names and enter `ItsoMdbQueue`.
- ► Click *Add* again and enter `ItsoResponseQueue`.
- ► Set the initial state to *START*.
- ► The completed Server Settings are shown in Figure 16-15.

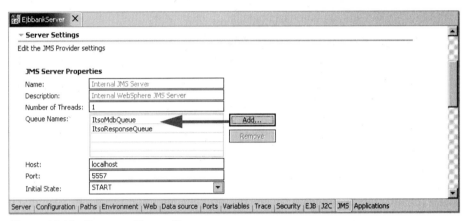

Figure 16-15   Server settings with queues

WebSphere MQ installation directory

The directory of the WebSphere MQ installation must be set in the server variables.

On the Variables page of the server configuration:

- ► Find the entry for `MQ_INSTALL_ROOT` and check that the value points to the WebSphere MQ installation directory, for example:

    ```
    d:/WebSphere MQ              <=== WebSphere MQ installation directory
    ```

- ► Find the entry for `WAS_PUBSUB_ROOT` and check the value:

    ```
    d:/WebSphere MQ/WEMPS
    ```

Save and close the server configuration.

Message-driven bean clients

We implement two clients that have very similar code:

- ▶ Servlet client (for testing)
- ▶ J2EE application client (for deployment)

Servlet client

The servlet client is easier to configure because we already have a Web project in the enterprise application:

- ▶ In the `ItsoBank5Web` project create a package: `itso.bank5.mdb.servlet`.
- ▶ Create a servlet named `MdbTester` in the new package. Select to have only a `doGet` method generated.
- ▶ Complete the code as shown in Example 16-1.

Example 16-1   MDB client servlet (abbreviated)

```
package itso.bank5.mdb.servlet;

import java.io.IOException;
import javax.servlet.ServletException;
import javax.servlet.http.HttpServlet;
import javax.servlet.http.HttpServletRequest;
import javax.servlet.http.HttpServletResponse;
import java.io.PrintWriter;
import javax.jms.*;
import itso.bank5.utility.*;
import java.math.BigDecimal;
import javax.naming.*;

public class MdbTester extends HttpServlet {

    private static final String QUEUECONNECTIONFACTORY="jms/ItsoMdbConnectionFactoryRef";
    private static final String SENDQUEUE          ="jms/ItsoMdbQueueRef";
    private static final String RESPONSEQUEUE      ="jms/ItsoResponseQueueRef";

    public void doGet(HttpServletRequest req, HttpServletResponse resp)
                        throws ServletException, IOException {
        String fromAccount = "101-1002"; // default accounts for transfer
        String toAccount   = "101-1001";
        BigDecimal amount  = new BigDecimal(10.00);
        String messageID = null;
        String selector  = null;
        boolean verbose = true;
        QueueSession session = null;
        QueueConnection connection = null;
        PrintWriter out = resp.getWriter();
        try {
```

```java
out.println("<html><body><h1>MDB Tester</h1>");
// Attempt to retrieve ConnectionFactory and Queues from the JNDI namespace
QueueConnectionFactory qcf = (QueueConnectionFactory)
                HomeFactory.singleton().getJMS(QUEUECONNECTIONFACTORY);
Queue outQueue = (Queue)HomeFactory.singleton().getJMS(SENDQUEUE);
Queue inQueue  = (Queue)HomeFactory.singleton().getJMS(RESPONSEQUEUE);
// Create a QueueConnection from the QueueConnectionFactory
connection = qcf.createQueueConnection();
connection.start();
// QueueSession: Not transacted, and acknowledge received messages
boolean transacted = false;
session = connection.createQueueSession( transacted,
                                        Session.AUTO_ACKNOWLEDGE);
QueueSender queueSender = session.createSender(outQueue);
// assemble our parameters
TransferDataObject transferMsg = new TransferDataObject
                                (fromAccount, toAccount, amount);
out.println("<br>Prepare msg "+fromAccount+"/"+toAccount+"/"+amount);
ObjectMessage outMessage = session.createObjectMessage(transferMsg);
outMessage.setStringProperty("BUSINESSMETHOD", "transfer");
selector = "CORR:TF"+ (new java.util.Random()).nextInt(999999);
outMessage.setJMSCorrelationID(selector);
out.println("<br>Sending message to "+outQueue.getQueueName());
queueSender.send(outMessage);
// get message id
messageID = outMessage.getJMSMessageID();
out.println("<br>Sent message "+messageID+"/"+selector);
// Message sent, let's read the response message.
selector = "JMSCorrelationID = '" + selector + "'";
QueueReceiver queueReceiver = session.createReceiver(inQueue, selector);
// Use the QueueReceiver to retrieve the message, a maximum of 5000ms.
out.println("<br>Waiting for response from "+inQueue.getQueueName());
Message inMessage = queueReceiver.receive(15000);
// Check to see if the receive call has actually returned a message.
if (inMessage == null) {
    out.println("<br>Failed to retrieve message");
    throw new JMSException("Failed to retrieve message.");
}
if (inMessage instanceof TextMessage) {
    // Extract the message content with getText()
    String replyString = ((TextMessage) inMessage).getText();
    out.println("<br>Reply: "+replyString);
} else {
    // Report that the incoming message was not of the expected type
    out.println("<br>Reply message was not a TextMessage");
    throw new JMSException("Tester: Retrieved the wrong type of message");
}
// Call the close() method on all of the objects.
queueReceiver.close();
queueSender.close();
session.close();
session = null;
connection.close();
connection = null;
```

```
        } catch (JMSException e) {
            System.out.println("Tester: JMS failed with " + e);
            out.println("<br>JMS failed with " + e);
            Exception le = e.getLinkedException();
            if (le != null) System.out.println("linked exception " + le);
        } catch (Exception exc) {
            System.out.println("Tester: Unexpected error " + exc);
            out.println("<br>Unexpected error " + exc);
        } finally {
            // Ensure JMS objects are closed
            try {
                if (session != null) session.close();
                if (connection != null) connection.close();
            } catch (JMSException e) {
                System.out.println("Tester: Unexpected error, failed with " + e);
            }
            out.println("<br>MDB Tester done</body></html>");
        }
    }
}
```

Servlet processing

The basic operation of the servlet is as follows:

► Retrieve the connection factory and the queues using the JNDI references

► Create a connection, session, and a sender

► Assemble a transfer object and put it into an object message

► Set the business method and a correlation ID

► Send the message

► Wait for a message on the response queue (with correlation ID)

► Display the reply message

► Close the connection

Deployment descriptor

We access the connection factory and the queues using references that must be defined in the deployment descriptor:

► Open the deployment descriptor of the Web project.

► On the References page, select the *Resource* tab. Click *Add* to define a resource reference for the `ItsoMdbConnectionFactory`:

  – Enter `jms/ItsoMdbConnectionFactoryRef` as the name

  – Click *Browse* for type and locate `javax.jms.QueueConnectionFactory`

  – Select *Container* for authentication

– Enter `jms/ItsoMdbConnectionFactory` as the JNDI name

Figure 16-16 shows the resource reference.

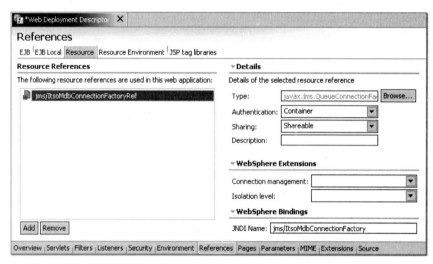

Figure 16-16   Resource reference for Web application

► Select the Resource Environment tab. Click *Add* and enter a resource environment reference named `jms/ItsoMdbQueueRef`. Click *Add* again and create a second reference as `jms/ItsoResponseQueueRef`.

For both references click *Browse* to locate `javax.jms.Queue` as the type and enter the correct JNDI name (`jms/ItsoMdbQueue` and `jms/ItsoResponseQueue`).

Figure 16-17 shows the two resource environment references.

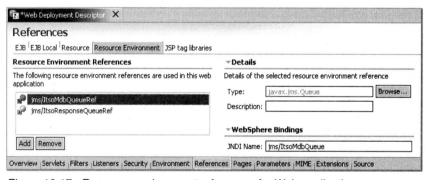

Figure 16-17   Resource environment references for Web application

► Save and close the deployment descriptor.

J2EE application client

This J2EE client runs inside a client container and accesses the message-driven bean in the same way as the servlet. The code is basically a duplicate of the servlet.

Refer to "Developing a message-driven bean client" on page 624 for details on how to develop and run the J2EE application client.

Testing the MDB

To test the MDB with the servlet client, start the `EjbbankServer` and wait until the server is ready.

> **Note:** We did install the embedded messaging component (WebSphere MQ) of Application Developer. However, the sample should work as well without WebSphere MQ; the built-in JMS server (MQ Simulator) provides a subset of the function that is enough for this example.

Running the servlet

Select the `MdbTester` servlet in the `ItsoBank5Web` project and *Run on Server* (context). A sample output is shown in Figure 16-18.

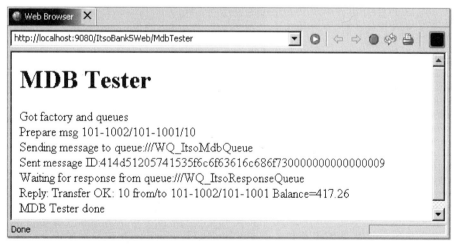

Figure 16-18   MDB client servlet output

The server console shows a number of test output lines that we included in the MDB and in the servlet to show the progress.

Transaction types

In "Creating the MDB" on page 567 we specified the transaction as *Bean*.

Specifying *Container* would have these consequences:

▶ The default container transaction type is *Required*. That means that a transaction is started for the onMessage method. The resources that are part of this transaction are the messages.

▶ This transaction would also be used for the database access in the CMP beans, and the database is another resource.

▶ The synchronization of multiple resources requires two-phase commit.

▶ For the CMP we used a regular JDBC driver, not the XA-compliant driver that supports two-phase commit.

▶ At the first database access, we get an error message that the resource cannot be added:

```
TransactionIm E WTRN0063E: An illegal attempt to enlist a one phase capable
resource with existing two phase capable resources has occurred......
while trying to enlist resources from datasource jdbc/ejbbank with the
Transaction Manager for the current transaction, and threw a Exception.
```

It is possible to use container-managed transaction with the MDB by changing the JDBC driver for the database to an XA-compliant driver:

▶ Open the EjbbankServer configuration on the JDBC page.

▶ Select the *Default DB2 JDBC Provider* and click *Edit*.

▶ Change the implementation class:

```
From: COM.ibm.db2.jdbc.DB2ConnectionPoolDataSource
To:   COM.ibm.db2.jdbc.DB2XADataSource
```

▶ Rerun the application and it works.

Another consequence of an MDB with container-managed transaction is that in case of an exception a rollback is issued. This rollback puts the input message back onto the queue, from where it is read again, and probably the same exception occurs again, and so forth.

For this reason, we chose to use bean-managed transaction. In the MDB bean we could explicitly start a transaction (this would require the XA-compliant JDBC driver as well), and handle exceptions, for example by discarding transactions that are duplicates.

We did not start a transaction; therefore the messages are not recoverable in our example.

Summary

In this chapter, we developed a message-driven bean as an asynchronous front end to the Transfer session bean.

We then developed a servlet client to test the MDB. In "Developing a message-driven bean client" on page 624, we will develop a stand-alone client that sends messages to the MDB for processing.

Client development

In this chapter, we describe how clients can access and use Enterprise JavaBeans in distributed applications. After introducing some basic concepts, we cover the main alternatives a developer has: direct access to entity beans, using access beans, and using a session facade.

We first describe simple applications to illustrate the concepts, but then we focus on using servlets as EJB client applications and give examples for each approach we present. At the end of the chapter, we compare these different approaches and provide guidelines for using them.

© Copyright IBM Corp. 2003. All rights reserved.

Type of clients

Clients that access EJBs are of different types:

▶ **Session beans**—A session bean can be looked at as being a client of the entity beans it accesses. In most cases, these beans run in the same EJB container and can use local interfaces.

▶ **Servlets**—Servlets can interact with EJBs through remote or local interfaces. A suggested approach is that servlets only interact with session beans, and the session beans interact with entity beans. To access session beans, the servlet can use either remote or local interfaces; for portability, remote interfaces are suggested.

▶ **J2EE application clients**—J2EE application clients run in a client container and have access to the services of EJBs running in an application server on a server machine.

▶ **Applet clients**—Java applets are embedded in HTML documents and can access EJBs running in an application server.

▶ **ActiveX application client** —ActiveX application clients use the Java Native Interface (JNI) architecture to programmatically access the JVM API. Therefore, the JVM code exists in the same process space as the ActiveX application (Visual Basic, VBScript, or Active Server Pages (ASP)) and remains attached to the process until that process terminates.

▶ **Pluggable and thin application clients**—The Pluggable and thin application clients provide a lightweight Java client programming model, thinner than the one offered by the J2EE application client. The pluggable application client uses the Sun Java Development Kit, and the thin application client uses the IBM Developer Kit For the Java Platform.

We already covered session beans in Chapter 14, "Session bean development" on page 519. In this chapter, we look at servlet and J2EE application clients.

References

References are defined in one module (EJB, Web, client) to access EJBs and resources contained in other modules (or in the same module).

References are basically of these types:

▶ EJB reference—For remote access to EJBs

▶ EJB local reference—For local access to EJBs in the same module or in the same JVM

- Resource reference—Access to external resources, such as databases and connection factories (for example, JMS)

- Resource environment reference—Access to an administered object accessed from an EJB (for example, JMS queue)

EJB references

Clients should access EJBs using references instead of the real JNDI name. References can be defined for remote access (`EjbRef`—remote EJB reference) and for local access (`EjbLocalRef`—local EJB reference).

References are configured in the deployment descriptors:

- EJB deployment descriptor—EJB references are defined for entity beans that access other entity beans through relationships, session beans that access entity beans, and message-driven beans that access other EJBs

   References for relationships are always local references, whereas other references can be remote or local references. Typically, EJBs running in one container use local references to access other EJBs.

- Web deployment descriptor—EJB references are defined at the Web application level for all servlets that require access to EJBs. Such references can be remote or local references. Local references require that the Web application run in the same server as the EJB container.

- Client application deployment descriptor—Remote EJB references are defined for all EJBs accessed by the client application.

Resource and resource environment references

Database resources are assigned a JNDI name and are accessed through a reference from EJBs:

- For CMP entity beans, this is almost automatic; we do not have to define a reference. When we define the data source, we specify that the data source is used for CMP beans, and in the CMP project we refer to the JNDI name of the database.

- For BMP entity beans, we define a reference that points to the JNDI name of the database. In the implementation code, we use the reference to access that database.

JMS resources are defined using resource references and resource environment references:

- Resource references are used for the queue connection factories

- Resource environment references are used for the queues

Using references in client code

Clients can use the global JNDI name of EJBs and resources, or they can use references. For portability, clients should always use references. A reference names is prefixed with `java:comp/env/` in the `lookup` method of the initial context.

Typical code to access a JNDI registered object using a reference:

```
javax.naming.InitialContext ctx = new javax.naming.InitialContext();

// remote EJB access
Object obj = ctx.lookup("java:comp/env/ejb/MyEJB");
MyHome ejbHome = (MyHome)javax.rmi.PortableRemoteObject.narrow
                                        (obj, MyHome.class );

// local EJB access
MyHome ejbHome = (MyHome)ctx.lookup("java:comp/env/ejb/MyLocalEJB");

// database access
DataSource ds = (DataSource)ctx.lookup("java:comp/env/jdbc/MYejbbank");

// JMS access
Queue q = (Queue)ctx.lookup("java:comp/env/jms/MYqueue");
```

Developing a servlet client

The first client application is a simple thin client Web application with HTML pages, servlets, and JSPs (Figure 17-1):

▶ Banking—The banking path consists of an HTML page and a servlet. From the `Banking.html` page, we invoke the `BankingServlet` servlet that executes the methods of the `Banking` session bean.

▶ Reports—The reporting path consists of an HTML page, two servlets, and three JSPs. From the `Reports.html` page, we invoke the `ReportServlet` servlet, which calls either the `ReportAccounts` or `ReportCustomers` JSP for output. The `ReportCustomers` JSP invokes the `ReportDetailServlet` servlet, which calls the `ReportDetails` JSP.

Both servlets execute the functions of the stateful `Reports` session bean. The `ReportServlet` stores the handle of the `Reports` session bean instance as session data. The `ReportDetailServlet` retrieves the instance, invokes multiple methods of the stateful session bean in sequence, and finally removes the instance.

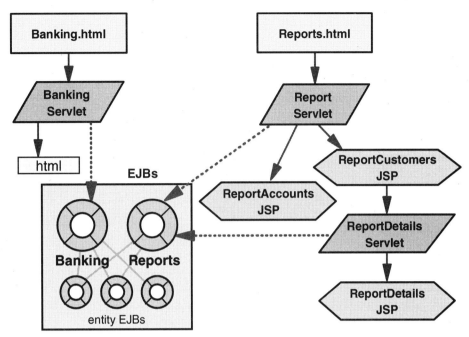

Figure 17-1   Web application design

Sample run

To illustrate the functions of the Web client, let's look at a sample run.

Figure 17-2 shows the banking HTML input page with parameter values and the output of four of the functions:

- ▶ Deposit of an amount (withdrawal would be similar)
- ▶ Transfer of an amount between two accounts
- ▶ List of customers that can access an account
- ▶ List the accounts of a customer with their transactions records

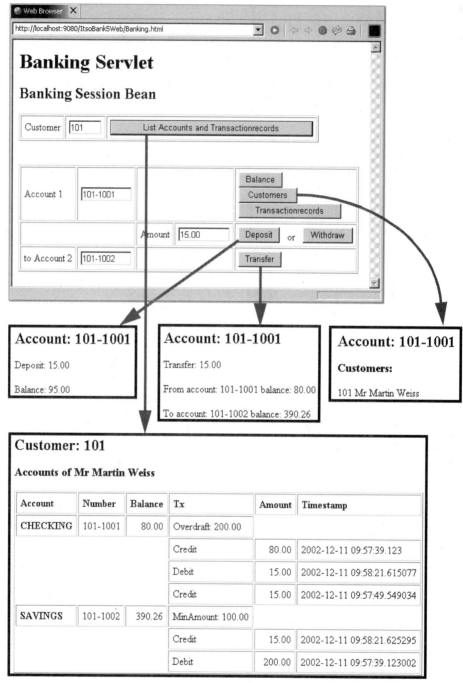

Figure 17-2 Web client run with banking output

Figure 17-3 shows the reporting HTML input page and sample output.

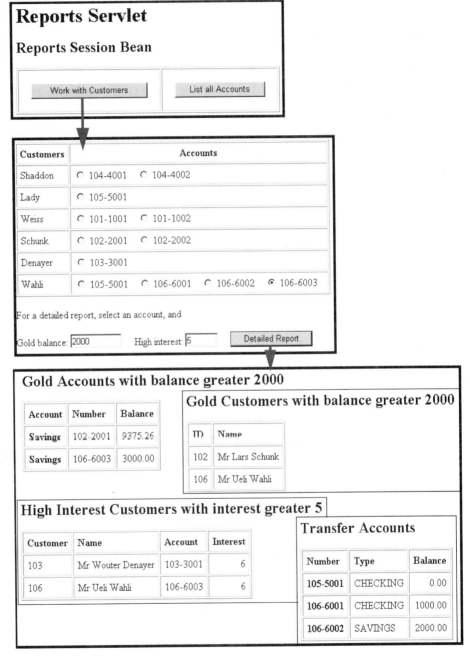

Figure 17-3   Web client run with reporting output

Web project

We use the ItsoBank5Web project created in "Creating the enterprise application" on page 383 for this Web client application.

We use an itso.bank5.servlet package for the servlets and store the HTML and JSP files under Web Content.

Creating the servlets

To create the servlets:

► Select the Java Source folder in the Web project and *New -> Servlet*. The New Servlet window opens (Figure 17-4).

► For the package, enter itso.bank5.servlet. For the class name, enter BankingServlet. Click *Next*.

► Select init, doGet, and doPost methods, leave *Add to web.xml* selected, and accept the default mapping. Click *Finish*.

► The editor opens with the skeleton code of the servlet.

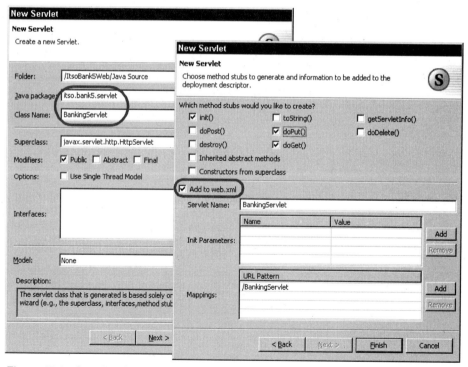

Figure 17-4   Creating a servlet

- ▶ Repeat the process twice and define the `ReportServlet` and the `ReportDetailServlet` in the same way.
- ▶ Close the editors for now; we will complete the code later.

Creating the HTML pages

To create the HTML page for the banking path:

- ▶ Select the `Web Content` folder and *New -> HTML/XHTML File*.
- ▶ Enter the name as `Banking.html` and click *Finish*.
- ▶ In the editor, replace the skeleton body with the content shown in Example 17-1.

Example 17-1   Web client HTML file for banking

```
<H1>Banking Servlet</H1>
<FORM action="BankingServlet" method="POST">
<h2> Banking Session Bean </h2>
<TABLE border="1" cellpadding="5">
    <TR>
        <TD>Customer</TD>
        <TD><INPUT name="customerid" size="3" type="text"></TD>
        <TD><INPUT name="custlist" type="submit"
                value="List Accounts and Transactionrecords"></TD>
        </TR>
</TABLE>
<br><br>
<TABLE border="1" cellpadding="5">
        <TR>
            <TD>Account 1</TD>
            <TD><INPUT name="account1" size="8" type="text"></TD>
            <TD colspan="2"> </TD>
            <TD><INPUT name="balance" type="submit" value="Balance"> <br>
                <INPUT name="customers" type="submit" value="Customers"><br>
                <INPUT name="trecords" type="submit" value="Transactionrecords">
            </TD>
        </TR>
        <TR>
            <TD colspan="2"> </TD>
            <TD>Amount</TD>
            <TD><INPUT name="amount" size="8" type="text"></TD>
            <TD><INPUT name="deposit" type="submit" value="Deposit">
                  or  
                <INPUT name="withdraw" type="submit" value="Withdraw"></TD>
        </TR>
        <TR>
            <TD>to Account 2</TD>
            <TD><INPUT name="account2" size="8" type="text"></TD>
            <TD colspan="2"> </TD>
            <TD><INPUT name="transfer" type="submit" value="Transfer"></TD>
        </TR>
```

```
</TABLE>
</FORM>
```

This HTML contains one form from which a number of banking transactions can be executed. The form invokes the BankingServlet for processing.

Define a second HTML file named Reports.html and replace the skeleton body with the content shown in Example 17-2.

Example 17-2   Web client HTML file for reporting

```
<H1>Reports Servlet</H1>
<FORM action="ReportServlet" method="POST">
<h2> Reports Session Bean </h2>
<TABLE border="1" cellpadding="20">
    <TR>
        <TD><INPUT name="custnames" type="submit" value="Work with Customers"></TD>
        <TD><INPUT name="accounts"  type="submit" value="List all Accounts"></TD>
    </TR>
</TABLE>
</FORM>
```

This HTML page contains one form from which accounts or customers can be reported. The form invokes the ReportServlet for processing.

Completing the servlets

The HTML pages invoke the servlets, BankingServlet and ReportServlet. The ReportServlet produces a customer list or an account list with transactions. From the customer list the ReportDetailServlet is invoked with a selected customer, an account, and two parameters.

Banking servlet
Example 17-3 shows the BankingServlet code.

Example 17-3   Servlet for banking transactions (extract)

```
package itso.bank5.servlet;

import .........

public class BankingServlet extends HttpServlet {

    private BankingHome bankingHome;

    public void doPost(HttpServletRequest req, HttpServletResponse resp)
        throws ServletException, IOException {
        processBanking(req, resp);
    }
```

```java
public void init() throws ServletException {
    try {
        bankingHome = (BankingHome)HomeFactory.singleton().getHome("ejb/Banking");
    } catch (NamingException ex) {
        ex.printStackTrace();
        throw new EJBException("Error looking up BankingHome: "+ex.getMessage());
    }
}

public void processBanking(HttpServletRequest req, HttpServletResponse resp) {
    try {
        PrintWriter out = resp.getWriter();
        out.println("<html><body><h1>Banking Servlet</h1>");
        BigDecimal amount = null;
        int customerid = 0;

        String custlistBut = req.getParameter("custlist");
        String balanceBut  = req.getParameter("balance");
        String customerBut = req.getParameter("customers");
        String trecordBut  = req.getParameter("trecords");
        String depositBut  = req.getParameter("deposit");
        String withdrawBut = req.getParameter("withdraw");
        String transferBut = req.getParameter("transfer");
        String account1    = req.getParameter("account1");
        String account2    = req.getParameter("account2");

        try {
            if ( !(req.getParameter("amount").trim().equals("")) )
                amount = new BigDecimal( req.getParameter("amount") );
            if ( !(req.getParameter("customerid").trim().equals("")) )
                customerid = new Integer( req.getParameter("customerid") ).intValue();

            Banking bank = bankingHome.create();

            if (custlistBut != null)
                out.println("<h2> Customer: "+customerid+"</h2>");
            else
                out.println("<h2> Account: "+account1+"</h2>");

            if (balanceBut  != null) {
                BigDecimal balance = bank.getBalance(account1);
                out.println("<p> Balance: "+ balance);
            }

            if (depositBut  != null) {
                BigDecimal balance = bank.deposit(account1, amount);
                out.println("<p> Deposit: "+ amount);
                out.println("<p> Balance: "+ balance);
            }

            if (withdrawBut != null) {
              try {
                BigDecimal balance = bank.withdraw(account1, amount);
                out.println("<p> Withdraw: "+ amount);
```

```
            out.println("<p> Balance: "+ balance);
          } catch (InsufficientFundException ex) {
            out.println("<p> Withdraw: "+ amount);
            out.println("<p> Sorry: Insufficient funds in account");
          }
        }

        if (transferBut != null) {
          try {
            BigDecimal balance = bank.transfer(account1, account2, amount);
            out.println("<p> Transfer: "+ amount);
            out.println("<p> From account: " + account1 + " balance: "+ balance);
            out.println("<p> To account: " + account2 + " balance: "+
                        bank.getBalance(account2));
          } catch (InsufficientFundException ex) {
            out.println("<p> Transfer: "+ amount);
            out.println("<p> Sorry: Insufficient funds in account");
          }
        }

        if (customerBut != null) {
          out.println("<h3>Customers:</h3>");
          Vector results = bank.getCustomers(account1);
          if (results == null)
            out.println("<p> No customers found ");
          else {
            for ( int i=0; i < results.size(); i++ ) {
              out.println((String)results.elementAt(i)+"<br>");
            }
          }
        }

        if (trecordBut != null) {
          out.println("<h3>Transactions:</h3><ul>");
          Vector results = bank.getTransrecords(account1);
          Enumeration enum = results.elements();
          while (enum.hasMoreElements()) {
            out.println("<li>"+(String)enum.nextElement());
          }
          out.println("</ul>");
        }

        if (custlistBut != null) {
          Vector results = bank.listAccountsOfCustomer(customerid);
          if ( results.size() == 0 )
            out.println("<p>Nothing found");
          else {
            String custdata[] = (String[])results.elementAt(0);
            out.println("<h3>Accounts of "+custdata[2]+"</h3>");
            out.println("<table border=\"1\"
cellpadding=\"6\"><tr><td><b>Account</b></td><td><b>Number</b></td><td><b>Balance</b></t
d><td><b>Tx</b></td><td><b>Amount</b></td><td><b>Timestamp</b></td></tr>");
            for ( int i=1; i < results.size(); i++ ) {
              String account[] = (String[])results.elementAt(i);
```

```
                                if ( account[0].equals("A") )
                                    out.println("<tr><td><b>"+account[1]+"</b></td><td>"+
account[2]+"</td><td align=\"right\">"+account[3]+"</td><td>"+account[4]+"</td></tr>");
                                else
                                    out.println("<tr><td></td><td></td><td></td><td>"+
account[1]+"</td><td align=\"right\">"+account[3]+"</td><td>"+account[2]+"</td></tr>");
                            }
                            out.println("</table>");
                        }
                    }

                    out.println("</body></html>");
                } catch (Exception ex) {
                    ex.printStackTrace();
                    out.println("<p>Error in banking session bean: "+ex.getMessage());
                }
            } catch (Exception ex) {
                ex.printStackTrace();
            }
        }
    }
}
```

Here are a few explanatory notes about the servlet code:

▶ The home of the `Banking` session bean is acquired in the `init` method using the home factory from the `ItsoBank5Utility` project.

▶ Depending on which submit button was clicked in the HTML page, one of the methods of the session bean is invoked.

▶ All the output is formatted by the servlet (we will use JSPs in the reporting path).

Reporting servlet

Example 17-4 shows the `ReportServlet` code.

Example 17-4   Servlet for reporting (extract)

```
package itso.bank5.servlet;

import ...

public class ReportServlet extends HttpServlet {

    private ReportsHome reportsHome;

    public void doPost(HttpServletRequest req, HttpServletResponse resp)
        throws ServletException, IOException {
        processReports(req, resp);
    }
    public void init() throws ServletException {
            reportsHome = (ReportsHome)HomeFactory.singleton().getHome("ejb/Reports");
        } catch (NamingException ex) {
```

```
            ex.printStackTrace();
            throw new EJBException("Error looking up ReportsHome: "+ex.getMessage());
        }
    }

    public void processReports(HttpServletRequest req, HttpServletResponse resp) {
        try {
            String custnamesBut   = req.getParameter("custnames");
            String accountsBut    = req.getParameter("accounts");
            try {
                Reports report = reportsHome.create();

                if (custnamesBut  != null) {
                    Handle handle = report.getHandle();
                    System.out.println("Handle class "+handle.getClass());
                    Vector customerList = report.listCustomerNames();
                    System.out.println("Servlet "+customerList.size());
                    req.setAttribute("customers",customerList);
                    HttpSession session = req.getSession(true);
                    session.setAttribute("reportEJB", report.getHandle());
                    getServletContext().getRequestDispatcher("ReportCustomers")
                                            .forward(req,resp);
                }

                if (accountsBut  != null) {
                    Vector accountList = report.listAllAccounts();
                    req.setAttribute("accounts",accountList);
                    report.remove();  // remove the stateful session bean
                    getServletContext().getRequestDispatcher("ReportAccounts")
                                            .forward(req,resp);
                }
            } catch (Exception ex) {
                ex.printStackTrace();
            }
        } catch (Exception ex) {
            ex.printStackTrace();
        }
    }
}
```

Here are a few explanatory notes about the servlet code:

► The home of the Reports session bean is acquired in the init method.

► When the customer list function is invoked, the handle of the session bean instance is placed into the session data for the next servlet.

► When the account list function is invoked, the session bean instance is removed after processing.

► Data is placed into the request block for formatting by JSPs.

► The JSPs are invoked using the forward method of the request dispatcher.

Reporting details servlet
Example 17-5 shows the `ReportDetailServlet` code.

Example 17-5   Servlet for reporting details (extract)

```
package itso.bank5.servlet;

import ...

public class ReportDetailServlet extends HttpServlet {

    public void doPost(HttpServletRequest req, HttpServletResponse resp)
        throws ServletException, IOException {
      processReports(req, resp);
    }
    public void init() throws ServletException {}

    public void processReports(HttpServletRequest req, HttpServletResponse resp) {
        try {
            BigDecimal balance = null;
            String accountID = null;
            int customerID = 0;
            int interest = 10;
            HttpSession session = req.getSession(false);
            Handle handle = (Handle)session.getAttribute("reportEJB");
            Reports report = (Reports)handle.getEJBObject();
            try {
                if ( !(req.getParameter("acctradio").trim().equals("")) )
                    accountID = req.getParameter("acctradio");
                if ( !(req.getParameter("balance").trim().equals("")) )
                    balance   = new BigDecimal( req.getParameter("balance") );
                if ( !(req.getParameter("interest").trim().equals("")) )
                    interest  = new Integer( req.getParameter("interest") ).intValue();
                customerID = (new Integer( accountID.substring(0,3) )).intValue();
                report.setCurrentCustomer(customerID);
                report.setCurrentAccount(accountID);
                report.setCurrentBalance(balance);
                report.setCurrentInterest(interest);

                Vector goldAccounts  = new Vector();
                Vector goldCustomers = new Vector();
                if (balance != null) {
                    goldAccounts = report.listGoldAccounts();
                    goldCustomers = report.listGoldCustomers();
                }
                req.setAttribute("goldAccounts",goldAccounts);
                req.setAttribute("goldCustomers",goldCustomers);

                Vector transferAcounts = report.listTransferAccounts();
                req.setAttribute("transferAccounts",transferAcounts);

                Vector highInterest = report.listHighInterest();
                req.setAttribute("highInterest",highInterest);
```

```
            String[] largestAccount = report.listLargestAccount();
            req.setAttribute("largestAccount",largestAccount);

            report.remove();        // remove the stateful session bean
            session.invalidate();   // remove session

            getServletContext().getRequestDispatcher("ReportDetails")
                                          .forward(req,resp);
        } catch (Exception ex) {
            ex.printStackTrace();
        }
    } catch (Exception ex) {
        ex.printStackTrace();
    }
  }
}
```

Here are a few explanatory notes about the servlet code:

► The Reports session bean is acquired from the handle in the session data.

► Using the parameters, multiple methods of the session bean are invoked in sequence.

► Data is placed into the request block for formatting by the JSP that is invoked using the forward method of the request dispatcher.

Creating the JSPs

To create a JSP:

► Select the Web Content folder and *New -> JSP File*.

► Enter the name of the JSP, for example, ReportCustomers.

► Go through all the panels and on the fifth panel (choose method stubs), select *Add to web.xml*. We are forwarding to the JSP from a servlet using a URL mapping.

► Click *Finish*.

Customer listing

The body of the ReportCustomers.jsp file is shown in Example 17-6.

Example 17-6   Customer listing JSP (abbreviated)

```
<%! String[] data = null; %>
<jsp:useBean id="customers" class="java.util.Vector" scope="request"></jsp:useBean>
<h1>Customers</h1>
<a href="Reports.html"> Go back </a>
<FORM action="ReportDetailServlet" method="POST">
<TABLE border="1" cellpadding="5">
    <TBODY>
```

```
    <TR>
        <TH>Customers</TH>
        <TH>Accounts</TH>
    </TR>
 <% if (customers != null) {
        for (int i=0; i < customers.size(); i++) {
            data = (String[])customers.elementAt(i); %>
    <TR>
        <TD> <%= data[0] %> </TD>
        <TD>
            <% for (int j=1; j< data.length; j++) { %>
                    <INPUT type="radio" name="acctradio" value="<%= data[j] %>"
                        checked>  
            <%= data[j] %> <br>
            <% } %>
        </TD>
    </TR>
    <%    }
 } else { %>
    <TR>
        <TD>No customers</TD>
    </TR>
 <% } %>
    </TBODY>
</TABLE>
<p> For a detailed report, select an account, and
<p> Gold balance: <INPUT name="balance" size="8" type="text">    
High interest: <INPUT name="interest" size="3" type="text">    
<INPUT name="details" type="submit" value="Detailed Report">
</FORM>
<p><a href="Reports.html"> Go back </a>
```

Here are a few explanatory notes about the JSP code:

► The useBean tag is used to access the data collected by the servlet.

► A loop formats the customer list into an HTML table for selection.

► Two fields for input are added at the bottom.

In the same way, define the other two JSP files, ReportDetails.jsp and ReportAccounts.jsp.

Details listing

The body of the ReportDetails.jsp file is shown in Example 17-7.

Example 17-7 Details listing JSP (abbreviated)

```
<%! String[] largestAccount = null; %>
<%! java.math.BigDecimal balance = null; %>
<%! int interest = 10; %>

<jsp:useBean id="goldAccounts" class="java.util.Vector" scope="request"></jsp:useBean>
```

```
<jsp:useBean id="goldCustomers" class="java.util.Vector" scope="request"></jsp:useBean>
<jsp:useBean id="transferAccounts" class="java.util.Vector" scope="request">
</jsp:useBean>
<jsp:useBean id="highInterest" class="java.util.Vector" scope="request"></jsp:useBean>
<% largestAccount = (String[])request.getAttribute("largestAccount");
    if ( !(request.getParameter("balance").trim().equals("")) )
        balance    = new java.math.BigDecimal( request.getParameter("balance") );
    if ( !(request.getParameter("interest").trim().equals("")) )
        interest   = new Integer( request.getParameter("interest") ).intValue();
   %>

<h1>Detail Report</h1>
<a href="Reports.html"> Go back </a>
<p>
<br>Number of Gold Accounts: <%= goldAccounts.size() %>
<br>Number of Gold Customers: <%= goldCustomers.size() %>
<br>Number of Transfer Accounts: <%= transferAccounts.size() %>
<br>Number of High Interest Customers: <%= highInterest.size() %>

<% if (goldAccounts.size() > 0) { %>
<h2>Gold Accounts with balance greater <%= balance %></h2>
  <table border="1"
cellpadding="6"><tr><td><b>Account</b></td><td><b>Number</b></td><td><b>Balance</b></td>
</tr>
  <% for ( int i=0; i < goldAccounts.size(); i++ ) {
        String data[] = (String[])goldAccounts.elementAt(i); %>
        <tr><td><b> <%= data[0] %> </b></td><td> <%= data[1] %> </td><td align="right">
<%= data[2] %> </td></tr>
  <% } %>
  </table>
<% } %>


<% if (goldCustomers.size() > 0) { %>
<h2>Gold Customers with balance greater <%= balance %></h2>
  <table border="1" cellpadding="6"><tr><td><b>ID</b></td><td><b>Name</b></td></tr>
  <% for ( int i=0; i < goldCustomers.size(); i++ ) {
        String data[] = (String[])goldCustomers.elementAt(i); %>
        <tr><td> <%= data[0] %> </td><td> <%= data[1] %> </td></tr>
  <% } %>
  </table>
<% } %>


<% if (highInterest.size() > 0) { %>
<h2>High Interest Customers with interest greater <%= interest %></h2>
  <table border="1"
cellpadding="6"><tr><td><b>Customer</b></td><td><b>Name</b></td><td><b>Account</b></td><
td><b>Interest</b></td></tr>
  <% for ( int i=0; i < highInterest.size(); i++ ) {
        String data[] = (String[])highInterest.elementAt(i); %>
        <tr><td> <%= data[0] %> </td><td> <%= data[1] %> </td><td> <%= data[2] %> 
</td><td align="right"> <%= data[3] %> </td></tr>
  <% } %>
  </table>
<% } %>
```

```
<% if (transferAccounts.size() > 0) { %>
<h2>Transfer Accounts</h2>
  <table border="1"
cellpadding="6"><tr><td><b>Number</b></td><td><b>Type</b></td><td><b>Balance</b></td></t
r>
  <% for ( int i=0; i < transferAccounts.size(); i++ ) {
      String data[] = (String[])transferAccounts.elementAt(i); %>
      <tr><td><b> <%= data[0] %> </b></td><td> <%= data[1] %> </td><td align="right">
<%= data[2] %> </td></tr>
  <% } %>
  </table>
<% } %>

<% if (largestAccount.length > 0) { %>
<h2>Largest Account</h2>
  <table border="1"
cellpadding="6"><tr><td><b>Number</b></td><td><b>Type</b></td><td><b>Balance</b></td></t
r>
      <tr><td><b> <%= largestAccount[0] %> </b></td><td> <%= largestAccount[1] %>
</td><td align="right"> <%= largestAccount[2] %> </td></tr>
  </table>
<% } %>
<p>
<a href="Reports.html"> Go back </a>
```

Here are a few explanatory notes about the JSP code:

► Multiple useBean tags are used to access the data collected by the servlet.

► A loop formats each result data object into an HTML table.

Account listing

The body of the ReportAccounts.jsp file is shown in Example 17-8. The result data is formatted into a table.

Example 17-8   Account listing JSP (abbreviated)

```
<%! String[] data = null; %>
<jsp:useBean id="accounts" class="java.util.Vector" scope="request"></jsp:useBean>

<h1>Accounts</h1>
<a href="Reports.html"> Go back </a>
<p>
<table border="1" cellpadding="6">
    <tr>
        <td><b>Account</b></td> <td><b>Number</b></td> <td><b>Balance</b></td>
        <td><b>Tx</b></td> <td><b>Amount</b></td> <td><b>Timestamp</b></td>
    </tr>
<% if (accounts != null) {
        for (int i=0; i < accounts.size(); i++) {
            data = (String[])accounts.elementAt(i); %>
            <% if ( data[0].equals("A") ) { %>
```

```
<TR>
    <TD> <%= data[1] %> </TD>
    <TD> <%= data[2] %> </TD>
    <TD align="right"> <%= data[3] %> </TD>
    <TD> <%= data[4] %> </TD>
</TR>
        <% } else { %>
<TR>
    <TD> </TD>
    <TD> </TD>
    <TD> </TD>
    <TD> <%= data[1] %> </TD>
    <TD align="right"> <%= data[3] %> </TD>
    <TD> <%= data[2] %> </TD>
</TR>
        <% }   %>
    <% } %>
<% } else { %>
    <TR>
        <TD>No accounts</TD>
    </TR>
<% } %>
</TABLE>
<p><a href="Reports.html"> Go back </a>
```

Figure 17-5 shows sample output of the ReportAccounts JSP.

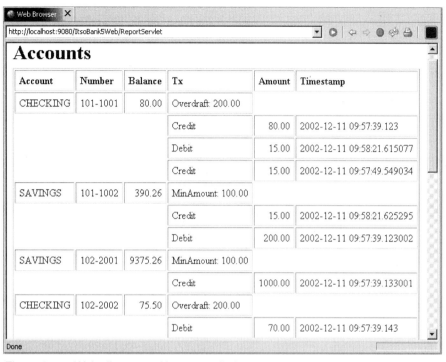

Figure 17-5   Web client run with account listing

Web application deployment descriptor

Before we can run the Web client, we have to configure the references that the servlets use to access the session beans:

▶ The `BankingServlet` uses `ejb/Banking` as the JNDI reference

▶ The `ReportServlet` uses `ejb/Reports` as the JNDI reference

Open the deployment descriptor editor for the `ItsoBank5Web` project. Double-click the project in the J2EE Hierarchy view or double-click `web.xml` in the J2EE Navigator view:

▶ On the Servlets page, you can see the three servlets and the four JSPs.

▶ Select the *References* page and select the *EJB* tab (top).

▶ Click *Add* to create a reference.

▶ Overtype the name (`New EJB Ref`) with `ejb/Banking`.

▶ Click *Browse* for the link entry and select the `Banking` session bean.

▶ Click OK and the rest of the fields are filled in correctly.

- ▶ Repeat the process and define a reference named `ejb/Reports` that points to the `Reports` session bean.
- ▶ Figure 17-6 shows the deployment descriptor with the references.

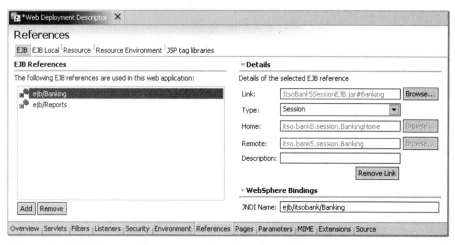

Figure 17-6   Web project deployment descriptor with EJB references

- ▶ Save and close the deployment descriptor.

Testing the Web client

Testing the Web client is straightforward:

- ▶ Start the `EjbbankServer` in the Servers view and wait until it is ready.
- ▶ Select the `Banking.html` file in the Web project and *Run on Server*.
- ▶ The first time, you are prompted to select which server to use. Select the `EjbbankServer` and also select *Set server as project default.* Click *Finish*.
- ▶ The HTML page appears and you can enter sample data and invoke one of the functions.
- ▶ A sample run is shown in Figure 17-2 on page 592.
- ▶ Select the `Reports.html` file and *Run on Server*.
- ▶ Sample output is shown in Figure 17-3 on page 593 and Figure 17-5 on page 607.
- ▶ Watch the Console view for test output written by the home factory and the servlets. Such output should not remain in the code for a production environment.

Developing a Struts-based Web client

Application Developer supports Web projects with built-in Struts support. In this section, we briefly introduce Struts and then develop the Web application using Struts.

What is Struts?

Struts is an open source framework for building Web applications according to model-view-controller (MVC) principles. Struts is part of the Jakarta project, sponsored by the Apache Software Foundation.

> **Note:** We do not describe Struts in detail. Refer to the official Jakarta project Struts home page and the official Struts user guide at:
>
> ```
> http://jakarta.apache.org/struts
> http://jakarta.apache.org/struts/userGuide/introduction.html
> ```
>
> You can also read the Struts concepts chapter in the redbook *Legacy Modernization with WebSphere Studio Enterprise Developer*, SG24-6806.

MVC framework with Struts

Struts provides these components to develop applications using MVC (Figure 17-7):

Model Struts does not provide model classes. The business logic must be provided by the Web application developer as JavaBeans or EJBs.

View Struts provides action forms to create form beans that are used to pass data between the controller and the view. In addition, Struts custom tag libraries assist developers in creating interactive form-based applications using JSPs. An application resource file holds text constants and error messages that are used in JSPs.

Controller Struts provides an action servlet (controller servlet) that populates action forms from JSP input fields and then calls an action class where the developer provides the logic to interface with the model.

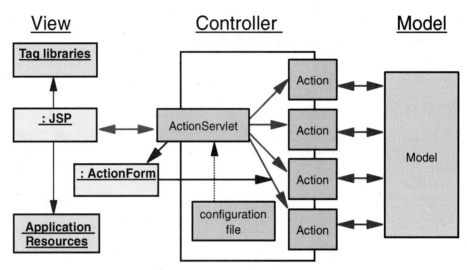

View	Controller	Model

Figure 17-7   Struts components in the MVC architecture

A typical Struts Web application is composed of these components:

► A single servlet (`org.apache.struts.action.ActionServlet`), which uses an XML configuration file. The action servlet invokes actions based on the JSP's *action* specification and it invokes JSPs based on the actions *forwarding* information.

► Multiple JSPs that provide the end-user view. Struts tag libraries make JSP coding easier.

► One application resources file that holds text constants and error messages and makes internationalization easy.

► Multiple action classes (extending `org.apache.struts.action.Action`) to interface to the model.

► Multiple action forms (extending `org.apache.struts.action.ActionForm`) to hold the data from the JSPs. The action forms are initialized by the action servlet and passed to the action classes. Action forms can be used to validate the data entered by end users.

Figure 17-8 shows the flow of information for an interaction in a Struts Web application.

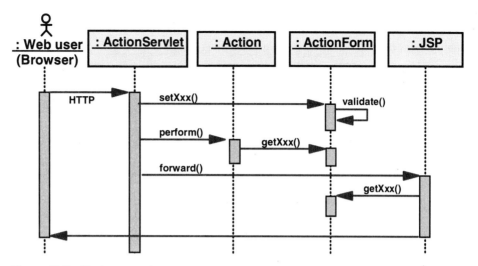

Figure 17-8   Struts request sequences

Application Developer support for Struts

Application Developer provides specific support for Struts-based Web applications:

- ► A Web project can be configured for Struts. This adds the Struts runtime, tag libraries, and action servlet to the project, and creates skeleton configuration and application resources files.

- ► A set of component wizards to define action form classes, action classes with action forwarding information, and JSP skeletons with the tag libraries included.

- ► A configuration file editor to maintain the control information for the action servlet.

- ► A graphical design tool to edit a graphical view of the Web application from which components (forms, actions, JSPs) can be created using the wizards. This graphical view is called a Web diagram.

To create our sample Web application with Struts, we start by creating the Web diagram and then we implement the JSPs, forms, and actions.

Creating a Struts Web project

Before we can start implementing the Struts application, we define a Web project with Struts support:

► Create a Web project named `ItsoBank5Struts` (Figure 17-9). Select *Add Struts support*. Click *Next*.

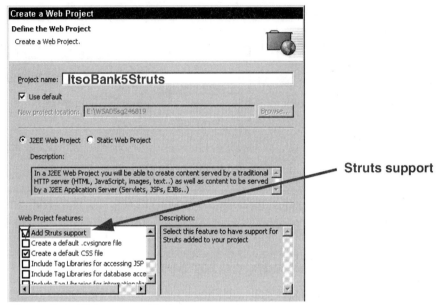

Figure 17-9   Web project with Struts support

► Use the existing `ItsoBank5EAR` project as enterprise application. Click *Next*.

► Select `ItsoBank5SessionEJB` and `ItsoBank5Utility` project as module dependencies. Click *Next*.

► Select *Override default settings*. Enter `itso.bank5.struts` as the Java package prefix. Select *Create a Resource Bundle for the Struts project*. Enter itso.bank5.struts.resources as the package for the resource bundle. Leave `ApplicationResources` as the resource bundle name. Click *Finish*.

► Click *OK* on the Repair Server Configuration window.

The new Web project is configured with an application resources file (`Java Source\itso.bank5.struts.resources.ApplicationResources.properties`), an action servlet (in `web.xml`), a configuration file (`struts-config.xml`) and four tag libraries (`struts-xxxx.tld`) in `Web Content\WEB-INF`, and the `struts.jar` file in `WEB-INF\lib`.

Creating the Struts Web diagram

We take a top-down approach to designing the Web application by lay ing out all the components in a Web diagram:

▶ Select the WEB-INF folder and *New -> Other -> Web -> Struts -> Web diagram*. Click *Next*. Enter itsobank5 as the name and click *Finish*.

▶ The Web diagram editor opens on the file itsobank5.gph (.gph is the file type for Web diagrams).

▶ Notice the icons in the tool bar:

The icons on the right are for placing new components into the empty diagram. The components are links, actions, forms, JavaBeans, JSPs, and subdiagrams.

Designing the flow of the application

Lay out three input JSPs, three actions, eight output JSPs, and three form beans. When you drop a form bean, you are prompted for a name and scope. Enter accountRequestForm and reportRequestForm as names and select *request* as the scope. Connect the components as shown in Figure 17-10.

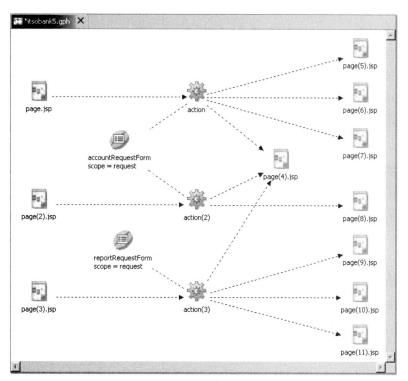

Figure 17-10   Web diagram with application design

Naming the components

Select each component and *Change Path* (context), then overtype the name (Figure 17-11):

► The three input JSPs are index.jsp, transfer.jsp, and reporting.jsp.

► The three actions are banking, transfer, and reports.

► The eight output JSPs are error.jsp, accountinfo.jsp, deposit.jsp, transactions.jsp, transferred.jsp, reports.jsp, accounts.jsp, and customers.jsp.

► The output links from the three actions carry a forward name. Select each link and *Edit the forward name* (context):

   – The three links to the error.jsp are named *fail*.

   – The three success links from the banking action are named *information*, *funds*, and *translist*.

   – The success link from the transfer action is named *transfer*.

   – The three success links from the reports action are named *reports*, *accounts*, and *customers*.

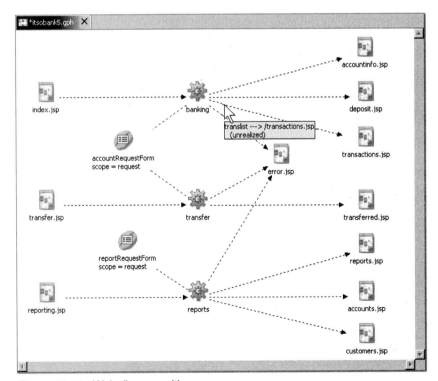

Figure 17-11   Web diagram with names

Defining application resources

Before implementing the components we configure the application resources. Open the `ApplicationResources.properties` file. Replace the content with the lines shown in Figure 17-12.

```
itso.heading=ITSO EJB Bank
itso.accounthead=Access Accounts and Perform Transactions
itso.accountinfo=Account Information
itso.account=Account number
itso.select=Select an action:
itso.info=Balance and information
itso.deposit=Deposit
itso.withdraw=Withdraw
itso.list=List transactions
itso.amount=Amount
itso.balance=Balance
itso.transact=Transactions
itso.type=Type
itso.interest=Interest
itso.transfer=Transfer
itso.submit=Execute
itso.errors=Error listing
error.noaccount=Account number missing.
error.noamount=Amount missing.
error.invalidamount=Amount value invalid.
error.insuffientfunds=Insufficient funds
error.required=Required field missing.
error.invalid=Invalid numeric value.
error.exception=Operation failed with exception
# Optional header and footer for <errors/> tag.
errors.header=<font color="red"><ul>
errors.footer=</ul></font>
```

Figure 17-12   Application resources file

Every line defines a key and a value. Some of the entries will be used as text in JSPs, and some entries are error messages. We did not define all the text constants used in all the JSPs.

Implementing the Web application

To implement a component, double-click the component and a wizard opens. You can implement components in any sequence, but a structured approach works best:

- We start with the form beans that hold the data that comes from the input JSPs and is passed to the action classes.

- Next, we implement the input JSPs. This sequence allows us to specify which fields from the form bean should be in the JSP.

- Next, we implement the actions, specifying which form bean to use and which output JSPs to call.

- Finally, we implement the output JSPs.

Implementing the form beans

Double-click the `accountRequestForm` form bean and the New ActionForm Class wizard opens:

- Leave the package (`itso.bank5.struts.forms`) and name unchanged and generate `reset` and `validate` methods. Click *Next* twice (we do not have JSPs to choose from).

- Add four access fields of type string `accountidS`, `accountidT`, `amountS`, and `selection`. Add one field of type `java.math.BigDecimal` named `amount`.

  The selection field is used to select the action: *balance*, *list*, *deposit*, *withdraw*, or *transfer*. Some actions require an amount.

- Select *Add new mapping* (for the configuration file).

The `AccountRequestForm` class opens in the editor.

- You can see the fields with getter and setter methods.

- The `reset` method resets all the fields before displaying the JSP.

- The `validate` method is used to validate input fields and return errors in case of invalid entries. Add the code in Example 17-9 to the validate method.

Example 17-9   Validating input fields

```
public ActionErrors validate(ActionMapping mapping,
                             HttpServletRequest request) {
   ActionErrors errors = new ActionErrors();
   ....
   boolean amountRequired = selection.equals("deposit") ||
           selection.equals("withdraw") || selection.equals("transfer");
   if ( accountidS.trim().equals("") )
      errors.add("account", new ActionError("error.noaccount"));
   if ( amountS.trim().equals("") & amountRequired )
      errors.add("account", new ActionError("error.noamount"));
   else
      if ( amountRequired ) {
         try {
```

```
                setAmount( new java.math.BigDecimal(amountS) );
            } catch (Exception e) {
                errors.add("account", new ActionError("error.invalidamount"));
            }
        }
        if ( selection.equals("transfer") ) {
            if (accountidT == null || accountidT.trim().equals("") )
                errors.add("account", new ActionError("error.noaccount"));
        }
        return errors;
    }
}
```

Note how error messages are returned. An `ActionError` object with a key of a value in the application resources file is added to an `ActionErrors` object that is returned to the caller. If the `ActionErrors` object is not empty, the original JSP is displayed again with error messages.

Implement the `reportRequestForm` in the same way, using the sample code that you downloaded.

Note that the implemented components show up dark in the Web diagram.

Implementing input JSPs

Double-click the `index.jsp` to implement the home page of the application and the wizard to define a JSP opens:

▶ The name is filled in already and the model is defined as Struts JSP.

▶ Skip the next three panels, since all the defaults are fine.

▶ Select *Add to web.xml*.

▶ Select the `accountRequestForm` from the pull-down; this adds the fields from the bean to the list of fields. Select the fields `accountidS`, `selection`, and `amountS`.

▶ For each field, you can set the label and size for the HTML definition. We will actually use Struts tag libraries to do a better job, but you can see what would be possible.

▶ Click *Finish* and the `index.jsp` opens in the page designer. The fields have been placed into a table and a Submit button is at the bottom.

▶ Note that the action link to `/banking` is reported as a warning because we have not implemented the action yet.

Using Struts tag libraries and application resources

Replace the body of the `index.jsp` with the code in Example 17-10.

Example 17-10   Home page of Web application

```
<BODY>
<h1 align="center"><bean:message key="itso.heading"></bean:message></h1>
<h2><bean:message key="itso.accounthead"></bean:message></h2>
<html:errors></html:errors>
<html:form action="/banking">
    <TABLE border="0" cellspacing="10">
        <TBODY>
            <TR valign="top" align="left">
                <TH><bean:message key="itso.account" /></TH>
                <TD><html:text property="accountidS" size="8" maxlength="8"></html:text>
                </TD>
            </TR>
            <TR valign="top" align="left">
                <TH><bean:message key="itso.amount" /><BR>
                (deposit or withdraw)</TH>
                <TD><html:text property="amountS" size="8" maxlength="8"></html:text></TD>
            </TR>
            <TR valign="top" align="left">
                <TH><bean:message key="itso.select" /></TH>
                <TD>
                    <html:radio property="selection" value="balance">
                        <bean:message key="itso.info" />
                    </html:radio><BR>
                    <html:radio property="selection" value="list">
                        <bean:message key="itso.list" />
                    </html:radio><BR>
                    <html:radio property="selection" value="deposit">
                        <bean:message key="itso.deposit" />
                    </html:radio><BR>
                    <html:radio property="selection" value="withdraw">
                        <bean:message key="itso.withdraw" />
                    </html:radio>
                </TD>
            </TR>
            <TR>
                <TD> </TD>
                <TD>
                    <html:submit>
                        <bean:message key="itso.submit"></bean:message>
                    </html:submit>
                </TD>
            </TR>
        </TBODY>
    </TABLE>
</html:form>
<hr>
<P><A href="transfer.jsp">Money Transfer</A>    
   <A href="reporting.jsp">Reporting</A></P>
</BODY>
```

Note the use of the Struts tag libraries:

- `<html:form>` tag is the Struts form with an action
- `<bean:message>` tags refer to text constants in the resources file
- `<html:text>` tags are input fields
- `<html:radio>` tags are radio buttons; they all point to the *selection* property
- `<hmtl:submit>` tag defines a submit button with a label from the resources file
- `<html:errors>` tag displays all error messages

Implement the `transfer.jsp` and the `reporting.jsp` in the same way, using the sample code that you downloaded.

Implementing actions

To implement an action, double-click the `banking` icon and complete the wizard:

- All the defaults for the action mapping are fine; you can see that the forwards are listed as defined in the Web diagram and the form bean is selected.

- For the action class the package (`itso.bank5.struts.actions`) and name (`BankingAction`) are prefilled. Leave the first `perform` method selected and click *Finish*.

- The `BankingAction` class opens in the editor. Note that a skeleton `perform` method is generated. This is where we implement the logic to interact with the `Banking` session bean to perform the requested selection. The method receives the form bean (`AccountRequestForm`) as input.

- Replace the code of the class with the code in Example 17-11.

Example 17-11   Banking action class

```
package itso.bank5.struts.actions;

import java.io.IOException;
import javax.servlet.ServletException;
import javax.servlet.http.HttpServletRequest;
import javax.servlet.http.HttpServletResponse;
import org.apache.struts.action.Action;
import org.apache.struts.action.ActionError;
import org.apache.struts.action.ActionErrors;
import org.apache.struts.action.ActionForm;
import org.apache.struts.action.ActionForward;
import org.apache.struts.action.ActionMapping;
import itso.bank5.struts.forms.AccountRequestForm;
// new imports
import itso.bank5.session.*;
import itso.bank5.utility.*;
import itso.bank5.exception.InsufficientFundException;
import javax.naming.NamingException;
import javax.ejb.EJBException;
import java.math.BigDecimal;
```

```java
import java.util.*;

public class BankingAction extends Action {

    public BankingAction() {
        super();
    }
    public ActionForward perform(
        ActionMapping mapping,
        ActionForm form,
        HttpServletRequest request,
        HttpServletResponse response)
        throws IOException, ServletException {

        ActionErrors errors = new ActionErrors();
        ActionForward forward = new ActionForward();
        // return value
        AccountRequestForm accountRequestForm = (AccountRequestForm) form;
        request.setAttribute("formbean",accountRequestForm);

        BankingHome bankingHome;
        try {
            bankingHome   = (BankingHome)HomeFactory.singleton().getHome("ejb/Banking");
        } catch (NamingException ex) {
            ex.printStackTrace();
            throw new EJBException("Error looking up BankingHome: "+ex.getMessage());
        }

        try {

            // do something here
            String accountID = accountRequestForm.getAccountidS();
            BigDecimal amount = accountRequestForm.getAmount();
            String selection = accountRequestForm.getSelection();

            Banking bank = bankingHome.create();

            if ( selection.equals("balance") ) {
                BigDecimal balance = bank.getBalance(accountID);
                request.setAttribute("balance",balance);
                forward = mapping.findForward("information");
                String[] result = bank.getAccountInfo(accountID);
                request.setAttribute("account",result);
            }
            else if ( selection.equals("list") ) {
                Vector results = bank.getTransrecords(accountID);
                request.setAttribute("trecords",results);
                forward = mapping.findForward("translist");
            }
            else if ( selection.equals("deposit") ) {
                BigDecimal balance = bank.deposit(accountID, amount);
                request.setAttribute("balance",balance);
                forward = mapping.findForward("funds");
            }
```

```
                   else if ( selection.equals("withdraw") ) {
                       try {
                           BigDecimal balance = bank.withdraw(accountID, amount);
                           request.setAttribute("balance",balance);
                       } catch (InsufficientFundException ex) {
                           errors.add("account", new ActionError("error.insuffientfunds"));
                       }
                       forward = mapping.findForward("funds");
                   }

               } catch (Exception e) {
                   // Report the error using the appropriate name and ID.
                   errors.add("account", new ActionError("error.exception"));
               }
               // If a message is required, save the specified key(s)
               // into the request for use by the <struts:errors> tag.
               if (!errors.empty()) {
                   saveErrors(request, errors);
                   forward = mapping.findForward("fail");
               }
               // Write logic determining how the user should be forwarded.
               // Finish with
               return (forward);
           }
   }
```

► The BankingAction class executes the methods of the Banking session bean,
  sets the appropriate forward action, stores the result data in the request block
  for the output JSP, and returns the forward.

Implement the transfer and the reports actions in the same way, using the
sample code that you downloaded.

Implementing output JSPs

Implementing the output JSPs is the same as for the input JSPs. Double-click a
JSP component and complete the wizard. No form bean has to be selected. Use
the sample code that you downloaded to complete the JSP code.

Completing Web diagram connectors

You can also draw connections from an action to an input JSP. When prompted,
select "input". Input connectors appear in red.

You can select a JSP and *Draw -> Draw All From*. This actions add the
connections between JSPs (hyperlinks).

Figure 17-13 shows the final Web diagram with all components implemented.

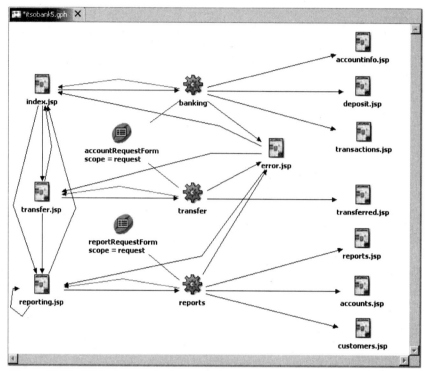

Figure 17-13 Web diagram implemented

Struts configuration file

Open the Struts configuration file (WEB-INF\struts-config.xml):

- On the Actions page select each action and enter the name of the input JSP into the Input field: /index.jsp, /transfer.jsp, or /reporting.jsp.

- Notice that the form bean and forwarding information is all specified.

- On the Form beans page, you can see the two form beans.

- On the XML Source page, you can see the file content in XML format.

Web application deployment descriptor

Open the Web application deployment descriptor editor. We have to complete the references to the EJBs:

- On the References page, select the *EJB* tab (top).

- Click *Add* and define a reference named ejb/Banking. Click *Browse* for the link and select the Banking session bean.

- ▶ Click *Add* and define a reference named `ejb/Reports`. Click *Browse* for the link and select the `Reports` session bean.

- ▶ On the Servlets page, select the `action` servlet. Look at the initialization parameters. The *config* parameter points to the `struts-config.xml` file, and the *application* parameter points to the resources file. The *debug* and *detail* parameters can be set to 0 to reduce the amount of test output in the server.

Testing the Struts client

Testing the Struts client is the same as testing the Web client.

- ▶ Start the `EjbbankServer` in the Servers view and wait until it is ready.

- ▶ Select the `ItsoBank5Struts` project and *Run on Server*.

- ▶ The home page appears and you can enter sample data and invoke one of the functions.

- ▶ A sample run is shown in Figure 17-14.

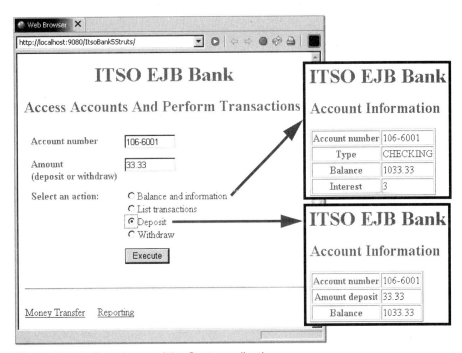

Figure 17-14   Sample run of the Struts application

J2EE client container

J2EE provides a client container to run client applications that access EJBs in a WebSphere Application Server. The client container can be launched inside the Application Developer for testing, or outside in a command window to access a server that runs inside the Application Developer or a WebSphere Application Server.

Developing a message-driven bean client

This J2EE client runs inside a client container and accesses the message-driven bean in the same way as the servlet we developed in "Servlet client" on page 579. The code is basically a duplicate of the servlet.

Creating an application client project

To create an application client project:

- Select *File -> New -> Project ->J2EE -> Application Client Project* and click *Next*.
- Select *Create J2EE 1.3 Application Client* project and click *Next*.
- Enter ItsoBank5Client as *name*. Select *Existing for Enterprise application project*, click the *Browse* button, and select the ItsoBank5EAR project. Click *OK* and then *Next*.
- Select ItsoBank5Utility from the *Available dependent JARs* list (it contains the TransferDataObject and the HomeFactory that we need). Click *Finish*.

Creating the MDB client class

To create the application client class:

- In the ItsoBank5Client project create a package, itso.bank5.client.mdb.
- In the new package, create a class named MdbClient. Select to create a main method and click *Finish*.
- Complete the code as shown in Example 17-12.

Example 17-12   MDB application client (abbreviated)

```
package itso.bank5.client.mdb;

import itso.bank5.utility.*;
import java.math.BigDecimal;
import java.util.Properties;
import javax.jms.*;
```

```java
import javax.naming.*;

public class MdbClient {
    private static final String QUEUECONNECTIONFACTORY="jms/ItsoMdbConnectionFactoryRef";
    private static final String SENDQUEUE            = "jms/ItsoMdbQueueRef";
    private static final String RESPONSEQUEUE        = "jms/ItsoResponseQueueRef";
    public MdbClient() {
        super();
    }

    public static void main(String[] args) throws JMSException, Exception {
        System.out.println("Client: Start");
        MdbClient testClient = new MdbClient();
        if (args.length == 3) {
            BigDecimal amount = new BigDecimal(args[2]);
            testClient.testMDB(args[0], args[1], amount);
        } else {
            System.out.println("Client: No parms supplied, using default");
            testClient.testMDB("101-1001", "101-1002", new BigDecimal("10"));
        }
    }

    private void testMDB(String fromAccount, String toAccount, BigDecimal amount) {
        String messageID = null;
        String selector  = null;
        boolean verbose = true;
        QueueSession session = null;
        QueueConnection connection = null;
        QueueConnectionFactory qcf = null;
        try {
            // Attempt to retrieve ConnectionFactory and Queues from the JNDI namespace
            Queue outQueue = (Queue)HomeFactory.singleton().getJMS(SENDQUEUE);
            Queue inQueue  = (Queue)HomeFactory.singleton().getJMS(RESPONSEQUEUE);
            qcf = (QueueConnectionFactory)HomeFactory.singleton()
                                          .getJMS(QUEUECONNECTIONFACTORY);
            if (qcf == null) System.out.println("Client: Failed to retrieve    ");
            // Create a QueueConnection from the QueueConnectionFactory
            connection = qcf.createQueueConnection();
            connection.start();
            // Create a QueueSession from the connection. not transacted
            boolean transacted = false;
            session = connection.createQueueSession( transacted,
                                              Session.AUTO_ACKNOWLEDGE);
            QueueSender queueSender = session.createSender(outQueue);
            // assemble our parameters
            TransferDataObject transferMsg = new TransferDataObject (fromAccount,
                                                        toAccount, amount);
            ObjectMessage outMessage = session.createObjectMessage(transferMsg);
            outMessage.setStringProperty("BUSINESSMETHOD", "transfer");
            selector = "CORR:TF"+ (new java.util.Random()).nextInt(999999);
            outMessage.setJMSCorrelationID(selector);
            // send the message
            queueSender.send(outMessage);
            messageID = outMessage.getJMSMessageID();
```

```
            if (verbose) System.out.println("Client: Sent message "+messageID+selector);
            if (verbose) System.out.println("Client: Receiving message from " +
                                            inQueue.getQueueName());
            selector = "JMSCorrelationID = '" + messageID + "'";
            QueueReceiver queueReceiver = session.createReceiver(inQueue, selector);
            if (verbose) System.out.println("Client: Retrieving the message");
            Message inMessage = queueReceiver.receive(15000);
            if (inMessage == null) {
                System.out.println("Client: The attempt to read the message failed");
                throw new JMSException("Client: Failed to retrieve message.");
            }
            if (inMessage instanceof TextMessage) {
                // Extract the message content with getText()
                String replyString = ((TextMessage) inMessage).getText();
                if (verbose) System.out.println("Client: Reply = '" + replyString + "'");
            } else {
                // Report that the incoming message was not of the expected type
                System.out.println("Client: Reply message was not a TextMessage");
                throw new JMSException("Client: Retrieved the wrong type of message");
            }
            // Call the close() method on all of the objects.
            queueReceiver.close();
            queueSender.close();
            session.close();
            session = null;
            connection.close();
            connection = null;
            System.out.println("Client: Done");
        } catch (JMSException e) {
            System.out.println("Client: JMS failed with " + e);
            Exception le = e.getLinkedException();
            if (le != null) System.out.println("Client: linked exception " + le);
        } catch (Exception exc) {
            System.out.println("Client: Unexpected error " + exc);
        } finally { //  Ensure JMS objects are closed
            try {
                if (session != null) session.close();
                if (connection != null) connection.close();
            } catch (JMSException e) {
                System.out.println("Client: Unexpected error, failed with " + e);
            }
        }
    }
}
```

Deployment descriptor

We access the connection factory and the queues using references that must be
defined in the deployment descriptor:

▶ Open the deployment descriptor of the client project.

- ▶ On the References page, click *Add* and select *EJB resource reference*. Define the reference for the `ItsoMdbConnectionFactory`:
  - Enter `jms/ItsoMdbConnectionFactoryRef` as the name.
  - Select `javax.jms.QueueConnectionFactory` as the type (pull-down).
  - Select *Container* for authentication and click *Finish*.
  - Select the reference and enter `jms/ItsoMdbConnectionFactory` as the JNDI name.
- ▶ Click *Add* again, select *Resource environment reference*, and define a reference for the `ItsoMdbQueue`:
  - Enter `jms/ItsoMdbQueueRef` as the name, `javax.jms.Queue` as the type (pull-down), and click *Finish*. Select the reference and enter `jms/ItsoMdbQueue` as the JNDI name.
  - Repeat this and define the `jms/ItsoResponseQueueRef` reference with `jms/ItsoResponseQueue` as the JNDI name.
- ▶ Figure 17-15 shows the references in the deployment descriptor.

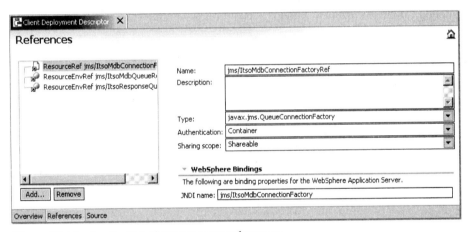

Figure 17-15   Application client resource references

Resource references

In Figure 17-15, we show how a resource reference is configured for the queue connection factory. In the current version of Application Developer, this configuration is not complete and does not work when running the application client.

One extra step using the application client resource configuration tool is required to make it work. We will cover this step before deploying the application (see "Application client resource configuration tool" on page 632).

> **Important:** The EJB resource reference (`jms/ItsoMdbConnectionFactory`) does not work when connecting to the server. To make the application work for testing, change the code to look up the connection factory with the real JNDI name instead of a reference:

```
try {
    // for deployment
    qcf = (QueueConnectionFactory)HomeFactory.singleton()
                                 .getJMS(QUEUECONNECTIONFACTORY);
    if (verbose) System.out.println("Client: deploy factory="+qcf.getClass());
} catch (Exception e) {
    // for testing
    String QUEUECONNECTIONFACTORYTEST = "jms/ItsoMdbConnectionFactory";
    initialContext = new InitialContext();
    qcf = (QueueConnectionFactory)initialContext.lookup(QUEUECONNECTIONFACTORYTEST);
    if (verbose) System.out.println("Client: test factory="+qcf.getClass());
}
```

- ► On the Overview page, click *Edit* for the main class. In the JAR Dependency Editor, click *Browse* and locate the `itso.bank5.client.mdb.MdbClient` class. Save and close the editor and the main class is set. This information is stored in the `MANIFEST.MF` file.

- ► Save and close the deployment descriptor editor.

Running the application client inside Application Developer

The application client requires access to JMS classes from embedded messaging to connect to the factory and queues through JNDI. We require the implementation classes in `com.ibm.mq.jar` and `com.ibm.mqjms.jar` for the MDB client.

> **Important:** A prerequisite for running the application client against the built-in server is that the embedded messaging client and server (WebSphere MQ) must be installed. Run this installation from the WebSphere Studio Installation Launcher even when you have installed WebSphere MQ as part of WebSphere Application Server on the same machine.

To run a J2EE application client, we have to define a launch configuration:

- ► Select the `ItsoBank5Client` project and *Run -> Run*. The Launch Configurations window opens.

- ► Select *WebSphere v5 Application Client*, click *New*, and complete the window (Figure 17-16):

  - Enter `MdbClient` as the name.

- Select `ItsoBank5EAR` from the enterprise application pull-down.
- Click *Apply.*

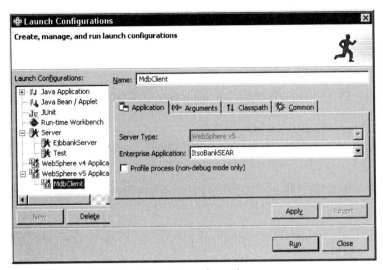

Figure 17-16   MDB client launch configuration

► Select the *Classpath* tab (Figure 17-17):

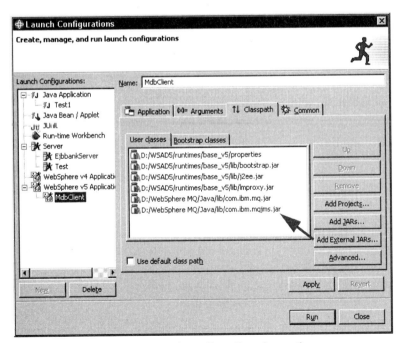

Figure 17-17   MDB client launch configuration classpath

▶ Add JAR files from the embedded messaging installation:
  – Click *Add External JARs.*
  – Locate the file `WebSphere MQ\Java\lib\com.ibm.mq.jar` and click *Open.*
  – Repeat for the file `WebSphere MQ\Java\lib\com.ibm.mqjms.jar.`

▶ Click *Apply.*

▶ Click *Run.*

▶ The Console view shows the output of the `MdbClient`:

```
IBM WebSphere Application Server, Release 5.0
J2EE Application Client Tool
......
WSCL0350W: Unable to create a resource for
    jms/ItsoMdbConnectionFactoryRefBad because the following error occurred:
WSCL0220E: An unsuccessful attempt was made to find the resource
        configuration information for jms/ItsoMdbConnectionFactoryRefBad.
......
WSCL0035I: Initialization of the J2EE Application Client Environment has
                                        completed.
WSCL0014I: Invoking the Application Client class
                        itso.bank5.client.mdb.MdbClient
Client: Start
Client: No parms supplied, using default
Client: Retrieving Queues from JNDI
Client: JNDI class=class com.ibm.mq.jms.MQQueue
Client: JNDI class=class com.ibm.mq.jms.MQQueue
Client: outQueue=class com.ibm.mq.jms.MQQueue
Client: Retrieving a QueueConnectionFactory from JNDI
Client: JNDI class=class com.ibm.mq.jms.MQXAQueueConnectionFactory
Client: test factory=class com.ibm.mq.jms.MQXAQueueConnectionFactory
Client: got connection
Client: connection started
Client: created queue session
Client: created sender
Client: created object message
Client: Sending the message to queue:///WQ_ItsoMdbQueue
Client: Sent message
    ID:414d51205741535f6c6f63616c686f73210ff53d20000601/CORR:TF482322
Client: Receiving message from queue:///WQ_ItsoResponseQueue
Client: Waiting for message
Client: Reply = 'Transfer OK: 10 from/to 101-1001/101-1002 Balance=50.00'
Client: Done
```

▶ For future runs, select *Run -> Run History -> MdbClient* or use the drop-down menu of the *Run* icon (   ).

Running the client outside Application Developer

We can run the client outside Application Developer by exporting the enterprise application and using `launchClient` to start the application client. The server must be started.

Runtime configuration changes

Some of the installed files in the internal Version 5 Application Server point to the wrong directories:

► Edit the file `<wsadhome>\runtimes\base_v5\bin\setupCmdLine.bat` and make the changes shown in Figure 17-18. Note that your installation directories may be different.

```
rem WAS_HOME=C:\Program Files\WebSphere\AppServer
SET WAS_HOME=D:\WSAD5\runtimes\base_v5

rem JAVA_HOME=C:\Program Files\WebSphere\AppServer\java
SET JAVA_HOME=D:\WSAD5\runtimes\base_v5\java

SET WAS_CELL=localhost
SET WAS_NODE=localhost

SET ITP_LOC=%WAS_HOME%\deploytool\itp
SET CONFIG_ROOT=%WAS_HOME%\config
SET CLIENTSAS=-Dcom.ibm.CORBA.ConfigURL=file:/%WAS_HOME%/properties/sas.client.props
SET CLIENTSOAP=-Dcom.ibm.SOAP.ConfigURL=file:/%WAS_HOME%/properties/soap.client.props

rem WAS_EXT_DIRS=%JAVA_HOME%/lib;%WAS_HOME%/classes;%WAS_HOME%/lib;%WAS_HOME%
/lib/ext;%WAS_HOME%/web/help;%ITP_LOC%/plugins/com.ibm.etools.ejbdeploy/runtime;C:\Pr
ogram Files\IBM\WebSphere MQ\lib
SET WAS_EXT_DIRS=%JAVA_HOME%/lib;%WAS_HOME%/classes;%WAS_HOME%/lib;%WAS_HOME%
/lib/ext;%WAS_HOME%/web/help;%ITP_LOC%/plugins/com.ibm.etools.ejbdeploy/runtime;D:/We
bSphere MQ/Java/lib

SET WAS_BOOTCLASSPATH=%JAVA_HOME%\jre\lib\ext\ibmorb.jar

SET WAS_CLASSPATH=%WAS_HOME%/properties;%WAS_HOME%/lib/bootstrap.jar;
%WAS_HOME%/lib/j2ee.jar;%WAS_HOME%/lib/lmproxy.jar

rem WAS_PATH=%WAS_HOME%\bin;%JAVA_HOME%\bin;%JAVA_HOME%\jre\bin;%PATH%
SET WAS_PATH=%WAS_HOME%\bin;%JAVA_HOME%\bin;%JAVA_HOME%\jre\bin;%PATH%;D:\WebSphere
MQ\bin;D:\WebSphere MQ\java\bin;D:\WebSphere MQ\WEMPS\bin

SET QUALIFYNAMES=
......
```

Figure 17-18   Changes to setupCmdLine.bat

▶ Edit the two files `sas.client.props` and `soap.client.props` in `<wsadhome>\runtimes\base_v5\properties` and make the changes shown in Figure 17-19.

```
...
com.ibm.ssl.protocol=SSL
com.ibm.ssl.keyStoreType=JKS
#com.ibm.ssl.keyStore=C\:/Program Files/WebSphere/AppServer/etc/
                                            DummyClientKeyFile.jks
com.ibm.ssl.keyStore=D\:/WSAD5/runtimes/base_v5/etc/DummyClientKeyFile.jks
com.ibm.ssl.keyStorePassword={xor}CDo9Hgw\=
com.ibm.ssl.trustStoreType=JKS
#com.ibm.ssl.trustStore=C\:/Program Files/WebSphere/AppServer/etc/
                                            DummyClientTrustFile.jks
com.ibm.ssl.trustStore=D\:/WSAD5/runtimes/base_v5/etc/DummyClientTrustFile.jks
com.ibm.ssl.trustStorePassword={xor}CDo9Hgw\=
...
```

Figure 17-19   Changes to properties files

Run the application client

Select the ItsoBank5EAR project and *Export* (context). Select *EAR file* and click *Next*. Set the output file to a known location, for example, `e:\ItsoBank5EAR.ear`.

Open a command window, set the current directory to the built-in application server, for example, `cd d:\<wsadhome>\runtimes\base_v5\bin`.

Start the application using the command:

```
launchclient.bat e:\itsobank5ear.ear
```

The same output as for the client inside Application Developer appears in the command window.

Application client resource configuration tool

To completely configure resource references for an application client, we have to run the application client resource configuration tool:

▶ Run the `clientConfig.bat` file (in `<wsadhome>\runtimes\base_v5\bin`) to start the tool. This requires that you made the changes in "Runtime configuration changes" on page 631.

▶ In the open window, navigate to the exported EAR file, for example, `e:\ItsoBank5EAR.ear`, and click *Open*.

▶ Expand the tree ItsoBank5Client.jar -> JMS Providers -> WebSphere JMS Provider, select *WAS Queue Connection Factories*, and *New* (context).

► Complete the window (Figure 17-20) and click *OK*.

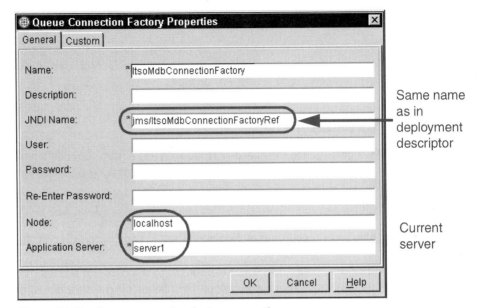

Same name as in deployment descriptor

Current server

Figure 17-20   Queue connection factory properties

► Select *File -> Save* to save the configuration (Figure 17-21).

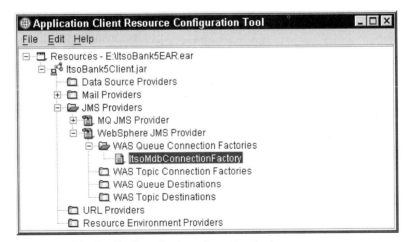

Figure 17-21   Application client configuration tool

► Close the tool.

A file named `client-resource.xmi` is added to the `ItsoBank5Client.jar` file inside the EAR file.

Rerun the application using the `launchClient` command. This time, no errors are reported and you connect to the proper queue connection factory.

> **Tip:** You can extract the `client-resource.xmi` file from the `ItsoBank5Client.jar` file inside the EAR file and import it into the `META-INF` folder of the `ItsoBank5Client` project. After that, the client runs without error inside Application Developer as well.

Deployment to WebSphere

After configuring the client JAR file with the application client resource configuration tool, the client can be run against a WebSphere Application Server where the message-driven bean is installed.

GUI client using access beans

In this application client, we demonstrate the use of the customer access bean (`CustomerData`) that we developed in "Developing a data class" on page 557.

This client is a J2EE application client with a GUI to maintain basic customer information (Figure 17-22).

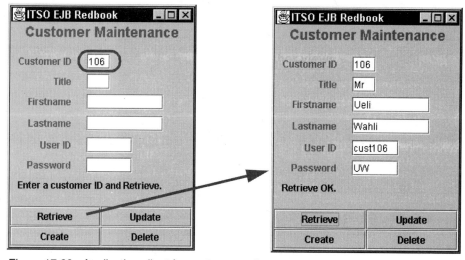

Figure 17-22   Application client for customer maintenance

Creating the GUI application client

We use the visual editor to create the GUI client:

▶ First we create a project for the client in the same way as described in "Creating an application client project" on page 624. We name the project ItsoBank5Client2. For dependent JAR files, select the ItsoBank5CmpEJB project.

▶ Create a package named itso.bank5.client2.

▶ Select the package and *New -> Other -> Java -> Visual Class*. Enter CustomerMaint as name, select *Frame, Swing*, create a main method, and a constructor. Click *Finish*.

▶ Create the layout shown in Figure 17-23.

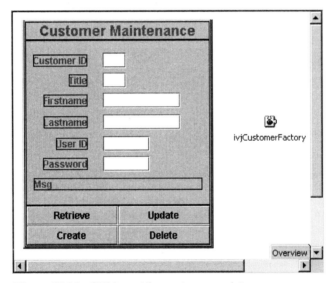

Figure 17-23   GUI layout for customer maintenance

▶ The layout consist of a label in the top area, a panel with a gridbag layout consisting of labels and data entry fields in the center area, and a panel with a grid layout consisting of four buttons in the bottom area.

▶ Drop a bean of type CustomerFactory next to the panel. We use the factory to connect to the Customer EJB.

Completing the code

To complete the code, we define the listeners for the buttons and implement the actions.

Listener class

The listener class is an internal class that monitors the actions.

```
IvjEventHandler ivjEventHandler = new IvjEventHandler();
class IvjEventHandler implements java.awt.event.ActionListener,
                                  java.awt.event.WindowListener {
    public void actionPerformed(java.awt.event.ActionEvent e) {
        if (e.getSource() == CustomerMaint.this.getJButton())    // Retrieve
            connRetrieve(e);
        if (e.getSource() == CustomerMaint.this.getJButton1())   // Update
            connUpdate(e);
        if (e.getSource() == CustomerMaint.this.getJButton2())   // Create
            connCreate(e);
        if (e.getSource() == CustomerMaint.this.getJButton3())   // Delete
            connDelete(e);
    };
    ... methods for WindowListener
}
```

Action methods

The action methods contains the logic to interact with the Customer EJB through the CustomerFactory and the CustomerData classes.

Retrieve

```
private void connRetrieve(java.awt.event.ActionEvent arg1) {
    try {
        System.out.println("CM-retrieve-start");
        int customerID = (new Integer(getJTextField().getText())).intValue();
        System.out.println("CM-retrieve "+customerID);
        CustomerKey customerKey = new CustomerKey( customerID );
        customer = ivjCustomerFactory.findByPrimaryKey(customerKey);
        customerData = customer.getCustomerData();
        getJTextField1().setText(customerData.getTitle());
        getJTextField2().setText(customerData.getFirstName());
        getJTextField3().setText(customerData.getLastName());
        getJTextField4().setText(customerData.getUserID());
        getJTextField5().setText(customerData.getPassword());
        getJLabel7().setText("Retrieve OK.");
        getJLabel7().setForeground(java.awt.Color.blue);
        System.out.println("CM-retrieve-end: "+customerData.getName());
    } catch (java.lang.Throwable ivjExc) {
        getJLabel7().setText("Retrieve failed.");
        getJLabel7().setForeground(java.awt.Color.red);
        handleException(ivjExc);
    }
}
```

Update

```
private void connUpdate(java.awt.event.ActionEvent arg1) {
    try {
        System.out.println("CM-update-start");
        customerData.setTitle(getJTextField1().getText().trim());
        customerData.setFirstName(getJTextField2().getText().trim());
        customerData.setLastName(getJTextField3().getText().trim());
        customerData.setUserID(getJTextField4().getText().trim());
        customerData.setPassword(getJTextField5().getText().trim());
        customer.setCustomerData( customerData );
        getJLabel7().setText("Update OK.");
        getJLabel7().setForeground(java.awt.Color.blue);
        System.out.println("CM-update-end");
    } catch (java.lang.Throwable ivjExc) {
        getJLabel7().setText("Update failed.");
        getJLabel7().setForeground(java.awt.Color.red);
        handleException(ivjExc);
    }
}
```

Create

```
private void connCreate(java.awt.event.ActionEvent arg1) {
    try {
        System.out.println("CM-create-start");
        int customerID = (new Integer(getJTextField().getText())).intValue();
        System.out.println("CM-create "+customerID);
        customer = ivjCustomerFactory.create(customerID);
        customerData = customer.getCustomerData();
        customerData.setTitle(getJTextField1().getText().trim());
        customerData.setFirstName(getJTextField2().getText().trim());
        customerData.setLastName(getJTextField3().getText().trim());
        customerData.setUserID(getJTextField4().getText().trim());
        customerData.setPassword(getJTextField5().getText().trim());
        customer.setCustomerData( customerData );
        getJLabel7().setText("Create OK.");
        getJLabel7().setForeground(java.awt.Color.blue);
        System.out.println("CM-create-end");
    } catch (java.lang.Throwable ivjExc) {
        getJLabel7().setText("Create failed.");
        getJLabel7().setForeground(java.awt.Color.red);
        handleException(ivjExc);
    }
}
```

Delete

```
private void connDelete(java.awt.event.ActionEvent arg1) {
    try {
        System.out.println("CM-delete-start");
```

```
        int customerID = (new Integer(getJTextField().getText()}).intValue();
        System.out.println("CM-retrieve "+customerID);
        CustomerKey customerKey = new CustomerKey( customerID );
        customer = ivjCustomerFactory.findByPrimaryKey(customerKey);
        customer.remove();
        getJLabel7().setText("Delete OK.");
        getJLabel7().setForeground(java.awt.Color.blue);
        System.out.println("CM-delete-end");
    } catch (java.lang.Throwable ivjExc) {
        getJLabel7().setText("Delete failed.");
        getJLabel7().setForeground(java.awt.Color.red);
        handleException(ivjExc);
    }
}
```

Constructor and initialization

The constructor allocates the `CustomerFactory` and creates the GUI through the `initialize` method.

```
public CustomerMaint() {
    super();
    System.out.println("CM-constructor");
    getIvjCustomerFactory();
    initialize();
}
private void initialize() {
    this.setContentPane(getJContentPane());    // create GUI layout
    this.setSize(246, 306);
    this.setTitle("ITSO EJB Redbook");
    getJButton().addActionListener(ivjEventHandler);    // button actions
    getJButton1().addActionListener(ivjEventHandler);
    getJButton2().addActionListener(ivjEventHandler);
    getJButton3().addActionListener(ivjEventHandler);
    this.addWindowListener(ivjEventHandler);
    getJLabel7().setText("Enter a customer ID and Retrieve.");
    getJLabel7().setBackground(java.awt.Color.white);
    getJLabel7().setForeground(java.awt.Color.blue);
    this.setLocation(100,100);
    this.show();
    System.out.println("CM-initialized");
}
```

Configuring the launcher

Open the deployment descriptor of the `ItsoBank5Client2` project and set the main class as `itso.bank5.client2.CustomerMaint` on the Overview page.

Create a launch configuration by selecting *Run -> Run*:

- ► Create a new configuration under WebSphere v5 Application Client.
- ► Set the name as `CustomerMaint` and select the `ItsoBank5EAR` enterprise application.
- ► On the Arguments page, add the program argument to indicate which client JAR file must be used:

```
-CCjar=ItsoBank5Client2.jar
```

Testing the GUI client

To test the GUI client, start the `EjbbankServer` and then launch the client from the *Run -> Run* menu. The GUI appears and you can invoke the four functions:

- ► To retrieve, enter a customer ID (101, 102, ... 106) and click *Retrieve*.
- ► To update customer data, change the data after retrieve and click *Update*.
- ► To creating a customer, enter all fields and click *Create*.
- ► To delete a customer, enter a customer ID and click *Delete*.

To test the GUI client outside of Application Developer, export the `ItsoBank5EAR` project as an EAR file and use the `launchclient` command:

```
cd <wsadhome>\runtimes\base_v5\bin>
launchclient e:\itsobank5ear.ear -CCjar=ItsoBank5Client2.jar
```

Note: This requires that `setupCmdLine.bat` has been changed (see "Runtime configuration changes" on page 631).

Client using a Web service

We only create a simple client that uses the Web service we created from the `Banking` session EJB. We already have a client project for Web service clients, `ItsoBank5WebClient`.

We mirror the servlet banking client from `ItsoBank5Web`, but instead of using the session bean, we use the Web service through the proxy:

- ► In the `ItsoBank5WebClient` project, create a package named `itso.bank5.servlet.client`.
- ► Create a servlet named `BankingServletClient`. In the editor, copy the code from the `BankingServlet`, and make these changes:

```
import itso.bank5.session.*;
import itso.bank5.exception.InsufficientFundException;
import itso.bank5.utility.*;
import java.io.PrintWriter;
import javax.ejb.EJBException;
import javax.naming.*;
```

```
import javax.rmi.PortableRemoteObject;
import java.math.BigDecimal;
import java.util.*;
import proxy.soap.BankingProxy;

public class BankingServlet extends HttpServlet {
public class BankingServletClient extends HttpServlet {

private BankingHome bankingHome;
BankingProxy proxy = null;                    // the proxy

public void init() throws ServletException {
    try {
        proxy = new BankingProxy();
    } catch (Exception ex) {
        ex.printStackTrace();
    }
}

// in all the business methods replace bank. with proxy. For example:
        BigDecimal balance = bank.getBalance(account1);
        BigDecimal balance = proxy.getBalance(account1);

// exception message
        out.println("<p>Error in banking session bean: "+ex.getMessage());
        out.println("<p>Error in banking client: "+ex.getMessage());
```

► Copy the `Banking.html` file and rename it as `BankingClient.html`. Change the action to point to the `BankingServletClient`:

```
<FORM action="BankingServletClient" method="POST">
```

Change the heading to indicate that the client uses Web services.

That's all. We converted the servlet to a Web service client. This client has no references to the EJB and can run anywhere.

Externalizing strings

Some of the strings we use in client methods contain important information, such as the PROVIDER_URL, the INITIAL_CONTEXT_FACTORY, the URL of the results page, and the JNDI name of the customer bean. You may want to keep other strings outside of the client code for internationalization, so that you can have the same client in multiple languages.

These strings would rather be placed into a properties file, making it easier for a developer to maintain the code. This is easily done in Application Developer.

Search for strings to externalize

Let us look at one example, the BankingServlet (in ItsoBank5Web). Open the BankingServlet source code and select *Source -> Externalize Strings*. The Externalize Strings wizard opens (Figure 17-24).

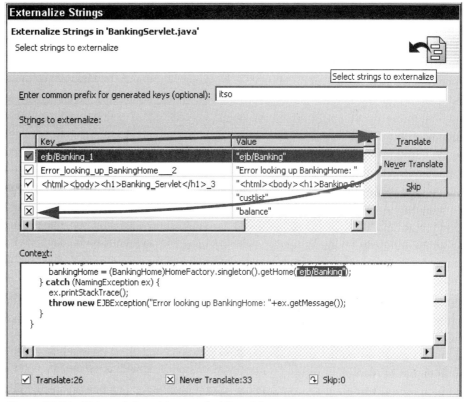

Figure 17-24   Externalizing strings: select the strings

In the first window step, you decide for each string if it should be externalized:

► Text constants should be externalized if you want to translate them into other languages (click *Translate*).

► JNDI names should be externalized so that you can change them without having to change the code.

► Attribute names from HTML forms should not be externalized; they will hardly change (click *Never Translate*).

► You can skip the decision and revise it later by running the wizard again (click *Skip*).

► You can enter a prefix (itso) for the generated keys in the properties file.

In the next window step, you decide in which files and classes to store the results (Figure 17-25).

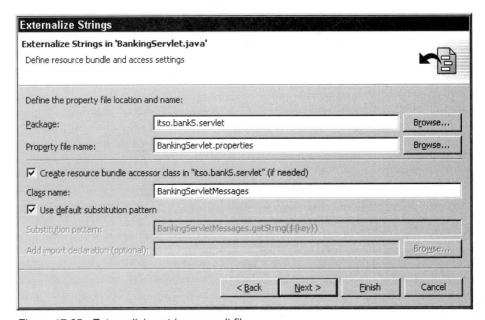

Figure 17-25   Externalizing strings: result files

A property file and a resource bundle accessor class are generated.

Skip the next window step, since there is nothing to verify or change. This step is used when rerunning the wizard after skipping decisions.

In the final window step, you can verify all the changes that will be performed (Figure 17-26).

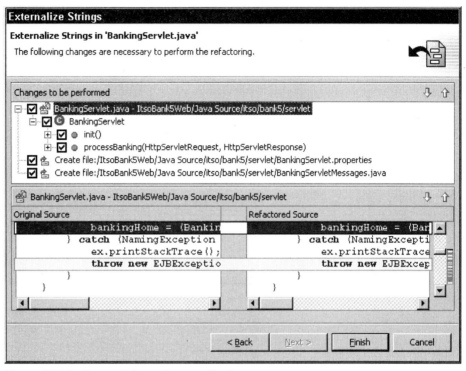

Figure 17-26 Externalizing strings: verify changes

For example, externalizing the string `ejb/Banking` changes the servlet code as follows:

```
bankingHome = (BankingHome)HomeFactory.singleton().getHome("ejb/Banking");
bankingHome = (BankingHome)HomeFactory.singleton().getHome
                (BankingServletMessages.getString("itsoejb/Banking_1"));
```

Click *Finish* to generate the code.

Result files of externalization

The result of externalization are two files and the changed servlet. The changes in the servlet were visible in the preview window step. Each externalized string is retrieved using a key from the `BankingServletMessages` class.

The `BankingServletMessages` class is shown in Figure 17-27. This class provides the interface between the servlet and the resource bundle.

```
package itso.bank5.servlet;
import java.util.MissingResourceException;
import java.util.ResourceBundle;

public class BankingServletMessages {
    private static final String BUNDLE_NAME =
                                "itso.bank5.servlet.BankingServlet";
    private static final ResourceBundle RESOURCE_BUNDLE =
                                ResourceBundle.getBundle(BUNDLE_NAME);
    private BankingServletMessages() {}
    public static String getString(String key) {
        try {
            return RESOURCE_BUNDLE.getString(key);
        } catch (MissingResourceException e) {
            return '!' + key + '!';
        }
    }
}
```

Figure 17-27   Externalizing strings: messages class

The resource bundle, BankingServlet.properties, is shown in Figure 17-28.

```
itsoejb/Banking_1=ejb/Banking
itsoError_looking_up_BankingHome___2=Error looking up BankingHome:
itso<html><body><h1>Banking_Servlet</h1>_3=<html><body><h1>Banking Servlet</h1>
itso<h2>_Customer___19=<h2> Customer:
itso<h2>_Account___21=<h2> Account:
itso<p>_Balance___23=<p> Balance:
itso<p>_Deposit___24=<p> Deposit:
itso<p>_Balance___25=<p> Balance:
itso<p>_Withdraw___26=<p> Withdraw:
itso<p>_Balance___27=<p> Balance:
itso<p>_Withdraw___28=<p> Withdraw:
itso<p>_Sorry__Insufficient_funds_in_account_29=<p> Sorry: Insufficient funds in ...
itso<p>_Transfer___30=<p> Transfer:
itso<p>_From_account___31=<p> From account:
itso_balance___32=\ balance:
itso<p>_To_account___33=<p> To account:
itso_balance___34=\ balance:
itso<p>_Transfer___35=<p> Transfer:
itso<p>_Sorry__Insufficient_funds_in_account_36=<p> Sorry: Insufficient funds in ...
itso<h3>Customers_</h3>_37=<h3>Customers:</h3>
......
```

Figure 17-28   Externalizing strings: resource bundle (abbreviated)

The resource bundle is the file that can be translated into other languages for a multi-language implementation of an application.

At this point you can rerun the servlet and it will work exactly the same way. You can make changes to the resource bundle and see the result in the output. For example, change the title to:

```
itso<html><body><h1>Banking_Servlet</h1>_3=
                     <html><body><h1>Banking Servlet Externalized</h1>
```

> **Note:** This resource bundle is similar to the Struts application resources file where we also keep the definition of text constants outside of the application code. See "Defining application resources" on page 615 for the Struts application resources file.

In our sample code, we kept both the original servlet and the externalized servlet, which we renamed as `BankingServletExternalized`. We also created a copy of the `Banking.html` file as `BankingExternalized.html` to invoke the servlet.

Summary

In this chapter, we developed a number of EJB clients using the session facade beans, the message-driven bean, and the Web service that was developed from a session bean.

Deployment of enterprise applications

This chapter describes how to deploy enterprise applications to a WebSphere Application Server.

To keep the discussion at a very simple level, we describe the process only in regard to our sample banking application, adding just a few notes about configuration management and deployment tools.

For detailed information about WebSphere Application Server, see the IBM Redbook *IBM WebSphere Application Server Version 5.0 Handbook*, SG24-6195.

© Copyright IBM Corp. 2003. All rights reserved.

Enterprise application

In this section, we discuss the configuration of enterprise applications in the Application Developer so that they can be deployed easily to a WebSphere Application Server.

Managing deployment descriptors with Application Developer

With Version 5 of the Application Developer, you can manage the deployment descriptors of EJB modules, Web modules, and application client modules. By specifying all the deployment aspects of an enterprise application in the Application Developer, you can bypass the Application Assembly Tool and install an enterprise application with little effort; all the deployment steps are seamlessly built into the development tool.

EJB module

An EJB module is contained in an EJB JAR file. The important deployment information for a WebSphere Application Server that you have to configure is contained in the WebSphere Bindings sections of the deployment descriptor editor:

► Overview page—Backend ID, JNDI - CMP Factory Connection Binding, and WebSphere extension of inheritance

► Beans page—JNDI name for each bean and possible WebSphere extensions such as caching

► References page—JNDI name for each of the references

► Access page—WebSphere extensions for access intent, security, and isolation level

► In addition, the mapping of CMP entity beans to tables must be performed before generating the deployed code

Web module

A Web module is contained in a WAR file. The WebSphere-specific options in the deployment descriptor are:

► Overview page—Virtual host name

► Servlets page—Markup language to mime type mappings

► References page—JNDI name for each of the references

► Extensions—A set of WebSphere extensions such as reloading, JSP precompile, file serving, and caching

Application client module

An application client module is contained in a client JAR file. The WebSphere-specific option in the deployment descriptor is the JNDI name for each of the references on the References page.

Configuring the WebSphere Application Server

In this section, we configure a base WebSphere Application Server to install and run the sample application.

There are two parts to the configuration that are required by the sample application:

▸ The JDBC driver and data source for the EJBBANK database that is used by the container-managed beans.

▸ The JMS listener, the connection factory, and the queues for the message-drive bean.

Start the server and the administrative console

To configure the server, we use the administrative console:

▸ Start the server (from the program group, from First Steps, or as a service).

▸ Start the administrative console (from the program group or from First Steps).

▸ Log in with your normal user ID (Figure 18-1).

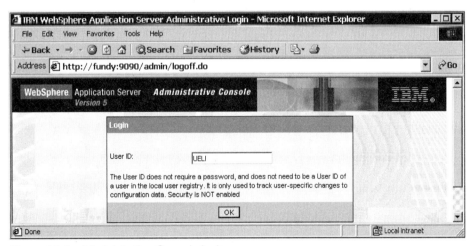

Figure 18-1   Administrative Console login

- ► Select *Servers* and *Applications* to expand the tree (Figure 18-2). Select *Application Servers* and you can see the default server (server1). Select *Enterprise Applications* and you can see the sample applications.

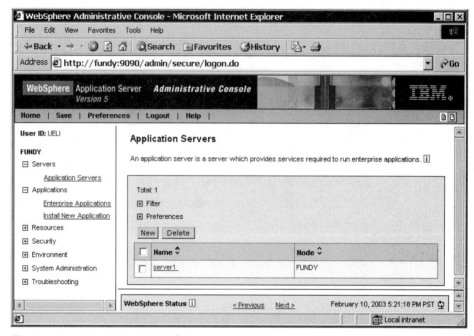

Figure 18-2   Administrative Console

Configuring a server

With WebSphere Application Server Network Deployment, we suggest that you configure a separate server and not use the default server.

With the base WebSphere Application Server, we use the default server (server1) for our sample applications.

Configuring a JDBC driver and data source

Now we will configure a JDBC driver for DB2 and the data source for the EJBBANK database.

JDBC driver

- ► Select *Resources* (left side) and select *JDBC Providers*.
- ► Select *Node* (should be preselected)

- ▶ Click *New* (under JDBC Providers):
  - – Select *DB2 JDBC Provider* from the pull-down and click *Apply.*
  - – All the defaults should be fine. Check that the implementation class is `COM.ibm.db2.jdbc.DB2ConnectionPoolDataSource`. Note that the classpath entry points to `${DB2_JDBC_DRIVER_PATH}/db2java.zip`. We have to check that this variable points to the DB2 installation (Figure 18-3).
  - – Click *Apply.*

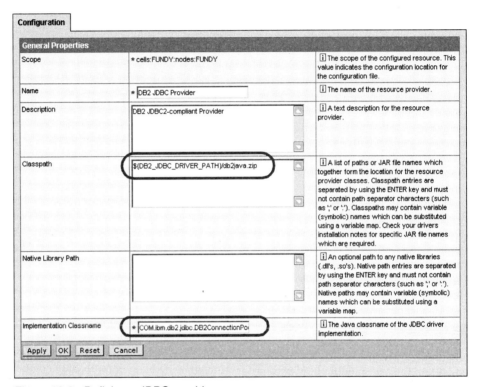

Figure 18-3   Defining a JDBC provider

Data source

- ▶ Under Additional Properties, select *Data Sources.*
  - – Click *New* (Figure 18-4).
  - – Enter `EJBBANK` as the name.
  - – Enter `jdbc/ejbbank` as the JNDI name (to match what we defined for testing).
  - – Select *Use this Data Source in container-managed persistence (CMP).*

- The data source helper class should be filled in as
  `com.ibm.websphere.rsadapter.DB2DataStoreHelper`.
- Click *Apply*.

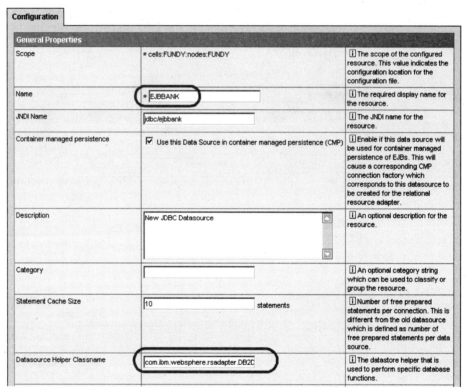

Figure 18-4   Defining the data source for the EJBBANK database

▶ Under Additional Properties, select *Custom Properties*, then select
  databaseName, enter `EJBBANK` as the value, and click *OK*.

▶ Go back to the data source (select *EJBBANK* at the top). Under Related
  Items, select *J2C Authentication Data Entries*, then click *New* (Figure 18-5):

  - Enter `DB2user` as alias.

  - Enter a valid user ID and password, for example what was used to install
    DB2.

  - Click *OK*.

  - The new alias appears in the list, prefixed with the node name.

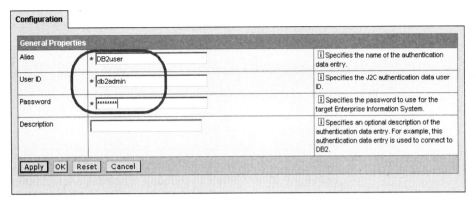

Figure 18-5   Defining an authentication alias

► Go back to the data source (select *EJBBANK* on the top):

   – For the container-managed authentication alias, select the DB2user from the pull-down (Figure 18-6).

   – Click *OK*.

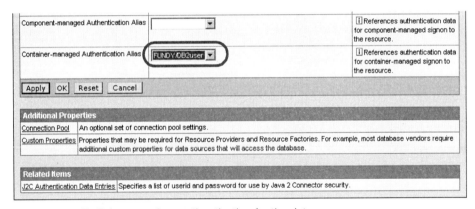

Figure 18-6   Defining container authentication for the data source

► If you select *Security* (left side) and *JAAS Configuration*, you can find the new alias by selecting *J2C Authentication Data*.

JDBC driver path

► Select *Environment* (left side) and *Managed WebSphere Variables*.

► Select *DB2 JDBC DRIVER PATH*.

► Enter the directory of the db2java.zip file, for example, d:\SQLLIB\java.

► Click *OK*.

Configure a message listener for the MDB

Next, we set up a message listener for the message-driven bean:

▶ Select *Application Servers* (under Servers), then select the server.

▶ Under Additional Properties, select *Message Listener Service*.

▶ Select *Listener Ports*, then click *New* (Figure 18-7):
  - Enter ItsoMdbListenerPort as the name.
  - Leave *Started* as the initial state.
  - Enter jms/ItsoMdbConnectionFactory as connection factory JNDI name.
  - Enter jms/ItsoMdbQueue as the destination JNDI name.
  - Leave the other values as defaults, since we are not building a high-performance system.
  - Click *Apply*.

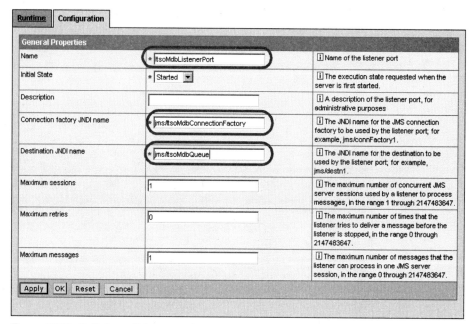

Figure 18-7   Defining a listener port

▶ Click *OK* for the listener port.

▶ Note that the status indicates that the listener port is not started.

Configure a connection factory and queues

To complete the JMS setup, we require a connection factory and queues:

▶ Select *Resources* (left side) and *WebSphere JMS Provider*.

- ▶ Select the node (preselected).
- ▶ Under Additional Properties, select *WebSphere Queue Connection Factories*, then click *New* ():
  - – Enter ItsoMdbConnectionFactory as the name.
  - – Enter jms/ItsoMdbConnectionFactory as the JNDI name.
  - – For the container-managed authentication alias, select the DB2user from the pull-down.
  - – Leave all other defaults.
  - – Click *OK*.

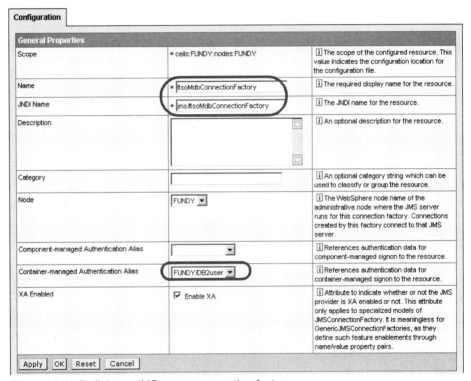

Figure 18-8   Defining a JMS queue connection factory

- ▶ Go back to the WebSphere JMS Provider, and under Additional Properties, select *WebSphere Queue Connection Factories* and ItsoMdbConnectionFactory.

  Under Additional Properties, select *Connection Pool* and make sure that the Purge Policy is set to *Entire Pool*.

- ▶ In the WebSphere JMS Provider, under Additional Properties, select *WebSphere Queue Destinations*, then click *New* (Figure 18-9):
  - – Enter ItsoMdbQueue as the name.

- Enter `jms/ItsoMdbQueue` as the JNDI name.
- Click *OK*.
- Repeat this for `ItsoResponseQueue` (`jms/ItsoResponseQueue`).

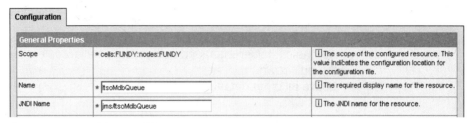

Figure 18-9   Defining a JMS queue

Activating the JMS server

We have to start the JMS server when the application server starts:

▶ Select *Application Servers*, then select the server.

▶ Under Additional Properties, select *Server Components*, then *JMS Servers* (Figure 18-10):

- For queue names, enter `ItsoMdbQueue` and `ItsoResponseQueue` on two lines.
- Select *Started* as the initial state and click *Apply*.
- Select *Security Port Endpoint* and note the port number that has been assigned to the JMS server, in our case, `5557`.

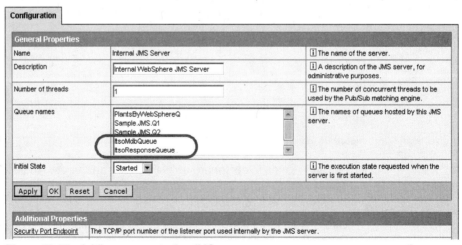

Figure 18-10   Adding queues to the JMS server

Save the configuration

Save the configuration. There should be no problems.

Stop and start the server

After stopping and starting the server, the `ItsoMdbListener` port is started.

Installing an enterprise application

The steps to install an enterprise application are:

► Create an EAR file
► Install the EAR file in the application server
► Start the server

Creating an EAR file

To create the EAR file for the sample application:

► Select the `ItsoBank5EAR` project and *Export* (context).
► Select *EAR file* and click *Next*.
► For the target location, click *Browse* and locate the WebSphere directory for installable applications, for example:

    d:\WebSphere\AppServer\installableApps\ItsoBank5EAR.ear

► Optionally, select *Export source files* (source is not required to run).
► Select *Include project build paths and meta data files*.
► Click *Finish*.

Installing the EAR file

To install the enterprise application, use the administrative console (log in if you are disconnected):

► Select *Applications* and *Install new application*.
► For a local path, click *Browse* and locate the EAR file (Figure 18-11):

    d:\WebSphere\AppServer\installableApps\ItsoBank5EAR.ear

Click *Next*.

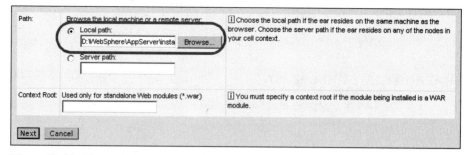

Figure 18-11   Enterprise application installation

▶ On the Preparing for the application installation panel, all the defaults should
   be fine:

   – You do not want to overwrite existing bindings; everything was configured
     in Application Developer
   – You can choose the virtual host (instead of `default_host`)

   Click *Next*.

Installation of the enterprise application is a 12-step process:

1. Provide options to perform the installation (Figure 18-12):

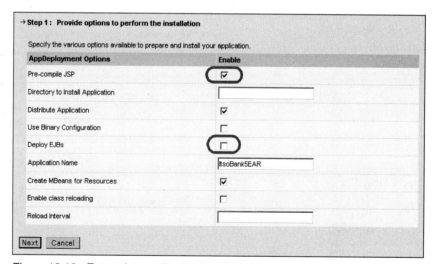

Figure 18-12   Enterprise application installation: step 1

   – You may want to select *Pre-compile JSP.*

   – Do not select *Deploy EJBs*; deployment code was generated in
     Application Developer.

In all the steps that follow, the correct information is predefined from the specifications we did in Application Developer.

2. Provide listener ports for messaging beans (Figure 18-13).

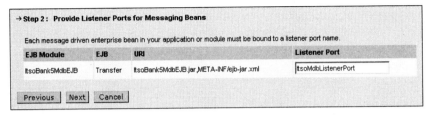

Figure 18-13   Enterprise application installation: step 2

3. Provide JNDI names for beans (Figure 18-14).

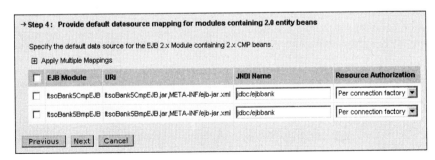

Figure 18-14   Enterprise application installation: step 3

4. Provide default data source mapping for modules containing 2.0 entity beans (Figure 18-15).

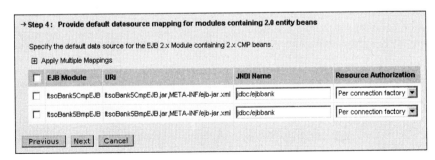

Figure 18-15   Enterprise application installation: step 4

5. Map data sources for all 2.0 CMP beans (Figure 18-16).

→ Step 5 : **Map datasources for all 2.0 CMP beans**

Specify an optional data source for each 2.x CMP bean. Mapping a specific data source to a CMP bean will override the default data source for the module containing the Enterprise bean.

⊞ Apply Multiple Mappings

☐	EJB	EJB Module	URI	JNDI Name	Resource Authorization
☐	Account	ItsoBank5CmpEJB	ItsoBank5CmpEJB.jar,META-INF/ejb-jar.xml		Container
☐	Customer	ItsoBank5CmpEJB	ItsoBank5CmpEJB.jar,META-INF/ejb-jar.xml		Container
☐	TransRecord	ItsoBank5CmpEJB	ItsoBank5CmpEJB.jar,META-INF/ejb-jar.xml		Container
☐	Checking	ItsoBank5CmpEJB	ItsoBank5CmpEJB.jar,META-INF/ejb-jar.xml		Container

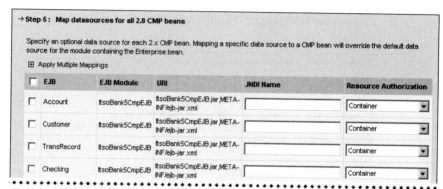

Figure 18-16 Enterprise application installation: step 5

6. Map EJB references to beans (Figure 18-17).

→ Step 6 : **Map EJB references to beans**

Each EJB reference defined in your application must be mapped to an Enterprise bean.

Module	EJB	URI	Reference Binding	Class	JNDI Name
ItsoBank5CmpEJB	Account	ItsoBank5CmpEJB.jar,META-INF/ejb-jar.xml	ejb/TransRecord	itso.bank5.cmp.TransRecordLocal	ejb/itsobank/T
ItsoBank5CmpEJB	Account	ItsoBank5CmpEJB.jar,META-INF/ejb-jar.xml	ejb/Customer	itso.bank5.cmp.CustomerLocal	ejb/itsobank/C
ItsoBank5CmpEJB	Customer	ItsoBank5CmpEJB.jar,META-INF/ejb-jar.xml	ejb/Account	itso.bank5.cmp.AccountLocal	ejb/itsobank/A

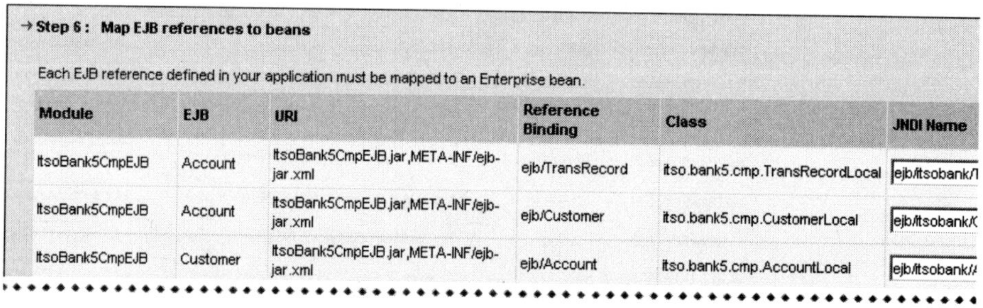

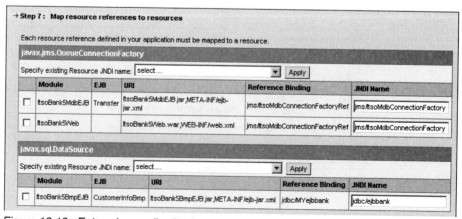

Figure 18-17 Enterprise application installation: step 6

7. Map resource references to resources (Figure 18-18).

→ Step 7 : **Map resource references to resources**

Each resource reference defined in your application must be mapped to a resource.

javax.jms.QueueConnectionFactory

Specify existing Resource JNDI name: select.... Apply

☐	Module	EJB	URI	Reference Binding	JNDI Name
☐	ItsoBank5MdbEJB	Transfer	ItsoBank5MdbEJB.jar,META-INF/ejb-jar.xml	jms/ItsoMdbConnectionFactoryRef	jms/ItsoMdbConnectionFactory
☐	ItsoBank5Web		ItsoBank5Web.war,WEB-INF/web.xml	jms/ItsoMdbConnectionFactoryRef	jms/ItsoMdbConnectionFactory

javax.sql.DataSource

Specify existing Resource JNDI name: select.... Apply

☐	Module	EJB	URI	Reference Binding	JNDI Name
☐	ItsoBank5BmpEJB	CustomerInfoBmp	ItsoBank5BmpEJB.jar,META-INF/ejb-jar.xml	jdbc/MYejbbank	jdbc/ejbbank

Figure 18-18 Enterprise application installation: step 7

8. Map resource environment entry references to resources (Figure 18-19).

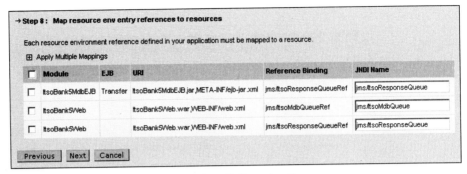

Figure 18-19   Enterprise application installation: step 8

9. Map virtual hosts for Web modules (Figure 18-20).

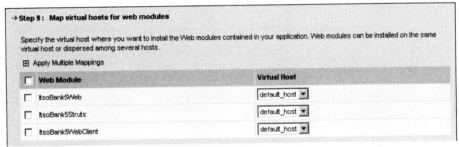

Figure 18-20   Enterprise application installation: step 9

10. Map modules to application servers (Figure 18-21).

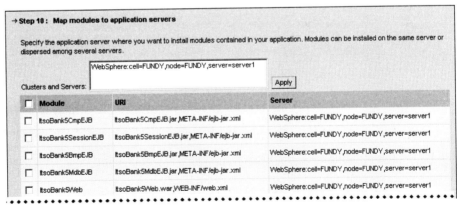

Figure 18-21   Enterprise application installation: step 10

11. Ensure all unprotected 2.0 methods have the correct level of protection (Figure 18-22).

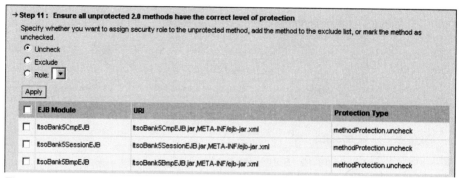

Figure 18-22   Enterprise application installation: step 11

12. A summary is produced (Figure 18-23).

→ **Step 12 : Summary**

Summary of Install Options

Options	Values
Distribute Application	Yes
Use Binary Configuration	No
Cell/Node/Server	Click here
Create MBeans for Resources	Yes
Enable class reloading	No
Deploy EJBs	No
was.policy.data	was.policy file does not exist
Application Name:	ItsoBank5EAR
Reload Interval	
Directory to Install Application	
Pre-compile JSP	Yes
Application Name	ItsoBank5EAR

[Previous]   [Finish]   [Cancel]

Figure 18-23   Enterprise application installation: step 12

– Click *Finish* and be patient. Messages are displayed in the console:

Check the SystemOut.log on the Deployment Manager or Server where the application is deployed for specific information about the EJB Deploy process as it occurs.

```
ADMA5009I: Application archive extracted at
                                C:\WINNT\TEMP\app_f1f643b6d3\ear
ADMA5003I: Jsps in wars ItsoBank5Web.war, ItsoBank5Struts.war compiled
                                                        successfully
```

```
ADMA5005I: Application ItsoBank5EAR configured in WebSphere repository
ADMA5001I: Application binaries saved in D:\WebSphere\AppServer\wstemp\
     ueli\workspace\cells\UELI\applications\ItsoBank5EAR.ear\ItsoBank5EAR.ear
ADMA5011I: Cleanup of temp dir for app ItsoBank5EAR done.
ADMA5013I: Application ItsoBank5EAR installed successfully.
Application ItsoBank5EAR installed successfully.
If you want to start the application, you must first save changes to the
                                              master configuration.
```

Click *Save to master configuration* to save the installed application. You can find the installed application in:

```
d:\WebSphere\AppServer\installedApps (under the node)
```

Starting the server with the application

You can start the `ItsoBank5EAR` enterprise application from the *Enterprise Applications* panel (under Applications). This may work, depending on the modifications you made to the configuration. Sometimes it is necessary to stop and start the server.

Stop the application server and restart it. This operation starts the server with the `ItsoBank5EAR` enterprise application.

Testing the ITSO banking application

With the server started ,you can try all of the sample applications inside the enterprise application.

> **Tip:** We can test the applications using the built-in Web server on port 9080. There is no need to configure and start the IBM HTTP server.
>
> To use the external IBM HTTP Server, we have to regenerate the plug-in:
> - Select *Environment* (left side) and *Update Web Server Plugin*
> - Click *OK* to regenerate the plugin
> - Stop and start the IBM HTTP Server

Web applications

The Web applications that use the EJBs can be started as follows:

```
http://localhost:9080/ItsoBank5Web/Banking.html
http://localhost:9080/ItsoBank5Web/Reports.html
http://localhost:9080/ItsoBank5Struts/index.jsp
```

The Web application that uses the Web service can be started as follows:

```
http://localhost:9080/ItsoBank5WebClient/BankingClient.html
```

Message-driven bean

The MDB sample is run by starting the application client:

▶ Open a command window and launch the client from the WebSphere Application server `bin` directory.

▶ You require the `ItsoBank5EAR.ear` file exported from the Application Developer.

▶ In our example, we use these commands:

```
d:
cd WebSphere\AppServer\bin
launchclient d:\websphere\appserver\installableApps\ItsoBank5EAR.ear
```

▶ Sample output is shown here:

```
IBM WebSphere Application Server, Release 5.0
J2EE Application Client Tool
Copyright IBM Corp., 1997-2002
WSCL0012I: Processing command line arguments.
WSCL0013I: Initializing the J2EE Application Client Environment.
WSCL0014I: Invoking the Application Client class
                        itso.bank5.client.mdb.MdbClient

Client: Start
Client: No parms supplied, using default
Client: Retrieving Queues from JNDI
Client: JNDI class=class com.ibm.mq.jms.MQQueue
Client: JNDI class=class com.ibm.mq.jms.MQQueue
Client: outQueue=class com.ibm.mq.jms.MQQueue
Client: Retrieving a QueueConnectionFactory from JNDI
Client: JNDI class=class com.ibm.mq.jms.MQXAQueueConnectionFactory
Client: factory=class com.ibm.mq.jms.MQXAQueueConnectionFactory
Client: got connection
Client: connection started
Client: created queue session
Client: created sender
Client: created object message
Client: Sending the message to queue:///WQ_ItsoMdbQueue
Client: Sent message ID:414d51205741535f55454c495f736572dbfef33d20000901/
                        CORR:TF57413
Client: Receiving message from queue:///WQ_ItsoResponseQueue
Client: Waiting for message
Client: Reply = 'Transfer OK: 10 from/to 101-1001/101-1002 Balance=137.50'
Client: Done
```

Application Assembly Tool

The Application Assembly Tool (AAT) can be used to create and modify EAR files. This tool can be used to complete the deployment information, such as JNDI references, before installing an enterprise application.

We do not cover the usage of the Application Assembly Tool in this document. With Application Developer Version 5, we can complete the deployment without the need to use the Application Assembly Tool.

Command-line tools

Command-line tools can greatly speed up deployment of applications and other WebSphere configuration tasks.

We only cover a small subset of the tools, those that seem useful to an application developer and tester. For a complete discussion of the tools, refer to the WebSphere documentation.

Command-line tools come in two sets:

► Batch commands (.bat files in `WebSphere\AppServer\bin`)
► Scripting tool (started with the `wsadmin.bat` file)

Batch command

Here is a list of a few of the commands:

► **backupConfig**—Creates a ZIP file of all the configuration information
► **restoreConfig**—Restores a configuration from a backup file
► **dumpNameSpace**—Lists all the JNDI names from the name server
► **ejbDeploy**—Generates deployed code for an EJB JAR file
► **firstSteps**—Launches the First Steps menu
► **startServer**—Starts a server
► **stopServer**—Stops a server
► **serverStatus**—Reports if a server is running
► **wsadmin**—Starts the scripting tool

Scripting tool

WebSphere provides a scripting tool, wsadmin, with which many of the configuration functions can be run in batch. For a description of all the functions, refer to the WebSphere documentation.

Wsadmin can be run with a single command, or you can interact with the tool:

► Single command example:

```
wsadmin -c "$AdminApp list"
```

A single command is passed to wsadmin using the -c option. The $AdminApp list command lists all the installed applications.

► To start wsadmin in interactive mode, enter wsadmin:

```
D:\WebSphere\AppServer\bin>wsadmin
WASX7209I: Connected to process "server1" on node UELI using SOAP
connector;  The type of process is: UnManagedProcess
WASX7029I: For help, enter: "$Help help"
wsadmin>
```

Example commands

Once the interactive mode has started, you can enter commands, such as:

```
$AdminApp list
$AdminApp install e:/itsobank5ear.ear
$AdminConfig save
```

Some commands work with objects that you have to retrieve first. For example, to regenerate the HTTP server plug-in:

```
set pluginGen [$AdminControl completeObjectName type=PluginCfgGenerator,*]
```

```
===> output:
WebSphere:platform=common,cell=UELI,version=5.0,name=PluginCfgGenerator,
mbeanIdentifier=PluginCfgGenerator,type=PluginCfgGenerator,node=UELI,pro
cess=server1
```

```
$AdminControl invoke $pluginGen generate "d:/WebSphere/AppServer
            d:/WebSphere/AppServer/config UELI null null plugin-cfg.xml"
```

```
===> output: plugin-cfg.xml file in d:/WebSphere/AppServer/config/cells
```

Stopping and starting an enterprise application:

```
set appManager [$AdminControl queryNames
        cell=mycell,node=mynode,type=ApplicationManager,process=server1,*]
$AdminControl invoke $appManager stopApplication ItsoBank5EAR
$AdminControl invoke $appManager startApplication ItsoBank5EAR
```

Example script

You can also write script files with multiple commands and run the file using:

```
wsadmin -f RunningApplications.script
```

The sample script in Figure 18-24 can be found in the Information Center. It lists all the applications running on all the servers on all the nodes.

```
# retrieve all cells
set cells [$AdminConfig list Cell]
foreach cell $cells {
    # retrieve nodes for each cell
    set nodes [$AdminConfig list Node $cell]
    foreach node $nodes {
        set cname [$AdminConfig showAttribute $cell name]
        set nname [$AdminConfig showAttribute $node name]
        # retrieve servers for each node
        set servs [$AdminControl queryNames type=Server,cell=$cname,node=$nname,*]
        puts "Number of running servers on node $nname: [llength $servs]"
        foreach server $servs {
            set sname [$AdminControl getAttribute $server name]
            set ptype [$AdminControl getAttribute $server processType]
            set pid   [$AdminControl getAttribute $server pid]
            set state [$AdminControl getAttribute $server state]
            set jvm [$AdminControl queryNames
                                   type=JVM,cell=$cname,node=$nname,process=$sname,*]
            set osname [$AdminControl invoke $jvm getProperty os.name]
            puts "  $sname ($ptype) has pid $pid; state: $state; on $osname"
            # retrieve applications
            set apps [$AdminControl queryNames
                           type=Application,cell=$cname,node=$nname,process=$sname,*]
            puts "  Number of applications running on $sname: [llength $apps]"
            foreach app $apps {
                set aname [$AdminControl getAttribute $app name]
                puts "     $aname"
            }
            puts "-------------------------------------------------"
            puts ""
        }
    }
}
```

Figure 18-24   Sample wsadmin script to list all applications

Summary

In this chapter, we described the basic steps for installing an enterprise application in WebSphere Application Server, including the configuration that is required in the server.

WebSphere Application Server has many performance and tuning options that we do not discuss in this redbook.

Application Developer team development environment

In this chapter, we describe software configuration management support in Application Developer Version 5.

The description provided here is in no way complete. We only scratch the surface of the team support capability of Application Developer. Also, we describe only how to work with Concurrent Versions System (CVS) and do not cover the support for ClearCase LT.

© Copyright IBM Corp. 2003. All rights reserved.

Introduction

Version control is critical to development. Even if you are working alone on a project, a version control system can save you a lot of time. You can freeze a project by creating a *version* in the version control system. Having multiple versions of a project enables you to go back and restore an older version into the Workbench.

Application Developer allows third-party Software Configuration Management (SCM) software vendors to plug into the Workbench environment. Application Developer ships with support for Concurrent Versions System (CVS) and with ClearCase LT. Both systems must be installed separately from the Application Developer installation. Note that the code for CVS is not shipped with Application Developer and must be downloaded.

For a list of third-party SCM adapters, see:

```
http://www-3.ibm.com/software/ad/studioappdev/partners/scm.html
```

Workspace

Application Developer maintains a local workspace where all the project data is stored. This workspace is file based.

The default location for the workspace is:

```
C:\Documents and Settings\<username>\My Documents\IBM\wsad\workspace
```

We advise you not to use this default location but create a custom location instead.

► You can then create multiple workspaces, one for each solution you are working on. This reduces the number of projects visible at any one time in the workbench.

► The directory where Application Developer maintains the workspace can be changed by specifying the -data <workspacedirectory> parameter on startup. The complete startup string could read:

```
D:\<wsadhome>\wsappdev.exe -data D:\WSAD5sg246819 -vmargs -Xms196M
```

We used D:\WSAD5sg246819 as the location of the workspace for this redbook.

Notice that you have to specify the full path name to the workspace and that the vmargs parameter must be last on the command line.

Projects

Projects are stored in folders within the workspace directory. Each project is stored in a main folder with subfolders. The subfolder structure is dependent on the type of project and user preferences.

All files in the project are exposed in the file system under the workspace root and project folder.

Local history

Local history of a file is maintained when you create or modify a file. Each time you edit and save a file, a copy of it is saved on the file system. This allows you at a future time to compare the current file state to a previous state, or to replace the file with a previous state. Each state in the local history is identified by the date and time the file was saved.

The local history can be accessed through the *Compare With -> Local History* option in the context menu of the file. Figure 19-1 shows a comparison between two states of a file. One line was changed and one line was deleted.

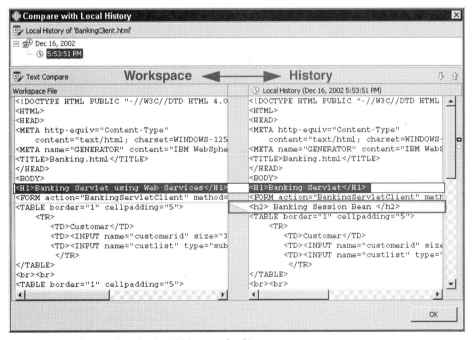

Figure 19-1 inspecting the local history of a file

Through the Workbench preferences (select Window -> *Preferences* -> *Workbench* -> *Local History*) you can control:

- ► The number of days to keep the files (7)
- ► The maximum entries per file (50)
- ► The maximum file size (1 MB)

> **Important:** Deletes are permanent. If a file is deleted, its local history is also deleted and the file is therefore unrecoverable.

Exporting

An EAR file can be exported with all the information needed by the workspace. This includes all necessary metadata so that the EAR file can be imported again and the workspace recreated.

In the J2EE perspective, select an enterprise application and *Export EAR File* (context). Specify the target location and select *Export source files* and *Include project build paths and meta-data files* (Figure 19-2). Click *Finish*.

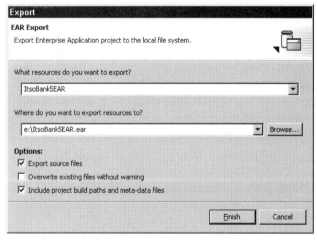

Figure 19-2   Exporting an EAR file

In the same way, you can export individual EJB, Web, and application client projects into EJB JAR, WAR, and application client JAR files.

Java and server projects can be exported as ZIP files.

Optimistic concurrency

In the optimistic concurrency model, any developer can change any code. This model is called optimistic because it assumes that conflicts are rare and that developers usually work on different files. When multiple developers do work on the same file, you have to deal with the conflict manually.

With EJB and Web projects, it is very likely that changes made by two developers result in updates to the deployment descriptor of the project. For example, adding an attribute to an EJB or defining a servlet invokes a change to the deployment descriptor.

Important: Merging the updates of a conflict can become a lot of work. It is a good idea to avoid conflicts by organizing an enterprise application into projects so that, in general, each project is maintained by one developer. If an urgent update must be done by another developer, then immediate synchronization can prevent conflicts.

In the case of EJB development, merging files can become quite a task. Just imagine a developer adding one method to the remote interface of an enterprise bean and configuring access intent for this method. Now the following files have to be merged:

► Remote interface source files
► Bean source files
► ejb-jar.xml
► ibm-ejb-jar-ext.xmi

Not only is this complicated work, but you also have to understand the file formats of the .xml and .xmi files. Wow.

Pessimistic concurrency

Application Developer also supports pessimistic concurrency through locking. This is supported in ClearCase LT. In this model, a developer actually obtains exclusive use of a file. The file is locked and cannot be changed by anybody else until the developer releases the lock. This can lead to unwanted bottlenecks when two people have to access the same file or when one developer simply forgets to release a lock. On the other hand, it also avoids having to merge the files, as is the case in the optimistic concurrency model.

Setting up a team repository

We will show how to set up an environment using CVS NT, which runs on Windows NT and Windows 2000. Please note that real production teams are advised to use CVS on a UNIX system.

The terminology used for accessing a CVS repository in Application Developer Version 5 is now aligned with the normal CVS naming. You will notice this difference if you are moving from Application Developer Version 4.

Concurrent Versions System

Concurrent Versions System (CVS) is an open-source network-transparent version control system. CVS is useful for everyone from individual developers to large, distributed teams.

CVS is not distributed with Application Developer, but support for CVS is integrated in Application Developer. CVS provides a team programming environment where team members do all of their work in their own Workbench, isolated from each other, and eventually share their work through a CVS repository.

CVS also can be used by a developer in stand-alone mode to keep versions of the code.

For general information about CVS and downloadable code for UNIX, go to:

```
http://www.cvshome.org/
```

For downloadable code for Windows, go to:

```
http://www.cvsnt.org/
```

CVS for Windows NT can use two protocols: pserver and ssh. Be aware that the pserver protocol will pass the user name and password information unencrypted over the network. If you need real security, you have to use the ssh protocol. In our example, we will use pserver.

CVS installation and configuration

We installed CVS for Windows NT (CVSNT) Version 1.11.1.2 for this redbook project.

After installation, the CVS server must be configured. Select *Programs -> CVS for NT -> Configure server.* In the CVSNT window, select the protocols that you want to support, and add the repository locations. You can set up multiple repositories for different development efforts. Start the server when done.

Figure 19-3 shows a sample CVSNT configuration window.

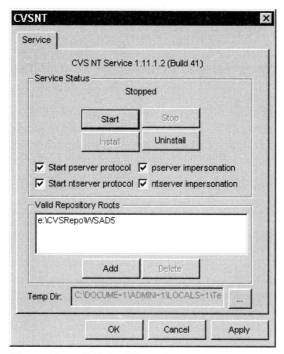

Figure 19-3   CVS for NT configuration

What is new in Application Developer Version 5?

The most important improvements in team support in Application Developer Version 5 are:

► CVS Repository Exploring perspective to browse the content of repositories

► CVS Console view shows messages returned from the CVS server

► Consistent CVS terms used throughout, for example, branch instead of stream

► File compression options for transferring files to the CVS repository

► New resources must be explicitly added to CVS control

► Text/binary support by identifying what file types are text or binary

- ▶ Synchronize outgoing change optimizations (only outgoing changes are synchronized, which reduces network traffic)
- ▶ CVS decorators are visual indicators next to resources

This list does not include all the new features, but points to the major differences compared to previous versions of WebSphere Studio products.

What changes could impact your work?

In Version 4, after adding an EJB project to CVS, you can delete the project from the workspace and when necessary import it again and all the components are reloaded.

In Version 5, this scenario will lead to many errors, such as missing classes, and you have to redeploy the EJBs. The reason is that some of the components, such as the deployed code, are not stored in the CVS repository in the default setup.

To store the deployed code in the CVS repository, you have to change the preferences of the Workbench:

- ▶ Select *Window -> Preferences -> Team -> Ignored Resources* (Figure 19-4).
- ▶ Remove the check marks to store EJB deployed code in CVS.
- ▶ Click *OK*.

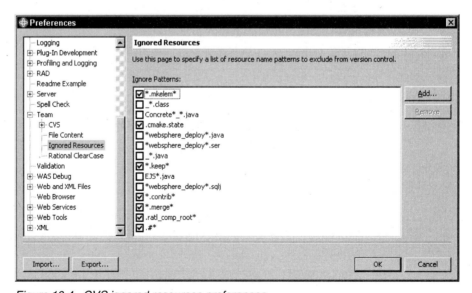

Figure 19-4   CVS ignored resources preferences

More details on ignored resources preference

On the Ignored Resources page, you can specify file name patterns to be excluded from the version control management system.

Files are matched against the list of patterns, before they are considered as version control candidates. A file or directory that matches any one of the patterns will be ignored during update or commit operations. The patterns may contain the wildcard characters * (any sequence of zero or more characters) and ? (any one character).

To add a file type to the ignore list, click the *Add* button. In the window, enter a file type (for example, *.class). To remove a file type from the ignore list, select the file type in the ignore list and click *Remove*. You can temporarily disable ignoring the file pattern by de-selecting it from the list; you do not have to remove the specified file pattern from the list.

Ignoring resources from version control

When synchronizing resources, you may not want to commit all resources to the repository. There are two ignore facilities provided, allowing the user to specify which resources should be excluded from update and commit operations:

► The first is a global ignore facility, provided by the Workbench as shown in Figure 19-4.

► The second is the CVS ignore facility, which reads the contents of a special .cvsignore file to determine what to ignore.

CVS ignore facility

The Eclipse CVS client recognizes a file named .cvsignore in each directory of a project. This is a standard CVS facility and many existing CVS projects may contain such a file.

This text file consists of a list of files, directories, or patterns. In a similar way to the global ignore facility, the wildcard * and ? may be present in any entry in the .cvsignore file. Any file or subdirectory in the current directory that matches any one of the patterns is ignored.

It is important to note that the semantics of this file differ from that of the global ignore facility in that they apply only to files and directories in the same directory as the .cvsignore file itself. A project may contain one .cvsignore file in each directory. For more information, visit http://www.cvshome.org.

Resources that have not been added to CVS control can be ignored by selecting *Team > Add to .cvsignore* from the context menu of the resource in the Navigator view. This menu option is also available in the Synchronize view.

Development scenario for a single user

In this section, we provide a short scenario using the CVS support in Application Developer. This scenario includes:

- ▸ Connecting to a CVS repository
- ▸ Adding a project to CVS
- ▸ Version a project
- ▸ Changing files and synchronizing a project

Connecting to a CVS repository

To connect the Workbench to a CVS repository:

- ▸ Open the CVS Repository Exploring perspective.
- ▸ Select *New -> Repository Location* from the context menu of the CVS Repositories view.
- ▸ Complete the window as shown in Figure 19-5.

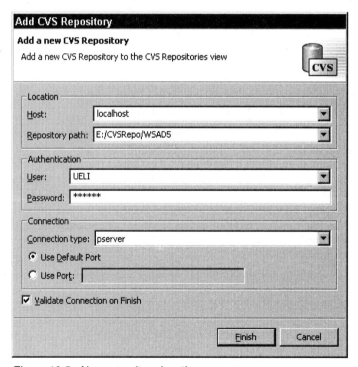

Figure 19-5   New repository location

You must know the repository path on the target machine. The *pserver* connection type validates your user ID and password with the Windows system.

► The repository location is added to the CVS Repositories view (Figure 19-6).

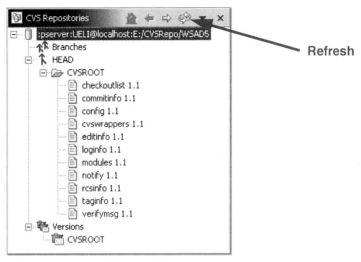

Figure 19-6 ICVS Repositories view after connecting

Adding a project to CVS control

The next step is to add projects to CVS control:

► Open the Web perspective, select the ItsoBank5Utility project and *Team -> Share Project* (context).

► Select *CVS* in the window, click *Next*, select the repository, click *Next* to go through the rest of the window, and click *Finish* (Figure 19-7).

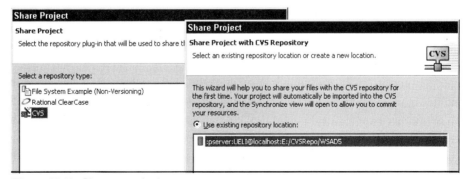

Figure 19-7 Share a project

- Refresh the CVS Repositories view to see the project name under HEAD and Versions (use the *Refresh* icon or the *Refresh View* context menu).

- Notice that no folders or files are visible; we have to add them to version control explicitly.

- In the Web perspective, select the folders of the Itsobank5Utility project you want to have under version control, for example, itso and META-INF, and *Team -> Add to Version Control* (context). Also select the project control files (.classpath, .project, .serverPreference) and *Team -> Add to Version Control* in a Navigator view.

- Now you can commit individual files, folders, or the whole project. Initially the easiest is to select the Itsobank5Utility project and *Team -> Commit*. You are prompted for a comment (enter Initial).

- Figure 19-8 shows the CVS Repositories view after adding the project to version control and committing the files. Notice that all files carry 1.1 as the revision number.

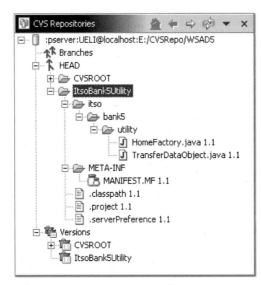

Figure 19-8   Project added to CVS

Note: If you look into the workspace file system for the ItsoBank5Utility project, you will see that a directory named CVS has been added to each folder that is under version control.

Create a version

Now we can freeze the initial code:

▶ In the Web perspective, select the Itsobank5Utility project and *Team -> Tag as Version*.

▶ You are prompted for a tag (Figure 19-9); enter V1-1, for example (periods are not allowed).

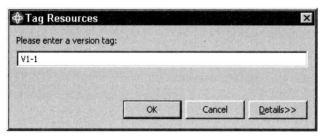

Figure 19-9   Version tag

▶ Refresh the CVS Repositories view and the project version is visible (Figure 19-10).

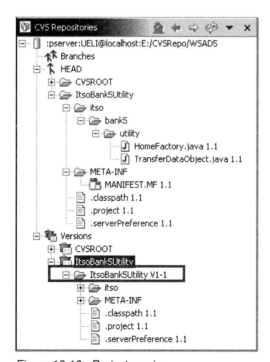

Figure 19-10   Project version

Making changes and synchronizing

The next step is to show how changes to the code are handled with CVS:

▶ In the `Itsobank5Utility` project change two files, for example:

  – Add a comment to the `HomeFactory.java` source and change some code.
  – Add line comments to the `TransferDataObject.java` source.

▶ After saving the files, select both files and *Team -> Synchronize with Repository* (context). The files are compared with the branch in the repository and the Synchronize view opens. Use the down arrow icon to display the first change (Figure 19-11).

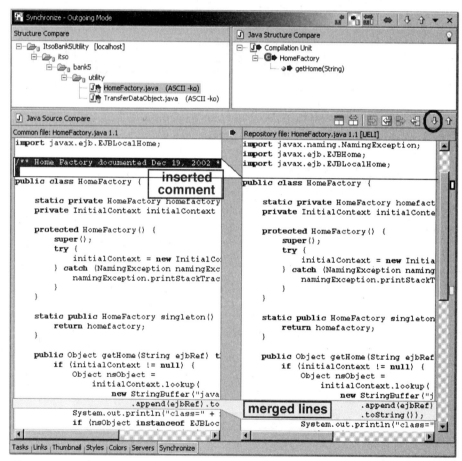

Figure 19-11   Synchronize view

▶ Move from change to change using the arrow icons and see the differences in the two files.

- Select the `ItsoBank5utility` project in the Structure Compare pane and *Commit* (context). This commits the changes to the repository. When prompted, enter `Change1` as comment.

- Refresh the CVS Repositories view and you can see that the two files carry 1.2 as the revision number.

- You could have committed the changes to the files by selecting *Team -> Commit* and the Synchronize view would have been bypassed.

- Select the project and *Tag as Version* and assign `V1-2` to the new version.

Synchronizing the project

When synchronizing a project, you may be prompted that the project includes files that have not been added to version control (Figure 19-12). Click *Yes* to add the files to version control.

Figure 19-12   Adding files to version control using synchronize

CVS console

In the CVS Console view, you can see all the interactions between Application Developer and CVS. Select *Window -> Show View -> Other -> CVS -> CVS Console* to open the view (Figure 19-13).

```
CVS Console
cvs ci -m "Change 1" "itso/bank5/utility/TransferDataObject.java" "itso/bank5/utility/Home
  Checking in itso/bank5/utility/TransferDataObject.java;
  E:/CVSRepo/WSAD5/ItsoBank5Utility/itso/bank5/utility/TransferDataObject.java,v  <--  Tr
  new revision: 1.2; previous revision: 1.1
  done
  Checking in itso/bank5/utility/HomeFactory.java;
  E:/CVSRepo/WSAD5/ItsoBank5Utility/itso/bank5/utility/HomeFactory.java,v  <--  HomeFacto
  new revision: 1.2; previous revision: 1.1
  done
ok (took 0:00.101)
***
***
cvs rtag -r "HEAD" "V1-2" "ItsoBank5Utility"
  cvs rtag: Tagging ItsoBank5Utility
  cvs rtag: Tagging ItsoBank5Utility/META-INF
  cvs rtag: Tagging ItsoBank5Utility/itso
  cvs rtag: Tagging ItsoBank5Utility/itso/bank5
  cvs rtag: Tagging ItsoBank5Utility/itso/bank5/utility
ok (took 0:00.070)
***
```

Figure 19-13   CVS Console view

Resource history

The Resource History view shows all the changes that have been applied to a file. Select the HomeFactory.java file in the CVS Repositories view and *Show in Resource History* (Figure 19-14).

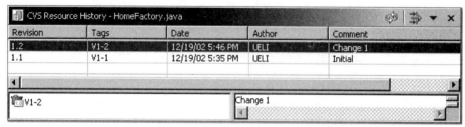

Figure 19-14   Resource history

File compare

There are a number of ways to compare two revisions of a file:

► Select two revisions in the Resource History view and *Compare* (context).

► Select a revision and a version in the CVS Repositories view and *Compare*.

► Select a file in any Navigator view and *Compare With*. In the window, select a repository version, repository revision, or a local history file for the compare operation (Figure 19-15).

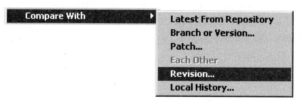

Figure 19-15   Comparing files

► The file comparison opens and you can step from change to change using the arrow icons (Figure 19-16).

Note: You can compare any two files with each other; we use revisions of one file as an example.

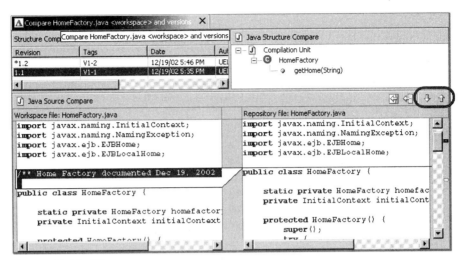

Figure 19-16　File compare

Disconnecting a project

You can disconnect a project from the repository. Select the ItsoBank5Utility project and *Team -> Disconnect*. You are prompted to confirm and also if you want to delete CVS control information (Figure 19-17).

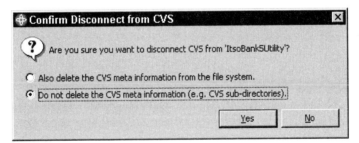

Figure 19-17　Disconnect confirmation

CVS adds special directories named CVS to the project and its folders. These directories can be deleted or kept on disconnect.

Reconnect

You can reconnect a project to the repository (*Team -> Share Project*). Reconnect is easier if the CVS folders are still in the project. If they were deleted, you are prompted to synchronize your code with the existing repository code.

Keyword expansion

It is interesting to get the versioning information that is inside of CVS in the Javadoc that is created for each file. One way to accomplish this is through keyword expansion.

► Select *Window -> Preferences -> Team -> CVS*. Set Default keyword substitution to *ASCII with keyword expansion (-kkv)*.

► Some of the available keywords (case sensitive) are:

► `$RCSfile$`—Will add the file name without the path

► `$Revision$`—Will add the latest version number

► `$Date$`—Will add the date and time when the last revision was checked in

► `$Author$`—Will add the name of the author

► `$Id$`—Will add all of the above in one string

► `$Log$`—Will add the comments written on every check in.

► These keywords will be expanded anywhere in the source file. There is unfortunately no way to selectively turn off keyword substitution.

► You can add the keywords to the Javadoc for the classes as in:

```
/**
 * class comment goes here.
 *
 * <pre>
 * Date $Date$
 * CVS History:
 * $Log$
 * </pre>
 * @author $Author$
 * @version $Revision$
 */
```

► If you want all your new Java files to contain this header, it is easy to add it to the default class level template. Select *Window -> Preferences -> Java -> Templates*. Now select the *typecomment* template. Click *Edit* and replace the text with this code (Figure 19-18):

```
/**
 * class comment goes here.
 *
 * <pre>
 * Date $$Date$$                    <=== $ must be written as $$
 * CVS History:
 * $$Log$$
 * </pre>
 * @author $$Author$$
 * @version $$Revision$$
 */
```

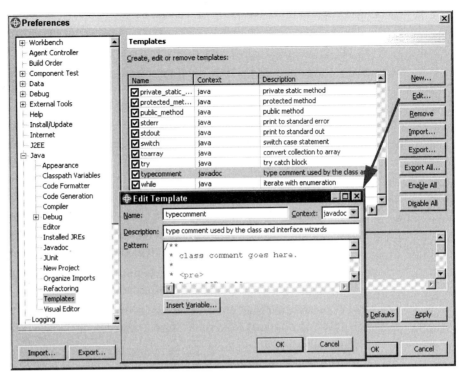

Figure 19-18   Using CVS keywords in Java comments

To make the same change for files generated by the wizards, also change the *filecomment* template.

After committing a new class to CVS, you can see the comments in the source:

```
/**
 * class comment goes here.
 *
 * <pre>
 * Date $Date: 2002/12/20 02:14:05 $
 * CVS History:
 * $Log: Test.java,v $
 * Revision 1.1  2002/12/20 02:14:05  UELI
 * Change 2
 *
 * </pre>
 * @author $Author: UELI $
 * @version $Revision: 1.1 $
 */
```

Development scenario for a team

In a team environment, the CVS server is placed onto a server machine. All members of the team connect to the same CVS server. You can have multiple repositories managed by the same CVS server.

We will not explore real team operation in this redbook, and will only outline a development scenario:

► All team members connect to the same repository.

► A team leader defines a new project.

► The project is added to CVS version control (*Team -> Share Project*).

► An initial version is created (*Team -> Tag as Version*).

► Team members load the project from CVS into their workspace. They select a project version in the CVS Repositories view and *Checkout as Project*.

► Team members add files and make changes to files. Periodically (frequently) they synchronize their work with the repository:

    – Commit their own changes to the repository
    – Pick up changes from other team members

► If the same file has been changed by two team members, a conflict exists and must be resolved by merging the changes.

► Periodically, the team leader creates a new version of the project.

► For maintenance work and new development in parallel, a branch can be created. By default there is only one branch, called *HEAD*.

Where to be careful

The dangerous areas in such a team environment are files that are changed frequently, for example, deployment descriptors (web.xml, ejb-jar.xml):

► Every time a servlet is added, the deployment descriptor is updated.
► Every time an EJB is added or modified, the deployment descriptor is updated.

The best way to handle this is to give such project updates to one team member, or to synchronize very frequently to minimize conflicts.

Appendixes

© Copyright IBM Corp. 2003. All rights reserved.

Setting up the environment

In this appendix, we describe the installation process for WebSphere Application Server (base) and WebSphere Studio Application Developer.

We also describe how to set up the EJBBANK database for the samples.

© Copyright IBM Corp. 2003. All rights reserved.

Installation planning

IBM WebSphere Application Server Base and Network Deployment have the same hardware and software requirements.

Hardware

Hardware requirements include:

- Any Intel-based PC running Windows NT Server V4.0, SP™ 6a or later, Windows 2000 Server, or Advanced Server SP 2 or later
- Intel Pentium processor at 500 MHz, or faster
- Support for a communications adapter
- Minimum 180 MB free disk space for installation (includes SDK)
- CD-ROM drive
- Minimum 512 MB memory; 784 MB recommended

Software

The installation requires the following software to be installed:

- Windows NT Server or Windows 2000 Server
- Netscape Communicator 4.7.9 or Microsoft Internet Explorer 5.5 SP 2 and 6.0
- Web browser that supports HTML 4 and CSS

For updated information about the hardware and software requirements, please refer to WebSphere Version 5 InfoCenter.

For the WebSphere installation, the database does not have to be configured. Cloudscape™ can be used in the test environment. However, other databases are required for the production environment. The following databases are supported with WebSphere Application Server V5 and WebSphere Network Deployment V5 on Windows platforms:

- Cloudscape 5.06
- DB2 UDB V7.2 Fixpack 7
- Informix® Dynamic Server Versions 7.31 and 9.3
- Oracle Enterprise Edition 8i Release 3 (8.1.7)
- Oracle Enterprise Edition 9i Release 2 (9.2)
- SQL Server Enterprise 7.0 SP 4 and 2000 SP 2

IBM HTTP Server is bundled with base WebSphere Application Server V5. However, the following HTTP servers can also be installed and configured to work with WebSphere Application Server V5:

► Apache Server 1.3.26

► HTTP Server 1.3.26 AIX®, Linux/390, Linux/Intel, Windows NT

► Internet Information Server 4.0

► Sun ONE Web Server, Enterprise Edition (formerly iPlanet) 6.0 SP 4

► Lotus Domino Enterprise Server (as HTTP Server) 5.0.9a

Before we start the installation, we also have to create the user with administrative rights on the local machine.

Installing DB2 UDB

To run our EJB examples, you must have a relational database system. All our testing was done with DB2 UDB Version 7.2 Fixpack 7.

Although it may be possible to run most of the examples with another relational database system, we only tested the examples with DB2 UDB.

Installation process

Installing DB2 UDB Version 7.2 is straightforward. Just follow the installation panels. You do not have to install all the components, such as data warehousing and performance tools.

After the base installation, you have to install Fixpack 7 or later.

Also, it is required that you run the command file `java12\usejdbc2.bat` to enable the JDBC Version 2 support for data sources.

Installing IBM WebSphere Application Server

The InstallShield Multi Platform (ISMP) is a new installer that is used to install the product on Intel, AIX, Linux, Linux/390, and Solaris. It checks the installation prerequisites. It also generates the uninstall program after the product has been completely installed.

The administrative database of WebSphere Version 4 does not exist any longer. All of the configuration information for the WebSphere Application Server Version 5 is now contained in XML files in the `${WAS_ROOT}\config` directory. There are many files that contain all the configuration information.

Installation process

First, we start the LaunchPad (`launchpad.bat`) to access the product overview, the ReadMe file, and installation guides.

► Select *Install the product* to launch the installation wizard (Figure A-1).

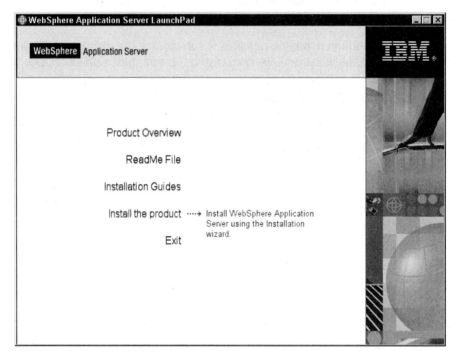

Figure A-1 WebSphere Application Server LaunchPad

► In the first window panel, select the language and click *OK*.

► Click *Next* in the Welcome panel.

- After confirming that we agree with the license agreement, we have to choose between two installation choices: *Typical* and *Custom*. Typical installs the entire product, whereas the Custom installation option allows you to deselect components you do not want to install. We chose Typical installation.

- The installation directories for the selected components are entered in the next panel. We chose:

  ```
  d:\WebSphere\AppServer
  d:\IBMHttpServer
  d:\WebSphere MQ
  ```

- In the following panel, we enter a node name and host name or IP address. In addition, we can select to install both WebSphere Application Server and IBM HTTP Server as a service on Windows NT or 2000.

- After the Summary window, the installation starts.

- The First Steps window is started automatically at the end of the installation.

Verifying the installation

Installation verification can be started from the menu. In Windows 2000, select *Start -> IBM WebSphere -> Application Server v5.0 -> First Steps*. Then select *Verify Installation*. We can also start the command ivc localhost.

If the install was successful, you should see messages similar to the following:

```
OS: Windows 2000
locale: en_US
hostname: NODENAME
cmd.exe /c "D:\WebSphere\AppServer\bin\ivt" NODENAME 9080
C:\WebSphere\AppServer
IVT0006I: Connecting to the WebSphere Server NODENAME on Port:9080
IVT0007I:WebSphere Server NODENAME is running on Port:9080
IVT0060I: Servlet Engine Verification: Passed
IVT0065I: JSP Verification: Passed
IVT0066I: EJB Verification: Passed
IVT00100I: IVT Verification Succeeded
IVT0015I: Scanning the file
D:\WebSphere\AppServer\logs\server1\SystemOut.log for
errors and warnings
IVT0020I: 0 Errors/Warnings were detected in the file
D:\WebSphere\AppServer\logs\server1\SystemOut.log
IVT0110I: Installation Verification is complete.
```

Installation of WebSphere Studio Application Developer

The installation of the Application Developer is a very straightforward process. Perform the following steps:

► Double-click `setup.exe` and the Installation Launcher window appears (Figure A-2).

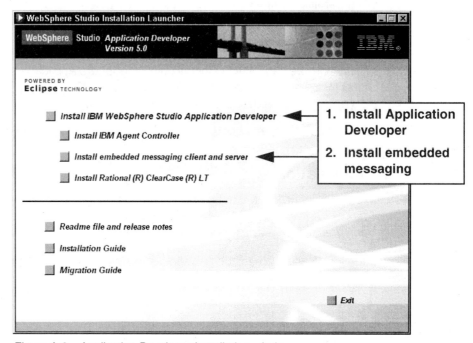

Figure A-2   Application Developer Installation window

► Select *Install IBM WebSphere Studio Application Developer*.

► In the Welcome page, click *Next*.

► In the *License Agreement* page, accept the agreement and click *Next*.

► In the *Destination Folder* page, browse to a folder of your choice and then click *Next*. We used `d:\WSAD5` as the installation folder.

► In the *Custom Setup* page, accept the defaults and click *Next*.

► In the next page, click *Install*.

► After a rather long time period, the next page tells you about the success of the installation. Click *Finish*.

► The last page allows you to specify the location of your workspace. We use `d:\WSAD5sg246819` for the workspace location.

Restart the installation launcher window and select *Install embedded messaging client and server*. This component is required for JMS messaging to feed a message-driven bean.

- ► If you installed WebSphere Application Server, installing the embedded messaging locates the existing WebSphere MQ installation and only tailors the Application Developer to use the existing code.
- ► If WebSphere MQ is not installed on this machine, then it will be installed now.

Setting up the EJBBANK database

To experiment with the EJB samples in this redbook, you have to set up the EJBBANK database:

- ► Download the sample code as instructed in Appendix B, "Additional material" on page 699.
- ► Unzip the sg246819code.zip file.
- ► Locate the directory c:\sg246819\sampcode_setup\database.
- ► Run the createbank.bat file. This command file uses the ejbbank.ddl file to create the EJBBANK database and the tables.
- ► Run the loadbank.bat file. This command file uses the ejbbank.sql file to load the tables with sample data. You can rerun this at any time to reset the data to the original content.
- ► You can run the listbank.bat file to see the content of the tables.

See Chapter 10, "Introducing and preparing for the sample application" on page 369 for a description of the tables.

Additional material

This redbook refers to additional material that can be downloaded from the Internet as described below.

Locating the Web material

The Web material associated with this redbook is available in softcopy on the Internet from the IBM Redbooks Web server. Point your Web browser to:

`ftp://www.redbooks.ibm.com/redbooks/SG246819`

Alternatively, you can go to the IBM Redbooks Web site at:

`ibm.com/redbooks`

Select the **Additional materials** and open the directory that corresponds with the redbook form number, SG246819.

© Copyright IBM Corp. 2003. All rights reserved.

Using the Web material

The additional Web material that accompanies this redbook includes the following files:

File name	Description
sg246819code.zip	Sample code for following the EJB samples throughout the book
corrections.txt	Corrections to the book after publishing

System requirements for downloading the Web material

The following system configuration is recommended:

Hard disk space	3 GB
Operating System	Windows 2000 or Windows NT
Processor	700 MHz or better
Memory	512 MB, recommended 784 MB

How to use the Web material

Unzip the contents of the Web material **sg246819code.zip** file onto your hard drive. This creates a folder structure **c:\SG246819\sampcode\xxxx**, where *xxxxx* refers to a chapter in the book:

_setup	Create the EJBBANK database and set up the home factory in the utility project.
devcmp	Develop container-managed persistence entity beans. Subdirectories for each step: Account bean, Customer bean, TransRecord bean, relationships, inheritance, finder methods, complete project.
devmapping	Mapping strategies with subdirectories for bottom-up, top-down, and composer.
devbmp	Develop bean-managed persistence entity beans.
devsession	Develop session bean, including creating a Web service.
devaccessbean	Develop access beans.
devmdb	Develop message-driven beans.
devclient	Develop EJB clients, with subdirectories servlet, struts, mdb, guiclient, webservice, and externalization.
zEARfiles	Exported EAR files for all enterprise applications. These files can be used to load all the code into Application Developer instead of developing the sample step-by-step.

Installing the ItsoBank5EAR.ear file

If you import the zEARfiles\ItsoBank5EAR.ear file into a workspace, some of the definitions are lost. Here are the guidelines for importing:

► Select *File -> Import -> EAR file*. Click *Next*.

► Browse to the EAR file:

    d:\SG246819\sampcode\zEARfiles\ItsoBank5EAR.ear

► Enter ItsoBank5EAR as the project name. Click *Next*.

► Select *Create a new Java project defined as a utility JAR or Web library*.

► Go through the remaining pages, or click *Finish* now.

Several errors are reported in the Tasks view. To fix the errors:

► Select the ItsoBank5Utility project and *Properties*. Select *Java Build Path*. On the Libraries page, click *Add Variable*. Select *WAS_50_PLUGINDIR* and click *Extend*. Locate lib\j2ee.jar and click *OK*. Click *OK* to close the Properties window. Errors in the ItsoBank5Utility project should disappear.

► Select the ItsoBank5Web project and *Properties*. Select *Java Build Path*. On the Libraries page, click *Add Variable*. Select SOAPJAR and click *OK*. Click *OK* to close the Properties window. Errors in the ItsoBank5Web project should disappear.

► Repeat the last step for the ItsoBank5WebClient project. All errors should disappear.

Installing the server

To install a WebSphere Version 5 test server with a valid configuration:

► Create a server project named ItsoServers.

► Select the new project and *Import -> Zip file*. Browse to the zEARfiles\ItsoServers.zip file and import it into the ItsoServers project.

► A server configuration named EjbbankServer appears in the Server Configuration view under *Unused Server Configurations*.

► Define a new server (not a server and configuration) named EjbbankServer. Select *WebSphere Version 5.0 -> Test Environment*.

► Select the new server and *Switch Configuration -> EjbbankServer*.

► You have now a fully configured EjbbankServer server with the ItsoBank5EAR projects attached.

Fix variables

The server configuration includes two variables that point to the WebSphere MQ installation with real directory names that may not match your installation:

► Open the server configuration (double-click `EjbbankServer`).

► Go to the Variables page (Figure B-1).

► Under Node Settings, scroll down in the variables list to the two entries:

```
MQ_INSTALL_ROOT = D:/WebSphere MQ
WAS_PUBSUB_ROOT = D:/WebSphere MQ/WEMPS
```

► Change the values to the directory of your WebSphere MQ installation.

► Save and close the server configuration.

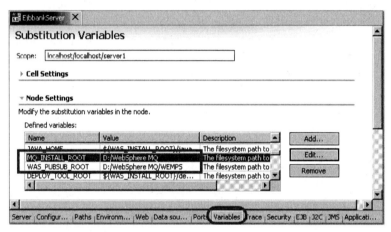

Figure B-1   Server configuration variables for WebSphere MQ

Abbreviations and acronyms

AAT	application assembly tool	**IIOP**	Internet Inter-ORB Protocol
API	application programming interface	**ITSO**	International Technical Support Organization
BMP	bean-managed persistence	**J2CA**	J2EE connector architecture
BMT	bean-managed transactions	**J2C**	J2EE connector architecture
CICS	Customer Information Control System	**J2EE**	Java 2 Enterprise Edition
CMP	container-managed persistence	**JAAS**	Java Authentication and Authorization Services
CMR	container-managed relationships	**JAF**	Java Activation Framework
CMT	container-managed transactions	**JAR**	Java archive
		JDBC	Java Database Connectivity
CORBA	Component Object Request Broker Architecture	**JDK**	Java Developer's Kit
		JMS	Java Messaging Service
COS	CORBA Object Service	**JNDI**	Java Naming and Directory Interface
CSIv2	Common Security Interoperability Version 2	**JSP**	JavaServer Pages
		JTA	JavaTransaction API
DBMS	database management system	**JTS**	Java Transaction Service
		JVM	Java Virtual Machine
DOM	document object model	**LDAP**	lightweight directory access protocol
EAR	enterprise application archive		
EIS	enterprise information system	**LTPA**	lightweight third-party authentication
EJB	Enterprise JavaBeans		
EJB QL	EJB query language	**MDB**	message-driven bean
EJS	Enterprise Java Server	**MVC**	model-view-controller
GUI	graphical user interface	**OMG**	Object Management Group
HTML	Hypertext Markup Language	**ORB**	object request broker
HTTP	Hypertext Transfer Protocol	**OTS**	Object Transaction Service
IBM	International Business Machines Corporation	**RAD**	rapid application development
		RAR	resource adapter archive
IDE	integrated development environment	**RDBMS**	relational database management system
IDL	interface definition language	**RMI**	Remote Method Invocation

© Copyright IBM Corp. 2003. All rights reserved.

SAM	Security Access Manager
SAX	simple API for XML
SCCI	source code control interface
SCM	software configuration management
SCMS	source code management systems
SDK	Software Development Kit
SOAP	Simple Object Access Protocol (also known as Service Oriented Architecture Protocol)
SQL	structured query language
SWAM	simple WebSphere authentication mechanism
TCP/IP	Transmission Control Protocol/Internet Protocol
TSO	TIme Sharing Option
UDDI	universal description, discovery, and integration
UOW	unit of work
URL	uniform resource locator
UTC	universal test client
WAR	Web application archive
WSDL	Web Service Description Language
WWW	World Wide Web
XMI	XML metadata interchange
XML	eXtensible Markup Language
XSD	XML schema definition

Related publications

The publications listed in this section are considered particularly suitable for a more detailed discussion of the topics covered in this redbook.

IBM Redbooks

For information on ordering these publications, see "How to get IBM Redbooks" on page 706.

- *WebSphere Version 5 Web Services Handbook*, SG24-6891
- *IBM WebSphere Application Server Version 5.0 Handbook*, SG24-6195
- *IBM WebSphere V5.0 Security WebSphere Handbook Series*, SG24-6573
- *Legacy Modernization with WebSphere Studio Enterprise Developer*, SG24-6806
- *WebSphere Studio Application Developer Programming Guide*, SG24-6585
- *Web Services Wizardry with WebSphere Studio Application Developer*, SG24-6292
- *Self-Study Guide: WebSphere Studio Application Developer and Web Services*, SG24-6407
- *WebSphere Version 4 Application Development Handbook*, SG24-6134
- *EJB Development with VisualAge for Java for WebSphere Application Server*, SG24-6144
- *Design and Implement Servlets, JSPs, and EJBs for IBM WebSphere Application Server*, SG245754

Other resources

These publications are also relevant as further information sources:

- *Enterprise JavaBeans*, Richard Monson-Haefel, published by O'Reilly, ISBN 0-596-00226-2

© Copyright IBM Corp. 2003. All rights reserved.

Referenced Web sites

These Web sites are also relevant as further information sources:

► EJB specification and J2EE

```
http://java.sun.com/products/ejb/index.html
http://java.sun.com/j2ee
```

► Eclipse workbench

```
http://www.eclipse.org
```

► Apache open source

```
http://jakarta.apache.org
```

► Struts

```
http://jakarta.apache.org/struts
```

► Common Versions System

```
http://www.cvshome.org
http://www.cvsnt.org
```

► Rational

```
http://www.rational.com
```

► SCM partners

```
http://www-3.ibm.com/software/ad/studioappdev/partners/scm.html
```

► Object Management Group

```
http://www.omg.org
```

► Backus Normal Form

```
http://cui.unige.ch/db-research/Enseignement/analyseinfo/AboutBNF.html
```

How to get IBM Redbooks

You can order hardcopy Redbooks, as well as view, download, or search for Redbooks at the following Web site:

ibm.com/redbooks

You can also download additional materials (code samples or diskette/CD-ROM images) from that site.

IBM Redbooks collections

Redbooks are also available on CD-ROMs. Click the CD-ROMs button on the Redbooks Web site for information about all the CD-ROMs offered, as well as updates and formats.

Index

© Copyright IBM Corp. 2003. All rights reserved.

B

C

X